EUI – Series A – 5

Daintith/Teubner (Eds.), Contract and Organisation: Legal Analysis in the Light of Economic and Social Theory

European University Institute
Institut Universitaire Européen
Europäisches Hochschulinstitut
Istituto Universitario Europeo

Series A

Law/Droit/Recht/Diritto

5

Badia Fiesolana – Firenze

Contract and Organisation:
Legal Analysis in the Light of Economic and Social Theory

Edited by

Terence Daintith and Gunther Teubner

1986

Walter de Gruyter · Berlin · New York

Library of Congress Cataloging-in-Publication Data

Contract and organization.
(Series A--Law = Droit ; 5)
Bibliography: p.
Includes index.
1. Law--Economic aspects. 2. Contracts--Economic aspects. I. Daintith, Terence. II. Teubner, Gunter. III. Series: Series A--Law ; 5.
K487.E3C66 1986 343'.07 86-4267
ISBN 0-89925-172-2 (U.S.) 342.37

CIP-Kurztitelaufnahme der Deutschen Bibliothek

Contract and organisation: legal analysis in the light of economic and social theory / ed. by Terence Daintith and Gunther Teubner. - Berlin ; New York : de Gruyter, 1986.
(European University Institute : Ser. A, Law ; 5)
ISBN 3-11-010705-8
NE: Daintith, Terence [Hrsg.]; Instituto Universitario Europeo ⟨Fiesole⟩: European University Institute / A

Dust Cover Design: Rudolf Hübler, Berlin. – Setting and Printing: Wagner GmbH, Nördlingen.
Binding: Verlagsbuchbinderei Dieter Mikolai, Berlin.
Printed in Germany

Table of Contents

Acknowledgements

This book is part of a larger research project of the European University Institute in Florence on the general theme of "Law and Economic Policy: Alternatives to Delegalisation" which has been conducted over the last three years under the direction of the two editors of this volume. The project aims to make a contribution from the legal standpoint to the current debate on the capacities and limits of the welfare state. This kind of work requires an interdisciplinary approach, and in particular an orientation of legal analysis towards economic and sociological theory. This perspective not only offers insights into the capacities of law to regulate social fields, but also demonstrates how legal norms can be changed if one incorporates social knowledge into legal analysis.

In a seminar series on the theme "Social Science Contributions to Legal Analysis" we asked distinguished scholars in law, economics and sociology from different countries to discuss with us their views on a possible transfer of knowledge from the social sciences to legal thinking. We invited them to present their specific "model" of the relations between law and the social sciences *in abstracto* and then to demonstrate the application of their model in the fields of Contract and Organisation. This book shows the results of the intensive discussions between these external experts and internal members of the Institute. The final versions of the papers have been considerably influenced by these discussions. We want to thank all participants, among them especially our doctoral students, for their valuable contributions.

The interdisciplinary method used in this book reflects a characteristic feature of the Law Department in the European University Institute. "Law in Context" is a specific approach to legal problems which is shared by all its members. In contrast to the technical and doctrinal style of legal analysis this approach insists on analysing legal phenomena in their social, political and economic contexts. General departmental discussions along these lines were of great help to our project, and we are especially grateful to Mauro Cappelletti, Werner Maihofer, Yves Mény, Patrick Nerhot and Joseph Weiler for their intellectual support.

We would like to thank Iain Fraser for his sensitive translation of the texts of some of our French and German contributors. For thorough and precise editorial assistance our thanks go to Thomas Abeltshauser, Tony Curran, Anne-Lise Strahtmann, and Elizabeth Webb, as well as to Brigitte Schwab, the Institute's Publications Officer, for her professional help in the final publication process.

Firenze, September 1985

Terence Daintith and
Gunther Teubner

I.
Introduction

Sociological Jurisprudence and Legal Economics: Risks and Rewards

Terence Daintith
Gunther Teubner
Firenze

Introduction

Contract and Organisation – these are two key concepts which link law and the social sciences. In contract law we find the legal reconstruction of economic exchange relations while at the same time, the legal principle of contractual liberty and the elaborate rules of contract law are the prerequisite for the development of complex economic market transactions. In an analogous fashion, the invention of the legal person, the variety of legal forms for associations and corporations, the complicated legal network of organisational competences and decision procedures have both reflected the emergence of organisations in the social and economic sphere, and decisively shaped the development of the "organisational society". Yet despite these interdependencies, the formation of legal concepts in the fields of contract and organisation was in the past an autonomous process in the legal system, whatever its socio-economic premises and consequences. The definition of principles, rules and concepts was the essential concern of legal processes: of court rulings, legislative procedures and doctrinal refinement. Questions about the appropriate rules governing contract and organisation had to be addressed to the professional lawyers. This monopoly of lawyers is effectively challenged today. Institutional economics, sociology of organisation, the theory of private government, the political economy of labour relations – just to name a few – make their claims on contract and organisation, not only in terms of empirical-analytical description, but of normative prescription as well.

If lawyers take up this challenge, not just as a threat to their professional identity, but rather as a chance for intellectual enrichment and practical improvement, then they should scrutinise the potential contributions of social science thinking to legal analysis of contract and organisation. More concretely, the question becomes twofold: (I) How does social science thinking in this field change the quality of legal argumentation? What are the methodological implications if one incorporates economic and sociological models in legal doctrine? (II)

What are the substantive legal results for contract and organisation? How do legal economics and sociological jurisprudence influence legal concepts, policies and rules relating to contract and organisation?

These are precisely the questions to which we give some tentative answers in this book. In order to reflect the broad spectrum of the discussion, the book presents various competing approaches to socio-legal thinking. All, however, concentrate on these two issues. Each analysis contains a distinct model of the relationship between legal and social science thinking. The models range – to give them somewhat fashionable labels – from "legal economics" via "law and society" to "legal critical studies". At the same time, in each contribution, the model is applied to problems in contract law, organisation law, or both, with the aim of elucidating concepts, interpreting rules, or formulating policies.

1. Social Science Models in Legal Doctrine?

1.1. Two Basic Approaches

In their programmatic statements, Hans Albert and Rudolf Wiethölter set the stage for a confrontation which is repeated throughout the book: social technology through law versus lawyers' reflection on law in society, legal incrementalism versus legal fundamentalism, instrumental rationality versus reflexive rationality. Albert presents a clear-cut socio-technical interpretation of law which opens the door to the instrumental approach in the social sciences. Rejecting the analytical and the hermeneutical tradition in modern legal theory, he proposes to redefine legal doctrine as a set of propositions concerning social effects of legal norms. Social knowledge thus becomes extremely important for legal argument: "Anyone wishing to define the meaning of the law must *ipso facto* do so thinking on the effects intended by it and the order it is aimed at. Such considerations necessitate the use of nomological knowledge, for the control effects of laws and interpretations are not simple logical consequences of the statements concerned". Law, as social technology, is supposed to design institutional arrangements that channel individual interests and motivations in such a way that certain social functions are realised.

This model of rational jurisprudence is strongly contested by Wiethölter. Legal socio-technics representing nothing but a "sociological natural law" have no effect whatsoever on legal practice. This is due to the self-definition of the legal *proprium* by the law itself. According to Wiethölter, legal practice has proved to be resistant to the challenges of the social sciences, although at the same time, legal practice is intrinsically committed to respond to the challenges of social development. The way out of this paradox is legal self-reflection. "Theoretical programmes applied reflectively must here always – reconstructively – follow up developments that have led to crises and – prospectively – investigate the possible conditions for overcoming the crises". Social science models become important in this process, but in a more indirect and complicated way. It is not so much the calculation of social consequences of norms that informs legal practice and theory but the interpretations of the world offered by "grand theories" in the social philosophical tradition, interpretations that challenge and respond to the "legal constructions" of social reality. The relationship between law and social science is, according to Wiethölter, "a relationship between autonomy and heteronomy about which, however, the law has still a co-determining role to play".

The basic tension between these two clearly defined positions is present – at least implicitly – in many (if not all) of the contributions to this volume. Some of them side with social technology, some with legal self-reflection. A third group tries to bridge the seemingly irreconcilable differences. David Trubek's contribution illustrates a possible synthesis. Dealing with the contemporary American debate in legal theory, the debate between "law and society" and "critical legal studies", he is concerned with the same basic issues of instrumental versus reflexive rationality, although the American fronts of the debate are not exactly the same as their European counterparts. Trubek proposes to infuse the empirical law and society research with critical consciousness and to ground the critical scholar's speculations upon some empirical foundation. He argues for systematic empirical analysis in order to identify properly the relation between legal constructions of social reality and the "law in action", its effects on social action in general. This seems to be a reasonable position similar to other attempts in this volume to mediate between the two extremes. Gotthold, for example, strongly criticises the normative implications of legal economics, but recommends the use of their methods in comparative studies.

Here we try neither to solve this controversy nor to find a synthesis between the antithetical positions. Instead we try a differentiating approach. Firstly, we seek to differentiate the ways in which "models" are constructed in legal doctrine, and in sociological and economic theory. This leads us to reject propositions of a simple transfer of scientific knowledge to law and to formulate the relations between law and the social sciences in a somewhat more complicated fashion. Secondly, we seek to differentiate various "levels" of legal analysis. This will allow us to spell out requirements for the collaboration of law and social sciences more clearly, defining a limited role for both instrumental and reflexive rationality. The contributions in this book show a large variety of methodological approaches to the cooperation of law and the social sciences which justifies such a differentiating explanation.

1.2. The Different Selectivity of Law and the Social Sciences

Most, if not all, of the authors in the volume agree that the relation between law and the social sciences cannot be seen as a simple transfer of "scientific" knowledge into the legal system. In particular, Gotthold points to the limited ability of scientific inquiry to assist in legal policy matters where moral questions are at stake. He thus criticises as illegitimate the imperialistic claims of social science models, especially in the "new" legal economics. Farjat, rejecting outmoded "scientism", defines scientific models, as well as legal doctrinal concepts, as competing "constructions of reality" none of which can claim superiority.

In our view, these considerations suggest that the different selectivity of law and the social sciences be taken into account. Selectivity refers to the fact that any scientific or practice-oriented model construction has to choose a limited set of variables which are supposed to grasp the "relevant" elements of "reality". The basically different selectivity of *social science research* on the one hand and of *decision-oriented legal doctrine* on the other brings about such a difference in the selection of the elements of models, construction procedures, the securing of information, verification and criteria of certainty, that the simple transposition of sociological or economic models of the outside world into legal analyses is excluded in principle (cf. Stachowiak 1973; Luhmann 1974; Krawietz 1978). Instead, the process should be analysed as a complicated "translation process" as shown by Joerges, whose translation rules have to be designed in function of the different contextual conditions of social science on the one hand and legal doctrine on the other (Teubner 1985). This distinction makes it possible to determine how to do justice to their differing selectivities, how to change, indeed to "manipulate", social science theories, thought patterns, concepts and methods in order to make them applicable to questions of legal doctrine.

It would thus be erroneous to describe the relation between social science models and legal models as a contrast between social reality and lawyers' ideology. There is no direct access to social reality, there are only competing system models of reality (Stachowiak, 1973:97). Therefore, one has to see this as a problematic relation between legal and social models of reality, each having its own rightful claims (Farjat). There is a fundamental difference between the analytical-empirical approach in science, with its more or less severe methodological restrictions, and the social constructions of legal practice and theory, which have quite different restrictions based on their orientation toward conflict resolution (Wiethölter).

The same holds true for the dynamics of motives. The motives and value premises of legal constructions of reality (e.g. case-orientation, principle of equality, procedures of legal evidence) are different from those of scientific constructions (e.g. scientific rationality, experience orientation, scientific discourse procedures). That means we have to accept different "cognitive conditionings" (Stachowiak, 1973:97) as premises of operational processes in law and in science. In general, the differences between scientific theories and legal models refer to the selection of the model variables, the procedures of model construction, the methods of testing, the criteria of certainty and the requirements for success. For example, it is not by chance that the rules of legal evidence differ from the rules of empirical research in social sciences and that there is no equivalent in science for the legal principle of *res iudicata*.

This implies complications for the relationship between scientific theories about law, and law's own models of reality. Though some would argue to the contrary, historical accounts of social developments, economic models of legal relations or results of empirical sociological analyses are not by reason of their closer access to social reality intrinsically superior to legal conceptualisations of law in society. Of two models, the one which is structurally and materially closer to the original is not necessarily better. In particular, science is not in a position to define authoritative models of external reality. Science produces only hypothetical models which can be tested in their capacity for strategic purposes. Science can serve only as stimulation not as notification (Habermas, 1976:107). In a precise sense, one cannot speak of a legal reception of social sciences. Rather, one has to see them as competing constructions of reality which allow for comparison of their relative strength.

It is possible to see this relation as a problem of power: who has the power to force his construction of reality upon others? (Farjat; Hejl, 1982:320). We, however, would prefer to see it as a problem of compatibility, of possibilities of drawing analogies and of mutual learning. Legal economics and legal sociology produce results which may either be rejected by lawyers or which may lead to profound changes in legal model construction. At best, there is a productive mutual exchange in the sense of social science "subsidies" (Luhmann, 1981:134) of legal concepts or vice versa.

The likelihood of mutual influence depends much on the congruence of the models' selectivity. Joerges raises this point when he observes that different economic theories have a differential chance of getting accepted in legal reasoning. Neo-classical competition theory and the individualism of the "new" economic analysis of law can much more easily be transformed into legal concepts and administered by the legal system than can concepts like that of workable competition. It is important to realise that this is not only a fortunate coincidence and a promising chance for interdisciplinary cooperation but also a "distortion of competition" between rival approaches. This leads to the conclusion that the transformation of theoretically grounded concepts into legal decisions must itself be made the object of interdisciplinary research. Another conclusion is that the social organisation of such a translation process is a matter beyond merely scientific interest: it becomes a matter of political concern.

The difference in selectivity has two main dimensions. One is empirical: what model variables are selected as relevant to describe social reality? The other is prospective: what social purposes are chosen to organise social knowledge? In both dimensions, the choices made by legal and social science may differ widely, and thus create problems for the translation process. Legal economics is a good example of such different choices in both the empirical and the prospective dimension. Schanze refers to the first dimension when he describes problem-prone interfaces between model and reality:

> Important limits to the economic model are in the conception of the individual wealth maximizer (who has in fact to deal with bounded rationality), in the problem of the initial assignment (or distribution of rights), and in the relative vagueness of the magic term of preferences which can be used not only to analyze, but also to justify odd ends. The price system does not always work. If it is brought to work under more complicated and more realistic model assumptions than those of complete information, free competition and costless transaction, results are frequently imprecise ...

Other authors refer mainly to the second dimension when they contrast the concept of economic efficiency with other legal values such as distributive justice or other non-efficiency related values. (Harris and Veljanovski; Romani; Gotthold). In particular, Buxbaum is quite explicit on this point. He demonstrates striking differences between an economic and legal analysis of the same object with the result that a legal analysis has to take more complex value considerations into account than just economic efficiency. It is very often the case that the law postulates political values to be balanced against economic values; sometimes it even postulates the primacy of political values. Buxbaum's assessment of economic theory in relation to law can easily be extended to any social science theory:

It can be an aid to understanding, and thus to the proper formulation of good doctrine; it can also be an aid for mystification, and thus to the legitimation of good, bad or indifferent doctrine. The one thing it probably cannot do is itself to prescribe the good; but at its most useful it should assist the law-maker and the law-applier in transforming the prescribed value into the prescribed action.

2. Levels of Socio-Legal Cooperation

Our second thesis also aims at transforming the somewhat rigid alternative between social technology and legal self-reflection into a differentiated approach. The thesis is that the conditions for making use of the social sciences in the law cannot be defined in general terms, but that it is only when different levels of the process of forming the law can be separated that the various requirements which the "translation" of economic and sociological models has to meet can be specified.

A number of varying approaches towards differentiation (Luhmann, 1974; Hopt, 1975; Hoffmann-Riem, 1977), can be developed further into a *multi-dimensional model of the integration of legal and social sciences.* Within this framework requirements for interdisciplinary work can be specified. Our distinction would pitch the translation processes on two main levels and then distinguish among several sub-levels: that of legal action, as expressed both by the formulation of general legal rules and by their activation in the form of specific legal decisions or actions, and that of the construction of fundamental concepts, where highly abstract relations are established between the development of society and the development of the law.

On the first main level, law can utilise the instrumental quality of the social sciences, their descriptive, explanatory and predictive potential. It is here that we can look to see what is the capacity of social science theories to generate indications for the content of legal action. On the second level it would be the social sciences' role to offer the potential of "grand theories" for the orientation of fundamental legal concepts. It has to be kept in mind, however, that both levels influence each other in the sense that decisions about rule formation and law application will have an impact on fundamental concept construction and *vice versa.*

2.1. Guiding Legal Action

We look first, then, at the contribution of social science theories in guiding legal action. This is an appropriate perspective in which to judge the utility and interest of these contributions: it is a familiar observation, touched on here by Albert, that *legal* analysis has as an essential feature the production of applicable results. This is most obviously the case where laws, regulations or existing judicial decisions are being analysed in the course of judicial process with a view to reaching a correct resolution of a dispute between litigating parties, but the same is true of most practical legal analysis, whether in the context of extra-judicial dispute settlement, dispute avoidance, or the framing of legal rules to govern a relationship between parties. The precise nature and object of the analysis will vary according to the circumstances and to the role of the lawyer involved. The judge will be concerned to reach a just decision which is in accordance with a correct interpretation of the relevant texts. In the context of a settlement negotiation, the professional legal adviser will be looking for texts and interpretations most favourable to the negotiating claims of his client; in the context of the design of legal relationships, he will be involved in the straightforward application of basic rules and the avoidance of pitfalls and ambiguities previously disclosed by litigation, practice, or doctrine. In all these cases, however, specific desired or undesired results constantly structure and guide the analysis.

Less obviously, perhaps, the same preoccupation with concrete results also guides and structures legal analysis connected with legislative activity. The legislator may normally be viewed by the lawyer as engaged upon the task of collective resolution of indefinite numbers of hypothetical future "cases", in a sense different from that which would, or might, obtain without his intervention. This is achieved through the introduction of a new and appropriately designed rule into the corpus which lawyers will be analysing in the course of the different individual legal activities (litigation, negotiations etc.) above described. It is worth stressing, perhaps, that we are not suggesting that legislation is necessarily designed with an eye to the litigation context: the aim may rather be one of providing facilities for more economical or productive private legal arrangements. In laying down new rules of conduct, or reshaping or reassigning rights or duties, the legislator's aim will be to avoid rather than foster litigation, producing a rule which is sufficiently clear, and which harmonises sufficiently well with the existing rules of the legal system, existing practice of its professionals and (perhaps) with existing perceptions of what is just or economically or socially acceptable to its addressees, to banish litigation about its interpretation to the extremes of its intended spectrum of application. To achieve this the legislator must be armed with the same kind of legal analysis – in terms of accurate interpretation of the relevant existing rules of the legal system, and accurate appreciation of their likely practical application – as must the individual practitioner, albeit on a wider scale.

For the normal purposes of the legislator, however, this kind of harmony and clarity, and the legal analysis that permits their attainment, are not enough. The legislator's interest in a changed result in a given range of cases may be purely qualitative, in the sense that his aim is confined to securing that as often as the circumstances envisaged in the new law arise, the new rule is applied or the new legal facilities offered are considered. His interest may also – and perhaps this is now the normal case, given today's penchant and possibilities for the statistical measurement of welfare – be quantitative in nature: that is to say, the motivations of the legislation will include some conception of the quantitative importance, in economic or social terms, of the range of cases addressed, and of the size of the aggregate change in the resolution of this range of cases that it is desirable to bring about. In this latter case, the legislation may appear simply as the instrument (or as one of several instruments) for the achievement of the relevant change in economic or social aggregates. Where the concerns are qualitative, and *a fortiori* where they are quantitative also, the analytical apparatus of the legislator needs to include some procedure for assessing whether the application of the new rule may not be vitiated, and if so in what measure, by irrelevance or by adaptive behaviour on the part of those to whom it is addressed. Irrelevance may occur because the legislator's understanding of the relevant social or economic circumstances is weak, or because the legislation is based on a false theory of social or economic action. Adaptive behaviour may involve such strategies as avoidance of the impact of the legislative provisions or the passing on of their benefits or burdens in unexpected directions. Traditional legal analysis of the interpretative and experimental type can say nothing about questions of relevance and provide only a small part of the solution to the problem of adaptive behaviour: it may indicate what scope the whole body of law, including the new rule, offers for adaptive behaviour, but by itself this is unlikely to be useful information. Unless the regime is truly draconian (as in Western societies is normally now only the case with tax laws) such scope will be virtually boundless in legal terms, being limited rather by economic and social factors which must be evaluated in order to identify the legal rules (if any) which will bear on the issue; and the legal analysis cannot in any event indicate how far the legal limits of adaptive behaviour, if constraining, will in fact be respected.

Here it is worth remarking that the needs of judge and legislator in this respect are not as different as might at first sight appear. Even under the appearance of deciding single cases, the judge may, of course, be acting as legislator. This is patent where the judge is entrusted with functions of legislative review, on a constitutional basis, as in the United States (Buxbaum), or on some other basis, such as that of international treaty, as in the case of the European Communities. It is less obvious, but no less true, where individual decisions are endowed with some determining authority over future cases under some version of the doctrine of *stare decisis*. Whether such judges will feel any consciousness of the inadequacy of traditional legal analysis for the discharge of their decision-making functions will depend, perhaps, on whether they view their legislative role as developmental or purely declaratory in nature. Whenever the judge needs more than pure legal analysis, so too do those lawyers whose activities involve the understanding of judicial decisions.

Even leaving aside the judge-as-legislator, problems of the actual effects of individual judicial decisions may arise. Parties may refuse, or be unable, to abide by the terms of decisions addressed to them, or may use the decision simply as a basis for further negotiations. Again, this step, between formal decision and effective result, can hardly be traced out through legal analysis alone, but demands resort to other techniques, which parties, or their advisers, will need to have mastered.

The inadequacy of traditional legal analysis to meet the lawyer's needs for understanding the economic and social fabric on which the law operates means that any legal system conceived of by its operators as being capable of change and development must, for the purposes of such development, have recourse to other types of analysis, such as those furnished by the social sciences which are the subject of this volume.

Acceptance of this requirement does not entail accepting that specific bodies of social science knowledge may be drawn upon by lawyers so as to produce "correct" results. One striking feature of the papers in this volume is that while most of them share the legal professional's interest in concrete results, the general tendency of this majority of papers is to warn against facile borrowings from social and economic theory, by drawing attention to restrictive assumption of such theory (Schanze), to their defective elaboration or application (Gotthold), to their inconsistency and consequent inability to suggest practical solutions (Joerges), to their capacity for "mystification" and concealment of real decisional premises (Buxbaum), or to the failure of results to conform to theory predictions (Teubner). If we put to one side the papers of the economists Romani and Schmid, we find that optimism about learning lessons for application in legal analysis is, to say the least, restrained. Only in the paper of Harris and Veljanovski do we find anything like an open espousal of a specific body of normative theory – in this case, welfare economics – as a guide to legal decision-making. The papers of Schanze and Daintith may also be characterised in terms of qualified optimism, rather than qualified pessimism, about the utility of economic theory. In using these terms, however, we are not so much identifying the intellectual propensities of the authors as the level and direction of the critique their papers contain. The optimists implicitly or explicitly criticise traditional legal analysis, indicating how decision-making may be improved by the application of social science knowledge; the pessimists assume that such knowledge will be applied, and address their critique to its selection and application.

With these caveats in mind, we can ask what these papers contribute to our understanding of the results of legal actions and decisions, whether on the part of legislators, judges or parties. The answer can best be ordered by reference to the extent to which, and the level at which, the various contributions aspire to indicate desirable results to actors in the legal system. For this purpose three broad approaches may be distinguished, each corresponding roughly to a different function of social science theory. The approaches overlap and we shall see that most of the relevant contributions contain elements of all three, but the distinctions are nonetheless valuable for the purposes of the translation process already described.

The first approach involves the descriptive and explanatory use of theory to produce empirical analyses of legally-regulated sectors of social or economic life. The German term *Normbereichsanalysen* ("norm area analyses", Müller, 1966) catches the essence of the enterprise. The aim of such analyses is to furnish empirically tested or testable theoretical statements about social structures, functions and developmental tendencies in such sectors and thus to clarify inter-relations between legal norms and social structures. In Selznick's language (1966,

1969), it is an institutional analysis which relates the "opportunity structure" of a social field to the "conceptual readiness" of the legal norms therein. The exponent of this approach thus holds back from offering explicit statements either of likely or of desirable legal action within the relevant field, making no assumptions about the values or objectives of legal actors. Implicit policy recommendations, based on the degree of fit disclosed between the regulated social sector and prevailing legal arrangements, may however often be discernible.

The second approach, that of legal impact analysis (*Folgenanalyse*, e.g. Rottleuthner, 1979), addresses itself explicitly to legal and social results. It is essentially socio-technical in character, in that it assumes that legal rules are designed to serve social and economic objectives and compares the intended effects of the rules with actual consequences and unintended side effects. The analyst may go on to make suggestions for the reinterpretation or reformulation of legal rules in the light of this demonstration, but does not question the objectives which the law sets out to serve. Here the translation process from social science to legal thinking is relatively easy, in that impact analysis works with the same assumptions as legal analysis but goes further: while the practitioner of the traditional legal approach would be content to interpret legal norms in the light of their purpose, the impact analyist explicitly seeks the social and economic consequences of legal arrangements which should, in principle, be open to empirical testing. In offering theoretically grounded explanations for discrepancies between legal purposes and actual or projected results, impact analysis utilises both the explanatory and predictive capacities of social and economic theory, offering employment for what Friedmann (1953) has termed "positive" as opposed to normative theory. Such theory may nonetheless incorporate powerful model assumptions: legal economics in fact tends to analyse legal institutions as economic incentive structures and employs the assumption of rational wealth maximisation in examining their impact on social behaviour. In contrast, sociological analyses of social functions and effects of legal norms rely predominantly on empirical research methods guided by some theoretical constructs like those developed in organisation theory, exchange theory etc. The difference, however, is only one of degree. Sociologists may make use of economic models, and economists of sociological research.

A third approach which it is helpful to distinguish for the purpose of characterising the contributions here is that of policy analysis (*Politikanalysen*, Hart and Joerges, 1980). Such analyses respond to or develop social policy conceptions and construct doctrinal statements from them. Unlike impact analyses, they are not primarily concerned with the economic and social consequences of specific legal arrangements, but rather analyse prescriptions of social and economic theory and attempt to draw out their legal implications. This kind of analysis is used when lawyers scrutinise the implications for law of competing theories, for example, theories of democracy. What are the institutional consequences of the elitist-pluralist concept of organisational democracy? How does law respond to a more participatory approach? Can a more complex concept of organisational democracy, grounded in systems theory, be translated into legal arrangements? This policy approach is used in a particularly highly developed form where legal concepts of competition law are influenced by the discussion of economic policy conceptions (e.g. Moeschel, 1975; Reich 1977), or where legal reform programmes are developed through the efficiency criteria of welfare economics (e.g. Posner, 1977).

As already indicated, these approaches are not tidy boxes within which to fit the relevant contributions here, particularly since only some of the papers set out to be examples of such approaches or combinations of them: others aim rather to survey or criticise such approaches over the whole or parts of one of our chosen fields of study. Let us try to summarise our view of the significance of these contributions, in terms of their approach and indications for substantive results.

In the sphere of contract, it is Romani on the one hand, and Harris and Veljanovski on the other, who tackle the fundamental economic issues, explaining how the legal enforceability of contracts (in particular, wholly executory contracts) promotes voluntary exchange productive of economic welfare (Romani), and how the existence of a body of contract law facilitates and simplifies the task of parties in making agreements. Both papers accept the argument that contract should function so as to offer parties the correct incentives to efficient behaviour in contractual formation, performance and non-performance. While Romani adopts what may be termed an orthodox stance, defending on economic grounds the enforceability of executory agreements and the non-enforceability of gratuitous promises, Harris and Veljanovski are more critical particularly of the literature which offers an economic concept of "efficient" breach of contract. They argue that this discussion neglects the external effect of general loss of confidence in contractual formulation of promises, and the fact that most contractual disputes are settled out of court, a factor which gives advantages to the breaching party which the law should take into account. They suggest that the legislative development of contract law in the United Kingdom in recent years has neglected this factor, introducing explicit judicial discretions which, while they may assist judges to do justice in the relatively few cases actually brought before them, add a further element of uncertainty to the many already existing, all of which work in favour of the breaching party in out-of-court negotiations. Specific alterations to contract law are suggested as a means of offsetting this imbalance, though at this point it becomes unclear whether the argument has moved from efficiency to distributional grounds.

The approach to the use of economic theory that these papers describe is essentially that of impact analysis, strongly tinged with normative elements. It is analysis of a rather specialised kind: with the exception of Harris and Veljanovski's discussion of out-of-court settlements, most of the work described involves little empirical investigation, but rather postulates consequences of legal rules and institutions – ranging from the very concept of enforceable contract to specific contractual remedies – by deduction from economic models of human behaviour. The comparison it is concerned to make is not so much between these consequences and the objectives of such rules and institutions – indeed what meaning is there in talking of the "objectives" of such basic common law rules? – as between the consequences and the results indicated by economic theory, employing these same models, as "efficient". One can see that the distance in such cases between a positive and a normative economic analysis of legal rules is small indeed.

In contrast, when judges or legislators set out to make specific changes in contract law with express policy objectives in view, legal impact analysis can occupy itself, more conventionally, with the confronting of intended with actual, or theory-predicted, results. This is what Harris and Veljanovski do in their section on the "out-of-court" aspect of contractual dispute resolution, as well as in a brief reference to contracting around the law, a theme taken up, in the same area of landlord and tenant law, by Schmid in a case-study of Michigan housing legislation. His study shows how landlords adapt their contracting behaviour to legislation protective of tenants. Experience and intuition would probably alert practising lawyers (though maybe not legislators) to this possibility in any event: what Schmid adds is an explanation of this adaptive capacity, and indications for its measurement, based on general economic concepts such as information costs. This, he argues, should make it easier for legislators to design rules which will be hard to circumvent and thus more likely to achieve their objective. Here an impact analysis is offered as an application of a general theory which will predict the impact and substantive consequences of alternative allocations of property rights. For Schmid, this is a better tool in the hands of legislators than reliance on the process of learning through experience which eventually brought the Michigan legislature to the same result.

Joerges might disagree. His paper on quality control law shows his scepticism about the capacity of economic theory to help in finding solutions to specific problems: such theories may be associated with given bodies of law, such as competition law, or consumer protection regulations, but when practical problems arise for resolution the relevant legal principles may themselves be in conflict. His example of car sales agreements in Germany shows how the protection of the consumer's interest depends not only on the legal regulation of the relationship between consumer and dealer but also on that between dealer and manufacturer and that the law offers possibly competing frameworks for determining the effective content of such regulation: competition law (restraints on vertical restrictions of competition); self-regulation (recognition of inter-organisation agreements); or general principles of contract law ("fairness" in manufacturer/dealer relationships). In thus stressing the complexity of legal decision-making and the partial character of economic as of other forms of social science analysis, Joerges indicates that all types of legal actors confront choices in the making, application or use of law, for whose guidance specific experience of the results of previous decisions is as important as predictions based on social theory. "Practice 'discovers', under the pressure of its needs to make decisions, paths to solutions where theory has got stuck in the search for concepts." He proposes a reformulation of the whole policy approach, which should no longer be seen as an exercise in pure interdisciplinary analysis, but as a socio-political process relating action and knowledge in the real world.

Returning for a moment to Schmid's paper, we may also see it as exemplifying the kind of institutional analysis which constitutes the first of our approaches.

His key concept is the "situation." Analysis of the "situation" (here, landlord-tenant relationships in a university town) reveals the type of social interdependence there existing and hence allows us to choose between legal alternatives: "It is the inherent features of goods which influence how one person's acts can potentially affect another. The instrumentality of law depends on the source of the interdependence." Schmid develops a typology of different "situations," which he has presented in more elaborate form elsewhere (Schmid, 1978), and here, as already noted, shows how it may serve as the basis for an impact analysis of a particular legislative initiative.

Another situational analysis is Daintith's study of long term contracts in the iron ore market. Daintith analyses the incidence and performance of these contracts in a concrete market and uses this material to discuss theoretical propositions by the economist Williamson and the sociologist Macaulay: what are the incentives for choosing long term contracts, instead of transitory contracts on the one side and organisational solutions (the purchase of ore mines by steel companies) on the other? What is the actual role of formal contract law in relation to economic practice? How did the parties adapt their legal regime to the abrupt changes in the market? While the primary aim of the paper is to carry out empirical tests of descriptive theories of contractual design and performance, it may also, by an inversion of perspective, be seen as offering an impact analysis. Unlike the studies so far discussed, the subject here is not the general (State) law relating to contracts, but the contract rules these parties have made for themselves, whose effects are examined at the level both of individual party behaviour and at that of the market as a whole.

Our contributors in the field of the law relating to organisations show considerable ambivalence in regard to the concrete results following from or to be expected of social science theory. The more specific the indications given by a contributor of points at which social science theories have influenced legal development, the more mistrustful he appears to be of their purposeful use to indicate legal results. Farjat, who like Harris and Veljanovski frames his contribution as a critical survey, devotes its first part to a number of examples of how economic science has reshaped the law relating to the enterprise: the redistribution of rights within it, the treatment of creditors and workers on bankruptcy, its competitive relationships with other firms. Yet in the "critical balance sheet" that follows he, like Joerges, stresses the competitive constructions of reality offered by different social science theories, and warns the lawyer against over-ready acceptance of any of them. It is still the lawyer (or law-maker) who is confronted with the necessity of choice, and theory cannot dictate results.

Farjat's point about the legitimising role of economic theory for legal development is driven home by Buxbaum in his policy analysis of U.S. Supreme Court decisions on corporation law. Using the rather less kindly epithet of "mystification" for the role of theory, Buxbaum analyses in detail the normative implications of three economic theories relevant to company law under federalism: the efficient capital market and corporate control market hypotheses, and the applications to economic federalism of public choice and public finance theory. He shows both that these bodies of theory have been applied by the Supreme

Court in rulings on State takeover statutes, and that their invocation may disguise shifts in the position of the Court on issues of division of legislative competence which are not, in his view, capable of determination by reference only to economic criteria.

The other four contributors on organisation law all tackle the theme of the "constitution of the firm", that is, the legal organisation of decision competences and income rights in the economic firm. All four are from West Germany, and the issue of co-determination either is their subject (as with Gotthold and Teubner), or looms large in their treatment of more general issues (as with Krause and Schanze). Albert, too uses this example to illustrate his general methodological point: his social technology programme includes sociological analyses which would elicit the effects of the regulations on the control of what happens in society and on the life situations of those concerned, as well as economic analyses which examine the efficiency of the institutional incentive structure. This combined socio-economic research programme avoids many of the shortcomings which one can find in purely economic or purely sociological analyses.

The pair of contributions by Schanze and Krause offer interesting contrasts. Both set out to offer general analyses of the firm. Both are generally optimistic about the applicability of economic theory, including its normative or policy applications. Schanze, the lawyer, seems the more cautious of the two. He argues both that economic analysis in general offers us "rules of prudence" in our evaluation of legal phenomena and, more specifically, that the theory of transaction costs suggests certain normative desiderata of an efficient legal system – equilibrium in the variety and standardisation of institutions, clear definitions of entitlements in decision-making units, a bias in institutional arrangements towards the inclusion of total costs of transacting (internalisation). In a section devoted to what he terms "extrinsic analysis" he goes on to use the first of these ideas as a means of legitimising the German co-determination law, arguing that it opens up new choices in the market for organisational forms for business activity. Proceeding, however, to an "intrinsic" analysis of the structure of the firm, Schanze offers only "a concept of positive inquiry" which might demonstrate the explanatory potential of economic analysis in the form of a refined version of property right theory. Once complete, however, Schanze's analysis could clearly have normative implications, at least in suggesting appropriate institutional designs to cater for a variety of enterprise needs. One might guess, however, that his preference would be to leave it to the market to test the appropriateness of the institutional structures proposed rather than to make forced marriages by legislation.

Krause, while he shares some of the same starting points – in particular, a reliance on property right and transactions costs theory – has a much more explicitly normative approach. Krause accepts efficiency as the primary goal for corporate organisation, operationalising it as profit-seeking in the service of consumer interests, and considers how this may be attained using an approach which, like Schanze's, is "neutral" as between different kinds of inputs into the organisation – and in particular, as between physical and human capital. This leads him to enunciate a series of normative propositions about which property right holders should be treated as "members" of organisations, about types of membership and the control rights that should attach to memberships of different types. Co-determination, seen as a "dualistic" approach because it recognises different kinds of interests in the firm as opposed to the single interest – the resources-based property right – recognised by Krause (hence his "monist" approach), is criticised as inefficient: among other things, it is likely to prejudice consumer interests and to absorb excessive productive energy in favour of interest mediation or social peace. Yet while the style is prescriptive, Krause insists that this is just a theoretical foundation and that he can give no guidelines on practical implementation, thus apparently leaving the way open for the interposition of non-economic values between theoretical prescription and practical results.

The treatments of co-determination in the contributions of Gotthold and Teubner shift the argument away from efficiency considerations towards questions about the distribution of power within the firm (Gotthold) and to its sociopolitical significance (Teubner). En route, however, these papers offer further insights about the uses lawyers can make of economic and social theory, about contrasts within and between the approaches we have outlined. Gotthold devotes the bulk of his paper to a sustained attack on the unrefined property right approach of Furubotn (1981): he raises objections as to its empirical foundation, its tautological character, and its selection of variables, and doubts whether it can be fruitfully used as a basis for a legal impact analysis of the co-determination phenomenon. At the same time, however, he suggests at one point that co-determination *can* be supported by reference to efficiency considerations, and is ready to draw on the descriptive resources of economic theory (adapting, as did Schanze, a "contractual nexus" model of the firm) to lay the basis for dicussion of distributive aspects of the topic.

Teubner, finally, sees the chief significance of co-determination in its functioning as an element of a neo-corporatist scheme of integration of a society increasingly differentiated along functional lines. After discussing empirical findings which suggest that co-determination has not achieved its intended effects of increasing individual worker satisfaction, and arguing, from theoretical premises and empirical evidence, that it has in fact redistributed power and provided more effective conflict-resolution procedures at enterprise level, he goes on to claim that at the societal level, co-determination performs a vital function of re-integrating political and economic systems, which it links – at the level of the firm – without subordinating either one to the other. This non-subordination is vouched by the fact that, in Teubner's view, co-determination contradicts both the political conception of class conflict and the economic rationality of the market. For him the question then becomes one of how the law may be formulated so as to exploit to the full this integrative potential. Ultimately, Teubner shows the same scepticism as do Farjat and Joerges about the capacity of established bodies of economic, social and political theory to furnish, of themselves, blueprints for adequate legal rules and organisation: but while Farjat is content to register this fact, and Joerges puts his faith in the capacity of lawyers to learn by experience in combining and balancing theoretical lessons, Teubner is looking for new theory which can itself guide this selection process.

2.2. Constructing Legal Concepts

We move now to the second level on which a process of translation between economic and sociological models on the one hand, and legal models on the other, needs to be conducted: that of the construction of fundamental concepts. Here we may distinguish two dimensions: basic doctrinal concepts of contract and organisation; and concepts of legal rationality.

Basic legal concepts of contract and organisation cannot, according to Wiethölter, be formulated without at least an implicit recourse to "grand theory". For him, the formation of legal concepts is inevitably committed to fundamental issues of historical and social philosophy, in models of the social world. "Using them, ideas can be related to interests in such a way that by *comparison* (with other models, with past reality, with limits of possibility, with the present as a future past or as a past future) historical and social consciousness can be brought into "constitution" no less than can social reality and the legal forms that define it and are defined by it." Wiethölter makes a rough distinction between different grand theory approaches which can be found – as the foundation of different concepts of contract and organisation – throughout this book: politico-social (substantive) programmes that challenge the developmental quality of law (e.g. Trubek), functionalist (systems theory) programmes that judge concepts by reference to their social adequacy (e.g. Teubner) and methodological programmes that test for scientific rationality (e.g. Albert).

Trubek represents the first tradition. Critical legal studies – in his analysis – interpret legal concepts as embedded in a "defensible scheme of human association" (Unger, 1983:565), in a coherent view about the basic relations between persons and the nature of society. This school of thought focusses on the structure of legal ideas, seeking to identify the deep principles of meaning that lie behind them and to relate these principles to social action and order. At the same time it offers a critical perspective. It identifies the legal system in capitalist societies as reification, presenting as essential, necessary and objective what is contingent, arbitrary and subjective. Capitalist legal systems are identified as hegemonic, that is they serve to legitimate interests of the dominant class alone. In this perspective, any legal operation can be analysed in terms of being part of a total world-construction and criticised in terms of its failure to keep the promise of universality, equality and freedom.

In contrast to these claims of human emancipation, the critical standard of a functionalist system analysis is "social adequacy" of legal concepts. Basic legal concepts like contract and organisation are seen as the result of a connected evolution of law and other social subsystems. Concepts are socially adequate if they satisfactorily reconcile the internal requirements of legal consistency with the external social demands on the legal system. (Luhmann, 1974; 1981:388). This school of thought analyses the function of legal concepts and institutions in relation to various system references. Teubner's paper is an example since it analyses the function of co-determination through law on different system levels: interaction, organisation, social subsystems, society in general. The theory of functional differentiation serves as a background to interpret the meaning of legal institutions, illuminating, in the case of co-determination its role as a "counter-institution" to the prevailing principle of economic rationality.

Finally, a scientific reformulation of dogmatic concepts is the goal of methodological programmes like that developed by Albert. Albert proposes to give up natural law versions as well as hermeneutical interpretations of fundamental legal institutions – like contract and institution – and to define them as a set of incentive devices the effects of which can be studied by the social sciences. Thus, a pervasive socio-technical conception of law would fundamentally alter the normative meaning of legal concepts in the direction of an instrumentalist view of the social world.

While Wiethölter stresses the embedding of legal concepts in models of social order, Farjat demonstrates the remarkable resistance to change shown by legal concepts once accepted as part of the lawyer's toolkit. The fact that specific changes to French company and commercial law are today, as he shows, consistently inspired and shaped by economic concepts of the firm or enterprise, has not led in France – or for that matter elsewhere – to the displacement of the legal concept of the company or corporation by a new legal concept of the firm. Rather, the old concept continues to be used, albeit with adjustments and extensions which permit its use in a way responsive to the changing economic and social demands being made on law. There may come a point where these adaptations are so profound that the original concept becomes a mere fiction, and can be sloughed off to reveal the new, coherent, concept that lies beneath; but the point is unlikely to be quickly reached.

In the case of the firm, a further restraint on a change of concept is suggested by Farjat's point that the economist's concept of the firm depends heavily in its turn on the legal concept of artificial personality – legal autonomy is what economists regard as the surest criterion of the firm. We might, indeed, be tempted to generalise on this insight and to see legal concepts as basic building blocks at least for economic theory. Support for this idea can be found in the way some economists find it helpful to decompose the firm into a set of contracts (Fama, 1980, Alchian and Demsetz, 1972), thus drawing on one legal concept – contract – even as they attempt to dispense with another – incorporation. The reservations to and refinements of this approach suggested by Gotthold and Schanze leave untouched this legal foundation. Further reflection on the papers in this volume will show that this is not a one-way process, either as between contract and organisation or as between legal concepts and economic theory. Fields of law may be reconceptualised in the light of economic or social theory, and to understand contracts we may need to theorise from organisational concepts like hierarchical authority (Macneil 1980; Williamson 1979, cf. Daintith). It does, however, appear that were we to invert the general question of this volume, and to ask what contributions legal theory can make to economic and social analysis, we might light first on the utility of basic legal concepts as shorthand descriptions of key social and economic relationships. Here again, it is important to remember that the process is one of translation, not of simple transposition (Aubert 1983:98). While the lawyer needs complex concepts, capable of practical application in a wide variety of familiar and unfamiliar circumstances, the economist or social theorist is interested in the core properties of such concepts, or perhaps in one only of such properties.

However, the very fact that lawyers have to shape their concepts in situations of practical decision-making furnishes them with a specific link with social reality which makes them appealing to social scientists. There are only a few social scientists in the field of contract and organisation who explicitly use legal conceptualisations in building theory (Selznick, 1969; Coleman 1974, 1982:69; Vanberg 1982:105). They are all aware, however, of the specific potential legal analysis can offer to social science analysis. Since the law has to deal with the factually emerging problems of social organisation, since it has to offer models of conflict resolution and for human cooperation, one can expect that legal concepts reflect typical structural problems of social reality. The problem-oriented case approach of lawyers to life offers them specific aspects of social reality which are not open in the same way to the theorising or fact-gathering social scientist. In this sense legal concepts of contract have recently been used to enrich exchange theory in the social sciences (Lempert, 1966), the concept of the legal person has been exploited for theories of collective action (Coleman, 1974, 1982, 1985) and legal distinctions in company law have aided in designing a sociological theory of "resource pooling" (Vanberg, 1982).

The final dimension of socio-legal cooperation concerns *legal rationality* – a concept which has been developed to describe the unity of internal structures of law, its external legitimation and its social functions. Drawing on Max Weber's famous analysis of formal rationality (Weber 1978), it has been proposed elsewhere that we distinguish three types of legal rationality: formal, instrumental and reflexive rationality (Teubner, 1983, 1985). To give a brief definition: formal rationality of law refers to setting a legal framework for autonomous social and economic action; instrumental rationality refers to socio-technology through legal norms; reflexive rationality refers to legal facilitation of discursive communication. In this volume, one can find many references to legal rationality, some explicit, some only implicit.

A large part of the contributions to this volume deal with instrumental rationality of law. In one form or another, they more or less follow the socio-technological approach to law which is programmatically circumscribed by Albert. Law is analysed as a device of social guidance which can be instrumentalised by political action to reach political goals. This is true for the legal economics describing legal norms as incentives for economic action, as well as for politically oriented approaches to law stressing more strongly the aspect of political purposes and goal conflicts.

Some elements of reflexive rationality can be found in the contributions by Trubek, Joerges and Teubner. To different degrees they stress the role of legal norms in facilitating processes of social discourse. However, there are remarkable differences among them. Joerges and Teubner have as a common starting point the problems instrumental law encounters in its efforts to regulate social life. Teubner argues for a retreat to a position where the law does not intervene directly by means of substantive regulation of behaviour, but relies on indirect means of control, as an internal stimulation of organisational self-reflection. In this sense, the law regulating the decision processs of the large organisation, sets rules for social discourse processes in which interests of different actors are weighed. Joerges, in contrast, focusses on the "reflexive" potential of the legal decision-making process as such. Since the social sciences have only a limited capacity to guide regulatory law, lawyers look to different sources of information. In this process a social co-operation emerges which Joerges calls "practice as a discovery process". The pressing legal and political problem becomes to organise this discovery process in such a way that claims to rationality can be fulfilled. In Trubek's analysis, a fundamental critique of legal concepts is supposed to set free the emancipatory potential of "reflection and a valid source of knowledge". Critical legal studies assume "that if the contradictions are uncovered, the "incoherences" demonstrated and the denied material brought to light, then the society can be transformed."

Finally, in a different fashion, the concept of reflexive rationality is elaborated by Wiethölter who opts for "legal reflection" in a context of theory of science, sociology of knowledge and history of science: "This reference triangle is mutually related: the social theory question of social action, taking into account the subject and object positions of (not solely academic) actors who all at the same time have their histories; the question from the theory of science as to the preconditions and effects of this work of discovery and interpretation, codetermined by both history and society; and the question from historical theory as to the possible meaning, possible goals, possible progress of social and scholarly action".

Bibliography

Alchian, Armon and Harold Demsetz (1972) "Production, Information Costs and Economic Information", 62, (I) *The American Economic Review* 777.

Aubert, Vilhelm (1983) *In Search of Law. Sociological Approaches to Law.* Oxford: Robertson.

Coleman, James (1974) *Power and the Structure of Society.* New York: W. W. Norton.

– (1982) *The Asymmetric Society.* Syracuse: Syracuse University Press.

– (1985) "Responsibility in Corporate Action: A Sociologist's View", in K. Hopt and G. Teubner (eds.), *Corporate Governance and Directors' Liabilities.* Berlin: De Gruyter.

Fama, Eugene E. (1980) "Agency Problems and the Theory of the Firm", 88 *Journal of Political Economy* 288.

Friedman, Milton (1953) "The Methodology of Positive Economics", in *Essays in Positive Economics* 3. Chicago: University of Chicago Press.

Furubotn, Eirik G. (1981) "Co-determination and the Efficient Partitioning of Ownership Rights in the Firm", 137 *Zeitschrift für die Gesamte Staatswissenschaft* 707.

Habermas, Jürgen (1976) *Zur Rekonstruktion des historischen Materialismus.* Frankfurt: Suhrkamp.

HEJL, PETER (1982a) *Sozialwissenschaft als Theorie selbstreferentieller Systeme.* Frankfurt: Campus.

HOFFMANN-RIEM, WOLFGANG (1977) "Rechtswissenschaft als Rechtsanwendungswissenschaft", in W. Hoffmann-Riem (ed.), *Sozialwissenschaften im Studium des Rechts.* Vol. II Verfassungs- und Verwaltungsrecht. München: Beck.

HOPT, KLAUS (1975) "Was ist von den Sozialwissenschaften für die Rechtsanwendung zu erwarten?", 11/12 *Juristenzeitung* 342.

KRAWIETZ, WERNER (1978) *Juristische Entscheidung und wissenschaftliche Erkenntnis. Eine Untersuchung zum Verhältnis von dogmatischer Rechtswissenschaft und rechtswissenschaftlicher Grundlagenforschung.* Wien, New York: Springer.

LUHMANN, NIKLAS (1974) *Rechtssystem und Rechtsdogmatik.* Stuttgart: Kohlhammer.

– (1981) *Politische Theorie im Wohlfahrtsstaat.* München: Olzog.

MACNEIL, IAN R. (1980) *The New Social Contract.* New Haven, London: Yale University Press.

MOESCHEL, WERNHARD (1975) *Rechtsordnung zwischen Plan und Markt.* Tübingen: Mohr.

MÜLLER, FRIEDRICH (1966) *Normstruktur und Normativität: Zum Verhältnis von Recht und Wirklichkeit in der juristischen Hermeneutik, entwickelt an Fragen der Verfassungsinterpretation.* Berlin: Duncker und Humblot.

POSNER, RICHARD (1977) *The Economic Analysis of Law* 2nd. ed. Boston: Little Brown and Co.

REICH, NORBERT (1977) *Markt und Recht. Theorie und Praxis des Wirtschaftsrechts in der Bundesrepublik Deutschland.* Neuwied: Luchterhand.

ROTTLEUTHNER, HUBERT (1979) "Zur Methode einer folgenorientierten Rechtsanwendung" 97 *Archiv für Rechts- und Sozialphilosophie* 118.

SCHMID, A. ALLAN (1978) *Property, Power and Public Choice. An Inquiry into Law and Economics.* New York: Praeger.

SELZNICK, PHILIP (1968) "The Sociology of Law", 9 *International Encyclopedia of the Social Sciences* 50.

– (1969) *Law, Society and Industrial Justice.* New York: Russell Sage.

STACHOWIAK, HERBERT (1973) *Allgemeine Modelltheorie.* Wien, New York: Springer.

TEUBNER, GUNTHER (1983) "Substantive and Reflexive Elements in Modern Law", 17 *Law and Society Review* 239.

– (1985) "After Legal Instrumentalism? Strategic Models of Post-Regulatory Law", in G. Teubner (ed.) *Dilemmas of Law in the Welfare State.* Berlin, New York: De Gruyter.

UNGER, ROBERTO (1983) "The Critical Legal Studies Movement", 96 *Harvard Law Review* 561.

VANBERG, VIKTOR (1982) *Markt und Organisation. Individualistische Sozialtheorie und das Problem korporativen Handels.* Tübingen: Mohr, Siebeck.

WEBER, MAX (1978) *Economy and Society.* Berkeley: University Press.

WILLIAMSON, OLIVER E. (1979) "Transaction-Cost Economics: The Governance of Contractual Relations", 22 *Journal of Law and Economics* 233.

II.
General Framework

Law as an Instrument of Rational Practice

HANS ALBERT*
Mannheim

1. Knowledge and the Problem of Social Norms

The course of social life is partly determined by a large number of norms of the most diverse nature, some of them usually classed as morals, others as law and others again as neither of these two types. It is difficult to make any plausible universally binding demarcation between these types of rule depending on content. In the various social formations that have arisen in human history very heterogeneous rules have been sanctioned in a similar manner. It is therefore perhaps more appropriate to start from the formation and application of these types of rule, and to call them law only where they meet certain minimum requirements such as the existence of secondary rules that regulate the identification, modification and adjudication of the various primary rules in a society (Hart, 1961:89). A contemporary legal system further presupposes the application of further secondary rules thereby ensuring that the possibility of private sanctions through the use of force is largely prohibited and replaced by official sanctions imposed and executed through more or less centralized social mechanisms (Hart, 1961:95; Geiger, 1947:108). The norms of the morals prevailing in a society or in one of its areas are by contrast customarily sanctioned in another manner – through "moral pressure" – although they may contain commandments or prohibitions which are regarded as extremely important – unless their content overlaps with that of the legal norms in force. On the basis of this concept formation, it immediately becomes clear that there may be quite different stages and forms of the formation of such types of rule, so that an analysis of specific societies necessitates a study of their peculiar structure and mode of function – and therefore, also of their importance for the course of social processes: their specific *control effects.* We shall return to this later.

To begin with, however, a few remarks on the kind of knowledge that can be expected about the problems arising here are perhaps appropriate. The theory of law and morality seems to show a certain similarity with the theory of knowledge and the theory of science. Like these it has evidently to deal with an area of socio-cultural *facts* that is difficult to delimit in detail and to clarify particular

* Translated from the German by Iain Fraser.

factual connections between them. On the other hand, one mostly expects *normative* findings from it, whose correctness is not dependent upon the mere factual validity of particular norms. The same is also true of the theory of politics, whose connection with the theory of law and morals is now indisputable, even if modern political science seems partly to have lost sight of it. If one has decided to distinguish the law actually in force, the prevailing morality and the actual politics – that is, real practice in the areas concerned – from what is acceptable from certain value viewpoints[1], then the question arises what contribution science – or knowledge at all – can make towards solving the problems concerned – whether they are normative or factual.

For anyone starting from the perspective of the justificatory thinking of classical rationalism, the question that science – the theory of law, morals and politics – has primarily to answer is the question of the justification of the norms concerned. This is a question of the *foundation of law, morals and politics,* just as the theory of knowledge has to answer the question of the foundation of knowledge, and in particular of science. But just as in the area of knowledge not every view can be taken as justified and therefore acceptable, thus, in relation to norms in the legal and moral sphere and to political measures, a distinction must be drawn in this respect. Here one would then have to distinguish between *justified* and therefore *legitimate* regulations and decisions, and those to which this characteristic cannot be ascribed. Whoever proceeds in this manner will not in general arrive at the conclusion that all actually existing norms and all decisions arrived at are also legitimate. At least he will therefore not reject in principle the possibility of a criticism of norms and on its basis, a criticism of political measures, as is the case in particular versions of legal and moral positivism.

This view of things can however only be immediately assumed if one approves the classical view of rationality, which has proved to be untenable. If instead one accepts the version sketched out above of critical rationalism and its interpretation of the cognitive practice, then, *in the first place* a *possible scientific* task, arising out of *specification of the programme of theoretical explanation* on the basis of laws follows. Anyone on the lookout for this kind of science – or for corresponding academic disciplines – must confront the fact that there is an abundance of investigations in legal sociology, moral sociology and political science studies that apparently belong to this species, so that one need not regard it as endangered. But much of the work in this area, on closer observation, is purely descriptive analysis of value attitudes and other facts that are in some kind of relationship to the norms mentioned. Analyses of this kind can hardly meet the requirements of the programme mentioned. They are *ad-hoc* studies of some questions or other that happen to occur to sociologists when they come to consider the theme of norms. Representatives of jurisprudence or other people interested in the systematic treatment of such questions not infrequently thereby gain the impression of being confronted with peripheral problems or – as also

[1] This distinction is one of the requirements of analytical jurisprudence which, in this respect, can hardly be refuted. See Hart (1971).

happens – with conceptual or classificatory studies that may deal with central categories but are essentially to be considered as preliminary studies. And this impression may be justified. I feel, in any case, that it is at least questionable to attribute this evaluation only to the normative approach of those concerned. Rather it is the case that the goal of explaining central facts has been relegated to the background in many of these studies.

Going back a little in history, we come to a sociophilosophical tradition within which the naturalistic analysis of law, morals and politics – detached from the Aristotelian-type cosmological metaphysics that previously prevailed in Western thought – was carried on in quite the sense of the programme mentioned above: namely, Scottish moral philosophy[2]. The representatives of this tradition searched for the natural bases of the phenomena concerned, and for the laws to which they are subject. In this way they endeavoured to include the sphere of human and therefore also social life in the programme of discovery of the theoretical empirical sciences. This does not mean that they neglected the normative side of the problems, but only that their naturalistic and empiricist approach induced them to include in their philosophical discussions contributions to a nomologically explanatory treatment of the problems. Above all, there emerged from this tradition a social science that arrived at a relatively highly developed theory – or better, a theoretical tradition – in which the idea of explanation uses in the natural sciences is transferred to the area of society: political economy. Here I cannot go further into the development of that discipline. What is most important for our purposes is the fact that it deals with a central range of problems for the understanding of the articulation of society, even if it only partly does so with regard to special phenomena, so that its general importance is difficult to discern: *the problem of social control.* What is more, it is approached in a theoretical manner, with laws being adduced[3].

However one might wish to characterise in detail the facts denoted by the terms law, morals and politics and delimit them from each other, anyone seeking to analyse them from the viewpoint of an explanatory science of social life will be well advised to seek to arrange them within the framework of the general range of problems of social control. This however means treating them in the manner customary in the tradition of political economy. This is by no means to be taken as assuming that the peculiarities of content and method of that tradition are still

[2] It is above all Friedrich August v. Hayek that we have to thank for penetrating references to the importance of Scottish moral philosophy for the analysis of social phenomena, along with some studies that lead further; on this cf. his essays on David Hume and Bernard Mandeville in his essay volume (1969), and also his work: *Die Verfassung der Freiheit* (1971).

[3] Ludwig v. Mises is therefore in my opinion quite right to assert that "it was only with the construction of political economy, which was a work of the 18th century, that the scattered pieces of sociological knowledge" became a *science,* and to see in it a general sociological approach that can be set against the usual type of sociology, even though the methodological apriorism that he represents is extremely disputable. Cf. v. Mises (1933:1). The behavioural approach in sociological thought is today operating quite along the lines of the economic tradition; on this cf. Homans (1961).

acceptable even in detail. Nor is it asserted that, theoretical tradition has so far brought into view all phenomena that can be approached in this way, nor that there are no alternatives to its attempts at explanation which might also be considered. It is intended merely to point out that the research programme of economics – by contrast with facile popular interpretations of the discipline – can appropriately be interpreted in a way that permits the phenomena of social control to be taken up theoretically, while in moral analysis, jurisprudence and older political theory they are normally treated from normative or hermeneutic viewpoints[4].

In such explanatory attempts the *specific norms* that are effective in the control of social life appear as *historically variable and culturally diverse facts* which are embedded in social operational structures. Actual morals and law in force depend, like politics, on all sorts of conditions of a natural and social character that have changed throughout history. This does not however mean that very general conditions of human existence expressed in universally encountered features of such regulations may not exist. The variable *norms* of social life *cannot* themselves be taken as laws in the sense of empirical science. They belong rather to the facts that must be taken into account for the *explanation* of social control processes, the *emergence and development* of which is itself to be *explained*. Since in the tradition of individualist sociology that reached its first culmination in classical economics all social phenomena are explained from the interplay of individual actions under certain conditions, the laws adduced in such explanations must be sought primarily in the area of modes of behaviour[5].

Norms come into question and must be explained to the extent that they take effect in individual behaviour and thereby play a part in determining the course of social processes. Their emergence and development is to be explained from the interplay of individual modes of behaviour. They come into consideration because of their *factual* validity, and *this* must be explained. In place of the *justification of normative validity*, which dominated in classical sociophilosophical thought, modern factual science must therefore find the *explanation of factual validity* and the *explanation of factual social control processes*, taking into account the *factual validity* of norms. Of course, this shift in the problem can scarcely satisfy the interest underlying the normative line of enquiry.

[4] This interpretation is, to be sure, *open* at one essential point to modes of procedure that depart from the normal explanatory practice of modern economics. Specifically, in my view a revision of the usual behavioural assumptions to take account of the results of psychological research should be considered.

[5] Naturally, all possible laws may be considered as aids that contribute to determining the structure of the various situations of action, by determining properties of the locations of the actions and the course of natural processes, even in technical aggregates. On the methodological problems of such explanations, cf. Lindenberg (1977:46).

2. The Nature of Jurisprudence: Dogmatics and the Problem of Social Embodiment

Jurisprudence as the science of the law in force seems at first sight to have scarcely any relationship with the problem of explaining factual validity, and therefore, with the programme of a theoretical science of the type outlined above. It stems from a different tradition that has developed in close relationship with legal practice and is defined above all by an interest in serving that practice directly, and not by an interest in theoretically based explanations. The character of legal science seems to be in complete and striking contrast with the research programme of the modern empirical sciences, guided as they are by the interest in explanation. One cannot therefore ignore the question of whether what we have to do with here is not a quite differently constituted form of knowledge, whose methodological peculiarities follow freely from the mode of its practical orientation. Here even the criticism inherent in modern thought seems to come up against a limit, since, as the leading representatives of this science stress, the core discipline of the field, systematic jurisprudence, is a *dogmatic* science of *normative* character, in relation to which one usually simply speaks of "dogmatics", so that the comparison with theology automatically imposes itself[6].

It has for long been noted that there are close connections and structural similarities between religion and law and between theology and jurisprudence[7]. One of the essential common factors between the theological and the legal mode of thought lies, I feel, in the fact that both offer a revelational model of knowledge, whereby the truth can be taken from pronouncements of bodies equipped with indubitable authority for the solution of the problems concerned. A consequence of this is that essentially only two types of problem can arise within this mode of thought: problems of *identification* of the relevant pronouncements and problems of their appropriate *interpretation*. In the first case the point is to select the valid sources, the "canons"; in the second, to interpret them validly, so that in both cases it is validity issues that arise, and moreover,

[6] Even such a defender of analytical jurisprudence and critic of natural law as Norberto Bobbio speaks of an *authority principle* "peculiar to jurisprudence and to theology", so that what one is concerned with here is a dogmatics that deals with a duty; cf. Bobbio (1965:102). And Julius Kraft, a philosopher of the Fries-Nelson branch of Kantianism says, with a critical stress, that jurisprudence is *de facto* a "part of theology", since it contains "the system of legal truths, true" because they are "proclaimed by a subject having internally derived or externally conferred autority". Its truth would then be "a truth of faith". It contains, he goes on, an "implicit belief in revelation", reducible "to the explicit system of belief in revelation, i.e. to theology", while theology can "recognise jurisprudence too only as its daughter discipline". This connection may, he continues, "be concealed, but not removed, by efforts at the definitional and organizational independence of jurisprudence", and would always remain "decisive for the basic nature of any form of jurisprudence"; Kraft (1957:50).

[7] Cf. e.g. Kelsen (1964:29); Schmitt (1934:49), where Kelsen is assigned the merit of "having pointed to the methodological relationship between theology and jurisprudence".

with solutions that tend to have a direct relationship with practice, since the content of the pronouncements concerned has a normative character[8].

Accordingly, with respect to style of thought, typical problem situations and probably also certain typical difficulties, there seems to be a not inconsiderable parallelism between the two disciplines. The mere fact that an authoritative entity has made particular pronouncements is recoined into a claim to unconditional universal recognition of their content and therby a simultaneous categorical requirement to follow them. That this entity is entitled to make such demands seems however to be an assumption that can merely be believed. Consequently, one can hardly avoid the conclusion that those concerned are evidently in both cases expected to show a faithful obedience that never arises in the normal interpretation of the practice of discovery in other sciences.

Certainly, the situation appears in a rather different light if actual interpretive practice in the two disciplines is looked at. In both cases there are obviously many ways the experts can go about solving the above-mentioned problems. Not only are there sometimes difficulties in identifying the authoritative pronouncements of the respective authorities, but furthermore it is frequently not immediately possible to define a particular interpretation as appropriate. This opens up room to manoeuvre for those role-bearers who have a monopoly of interpretation and identification for the "revelations" concerned. In this context it is a not an unimportant fact that the entity that allegedly stands behind them may on closer investigation prove to be fictitious[9]. Thus, the "dogmas" that these experts have to start from in their mediatory activity may to a not inconsiderable extent in each case be taken as their own product. To that extent, the comprehension and transmission of dogmatically alleged pronouncements of others is replaced by the voicing of dogmas created by themselves. While this may contribute to the flexibility and adaptability of the modes of thought concerned and the institutions connected with them, it not infrequently led on the other hand to grave doubts as to the legitimacy of this style of thought.[10] For the authority of the theological and legal experts is barely sufficient if it is no longer supported by a corresponding belief in revelation, or is not able to find any other form of legitimation.

It looks at any rate as if the dogmatic, normative structure habitually ascribed to legal thought even by critical representatives of the discipline can scarcely be changed. It seems to be connected with the requirements placed on practical

[8] For the religious area this is true at least to the extent that ethical references arise in it.

[9] Thus, the supra-individual will of the state alleged to lie behind legislation has proved to be a fiction. Carl Olivercrona takes this as a starting point for revising the so-called imperative theory and defining a concept of a "freestanding imperative", under which even the laws can be subsumed; on this cf. Olivercrona (1942:27 and 1940). In theology there would seem to be a wish to make God, something even theologians today seem to find difficulties believing in, partly *per definitionem* into a "freestanding interrogative": "God, then, means", as for instance Herbert Braun puts it, "the whence of my unease"; cf. Braun (1971:341).

[10] On this cf. e.g. Buchanan (1975:105); also v. Hayek's criticism of legal positivism in his own work (1976:44).

lawyers[11]. It is from them that the representatives of jurisprudence must evidently start if they are to convey to aspiring lawyers the knowledge they will later have to apply in their legal practice. Jurisprudence would then appear from its very origin to be a strongly practice-oriented science, and a theory of science oriented to the attainment of pure knowledge would scarcely be of interest to it. Looking at the teaching practice in law faculties, one's first impression is that the one thing of supreme importance for the aspiring practitioner is to learn *to use* particular *texts* – texts of laws, commentaries, collections of court decisions – so that with their help they can reach practical *decisions* that accord with *valid law*. The link to valid law seems to predetermine the simultaneously *dogmatic and normative* and – at least to the extent that it must be based on texts – *hermeneutic* character of this cognitive practice. Already the *cognitive interest* that underlies it would seem to distinguish jurisprudence from the empirical sciences, defined through a programme of theoretical explanation. When efforts are nonetheless made to subject this discipline to the ideal of the scientific method or to a revision of its image of itself in that direction, these are always customarily rejected by pointing out that they fundamentally misapprehend the true character of this science[12].

It is nevertheless by no means the case that the representatives of jurisprudence are agreed on the interpretation of their cognitive practice and in the rejection of such revisionist endeavours or that there is any consensus on their position regarding natural law and its importance for positive law and the legal science that deals with it. There are, rather, among its representatives very divergent views on the nature of this discipline.

One can still find natural-law positions in which positive law is seen as constituted and bound by a normative reality of an absolute nature, a kind of higher law (Verdross, 1966:307; Auer, 1966:463), a reality that is discernible and independent of human institutions, but binding upon them.

The idea of such as reality is of fundamental meaning only within a sociomorphic cosmology (Kelsen, 1964; Topitsch, 1958) – within which it did in fact arise – i.e., a view in which the total context of nature, including the human world that is embedded in it, is interpreted as a meaningful whole established by divine powers. These powers are then to be regarded as the source of those absolutely binding norms that on this view permeate reality and that the positive law of human communities also has to follow. If the existence of such norm-creating powers is not assumed, then there is no basis at all for the normative interpretation of reality characteristic of natural law[13]. This law has, from its origin, a

[11] On this cf. Ballweg (1972:45): "In legal dogmatics, what we have is an opinion structure placed beyond question, to bring about decidability in the area of legal evaluation". In this connection it is a matter of "obligation to justify", "obligatory interpretation" and "obligatory decision", but a cognitive function is explicitly denied (p. 46).

[12] On this cf. in particular: Kantorowicz (1962a:101) and v. Savigny (1972:97) and Albert (1972:109).

[13] This is not to deny that this view may have certain advantages from practical standpoints; on this cf. De Jouvenel (1972:237); but the crisis of faith leads to its undermining, so that even these advantages disappear; cf. de Jouvenel (1972:250).

sacred character, and its use to legitimate positive law must lead to the *sacralisation* of the latter, as did in fact happen (Arndt, 1966:116). The possibility of such a legitimation effect follows from the origin of these supra-positive norms. The problem of legal cognition consists then, in simply identifying the revelations of the norm-creating entities, appropriately interpreting them and suitably applying them. Accordingly, in jusnaturalist thought, it is still the *unity of theology and jurisprudence* and not their mere *structural similarity* that is presented[14].

In this form, the jusnaturalist view is a version of the absolute justificatory thinking that today we may consider as outmoded. It is, moreover, a version which is burdened with the hybrid concept of a normative reality and the complementary concept of a normative cognition. These concepts do little more than disguise the fact that in this thinking there is an ultimate recourse to the simple factual existence of a norm-setting entity, to a kind of *metaphysical fact* which may perhaps be outside normal cognition, but does not thereby become immune to the question of its legitimation. The jusnaturalist critics of legal positivism too often forget that their constructions are exposed to criticism at the same point, since they themselves tend to criticise a particular version of positivism, namely that in which a *fact* – such as the efficacy of a legal system – is equipped with *validity in the normative sense*[15]. Even on the plane of theology and metaphysics, concluding the normative validity of an established norm from its actual existence must remain a fallacy.

The regression to natural law is therefore incapable in principle of remedying the deficiency that the positivist view is accused of here. Furthermore, the sociomorphic cosmology without which this kind of jusnaturalist thinking becomes meaningless, is incompatible with a world-view that fits in with modern scientific knowledge. A further objection to this kind of thinking can follow from this[16]. The view that today legal science again needs this supra-positive variant of dogmatic thinking[17] seems to me to rest on a misunderstanding of the fundamental objections to it, which arise from the influence of an evaluation stemming from a disputable account of historical circumstances[18].

[14] It is therefore not surprising that the mode of thought that prevails here has a simultaneously dogmatic, normative and hermeneutic character, since the point is after all to understand the normative content of dogmatically alleged revelations. In this connection Hans Dombois's statement is also understandable, to the effect that "the structure of the problem of law essentially coincides with the structure of the theology of revelation", cf. Dombois (1966:456).

[15] Alf Ross subjected this version of positivism as quasi-positivism of a jusnaturalist character to criticism, on the example of Kelsen's "basic norm"; cf. Ross (1961:IV, 46 and 78). The same example is, interestingly enough, used by a representative of natural law to disclose the "Achilles heel of modern positivism" in order to draw therefrom positive consequences for natural law; cf. d'Entreves (1951:106).

[16] Namely, if one is prepared to let advances in knowledge enrich the shaping of one's own world-view and therefore also one's criticism of traditional concepts of the world; something that, to be sure, can by no means be taken as "necessary".

[17] For a criticism of an attempt to show that legal positivism is "logically contradictory", cf. Hoerster (1970:43).

[18] For a criticism cf. Arndt (1966) and Knoll (1962).

The *sacralisation* of the law need have nothing to do with its *humanisation*. That this criticism does not apply to all forms of legal thinking that use the language of natural law scarcely needs emphasising[19].

Anyone who abandons the jusnaturalist position has the possibility of treating *positive law* as a human *cultural achievement*, more specifically as a phenomenon from the area of *social control*, the control of the conduct, towards each other, by the members of society. This area, as already suggested above, also includes the phenomena of ethics and morals. The phenomenon in question, and here there seem to be essentially no differences of opinion, generally involves the use of very specific types of norms in modern complex societies by specifically qualified role-bearers – judges, lawyers and administrative officials – for interpreting particular situations, and to a large extent these rules may be found in official texts[20]. It is these texts that form the basis of what is taught in the core discipline of legal science, so-called "dogmatic" jurisprudence.

This view, however, by no means leads to an unambiguous definition of the nature of the discipline. Instead, one can distinguish at least two major trends in legal thinking, which arrive at differing interpretations: a *realistic, sociological* one and a *normative, analytical* one. According to the former, jurisprudence as an *empirical* science deals with *social facts*. The latter, instead, holds that it can be treated only as a *normative* science, which aims at discovering social rules[21]. Here an attempt is evidently made to abstract from both jusnaturalist and sociological viewpoints and to define positive law as an *autonomous cosmos of valid norms*, which is to be *cognitively grasped* by a pure jurisprudence of a non-empirical nature.

This view of things indubitably suits the practice-oriented self-conception of the normal lawyer, as that practice largely consists in using such norms to deduce or to legitimise decisions. It also suits the basic orientation of both analytical and hermeneutical thinking, since the norms to be applied must in each case be elicited through interpreting relevant texts. Therefore the *methodology* of pure jurisprudence seems to be better equipped and to have recourse to the *analytical* or hermeneutical *procedures* stressed in those philosophical tendencies than to the methods of the theoretical empirical sciences. The normativists' argumentation sounds most plausible against realism, characteristically, when it, for instance, refers to the activity of the judge, who cannot after all base his decisions solely on descriptions and explanations of social facts, but must always here have recourse to normative rules to justify them[22]. Were jurisprudence to confine itself to predicting the behaviour of judges, as some versions of realism seem to suggest, then obviously the judge himself in his decision-making could find no use for it, since what he wants is not to predict his own behaviour but to reach a practical decision.

[19] It does not, for instance, apply to v. Hayek's preferred interpretation, which as far as I can see shows none of the above-mentioned shortcomings; cf. v. Hayek (1976:59).

[20] At least that is the way the present situation, which is our primary interest here, looks.

[21] For the first view cf. for instance, Ross (1958); for the second, cf. Kantorowicz (1962b:38) and Kelsen (1954:133).

[22] On this cf. Kantorowicz's arguments against American realism (1962a:110).

Starting with such arguments, one can, certainly, also question the starting-point of normativism in the lawyer's self-conception. For it is by no means obvious that jurisprudence as a science can, without elaboration, identify itself with the judge in a decision-making situation. Its pronouncements *about* law can in the first place, be distinguished from the norms of law and the texts that contain them – the propositional systems of legal documents (Ross, 1958:9). If the rules of positive law themselves have a normative character, this need in no way also apply to the statements of jurisprudence about these rules.

If one puts this distinction into effect, then, instead it is the remarkable idea of a *cognitive* understanding of norms which is supposed to be reflected in *normative* pronouncement that disappears. What is hardly disputed is that statements of legal parlance to a large extent have a normative character. The application of *these* statements to legally relevant situations by the judge or other role-bearers leads to decisions with corresponding social effects. By contrast, the statements of jurisprudence *refer to* statements of the first kind and the rules formulated in them. They need not therefore have this character.

One can of course treat these rules *as if* one were dealing with that autonomous cosmos of valid norms the existence of which the normativist, analytical view believes it can take as a starting-point. But this fiction disappears when the question is asked what is meant by "validity" here and what space-time region this validity refers to. For it immediately becomes clear that in some way account must be taken of the social anchorings and the effectiveness of those norms[23]. The question of the existence of such a system of norms – of positive law, or of positive morals – cannot be decided without reference to social facts. If, however, one does not condescend to consider this question, than one can no longer find any essential difference between the positive law in force in a particular area – a specific region of space-time – and an imaginary system of rules of a similar type[24]. A pure jurisprudence that abstracted from social facts to such an extent would thus degenerate into formalism.

3. The Nature of Jurisprudence: The Social Technology Conception

Knowing the valid norms of positive law – indubitably an essential element of knowledge in legal science – is as we have seen of great importance also for the analysis of social reality, precisely because these norms are to a certain extent

[23] Even H. L. A. Hart, who in his analysis mainly stresses the *internal* aspect of legal rules – their pretension to be followed by those to whom they are addressed – is nevertheless forced, in order to answer the question of the *identification* of the legal system valid in a particular area, to an actually *recognised* rule (rule of recognition); cf. Hart (1961:97). This rule corresponds in many respects to Kelsen's basic norm, but the problem of its existence is in each case a question of fact; cf. Hart (1961:245); cf. also the review by Ross (1962:1185).

[24] The view by v. Hayek also seems to me to be a version of realism to the extent that the primary point in jurisprudence is for him to identify the legal rules that have been handed down, i.e., to solve a cognitive problem. A further problem is then to test the system of these rules for consistency and appropriately modify, supplement and thereby develop it; cf. v. Hayek (1976:15 and 38).

effective and therefore must be adduced in *explaining social phenomena.* The issues of *social control* and of the *mode of functioning of the control mechanisms* that help to determine the course of social life cannot be understood without taking the norms that are actually effective into account.

The starting-point for dealing with these problems may be the theoretical idea that the cognitive and normative convictions of the people engaged in action have, along with motivational factors, constitutive importance for their opinion-forming process and therefore for their decisions and the establishment of their behavioural habits[25]. *Inter alia,* they lead in each case to a specific mode of perceiving a situation and – within its framework – to expectations, including those as to the conduct of others, which should be regarded as relevant to decision-making. It is obvious that norms regarded as valid in this connection – including those of positive law – may play an important part, as constituents of not only normative but also cognitive components of the belief systems concerned. For the assumption that other people follow such norms plays a part in determining the range of expectations of the person whose behaviour is in any particular case to be explained. Thus, knowing the norms effective in society becomes relevant to explaining social processes[26]. This knowledge is utilised in constructing the applicability conditions of the descriptive laws in question.

Assume, for instance, that a particular judicial decision is to be explained. Here even the identification of this behaviour as a meaningful action is an act of understanding that presupposes a certain legal knowledge. And the explanation cannot of course ignore its meaningful character. But this does not mean that the norms concerned are the only causally relevant factors. On the contrary, an explanation is required of how far the person concerned has been guided specifically by them and specifically in such and such a way, i.e. of how far they are relevant to control. This may lead back to very complex interconnected phenomena in which motivational and situational factors also play a part, so that it may be extremely difficult to throw theoretical light on them. The individualistic tradition of sociology embodied in economic thinking will, precisely in respect of such problems, be dependent on relevant findings of psychological research. To solve them, one must evidently have nomologically grasped the structure of a partially norm-governed piece of behaviour.

It can therefore be seen how important the reconstruction of the beliefs of the persons is in explaining actual behaviour. This applies not only to the judge whose verdict is to be explained, but also, for instance, to the entrepreneur, whose decisions have to take account of valid legal rules. The reconstruction will

[25] Max Weber's works already contain approaches in this direction; cf., for instance, the relevant passages of his article (1951:322), where his conception of the "understanding explanation" is particularly convincingly exemplified. On the problem of the possibility of explaining human action – or more meaningfully, the understanding of accessible modes of behaviour – on a theoretical basis.

[26] Knowing them gives starting-points for the reconstruction of the cognitive systems of persons engaged in action. By "understanding" Weber generally seems to have meant such acts of reconstruction. His solution of the problem of explanation on this basis is, however, probably insufficient in detail.

utilise knowledge about the valid norm system – positive law or positive morals. In most cases indeed one will *de facto* even have to be content with an explanation sketch in which the *interpretation* of the situation in each case, using the norm system, by the *explainer* must take the place of an *explicit description* of the circumstances in accordance with the *usual explanatory scheme*. It is therefore quite understandable that the idea could arise that one could do entirely without an explanation, because the whole circumstances were adequately comprehensible through understanding, and that it was further believed that this understanding could be seen in the sense of hermeneutics, although this discipline can only count as a technology of the interpretation of texts[27]. Under certain normal conditions, the application of the relevant interpretive scheme on the basis of the use of relevant texts – e.g. the laws, commentaries and collections of decisions – is to some extent a usable surrogate for an adequate explanation, so that text interpretation is the essential heuristic means of such a substitute solution of the problem of explanation. This can very easily lead to the fallacious view that legal sociology, as well as so-called dogmatic jurisprudence, are basically hermeneutic disciplines, since both essentially deal with the interpretation of texts in order to deduce adequate decisions. But *de facto* in legal sociology – and in theoretical social science in general – the point is to analyse phenomena in which the law is a partially constitutive element. Text interpretation is only an aid within this explanatory process, so as to reconstruct the context of the problem-solving behaviour of the individuals involved. Anyone who can bring himself to regard valid law as a constituent of the "objective spirit" can thus find a hint of how that spirit influences what actually happens: by helping to structure the problem situation of people engaged in action. That a science of social control is dependent on text interpretation, among other things for the reconstruction of the institutional arrangements relevant to the social course of things is obvious to me[28].

Let us now come back again now to the core discipline of legal science, the so-called "dogmatic jurisprudence", to clear up the question of whether this discipline cannot in fact have an essential relationship to the cognitive practice of the empirical sciences. We have seen that the thesis of the normative character of the discipline, taken for granted by many, is problematic even though the normative character of legal language – or at least of the texts written in it – is not disputed. It is, as we saw, not directly possible to deduce from the character of such language the character of jurisprudence, which speaks *about* statements made in that language, and about their *meaning*, that is, the *norms* expressed in them. To the extent that that is the case, jurisprudence would at first appear to be, while not a normative, at least a hermeneutic discipline, and as far as the term "dogmatic" is concerned, the justification for it is not entirely clear[29].

[27] Not only Dilthey but earlier even Schleiermacher came close to this view. It can in no way be regarded as outdated by the universal hermeneutics of more recent date.

[28] Theoretical economics will therefore presumably have to deal more than hitherto with such questions in the context of the "institutionalist revolution" that is at present taking place.

[29] In Kantorowicz it evidently results from his calling the rules it analyses "dogmas"; cf.

But the interpretive procedures practised in it are evidently intended to reconstruct "valid law". If one understands by this, as is generally the case, that the legal system is actually valid and therefore is also effective in a particular space-time region, then what is being talked about is presumably facts of social reality[30]. Accordingly the interpretive hypotheses for the legal texts in question would again be mere aids in formulating normal hypotheses about social facts – specifically abut particular control phenomena – in particular socio-culturally delimitable space-time regions. This would bring us to that realistic, sociological view of jurisprudence so long rejected by the normativists as inadequate because it makes the discipline unusable in legal practice. But it is hard to see what there is to say against this view if it is put forward in a way that seeks to do justice to the normative character of legal texts.

Be that as it may, difficulties seem to arise from the fact that the relevant texts leave a more or less wide margin for interpretation, and that furthermore the idea that the legal system is a complete system has proved to be untenable. It is therefore evidently necessary to supplement the valid norm system by appropriate interpretive practices. To begin with, this means merely that it is not so simple to find the actually valid legal system as might have been assumed (Hart, 1971:29). But that is no reason to abandon the realistic viewpoint. It is certainly understandable that a jurisprudence that wishes to give guidance and assistance to legal practice should seek at this point to bring normative positions into play. For here the question arises of "how the laws *ought* to be interpreted and their lacunae filled"[31], and how the regulation of the social relationships concerned is to be *adequate* in the sense of valid law. In practice answering this question often leads to the procedure known as "judicial law-making". This would seem to play a part in each case in creating the legal system, so that simply finding the valid system would not seem to be much help in solving the problem arising here. Were one to immediately seek to leave that solution to legal practice, then obviously jurisprudence as a science would, on a very important point, have scarcely anything to offer practice. Does one then have to abandon the realist view and go over to normativism if one is to give jurisprudence the task of not only *establishing* what the valid legal system is, but also helping to *shape* it through adequate proposals?

Interestingly in this connection the representatives of normativism tend to bring into play the *teleological* viewpoint, by pointing to the purposes by which the interpretive suggestions of jurisprudence ought to be guided (Bobbio, 1965). Irrespective of whether it is believed that such *purpose or value viewpoints* can be derived from the law itself or from other sources, it is at any rate not clear why

Kantorowicz (1963:45); but even if one accepts this remarkable usage, one still cannot directly transfer this characterisation of the *object* of the discipline to the discipling *itself*.

[30] On this cf. Ross (1958:9), which puts forward the thesis that the representatives of jurisprudence that describe this legal system can formulate their conclusions in statements of the following type: "such and such a directive is valid German law", with such statements being taken as statements of fact.

[31] Thus Kantorowicz in his article (1962b:137), dealing with a regulation on boycott in keeping with the "intentions of the law".

they should not be made explicit, so as to make them accessible to common evaluation. The same is true of the *consideration on causal relationships*, which are relevant for the formulation of particular proposals; for instance on the effects of applied norms or proposed interpretations on social life. Admittedly these considerations have an important role to play[32]. Anyone wishing to define the *meaning* of the law must *ipso facto* do some thinking on the *effects* intended by it and the *order* it is aimed at. Such considerations neccessitate the use of *nomological knowledge*, for the *control effects* of laws and interpretations are not *simply* logical consequences of the statements concerned. Furthermore they make it necessary, of course, to consider the *system context* of the norms concerned, to the extent that these effects are conditioned by that context.

If one can accept that all this should be made as explicit as possible – and it is precisely a *practice-oriented* jurisprudence that has every reason to do so if it really wants to *aid* practice – there then follows the possibility of treating this discipline as a social technology – oriented towards particular value positions, which may in some circumstances also be alternative ones. It would be aimed at formulating, under these hypothetically presupposed viewpoints, particular *interpretive proposals* for the *recognised sets of norms* in valid law, particular *proposals* for *modifying* the system of valid norms so as to remove norm conflicts, and also *proposals* for *developing the system* by introducing new norms through legislation. We shall come back later to the problem of the value perspectives that may play a part here. The incorporation of the interpretations or norms concerned into the body of valid law would then be a matter for the role-bearers of legal practice who are authorised to do this task – the judges and the legislative bodies – who could take their decisions in the light of the findings supplied by jurisprudence. The latter would itself be practice-oriented without having a normative character. It would not be dogmatic, but would operate with hypotheses which above all would utilise the relevant sociological knowledge. And it would not be a hermeneutic discipline, although it would *inter alia* also operate with methods for interpreting texts.

4. Political Economy as Rational Jurisprudence: The Basis of Politics in Social Technology

Theoretical economics can as we have seen be treated as a sociological approach having as its task the study of the problems of social control within a naturalistic research programme. This means, however, that in this theoretical tradition the institutional conditions of such control phenomena and therefore the norms

[32] v. Hayek too admits into his conception inclusion of intentional viewpoints and factual situations; on this cf. v. Hayek (1973:105), where he states interalia "that there can never be a science of law that is purely a science of norms and takes no account of the factual order at which it aims" and then brings up the problem of the *factual compatibility* of the norms of a system – on this cf. the section on the compatibility issue in my contribution to the Kraft Festschrift, Albert (1960:223). See also v. Hayek (1976:38), where the total context of the norm system is again stressed.

effective in this context must also be considered. In classical economics this was largely the case[33]. With the neoclassical phase, the problems began to be shifted in the direction of a decision-oriented – and therefore formalist – position under the influence of which the tendency to construct economic models in an institutional vacuum and to make their fundamental behavioural assumptions as content-free as possible spread[34]. It is only recently that a theoretical institutionalism within the economic tradition has been developed by taking account of the importance of legal regulations for the control of social processes, and thus theoretical institutionalism has allowed one of the central ideas of classical economics come back into its own[35].

The *economic research programme* is, in its essential features, precisely so constituted that the results of theoretical research in this tradition can be the *foundation of a rational jurisprudence* that would be a discipline of social technology in the way sketched out above and would have to contain, as one of its most important elements, a *theory of legislation*[36]. It may sound astonishing to characterize theoretical economics as a sociological tradition and to simultaneously call it a possible foundation for this kind of jurisprudence. But the appearance of confusion that this may create arises only from our inclination to take the institutionalised academic division of labour and the discipline boundaries connected with it more seriously than the structure of our theoretical and practical problems. Those who – failing to see the generality of its theoretical approach – seek to confine economics to the so-called economic sphere, assign to sociology the remaining problems it has hitherto not solved and the remaining areas of society, and limit jurisprudence to the interpretation of texts, can in fact only regard the merger proposed above, which springs from the specific nature of the problems arising here, as an illegitimate attempt to break through the tradition-hallowed barriers between established disciplines. But they will have difficulties in understanding in what respect Adam Smith's economic major work can be classed as a contribution to the theory of legislation, and likewise,

[33] This is true above all of the work of Adam Smith, who as Hutchison rightly states – cf. Hutchison (1976:507) – was a philosopher in a broad sense of the word; above all a social philosopher, who in his economic investigations attributed the greatest importance to the legal framework of social events.

[34] This tendency, which I had repeatedly attacked as "model-platonism", has for some time – at least as regards the institutional deficit in the constructions that result from it – been sharply criticised by Harold Demsetz and other representatives of the property-rights school as a "nirvana approach". Other theoreticians are endeavouring to exploit the findings of psychological research to revise the behavioural assumptions; on this cf. Scitovsky (1977); Leibenstein (1976).

[35] On this cf. Furubotn and Pejovich (1972:1137), as well as the volume of essays edited by these two economists (1974).

[36] Dugald Stewart, the editor of Adam Smith's works, clearly sets out the relationship of political economy to this kind of jurisprudence in his biographical appendix. For him, Smith's work – *An Inquiry into the Nature and Causes of the Wealth of Nations*, 1776 – was "... the most comprehensive and perfect work that has yet appeared, on the general principles of any branch of legislation", cf. Stewart (1963: Vol. V, 484).

they will not be able to properly appreciate the close relationship between Bentham's principles of legislation and the fundamental issues of economics.

Utilitarianism, which strongly influenced economic thinking in the neoclassical phase, has been criticised for many varied reasons – some of which are justified[37]. But this does not mean that all its ideas are unusable. The differences between Scottish moral philosophy and Bentham's philosophical radicalism should not be underestimated[38], as they have in common one essential element that specifically concerns our problem. Bentham, like Hume and Smith, wished to transfer the programme of theoretical explanation that had proved itself in the natural sciences to the moral sphere[39] – i.e. the sphere of social life – and on this basis to build an art or technology that could be used as the basis of a rational politics. And he saw the importance of a general theory of behaviour for the achievement of this goal; a theory that in his view would have to refer back to human endeavour after the satisfaction of needs in order to explain their modes of conduct. He sought to sketch out this theory (Bentham, 1833), and did so in a way that prefigured much of what later became effective in psychological research. He saw that the expectation of rewards and punishments of the most varied nature that is connected with the striving to satisfy needs is of great importance for behaviour[40] and that the theory of the art of legislation – as a part of social technology – has to link up with the relevant knowledge if it is to act realistically[41].

Any effective legislation is really a restructuring of the social order and therefore directed at changing the course of social events in particular areas. This change of course becomes possible because different modes of behaviour, i.e. different from previous modes are designated as positive or negative – by positive and negative sanctions in the broadest sense of the word – thereby bringing about a change in the interest position of the members of society. This is of course true not only of acts of legislation but also of other interventions in social life. The individualist research programme that seeks to explain all social processes from the interplay of the modes of behaviour of individuals seeking to solve the problems constituted by their needs and expectations is by virtue of its structure particularly suitable for acting as a basic for this kind of social technology[42].

An applied science of this kind can only point to possibilities of action, and thereby to possibilities for achieving particular goals or combinations of goals through the use or avoidance of particular means. It can – as regards the

[37] On this cf. Albert (1978: Ch. V.).

[38] On this cf. above all the relevant works of v. Hayek (1976:17).

[39] Cf. Halevy (1928:9). The aim was to introduce Newtonian methods into the analysis of morals.

[40] This is not so trivial as it may *prima facie* sound, since "rewards" and "punishments" are understood in a very general fashion in connection with the structure of needs.

[41] This is of course also true of other parts of social technology, e.g. the theory of education; on this cf. Lewin (1931).

[42] This is of course not intended to mean that the explanatory approaches available today within this programme are without weaknesses.

problems of the social order – characterise possible types of institutional measures and their general mode of operation, thereby analysing the effects of such systems in respect of the performance characteristics formulated on the basis of certain postulated value positions, as for instance Adam Smith sought to do with the means available at the time[43]. It cannot of course, supply any *legitimation* to a social order in the sense of the classical idea of justification, and any attempt to do so would, as we have seen, be utopian[44]. If one accepts the critics' standpoint, then justifications of this kind must be replaced by *comparative evaluations of alternative solutions to the problem*, and this is precisely what is possible with the resources of an applied science of the kind indicated, if the necessary value positions can be made available. There the method which goes back to Adam Smith therefore not only corresponds to the methodological style of the research practice of a science aiming at explanation, but goes on to make an important contribution towards answering the *question of how rational politics is possible*. This type of politics would use scientific findings and also meet the requirements of rational practice, by starting from the analysis and evaluation of the pros and cons of alternative solutions to problems in order to arrive at a decision.

As far as the value positions to be taken into account here are concerned, it is by no means obvious that they can be traced back to one uniform principle[45]. A multiplicity of acceptable positions naturally leads to a balancing problem, which in some circumstances has to be solved not *in abstracto*, but only by considering actual historical conditions. The various political tendencies that influence legislation sometimes differ more in how they seek to solve such balancing problems than in the value positions that they regard as authoritative. Since their notions in this connection are additionally bound up with differing views on the facts and trends of social life, the problem situation becomes much more complex for all concerned than the political rhetoric of the advocates of various solutions, calculated for effect, would suggest[46].

The utilisation of scientific knowledge in an analysis of alternatives which may be used as the basis of rational politics means answering the important question of feasibility that is important for any rational practice, and thereby marks off the limits of what is possible. Answering such questions of course depends

[43] Cf. Vining (1956:14), and Buchanan (1976:8), which stresses that apart from the standpoint of efficiency, justice also played a part.

[44] Even Peter Graf Kielmannsegg, who in his interesting historical study of constitutional problems (1977) explicitly sets up justificatory requirements and occasionally also brings out the justificatory idea critically against other proposed solutions (1977:214) in his own proposal then *de facto* abandons the idea and replaces it by a less ambitious construction op. cit. p. 256 ff. – which, as far as I can see, is compatible with the view put forward here.

[45] The principle, stemming from Cesare Beccaria and taken over by Jeremy Bentham, of the greatest happiness of the greatest number, which long continued to influence welfare economics formulations, has rightly fallen into disrepute.

[46] On this cf. Luebbe (1967), where the special *ratio* of this rhetoric is elaborated.

among other things on the specific situation and therefore on the actors – the bearers of social roles – that they relate to. Technological systems of statements tend to relate to possible starting-points for human action. Their application calls for the identification of such starting-points in the specific situation, so as to work out the *feasible* alternatives among the *relevant* ones. Since value positions are needed to define relevance, the analysis of options itself cannot manage with only the findings of pure knowledge. In applying technological knowledge to specific situations, valuations are unavoidable, even in seeking relevant alternatives, for these are determined by the practical problem situation and the evaluations inherent in it. There is as it were, a prior filtration – and this is, as we have seen, also true of the cognitive practice of science – in order to secure a graspable range of alternatives. As with cognitive practice, here too the method of problem-solving behaviour is underlain by a *rational heuristics* which in some circumstances is characterized by long-term *programmes*, in which the *nature of the solutions sought* is sketched out in advance – by the requirements that have to be based on adequate solutions.

5. Market and Organisation: Alternative Control Mechanisms and Incentive Patterns

A social technology which intends to serve as a basis for a rational politics must start from an analysis of the relevant social control mechanisms and the incentive patterns effective in them, the systems of reward and punishment, on which they are based. Studies of such control mechanisms based on the individualist research programme have in the meantime led to a fundamental correction of the view that it is appropriate from the viewpoint of efficiency and welfare to correct every alleged failure of the market mechanism through the state's ensuring of compensatory change using bureaucratic means. The problems seem often to be soluble without the direct use of state compulsion and consequent discretionary decision of government officials (On this cf. the third part of the book by Hayek 1973/78; cf. also Peacock, 1975:160).

The problem of social technology which is to be solved in each case can be reduced to the question of how particular functions can be institutionally embodied by channelling individual interests. Institutional arrangements must therefore be constructed and installed, with the help of which the personal interest of the individuals concerned – their motivation – is used to bring about the performance of particular functions. The social technology approach thus involves a kind of functionalism, which, to be sure, presupposes the analysis of causal connections and thereby, explanations of the usual type, while functionalism in theoretical thought generally amounts to methodologically faulty explanations, if it is not limited to heuristics. The ideal case, in the sense of a liberal arrangement, is of course the one where the functions concerned are performed because those doing the relevant work find that work itself satisfying. To be sure, the problem of coordinating such work still remains. A further possibility consists in the provision of rewards as an incentive to do the work concerned. In this case it must be ensured that the reward is closely connected with the performance called for, so that it cannot be obtained while avoiding the relevant requirements. Another possibility is to put a person in a situation of compulsion, whereby commands and prohibitions bound up with threats of punishment are used to bring about an appropriate performance[47]. One must of course set up appropriate limits here, of a physical, social or moral nature, to bring about the performance. From the viewpoint of freedom, and in general also from that of efficiency, this authoritarian method is in comparative terms the worst one.

In social life today there are essentially two types of regulatory forms: those that have the character of an *organisation,* and those that have that of a *market* (Zetterberg, 1962:61; Albert, 1967:392). Structures of the first type are subject to control by a common management, while the others function without any such authority. From a social technology point of view, these are alternative ways of controlling social processes, between which a choice can be made according to the performance characteristics concerned and the value positions underlying them[48]. There may of course exist, within market networks, organisations of all types – for instance firms, hospitals, parties, associations – and on the other hand, even within organisations there may be structures operating in a market fashion. Markets tend to be organised in such a way that in them, the first two types of motivation dominate, although of course the protection of market dealings by the legal system works with the threat of punishment. In organisations, by contrast, commands and prohibitions play a larger part, notwithstanding the great differences in the extent of the compulsion applied. In organisations the coordination of activities takes place largely through directives; in markets through free agreements made on the basis of supply and demand. The recruitment of staff for organisations may in turn be effected through market mechanisms or by organisational compulsion[49]. The same is true in relation to the provision of physical equipment and financial means.

From the viewpoint of freedom, then, market mechanisms would always be preferable for the coordination of individual actions and therefore for the control of social processes, were it not for the fact that the great differences in power among those involved could in turn lead to situations which are characterised by compulsion[50]. The value of freedom for the individuals depends above all on the extent and the nature of the available alternatives – i.e., on the room for manoeuvre in action. This is one of the essential reasons why liberal theoreticians stress the need for free competition. That state compulsion can be used to protect

[47] The subdivision of cases corresponds to the one made by Lewin (1974).

[48] They have been analysed as alternatives for the economics sphere above all by Coase (1937). He elaborates on the role of transaction costs and of efficiency considerations for the choice between the two forms. This position also dominates in the property-rights approach, which was heavily influenced by Coase's article.

[49] For instance, we have the first case with a mercenary army or a capitalist firm, and the second with a conscript army or a forced labour camp.

[50] An extreme case might be for one of the market partners, alone to control a large part of the goods vitally necessary to the others.

free competition is therefore among the essential principles of a policy aimed at bringing about a free system. Another is that the resulting application of compulsion needs to be regulated by general laws in order to render arbitrary intervention impossible.

The fact that in free market dealings organisations of all types are formed on the basis of contractual agreements between the participants arises presumably because of efficiency advantages that may be associated with a centrally coordinated division of labour (Coase, 1937). As long as governmental compulsion is not exercised in order to keep such organisations alive, it is probably in the interest of increased welfare to allow them to function. Nevertheless, a liberal policy cannot be disinterested in the fact that authority structures of this nature impose as a consequence certain restrictions on self-determination, which essentially contradict the idea of liberty[51]. Not only can it apply general protective provisions for the members of such organisations[52], but furthermore it can lay down general rules for their structure, which limit the compulsive character of the hierarchical relations existing within them. However, it ought to be clear as to how far it thereby renounces an otherwise possible increase in efficiency in the interests of freedom. The *fact* that in some circumstances it may be necessary to choose between higher efficiency and greater freedom is not to be denied.

Furthermore, the increase in competitive pressure also seems to be able to contribute to a reduction in the arbitrary exercise of power in the organizations concerned, because it works to reduce efficiency and thereby endangers their survival (Leibenstein, 1976:207; also Rowley and Peacock, 1975:167). Under conditions of effective competition, organisations of all kinds also develop an interest in more efficient methods of controlling the work process, and these methods not infrequently go hand in hand with a mitigation of compulsion situations and with motivation based on positive incentives.

Relevant studies in recent years ought to have made it clear that many cases of alleged failure of the market mechanism are connected with the fact that property rights in scarce goods are not defined in a way that could have brought about a functioning market mechanism[53]. The problems of environment protection, land use, use of the electromagnetic spectrum for broadcasting and television and other problems of this nature can obviously, if property rights are suitably limited, be solved without bureaucratic arrangements, i.e. without recourse to

[51] On this cf. the above cited book by Rowley and Peacock (1975:163). It is clearly not possible to dispute the fact that these are authority structures on the ground that the subordination relations concerned are based on contractual agreements between the participants. This is, after all, true also of a mercenary army or for the active officer corps of a conscript army. In these cases scarcely anyone would deny the power character of the social formation concerned.

[52] As v. Hayek states, a free system by no means rules out general regulations, such as worker protection legislation; cf. v. Hayek (1973:78).

[53] The clarification of these problems is due, above all, to the property-right approach in economic thinking, which has brought back recognition of the crucial importance for the economic research programme of institutional components; on this cf. e.g. Furubotn and Pejovich (1972:1137).

the discretionary decisions of functionaries. The assumption that such decisions in these cases are necessary because the market will inevitably fail was evidently founded on insufficient analysis, and moreover, started from the false assumption that bureaucratic arrangements through state power would be bound to involve fewer difficulties. A comparative analysis of alternative control mechanisms clearly leads to other consequences, especially when, apart from efficiency viewpoints, it also makes use of the idea of liberty.

The close connection between liberty and property had already been worked out in the Scottish moral philosophy of the eighteenth century. Under the influence mainly of socialist views in the nineteenth century, the idea of private property as a rigid legal entity with its form laid down once and for all developed; a kind of property essentialism that has contributed to the burdening of the discussion about capitalism with the confrontation of radical alternatives. Abolition of private property in the means of production became a fetish of the Marxist attack on capitalism, so that socialism was in a position to present itself as the sole alternative.

In the meantime, not only has this alternative been discredited through the totalitarian developments connected with it (Albert, 1978: Chap. IV and Chap. VIII), but it has further become clear that private property is not a static entity, but is a very flexible complex body of rights, caught up in continual change. The word "property" has certain connotations which may signify the complete unrestricted disposal of a piece of land, a house, furniture or machines, or even, as in the case of slavery, of people. But anyone who knows anything about the law knows that at various times, numerous, diverse restrictions on the power of disposal existed, some with a legal basis – e.g. planning restrictions – and some based on contractual agreements – e.g. contractually guaranteed utilization rights. The content of the right to property was changed sharply through labour protection legislation and through the development of company structures involving liability restrictions. The "property" of the shareholders, which relates to the share certificate, is bound up with administrative rights and rights to the receipt of a share in profit which can also be counted towards the complex of private property. Private property as a fixed arrangement, unchanged over time, is just as much a fiction as the idea that there is only *one* capitalism, even if it is divided into early, middle and late capitalism[54]. In short, though these terms are useful in many contexts, they are of limited value for analytical purposes.

The legal arrangements which in a society serve to guarantee individuals an area of autonomous decision-making may be very different. They go far beyond what is laid down in the ownership rights contained in the law of property. From the sociological viewpoint, it seems advisable to use a concept of property that covers all legal arrangements that delimit individuals' area of free decision. Such decisions are those where normally no governmental compulsion is possible, while private compulsion can be resisted by recourse to the state power by legal

[54] On the problems of such concepts of development theory with a background in philosophy of history cf. the critical study by Watrin (1968:40).

means[55]. Among such legal arrangements one must count membership rights in the organisation that takes central political decisions, i.e. in the state[56].

It is only when these political rights are also included in the analysis that the extent and nature of the individual's freedom to manoeuvre in legitimate action can be measured and thereby various systems of society be evaluated in comparative terms with regard to the regulative idea of freedom. The actual "constitutions" that come into this evaluation contain all the norms laid down for human actions that are effective in this respect. The constitutional document of a modern state, however, usually contains only a small part of these norms, though it sometimes includes the incorporation of a legislative programme that expresses the principles that should be decisive for legislative activity[57]. It is only when legislative practice is oriented in this or another way to regulatory ideas, and if in so doing it adequately employs available knowledge of social technology, that one may not expect it to get lost in a maze of short-sighted ad-hoc regulations – the effect of which is to interfere with each other.

6. Company Constitutions

As already stated, firms, even when they appear in the context of a free market economy, are authority structures that within such a system recruit their employees through the market and retain them by free agreements. That authority is exercised inside them is, as already mentioned, a fact that must be evaluated negatively from the viewpoint of freedom, even if the needs of the employees have become so adjusted to this actual state of affairs that they are content with it. The actual constitutions of the firms appearing in a market economy are the result of decisions taken by those concerned having regard to the existing normative regulations – primarily, the laws in force. Therefore, it cannot be doubted that legislation is capable of exercising considerable influence on company constitutions and in the course of the decision processes in such organisations. It is therefore, also in a position to affect the nature of the authority existing in them. It can therefore try to promote those forms of companies in which those aspects of domination, that are negative as regards the idea of freedom, are mitigated by influencing the firms' market environment – for instance in the direction of an increase of competitive pressure – and by regulations that apply directly to the constitution of firms. However, one must be clear that such influence may negatively affect the performance characteristics of firms which are relevant from other value viewpoints – especially that of efficiency in the sense of the increase of prosperity.

[55] In this case, as Buchanan states, no categorical distinction between human rights and property rights is any longer possible; cf. Buchanan (1975:10).

[56] Consistently, they are included by Buchanan in his study; cf. Buchanan (1975:41).

[57] On this cf. v. Hayek (1976:225), where it is pointed out that the revolutionary colonists in North America towards the end of the 18th century were the first to put into practice the idea that such a superordinate law ought to be codified and thereby made clear and enforceable.

The participation question can also be looked at in this perspective. It is well known that there are many different codetermination arrangements in company constitutions, and that different positions have been taken on item (Pejovich, 1978; Backhaus/Nutzinger, 1982). These arrangements were arrived at partly on a voluntary basis, partly promoted or compelled by the legislation of the state concerned. Behind the relevant legislation there are in each case various interests, that also affect the evaluation of the regulations concerned. This does not mean, however, that there cannot be an objective analysis made of these.

To the extent that appropriate sociological findings are available, one can indeed elicit the *effects* of the regulations on the *control* of what happens in society and on the *life situation* of those concerned, and these results can be assessed on the basis of various *hypothetically* assumed *value standpoints*, and this assessment can be valid even for those who deny one or other of these standpoints[58]. Of course the social sciences cannot of course themselves seek to make those value standpoints, hypothetically assumed by them, binding, as the result of objective knowledge[59]. Thus, for instance, economic analysis cannot declare the efficiency standpoint to be binding, though it can quite legitimately advance it by analysing the effects of the regulations concerned on social events, by, for example, finding that particular institutional arrangements lead to an inefficient incentive structure in the area concerned and thereby to a reduction in prosperity in the society concerned (Furubotn, 1978:131; 1982:203; Backhaus and Nutzinger, 1982:127; Backhaus, 1982:183; 1982a:281).

As far as the question of reduced efficiency is concerned, one may in analysing abstract from the fact that efficiency is normally evaluated positively as a performance characteristic of social regulatory systems. However as regards the material problem arising here, two things should be stated at the outset. First, the relative prices and therefore also costs – including transactional costs – are dependent on the particular distribution of property rights, so that an efficiency evaluation in fact is meaningful only in relation to such a distribution (Schmid, 1976). Secondly, the question of the effect of particular participation regulations on efficiency is still rather controversial today (Backhaus, 1982:241). However, the same thing also seems to me to be true as regards the effects of such regulations on the freedom of those involved.

However, generally speaking, it would seem to be necessary to draw two conclusions from the debate so far on the social technology issue. First, for each such analysis it is absolutely essential to specify precisely the *institutional arrangements* brought about by the participation regulations concerned[60]. Secondly, the *behavioural assumptions* that economic analysis has hitherto worked with – the individual utility functions which in any particular analysis are usually

[58] The assessment concerned is valid, at any rate, *relatively* to the standpoints concerned, and therefore *objectively*, irrespective of whether one takes these standpoints as one's own.

[59] This is all reconcilable, as will easily be seen, with the principle of the value-freedom of science postulated by Max Weber; on this cf. Albert (1968: chapter III).

[60] Backhaus especially has drawn attention to this (1982:241).

specified in detail in each case *ad hoc* – are often not adequate to determine the precise *incentive situation* resulting from the institutional and other circumstances of individual behaviour. One is therefore frequently forced to work with plausible ad hoc assumptions, thereby exposing oneself to the reproach of barely concealed *a priori* reasoning[61], though *de facto* this may in certain circumstances be motivated by definite evaluations. It may therefore be said with some justification that the question of the actual effects of participation regulations, which is decisive from the social technology point of view, has hitherto remained inadequately clarified[62], and this is an unsatisfactory situation for all concerned.

Turning now to the question of the extent to which legislation ought to compulsorily introduce such regulations (to dictate to firms), the objection is sometimes raised that regulations which are not arrived at in a voluntary manner are in any case inefficient and therefore ought not to be made binding through the law. This objection starts from the assumption that all acceptable institutional arrangements must develop spontaneously without legislation; an assumption which can hardly be accepted as an obvious one, especially since it cannot even cope with the constantly arising situations that are in the nature of a prisoner's dilemma. Nor does it cope with the fact that apart from the efficiency standpoint other value standpoints for evaluating institutional measures also exist. Moreover, Pareto's criterion that underlies the efficiency standpoint is itself open to certain objections that make its applicability doubtful (Albert, 1978:127; Schmid, 1976:24). The idea that one can by using this criterion cope with the fact that economic analysis has not satisfactorily solved the problem of the interpersonal comparability of utility, while nevertheless arriving at economically based minimum value judgments that are adequate for political recommendations, is not sustained. The methodological individualism of economic analysis does not provide the means to evaluate total social magnitudes. In order to apply sociological knowledge in support of rational politics, one is therefore dependent on a combination of social technology analysis and explicitly introduced value standpoints that cannot be deduced from knowledge.

Bibliography

ALBERT, HANS (1960) "Wissenschaft und Politik", in E. Topitsch (ed.) *Probleme der Wissenschaftstheorie*. Vienna: Springer.
– (1967) *Marktsoziologie und Entscheidungslogik*. Neuwied/Berlin: Luchterhand.
– (1972) "Normativismus oder Sozialtechnologie?" in H. Albert, N. Luhmann, W. Maihofer, O. Weinberger (eds.) *Rechtstheorie als Grundlagenwissenschaft der Rechtswissenschaft*. Bielefeld: Bertelsmann.
– (1978) *Traktat über rationale Praxis*. Tübingen: Mohr.

[61] On this cf. Nutzinger's critique (1982a:39).
[62] Nutzinger points out (1982b:43) where the question of speed limits on road vehicles is analysed in this sense.

– (1980) *Traktat über kritische Vernunft*. Tübingen: Mohr.
ARNDT, ADOLF (1966) "Die Krise des Rechts", in W. Maihofer (ed.) *Naturrecht oder Rechtspositivismus?* Darmstadt: Wissenschaftliche Buchgesellschaft.
AUER, ALBERT (1962) "Der Mensch und das Recht", in W. Maihofer (ed.) *Naturrecht oder Rechtspositivismus?* Darmstadt: Wissenschaftliche Buchgesellschaft.
BACKHAUS, JÜRGEN (1982) "Information und Technologie in der mitbestimmten Unternehmung", in J. Backhaus and H. Nutzinger (eds.) *Eigentumsrechte und Partizipation*. Frankfurt a. M.: Haag & Herchen.
– (1982a) "Die mitbestimmte Großunternehmung: Eine effiziente Unternehmensform", in J. Backhaus and H. Nutzinger (eds.) *Eigentumsrechte und Partizipation*. Frankfurt a. M.: Haag & Herchen.
BACKHAUS, JÜRGEN and HANS G. NUTZINGER (1982) *Eigentumsrechte und Partizipation*. Frankfurt a. M.: Haag & Herchen.
BALLWEG, OTTMAR (1972) "Rechtsphilosophie als Grundlagenforschung der Rechtswissenschaft und der Jurisprudenz", in H. Albert, N. Luhmann, W. Maihofer, O. Weinberger (eds.) *Rechtstheorie als Grundlagenwissenschaft der Rechtswissenschaft*. Bielefeld: Bertelsmann.
BENTHAM, JEREMY (1833) *Des englischen Juristen, Prinzipien der Gesetzgebung*. Cologne: Arend.
BOBBIO, NORBERTO (1965) *Die ontologische Begründung des Rechts*. Darmstadt: Wissenschaftliche Buchgesellschaft.
BRAUN, HERBERT (1971) "Die Problematik einer Theologie des Neuen Testaments", in H. Braun (ed.), *Gesammelte Studien zum Neuen Testament und seiner Umwelt*. Tübingen: Mohr.
BUCHANAN, JAMES M. (1975) *The Limits of Liberty. Between Anarchy and Leviathan*. Chicago/London: University of Chicago Press.
– (1976) "The Justice of Natural Liberty", V *The Journal of Legal Studies* 8.
COASE, RONALD H. (1937) "The Nature of the Firm", 4 *Economia* 386.
D'ENTREVES, ALESSANDRO P. (1951) *Natural Law, An Introduction to Legal Philosophy*. London: Hutchinson's University Library.
DE JOUVENEL, BERTRAND (1972) *Über die Staatsgewalt. Die Naturgeschichte ihres Wachstums*. Freiburg: Rombach.
DOMBOIS, HANS (1966) "Das Problem des Naturrechts. Versuch eines Grundrisses", in W. Maihofer (ed.) *Naturrecht oder Rechtspositivismus?* Darmstadt: Wissenschaftliche Buchgesellschaft.
FURUBOTN, EIRIK G. (1978) "The Economic Consequences of Codetermination on the Rate and Sources of Private Investment", in S. Pejovitch (ed.) *The Codetermination Movement in the West*. Lexington/Toronto: Lexington Books.
– (1983) "Information, organisatorische Struktur und die möglichen Vorteile der Mitbestimmung", in J. Backhaus and H. Nutzinger (eds.) *Eigentumsrechte und Partizipation*. Frankfurt a. M.: Haag & Herchen.
FURUBOTN, EIRIK G. and SVETOZAR PEJOVICH (1972) "Property Rights and Economic Theory: A Survey of Recent Literature", X *Journal of Economic Literature* 1137.
– (1974) *The Economics of Property Rights*. Cambridge/Mass.: Ballinger.
GEIGER, THEODOR (1947) *Vorstudien zu einer Soziologie des Rechts*. Aarhus: Universitetsfarlaget.
HALEVY, ELIE (1928) *The Growth of Philosophical Radicalism*. London: Faber.
HART, HERBERT, L. A. (1961) *The Concept of Law*. Oxford: Clarendon.
– (1971) "Der Positivismus und die Trennung von Recht und Moral", in H. L. A. Hart, *Recht und Moral*. Göttingen: Vandenhoeck & Ruprecht.
v. HAYEK, FRIEDRICH A. (1969) *Freiburger Studien*. Tübingen: Mohr.

– (1971) *Die Verfassung der Freiheit.* Tübingen: Mohr.
– (1973–78) *Law Legislation and Liberty, Vol. I–III.* London: Routledge & K. Paul.
HOERSTER, NORBERT (1970) "Zur logischen Möglichkeit des Rechtspositivismus", XVI *Archiv für Rechts- und Sozialphilosophie* 43.
HOMANS, GEORGE C. (1961) *Social Behaviour.* London: Routledge & K. Paul.
HUTCHISON, TERENCE (1976) "Adam Smith and the Wealth of Nations", XIX *The Journal of Law and Economics* 507.
KANTOROWICZ, HERMANN (1962a) "Rationalistische Bemerkungen über Realismus", in H. Kantorowicz, *Rechtswissenschaft und Soziologie.* Karlsruhe: Müller.
– (1962b) "Rechtswissenschaft und Soziologie", in H. Kantorowicz (ed.) *Rechtswissenschaft und Soziologie.* Karlsruhe: Müller.
– (1963) *Der Begriff des Rechts.* Göttingen: Vandenhoeck & Ruprecht.
KELSEN, HANS (1954) "Kausalität und Zurechnung", VI *Österreichische Zeitschrift für öffentliches Recht* 133.
– (1964) "Gott und Staat", in H. Kelsen, *Aufsätze zur Ideologiekritik.* Neuwied/Berlin: Luchterhand.
KIELMANNSEGG, PETER GRAF (1977) *Volkssouveränität. Eine Untersuchung der Bedingungen demokratischer Legitimität.* Stuttgart: Klett.
KNOLL, AUGUST (1962) Katholische Kirche und scholastisches *Naturrecht. Zur Frage der Freiheit.* Vienna/Frankfurt a. M./Zürich: Europa Verlag.
KRAFT, JULIUS (1957) *Die Unmöglichkeit der Geisteswissenschaft.* Frankfurt a. M.: Verlag Öffentliches Leben.
LEIBENSTEIN, HARVEY (1976) *Beyond Economic Man. A New Foundation for Microeconomics.* Cambridge, Mass./London: Harvard University Press.
LEWIN, KURT (1931) *Die psychologische Situation bei Lohn und Strafe.* Leipzig: Hirzel.
LINDENBERG, SIEGWART (1977) "Individuelle Effekte, kollektive Phänomene und das Problem der Transformation", in K. Eichner und W. Habermehl (ed.), *Probleme der Erklärung sozialen Verhaltens.* Meisenheim: Hain.
LÜBBE, HERMANN (1967) *Der Streit um Worte, Sprüche und Politik.* Bochum.
v. MISES, LUDWIG (1933) *Grundprobleme der Nationalökonomie. Untersuchungen über Verfahren, Aufgabe und Inhalt der Wirtschafts- und Gesellschaftslehre.* Jena: Fischer.
NUTZINGER, HANS G. (1982a) "Die Mitbestimmungsbewegung in den westlichen Demokratien aus der Sicht der ökonomischen Theorie der Eigentumsrechte", in J. Backhaus and H. Nutzinger (eds.) *Eigentumsrechte und Partizipation.* Frankfurt a. M. Haag & Herchen.
– (1982b) "Die ökonomische Theorie der Eigentumsrechte – Ein neues Paradigma der Sozialwissenschaften?", in J. Backhaus and J. Nutzinger (eds.) *Eigentumsrechte und Partizipation.* Frankfurt a. M. Haag & Herchen.
OLIVECRONA, KNUT H. C. (1940) *Gesetz und Staat.* Copenhagen: Munksgaard.
– (1942) *Der Imperativ des Gesetzes.* Copenhagen: Munksgaard.
PEJOVICH, SVETOZAR (ed.) (1978) *The Codetermination Movement in the West.* Lexington/Toronto: Lexington Books.
ROSS, ALF (1961) "Validity and the Conflict between Legal Positivism and Natural Law", *Revista Juridica de Buenos Aires* 46.
– (1962) "The Concept of Law, by H. L. A. Hart", 71 *Yale Law Journal* 1185.
– (1974) *On Law and Justice* Berkeley: University of California Press.
ROWLEY, CHARLES R. and ALAN T. PEACOCK (1975) *Welfare Economics. A Liberal Restatement.* London: Robertson.
v. SAVIGNY, EIKE (1972) "Die Jurisprudenz im Schatten des Empirismus", in H. Albert, N. Luhmann, W. Maihofer, O. Weinberger (eds.) *Rechtstheorie als Grundlagenwissenschaft der Rechtswissenschaft.* Bielefeld: Bertelsmann.

SCHMID, ALLAN (1976) "The Economics of Property Rights: A Review Article", 10 *Journal of Economic Issues* 159.

SCHMITT, CARL (1934) *Politische Theologie, Vier Kapitel zur Lehre von der Souveränität.* Munich/Leipzig: Duncker & Humblot.

SCITOVISKY, TIBOR (1977) *Psychologie des Wohlstands. Die Bedürfnisse des Menschen und der Bedarf des Verbrauchers.* Frankfurt a. M.: Campus.

STEWART, DUGALD (1963) "Account of the Life and Writings of Adam Smith, LL. D.", in D. Stewart (ed.) *The Works of Adam Smith.* Vol. V. Aalen: Zellor.

TOPITSCH, ERNST (1958) *Vom Ursprung und Ende der Metaphysik. Ein Studie zur Weltanschauungskritik.* Vienna. Springer.

ÜBBE, HERMANN (1967) *Der Streit um Worte, Sprüche und Politik.* Bochum.

VERDROSS, ALFRED (1966) "Was ist Recht? Die Krise des Rechtspositivismus und das Naturrecht", in W. Maihofer (ed.) *Naturrecht oder Rechtspositivismus?* Darmstadt: Wissenschaftliche Buchgesellschaft.

VINING, DANIEL R. (1956) *Economics in the United States of America.* Paris: UNESCO.

WATRIN, CHRISTIAN (1968) "Spätkapitalismus", in E. K. Scheuch (ed.) *Die Wiedertäufer der Wohlstandsgesellschaft.* Cologne: Markus.

WEBER, MAX (1951) "R. Stammler's 'Überwindung' der materialistischen Geschichtsaufassung", in M. Weber (ed.) *Gesammelte Aufsätze zur Wissenschaftslehre.* Tübingen: Mohr.

ZETTERBERG, HANS L. (1962) *Social Theory and Social Practice.* New York: Bedminster Press.

Social Science Models in Economic Law

RUDOLF WIETHÖLTER*
Frankfurt

The subject matter of this paper may give rise to the expectation that a social science model (or even several models) and its influence on economic law will be reconstructed. I adhere to a "model" of a Criticial Theory of society, for which there can be no directly decisive effect on decisions. Consequently I have to disappoint such expectations. In this paper, I am only concerned with estimating the chances of such an influence, especially in terms of law itself. Following an outline of the issues in part I, I discuss in part II the relationship between the construction of models, the phenomenon of legalisation and the legal principle of proportionality in the analytical framework of paradigm change and social and system integration. Part III deals with the consequences for legal methods. In part IV a number of examples are discussed and the main conclusions are presented.

I.

Natural law and legal positivism are the two quarrelling brothers that have determined our inheritance as far as legal culture goes over the last 200 years. Their – sole? – successor seems to be turning out to be a "sociological natural law" which is able – to use Voltaire's felicitous phrase – to kill a whole herd of sheep when used as a magic word, provided a sufficient quantity of arsenic be added to it. Retaining this image for the moment, it is the quantity of arsenic that I shall be dealing with in this paper. Departing from the image, I wish to deal with the paradox that the social sciences are now concerning themselves with "law" (as hardly ever before) in the same manner as jurisprudence is concerned with "society", but with little or no impact on either law or society. More precisely, social sciences and jurisprudence are concerning themselves – newly, explicitly and certainly not without reason – with the rationality(ies) of law as rationality(ies) of society; that is, using traditional language, under the double aspect of justificatory normativity and sociology of domination *(Herrschaft-*

* Translated from the German by Iain Fraser

ssoziologie). These efforts are aimed at nothing less than objectivisable criteria of justice itself. Hand in hand with all these efforts goes the idea that increasing rationality in ever smaller, more remote, decentralised units only makes the irrationality of the "whole" grow even more. A historical anathema seems to afflict the divisions of labour, class and system, so that a synthesis over the whole of society, a "rational identity for modern societies", (Habermas) is no longer within reach. The offers by social theory become increasingly abstract, radical and complex, only to fall in turn to the anathema of the division of labour, class and system that they all attempt to oppose. Is it any wonder then that the law can prove untouched by this, while at the same time completely imprisoned by it? In my opinion the dominating phenomenon of the last 10 to 15 years is that the *work of lawyers* as socially-oriented and -exercised practice has remained almost untouched by all the more fundamental challenges facing our legal system, jurisprudence and legal doctrines. Nevertheless, at the same time, the need for reflexivity in relation to these developments in society as a whole has increasingly entered our awareness. Ultimately, of course, this reflexivity can – as hitherto has always been the case – advance only furtively, insidiously, indirectly; in brief, in praxis itself. This finding suggests that such theories will have some influence, but this will be both less than and different from what their modellers think and wish. Among such challenges one may distinguish crudely between: politico-social (substantive) programmes with the characteristic (or defect) of the absence of contemporary developmental quality, functionalist (systems theory) programmes with the characteristic (or defect) of the lack of social adequacy, and methodological programmes with the characteristic (or defect) of the lack of scientific rationality. All these transitions have been resisted in every quarter, but have not led to any significant reconstruction of self-awareness. This stability probably justifies the assumption that legal work is public action under justificatory requirements (conditions of justification) – these are what allow it to be characterised as distinctively legal – however it cannot be simply assigned to one single theoretical camp.

My thesis is as follows. The distinctively legal aspect, the legal *proprium*, is in part obvious, in part doubtful, but in practice always present or at least active. It always requires definition, yet goes on defining itself as long as other definitions cannot be justified, realised or implemented. The observer's attention has therefore to be focused initially on a central circle since he is always also a participant. What is the distribution of the chances for success of possible legal science; as "criticism" and as "growth of knowledge", will make it "positive law" – and that is our perpetual legal destiny for an unforeseeable period – also "right law"? For that is, no doubt, the expression in thought for a given epoch of justice itself, the search for which is everlasting. Here one must risk revealing one's criterion of inquiry. For myself I denote it as *self-reflection of legal science* in a context of theory of science, sociology of knowledge and history of science. The elements of this reference triangle are mutually related: they comprise the social theory question of social action, taking into account the subject and object positions of (not solely academic) actors who all at the same time have their histories; the question from the theory of science as to the preconditions and effects of this work of discovery and interpretation, codetermined by both history and society; and the question from historical theory as to the possible meaning, possible goals, possible progress of social and scholarly action. This framework can be indicated more precisely by referring to the most important constituents. Particular elements, tasks and characteristics of individual disciplines involved in a division of labour stand in the foreground. On the one hand it will be a social and scientific model that orients a tradition of academic research, that is from accepted issues, approaches and principles of interpretation via the lifestyles of the professional worlds concerned to regulative practice itself that characterises an area of work. On the other hand, it will be a standard of skills and work procedures as everyday know-how, social efficiency, the standing of those concerned, and their share in dealing with problems arising. Briefly, we may term these three consciousness, orientation, and methodology.

Legal relationships can in fact be understood neither from themselves nor from eternal ideas, but on the basis of historical and social conditions. Putting it more fashionably, our societies depend for the solutions to their problems on themselves, for the orientation, legitimation and sanctioning of such solutions they depend on more abstract references which admittedly are in turn themselves produced. What the law is, then, concerned with is a relationship between autonomy and heteronomy about which, however, the law has still a (co-) determining part to play. Theoretical programmes applied reflectively here must always – reconstructively – follow up developments that have led to crises and – prospectively – investigate the possible conditions for overcoming the crises. All this sounds like a Promethean grasping after a world-embracing formula (covering the law too). It is a world-embracing formula, for three reasons: because the point really is the renewable universality of the category of law or else its overcoming, transcending, replacement, and because, moreover, major evolutionary programmes can no longer take refuge in traditional transcendence; and finally because universal history can presumably no longer be treated with impunity as being about "western" (particularist) development of culture and civilisation. Hence the presumptuousness of the attempt. But not to dare it today would at the same time mean finally detaching reflexive programmes that (still) cover a whole from science programmes that make plausible explanations under consent obligations possible. In addition, it would also mean detaching them from those action programmes that transform acceptable proposals (under laws of freedom) into decisions. That would in turn mean a final and momentous separation between our advances and our heritage in social philosophy and cultural history on the one hand, and industry and technology on the other.

II.

In order to deal with the problem in manageable parts, I shall choose as a characteristic phenomenon "*legalisation*", as a typical all-purpose magic weapon of legal dogma the "*legal principle of proportionality*", and as characteristic of the scholarly apparatus the concept of the "*model*". I shall also choose for the reflexive explanatory reference – as analysis of the formation of a criterion – two concepts that occupy a central position in the contemporary debate on the theory and practice of the social sciences: the concept of *paradigm change* and the concept of *system and social integration.*

1. a. Following *Thomas Kuhn*, "paradigm" means, without going into details here on the origin and use of the term, the set of prevailing fundamental patterns in theoretical concepts, methods of working, value orientations, dogmatic categories, evaluations of problems and practical orientations in decision-making applied by a research- or a decision-making community; it both facilitates work but also delimits it. The underlying belief patterns making up a paradigm are inescapably imbedded in social relationships, social *(Welt-)Anschauungen* and rival party positions. Circularity is unavoidable here – and it increasingly becomes the major problem. Social relationships which we know something about and want to do something about do not rise and fall without our knowledge and action, just as we are not in a position to know or to do anything apart from them. Here lies the unity of "theory" and "practice" in a society (with its history, its science, its morals and its art, and not least its law). Academic practice (and correspondingly, legal practice) "regulates" its theory of rationality through institutionally organised processes no less than this theory "regulates" that practice through methodology. Instead of paradigm one might also speak of the "third world" or of the "life-world". What is meant in each case is a relationship between cultural reproduction, social identification and professional socialisation that dominates us *in practice.*

b. The two terms *system and social integration* (which go back to *D. Lockwood*) cover the perpetually problematic relationship between individuals and collectives (between "freedom" and "institutions"). Societies that seek to keep their social functions independent of the ideas of justice in the minds and hearts of their citizens, end up in permanent crisis (in the most recent expression for this, become "ungovernable") no less than do those that attempt to rigidly impose such ideas against demands and needs for change. Contemporary debate in social theory seems here to be tending towards a late *mariage de convenance* between philosophies of action and systems sociologies. Theories of society, as evolutionary theories, at least agree that modern developments are bound up with systems divisions, demarcations and differentiations. The extent and effects of such differentiations are the object of dispute. The main conflicting camps can probably be distinguished as functionalist evolutionary theories on the one hand and normative, critical evolutionary theories on the other. As representatives of each of them one may adduce the recent *magna opera* by Niklas Luhmann (Gesellschaftsstruktur und Semantik, 2. vol. 1980, 1981; and Soziale Systeme, 1984) and Jürgen Habermas (Theorie des kommunikativen Handelns, 2 vol. 1981; and Der philosophische Diskurs der Moderne, 1985).

c. It is not so much the details of the use of the two terms that can be useful to us, as the overall explanatory power and the guidance they may give as to the position of "law". The paradigm concept makes it easier for us to understand a number of things: the fact and the reason(s) why more fundamental changes are bound up with extremely stringent conditions; that even in the case of very fundamental change, the old forms long continue to conceal new contents; and the fact and the reason(s) why "ideas" indeed become a "material force", though in a different way than Marx meant, when they "seize the minds of the masses". The analysis of system and social integration makes it easier for us to understand the reason why system crises do not affect social crises either not at all or only by roundabout ways, via crises of consciousness, motivation or legitimation; why such mediation crises are still determined more by the "system" than by "sociality"; and why practical, moral, life-world efforts are more likely to be overtaken or overrun than moved onward by the "train of history".

2. Using these two criteria, I hope to combine in a single theme the differences in the legalisation debate, practical dominance in decision-making through norms of legal proportionality, and the selectivities of model-building, so as to throw light, with the aid of representative examples, on the effects of social science models on the law, which are ordinarily unclear and may only be understood reconstructively.

Today anyone seeking to renew fundamental issues of historical and social philosophy, while at the same time coping with the increased demands pressing upon theoretical programmes and the complexification of control models, and the transformation of the law, which is itself likewise being transformed, has to have recourse to a general *model theory*. Using a general model theory facilitates the following tasks: for instance, the discussion of the transformations of social relationships into legal relationships, the definition of the productive qualities of legal doctrine, and also of course the description of the status of the model, the modelling of the areas of the law, and finally the reduction of society and "modern" law to correspondences (covariances). It is striking here that the theoretical status of models remains mostly in a state of fruitful darkness. Still, at least since the modelling of model theory by Max Weber, one thing has become clear. Model theory may well (in theory) explicitly abandon both a discovery programme aimed at mirroring reality and a socio-historical descriptive programme aimed at determining the future. In practice it can nevertheless be both, i.e. as a pattern of offered interpretation and reflection from the stock of sovereign overviews and surveys. Models are pictures (of the world), though admittedly not in the way land-scapes are represented in maps, nor are they even of the kind with which prophets lead their peoples, but they are mental constructions and games. Using them, ideas can be related to interests in such a way that by *comparison* (with other models, with past reality, with limits of possibility, with the present as a future past or as a past future etc.) historical and social consciousness can be brought into "constitution" no less than can social reality and the legal forms that define it and are defined by it. The advantage of reflective programmes, is that they can relate everything to everything else, but this is of course also their drawback, i.e. that they always arrive too late to open up any future (far less help in planning it). Scepticism (at least on my part) is – since and with Max Weber – appropriate for those programmes which, beyond the socially adequate analytical technologies, are no longer capable of promising an "adequate society".

3. *Legalisation* is today, no doubt, the issue most widely dealt with among legal and social scientists involved with law and society. In Germany it appeared at the end of the 20s *(Otto Kirchheimer)* as a critical term. Legalisation then meant picking out and combating the petrification of political freedoms and social emancipation, that is, opposing those strategies which in the name of whatever legal *status quo* sought to block social conflicts and/or to keep them in a state where they could be decided unilaterally. That – disputed – conception of legalisation is therefore a particular (conservative) materialisation of formal law, and of course as such is still of a great importance today.

Today, quantitative (naturally never without "quality"!) problems are often discussed under the heading of legalisation, i.e. the extension of law to more (and new) areas and the intensification of law in areas already occupied. In this paper I do not intend to place this phenomenon in the foreground. That ground should in my opinion be occupied by three distinguishable modes of application, and therefore three problem contexts.

a. Legalisation as an Ambivalent Strategy

Here the development of bourgeois legal culture, in itself ambivalent (on the one hand, the law as a philosophical goal for society, as the realisation of legal freedom; on the other, the law as the protection of "*Vermögen*", in the double sense of "property" and "ways of action") is maintained. The law can be referred to above all for exploitive and protective sanctions. Against this, it is in principle unusable for the initial success of "newcomers". It is in connection with this that the ambivalence of critical and affirmative hopes and invocations is based, among both the left and right. The usual polemics go from "emancipation from law" as "law" ("on the left" as, for example, hopes against "capital" or "politics", "on the right" as hopes against "the state" or "the unions") to such abstract formulas as "no freedom for the foes of freedom". This, of course, gives rise to confusion, which is in some cases intentioned and achieved with different degrees of success. Thus it may seem plausible to suggest that de-legalisations (e.g. contractual freedom to divorce or school supervision law) is in fact legalisation (as freedom under law), or that legalisation (e.g. trade-union organisational autonomy) is really de-legalisation (the gagging of minorities). Uniform, guaranteed *legal rationality* can at any rate no longer be found here. Clarification can be provided only through the historical and social reconstruction of the form-content-problem of bourgeois law and through conscientiously systematising the social guarantees and securities producible under forms of law.

b. Legalisation in the context of "sociological" theories of society that include but overlap the law, of the type of *systems theory* (in Germany the key figure is Niklas Luhmann). Here the object of concern is functional prerequisites of law, which are mostly, as system performances, limited to systematisations of decisions. Luhmann considers, for instance, that such questions (and answers) as those about the nature of the law and of the person, of the sources of the law, of principles of justice etc., are hopelessly "old European" and are no longer relevant. His succinct approach is to subject all under legal theory to the question of whether it can formulate law, independently of old European handicaps, as a self-referential, self-reproducing system. The promises and the demands of such a system programme can be seen more clearly only when one has gone through it thoroughly. Then one sees that the complete redefinition of social and legal rationality as specifically *system rationality* (with many indubitably modern and successful adaptations) dismisses the human being (as individual and as citizen) from the centre of social theory. Instead, it finds its centres in "administration" and "economy" and – convincingly – allows "positive law" unlimited functions of application and of intensification (in total contrast to, for instance, left or left-liberal system theoreticians, who regard the rationality and productivity of law as exhausted, not extendable and incapable of self-transcendence).

c. Legalisation in the context of historical, genetic *reconstructions of social developments as levels of learning* (in Germany the key figure here is Jürgen Habermas). Here the point is the transformation of the philosophy of history into (critical) social theory, which seeks to understand both law and society in order to perceive and to overcome (avoid) "pathological" developments by those affected and involved.

d. The viewpoint I support, with Jürgen Habermas, is that modernity is an uncompleted project. While a substantive rationality expressed in religious and metaphysical "*Weltbildern*" has long been separated into elements of (objectivising) science, (universalistic) morality, and (formal) law, and (autonomous) art, the project of modernity is and remains the endeavour to take these autonomisations seriously in their historical right and develop them further. The connection between them, which perpetually needs and is capable of renewal, must however at the same time be used on behalf of practice in the life-world, as a rational shaping of the conditions of life.

As far as the rationality pattern goes, historical rationalisations have led to an irreversible system rationality (in and for political administration and the economy). However, it is possible to reconstruct the reason that founded this rationality, and this should make us determined not to let our "life-world" be dominated ("colonized") by the rationality imperatives of the "system".

4. It will perhaps have become clear in outline that and how the theoretical camps, precisely in the nature of their model building, must combine (model) both system and social integration and the paradigm change, as also the participation and involvement of the human being (as individual and as citizen) into an object of investigation *and* a presentation of subjectivity.

5. The *legal principle of proportionality* represents – in proportion to its suitability, requisiteness and appropriateness – the connecting piece which *in practice* chooses between social theories – even if unexpressed – and legal decisions. It does so by simultaneously – in accordance with the paradigm and system-social integration analysis – "opening up" historical and social transformations, contemporary modes of functioning and, not least, model patterns and model builders.

The principle is age-old, of venerable descent from the virtue of justice itself, that major virtue – beside courage, wisdom and prudence – among the classical philosophical cardinal virtues. It was later amalgamated with the Christian virtues of faith, hope and love and still later with the bourgeois revolutionary promises of freedom, equality and fraternity (security, solidarity). As *iustitia distributiva* and as *iustitia commutativa* it was certainly involved in vicissitudes, but with the modern bourgeois *Rechtsstaat* law took on its clearest lines. *Commutative* justice is fully utilised in the legal principle of contractual parity, which as guaranteed and guaranteeing contractual justice provides general justification of the indifferent – in both senses of unconcerned and impartial – content of formal legal definiteness (as *freedom under law*). *Distributive* justice reaches its culmination in the constitutional (p)reservation in favour of universal freedom and against private abuse of freedom and in this function is linked to *equality before the law*. This philosophical legal system, as the founding idea of bourgeois society, is "proportionality" itself. Interventions are legally proportionate if, because and insofar as they are appropriate and necessary, they keep freedom within limits, equal for all, through means of a universal law.

The extent to which everything has changed here is well known, and is not disputed in detail. Law is today supposed to make the free pursuit of goals (with controllable use of means) possible and thereby to prove its usefulness, and in turn to be a socially purposeful institution. Law consequently becomes both the producer and the product of society. Therein lies the double reconstruction (transformation) of law, on the one hand vis-a-vis the philosophical founding idea of civil society under the rule of law (whereby society is to be realised by the criterion of law) and vis-a-vis the antibourgeois movement (law is the "superstructure" of a "base" that is to be understood as a contradictory relationship between the forces of production and the relations of production, and is to be removed by way of the revolutionary disruption of society, and till then merely made use of). It would seem, no "model" can cope with this double reconstruction. Systems-theory models cannot "free" people (at least not quickly and effectively enough) from their faith in law, nor lawyers from their work, nor institutions from their dysfunctional structure, and so on. Critical theories of society cannot revolutionise, and do not seek to be constructively affirmative. The more "internally legal" models of law fall between invocations of their environments and promises of their internal worlds.

In such a situation, the triumphal course in practice of the proportionality principle of law is hardly surprising. Just as social models simultaneously deny and assume functions of depiction and exemplariness, so too can this (higher) principle serve all social models without needing to be subordinate to any; not mysterious, but hardly surmountably, mute; a feudal relationship between society and law through investiture (legitimation for decision-making and potential for sanctioning) against commendation (achievement of social goals through the law); more traditionally "the thinking obedience" of all lawyers. To be sure, the dilemma cannot simply be argued out of the way. The principle has been transformed (specifically, of course, by thinkingly obedient jurists in the service of society) from a freedom/causality to a purposefulness/utility functionality. A third core element which was, certainly, its inner element from the start, has taken over the major role beside suitability and requisiteness: that of adequateness, proportionality (there are other terms, such as prohibition of abuses etc.) which in older classical form appears as *"suum cuique"* or as *"aptum"*, in more recent classicism as *"proprietas"*, and contemporaneously as the "positive *and* right" (social *and* legal). *Definition of proportion* by way of justification of a decision in no longer consented, obvious, problem-free, harmonious, "contractual" legal situations. Some more detailed observations are in order.

a. The modern rationality of causality has, with the link that can be made between cause and effect, reason and consequence, means (ways) and aims (purposes), by using the category of (natural and technological) law, made possible specifiable forecasts and technologies. Forecasts and technologies in the area outside the natural sciences constitute potential strategies. The element missing from science – the normative, social, historical one – (the category of law, causality itself) has – with the exhaustion of idealistic philosophy – been found ultimately in the *"value" concept* through adaptation of the conception of causality (for some as a real abstraction, for others as an ideal or real type etc.). Karl Marx regarded the logical basic category of labour and the historical basic category of class struggle as real abstractions. Max Weber sought with the basic category of "ideal type" to save the cultural sciences vis-a-vis the natural sciences, by simultaneously avoiding political positivism and historical materialism. And yet both merely built (selective) models. They constructed sentences that were neither purely and completely descriptive and empirical, because there is no possibility of complete refutation, nor purely and completely normative, because they remained assertions, about given situations which instead claimed to count as an *offer* of an objectively possible and therefore correct interpretation (to that extent "science") and a correspondingly possible (and therefore right) mode of action (to that extent politics). It is unavoidable here and it is indeed the aim that the detailed evaluations made should make credible the preliminary design of the *whole* (for the whole) which in turn is therefore never entirely refutable, because – as a guideline for confirmations (i.e. nonrefutations) – it plays a part in arranging the data (observations, *cases*). The difference (in the case of so-called non-nomological hypotheses) between explanations and prognoses on the one hand and estimates of trends and tendencies, model building, plans, programmes and goal projections on the other is therefore transcended in *practice,* because normative decisions (bans on anything contradictory) are always involved in uncertain conditions, so that the difference between is and ought to be avoided. *Practice* therefore becomes *the* area of (theoretical) confirmation, because the object of theory here is never the generally repeatable (a "law"!), but in each case the *specificity* of a case (the task!) in the "light" of the guideline programme. The proximity of such "science" to "case law" is immediately obvious.

b. Sociological models that relate will-mediated causality, i.e. intentional action, to goal preferences – and vice versa – simultaneously make it possible to relate the value distinctions of goals back to the serviceability of the means for realising the values (and vice versa). The classical description that the end justifies the means is followed by the contemporary description whereby whoever regards the ends as valuable, or at least pursuable, must declare admissible those means whereby they (the ends) can be achieved. From the legal point of view, this leads to very considerable difficulties. In the classical idea of the rule-of-law freedom was freedom as to ends (contents) plus legal supervision over *forbidden* means (to achieve them). We have in the meantime been tormented by the randomness of ends, the confusion between means and ends, the problems that have to do with consequences of human action which are not simultaneously consequences of human intent (such consequences are unavoidable, unplannable, and not prohibitable). In brief, the conflict potential of "free", even if legally bound, pursuit of goals has for long compelled legal, because of the social, *control of ends*. One therefore needs criteria to measure ends (to evaluate them) in relation to disproportionate costs bound up with the use of suitable and necessary means, and to measure means (to evaluate them) in respect of the consequences they (may) lead to, the side-effects of the consequences, and the consequences of consequences etc. This work cannot be done "legally" (at least in the sense of traditional criteria and instruments). It is not the application of calculable *norms of prohibition* but appropriate (proportional) balancing between (and feeding back from) situational causes in the light of general programmes of guidelines. Here there is revealed a (not reference-free, but reference-diffuse) – "relational" (proportional) administration of general legal reservations on behalf of both subjective, individual and general freedom, of usefulness for the whole and for the parts, etc. More precisely: a general legal reservation for the whole of society, which by way of the recallable "positivity of law" and of the appealable "rightness of law" seems to legitimize nothing less than a universal *legal appropriateness* of – old and new – measures in situations. Sociological natural law in being? Rule through state of emergency? In any case, and at least, a transformation of delegated authority of free action within (legal) limits: into delegated authority to determine free action itself. To use an earlier formula: self-righteous law of conflict *(selbstgerechtes Kollisionsrecht)*.

c. It is therefore worthwhile looking into the mode of action of the proportionality principle through which, eternally and inescapably, "law" and "non-law" become tied together into "law". At any rate, the principle is a suitable, necessary and appropriate object for those approaches to reconstruction that relate social "normativity" (as legal rationality) to social power relationships (as in need of social rationalization).

d. It has, no doubt, become clear by now that the "proportionality" in the proportionality principle – in its function of evaluating costs arising in relation to benefit aimed at – can easily and endlessly be translated into other language games: expense – yield, cost – benefit, zero-sum-game – optimum need – satisfaction, society of expectations – all-providing state, majority – minority, feasible – unfeasible, objective compulsion – priorities. Here we find an opportunity for the use of social (social science) "calculations" as the definition of social relationship in law.

e. Finally, it should not be overlooked that in almost all important decisions of superior courts the "economically reasonable man (citizen)" appears, the normative configuration – as it were, the ideal general manager for invisible hands – which always symbolized the right path of virtue, the proper end-means-balance; in brief the measure and the mean, that is, *proprietas* itself.

At any rate, the practice of law application reaches preference decisions on conflicting "interests" by the legal application of a conflict norm (more precisely: conflict rule) which is developed, interpreted and applied. Such work therefore hits upon "the right" (more exactly, one possible right) by bringing it about. If one wishes to trace the magic of this "positive" law as "right" law, then one must reconstruct the underlying conflict rules on the basis of decisions. One comes upon them mostly by exposing the *"thing"* that has – explicitly or in a concealed manner – been taken as a basis in decisions. In the "thing" as content and the conflict rule as form, legal rationality is constituted as social rationality.

III.

The consequences for legal method (more precisely: for a unity between legal dogma and legal method as legal practice itself that can always only be reconstructed by theory) are obvious.

1. The classical civil-law method consisted – in the context in which universal laws and equal freedoms were rooted i.e. the calculability of action that was wrong because it was identifiable by forbidden use of means) – in the control of legal form, initiated through disruptions (major examples: infringement of contractual promises and tort damage to property). Contemporary legal method ought in the first place to pay attention to the degree to which these requirements have changed. I shall now briefly characterise these (for civil law in the broader sense, that is, including labour and economic law).

a. Thorough transformations of causality (legally for example, adequate causality, social adequacy etc.) into proportionality, i.e. "functionalities" in the sense of objective possibilities which within system constraints replace, complement, surpass, the hitherto constituted subjective possibilities in the legal world (life on the basis of subjective rights). This means above all bringing the total social preconditions for the development of private autonomy, of markets, of plans etc. to the fore.

b. Norm-purpose strategies indicate the pervasive dependence of legal strategies on extra-legal, social system-references. This means above all bringing to the fore methodologically the dependence of the production of legal rules on the assumed social theories.

c. Reflexion on the consequences demands the inclusion of future orientation (planning) into the legal world, which is in itself freed of consequence. "Purposive programmes" instead of "conditional programmes" are a slogan for this extremely controversial trend. This means above all relating decision-making work to the intermeshings of effects. It may mean that legal work as isolated individual case-work, recedes more into the background.

d. Legitimation through procedure is also – a controversial, but successful – slogan under which the retreat of legal decision-making programmes from the normative (justice as ideal) into an effect perspective (successful social aid as social performance) is proclaimed. This means above all asking the question of whether we have not been doing this for a long time, and perhaps, more precisely, whether it has been done "successfully" or not?

2. Under attack contemporary legal method has taken refuge in a self-righteous procedural virtue. It "practices" a general "logic of the particular". This means above all that it is no longer the *discovery* of facts under specifiable norm-hypotheses (which traditionally was always the exercise of freedom under general, formal prohibitory ground rules) that regulates application of the law but *definitions* of various units of "normative" and "social" problem material under perspectives of legal principles. Legal principles in turn are arrived at in the light of "system" conditions, especially of the legal system and even more of the judicial system. On the whole this does, to be sure, express – methodologically too – a radical shift from a civil-law to a social-constitutional orientation of standards. But the "thing" – a mean between normative guidelines and social relationships – is of course not thereby affected. Brief mention should be made here of the extent to which methodology, which is, moreover, unavoidably linked to procedures and strategies, is dependent on the reference back to substantive theory. Methodologically, it is undisputable that in the so-called syllogism model, in a tautological transformation, i.e. in the concretization of norms in the light of factual situations and in the abstraction from factual situations in the light of norms, the identical work effort of subsumption and interpretation, application is revealed. Here it is the defining and reflecting judgemental powers that are at work. The precondition here is always a split between "legal" and "social" subsumption (interpretation, application) on which, in the first place the possibility of making law definable as law in the form of situations and thereby separating it from the rest of the social field is dependent. However, today nobody any longer thinks and works in this (Kantian) way. Nor shall I go into the amount of professional schizophrenia that we would meet with if either, the lawyer had himself to formulate the social, i.e. non-legal, issues that are preconditions for this work by way of translation, which he is unable to and need not do, or correspondingly the non-lawyers had to take over the legal points, which they likewise are unable to and need not do. This is the old familiar problem of expert compartmentalisation which however is not sufficiently understood in a systematic way. Here I am concerned only with a more precise characterisation of the problem. It is rooted in the traditional conception that in spite of differing ("pluralist") value judgements in all social problem areas, a *uniform* (indeed, "right") (value) judgement can be possible in the specific legal problem area. It is this split that justifies the stylization of all controversial judgement in the social area as situational ("facts") elements of non-controversial judgement in the legal area. As far as content goes, this model presupposes that there is something like a fixed core area of law – as *form* of social *material*. This connection is ultimately the question of "formality", "materiality", "procedurality", "functionality", "relationality", and one could easily multiply these terms of law. Here too, the point is selective recourse to social material in the form of law. Applying it more generally: no theory, no model, is possible without such selection. Selectivity constitutes the academic mode of working. The results of selection constitute our theories and models.

3. The legal method has for long been moving between rationalities of rule and exception and that of interest-weighing. The rationality of rule-exception can only be guaranteed when one has precise predefinitions of the consequences of infringing legal goods as an indispensable conditional programme (in this case, for instance, the proportionality criterion could be applied at least to define the proportionality of a law X that has hitherto been protected – say so far without exception – to a – say not yet, or almost already or at least in the particular case justified in principle – offensive act Y.) Interest-weighing can absolutely not be done by legal means, because one needs a forum, where the interest conflict can (as a legal conflict) be dealt with according to binding conflict rules. In the case of socially (not "legally") defined conflicts both must be produced and re-produced, but can no longer be presupposed. It is precisely such difficulties that, for instance, systems theories – in an attempt to replace action theories – attack. Admittedly, little then remains of classical legal rationality as rationality of freedom.

IV.

Verba docent exempla trahunt. However, examples may also be tempting. I shall choose three examples that are claimed to be exemplary from the field of economic law, as understood in a broad sense.

1. However, we will begin with an example of explicit transformation. It has found no successor, and is therefore regarded in all fields as an absolutely horrifying example (RGZ 106, 272–277 (6. 2. 1923)). The Kiel town tram system was temporarily out of service due to lack of electrical current. The power station had been stopped by striking workers organized in the metalworkers union. Drivers, conductors and inspectors of the trams organized in the transport workers union, who where not on strike, turned up for work and demanded the payment of their wages. From the legal and sociological viewpoint the Reichsgericht performed a transformation (translation) of exemplary charm. I shall briefly reconstruct it.

a. Level of current law: according to the general contract law, this would amount to creditor's default of acceptance or creditor's bearing the risk (§ 615 BGB);

accordingly the workers should receive their wages, though they had not worked.

b. "In order, however, to reach a satisfactory solution to the dispute, one should not base oneself on the provision of the Civil Code, but instead consider the social relations as they have since developed ...". There follows a social subsumption, to the effect that there are two groups in society, the employers and the workers. The workers are members on the one hand of the worker class and on the other – by their labour contract – of an enterprise and work community (of employer and workers). If the latter community failed for reasons not the fault of the employer (as in this case), the workers would have to accept the refusal of wages.

c. A renewed (second) level of law: "This finding derived from the social circumstances can however, also, without difficulty, be incorporated in the provisions of the Civil Code". The Reichsgericht then applied § 323 BGB (where there is impossibility of performance, the corresponding counterperformance cannot be claimed. The workers are not entitled to wages.

What is acting as a "thing" in this decision are social classes (employers and workers) and social communities (the work community), and the conflict rule is forced solidarity.

Brief commentary: Right up to the present, in the law of industrial risk distribution both the community ideology (where the firm suffers, the burden should be distributed over both groups) and the class ideology (depending upon which sphere is hit, the burden is allocated one of the two groups) can be used as approaches in legal doctrine.

2. In the law of price control the point there is the abuse of market power. The criteria for this are defined by *comparison* – historical (earlier price policy) and spatial (price policy, say, abroad). In a series of decisions the Bundesgerichtshof has discovered and "transcended" the following dilemma. No comparison without addition and deduction in the case of the items compared, but it is precisely these changes that disrupt comparability. The consequence is: no price control.

In this case-law (under the indirect influence of the uncertainty theory of physics and the position of the entrepreneur in competition theory) what is acting as a "thing" is the impossibility of defining competition; the conflict rule is a sociological – historical assumed law of self-perpetuating developments (pattern predictions).

Brief commentary: Freedom of competition (as law) is therefore in need of protection and capable of being protected only against distortions of competition through "political systems" but not in the "economic system".

3. The Springer group is an important media empire. A well-known journalist (Guenter Wallraff) worked there for a long period under a false name as a participating observer and subsequently published his experiences and views. The Bundesgerichtshof (BGHZ 80, 25–43; 20. 1. 1981) justified his action in principle (in view of the proportionality principle) as an appropriate disclosure of press abuses in the interests of press freedom.

In this example of case-law what is acting as "thing" is a notion of the "true" press and of the "true" public opinion; the conflict rule is the presumption that the journalist was acting as a social agency and that his action was justified by success.

Brief commentary: If and because breaches of the law can be justified by any kind of success that they achieve, then high treason can indeed, even in positive law, be a question of the date.

4. Trade unions, like other associations, have for various reasons problems with members. The German system of interest representation is organized in a dual way for workers: central industrial trade unions and decentralized works councils. For works councils elections – as for all elections – electoral freedom applies (with sanctions against its infringement). Are trade union prohibitions on members from being candidates on other lists infringements of electoral freedom or the realisation of freedom of association? The law of the highest courts has consistently decided in favour of electoral freedom within the plant, which they preferred on the basis of the proportionality principle.

What is acting as a "thing" here is the welfare within the plant of workers and firm, with as conflict rule an unambiguousness doctrine of damage to goods (in the specific case: trade unions are unambiguously infringing plant electoral freedom, while union candidates on non-trade-union lists do not unambiguously infringe union freedom of association).

Brief commentary: Corporatism analysts study the tripartite system of "politics" (state), "economy" (employers) and "labour" (unions) in terms of their activities which promote or endanger social stability. Critics feel that unions are too weak for a successful corporatism project, because state and employers are less dependent on unions than on the rank and file in the plants. Reflection on consequences (not by the judiciary but on the results which have been decided): Cui bono?

V.

In the fundamental legal principle of proportionality I have sought to define the most influential machinery of transformation for the osmosis, translation, covariance of law and society, as the supreme and most general productive principle of an – admittedly silent and absolutely unavoidable – justification of conflict rules for the decision of conflicting rights, interests and needs. Legal relations are in fact (in Germany since the days of Savigny) neither pure objects of evaluations nor pure evaluations of objects, but have always been premediated general decisions on the assignments of facts to a particular law by way of connection, the qualification of legal answers to social questions. Legal relationships do not presuppose (already) defined legal principles but produce these legal principles (more correctly, of course: lawyers are regarded as being authorized to effect this production). In the concealed application premises of the qualification theory itself, i.e. in the mode of application of the proportionality principle, a complete social science theory programme (*sub verbo* proportionality, justice or the like) is concealed. For the qualification theory (not the norm) defines the selection of object areas, and is in turn defined (not by norms, but) by the selection among the supreme alternatives in evaluation; accordingly, the mediatory definitions of (links between) objects of (say, economic) law and a methodology guided by a substantive theory (social goals, system performance: the different ways of saying do not enter in here) are therefore in need of explanation and justification (proportionality qualifications as theory of/for/in practice itself). This critical work is however lacking. Whether and how it could be done cannot be answered by the means of law, jurisprudence and lawyers. I should like to make my contribution thereto in the debate on materialisation and proceduralisation.** Here I shall accordingly merely state the following thesis: it is on the "projects" for the whole of society that are in each case to be implemented and realized that – reconstructively – the way "criticism" and "constructions" can react towards the law and from the law to each other, depends. The thing affected is always the justification of conflict rules for the sake of a "thing".

** See WIETHÖLTER, RUDOLF (1985). "Materialization and Proceduralisation in Modern Law," in G. Teubner (ed.). *Dilemmas of Law in the Welfare State*. Berlin: de Gruyter.

Where the Legal Action is: Critical Legal Studies and Empiricism

David M. Trubek*
Wisconsin-Madison

Introduction

Critical legal studies is a scholarly project of recent vintage. It has attracted wide interest. But the nature of the project is not fully understood, and the implications of a "critical" approach to legal studies have not been fully realized even by those who participate in the movement. Critical legal studies rests on a set of notions about relationships among the ideas we hold about law and society, the structures of social life we are engaged in, and the actions we take. These ideas present a challenge to legal scholarship as it is currently practiced, as well as to the organization of American society. The ideas on which the critical studies movement is based derive from a variety of sources in legal and social theory; not all are fully worked out or easily understood. This essay is an effort to clarify some of these ideas, and to draw out some of their implications for research on the history, meaning and impact of law.

* This essay could be seen as an effort to resolve some of the questions left unanswered in an earlier piece I wrote (Trubek, 1977: 529).It was inspired by debates with several of my colleagues in the Conference on Critical Legal Studies and by discussions with Lawrence Friedman, Joel Handler, Austin Sarat and Bill Whitford about the relationship between CCLS and the "law and society" movement. Many people provided helpful comments on earlier drafts: these include Richard Abel, Kristin Bumiller, Willard Hurst, Leonard Kaplan, Duncan Kennedy, Karl Klare, Mark Lazerson, Deborah Rhode, Austin Sarat, John Henry Schlegel, Ted Schneyer, Gunther Teubner and Mark Tushnet. I am especially indebted to Stewart Macaulay, with whom I exchanged ideas at every stage of the project, Joel Rogers who read the manuscript with painstaking care and provided numerous critical comments and suggestions, and Carroll Seron and Frank Munger who shared a draft of their paper on the same subject. Opportunities to present tentative versions of the paper to the University of Wisconsin Interdisciplinary Legal Studies Colloquium and Legal History Program, the Center for European Legal Policy (Bremen), the European University Institute (Florence) and the University of California-Berkeley Program in Jurisprudence and Social Policy, helped me clarify the ideas. Lee Karlin assisted in the early stage of the research. Mark Cammack participated throughout the project and provided invaluable assistance both in formulating issues and in the conduct of the research. No one but me is to blame for what resulted from all this interaction. A first version of this article has been published in the Stanford Law Review I (1984).

In a sense, this could be seen as an essay on "method." Part of the polemics within and about critical legal studies has to do with what appear to be questions of scholarly method.[1] Some question whether critical scholarship can produce valid knowledge about law in society, since the scholarly method employed stresses the study of appellate cases and other indicia of legal doctrine, and seems to overlook "empirical" evidence of the social "impact" of law or the behavior of legal actors. On the other hand, people within the critical legal studies movement sometimes attack the sort of research that does focus on attitudes, behavior, and impact as a form of "social science mystification" which hides the true nature of social relations and the real importance of law in society. These people seem to be arguing about method, and particularly about the value of "empiricism" in legal studies.

I am sure one could construct a full latter-day *methodenstreit* out of these debates, and find in it echoes of the arguments that have split the German social science community from Max Weber's day to the present (Adorno et al., 1976). That, however, is not my purpose. Behind the current discussion of method, I believe, lies a much more interesting set of questions about the nature and function of law in modern society, and the relationship between legal ideas and social action. Critical legal studies has contributed to the eternal debate on these matters, and one can learn something about that contribution by starting with what appear to be questions of method.

1. The Critique of Legal Order

I shall argue in this essay that Critical Legal Studies is both a continuation of, and a challenge to, an older tradition in legal studies. I call this tradition the "critique of legal order." This tradition can be seen as the outgrowth of American legal realism, one of the sources of the "law and society" movement that has produced so many valuable studies of what actually occurs in our legal life, and the starting point for the movement in thought that is associated with the Conference on Critical Legal Studies.

The idea of a legal order is a central part of the Western tradition of social thought about law, but it has been given many names. As I use the term, it is similar to Weber's concept of formally rational modern law (Weber, 1968:654).

[1] While there is a lively debate about the relationship between critical legal studies and empiricism, it is extremely difficult to document the various positions that have emerged. This is largely because very little has been written and nothing as yet published which explicitly deals with the questions canvassed here: people talk about these matters extensively, but rarely write about them. (For one exception, see Munger and Seron 1983). Partly because of the paucity of texts, but also because of the nature of the issues, I have relied very heavily on extended conversations with proponents and opponents of CLS to develop the ideas presented here, but make no attempt to document these discussions. There has been more explicit attention to these questions in Great Britain, and readers interested in these issues will find a useful analysis in Cain and Finch. (1981:105). For one critical scholar's views of "social science" in American legal studies, see Tushnet (1980:1383).

Mensch and Kennedy's classical legal consciousness (Mensch, 1982; Kennedy, 1980:3) and Selznick and Nonet's concept of autonomous law (Nonet, and Selznick, 1978: part III). Following Unger, (Unger, 1976) I use the term "legal order" to describe the view that four conditions prevail in a society. First, the law is in some sense a system, that is, a body of concepts ("doctrine") which, properly interpreted, provides an answer to all questions about social behavior (including the answer that the law does not affect that behavior). Secondly, there is a form of reasoning which can be employed by specialists that will generate the necessary answers from doctrine when such answers are required. Thirdly, that doctrine reflects a coherent view about the basic relations between persons and of the nature of society; Unger calls this a "defensible scheme of human association." (Unger, 1983:561). Finally, to a significant degree, social action in the society is oriented toward the norms that are generated by the legal system, either because these legal norms have been internalized by the actors or because by threat of or actual coercion the actors come to abide by them.

The critique of legal order is based on four principles, which I call indeterminacy, antiformalism, contradiction and marginality. Taken together, these principles challenge the idea that a legal order (in this sense) exists in our (or any other) society.[2] First, the critics assert that while there is clearly a body of stuff we can call legal doctrine, it is not a "system." That is, the doctrine neither provides a determinant answer to questions nor covers all conceivable situations: that is the principle of indeterminacy (Kennedy, 1976:1685; Kennedy, 1973:351). Secondly, the critics reject the idea that there is a distinct form of legal reasoning which can be applied to the doctrinal materials by neutral specialists to yield concrete results: this is the principle of antiformalism (Unger, 1983:561). Thirdly, the critics reject the view that the doctrine contains a single, coherent and justifiable view of human relations; rather they see the doctrine as reflecting two or even more different and often competing views, no one of which is either sufficiently coherent or pervasive to be called dominant (Kennedy, 1976 and 1979:205; Macaulay, 1966; Tushnet, 1979:1307). This is the principle of contradiction. Finally, the critics note that even under those circumstances in which a consensus can be formed about the norms of the law, and thus the potential for internalization of legal norms or legal coercion, there is no reason to believe that the law as such often or even frequently is a decisive factor in social behavior: this is the principle of marginality (Macaulay, 1963; Galanter, 1974:95).

The critique of legal order presents a challenge to legal scholarship as it traditionally understood itself. If law is indeterminant, all scholarship on what the law is must appear to be a form of advocacy, rather than a "neutral" or "scientific" activity. If there is no distinct form of legal reasoning, scholarly argumentation about the law blends into political and ideological debate. If the

[2] For a general introduction to the critique of legal order, see, Kennedy (1980); Mensch (1982); Gordon (1981:1017); Tushnet (1981). If one reads Stewart Macaulay (1963:55), Macaulay (1966:1051), one can see why it might be possible to claim that all the elements of the critique of legal order were understood over twenty years ago. Kennedy (1976:1685).

stuff of legal doctrine is, by its nature, contradictory, then legal argumentation can find no grounding in the materials of law itself; given good advocates and limiting argumentation to materials in the doctrine, all lawsuits and all scholarly debates about the law should end in a tie. And if law is marginal, then whatever normative arrangements govern social life must be worked out extralegally, or at best "in the shadow of the law." Moreover, since the law that casts that "shadow" is itself indeterminant, contradictory, and a part of political and ideological debate and struggle, "law" itself is not something hard but rather an obscure and vague source of normative guidance, so that social arrangements are shaped in the shadow of a shadow, as it were.

Those who accept the critique of legal order can find it paralyzing or exhilarating. While the critique seems to deny the validity of some kinds of legal scholarship, it opens up multiple possibilities for new scholarly directions. In a sense, this essay is about some of these possibilities, and the relations among them. In analyzing the debate about "empiricism" within Critical Legal Studies, and the claims made by critics of CLS that it is "anti-empiricist." I am discussing arguments between people all of whom have bitten of the fruit of the critique of legal order, but who have taken different paths as they try to work out its implications for their lives and their work.

One of the themes of the essay is the importance of holding all the elements of the critique together as one pursues its implications. I fear that many have latched onto one or two of these ideas and forgotten about the rest. To do that would, in my view, be to go down a dead end. So this essay is really about what it would mean seriously to follow out the full implications of indeterminacy, antiformalism, contradiction and marginality all at once.

2. What Is the Meaning of "Empiricism" in the Debate over Critical Legal Studies?

In using the debate over something called "empiricism" as the thread into the cave, I will restrict myself to the uses of this term within the particular argument that has sprung up within and about the Conference. Whatever meanings empiricism may have to outsiders, it has taken on particular – and often polemic – meanings in the arguments among critical scholars and between them and others who work within the broad framework set by the critique of legal order. Moreover, as we look more closely at the debate itself, we can see that "empiricism" is used in at least three distinct ways. The first task is to sort out these meanings.

This debate takes place among people who are studying the law; one can imagine that when they talk about "empiricism" they are referring to certain techniques to be used in this effort, e.g. surveys, interviews, multivariate analysis. To be sure, that is what they are doing. But the debate seems to be about something else as well: something larger seems to be at stake.

This is clear when we look at the way some people in critical legal studies think about the techniques of empirical inquiry. These people express hostility towards empiricism because they think it is associated with (a) determinism and (b) positivism.

Determinism is the view that the social world is governed by fundamental laws. Social life, like the interaction of molecules and the rotation of planets, obeys certain laws. These laws, which give society its deep logic, exist irrespective of our wills. Social science, in this view, brings to light the objective conditions which determine our fate.

Positivism is the view that there is a radical distinction between statements about facts and other statements, and that empirical social science can only consist in statements about facts (See Alexander, 1982). Positivists include those who favor grand theory, as well as those who set their sights on more modest propositions of the middle range (Alexander, 1982:5). It may include those who style themselves as structural functionists and those who espouse some version of Marxism.[3]

For those who share the "positivist persuasion" scientific knowledge is a set of generalizations about facts. The ultimate arbiter of any theory is the facts: Knowledge is built up through an iterative process in which general statements are tested against what we can demonstrate to be the case using methods of empirical inquiry which allow us to determine if the laws we hypothesize adequately describe the facts we can apprehend. Theory and method are defined in this context. We have to state laws in ways that allow them to be falsified by factual inquiry (theory), and we must have ways to measure the facts against the relationships posited by the theory (method). The task of empirical social science in this sense is demanding. The first challenge is getting the right facts: there is always the problem of whether something we know about social life is central and representative, or peripheral and unusual. We also have to be sure to separate out what the observer wants to believe (bias) from the real facts. A second problem is to set forth knowledge of the facts with parsimony; there must be some way to reduce the information we receive about empirical reality to a comprehensible and testable set of propositions.

When some people in CLS attack something they call "empiricism," they think they are challenging *both* positivism and determinism. They think that the search for the facts, and the use of various methods to get the facts, reveals a commitment to reduce all knowledge to statements about an empirical world and an acceptance of some form of determinism.

Few who defend the search for facts and the empirical method accept this vision of what they are doing. While there are many alternative accounts of empiricism employed by defenders of the methods in question, one worthy of special note might be called "pragmatism."[4]

The pragmatic approach accepts the view that to understand social life we must be in touch with what is going on now in our culture. This leads them to support, and engage in, much the same sort of inquiry which might be carried

[3] For a critique of positivism in Marxist thought see Albrecht Wellmer (1974).

[4] This category was suggested to me by my colleague *Bill Whitford* who is a leading practitioner of what I would call pragmatic empiricism in legal studies. Rorty (1982).

out by positivists, including those whose positivism includes determinism. The difference is not in "method" in the sense of surveys versus texts, data versus doctrine. The difference is in the understanding the pragmatists have about why they are conducting surveys or observing all that behavior. Where positivist determinists see themselves as mapping some underlying reality and constructing iron laws of social life, the pragmatists are concerned with conducting an inquiry that will advance some end they have in view (Rorty, 1982:160).

Let us assume that I want to be sure that my faculty hires more women. To further this interest, I will want to learn how the appointments process really works: to do this I will conduct what we should properly call an "empirical" inquiry. I will listen to debates, identify various coalitions, understand how they react to various arguments, and plan my strategy accordingly. I do not hope to develop any "iron law of faculty politics" but if I get my candidate appointed, who cares? Or assume that I favor broad access to the courts by social movements who are using various strands of legal doctrine to advance what I consider to be worthy aims. Someone comes along and claims that our litigation rates are soaring and are now the highest in the world, that our courts are being called on to handle issues never before resolved in litigation and beyond their inherent capabilities, and that as a result we should deter the use of courts by various litigants. I will want to test these claims using what evidence I can gather: I may analyze the litigation statistics over time and in comparison with other nations, I will look for historical precedents for the kinds of litigation I support, I may interview judges, lawyers and court administrators to see how they see what is going on: all this "empirical" inquiry may produce a counterpicture of what is going on that I can use to defend policies I favor (Galanter, 1983). Finally, assume I find it distasteful that sellers bilk consumers and someone says the solution is to pass the sort of consumer protection law that is in force in Alabama. Before I sign on, I may want to go to Alabama and find out what is going on. I will want to talk to lawyers, people in the Attorney General's office, and consumers. If I want to be sure consumers can and do use the law, I may want to conduct a statistically valid survey of Alabama consumers. If I find the systems work, I may go along, but if I discover that no one knows about the law, or that it is too expensive to use it, or that lawyers dissuade consumers who want to sue local merchants, I will decide that this law does not foster the interests I favor (Macaulay, 1979:115). In all these examples, empirical methods have been used pragmatically to advance a chosen goal.

In the debate over critical legal studies there is yet a third way in which "empiricism" is used. This is a usage designed to distinguish different ways of studying the law. In this "legal studies" sense the term empiricism describes an approach to the study of law which is distinguished from traditional scholarship on the law as such. Such traditional research seeks to state what the prevailing legal norms are: Research of this sort focuses on doctrine; the authoritative texts, i.e. constitutions, statutes, rules, and cases. Other materials including history and information about society may, and frequently are, introduced, but only to aid in normative interpretation. In the legal studies sense "empirical" is used to distinguish a type of study of law whose aims differ radically from doctrinal legal research. Where doctrinal research focuses on what the law "is" the "empirical" legal tradition examines what has brought the law about, what the actors in the legal system do, how law actually works, what effect it has on people.[5] I call this "empirical legal studies."

The successful creation of a tradition of research which examines law from the outside, examining its history, meaning and impact, has been a heroic achievement. It has long been clear that doctrinal studies alone cannot give an adequate account of the operation of law, and that exclusive reliance on doctrinal studies can mislead us about what really matters. Yet it has not been easy to go beyond doctrinal studies: the effort has been hampered by the recalcitrance of traditional legal scholars, the unwillingness of law schools to support risky (and often costly) research endeavors, the indifference of most social scientists to legal institutions, and the absence of any permanent institution designed to foster this kind of work.[6] Despite these barriers, the movement to expand legal studies from doctrine to the study of what law does (or doesn't do) has been relatively successful, creating new alliances between lawyers and scholars in other disciplines, spawning numerous "law and ..." subfields (e.g., law and society, law and economics, legal history) and generating a substantial literature.

In the struggle to construct a nondoctrinal tradition in legal studies, many came to see what they were doing as "empirical," and to believe that this term defined a bright line between their activities and those of the traditionalists against whom they were rebelling. It is easy to understand how this occurred. Although the nondoctrinal tradition can be seen as one of the fruits of the general critique of legal order, many who pioneered in the nondoctrinal movement tended to put greatest stress on the principle of "marginality," that is, the idea that legal norms influence what goes on in society at best in an indirect and uncertain fashion. They felt that to study what really goes on in the shadow of a shadow it was necessary to get out of the library and get "the facts"; i.e. to see

[5] See, e.g., Abel (1973:175). The purpose of what Abel calls "law books" is to rationalize (in the Weberian sense) legal doctrine, i.e., to state, explain, organize and criticize legal rules according to currently acceptable legal criteria. Such legal rationalization is a part of the professional legal enterprise. Law books are legal scholarship produced to meet the demands of the functioning legal system.
By contrast, the common feature of all "books about law" is their detachment from the professional enterprise; their objectives lie outside the legal system. Books about law are a reflection upon the whole activity of which law books are a part.

[6] John Henry Schlegel has provided us with a fascinating account of the early struggles to establish empirical legal studies in America. He notes that the law schools were not prepared to support an endeavor that would require long periods of collaboration between lawyers and social scientists, and could lead to results that would challenge, rather than confirm, the reformist ideas that initially led the schools to dabble in social science. (Schlegel, 1980:459). Robert Gordon has noted that legal scholarship is particularly resistant to what he calls "historicism," i.e., the idea that legal ideas, institutions and structures are changeable. (Gordon, 1981:1017). Recently,scholars as diverse as Stewart and Macaulay and Richard Posner have lamented the continuing hostility of the law schools to the empirical and social scientific temperament. See Macaulay (1982); (Posner, 1981:1113).

what really went on in areas allegedly affected by legal rules. It is part of the folklore of the University of Wisconsin Law School, where this tradition has flourished, that Frank Remington argued that criminal law should be studied in the patrol car, and Stewart Macaulay echoed him by saying that business contract law should be looked at in the offices of corporate purchasing agents. Riding in the patrol car, or visiting the GM purchasing agent, was empirical; parsing cases on the Miranda rule or analyzing the doctrine of consideration was not. In addition to the effect created by their acceptance of the principle of marginality, the creators of the nondoctrinal tradition were influenced by the American social scientists with whom they formed an initial alliance. Then, as today, many of the social scientists who became interested in the study of law accepted some version of the positivist account of social knowledge. This naturally led them to define "theory" as empirical theory in the positivist sense, and to place great emphasis on the need to employ standard "empirical" methods (surveys, interviews, analysis of statistics) to validate theory. So at least for some, the term "empirical legal studies" came to be equated with the nondoctrinal tradition and thus in this third sense has entered into the debate over critical legal studies.

3. Confusion in the Discussion of Empiricism in Legal Studies

One reason that the debate over empiricism and critical legal studies is so confused is because these three senses of empiricism get mixed up. Some who don't like critical legal studies and do like "empiricism" in the third (legal studies) sense note that critical scholars seem to be studying legal doctrine, as, in a sense, they are. Since by definition the study of doctrine is excluded from empirical legal studies, these people feel they can reject the critical legal studies movement as "nonempirical," and for this reason incapable of providing an adequate account of law in society. On the other hand, some who like critical legal studies but do not like positivism and determinism conclude that all the people who are doing interviews, analyzing statistics, conducting surveys, coding records and so on must be positivist determinists. Since the critical scholars see the reductionist view of knowledge as a mystification of social life and the determinist account of society as a barrier to transformative politics, they reject what they take to be empirical legal studies.

It seems to me that most of this argumentation is just wrong. On the one hand, there is no reason to identify nondoctrinal methods of research in legal studies with positivist determinism. That doesn't mean that positivists do not exist,[7] or that some people who analyze litigation rates may believe they are in

[7] Donald Black, a leading practitioner of empirical legal studies, identifies himself as "an uncompromising adherent of the positivist approach." See Black (1972a:709). Black asserts that "law can be seen as a thing like any other in the empirical world." (Black, 1972b:1086). He lists the basic principles of a positivist social science of law as, first, "science can know only phenomena and never essences. The quest for the one correct concept of law or anything else 'distinctively legal' is therefore inherently unscientific." Second, "every scientific idea requires a concrete empirical referent of some kind . . .

touch with unalterable aspects of reality. It just means that most people who do that sort of thing are probably aware of the limited, provisional and pragmatic nature of the knowledge it yields. On the other hand, it is silly to say that critical legal studies is doctrinal, in the sense in which that term is used in the debate. This argument confuses the object of study with the purpose of study. Certainly, critical legal scholars spend a lot of time reading doctrinal materials and writing about cases and statutes. But they are not trying to find out what the law "is"; nothing, I submit, is further from either their intentions or the results of their work. To suggest that somehow Duncan Kennedy and Karl Klare are doing the same thing as Langdell and Williston is just nuts.

On the contrary, if we are to classify the critical scholars in the terms employed by the debate over legal scholarship, then they clearly fall on the empirical side of the line as the term is used to distinguish forms of legal studies. That is, if we accept as valid the definition of empirical legal studies as research on what the law does in society, in contrast to studies of what the law on a given question "is," then critical scholars are doing empirical research. While at a later point I will seek to question the doctrinal-empirical dichotomy itself, first I want to defend the claim that, at least in the terms of the distinction, critical legal studies is empirical.

What is the basis for differentiating empirical and doctrinal legal studies? One might see the distinction as similar to that between theology and the sociology of religion. Theologians develop ideas about the world and humanity from within an authoritative tradition: a sociologist of religion would look at theological production from without, attempting to account for it and to trace its impact on society (Weber, 1968:339). Similarly, empirical legal studies looks at the operations of the law from the outside, asking what brings the law about and what impact it has. Moreover, empirical legal studies, like the sociology of religion, has a potentially subversive effect on the object of study. Because these enterprises question the self-understanding of the activity they study, they may appear to threaten it.

Empirical legal studies not only look at law from the outside; they also make problematic what is taken for granted by those whose activities they study. It is no accident that Stewart Macaulay's study of "Non-Contractual Relations in Business" is one of the classics of the empirical legal studies tradition (Macaulay, 1963:55). This study juxtaposes the assumptions built into the law of contract with an empirical investigation of what businessmen do. Where the law of contract presupposes that commercial relations are explicitly established in

Accordingly, insofar as such ideal as justice, the rule of law, and due process are without grounding in experience, they have no place in the sociology of law." And finally, "value judgments cannot be discovered in the empirical world and for that reason are without cognitive meaning in science ... Science is incapable of an evaluation of the reality it confronts." (p. 1092). The aim of the sociology of law should be to develop a general theory of governmental social control, "a theory that would predict and explain every instance of legal behavior." (p. 1087). Black himself offered such a general theory in his book (Black, 1976).

advance, Macaulay found businessmen rarely plan for the long-term implications of their transactions in advance (Macaulay, 1963:56). Where the law of contract presupposes that breakdowns in business relations will be resolved in courts through the application of the rules of contract law, Macaulay found that courts were rarely used by businessmen with disputes (Macaulay, 1963:60).

Critical legal studies follows this tradition: it looks at law from the outside; makes problematic things taken for granted by the object of study, and examines relationships between legal ideas and social action. The focus of these studies, however, is rather different than much of the "empirical" work done heretofore: this difference of focus helps explain the confusion over how to label this newer tradition.

4. The Critique of Legal Thought

Critical legal studies in the United States includes a wide range of scholarly activity, but much of the writing produced by CLS focuses on the ideas in legal doctrine or legal scholarship. Since it is this work – the critique of legal thought, if you will – which has generated the debate I am analyzing, I shall focus on it. Critical scholars write articles about major legal decisions in areas like labor (See generally Cloke, 1976:159; Klare, 1978:265, 1981: 450, 1982; Stone, 1981:1515), and anti-discrimination law (Freeman, 1978:1049, 1982), about doctrinal concepts in tort (Abel, 1981:59, 1982; Kennedy, 1982:563), contract (Gabel, 1977:601; Gabel and Feinman, 1982), and public law (Tushnet, 1979:1307; Frug, 1980:1057), and on the presuppositions of legal scholarship itself (Tushnet, 1980:1383, 1981:1205; Kennedy, 1979:205; Gordon, 1981:1017; Gabel, 1980:25). Unlike the judges and scholars whose work they study, however, those who *critique* legal thought do not try to determine what are the appropriate rules for wildcat strikes or whether it is necessary to prove discriminatory intent as a condition of liability under antidiscrimination laws: rather they seek to expose the assumptions which underlie judicial and scholarly resolution of such issues, question the presuppositions about law and society of those whose intellectual product is being analyzed, and examine the subtle effects these products have in shaping legal and social consciousness.

Critical legal scholars take doctrine seriously. But they also think they are examining the social role of law. The critical scholars clearly believe that when they conduct a critique of legal thought they are not doing doctrinal research but are looking at law from the outside, and tracing relationships between law and social action. Moreover, they see themselves as working out the implications of indeterminacy, antiformalism, contradiction and marginality.

All this seems to be a puzzle to those who visualize a clear boundary between doctrinal and empirical legal studies. All the legal empiricist can see is that the critical scholars have abandoned the patrol car for the library. Instead of studying the gap between the law in the books and the law in action (Abel, 1980:805; Sarat, 1983) or looking for extralegal sources of normative order (Galanter, 1981:1), the critical scholars are just studying the law (or even worse:

they are studying *studies* of the law). So how can they claim to be part of the nondoctrinal tradition, to continue a critique of legal order which includes the principle of marginality?

4.1. Law, Meaning, and the Construction of Society

The answer lies in a view of social relations. For those who engage in the critique of legal thought, ideas in some strong sense can be said to "constitute" society. That is to say, social order depends in a nontrivial way on the fact that the actors in a society share "world views": basic notions about human and social relations which give meaning to their lives. Ideas about the law – what it is, what it does, why it exists – are part of the world view of any complex society like ours: these ideas form the legal consciousness of society. The critique of legal thought is the analysis of the world views embedded in modern legal consciousness.

Karl Klare states this program with clarity. He describes capitalist society as a "constructed totality" in which ideas, institutions and power relations interrelate in complex ways. Looking at his own specialty, American labor law, Klare describes this body of thought as the embodiment of a "moral and political vision," which contains a "powerfully integrated set of beliefs, values and political assumptions" (i.e. a world view) which serves as a "legitimating ideology that reinforces the dominant institutions and hegemonic culture of society" (Klare, 1982:73). The task of "critical labor law," he suggests, is to bring to light the world view encoded in labor law doctrine (Klare, 1982:66).

One could see this project as the analysis of ideology: indeed, Klare and other critical legal scholars define their work largely in this fashion. Looking at critical legal studies as the analysis of ideology makes it possible to see in what way it would be proper to characterize it as empirical legal studies. By studying legal doctrine from this perspective, the critical scholars are examining the ways in which lawyers produce ideological pictures, and how these pictures influence social relations. Seeing the critique of doctrine as the study of ideology should clear up, for those who haven't been able to work it out, the difference between *Corpus Juris Secundum* and *The Politics of Law*[8]. It might even lead one to conclude that critical legal studies is really in the mainstream of social science, for ideology is a well-recognized field of social research.

But things are not quite that simple. There is a world of difference between the typical product of critical legal studies and much sociological research on ideology. Take as an example of the latter Max Weber's classical study of the relations between world views and domination in his monograph *The Religion of China* (Weber, 1968). This study analyzes the relationship between the world views of Confucianism and Chinese political and economic structures. Weber accepted the view that societies are held together by constructed realities of meaning. In *The Religion of China* he shows that the most basic religious and ethical ideas of Confucianism created a world of social meaning in which the domination of the gentry or mandarin class could be seen as self-evident and

[8] See Kairys (1982). This book contains a series of essays by members of the Conference on Critical Legal Studies and the National Lawyers Guild.

necessary. To put it in the language of critical legal studies, Weber saw Confucianism as a "moral and political vision" and demonstrated how it "legitimated the hegemony" of the gentry who were the dominant "class" in Imperial China. But while Weber's analysis of the relations among world views and sociopolitical domination helps us understand traditional Chinese society, he is obviously uninterested in *criticizing* Confucianism's cosmology or its related ideas about social structure and state. The project of critical legal studies is very different: while critical legal scholars seek to show relationships between the world views embedded in modern legal consciousness and domination in capitalist society, they also want to *change* that consciousness and those relationships. That is the *critical* dimension in critical legal studies. In this scholarly tradition, the analysis of legal consciousness is part of a transformative politics.[9] This is what distinguishes critical legal studies from much of "social science" as we normally understand it.

4.2. The Critique of Legal Consciousness and the Transformation of Society

The idea that legal scholarship can be a kind of transformative political action is central to what I have called the critique of legal thought. It represents an important part of the critical legal studies tradition. But it is an idea that is not well understood. And the views it rests on have not been fully worked out, even by those who engage in this practice.

In this section, I shall set out a provisional account of the views that underlie such scholarly practice. I consider this account provisional for two reasons. First, although it is based on a study of the work of the critical scholars, it is strictly my own, not a collective view to which all currently adhere. Secondly, and more importantly, the account leaves many issues unresolved. But it does help us see how the critical analysis of legal thought might contribute to social change.

It will be useful to start with a more familiar notion of the relationship between legal scholarship and politics. There is an old tradition of instrumental radicalism in the law schools; legal scholars who sympathize with specific social movements (unions, blacks, women) have helped foster the goals of these movements by lending their legal talents to specific struggles. These radical instrumentalists may participate in litigation or write doctrinal articles justifying results thought to provide instrumental gains for the movements in question.

Critical legal scholars do not reject this kind of radical instrumentalism; indeed, many engage in it. But the movement also involves a very different set of practices: these aim at changing society through the transformation of legal consciousness.

The consciousness of any society rests on a set of world views: basic (and sometimes implicit) notions about what is natural, necessary, just, and desirable. These world views provide an explanation for what would otherwise be inexplicable or intolerable. They lie behind all specific justifications of unequal power, social hierarchies and differences in life-chances. They give to society what is

[9] For an extended discussion of the relationship between critical legal studies and transformative politics, see Unger (1983:561).

most fundamental: meaning. Social actors are like fish; they can only survive in a sea of meaning. The worlds of meaning we construct shape and channel what we do and do not do. In this view, it is not possible fully to separate social relations and the world views on which they rest: they are the same thing. That is why critical scholars sometimes say that consciousness *constitutes* society, rather than merely mirroring or distorting social relations.[10]

By legal consciousness, I mean those aspects of the consciousness of any society which explain and justify its legal institutions. Taken most broadly, legal consciousness includes all the ideas about the nature, function, and operation of law held in society at a given time. It incorporates and is largely shaped by, but is not limited to, the ideas held by the legal profession: public understanding and evaluation of law is as much a part of our legal consciousness as are the most refined views of the most eminent scholars or the most comprehensive decisions of the Supreme Court. The legal consciousness of our time and place is the way in which we integrate our understanding of legal order with other ideas which give meaning to our social world.

If society is in some sense constituted by the world views that give meaning to social interaction, then to change consciousness is to change society itself. That is the central tenet of the critical legal studies creed, the grounding for the belief that scholarship is politics. For if scholarship can change consciousness it is not merely a move toward an ultimate transformation; it is the real thing.

But how can scholarship affect consciousness? What can scholars hope to do to change the way we see and value the world? Critical scholars base their answers to these questions on two assumptions: First, that world views rest on claims to truth; it is the claim to truth that gives meaning to a world view and thus gives it constitutive power. Secondly, while world views may be partially false, they contain within them a kernel of truth that can be uncovered. Because every world view is hostage to its claim to be true, its constitutive force can be undermined if these claims can be refuted. Because there is a kernel of truth in any world view that has become dominant in any society, the refutation can take place within terms partially set by the existing tradition itself. Albrecht Wellmer, a leading exponent of the Frankfurt School critical theory of society, says:

> Critical theory is derivable from a notion of the "good life" already available to it as part of the socio-historical situation it subjects to analysis; which, as the notion of an acknowledgement of each individual as person by every other individual, and as the idea of a non-coercive communal human life of dialogue, is a draft meaning of history already fragmentarily embodied in a society's traditions and institutions: a draft meaning which it applies critically in opposing a society and its dominant forms of self-understanding. (Wellmer, 1974:40. See also Unger, 1983:561).

If one examines the work of critical legal scholars, one can find evidence that they share this view of the relationship between scholarship and transformation. Karl Klare is most explicit when he argues for critical examination of the ideological (i.e., false) aspects of labor law doctrine:

[10] For a general statement of this perspective on consciousness and society see Gordon (1982:291).

The mission of all critical social thought is to free us from the illusion of the necessity of existing social arrangements. The more total the criticism, the greater the emancipation ... The critique of labor law as ideology is therefore an indispensable component of the utopian project of experiencing in thought and in social life the radical disintegration of the intellectual and institutional constraints of capitalist society. (Klare, 1981:450, 482).

Klare and others share the view that scholarship can bring to light the world views encoded in modern legal consciousness, so that we can understand what in it is false and what contains a "draft meaning of history" in Wellmer's sense. When this is done, the scales will fall from our eyes, and we will be free to create new systems of meaning and thus new relationships.

A good example of this sort of research is the collective effort by people in the Conference on Critical Legal Studies to describe the rise and fall of a "classical legal consciousness" in America. This project was initiated by Duncan Kennedy, who has contributed several major published (Kennedy, 1979:205, 1980:3) and unpublished works to the effort. It is ably summarized by Elizabeth Mensch in a recent essay on "The History of Mainstream Legal Thought." (Mensch, 1982). Mensch's essay tells the story of the rise and fall of classical legal consciousness, seen as a coherent set of ideas about law and society which Mensch asserts held sway among leading legal thinkers in the latter part of the 19th century. As Mensch describes it, "classical legal consciousness" provided answers to basic questions about the relationship between individuals and society, the relationship between the state and private actors, and the nature and operation of the law.[11]

Like Confucianism in Imperial China, classical legal consciousness legitimated a structure of hierarchy and domination, in part by justifying it and in part by deflecting attention from its nature and operation. The story Mensch tells is of

[11] In this view, the distinguishing feature of elite legal thinking from roughly 1885–1935 was its ardent faith in the possibility of a rationalist ordering of the entire legal universe. During the classical age, jurists presumed to transcend the uncertainty of philosophical speculation for the hard and sure world of science. The basic premise was that there is a unique legal structure which corresponds to a market economy and a republican form of government. It was the task of the jurist to discover and elaborate that conceptual structure.

As fully developed, the theory conceived the world not as a multitude of particularized social relationships but as instances of a single general legal relation. The relations of private parties to each other and to the state, and of the states to each other and to the federal government, were all qualitatively analogous. The legal world was viewed as a structure of nonoverlapping bounded spheres of protected rights and powers. These rights and powers were absolute within their protected domain. Disputes arose only over the contours of the bounded spheres. Thus, the judicial task was to define and police boundaries. Moreover, the precise limits of a legal actor's powers were thought to be discoverable through the application of an objective methodology.

Realist scholarship of the early twentieth century demolished the premises of classical legal consciousness. But as Mensch notes, and this is the key point, " [the] basic model, although in bankrupt form, is with us still. The message the model conveys is that actual power relations in the real world are by definition legitimate and must go unchallenged." p. 26.

the rise of a series of challenges to the world views encoded in this mode of legal thought, launched largely by the American legal realist movement, followed by a series of counterattacks to these challenges by other post-realist modes of thought about law (e.g. law and economics, legal process) all of which sought to contain the realist critique and preserve dominant features of the classical synthesis. While these post-realist movements are quite diverse, they seem to be tied together by a common ideological intent, namely the effort to blunt challenges to the world view of classical legal thought (Tushnet, 1980:1383; Mensch 1982).

In her effort to unmask the ideological nature of the post-realist "counterreformation," Mensch uses a device that appears in other critical scholarship – the analysis of the incoherence of particular legal ideas or views.[12] Critical scholars have devoted substantial efforts to demonstrating the existence of contradictory ideas in modern legal doctrine. One might argue that one of the movement's major scholarly contributions has been to expand and deepen the insight, first expressed by writers in the realist tradition like Karl Llewellyn (Llewellyn, 1960:521) and Stewart Macaulay (Macaulay, 1966:1051), that legal doctrine contains radically contradictory principles, and thus to work out the implications of the principle of contradiction mentioned earlier. Kennedy's essays on private law doctrine (Kennedy, 1976:1685) and his study of Blackstone's Commentaries (Kennedy, 1979:205) illustrate this mode of analysis. In his study of "Labor Law as Ideology," Klare identifies contradictory principles in labor law doctrine. These include ambivalence in the use of the distinction between what is public and private (Klare, 1981:470), and contradictions in the conceptualization of workers' rights, which are alternatively treated as individual or collective, inalienable or waivable (Klare, 1981:473). "The decisional law of collective bargaining," he says, "has generated a number of frameworks and hierarchies of workplace rights, each of which is so ambiguous and internally contradictory that the courts may, and do, brutally manipulate these rights frameworks in particular cases." (Klare, 1981:469).

4.3. Legitimation and Truth

The amount of energy critical legal scholars devote to demonstrating that liberal legal doctrine is "incoherent" suggests that they believe that more is at stake than mere repetition of the insights of legal realism. For it is partly by the demonstration of the *internal* inadequacies of liberal legal thought that, it is believed, *critique* will undermine its power over men's minds. So it is not enough to develop a general "proof" of doctrine incoherence: manifestations of the contradictions in liberal legal doctrine must be studied in their particularity, so that we can come to see that they contain no immanent legal or social rationality, other than that of cloaking power in the garb of right.

[12] Thus, the period from 1940 to the present is described as a series of "efforts to reconstruct American legal thought"; all of these, however, she asserts contain fairly obvious "intellectual incoherences." (1982:37).

It is no surprise that this approach worries some on the left, who see liberal rights theory as a possible source of instrumental support for left social movements (Sparer, 1984). Although critical scholars recognize this concern, most in the end come down on the side of the argument reflected by the work of Klare, Kennedy and Mensch. Why is this so? The scholars who take this position are politically sophisticated; they recognize the force of the arguments of those who see rights theory as a shield for left social movements. I submit that they reject this line of argumentation because of a belief in the liberating value of the truth. The critical scholars see within liberal doctrine a core of truth and a periphery of mystification: the task is to bring the truth content of liberal rights thinking to the surface by demonstrating the mystifying and ideological content of the periphery. Commenting on this issue, Duncan Kennedy says:

> ... the argument that there will be bad consequences for the left if liberal rights theory loses its plausibility is a weak one. The point is that the theory is wrong and incoherent. This is just *true*, as far as I can tell, and no amount of lamenting the consequences of his fall will put Humpty Dumpty together again. (Kennedy, 1981:503).

This does not mean that rights theory should be ignored; quite the contrary, the critical scholars see it as the essential starting point for critical work in part because there is a vital core of truth embedded in what must be seen as a complex and contradictory body of thought. "Embedded in the rights notion," Kennedy says, "is a liberating accomplishment of our culture: the affirmation of free human subjectivity against the constraints of group life, along with the paradoxical countervision of a group life that creates and nurtures individuals capable of freedom. We need to work at the slow transformation of rights rhetoric, ... rather than simply junking it." (Kennedy, 1981:503).

It is at this point that critical legal studies diverges from the conventional social science approach to the study of ideology. Because conventional research on ideology accepts the radical distinction between is and ought, fact and value, the concept of "truth value" would appear alien to its practitioners, and the notion that a demonstration of something called "falseness" would lead to social change would seem curious to say the least. And it is for this reason that we must now reconsider the dichotomy between doctrinal legal research and empirical studies of law which was introduced above. To the extent that this distinction also rests on the radical separation of a normative realm (legal doctrine) and a realm of social behavior that is pure facticity (empirical reality), it is incoherent to anyone who accepts, as I do, the vision of knowledge and politics on which critical legal studies is based (Unger, 1975).

This problem becomes very clear if we look more closely at the concept of "legitimation," which is frequently employed by critical scholars. Critical legal scholars believe that the world views embedded in legal consciousness "legitimate" unjust social relations by making these relations seem either necessary or desirable. "Every stabilized social world," Roberto Unger says, "depends for its serenity, upon the redefinition of power and preconception as legal right or practical necessity." (Unger, 1983:561). Critical studies research begins with that insight, seeking to discover the false but legitimating world views hidden in complex bodies of rules and doctrines and in legal consciousness in general.

The concept of legitimation is complex and to a degree ambiguous. If we go back to Weber, who first introduced "legitimation" as a central concept in social theory, we find that while he classifies legitimation he never really explains the legitimation process itself. That is, Weber tells us that all forms of domination, i.e. the power to issue commands that will be obeyed, rest in part on the "legitimacy" of that power, and that legitimation may be based on traditional, legal-rational or charismatic grounds (Weber, 1968, Vol. I:212). He says that the degree of legitimation will depend on the extent to which the appropriate beliefs are held in a society, but he does not tell us what brings about these beliefs or how they change.

In the critical theory of society originally developed by the Frankfurt School and currently represented by the work of Jürgen Habermas, one can find a different view of legitimation. Raymond Geuss defines the meaning of legitimation in this theory:

> To say that the members of the society take a basic institution to be "legitimate" is to say that they take it to "follow" from a system of norms they all accept; agents think the norm-system capable of conferring legitimacy because they accept a set of general beliefs (normative beliefs and other kinds of beliefs) which are organized into a world-picture which they assume all members of the society hold. So a social institution is considered legitimate if it can be shown to stand in the right relation to the world-picture of the group. (Geuss, 1981:59).

Habermas contrasts the use of legitimation in critical theory with Weber's concept. While for Weber "legitimation" is an "empirical phenomenon without an immanent relation to truth" (Habermas, 1975:97). Habermas wants to hold on to the idea that world views by their nature make claims to truth and are in a sense hostage to these claims. (Habermas, 1975).

It is this view that relates the critical theory of society to the process of social transformation. If it is the case that world views in some sense define social relations, but that their constitutive force depends on their "truth value," then it is possible to change world views and thus society by subjecting world views to critical analysis. A world view legitimates a given social institution by presenting it as a necessary or efficient way of satisfying interests actors know they have; once they see that the institution is in no sense necessary nor fosters these interests their attitudes towards it will change: Geuss suggests that if actors are suffering from this sort of "ideological delusion," they can:

> ... be enlightened by the "self reflection" which critical theory sets off. In the initial state their wants and desires were seriously frustrated by a social institution they thought they had an interest in maintaining. Reflection shows them that this is a mistake and that they actually had an interest in abolishing the social institution in question, which not only frustrates perfectly legitimate wants and preferences, but prevents free communication and discussion. (Geuss, 1981:73).

My provisional account of the practice of critical legal studies suggests that these scholars employ some version of this approach, and that the critique of legal thought is designed to challenge the legitimacy of our current legal consciousness, thus setting in motion processes of self-reflection. I do not mean to suggest that the American scholars have consciously tried to follow in the footsteps of the European critical social theorists: despite the appropriation of the label "critical" the Americans have paid scant attention to the Frankfurt School tradition or to the work of its contemporary interpreters like Habermas.[13] Rather, I merely want to note some parallels between the American discussion and the ideas of those who first introduced the idea of a "critical theory."

Not only is my account merely a provisional description of the current practices of the critical scholars; to the extent that it is descriptively valid it leaves many questions unanswered. As presented the account relies on a very strong "cultural" view of social relations, in which society is in some real sense "constituted" by systems of meaning – what Habermas has called "world-maintaining interpretive systems" (Habermas, 1975:118). To the extent this strong culture view is accepted, the efficacy of critique as a transformative practice depends on the continued significance of world-maintaining interpretive systems in modern society. Yet it is the critical theorists of society, from Adorno to Habermas, who themselves have raised the spectre of the gradual destruction of such meaning systems under conditions of modernity.[14]

Furthermore, the nature of "truth" in this account is problematic. The American critical scholars have certainly not mastered Habermas' complex notion of the truth value of critical theory, and would undoubtedly have difficulty with its transcendental elements if they did. Yet they have not produced one of their own. Moreover there is some tension betwen the strong "cultural" view of society in which society is constituted by its existing world views, and the notion that critical theory can demonstrate the falseness in current world views.[15] The critique of legal thought depends on a concept of truth, but this concept has yet to be fully explained.

5. Critical Legal Studies and Interpretivist Scholarship

I have argued that there is a way to see critical legal studies which makes it part of a continuous tradition of nondoctrinal research on law, and thus as a kind of

[13] For example, one will find scant reference to Habermas in the writings of the American critical scholars. For two recent exceptions see Baker (1982:293); Hyde (1982:1031).

[14] The idea that the process of capitalist modernization destroys symbolic systems that give life meaning goes back at least to Max Weber, who described modernization as a process of increasing rationalization and "disenchantment of the world." Weber saw the increasing rationalization of modern life as a process by which mechanical and impersonal systems come to replace symbolically mediated structures of meaning. Wellmer describes these as processes which: "tend to depersonalize social relationships, to dessicate symbolic communication and to subject human life to the impersonal logic of rationalized, anonymous administrative systems; historical processes, in short, which tend to make human life mechanized, unfree and meaningless." (Wellmer, 1983:13). Wellmer argues that the Weberian notion that the capitalist modernization process leads to a "closed system of instrumental and administrative rationality" and threatens to destroy the "life world" of symbolically structured meaning was incorporated into the critical theory of society as the "Negative Dialectics of Enlightenment." (Section III.). Habermas takes up this issue in "Legitimation Crisis," (1975:Chap. 4).

[15] This point was suggested by Joel Rogers (private communication to the author).

empirical research. I have suggested that critical legal studies and some other forms of nondoctrinal research on law share a common tradition, which I have called the critique of legal order. In making these claims, I have tried to clear away some of the shallower criticisms of the critical legal studies movement and to stress that there is continuity in the nondoctrinal tradition, in contrast to the view of those who only see rupture and division. But this effort is only a preliminary one: while there are continuities and areas of agreement between the critical legal scholars and others in that capacious mansion I have called the nondoctrinal tradition, there are also profound differences as well.

It is obvious that if critical legal studies is a form of "empiricism," it rests on a very different conception of that term than is usually employed by many who have urged more research on the behavior of legal actors or the actual operation of the legal system. My effort to characterize critical legal studies as "empirical research on law" will sound strange to those for whom that term derives from a bright line between the realms of doctrine and behavior, and between values and facts. For it is true that critical legal studies, properly understood, represents a strong challenge to the self-understanding of many who think of themselves as practitioners of "empirical legal studies."[16]

More fully to explore this, I have constructed two polar models of social knowledge about law. I call one of them "behaviorist" and the other "interpretivist" legal studies. These models are "ideal types" in the pure sense – one-sided accentuations of views which are meant to highlight salient dimensions of scholarly belief and practice. These constructs are not meant to describe views held by any one scholar, let alone to serve as sociological accounts of competing scholarly camps. There is no suggestion that anyone holds either of these sets of views as a whole, or that the scholarly community is made up of two neatly demarked camps that stand, like teams on a field, separately labelled and in struggle with one another. Rather, these constructs are useful only to sort out issues and initiate more detailed and contextual studies of research traditions and kinds of scholarly self-understanding.

To create these constructs, I sought to identify contrasting presuppositions on what seemed to me to be the basic issues for any body of social thought about law: (I) what creates social order; (II) what is the nature of social action; (III) what is the role of law in society; and (IV) what constitutes valid knowledge in general and of law in particular. The analysis is summarized in Figure 1.

5.1. Behaviorist Legal Studies

Behaviorism is a form of positivism applied to the study of law in society. It stresses empirical validation of theories about the behavior or conduct of actors in or affected by the legal system. For the behaviorist, the focus of study is externally observable indicators of legally relevant individual or group conduct like the decision to litigate or not. A behaviorist would believe that it is possible to provide causal explanations of such conduct. A causal explanation consists of a proposition concerning the relationship between two or more observable indi-

[16] For an effort to grapple with this challenge, see Sarat (1983).

Figure 1
Two Modes of Legal Studies

	Behaviorist	*Interpretivist*
SOCIAL ORDER	Structures of constraint which impose on actors external limits dictated by objective necessities	Consciousness, culture and organization form mutually reinforcing structures of meaning which define what is possible
ACTION	Conduct in accordance with arbitrary individual desires, internalized norms (roles), objective constraints and external sanctions	Conduct in accordance with socially created systems of meaning
LAW IN SOCIETY	Behavior of subset of individual actors and institutions in society which constrain or facilitate action	A complex cultural code which explains the social world and how it fits together, and a part of the structure in which action is embedded
SOCIAL KNOWLEDGE ABOUT LAW	Empirically validated objective knowledge of causal laws governing law-related social behavior	"De-coding" or explicating the deep structures of law and demonstrating the relationship between these structures of social action and order

cators of behavior, plus an empirical validation of the proposition using representative data. Thus a behaviorist might assert that "people in long-term continuing relationships litigate less frequently than those whose contacts are episodic" and this proposition would be proven if a representative sample of people in disputes showed higher litigation rates for those whose contacts were fleeting.

What are the presuppositions of behaviorist legal studies? We must explore how behaviorism deals with order, action, law and knowledge. These are the four principal theoretical axes on which my construct and comparison are built.

The problem of social order is that of explaining how social behavior is organized in nonrandom patterns. Behaviorism sees social order as the result of the interaction of an arbitrary volition, an individual rationality, and collective constraint. Order is maintained because individuals seek their own separately determined and arbitrarily chosen ends but do so in accordance with a rational calculation of constraints imposed by external social sanctions. These sanctions are imposed by structures external to the actor and reflect underlying functional "necessities" of society. Social action, that is, what actors do in social life, is in this point of view at once voluntary, yet in the last analysis determined since it is constrained by external structures which obey an objective logic of functional necessity. The "soft" voluntaristic possibilities of action are constrained by a hard reality of roles and sanctions.

Behaviorism equates law with external constraint on action. For the behaviorist, what is socially significant about the law is its impact on decisions of those it affects. In this sense, the most important dimension of social knowledge about the law is knowledge about the relationship between legal behavior and social behavior. Legal behavior is part of the hard structure of constraint and facilitation that gives action its direction and society its order. Whatever it is about "law" that affects social behavior is relevant; whatever does not have such an effect is not.

For our purposes, it is especially important to understand how behaviorism deals with legal doctrine. A behaviorist would not deny the importance of legal doctrine for the understanding of the social role of law, any more than they deny the relevance of the judge's prior political affiliations. She simply would see doctrine as one of the things that influences the behavior, present or future, of actors in the legal system. To twist an old *canard*, behaviorism is not more interested in what the judge had for breakfast than what the law says; it is concerned with both if it looks as if either might influence what the judge *does*.

Behaviorism is based on a belief in objective knowledge of causal relationships. In the behaviorist model "law" may be either a dependent variable, to be explained by social variables, or an independent variable, explaining them. But in either case the ideal of knowledge is a statement that X causes Y. In what sense is this knowledge objective? Behaviorism would make two claims to objectivity. Since it is on these points that interpretivism and behaviorism diverge most significantly, it is important to develop this point.

Behaviorism would see social knowledge as objective because it is knowledge about facts. (This is the weak sense of objectivism.) Facts are neutral and external to the observer. If we know something about the relationships between facts X and Y, (e.g. litigation rates and social relationships) this knowledge exists independently of our values. Of course, the facts we are talking about must be representative, so we have to worry about things like sampling and statistical significance, and thus with demonstrating that others are likely to get the same results. But as long as these tests are met, there is no further bar to objectivity.

There is, however, a stronger sense of objectivity in the view of knowledge I am calling behaviorism. This is the view that behavior is determined by objective "laws," social factors external to the individual which can be shown to account for his conduct. In this stronger sense, behaviorist knowledge is objective because it reflects the deep logic of society, the basic and general principles which explain constraint and thus determine action. To the extent that behaviorists were to accept this view of objectivity, they would be both positivists and determinists.

5.2. Interpretive Legal Studies

Interpretivism is the study of relations among legal ideas, social beliefs, action and order. Like behaviorism, interpretivism seeks to account for action and order, but does so by stressing the role of consciousness in action and beliefs in consciousness. An interpretivist would not see beliefs as random nor individual action as arbitrary. Rather, beliefs from coherent wholes, systems which are structured by principles of meaning. A structure of beliefs reflects a world view: some vision of the world and man's place in it. Since beliefs constitute consciousness, they influence action and explain order. And since beliefs are organized into distinct and interrelated structures, they are neither arbitrary nor random. Law is both a set of beliefs and a constituent part of consciousness. Interpretivist scholarship would, therefore, focus on the structure of legal ideas, seeking to identify the deep principles of meaning that lie behind them, and to relate these principles to social action and order.

An interpretivist would emphasize the role of meaning in the maintenance of order. For the interpretivist, consciousness, culture and social organization would be seen as mutually interrelated and reinforcing systems of ideas about man and society: together they make up a meaningful whole. Individuals understand the world in terms of these structures of meaning, and this understanding affects their actions. In contrast to a behaviorist, *an interpretivist* would not split action into a soft and arbitrary core of individual volition and hard shell of external constraint. Rather, they would see action as the result of socially constructed systems of meaning which constitute the individual, providing the grounds for behavior and defining the channels of conduct.

The concept of law in my account of interpretivism derives from this view of action and order. Law on this view is one of several important interlocking systems of belief or complex cultural codes: part of the system which explains why the social world is as it is and how each individual fits within it. Law, like other aspects of belief systems, helps define what it means to be an individual and what relations with others make sense. In this way law forms part of consciousness and influences outcomes. At the same time that law is a system of belief, it is also a basis of organization, a part of the structure in which action is embedded.

An interpretivist would see law as a set of interrelated ideas and practices whose deep structures reflect an effort to order social existence and its puzzles in meaningful ways. Interpretivism leads naturally to the internal analysis of systems of legal ideas, not simply to set forth the ideas themselves but also to see how these ideas shape the society and are shaped by it. An interpretivist would seek to identify the relationships between the structures of legal belief and practice, on the one hand, and social order and the springs of action on the other. An interpretivist would seek to explain legal ideas and practices in light of systems of belief and principles of order, and to identify the points at which law forms part of the cultural and organizational whole which determines the shape and trajectory of society.

5.3. Critical Legal Studies and Interpretivism

While there are probably no pure behaviorists or interpretivists in the world, many within critical legal studies would undoubtedly accept much of the interpretivist approach outlined and reject much of what I have called behaviorism. I have already suggested that critical scholars have focused on the analysis of legal consciousness, and that their view of the relationship between scholarship and politics rests on an interpretivist notion of how meaning affects action. Further, most critical scholars would reject the positivism and determinism they see in behaviorist legal studies. Indeed, in his masterful summary of theoretical developments in critical legal studies, Robert Gordon argues that the central thrust of the movement is interpretive and *therefore* as antideterminist. He stresses the importance of critical studies rejection of all instrumental accounts of law:

> Positivist social scientists (who would include both liberal and Marxist "instrumentalist" legal theorists) are always trying to find out how social reality objectively works, the secret laws that govern its action; they ask such questions as, "Under what economic conditions is one likely to obtain formal legal rules?" Anti-positivists assert that such questions are meaningless, since what we experience as "social reality" is something that we are constantly constructing; and that this is just as true for "economic conditions" as it is for "legal rules." (Gordon, 1982:287).

To the extent that critical legal scholars stress an interpretivist view of law and social knowledge, and seek to make a clean break with positivism and determinism, the movement represents a distinct vision of what it means to carry out nondoctrinal research or empirical legal studies. For while it would be misleading to classify all other forms of empirical legal studies (e.g., law and society, law and economics) as either positivist or determinist (or both), their practices often reveal a tacit acceptance of one or both of these elements of behaviorism.[17]

6. Critical Legal Studies and the Interpretation of Law in Capitalism

Understanding critical legal studies as an interpretative mode of scholarship can help us understand a lot about the movement's intention and understand more fully the rationale for the study of legal doctrine as ideology. But to treat critical legal studies merely as part of a wide movement in scholarship that rejects behaviorism and stresses the importance of interpreting systems of social meaning would be to truncate the account.[18] For what is most important is that the critical scholars are concerned with the interpretation of the legal consciousness of *capitalist* societies, and that they believe that their interpretative scholarship will contribute to social transformation. Critical legal studies is interpretative scholarship with a particular subject and a distinct intent.

[17] For example, a large number of law and society studies seek to discover or quantify the causal effect or impact of law in the "real world," e.g., the effect of police activity on the crime rate; the impact of a supreme Court decision on public attitudes; the impact of the death penalty on the murder rate; the effect of racial, social or economic factors on sentencing or the exercise of police discretion. The general commitment of these scholars to causal explanation is attested by the widespread use of statistical methods for the analysis of data. In explicit recognition of the complex nature of causation, results are usually framed in probabilistic rather than simple causal terms. Nevertheless, such studies exhibit some of the general features of what I have called behaviorism: a belief in external constraints on action and in the possibility of objectively verifiable knowledge about the operation of such constraints.

[18] For an evaluative discussion of recent trends and moods in social scientific thought see Bernstein (1978).

This brings me to one of the most difficult aspects of any account of critical legal studies, namely the relationship between this mode of scholarship and the "Marxist" tradition. It is not my intent to determine either if it still makes sense to speak of a coherent "Marxist" tradition in social thought, or to canvass the relationships between the ideas of the critical scholars and the history of Marxist scholarship. What I do want to do is identify some of the key ideas used by critical scholars in their project of "decoding" the legal consciousness of capitalism, as they relate to the question of empiricism or method. Some of these ideas, and particularly the Gramscian notion of "hegemonic consciousness" and the Lukasian concept of "reification" figure heavily in the CLS account of law in capitalism and derive from the Marxian tradition. These ideas provide a clue to the theory of law in society used by critical scholars and have implications for the question of method.

Critical scholars see social order as maintained by mutually reinforcing systems of belief and organization. But these beliefs are not in any sense "true." Quite the contrary, the belief systems which structure action and maintain order in capitalist societies present as eternal and necessary what is only the transitory and arbitrary interest of a dominant elite whose unequal and unjust power is justified by what appear to be a commonly acceptable body of ideas. Thus systems of ideas are *reifications*, presenting as essential, necessary and objective what is contingent, arbitrary and subjective. (Gabel, 1980; Kennedy, 1979:205; Gordon, 1982). Furthermore, they are *hegemonic*, that is, they serve to legitimate interests of the dominant class and it alone. (Freemann, 1978:1049; Gordon, 1982; Klare, 1981:450).

In addition to classifying modern legal consciousness as reifying and hegemonic, critical scholars see legal thought as *denial*. (Kennedy, 1979:205). Like the Frankfurt School, the American critical legal scholars have incorporated concepts from Freudian psychology into social theory.[19] Legal thought is a form of denial, that is, a way to deal with perceived contradictions which are too painful for us to hold in consciousness. What legal thought *denies* is the recognition of the contradiction between the promise of universality, equality and freedom and the reality of a legal order that benefits some over others, maintains hierarchy, and constrains the possibilities of action.[20]

[19] The similarity of the epistemic structure of the Frankfurt School's theory of society to psychoanalytic theory should be apparent. As Geuss points out, both theories "have special standing for human action in that: (a) they are aimed at producing enlightenment in the agents who hold them" permitting them to determine their true interests and "(b) they are inherently emancipatory, i.e., they free agents from a kind of coercion which is at least partly self-imposed." (Geuss, 1981:1).
Moreover, whereas traditional theories are "objectifying," critical theories are "reflective." Thus the revolutionary contribution of Freud and the Frankfurt School lies in reestablishing reflection as a valid source of knowledge and connecting that which traditional theory assiduously separates: knowledge and interests.

[20] In "Blackstone's Commentaries," Duncan Kennedy argues that we experience a fundamental contradiction between our desire for individual freedom and our participation in a social community. The contradiction lies in the fact that our "freedom is at the same

By employing the concepts of reification, hegemony and denial, critical scholars adopt what I want to call an "action perspective." That is, they believe that there are definite relationships between systems of ideas, social structure and social change.

All these ideas imply contradictory relationships between world views in capitalism and the structure of domination. That is, there is a difference in the way we decode the world view of capitalism and the way we might go about interpreting some other society, say Bali or Imperial China. It is the nature of social ideas in capitalism that they not merely *justify* capitalist social relations, but that they do so by making them appear as something other than they are. Reifications are something other than we really are as human beings: they constitute an alienation from something more fundamental. A hegemonic consciousness is a way of masking and hiding hegemony. Denial is just that: a mechanism that permits us to avoid admitting or facing something we know, in some way, to be true.

It is this very contradictory quality of world views in capitalist culture generally, and in particular instances like legal consciousness, that create an action framework. For the contradictions can be uncovered, the "incoherences" demonstrated, the denied material brought to light. And if that occurs, then the society can be transformed. Like the Freudian analyst, the critical scholar can bring to "consciousness" what is hidden by hegemonic world views. The truth inheres in the very system that serves to hide it: the present contains a draft history of the future. That is the basis of the emancipatory hope expressed by scholars like Kennedy and Klare. By interpreting the world, we set in motion forces that can change it.

time dependent on and incompatible with the communal coercive action that is necessary to achieve it" (p. 211). Our universe of others both "forms and protects us" and "imposes on us" (and we impose on others) "hierarchical structures of power, welfare and access to enlightenment that are illegitimate" (p. 212).

Legal thinking, the enterprise of categorizing, analyzing and explaining legal rules, has as one of its motives the aim of denying or mediating our feelings of contradiction. The most recently dominant mode of legal categorization and thought, the one which Blackstone helped establish, is generally called liberalism. Liberalism accomplishes its mediating function by dividing the social world into two opposed entities. One entity, called "civil society," is an arena of free interaction among private individuals. Individuals acting in civil society are rendered unthreatening to each other because the other entity, "the state," forces people to respect one another's rights. Thus, the message of liberalism is that "in civil society, others are available for good fusion as private individual respectors of rights; through the state, they are available for good fusion in the collective experience of enforcing rights" (p. 217). One who adopts such a view can effectively deny the fundamental contradiction.

In addition to its mediating function, legal thought can also serve an apologetic function. "The element of apology comes in because legal thought denies or mediates with a bias toward the existing social and economic order." (p. 217). It tells us that through the existing order, either as it is or with some minor adjustments, we can overcome the contradiction.

The idea that critique of consciousness may contribute to social transformation derives from the view of society as a constructed totality of meaningful relationships. To understand this, it is useful to contrast the critical legal studies approach with traditional Marxist notions of the nature of law and legal thought: that idea was expressed in Marx' metaphor of the "base and the superstructure."[21] At least as understood by most Marxist scholars, this meant the existence of a material base ("relations of production") which in some more or less direct way determined the realm of ideas; in the legal area the relationships of production are seen to determine the legal ideas. The metaphysics of the base/superstructure metaphor make social relations the "reality" and ideas the "reflection" of reality. What critical legal studies has tried to do is not *reverse* this polarity: that would make the movement pure idealism. Rather, it has sought to simply eliminate the dichotomy altogether. In critical legal studies neither ideas nor structures are the reality.

The transcendence of this dichotomy is one of the central features of critical legal thought.[22] For scholars in this tradition, it is incorrect to say that there is a

[21] "The general result at which I arrived and which, once won, served as a guiding thread for my studies, can be briefly formulated as follows: In the social production of their life, men enter into definite relations that are indispensable and independent of their will, relations of production which correspond to a definite stage of development of their material productive forces. The sum total of these relations of production constitutes the economic structure of society, the real foundation, on which rises a legal and political superstructure and to which correspond definite forms of social consciousness. The mode of production of material life conditions the social, political and intellectual life process in general. It is not the consciousness of men that determines their being, but, on the contrary, their social being that determines their consciousness. At a certain stage of their development, the material productive forces of society come in conflict with the existing relations of production, or – what is but a legal expression for the same thing – with the property relations within which they have been at work hitherto. From forms of development of the productive forces these relations turn into their fetters. Then begins an epoch of social revolution. With the change of the economic foundation the entire immense superstructure is more or less rapidly transformed. In considering such transformations a distinction should always be made between the material transformation of the economic conditions of production, which can be determined with the precision of natural science, and the legal, political, religious, aesthetic or philosophic – in short, ideological forms in which men become conscious of this conflict and fight it out." (Marx, 1969:503).

[22] It could be argued that, at least as I have presented it, the critical legal studies approach to the base-superstructure issue is not a transcendence but a rejection, and that critical legal studies appears in my account to be pure idealism and thus as a complete rejection of Marxist notions. In his essay on "Hegemony and Consciousness in the Thought of Antonio Gramsci," Femia (1975:35) identifies four ideal-typical models of this relationship:
(a) consciousness determines base (idealist view)
(b) consciousness and base interact on an equal basis (conventional view)
(c) base determines consciousness (classical, scientific Marxism)
(d) base determines what forms of consciousness are possible (Gramscian Marxism).

real world which is mirrored, directly or indirectly in legal ideas. Ideas and structures are mutually constituting, and neither is real or not real; in some way both are real and unreal at the same time. Law creates society and society law; the relationships are complex and multidirectional. The resulting systems of action and order must be seen as a totality; nothing more or less.

If law and society are mutually constituting, then in a sense the distinction law versus society itself makes no sense. The effort to maintain this distinction, like that between a "public" and a "private realm" is just one more feature of a hegemonic consciousness and one more instance of reification.[23] And if law and society are mutually constituting, there is no *a priori* barrier to a transformative politics that employs the methods of critique and what Unger calls "deviationist doctrine" (Unger, 1978:561). Critique can create the possibility to imagine new forms of social relations and derive some basis for utopian vision from the core of truth in legal consciousness; deviationist doctrine can carry forward that effort by reconstructing the core and moving beyond our current understanding of what is possible and desirable in our institutional arrangements.

The key idea is that legal consciousness has an effect on those who live in it, and legal consciousness is vulnerable to attack and reconstruction. (Kennedy, 1979:220).

Femia argues that only models (c) and (d) can be considered Marxism, and that Gramsci's revision of the classical Marxist formulation did not reject the determining force of the economic base or mode of production, but rather weakened the direct causal relation between changes in economic relations and changes in consciousness on which the classical account rested. In this view, Femia says, "... the economic base sets, in a strict manner, the range of possible outcomes, but free political and ideological activity is ultimately decisive in determining which alternative prevails. There is no automatic determination: only the creation of a more or less favorable atmosphere for the diffusion of a new ethos. (p. 38)" (I am indebted to Mark Lazerson of the UW Department of Sociology for drawing this study to my attention.)

I think it is fair to say that by now most of the active scholars in the critical legal studies movement would reject the view Femia attributes to Gramsci, since they would reject the very terms of the analysis, namely that there are separate realms that can be called the "base" or the "superstructure." This does not mean, as Lazerson has pointed out in a personal communication, that we cannot find passages or whole articles in which some of the critical scholars seem to adhere to the "Gramscian" view. Critical legal studies is a project in formation, and there is no doubt that it has been influenced by Marxist thought in general and by Gramsci in particular. But as the passage from Robert Gordon (1982:287) suggests, the interpretist strand in CLS at least has firmly broken with all forms of determinism, whether direct or "in the last instance."

[23] For example, Gerald Frug has shown how the construction of the legal categories of public and private and the categorization of the city as a public entity and the corporation as a private entity makes the power of the latter and the powerlessness of the former seem natural, right and necessary. We are prevented from recognizing that the present powerlessness of cities is the result of an historical choice which can be overturned. (Frug, 1980:1057).

7. Reading Ideologies: Where Are the Messages, Who Are the Recipients?

Critical legal scholars are reading ideologies. They see legal consciousness in capitalism as a complex set of messages which, taken together, construct a social reality that denies immanent possibilities of human action and freedom. They believe that by demonstrating the falseness or incoherence of the ideas critique can open new possibilities and provide a grounding for imaginative reconstruction. This approach assumes that social actors, like psychoanalytic patients, can be freed of the constraints of delusions through a therapeutic technique which identifies the nature of the delusion.

The question then arises: where do these processes occur? If legal consciousness is a code containing partially false messages, who are the recipients of these messages? If critique consists of an alternative set of messages, to whom is critique addressed? If social actors are like patients suffering from a delusion, how do we know that the therapy is valid? How can the critical scholars be sure that the messages they send are less illusory than the ones they attack?

Critical legal scholars have barely addressed these issues. One can find some general ideas about this process in chance remarks made in the course of extended criticism of legal ideas, but nowhere can one find any description of how critical "method" is expected to work in practice. Perhaps Karl Klare has gone furthest toward providing an explanation. In "Labor Law as Ideology" he tries to explain the relationship between liberal labor law doctrine, which is explicitly labelled as an elite ideological product, and the behavior of the union movement. To demonstrate the existence of labor law ideology, Klare concentrates exclusively on appellate court opinions and academic commentary. In his interpretation he draws on his own analyses and those of other critical labor law scholars like Katherine Stone (Stone, 1981:1515) to show how labor law doctrine denies the desirability or the possibility of extended worker control of the workplace, and thus justifies managerial prerogative. Because Klare *assumes* that the justificatory messages in this elite literature have a direct influence on worker and union decision making, he is able to assert that there is a relationship between the creation of a labor law ideology and the relative passivity of American unions in the post-war period.

There is, however, no effort to demonstrate this process or explain why workers or union officials might accept labor law's justificatory rhetoric. Klare himself is uneasy about this: in a footnote which reveals more than may have been intended, he confesses that:

> ... an important limitation of the critical labor law approach is its relative neglect, thus far, of the important task of drawing out empirically the interrelationships and connections between the intellectual history of collective bargaining law and the social history of the post-World War II labor movement. (Klare, 1981:452).

Kennedy makes a similar confession in his study of Blackstone's Commentaries:

> ... what I have to say is descriptive, and descriptive only of thought. It means ignoring the question of what brings a legal consciousness into being, what causes it to change, and what effect it has on the actions of those who live it. (Kennedy, 1979:220).

These and similar disclaimers in the critical literature cause some disquiet. If Klare recognizes that there is no systematic empirical evidence for the propositions he asserts about the legitimating effects of labor law doctrine in the post-war period, how can he be so sure that critique will pay off in transformative terms? Maybe nobody in the labor movement believes a word of liberal labor doctrine; if that were the case it might make no difference to anyone if critical labor law scholars uncovered the world views in this doctrine, or show its incoherence. If Kennedy omits any discussion of the effects of legal consciousness in a 173-page article on Blackstone's legal thought, how confident can we be that his method bears any relationship to his political intent? We might find Kennedy's superb but complex analysis of the structure of Blackstone's thought inherently interesting, but how can we be confident that once we have struggled through it our lives will be changed any more than they will be by grasping the structure of Confucianism?

These doubts lead some to question the whole project of transformation through the critique of doctrine as ideology. For these commentators, the dominant interpretivist tradition in critical legal studies has failed to grasp the lessons of legal sociology. At least since Stewart Macaulay's research on contract law, it has been a commonplace in the law and society tradition that relations between elite doctrinal production and social behavior cannot be assumed *a priori*. Indeed, one might go so far as to say that law and society scholars assume that the burden of proof lies with those who would assert that any relationship exists at all. Thus in a recent paper delivered at the annual meeting of the Conference on Critical Legal Studies, Carroll Seron and Frank Munger argue that interpretivist critical legal scholarship simply replicates the errors of the liberal doctrinal tradition it attacks, for it starts with the assumption that legal doctrine is produced autonomously and directly influences social life. (Gerd and Unger, 1983). At least until critical legal studies meets the sociologist's "burden of proof" and provides evidence that legal consciousness does affect what goes on in society, these authors remain skeptical of claims that doctrinal critique can have a transformative effect.

I think this is a challenge which critical legal studies must meet. Until we can produce convincing maps of the relationships between elite ideological production, the social definition of meaning, and the history of social relations, it will be hard to sustain the claims made for critical studies. But *contra* Seron and Munger, I do not see that this means that critical studies should reject the project of reading ideologies by analyses of texts. Rather, I think the lesson to be taken is that this process must be extended to encompass studies of the construction of meaning and its relationship to action at all levels. What we need in the labor law field, for example, are studies that go beyond the analyses of texts to investigate the social construction of meaning through law in law firms, board rooms, union halls and on the shop floor, as well as historical studies that demonstrate how conceptions of what is possible and desirable affected decisive decisions in labor relations.

All of this would be quite consistent with the critical studies tradition. While it is true that critical scholars have not paid much attention to the study of everyday legal consciousness, there is one area in which critical studies has contributed a great deal to our understanding of how the social meaning of legal life is constructed in daily life: the law school. Because critical scholars consider that the transformation of the law schools themselves is a central feature of their political project, they have devoted substantial attention to what might be called the "interpretivist sociology" of legal education. Kennedy's analyses of the social psychology of legal education are masterful studies of how consciousness is created in micro-settings: one need look no further than his essays on legal education for models of how to study legal consciousness in action. (Kennedy, 1970, 1980, 1982, 1983). The challenge of meeting the "sociologist's burden of proof" must be met, but the tools are already at hand within the critical legal studies tradition.

What will we learn when, for example, we turn the study of labor law from the Supreme Court to the shop floor? I am too much of a pragmatic empiricist to speculate on something about which so little is known. But I would not be surprised if we will discover something very different than the simple "transmission belt" model which one might derive from the critical labor law literature. Anyone who is familiar with the literature of the sociology of meaning systems in capitalist societies will know that these societies tend to produce a multiplicity of world views. Surveying the extant literature on social stratification and value consensus in liberal democracies, for example, Michael Mann observes that members of the working class are more likely to reject dominant beliefs about social relations than are the middle class, especially when questions are posed in terms of concrete issues of daily life. This analysis leads Mann to question both liberal notions of consensus and Marxist theories that posit the existence of a single hegemonic consciousness. He notes:

> While rejecting more extreme versions of harmonistic theories, we must also do the same with Marxist ones. There is little truth in the claims of some Marxists that the working class is systematically and successfully indoctrinated with the values of the ruling class. Though there is a fair amount of consensus among the rulers, this does not extend very far down the stratification hierarchy. (Mann, 1970:435).

Although Mann's paper relies on very fragmentary evidence, it does suggest that labor law ideology on the shop floor may be rather different than it appears when we read the elite texts.

Exploration of these questions will take us further on the path of reading ideologies already charted by the critical scholars: what we should learn from this will be more complex than the simple transmission-belt theory, but that does not mean that studies of labor law on the shop floor, for example, will refute what the critical scholars have discovered. Once we have successfully mapped the universe of labor law ideologies, we may find countertrends and "counterhegemonic consciousness," but it is likely that these will appear along with dominant views in a complex and contradictory amalgam. One of the most interesting findings in Mann's study is that working class consciousness is split between a concrete realization of injustice and inequality in day-to-day matters, and an acceptance of broad propositions about the necessity and justice of existing social relations. (Mann, 1970:429).

Joseph Femia comes to a similar conclusion. Analyzing a wide range of surveys of mass consciousness in the U.S. and Great Britain, Femia finds that workers tend to accept dominant images of society when these are stated in very general terms, but to manifest dissensus in specific actions and in the application of general beliefs to everyday situations. He reads the survey data as suggesting that: "the average man tends to have two levels of normative reference – the abstract and the situational. On the former plane, he expresses a great deal of agreement with the dominant ideology; on the latter, he reveals not outright dissensus but nevertheless a diminished level of commitment to the bourgeois ethos, because it is often inapposite to the exigences of his class position." (Femia, 1975:46).

If these general analyses hold true for the mass legal consciousness as well, it is clear that the initial insights of critical scholars like Klare are partially correct: mass consciousness does reflect elite consciousness to a degree. Moreover, the identification of areas of dissensus should provide a basis for the development of alternative visions of social relations, thus realizing the full program of critical legal studies. Finally, it is important to recognize that elite consciousness may be an important part of a system of control, even if it is rejected by the mass. For to the extent that an elite accepts a favorable view of its own role in society, its self-confidence is enhanced: the labor law ideology Klare and Stone are examining may be important not simply because it justifies the system to the workers, but also because it justifies it in the minds of the managers.

8. Critical Legal Studies and the Nondoctrinal Tradition: Rupture or Reconciliation?

I have shown that there is continuity between the work of the critical scholars and those of others interested in nondoctrinal legal studies. The critical scholars share with others a concern to show how the law works and what impact it has; they, too, look at law from the outside, as it were, questioning its own self-understanding. I have suggested that critical legal studies is part of a broad movement in nondoctrinal thought on law that rests on the critique of legal order and accepts the principles of indeterminacy, antiformalism, contradiction and marginality.

Yet at the same time I have suggested that critical legal studies has rejected some of the views that animated many studies to date. Moreover, I think it is fair to say that critical scholars have ignored the implications of what I called the principle of marginality: as my discussion of critical labor law doctrine suggests, CLS scholars assume rather than investigate the relationship between elite legal ideological production and social action. Not only does their work in this sense fail to meet the "sociologist of law's burden of proof"; they seem relatively indifferent to most of the literature on law and society that does try to explore the impact (or lack thereof) of legal rules, doctrines and institutions.

What explains the failure to examine assumed mechanisms for the social construction of meaning, and the indifference toward, or even hostility to, so much of what is normally understood as "empirical legal studies." I can offer two explanations. First, a major theme in critical legal studies is the hostility to what the CLS scholars call "positivism." Since critical scholars identify empirical legal studies with positivism they are suspicious of its methods and dubious about its results. Secondly, critical legal studies is the product of the law schools; it is legal scholarship first and foremost. There are strong forces within the legal academy that channel scholars toward the study of legal doctrine, even if the result of the study is a critique of doctrine. These forces have influenced the critical scholars as they have shaped the scholarly tradition of their less radical colleagues.

8.1. Antipositivism

When critical legal studies scholars start talking about empirical research, the word "positivism" immediately comes up. When asked why there is so little empirical research, in the traditional sense, done by critical scholars, or why empirical studies are so rarely cited in CLS literature, the answer given is that work of this type is "positivist." What does this mean and why do critical scholars react so vehemently when they think they have found a positivist in their midst?[24]

The critique of positivism in CLS has three general themes. First, it is thought that positivism necessarily entails determinism. In the introduction to this article, I separated positivism (a theory of knowledge) from determinism (a metaphysics of society). CLS discussions conflate the two, and since most CLS scholars believe that the world is made by willing subjects and can be remade by willing subjects, they are as opposed to determinism in social thought as they reject determinacy as an adequate description of legal doctrine (the principle of indeterminacy). Indeed, one CLS scholar described the movement as an attempt to do for social thought what the legal realists did for legal thought: to frankly recognize that society, like law, is constantly made and remade by human actors with concrete intentions, and to build a body of scholarship around this recognition of indeterminacy.[25] As Robert Gordon has pointed out, (Gordon, 1982). CLS scholars are as hostile to statements from the left like "this is an inevitable development of the logic of monopoly capital" as they are to statements like "this set of arrangements for operating the factory, or this set of property rights, is functionally necessary to achieve maximum output or efficiency."

The second dimension of the critique of positivism is the view that it is

[24] Once again, in setting forth CLS views on method I must draw heavily on oral sources. The views set forth in this section are derived from several sources, including extended conversations with Mark Tushnet, Duncan Kennedy, Morton Horwitz, and Robert Gordon. For general discussion of the views of two CLS scholars on these questions, see Gordon (1982); Tushnet (1980).

[25] This point was made by Karl Klare at the first Critical Legal Studies Summer Camp, Santa Cruz, CA, July 1980.

reductionist. CLS scholars think that the behaviorist approach to law in society reduces the law to an external force acting in social life, and thus ignores the complex relationships between action on the one hand, and subjective meanings and sets of beliefs on the other. Behaviorism, it is feared, leads necessarily to methods which relate objective indicators of behavior with variables external to the actor, while a central theme of critical legal thinking is that the actor's ideas about the meaning of the relations she is embedded in are the most important thing a social explanation should account for.

The third critique of positivism or behaviorism relates to the first two: behaviorism is thought to be *politically conservative* in part because all determinist and reductionist thought is conservative and in part because of the particular form which behaviorism in legal studies has taken in the United States. Any form of determinism is conservative because it suggests that the real springs of social change lie outside the individual or the group. If society only changes because of some external, objective, deep logic like the needs of the economy or the logic of monopoly capitalism, then there seems to be no room for political action. Determinism of the right reifies the status quo while determinism of the left encourages a quiescent waiting for the inevitable turn of the wheels of history. Similarly, reductionism is conservative because it hides from view what critical scholars see as a central instrument for social transformation: the change of consciousness through the critique of belief systems.

If all forms of positivism, whether of the right or the left, are seen to be politically conservative, I think that CLS believes that much of the actual practice of empirical research on law in the U.S. is politically conservative in a more direct and concrete way. That is, the way that topics are defined and studies conducted, it is alleged, tends to reify the existing system of law and existing beliefs.[26] Survey research, critical scholars would probably argue, can only tap the very belief systems or false consciousnesss which it is the task of the scholar to unmask. In their view, empirical researchers spending years analyzing the answers to complicated surveys about disputes are like madmen wandering around in an asylum they themselves have constructed. Believing they are really in touch with "reality," these scholars are simply living in a set of false constructs whose pernicious social effect they themselves have strengthened.

But the attack is not on methods, in the narrow sense: behaviorists could shift to participant observation or in-depth interviews or other data collection efforts without saving themselves from the attack of the critical scholars. The real problem is that all these methods accept the world as it seems to be, both to the observer and the observed, but for the critical scholar this world is a dream, and the task of scholarship is not simply to understand the dream, but to awaken the dreamers.

One of the tenets of behaviorism which merits particular scorn from the antipositivist school is the notion that social knowledge of a positive nature is objective. For the critical scholar, the pretense that social science methods lead to objective and value neutral knowledge is perhaps its most offensive feature. This way of describing knowledge hides an implicit and conservative political message behind a neutral, technocratic facade.

8.2. Legal Education

Because they erroneously think that all studies using methods of empirical inquiry are positivistic and thus determinist, critical scholars may feel justified in ignoring their findings and rejecting their methods. But these tendencies are strengthened by other, perhaps stronger, forces. Most critical legal scholars are legal educators. They are paid to train students to read the law and argue about it. They spend their working lives in settings which stress the importance of legal texts. Many work in schools which are largely isolated both from the day-to-day world of legal practice, and from other academic disciplines. All these factors help explain why, even though contextual studies of law and legal thought in action seem to form a necessary part of a genuine program of critical thought on law, such studies are rarely produced. The chief exception, namely analyses of how the law school itself works as a social process, only proves the point.

There are many studies which demonstrate the strong impact of the professional education mission on legal scholarship, and the "tilt" this creates toward studies of legal doctrine (Macaulay, 1982). This is not the place to analyze this question in depth; suffice it to say that the scholarly practice of critical legal scholars shares with legal scholarship generally a concern with analysis of doctrine. Seron and Munger note the paradox that this most radical of legal studies movements tends to share the same domain of study that its conservative opponents occupy, contrasting this trend in law with the tendency of radical movements in other social studies to break more fundamentally with the scholarly traditions of their field (Seron and Munger, 1983).

I have tried to show that it is a mistake to treat critical legal studies as the replication by the left of conventional studies of legal doctrine. But at the same time, there is validity in the point. For while critical legal studies reads doctrine as ideology, thus distancing itself from mainstream legal scholarship, it has limited itself to the study of ideology *in doctrine*.

8.3. Beyond the Study of Ideology in Doctrine

It is that barrier that I hope will be breached. If this essay has any purpose beyond self-clarification, it is to make the case that critical legal studies should extend its study of legal consciousness beyond the study of doctrine. When it does that, it will find the ground has already been laid. For in the tradition of empirical studies of law, one can find exemplary research by empiricists who want to know how the world works, but who share the critical scholar's fears of positivist determinism.

Look, for example, at Stewart Macaulay's recent study of "Lawyers and Consumer Protection Legislation." (Macaulay, 1979:115). This study purports to be an empirical study of how lawyers handle consumer complaints: but it can be read as both more and less than that. What Macaulay tries to explain is why lawyers who are asked to assist aggrieved consumers behave as they do. What the lawyers do, Macaulay tells us, is to attempt to seek an accommodation between the consumer and the provider of goods and services. They neither litigate nor tell the clients to go away: they seek to persuade the provider to provide redress if the client is aggrieved, but if informal methods fail to achieve this goal the lawyer shifts to persuade the client that the grievance doesn't exist or is unworthy of further effort. This study isolates a "moment" of social action, i.e. of meaningful behavior. This moment is influenced by a set of overlapping and potentially conflicting sets of beliefs and by what are seen as structural constraints the attorney faces. Consumer law and consumerism create a set of beliefs that press the client toward vindication of "rights"; the client is influenced by these cultural factors and names and blames the provider. The lawyer is influences to a degree by the same set of beliefs, as well as the popular image of the attorney as a zealous advocate for the client and the reinforcement of these notions in professional ethics. But the attorney is also influenced by an ethic of individualism which runs contrary to the ideals of consumerism, an ethic which the attorney may hold because he/she is a small businessperson and capitalist entrepreneur and which is the dominant ethic of the providers which are at once the other side in this dispute and people with whom the attorney maintains long-term continuing and potentially profitable relationships. The actual conduct of the attorney is the result of these competing forces, which derive from the ideals and beliefs of the actors, as well as the economic relations between them (you can't make money litigating small claims; you can't have a successful law practice in a small town if you make too much trouble for the merchants).

There is no reductionism in Macaulay's story as I have reconstructed it. The attorney is not reduced to a puppet of some general deep logic nor presented as the embodiment of some universal cultural ideal. Interests, material and ideal, impel behavior, but behavior is defined and mediated by the cultural situation. The account is interpretivist and empirical at the same time. It is based on the minute observation of a moment of action, yet it relates that moment to the whole in a way that unites beliefs and conduct, individual consciousness and cultural ideals.

The pragmatic tradition in empirical legal studies, illustrated by Macaulay's essay on consumer law, offers a possibility for the reconciliation of the critical impulse, the need to know what is going on, and the study of legal consciousness in action. There are a vast number of questions that need to be explored using this approach. How, for example, do the ideas about what is the proper organization of society, encoded in legal beliefs, affect the way the legal profession behaves? How do lawyers' views of what is possible get shaped by legal ideas, and how do these views come to influence other actors in society? Does the fact that law draws lines between a public and a private sphere influence political struggles? Does the possibility of a legal remedy – or the lack of one – make a difference in the organization and expression of social conflicts?

These issues have already been explored by scholars who study the process of dispute transformation, i.e., the way the nature, intensity and trajectory of social conflicts are affected by the intervention of various actors, including lawyers.[26]

[26] For a general introduction to dispute transformation see Felstiner, Abel and Sarat (1981:631); Mather and Yngvesson (1981:775).

As I have pointed out in an earlier essay (Trubek, 1981:727), the study of dispute transformation offers a rich field for concrete studies of how legal ideas and legal organization affect social order and disorder. Numerous studies have shown how the lawyer's image of what sorts of claims are valid influences the kinds of disputes that emerge and do not emerge (Macaulay, 1979:115). The lawyer's views of what is a "legitimate" grievance are in turn influenced by ideas and values drawn from the law itself and legal consciousness generally, as well as from social norms and ideals. The lawyer's perception of conflict is influenced by her own position in the social structure, by the structure of legal representation and the incentive system of legal practice.[27]

These illustrations lead me to believe that the time has come for critical scholars to stop berating all empiricists for an alleged positivism, and for the legal sociologists to stop calling the critical scholars neo-Willistonians. These people think they are arguing about methods, but the claims they make suggest they are arguing about nothing at all. Clearly there are many real questions posed by critical legal studies that are worthy of serious debate, and clearly critical legal studies poses serious challenges to our understanding of what we are doing when we study law from the outside and examine its social impact. It is time to move on to the real questions.

Bibliography

ABEL, RICHARD (1973) "Law Books and Books about Law", 26 *Stanford Law Review* 175.

– (1980) "Redirecting Social Studies of Law", 14 *Law and Society Review* 805.

– (1981) "A Critique of American Tort Law", 8 *British Journal of Law and Society* 59.

– (1982) "Torts", in David Kairys (ed). *The Politics of Law.* New York: Pantheon Books.

ADORNO, THEODOR (1976) *The Positivist Dispute in German Sociology.* New York: Harper & Row.

ALEXANDER, JEFFRY (1982) *Theoretical Logic in Sociology. Positivism Presuppositions, and Current Controversies.* London: Routledge & K. Paul.

BAKER, EDWIN (1982) "The Process of Change and the Liberty Theory of the First Amendment", 55 *Southern California Law Review* 293.

BERNSTEIN, RICHARD (1976) *The Restructuring of Social and Political Theory.* Oxford: Blackwell.

BLACK, DONALD (1972a) "Law, Society and Industrial Justice by Ph. Selznick, Ph. Nonet and H. W. Vollmer – Book Review", 78 *American Journal of Sociology* 709.

– (1972b) "The Boundaries of Legal Sociology", 81 *Yale Law Review* 1086.

– (1976) *The Behavior of Law.* New York: Academic.

CAIN, MAUREEN and KALMAN KULCSAR (1982) "Thinking Disputes: An Essay on the Origins of the Dispute Industry", 16 *Law and Society Review* 375.

CAIN, MAUREEN and JANET FINCH (1981) "Toward a Rehabilitation of Data", in

[27] For an illustration of a similar mode of analysis, see Robert Gordon's essay on the way elite New York lawyers sought to reconcile their ideals and their practices at the turn of the century. See Gordon (1983).

P. Abrahams et al. (eds.) *Practice and Process: British Sociology 1950–1980*. London: Allen & Unwin.

CLOKE, KENNETH (1976) "Political Loyalty, Labor Democracy and the Constitution", 5 *San Fernando Valley Law Review* 159.

FELSTINER, WILLIAM, RICHARD ABEL and AUSTIN SARAT (1981) "The Emergence and Transformation of Disputes: Naming, Blaming, Claiming ..." 15 *Law and Society Review* 631.

FEMIA, JOSEPH (1975) "Hegemony and Consciousness in the Thought of Antonio Gramsci", 22 *Political Studies* 35.

FRAY, GERALD (1980) "The City as a Legal Concept", 93 *Harvard Law Review* 1057.

FREEMAN, ALAN (1978) "Legitimizing Racial Discrimination Through Anti-Discrimination Law: A Critical Review of Supreme Court Doctrine", 62 *Minneapolis Law Review* 1049.

– (1982) "Antidiscrimination Law: A Critical Review", in David Kairys (ed.) *The Politics of Law*. New York: Pantheon Books.

FRUG, GERALDE E. (1980) "The City as a Legal Concept", 93 *Harvard Law Review* 1057.

GABEL, PETER (1977) "Intention and Structure in Contractual Conditions: Outline of a Method for Critical Legal Theory", 61 *Minneapolis Law Review* 601.

– (1980) "Reflection in Legal Reasoning", 3 *Res. in Law and Society* 25.

GABEL, PETER and JAY FEINMAN (1982) "Contract Law as Ideology", in David Kairys (ed.) *The Politics of Law*. New York: Pantheon Books.

GALANTER, MARC (1974) "Why the Haves Come Out Ahead: Speculations on the Limits of Legal Change", 9 *Law and Society Review* 95.

– (1981) "Justice in Many Rooms: Courts, Private Ordering, and Indigenous Law", 19 *Journal of Legal Pluralism* 1.

– (1983) "Reading the Landscape of Disputes: What we Know and don't Know (and think we know) about our Allegedly Contentious and Litigious Society", 31 *UCLA Law Review*.

GEUSS, RAYMOND (1981) *The Idea of a Critical Theory*. Cambridge: Cambridge University Press.

GORDON, ROBERTO (1981) "Historicism in Legal Scholarship", 90 *Yale Law Journal* 1017.

– (1982) "New Developments in Legal Theory", in David Kairys (ed.) *The Politics of Law*. New York: Pantheon Books.

– (1983) "The Ideal and the Actual in the Law: Fantasies and Practices of New York City Lawyers, 1870–1910", unpublished paper. University of Wisconsin Legal History Program Summer Workshop.

HABERMAS, JÜRGEN (1975) *Legitimation Crisis*. Boston: Beacon.

HYDE, ALAN (1982) "Is Liberalism Possible?" *N.Y.U. Law Review* 1031.

KAIRYS, DAVID (ed.) *The Politics of Law*. New York: Pantheon Books.

KENNEDY, DUNCAN (1970) "How the Law School Fails: A Polemic", 1 *Yale Review of Law and Social Action* 71.

– (1973) "Legal Formality", 2 *Journal of Legal Studies* 351.

– (1976) "Form and Substance in Private Law Adjudication", 89 *Harvard Law Review* 1685.

– (1979) "The Structure of Blackstone's Commentaries", 28 *Buffalo Law Review* 205.

– (1980) "Toward an Historical Understanding of Legal Consciousness: The Case of Classical Legal Thought in America, 1940–1950", 3 *Research in Law and Society* 3.

– (1980) "First Year Law Teaching as Political Action", 1 *Law and Social Problems* 47.

– (1981) "Critical Labour Law Theory: A Comment", 4 *Industrial Relations Law Journal* 503.

– (1982) "Distributive and Paternalist Motives in Contract and Tort Law, with Special Reference to Compulsory Terms and Unequal Bargaining Power", 41 *Maryland Law Review* 563.
– (1982) "Legal Education as Training for Hierarchy", in: David Kairys (ed.) *The Politics of Law*. New York: Pantheon Books.
– (1983) *Legal Education and the Reproduction of Hierarchy*. Cambridge: Cambridge University Press.
KLARE, KARL (1978) "Judicial Deradicalization of the Wagner Act and the Origins of Modern Legal Consciousness 1973–1981", 62 *Minneapolis Law Review* 265.
– (1981) "Labour Law as Ideology: Toward a New Historiography of Collective Bargaining Law", 4 *Industrial Relation Law Journal* 450.
– (1982) "Critical Theory and Labour Relations Law", in David Kairys (ed.) *The Politics of Law*. New York: Pantheon Books.
KIDDER, ROBERT (1981) "The End of the Road? Problems in the Analysis of Disputes", 15 *Law and Society Review* 718.
LLEWELLYN, KARL N. (1960) *The Common Law Tradition: Deciding Appeals*. Boston: Little Brown.
MACAULAY, STEWART (1963) "Non-Contractual Relations in Business: A Preliminary Study", 28 *American Sociological Review* 55.
– (1966) "Private Legislation and the Duty to Read – Business Run by IBM Machine, The Law of Contract and Credit Cards", 19 *Vand. Law Review* 1051.
– (1979) "Lawyers and Consumer Protection Laws", 14 *Law and Society Review* 115.
– (1982) "Law Schools and the World Outside Their Doors II: Some Notes on Two Recent Studies of the Chicago Bar", 32 *Journal of Legal Education*.
MANN, MICHAEL (1970) "The Social Cohesion of Liberal Democracy", 35 *American Sociological Review* 423.
MARX, KARL and FRIEDRICH ENGELS (1969) *Selected Works*. Vol. I. Moscow: Progress Publishers.
MATHER, LYNN and BARBARA YNGVESSON (1981) "Language, Audience and the Transformation of Disputes", 15 *Law and Society Review* 775.
MENSCH, ELIZABETH (1982) "The History of Mainstream Legal Thought" in David Kairys (ed.) *The Politics of Law*. New York: Pantheon Books.
MUNGER, FRANK and SEREN CARROL (1983) "The Role of Empirical Research in the Future of the Conference on Critical Legal Studies", 7th Annual Conference on Critical Legal Studies, Camdon NZ.
NONET, PHILIPPE and PHILIP SELZNICK (1978) *Law and Society in Transaction: Towards Responsive Law*. New York: Harper & Row.
POSNER, RICHARD (1981) "The Present Situation in Legal Scholarship", 90 *Yale Law Journal* 1113.
RORTY, RICHARD (1982) *The Consequences of Pragmatism*. Brighton: Harvester.
SARAT, AUSTIN (1983) "In Justice in the Name of the Law". Unpublished plenary speech delivered at the Law and Society Association. Denver.
SCHLEGEL, JOHN H. (1980) "American Legal Realism and Empirical Social Science: From the Yale Experience", 28 *Buffalo Law Review* 459.
SPARER, ED (1984) "Fundamental Human Rights, Legal Entitlement and the Social Struggle: A Friendly Critique of the Critical Legal Studies Movements" 36 *Stanford Law Review* 509.
STONE, KATHERINE (1981) "The Post-War Paradigm in American Labour Law", 90 *Yale Law Journal* 1515.
TRUBEK, DAVID M. (1977) "Complexity and Contradiction in the Legal Order: Dalbus and the Challenge of Critical Social Thought about Law", 11 *Law and Society Review* 529.

– (1981) "The Construction and Deconstruction of a Dispute – Focused Approach: An Afterward", 15 *Law and Society Review* 727.
Tushnet, Mark (1979) "Truth, Justice and the American Way: An Interpretation of Public Law Scholarship in the Seventies", 57 *Texas Law Review* 1307.
– (1980) "Post Realistic Legal Scholarship", 1980 *Wisconsin Law Review* 1383.
– (1981) "Legal Scholarship: Its Causes and Cures", 90 *Yale Law Journal* 1205.
Unger, Roberto M. (1975) *Knowledge and Politics*. New York: Free Press.
– (1976) *Law in Modern Society*. New York: Free Press.
– (1983) "The Critical Legal Studies Movement", 96 *Harvard Law Review* 561.
Weber, Max (1968) *The Religion of China*. New York: Free Press.
– (1978) *Economy and Society*. Berkeley: University of California Press.
Wellmer, Albrecht (1974) *Critical Theory of Society*. New York: Herder.
– (1983) "Reason, Utopia and the Dialectic of Enlightment". Unpublished paper.

III.
Contract

The Use of Economics to Elucidate Legal Concepts: The Law of Contract

DONALD R. HARRIS
CENTO G. VELJANOVSKI
Oxford

Introduction

The purpose of this paper is to illustrate the value to lawyers of using economic perspectives to obtain a deeper understanding of the law.[1] There is some affinity between economics and law which often makes collaboration between economists and lawyers easier than between lawyers and other social scientists. Lawyers have, often without knowing it, been forced to face many economic issues when developing legal principles, and their discovery of economic theory frequently enables them to perceive more clearly issues of which they were only dimly aware. Economic theory can give lawyers an external view of the law, a new perspective from which to appraise the law. But there are limitations to the economic viewpoint, which normally assumes the existing distribution of wealth and income. Legal rules must often take account of concepts of justice ('fairness') and ethical standards, which are factors beyond those used by economists; nevertheless, lawyers should still benefit from the insights of economics – they may see more clearly the situations in which they are allowing distributive justice to override economic efficiency.

This paper will take its illustrations from the law of contract; all legal systems must have a set of rules to govern the making and enforcement of agreements, and we hope that much of what we say about the English law of contract will have parallels in the law of contract in other legal systems. We consider in turn various economic approaches to contract law.[2]

[1] For a general introduction to the law-and-economic literature see Posner (1977); Veljanovski (1982); Bowles (1983); Polinsky (1983).

[2] The economic literature on contract and contract law is now vast. Some idea of this work can be gained by consulting Posner (1977: chap. 4); Polinsky (1983: chaps. 5 and 8); Kronman and Posner (1979); Ogus and Veljanovski (1984: chap. 4). See also Veljanovski (1984); *cf.* MacNeil (1981).

1. Contract Law Viewed as a Framework for the Making of Voluntary Transactions

The economist offers explanations for the overall purpose of the law of contract. He says that parties enter into legallybinding contracts because they expect to obtain a benefit from doing so. The law makes promises in contracts legally binding because that enables parties to improve their "welfare": the ability to make binding promises decreases future uncertainty and generates beneficial reliance on each other's promise. Formal rules of law are needed to facilitate the making and enforcement of promises, because the parties cannot themselves make arrangements which adequately guard against the risk of a promise being broken.

By the use of an ideal "model" of contract, the economist can also explain the need for external pressure (for example, courts) to enforce contractual promises. In the hypothetical, ideal world in which each party was fully informed about all the circumstances and could accurately predict the future, and the costs of negotiating were negligible, the parties would draw up a "complete contingent contract", that is, one which exhaustively specified all the parties' rights and obligations in every possible situation, and which provided a set of procedures and penalties to deal with every conceivable aspect of non-performance (Shavell, 1980). In practice, such a contract would be very costly (in both time and expense) to draw up and to enforce; and even if the parties had made such an "ideal" contract, they could still encounter two principal difficulties in the course of performance of the contract – verification of the relevant facts, and enforcement of the promise against an unwilling party. First, the contract may contain a clause purporting to deal with a particular contingency but one party may dispute that the facts specified in the clause have occurred. If this dispute cannot be settled by agreement, some third-party resolution (by a judge or arbitrator) will be needed to decide it. Secondly, many contracts are not self-enforcing, in the sense that each party could "enforce" the other's promise without assistance from third parties. Most contracts require some third-party mechanism (such as courts) to be organised by society in order either to induce the party contemplating a breach to perform his promise or else to force him to pay the penalties for breach agreed in the contract. Frequently, market or other forces, such as fear of the loss of business reputation, will be sufficient to induce performance of contracts (Macaulay, 1963; Beale and Dugdale, 1975; Wilson, 1980), but in some cases of breach of promise an external enforcement mechanism would be needed even with the ideal, model contract. Accordingly, the law of contract provides a framework within which voluntary arrangements agreed between the parties can, if the parties so wish, be turned into binding arrangements subject to external or third-party enforcement. The law thus facilitates the making of arrangements which the parties could not achieve on their own, without the assistance of the law.

2. Minimisation of Transaction Costs

In the context of contract, "transaction costs" is a term used by economists to cover the time, effort, trouble, and other costs incurred by the parties in negotiating agreement upon the terms of their contract, or in negotiating the settlement of, or litigating the adjudication of, a contractual dispute. The economist assumes that rational men will strive to avoid or minimise transaction costs (Kronman and Posner, 1979: chap. 1; Williamson, 1979).

Although the economist may, for some purposes, use the idea of a complete contingent contract (see section 1 above), he accepts that in practice most contracts are incomplete, in that they fail to provide expressly for many contingencies which even a layman could anticipate. A simple reason for this is that it would be too costly for the parties to negotiate agreement on a comprehensive set of precisely-defined obligations for many situations when they know that most of these situations would never occur; another reason is that it would often be beyond the capacity of the parties to anticipate the less likely contingencies. Usually the parties specify only the main aspects of their relationship and leave unspecified many less important aspects. By doing this, they tacitly agree that, if in the course of performance a secondary aspect does become important and they cannot then agree on how to deal with it, they will rely on the law to resolve the problem. From this point of view, a vital function of the law of contract is to provide a set of standard clauses or rules to cover the contingencies for which the parties have not made precise arrangements in their contract. The legal rules are a ready-made or standardised set of clauses which the parties can use if they do not want a completely "tailor-made" or "custom-built" contract. Use of the standard clauses saves the parties much time in negotiating contracts, thus minimising transaction costs. If a dispute about the contract later arises between the parties, their attempts to negotiate a private settlement of the dispute out of court will also be explained by their self-interested desire to minimise transaction costs (see section 8 below).

3. The Cost of Information

The economist also views the institution of contract and the provisions of contract law as encouraging the production of the optimal amount of information. There is a general tendency among lawyers and legislators to assume that information is costless, but economists understand that it is very costly to acquire information (new facts) and to minimise mistakes. Contract law can be seen as part of the incentive system designed to encourage people to acquire and produce new information about market opportunities and mutually beneficial exchanges. (The notion of 'efficient' breach is closely linked to these goals: see section 7 below.) The cost of supplying correct information and the corresponding cost of relying on incorrect information underlie the legal rules on representations made by one party to induce the other to enter the contract, and the rules on the effect of mistakes (where one or both parties have entered the contract on the assumption of incorrect facts). It has been argued that the legal rules should be designed to impose liability on the party best able to avoid such mistakes in future, viz. the party who can more cheaply gather or produce the relevant information (Kronman, 1978a).

4. Bargaining around the Law

Another insight to be gained from the economist is that laws which regulate specific terms of a contract may be circumvented by adjustment in other terms by the parties. If a term is regulated by the law, the beneficial effects of the regulation may be offset by adjustments in other terms so that the net improvement in the welfare of the favoured party will be less than initially anticipated by the legislator, and may even be negligible (Coase, 1960). For instance, legislation designed to protect consumers may prohibit special clauses which exclude the normal legal liability of the other party, or, on the other hand, may require the other party to undertake a liability which he would not voluntarily undertake (e.g. legislation requiring manufacturers to provide guarantees with the products they sell); but consumers may not benefit much since the price may be adjusted to offset the increased costs which these legal requirements impose on the other party. In general, there will be a tendency for the parties to bargain around a legal requirement when it does not encourage value-maximizing (i.e. efficient) contracts; in other words, the party bearing the higher costs will have an incentive to shift them on to the other party. Thus it is not possible to assume (as most lawyers tend to) that, because a law is designed to favour one party, its ultimate impact will also be beneficial to that party.

Perhaps the best documented example of a law designed to favour one group which rebounded to their disadvantage is rent control. The belief underlying rent control legislation appeared to be that controlling the price of a commodity will not lead to adjustments in the behaviour of the supplier. But economics informs us that controlling the price of a commodity such as rented accommodation, so that the real rate of return to investment in it falls, will merely encourage landlords to seek other ways of increasing the income from their properties. They will try, for example, to demand key or deposit money, or will require the tenant to pay for repairs and other expenses. If these clauses are also controlled, landlords will either withdraw their properties from the rented accommodation market or allow the quality of their properties to fall by not maintaining them. The result of this type of legal intervention is that tenants as a group are harmed by shortages in rented accommodation or by the poor quality of the accommodation which is available.

5. Contract Law Viewed as a System of Incentives

Another way in which economists can teach lawyers to view the law of contract is as a system of incentives and disincentives to influence decisions whether or not to make, and whether or not to perform contractual promises. The law is seen as an important influence on the behaviour of the parties, particularly in the decisions which they take in the course of the contractual period: the legal rules will affect their choices between the different courses of action open to them. Although the law-maker may not have thought of the influence which the rules of contract law might have on the behaviour of citizens, once those rules exist and are known to the parties, they will function as incentives to behave in certain ways and *not* to behave in other ways. (It is easy to think of the penalties of the criminal law as a system of incentives *not* to commit crimes. The economist considers that all civil law can function in a similar way – to the extent that citizens know the legal rules, that knowledge will influence how they decide to act.)

The sorts of questions which this approach poses for the contract lawyer are: Do the rules on breach of contract and on the remedies for breach provide sufficient incentives to promisors who may be deciding whether or not to perform their promises? Here, the promisor's anticipation of what the legal consequences of breach might be, and of the cost to him of those consequences, may be the crucial factor in influencing his decision one way or the other (Barton, 1972; Shavell, 1980; Polinsky, 1983a). (This approach assumes that society does not wish every contractual promise to be performed exactly according to its terms: see below under section 7.) Once this approach is followed further questions arise. In which types of situation do we wish to have a legal remedy which compels the promisor actually to perform his promise according to its terms (in English law, the remedies of specific performance (Kronman, 1978b; Schwartz, 1979) and injunction)? In which types of situation is it sufficient for the disappointed promisee to be confined to money compensation for the net loss which he has suffered as a result of the breach[3] (after taking account of his ability to obtain substitute performance from a third party – the doctrine of mitigation which has a ready application in the market situation)? If there is no available market (e.g. because the contractual performance was designed for the unique requirements of the promisee, as in the building of a house to specified plans on a specific site), in which circumstances should the legal remedy give the disappointed promisee the full cost of his getting substitute performance from a third party who contracts to complete the work (e.g. building the house) which the contract-breaker undertook but failed to complete?

6. The Concept of Risk-taking

Often, of course, contractual promises cannot be fulfilled despite the best efforts of the promisor, and in this situation the concept of the law as an incentive system will obviously not apply. But another economic concept is available to the lawyer to clarify his thinking about involuntary breach of contract – the concept of risk-taking. Much of the future we face is uncertain, but one way of partially reducing that uncertainty is to obtain binding promises from other people that they will perform (or refrain from performing) certain acts in the

[3] There is, however, still considerable confusion about what is the appropriate level of compensation. See Goetz and Scott (1977); Harris *et al.* (1979); Rea (1982).

future. A contract is often a reciprocal allocation of specified risks and an efficient system of contract law should facilitate risk-sharing by upholding the allocation of risks made by the contract (Polinsky, 1983a; Polinsky, 1983b, chap. 8). This approach justifies the result that, even where the failure to perform was an event beyond the control of the party in breach, the loss should nevertheless be imposed on him (Posner and Rosenfield, 1977). It must be assumed that in the usual case, where both parties are risk-averse, they will have allocated the risk of an anticipated loss caused by nonperformance to the party better able to bear it or to insure against it, who will typically be the party making the promise. The only exception to this approach would be where the event preventing performance was an unusual one, beyond the scope of the normal risks contemplated by the parties, in which case the doctrine of frustration will operate under English law to terminate further performance of the contract (thus making the parties share the risk).

7. The Economic Concept of Efficiency

Economic efficiency in this context requires that resources be allocated and risks assigned so that the value of resources, as measured by the parties' willingness-to-pay, is maximised (see Posner, 1977: chap. 2). The economic approach based on efficiency examines the incentive effects of law and the costs and benefits of alternative courses of action open to the parties. The economist assumes that, at the moment of making the contract, each party (as a rational person) values the promise of the other more than (or at least as much as) any alternative which he could then find in exchange for his own promise. At that time, the contract is "efficient", but circumstances may change thereafter. A promisor will break his contract if, at the time of the breach, he can find a better opportunity for his labour and resources, under which he will make (after fully compensating the promisee for the loss caused by the breach) a greater profit than he would have done if he had performed his promise. The Chicago school of law and economics, led by (former Professor) Richard Posner, claims that this result is 'efficient' and should be encouraged by the law, because, by maximising the total value or utility of the two parties, it benefits society. Remedies under contract law should aim (it is said) to discourage "inefficient" breaches, by which is meant breaches which impose total costs on the parties in excess of any benefits accruing to the breaching party. Thus, if the breach of contract was avoidable, the promisor should be required to make good all the loss suffered by the promisee, which is a rule providing a test of the economic efficiency of the breach. If, in anticipation of paying full compensation (damages) under this rule, the promisor still decides to break his promise, the implication is that the resources released by the breach are being allocated to more efficient uses, and that society as a whole therefore benefits. The law is, in effect, permitting the promisor to break his contract, provided he pays the promisee the monetary equivalent of the lost benefit which performance would have given him.

In our view, however, this approach is not always correct. When the promisor is deciding whether or not to break his promise, we cannot calculate efficiency from society's point of view by putting together two valuations of utility made at different times: it is not legitimate to take the re-valuation of the use of his labour and resources made by the promisor at the time of the breach, while holding the promisee to his valuation made at the time of making the contract. The theory of economic efficiency would require us to allow the promisee also to revalue at the later time, and if he then increases his valuation of the utility to him of the other party's performance, the question should be whether the extra profit expected from the promisor's alternative activity is more than sufficient to compensate the promisee for the revised valuation of the loss which breach would cause him. The argument in terms of justice would be similar: why should the law permit one party to a contract to use later information to his advantage, while refusing the other party the opportunity to counter by doing the same? There may be insuperable practical problems for the court if it had to decide whether the promisee's revaluation was genuine, and not opportunist behaviour in a situation of bilateral monopoly (Williamson, 1979; Muris, 1981) where the contract locks the two parties into such a relationship. But we should not claim that the result achieved by the present law is always "efficient".

The concept of "efficient breach" of contract may also be criticised by using another economic concept, that of an "externality". In this context, an externality is a third-party effect, an external cost suffered by a third party which is not taken into account by the contracting parties when they agree the terms of their arrangement; or an external cost caused to a third person by the breach of contract, and for which no compensation need be paid by the contract-breaker. If the contracting parties are able to ignore external costs when deciding how to act, there may be economic inefficiency, because the social costs (viz. the costs to society as a whole) may exceed the social benefits (again, to society as a whole). In the context of breach of contract, it can be argued that society needs a high level of reliance on the fulfilment of contracts. Business and the ordinary life of individual citizens could not be carried on in the present way, if it was not possible to rely on most contractual promises being performed. A certain level of contractual breaches may be tolerated by society (indeed, must be tolerated in those situations where circumstances beyond the control of the promisor prevent the performance of his promise). Each breach of contract tends to weaken public confidence in the reliability of contractual promises, especially since most breaches will come to the knowledge of third parties. To the extent, therefore, that a failure to fulfil a promise is a voluntary and deliberate failure on the part of the promisor, it will tend to undermine general reliance on contracts and thereby cause an external cost (which is not taken into account – at least in English law – in the assessment of damages for the loss caused to the promisee). Those writers who have supported the concept of the "efficient breach" of contract have ignored this externality.

8. The Use of Contract Law in Negotiating out-of-Court Settlements[4]

Most of the writers who apply economic perspectives to the law of contract have implicitly assumed that a breach of contract immediately and automatically brings a legal sanction into operation. But lawyers know that, although there are many occasions in which disputes arise between parties to contracts, there are relatively few occasions when these disputes are settled in the formal setting of the courtroom, by judges applying the rules of the law of contract. The vast majority of contractual disputes are settled by direct negotiations between the parties (with or without the assistance of lawyers), in which compromises are reached in the light of all the factors which the parties consider relevant, especially any desire on their part to maintain an existing relationship between them; they are not limited to the "legal" considerations which the judge may properly take into account when reaching a judgment. The contract-breaker knows that the procedure for taking the claim to a full hearing in court involves cost and delay, which he can exploit to his own advantage in the negotiations. If the claimant is under financial pressure, he will obviously be more willing to accept the immediate payment of a lower sum, than to face continuing pressure and uncertainty in the hope that a court will award a greater sum (often an unknown amount) at some unknown time in the future. Fear of the expense of pursuing or defending a claim may obviously induce a compromise. Again, people differ greatly in their psychological make-up, and in their ability to face uncertainty (which economists call their attitudes towards risks). The emotional strain of a dispute, or the fear of being involved in a public court hearing, may also exert some pressure on one or both parties to settle. Thus, the parties' imperfect appreciation of what the formal law of contract would say about their problem is usually only one of many relevant factors, and its force is often outweighed by other factors. The formal legal rules, and the anticipated costs of litigation if the dispute were taken to court, provide only the background to the parties' negotiations: the law merely casts a distant shadow on their negotiating positions.

It will be argued by some that the possibility of a judicial resolution of the dispute offers adequate protection to a party who feels that the pressure of these extra-legal factors is unfair to him. Empirical studies, however, show that the fear of delay, expense and uncertainty in using the courts frequently outweighs the apparent advantage that the eventual judgment should, in theory, ignore all extra-legal considerations. A party must make a crude cost-benefit analysis of the pros and cons of an early compromise of his dispute, and it is not surprising that the other advantages of a compromise usually outweigh the disadvantage that the impact of extra-legal factors cannot be avoided. One consequence is that, even where lawyers are involved in negotiating the settlement, the legal rules are often applied by them without any precision, because if other factors are likely to prevail, it is a waste of time and expense to investigate the precise legal position.

[4] This section is based on ideas originally developed in Harris and Veljanovski (1983).

The economist explains this situation by saying that the disputing parties realise that extra-legal methods of resolving contractual disputes are usually much cheaper, and that rational individuals will always choose the cheapest method of dealing with a dispute (minimising transaction costs: see section 2 above). The relevant question is then whether each mode of dispute resolution (renegotiation, arbitration, settlement or compromise, litigation, etc.) is designed so that it imposes the minimum necessary costs on each party and does not distort the incentives to perform. It would clearly not make economic sense either to settle all contractual disputes out-of-court, or to refer all to adjudication. In theory, there will be an 'optimal' level of litigation which reflects the social costs and benefits of using the courts compared with using other settlement processes. An appreciation of this situation should lead contract lawyers to the conclusion that legal rules on remedies for breach of contract should be designed to take into account the fact that in the vast majority of cases the rules will be used to guide out-of-court settlements and to induce compromises. This means that the law-maker (whether judge or legislator) should consider the effect of any proposed rule on the relative negotiating strength of the parties, and, in particular, how the rule will affect the distribution of the "bargaining chips" or advantages between the parties. In particular, he should aim primarily at the potential use of the rules in a two-party, "direct negotiations" situation, rather than at their use by an impartial, third party arbitrator or judge.

The law-maker, at least in England, has assumed that the rules of contract law will be applied in an independent way, and that the impartiality of the judge will prevent any apparent inequality between the parties in court; it is assumed that the ideal of equality before the law will be achieved by the judge ignoring the relative wealth of the parties, their business or financial strength, their reputations, political support, or other extra-legal circumstances. The independence of the judiciary is avowedly designed to neutralise the inequalities of the parties' negotiating strength in the market-place outside the court. But if contract law is used in out-of-court negotiations much more frequently than in court, the law-maker should realise that the assumption of impartial, third-party application of the rules will seldom apply, and that his rules will usually be applied in a "dirty" world where extra-legal factors may predominate. Relative bargaining strength is the crucial factor here, and, if there is an inequality, there is no third party to protect the weaker party.

We can illustrate the problem by reference to some English rules on contract law. In the last fifty years, there has been a tendency for new rules of law to give discretion to the judge, by enabling him to decide what is "fair" or "just" or "reasonable". These rules may work well in disputes which are resolved by judgment in court. But when they are used in out-of-court negotiations between the parties, they obviously create uncertainty in predicting how a judge would decide. In these negotiations this uncertainty gives an advantage to the contract-breaker (the defendant to the claim). Because there is no assurance that the judge would award any particular sum of money as compensation for breach, the defendant can usually persuade the claimant to accept a much lower sum than he claims as representing his loss. The uncertainty is very likely to lead to a "discount" or reduction in the agreed compensation. Unfortunately there will be other discounts in addition, because there will usually be other uncertainties facing the claimant – uncertainty about the facts, if there is a dispute over the evidence; uncertainty about the length of the delay before the dispute could be settled by a judge; and uncertainty about the legal costs of going to court. The contract-breaker can use each uncertainty and the delay involved in litigation to extract from the other party a settlement for a sum which is substantially less than the courts would award. Rules which may work well when applied by an impartial third-party, may confer unfair advantages on one or other party in the context of direct, two-party negotiations.

The law-maker could influence the level of out-of-court settlements by changes in rules of evidence and procedure. Rules of evidence obviously affect the bargaining strength of the parties. Under present English law, the promisee, the innocent party, must bear all the responsibilitiy of proving that the contract has been broken, and of proving the extent of the loss caused to him. If he cannot find sufficient evidence on these issues, his claim will fail. This risk creates another uncertainty which the contract-breaker can exploit in negotiations. The balance of relative advantage could be altered by changing the onus of proof in some situations, so that the contract-breaker bore more of the risks and costs of proof. For instance, the promisor could be made liable in some circumstances unless *he* could prove full performance of his promise. A businessman who sold an article to an ordinary citizen for his own use (a "consumer" in economic terms) might be made responsible, if there was a dispute about the quality or standard of the article, for proving that the article was up to the required standard. Any doubt or uncertainty on this question would then benefit the consumer. In view of the parties' relative bargaining strength outside the court, it might be fair to shift this responsibility from the weaker to the stronger party. Similarly, rules of procedure which permit the defendant to delay a court hearing in order to give him adequate notice of the claim against him, and adequate time to prepare his defence, obviously give him an advantage in negotiations. But they could be balanced by rules enabling the courts to award high rates of interest on any judgment against a defendant who finally loses the case in court. If the court could award interest on the compensation running from the date of the breach of contract, the higher the rate of interest, the less the advantages which the defendant would gain from using the risk of delay as an argument in negotiations for a settlement. Finally, rules on the allocation of legal expenses will affect the bargaining advantages of the parties in direct negotiations. A rule that each party must pay his own expenses of the court hearing, whether he wins or loses, will improve the defendant's position in negotiations because he is then in a position to threaten to impose a further cost on the claimant. If the party who wins in court can recover all his legal expenses from the losing party, this rule will widen the range of possible outcomes in court: it will therefore discourage weaker or risk-averse claimants. Each rule should therefore be evaluated in the light of its likely effect on negotiations out-of-court, as well as in the light of its expected use in court.

9. Conclusions: the Social Objectives of Contract Law

For the economist, the first question to be asked in relation to any legal rule is "What is the rule trying to achieve?" The economist forces the lawyer to attempt to formulate the social objective of the rule, so that the question can then be asked whether the rule is "efficient" in achieving that objective. This paper has considered many different objectives of contract law, such as facilitating voluntary exchanges of promises; the efficient allocation of resources and of risk-bearing; the encouragement of reliance on promises, and of the production and exchange of information; the avoidance of mistakes; the minimisation of transaction costs; and the incentive to perform promises wherever that produces an efficient result. But "efficiency" for the economist can be consistent with any of these objectives. With so many goals to be met it is evident that the law is unlikely to achieve them all simultaneously and thus is unlikely to achieve optimal results in all situations. The law should adopt the "second-best" approach and choose which objective is to have priority in a given situation, and then choose which rule is most likely to achieve that objective in that situation. Economic theory does not require perfection in achieving a goal: the choice will normally be a comparative one – is rule A more likely than rule B to achieve a given objective in a particular situation? In a "second-best" world in which information is costly to obtain and the legal system is costly to operate, a rule may be "optimal" although it is not fully efficient in achieving a stated goal.

Bibliography

BARTON JOHN H. (1972) "The Economic Basis of Damages for Breach of Contract", 1 *Journal of Legal Studies* 277.

BEALE, HUGH and TONY DUGDALE (1975) "Contracts between Businessmen: Planning and the Use of Contractual Remedies", 2 *British Journal of Law and Society* 45.

BOWLES, ROGER A. (1983) *Law and the Economy,* Oxford: Martin Robertson.

COASE, RONALD H. (1960) "The Problem of Social Cost", 3 *Journal of Law and Economics* 1.

GOETZ, CHARLES J. and ROBERT E. SCOTT (1977) "Liquidated Damages, Penalties and the Just Compensation Principle: Some Notes on the Enforcement Model of Efficient Breach", 77 *Columbia Law Review* 554.

– (1980) "Enforcing Promises: An Examination of the Basis of Contract", 89 *Yale Law Journal* 1261.

– (1981) "Principles of Relational Contracts", 67 *Virginia Law Review* 1089.

HARRIS, DONALD, ANTHONY I. OGUS and JENNY PHILLIPS (1979) "Contract Remedies and the Consumer Surplus", 95 *Law Quarterly Review* 581.

HARRIS, DONALD and CENTO G. VELJANOVSKI (1983) "Remedies for Breach of Contract: Designing Rules to Facilitate Out-of-Court Settlement", 5 *Law and Policy Quarterly* 97.

KRONMAN, ANTHONY T. (1978a) "Mistake, Disclosure, Information and the Law of Contract", 7 *Journal of Legal Studies* 1.

– (1978b) "Specific Performance", 45 *University of Chicago Law Review* 351.

Kronman, Anthony T. and Richard A. Posner (eds) (1979) *The Economics of Contract Law,* Boston: Little Brown.

Macneil, Ian R. (1981) "Economic Analysis of Contractual Relations: Its Shortfalls and the Need for a Rich 'Classificatory Apparatus'" 75 *Northwestern University Law Review* 1018.

Macaulay, Stewart (1963) "Non-contractual Relations in Business: A Preliminary Study", 25 *American Sociological Review* 55.

Muris, Timothy J. (1981) "Opportunistic Behavior and the Law of Contract", 65 *Minnesota Law Review* 521.

Ogus, Anthony I. and Cento G. Veljanovski (1984) *Readings in the Economics of Law and Regulation,* Oxford: Oxford University Press.

Polinsky, A. Mitchell (1983a) 'Risk Sharing through Breach of Contract Remedies', 12 *Journal of Legal Studies* 427.

– (1983b) *An Introduction to Law and Economics,* Boston: Little Brown.

Posner, Richard A. (1977) *Economic Analysis of Law,* Boston: Little Brown.

Posner, Richard A. and Anthony M. Rosenfield (1977) "Impossibility and Related Doctrines in Contract Law: An Economic Analysis", 6 *Journal of Legal Studies* 83.

Rea, Samuel A. (1982) "Non-pecuniary Loss and Breach of Contract", 11 *Journal of Legal Studies* 35.

Schwartz, A. (1979) "The Case for Specific Performance", 89 *Yale Law Journal* 274.

Shavell, Steven (1980) "Damage Measures for Breach of Contract", 11 *Bell Journal of Economics* 466.

Veljanovski, Cento G. (1982) *The New Law-and-Economics: A Research Review,* Oxford: Centre for Socio-Legal Studies.

– (1984) *Economics of the Common Law: A Bibliography.* Oxford: Centre for Socio-Legal Studies.

Williamson, Oliver E. (1979) "Transaction Cost Economics: The Governance of Contractual Relations", 22 *Journal of Law and Economics* 233.

Wilson, James A. (1980) "Adaptation to Uncertainty and Small Numbers Exchange: the New England Fresh Fish Market", 11 *Bell Journal of Economics* 491.

Some Notes on the Economic Analysis of Contract Law

Franco Romani
Roma

1. Contract in Economic Analysis

The purpose of this paper is to try to explain how and why economists, in the pursuit of their own subject, came to be interested in legal problems and more specifically in contract law, and to try to suggest that they may have something useful to say to legal scholars. The interest of economists in legal problems started with the increasing attention given by economic theory to what have been called externalities, or external effects. The external effect of an economic decision is an effect, whether beneficial or harmful, upon a person who was not a party to the decision. If a decision maker in his decision does not take these effects into consideration, if, that is, he does not calculate the costs and benefits his decisions impose upon third parties, he may undertake activities which although useful to him are harmful for society; and inversely he may limit activities which are socially useful. This very simple idea has been the theoretical basis of a great part of the theory of the economic intervention of the state, a theory which may be reduced to the basic proposition that the state should intervene when the market does not work.

Around the sixties this approach came under attack mainly by economists of the Chicago School. In a now famous article (Coase, 1960), Ronald Coase showed how in a world without transactions costs the inefficiencies caused by external effects could not exist. Coase, in effect turning upside down the traditional point of view, maintained that so called external effects did exist because the market (i.e. the negotiation between the parties) was not working, mainly because of the existence of transaction costs, not that the market does not function because there are external effects. This result, which like all good theoretical results seems obvious once understood is nicely (and critically) summarised by Calabresi (1968:68).

Thus, if one assumes rationality, no transaction costs, and no legal impediments to bargaining, *all* misallocations of resources would be fully cured in the market by bargains. Far from being surprising, this statement is tautological, at least if one accepts any of the various classical definitions of misallocation, These ultimately come down to a statement akin to the following: a misallocation exists when there is available a possible reallocation in which all those who would lose from the reallocation could be fully compensated by those who would gain, and, at the end of this compensation process, there would still be some who would be better off than before.

This and other similar definitions of resource misallocation merely mean that there is a misallocation when a situation can be improved by bargains. If people are rational, bargains are costless, and there are no legal impediments to bargains, transactions will *ex hypothesi* occur to the point where bargains can no longer improve the situation; to the point, in short, of optimal resource allocation. We can therefore, state as an axiom the proposition that the externalities can be internalised and all misallocations, even those created by legal structures, can be remedied by the market except to the extent that transactions cost money or the structure itself creates some impediments to bargaining.

The so-called Coase theorem could well be a tautology, but this tautology has not been useless insofar as it has forced economists to look for the more fundamental explanations for the presence of situations usually identified with the term externality i.e. transaction costs. And in studying transaction costs economists began to study legal problems. As George Stigler very aptly put it (1972:12).

The Coase analysis has emphasised the urgent need in economics for a general theory of transaction costs. The development of a theory of costs is a task for economists, but an integral part of that task is the understanding of the legal processes which may be employed. Economic life requires reliable commitments by the transactor and economic disagreement calls for methods of solution... It comes as more of a surprise to the theoretical economist, I am sure, than to his legal brethren that economic order has a deep relationship to legal order.

In connection with the problem of externalities the main categories of transaction costs which are analysed are:

i) the costs of defining and policing the right of exclusion (the cost of defining property rights);

ii) the costs associated with negotiating and enforcing contracts for the exchange of property rights.

As a legal student will immediately realise this categorisation refers to the two main characteristics of the property right, i.e.

i) the right to use, or to decide how and by whom a thing shall be used; which implies the right to exclude other individuals from its use;

ii) the right to transfer, or freely alienate, the ownership of the good to any person the owner sees fit. This right implies the right to enter into contracts with other individuals and to choose the form of such contracts (freedom of contract).

The attention of economists, when dealing with externalities, has been mainly directed towards the right of exclusion. The so-called problem of the "commons" (fishing in the ocean, the congestion of a road, the overgrazing of a pasture) is the main example of it. As is well known the problem of the commons arises when, due mainly to the impossibility of exclusion, no rent is imputed to a scarce fixed factor such as land, fishing grounds or roads. The consequence is that the resulting free access equilibrium is inefficient because the average product of the variable factor, instead of the marginal products is equated across alternative uses.

Or, to avoid any technical jargon, we could say that a resource which is in fixed supply is very likely to be over used if available free of charge. Ownership of the scarce resource is one way of insuring that a charge will be levied which reflects the scarcity of the resource. The possibility of excluding those who are not willing to pay is the precondition for being able to obtain the price required for efficiency purposes.

The reason for stressing this problem of exclusion lies in the obvious fact that exclusion is the precondition of transfer (what is the sense of selling a piece of land which everybody can use?). Once the right to exclude is established, the good or the asset is, from the economic point of view, clearly specified and so it can be transferred. The right to transfer (freedom of contract) has the function of insuring that the good or the asset is put to the best use. From the point of view of efficiency this is the main function of the institution of property.

Very frequently it is the difficulty of making exchanges, i.e. of contracting, which may explain why a system of private property has not emerged[1]

Take for example the case of pollution, which is the typical case discussed in connection with externalities. It is frequently asserted that pollution is due to the difficulty of enforcing property rights in air or water. I think the assertion is correct. However I would like to stress that these property rights are difficult to enforce not so much because there is a difficulty of exclusion but mainly because the difficulties and costs of contracting are very high. The demand for water by someone dumping garbage into a river is clearly measurable by the amount of garbage he wishes to dispose of in this way. If dumping garbage is forbidden there is an exclusion from the use of the water. The cost of exclusion is not thought to be really relevant (we have serious and competent people proposing to tax garbage per ton). The real trouble, as perceptive economists have been quick to realise (Baumol, 1972) lies in the nature of the "public bad" of pollution; while the polluter demands a precise amount of water (from which he could easily be excluded) he would, if the water rights in the river belong to a large number of people (as is commonly the case) have to negotiate with each one of them. It is obvious that the costs of contracting would be really prohibitive (above all if we consider that each one of the owners would have a veto power). In situations of this type it is therefore difficult for a market to operate.

In consequence, as Calabresi and Melamed (1972) explain, certain "entitlements", like the right to clean water, may be protected by liability rules instead of what they call property rules. The distinction between these two regimes of legal protection clearly reflects our distinction between the right to exclude and the right to transfer. If there is a right to exclude there is clearly an entitlement. However there are situations, like that of water rights, in which the right to transfer this entitlement by contract is difficult, costly or deemed to be inconve-

[1] We must note that there is an interaction between the two different types of transaction costs. For instance if the cost of negotiating contracts is very high it may render worthless the effort to define exclusivity even if its costs would be very low. Conversely if the costs of contracting were very low it could be convenient to enforce exclusivity even if the costs of defining it were much higher than in the preceding case.

nient. Here the legal system offers a particular kind of protection, through liability rules. An example given by Calabresi and Melamed of an entitlement protected by liability is the case of "eminent domain" which is a case where, as in our previous example of pollution, the seller may have a veto power (the hold-out problem) and so contracting becomes difficult and therefore it is better to resort to a liability rule. Another example given is the case of "accidents". "If we were to give victims a property entitlement not to be accidentally injured we would have to require all who engage in activities that may injure individuals to negotiate with them before an accident, and to buy the right to knock off an arm or a leg" (Calabresi and Melamed, 1972:1108).

It can be seen that problems of contracting are taking the centre of the stage of economic analysis of externalities and of the law. For instance economists have used the cost of contracting to explain the existence of the firm, which may be defined as an organisation within which the allocation of resources is done not by the price system but by authority. Once again the problem was clearly posed by Coase (Coase, 1937) who explained the existence of the firm by reference to the cost of using the market to form contracts.

But how are we to explain the existence of situations in which the costs of using the market are greater than the costs of internal organisation? An interesting attempt at a solution is given by Alchian and Demsetz (1972). They introduce the concept of team production, whose main characteristic is that the output yielded by the team is not simply the sum of the separable output of each of its members. With such team production it is difficult, solely by observing total output, either to define or determine each individual contribution to the output of cooperating inputs. In consequence it is difficult to set up a structure of individual rewards related to the contribution to joint output of each member of the team. Clearly if rewards are unrelated to efforts there will be no incentive and each member will have a tendency to reduce his effort by shirking as he will not bear the full cost of it. Thus in Alchian's and Demsetz's view the two key demands placed on economic organisation are those of metering input productivity and metering rewards. Team production, therefore, needs monitors. But who monitors the monitors? Quis custodiet custodes? According to Alchian and Demsetz the classical capitalist firm is an institution which provides an efficient solution to this kind of problems. At the basis of this explanation of the existence of the firm there are the difficulties and costs connected with what we called the right to exclude and the right to contract. The right to exclude, as we said, has the function of specifying clearly the goods or the assets which can be transferred. In the situation described by Alchian and Demsetz the good which is sold is the effort of the members of the team. If individual effort could be easily measured (for instance by reference to output) there would be no problem in setting up a market as exclusion could be easily carried out (each would be paid according to the output he produced) but when there is a team production this is no longer possible, exclusion becomes difficult, and the market cannot work properly.

A very important work, along a similar line of thought, has been undertaken by Williamson on markets and hierarchies (1975) in which he tries "to identify a set of *environmental factors* which together with a related set of *human factors* explain the circumstances under which complex contingent claims contracts will be costly to write, execute and enforce. Faced with such difficulties, and considering the risks that simple (or incomplete) contingent claims contracts pose, the firm may decide to bypass the market and resort to hierarchical modes of organisation. Transactions that might otherwise be handled in the markets are thus performed internally, governed by administrative processes instead" (Williamson, 1975).

Enough has been said, I hope to show how economists have come to appreciate the central role of a study of contract within economic analysis. I turn now to consider how economists approach certain problems about contract which are central to legal analysis.

2. Executory Contracts

Economists have always been familiar with the theory of exchange. When they talk of exchange, however, they have in mind a *simultaneous* exchange. Simultaneous exchange, though, is not particularly interesting for the student of contract. To him, the contract is in essence an *exchange extended into the future.* The contract is *a promise* of doing something in the future in exchange for something else. Now the future is uncertain and therefore there is the possibility that the costs and benefits of the exchange will turn out differently from what the parties expected. What contract law does is to use the machinery and the authority of the state to enforce, as the future unfolds the original agreement.

But why should the original agreement be enforced? This is the traditional problem, for lawyers and philosophers, of explaining why a promise should be binding. The economist may have something sensible to say about this. In the absence of sanctions one who promises to do something in the future may find it in his interest not to. It may well be that if this possibility is taken into consideration the system of future exchanges will collapse with a loss of welfare for everybody.

We can express this situation in terms of the theory of games. The pay-off structure of a market exchange is that of a game that the theorist calls a Prisoner's Dilemma. By way of example, take two individuals, Tizio and Caio. Tizio has the good A, whose value to him is one dollar while Caio values it at two dollars. Caio has the good B whose value to him is one dollar, while Tizio values it at two dollars. It is clear that both Tizio and Caio would gain from exchanging the goods. However, let us introduce into this simple world the possibility that one of the parties, once he has received the good from the other, does not fulfil his part of the obligation. All the possibilities may then be summarized by the following matrix (see p. 126).

If Tizio and Caio do not make the exchange. (i.e. Tizio keeps A and Caio keeps B) each retains a good worth one dollar (quadrant IV). If they make the exchange (Tizio gives A and Caio gives B) each ends up with goods worth two dollars (quadrant I).

However if Tizio gives A but Caio keeps B Tizio will end up with nothing

	Caio gives B	Caio keeps B
Tizio gives A	(I) T2 C2	(II) T0 C3
Tizio keeps A	(III) T3 C0	(IV) T1 C1

while Caio gets three dollars worth (quadrant II). The same reasoning, symmetrically, could be applied to Caio (quadrant III).

One can intuitively see that, if Tizio and Caio distrust each other, the more rational solution for each of them is to keep his good in order to avoid the risk of ending up empty handed. This means that there will be no exchange. As we have seen, however, each would have gained if the exchange had taken place. Moreover, the exchange is the value-maximising solution for society in dollar terms. The value of the goods in their new hands is four dollars whereas it was two dollars before. Making the promises between the parties binding is a way of insuring that both parties enter, in a situation of this type, into exchange, therefore increasing the welfare of both.

We therefore suggest that contract may be explained as a solution to a prisoner's dilemma.

The example of how a binding promise solves a prisoner's dilemma problem refers to contracts which are only partially executory, that is, where Tizio performs and the question then is whether Caio is to be held to his promise (or vice versa). The case of wholly executory contracts does not fit easily into a prisoner's dilemma situation. If Tizio and Caio exchange promises but Caio then wishes to withdraw before Tizio has performed we may ask why the rule of contract should enable Tizio to enforce Caio's promises. The usual answer would be that the main function of executory contracts is to allocate the risks of changes in events before the date for performance arrives. This shifting of risk means a gain for both parties. If however anyone is free to renege on his engagement this utility-increasing reallocation of risk would become impossible for the prisoner's dilemma reasons illustrated above.

It has been suggested however that there may well be executory contracts whose function is not to allocate risk. Atiyah, for instance in a recent review article (1981), offers a simple example

> where A contracts to sell an orange to B for 10p, and B contracts to buy it at that price. The agreement is that the contract is to be performed on both sides tomorrow: because this is a free and voluntary agreement we can assume that A values the orange at less than 10p, otherwise he would not sell it for that price. Let us assume that he values it at 8p. B, on the

other hand, must obviously value it at more than 10p otherwise he would not pay 10p for it. Let us assume B values it at 12p. Clearly a simultaneous exchange now will improve the position of both parties.

But when the time for performance arrives, A changes his mind and now values the orange differently. Professor Atiyah considers two possibilities: the first is that A values the orange at 11p, the second that he values it at 13p. The principle of efficiency requires that the orange should go to the party who values the orange more i.e. to B when A values the orange at 11p and to A when he values the orange at 13p. It is easy to show that without transaction costs, this is the result that would be reached either if the promise is binding or if it is not (it is a straightforward application of the Coase Theorem)[2]. However Professor Atiyah maintains that in the presence of transaction costs the solution is not so clear cut. He shows in fact that the only case in which the presence of transaction costs seems to make no difference is the case where there is no liability for the breach of the contract and A has revalued his good to 13p i.e. the case in which there is no liability rule, A breaches the contract and keeps the orange. The conclusion he draws from his example is that economic analysis has not yet provided reasons why it is efficient to enforce wholly executory contracts.

I do not think this conclusion is correct. What Professor Atiyah really proves with his examples is that in certain legal systems, there is the possibility that the expected costs of transactions may be higher than the expected gains of winning a case. It is clear that in a situation of this type if A does not perform B is not going to sue. But the examples of Atiyah depict a situation in which, from an economic point of view, the rule in operation is the absence of liability *de facto* for the party that does not perform. It is therefore a *non sequitur* to infer from the examples that the efficiency of the liability rule for the breach of an executory contract from an economic point of view has not been proved. What Atiyah shows is simply that it might be difficult (or even impossible) to implement a liability rule in practice. From an economic point of view the right question is the following: if a liability rule could be implemented in practice is it preferable to a no liability rule? With such formulation of the question we are practically back to the Coase theorem. From an allocational point of view it should be a matter of indifference which rule is adopted.

From a distributional point of view of course there will be a difference. In the example chosen by Atiyah we are allowed, though, to consider some distributional question. In fact, as Atiyah says, "parties who make contracts today for

[2] The proof is very simple indeed. If A values the orange at 11p, with a liability rule in operation which would force him to pay 2p to B in case he does not perform (12p–10p) it would be his interest to perform. If, however, A now values the good at 13p he would pay the 2p to B and not perform. In both cases the orange will go where it is most valued (the efficiency principle). In the case where there is a no-liability rule if A values the orange at 13p he will not perform and this is the efficient solution. If he values the orange at 11p he will not perform either. But now B will make a new offer at a price higher than 11p and, assuming the absence of transaction cost, he will therefore and up with the orange. Therefore also in this case the efficient result is still insured.

performance may not be doing so to allocate risks tomorrow at all: they may be doing so because they cannot perform today, although they would if they could. In my example perhaps A does not have his orange available, or B does not have his money available today" (Atiayh, 1981:205).

It seems that in Atiyah's example the executory contract is made due to the unfortunate impossibility of making a simultanoues exchange immediately. Therefore a comparison should be made between a simultaneous exchange done today and a simultaneous exchange postponed to tomorrow (the executory contract has been made to make sure that what is impossible today will be done tomorrow). Suppose that the parties had nonetheless succeeded in making a simultaneous exchange today. When tomorrow arrives A may have changed his mind and may value the orange either 11p or 13p. Of course in both cases he regrets having made the exchange. Should he value the orange at 13p he can buy it back again: the good will then go where it is most valued, and efficiency is insured. But this from a distributional point of view is exactly the situation in which the parties would have found themselves if they had signed an executory contract with a rule of liability effectively implemented.

Following Atiyah's reasoning through, therefore, we should conclude that any exchange is inefficient insofar as a party may subsequently change his mind. This is a step that as a dull, mainstream economist, I am not yet ready to take without further analysis.

To sum up the argument, I believe that executory contracts are usually made for shifting risks (they are mainly a form of insurance) and this is an economic activity which legal rules should encourage in order to avoid prisoner's dilemma situations. There may well be a few cases in which this is not true but there are no reasons from an economic point of view why in these cases we should change the legal rules. From the efficiency point of view both types of rules (liability and non-liability) are more or less equal, but from a fairness point of view, it is better to have a liability rule for the breach of contract. Moreover, to have the same rule for all cases saves the costs, for the courts, of finding out whether an executory contract is or is not a way for allocating the risks.

3. Binding Promises

Viewing the contract as an attempt to deal with a prisoner's dilemma may help in understanding the structure and the development of the contract law. It explains, first of all, the emphasis of the traditional theory on looking at the will of the parties. This is a way of seeing, through the eyes of the parties themselves, what is the original matrix of the pay-offs on the basis of which they entered into a contract. A legal system should never allow that a party be damaged for having believed that a promise was binding. To ensure that this is not happening one needs to know what the parties intended. However the need to maintain trust in the institution of contract does not imply that promises should be *absolutely* binding. For instance, the unfolding of time may change the matrix of pay-offs (in our example Tizio and Caio change their valuation of the goods) and therefore the exchange could cease to be value maximising. In this case it could be sensible and economically efficient to allow a promise to be broken. To keep the trust in the institution of contract, this should be allowed, however, only if:

a) the party who breaks the promise is not going to benefit by the behaviour of the other party while executing his part of the obligation (there should be restitution). It is obvious that if this were not so there would be built into the system an incentive to break promises;

b) the party who has not broken the promise should be as well off as he would have been if the promise had not been broken; and in any case he should never be damaged for having relied on the contract.

Of cource to insure that, when a promise is broken, these two conditions are respected we need an independent third party (the court). This need also arises because the parties, when making a contract, are not able (either because it is too costly or just for sheer lack of imagination) to foresee all the possible contingencies that could appear in time. In this case they trust that should unexpected contingencies emerge there are rules and an independent third party that would provide a fair solution. As a matter of fact, as has been said (Kronman and Posner, 1979:4):

> many substantive rules of contract law are simply specifications of the consequences of some contingency for which the contract makes no express provision. If the parties are satisfied with the way in which the rule allocates the risk of that contingency, they have no need to incur the expense of writing their own risk allocation rule into the contract.

In general we can say that, when, for whatever reason, it appears that on a particular contingency there has not been a specific promise and there is not a specific substantive rule implicitly accepted by the parties, it is not surprising that a court will decide the case according to the residual general principles of law, such as the tort principle of compensation for harm done, the restitution principle for benefits conferred and so on. This may be the reason why even some shrewd observers of legal reality may have got the impression that, in practice, the will of the parties is not really the basis of the contract and that the emphasis given to this element is just a transitory and soon-to-disappear episode of liberal ideology. I do not feel, however, that this impression is correct. If the interpretation of the contract as a solution to a prisoner's dilemma is sound, the main function of contract law is and remains to insure that *ex ante*, and not *ex post* all parties gain from the fact that the institution of contract exists. But the main way of seeing what was the situation *ex ante* is to look at the valuations and expectations of the parties themselves at the moment the contract was made. This interpretation offers a good explanation of (or is warranted by?) the rationale behind the common law doctrine of consideration, which sometimes is taken as an indication of the relative relevance of the will of the parties in making a promise binding.

In fact if, when the contract is made, there is not an exchange of something for something and thus, a gain for all the parties concerned, the possibility of a situation of the prisoner's dilemma's type does not emerge and therefore there is no need to look at the will of the parties. To make gratuitous promise binding, therefore, would be purely a waste of time and resources, that is economically inefficient. The parties are themselves quite capable of giving force to their wills if they want.

In an influential article Richard Posner (1977), has put forward some interesting ideas on the problem of gratuitous promises which are worth discussing in the present context. The problem of these promises is why they are made. The purpose of a promise in an ordinary exchange is to induce performance, but if reciprocal performance is not desired, why promise at all? Why promise to make a gift, rather then waiting until one is ready to make the transfer and then just making it? According to Posner:

a gratuitous promise, to the extent it actually commits the promisor to the promised course of action, creates utility for the promisor over and above the utility to him of the promised performance. At on level this proposition is a tautology: a promise would not be made unless it conferred utility on the promisor. The interesting question is how it does so (Posner, 1977:412).

Richard Posner argues

that it does so by increasing the present value of an uncertain future stream of transfer payments (Posner, 1977:412).

To give a simple example: A promises to give one hundred and ten dollars to B next year. Suppose the current rate of interest is ten per cent. If the promise is binding, B could today borrow one hundred dollars and use the money sure in the knowledge that he will be able, next year, to pay with the gift principal and the interest (i.e. at a rate of interest of ten per cent the present value of one hundred and ten dollars next year is one hundred). However, Posner maintains that a non-binding promise of one hundred and ten dollars has a lesser value for the promisee (therefore for the promisor it is as if his gift were reduced in size). Suppose he calculates that the promisor will just give half of what he promised i.e. fifty-five dollars. In this case the promisee, if he wants to play safe, could only borrow fifty dollars, the present value of the promise. Therefore Posner argues, the difference between the two present values (fifty dollars) represents the social cost of not having the institution of a binding promise. More precisely the promisor who intends to keep the promise will, if the promise is legally binding see the size of his gift increased at no cost to him and "here is a clear case where the enforcement of gratuitous promise would increase net social welfare" (Posner, 1977:412). The suggestion is clever but not quite right.

In fact if A keeps his promise, although not binding, next year B will find himself with fifty-five dollars that he did not expect, i.e. he will find himself in a situation as if he had last year saved fifty dollars and invested them at the rate of interest of ten per cent. And this is clearly a benefit to B and by consequence, according to the premise of Posner, an increase of utility for the promisor.

There is however a grain of truth in what Posner says. Of course, if B had relied on the promise he would probably have planned his expenditure differently (there is no reason for him to choose to save fifty dollars) and therefore there is a loss of utility for the promisee for the reason that the promise was not legally binding. But this loss is not at all represented by the difference in the present values of gifts in the alternative systems of liability. So the point made by Posner is really much less weighty than it may seem at first sight.

Probably one of the purposes of making a purely gratuitous promise is to give, out of benevolence, information to the promisee in order that he may plan his activities better. It is not logically impossible for the promisor not to care whether the promise is believed or not. The benefit for him is of having given the information. If, however, we think that not the gift, but the change in planning is really what the promisor cares about we are in a sense abandoning the idea of a purely gratuitous promise and we begin to see the promise as a way of inducing the promisee to do something in which the promisor is interested. The greater his interest, the closer we are to a prisoner's dilemma situation. This then becomes the reason why we may wish to make the promise binding.

This discussion on the enforceability of promises may serve as an example of how an economist's mind may work when faced with a legal problem. I am not suggesting that this is the correct, or best approach to such contractual questions: only that this is a creditable approach which, for certain purposes, may be the most useful.

Bibliography

Alchian, Armen A. and Harold Demsetz, (1972) "Production, Information Costs and Economic Organization", 62–1 *American Economic Review* 777.

Atiyah, Patrick S. (1981) "The Theoretical Basis of Contract Law – An English Perspective", 1 *International Review of Law and Economics* 183.

Baumol, William J. (1972) "On Taxation and the Control of Externalities" 62–1 *American Economic Review* 307.

Calabresi, Guido (1968) "Transaction Costs, Resource Allocation and Liability Rules – A Comment", 11 *Journal of Law and Economics* 68.

Calabresi, Guido and Douglas A. Melamed (1972) "Property Rules, Liability Rules, and Inalienability: One View of the Cathedral" 85 *Harvard Law Review* 1089.

Coase, Ronald C. (1937) "The Nature of the Firm" 4 *Economica* 386.

– (1950) "The Problem of Social Cost" 3 *Journal of Law and Economics* 1.

Kronman, Anthony, T. and Richard A. Posner (1979) *The Economics of Contract Law*. Boston: Little Brown.

Posner, Richard (1977) *Economic Analysis of Law*. Boston: Little Brown.

– (1977) "Gratuitous Promises in Economics and Law", 6 *Journal of Legal Studies* 411.

Stigler, George J. (1972) "The Law and Economics of Public Policy: A Plea to the Scholars", 1 *Journal of Legal Studies* 1.

Williamson, Oliver E. (1975) *Market and Hierarchies: Analyses and Antitrust Implication*. New York: Free Press.

Neo-Institutional Economic Theory: Issues of Landlord and Tenant Law

A. ALLAN SCHMID*
Michigan State University

Introduction

Neo-institutional economic theory has as its purpose to formulate testable hypotheses predicting the impact and substantive consequences of alternative property rights. Its practice should also serve the client who specifies an economic performance and asks what law would help achieve it. Classical institutional economics, brought to its apex by John R. Commons, focused on the transaction as the unit of analysis. People are interdependent and their actions create conflict as well as opportunities for accomplishment beyond that reachable by the individual. They have at their disposal physical, emotional and perceptive capacities. Their access to resources and the use of their potential capacities are shaped by property rights.

Property rights are used here in a broad sense to refer to the understandings we carry in our heads of the relationships of one person to another with respect to a resource or any line of action. Rights are the instrumentality by which any society controls and orders human interdependence and resolves the question of who gets what. The terms institutions, rights, and rules of the game are used here interchangeably. In the words of Commons (1950:21) "an institution is collective action in control, liberation and expansion of individual action" or as Kenneth Parsons (1942) says "Property is a set of social relationships which ties the future to the present through expectations of stabilized behavior regarding other persons and things".

In an interdependent world, the opportunities of one person are shaped by the opportunities of others (Samuels, 1981). And it is rights that define the potential for these interacting opportunities. One person's *duty* that must or must not be performed is anothers's *right* and that person can ask for the collective's help in achieving the desired acts of others. If one person has a *liberty* and may choose an opportunity, the other person is *exposed* and cannot interfere (Hohfeld, 1913).

* Research funded by the Michigan Agricultural Experiment Station and referenced there as Journal Article Number 10795.

A key concept for neo-institutional economic theory is the classification of the characteristics of goods which are sources of interdependence. It is the inherent features of goods which influence how one person's acts can potentially affect another. The instrumentality of law depends on the source of the interdependence. If you do not know where the ability of one person to affect another is coming from, you cannot control the opportunities of the parties to potential transactions. The section headings of this chapter illustrate this goods classification which is referred to as the "situation".

Thus the first component of the neo-institutional economic theory is classification of the situations of interdependence. The next component is the structural or institutional alternatives. Most institutional economists begin with contrasting bargained (market), administrative, and status/grant transactions (Heilbronner, 1962:chap. 1 and Polanyi, 1957:250). This is a good place to start, but more complex and necessarily *ad hoc* variations must be added for the case at hand. The final component of the neo-institutional paradigm is performance. The performance variables chosen depend on the analyst's perception of the concerns of the groups in society (or the analyst's clients). A positive theory limits these to substantive and observable measures of who gets what rather than the abstractions of efficiency, productivity, justice or freedom which are often value implicit and presumptive.

A scientific theory must identify variables and specify the relationships among them, and formulate hypotheses which are potentially falsifiable. In social science experimentation, it is particularly important that theory can identify problem situations as to their essences and instruments as to their functional equivalents. When a legal change is proposed, it may never have been tried before. There is nothing extant to observe. In that case we need a theory to organize our previous experience in situations which had the same functional ingredients, even though they were wrapped in different exteriors.

In the balance of this chapter a neo-institutional theory will be described. Rather than simply being an abstract theoretical statement, the treatment here will outline the theory with reference to a particular set of interdependencies growing out of landlord-tenant transactions in rented housing. The specific references to law are to the *Michigan Compiled Laws Annotated* (M.C.L.A.) section 544.601, referred to as the Security Deposit Law, and M.C.L.A. section 544.631, known as the Truth in Renting Act. The 1972 Security Deposit Law provides that a deposit to cover damages to the premises may be required and held by the landlord, but it is the property of the tenant. An inventory checklist of the condition of items on the premises is signed by both parties at the beginning of the tenancy. If the landlord claims any part of the deposit for damages after the tenant departs, and the tenant disputes the claim, the landlord must commence a court action to obtain possession of the money. If the landlord keeps the deposit without court action, he is liable to the tenant for double the amount of the deposit retained. Any contract provision waiving these rights is unenforceable at law. The framers of the Act hoped for a performance whereby tenants paid only for damage done and thereby had a larger proportion of their deposit money returned to them than had been common in the past.

The 1972 Act did not achieve its hypothesized performance, so in 1978 an additional law was passed, referred to as the Truth in Renting Act. Among other things it not only made contract provisions waiving tenant rights to security deposits unenforceable, but made their inclusion in a contract illegal and subject to recovery of damages resulting therefrom.

The discussion is aimed at explaining why the first law failed to perform and to suggest that an adequate theory should have been able to organize experience to have designed a law sufficient to the purpose. While the case is of interest in itself, it is chosen primarily to illustrate the potential of a theory with general application[1].

The commonest class of ways that one person can affect another is when one person's use of a resource is incompatible with another's. With respect to the apartment the first question we ask the law to answer is: who has the rights to use it and decide conditions for others to use it. Persons A and B cannot make full use of it at the same time. So the first question of legal structure is, who is the landlord, i.e. who is able to receive bids form others; and who must make a bid if they want a place to live. The law in question did not do anything to redistribute factor ownership. Use of the property in a manner unauthorized by the owner is a legal wrong. It might be a matter of criminal law if the unauthorized use is arson, or civil law if the unauthorized use damages the apartment or its contents.

While landlords are entitled to sue for damages, they have found that the right is of little value if the damaging tenant has moved away quickly and is costly to trace. Also even if found, the tenant may not have the capacity to pay for the damage done. With this experience, landlords have exercised their right of contract to collect a damage deposit prior to occupancy. So in a sense the exercise of one's right to be free of damage is itself a type of good whose salient feature is its high transaction (information) cost – more on this below. The damage deposit as a sum of money is an incompatible use good. Both before and after these Acts, landlords used the deposit money to earn interest for themselves until it was time to return it. Some law reformers contemplated declaring that the deposit and its interest earning power remained to the benefit of the tenant and its only function could be to guarantee the capacity to repay damages, but this was not enacted. The money was freely tradeable and if the landlord could bargain for use of it as a term of the lease, the law did not prevent its alienation for the purpose of earning interest. The issue of use as opposed to exchange rights is fundamental to definition of the prevailing structure. The ownership of the deposit was fractured into several complex parts.

Of major interest to economists is the relative bargaining power of the parties to a transaction (i.e., the ability of any one person to affect price). The interdependence created by bargaining power is controlled by rights related to the degree of competition. Under conditions of fewness, one party can exact a one-sided bargained exchange. The legal variables suggested by neo-classical economics are those related to antitrust law and illegal restraint of trade, which

[1] For more detailed exposition of the theory and further applications see Schmid (1978 and 1981) and Samuels and Schmid (1981).

prevent suppliers (or buyers) from setting prices above the cost of production where unusual profits are earned. This does not seem to be a major issue here. There is no apparent collusion among landlords to restrict the supply of housing. Nor are tenants forming collective bargaining associations and preventing other would-be tenants from framing bids at market prices.

So far the two main property right alternatives identified by neo-classical economics have been discussed – namely factor ownership controlling incompatible use and rules of competition controlling bargaining power. In the discussion to follow it will be seen that instrumental as these two types of rules may be, they do not begin to control all sources of interdependence. Knowledge of these other sources will help to suggest additional institutional alternatives and to interpret the results of new experiments.

1. Transaction and Information Costs

To make a good transaction, each party needs good information and access to the relevant parties. Thus, the making of agreements must not be too costly: if it is, nothing happens. The party which faces higher information costs will be at a disadvantage in making the transaction. The kinds of information needed are varied and complex. First, there is the matter of knowledge of price and quality of apartments available. This is very much related to the classical interest in the functioning of markets, but did not seem to be much of a problem in the present case.

Very much at the heart of the landlord-tenant transaction is the matter of the cost of establishing the extent of damage if it occurs. The original condition and value of the apartment and its contents are at issue. The landlord says everything was perfect and of the highest quality while the tenants say the table was already scratched and the leg already broken when they moved in. If this must be proven in a court of law, there are information and transaction costs to bear. If a damage deposit is in the hands of the landlord, then he makes the appraisal and returns the remainder after deducting any damages as he sees it. If the tenant disagrees, he must bear the costs of initiating court action to recover the excessive deductions. Since court actions of even a minor sort are not free, the tenant may accept a damage deduction when the cost of the transaction is greater than the value of the loss. If the tenant has the right to refuse the claim, then the landlord must bear the transaction costs to pursue relief in the courts. The result is the same, only the shoe is on the other foot. The landlord accepts damages when the transactions costs of collection are greater than the damage. Depending on the bargaining strength of the parties, the landlord may include the average of these small losses into the rental charge to the disadvantage of the tenant who is truly careful and causes no damages at all.

The bargained outcome of this when money for deposits was freely exchangeable (prior to the 1972 Security Deposit Law) was that landlords contracted for damage deposits paid in advance and from which they made deductions at will. The performance results of this right (liberty) in the context of high information and transaction costs were judged unacceptable by the government. A law was passed which changed factor ownership of the deposit with reference to who must initiate court action to alter any division of the deposit not agreed to mutually. The deposit was declared the property of the tenant (but not the interest thereon). If the landlord claimed any part of it, he had to bear the transaction costs of getting a judge's consent. Further this right was declared non-exchangeable, even if the tenants thought they might receive fair value by giving up this right (perhaps a reduction in rent), no such contract provision waiving the right was enforceable at law. The rationale might have been that because of unequal bargaining power or information costs, the tenants would not be able to make fair bargains and would exchange rights to their deposit money too cheaply.

The framers of the legislation must have hypothesized that they were dealing strictly with an incompatible use good controlled by factor ownership. When they changed the factor ownership and made it non-exchangeable they predicted that tenants would be able to retain more of their deposits unless substantial and clear damage had occured. But in fact, the hypothesis proved incorrect. Many landlords still included provisions in their contracts giving them the right to make deductions at will. While these would have been unenforceable in court, uninformed tenants accepted them. Property rights are themselves a type of good. Landlords may be able to take advantage of tenants for whom the costs of information about their rights are high. Misinformation would have little effect if information were cheap.

To off-set the information costs, a new law was passed which made waiver of ownership of deposits not only unenforceable but illegal. Further, a duty was placed on the landlord to inform the tenant that the tenant had some unspecified rights in such things as deposits.

Each rental contract must contain the following notice:

Michigan law establishes rights and obligations for parties to rental agreements. This agreement is required to comply with the Truth in Renting Act. If you have a question about the interpretation or legality of a provision of this agreement, you may want to seek assistance from a lawyer or other qualified persons.

It might be thought that the law might have required that a copy of the law itself be distributed to tenants. This, however, may not have solved the problem of information cost. Too much information can be as bad as too little and confused tenants might still not understand their opportunities under the law.

The new law went even further in recognizing interdependence created by high information costs. An unscrupulous landlord might still be tempted to include a prohibited clause in the rental contract hoping that if a few knowledgeable tenants overcame the transaction costs of seeking court removal and fines for the offending clause, others would still be misled by its provisions.

First, the law requires the tenant to give written notice of the offending clause to the landlord who then has 20 days to give notice to all other tenants that the clause is void and unenforceable. If notice of the prohibited clause is not given by the landlord, a single tenant may enjoin the landlord to exclude it from future contracts and the court will order the landlord to give the required notice. This applies to all leases to which the landlord is a party at all housing sites. The law recognizes the role that court transaction costs might play in deterring a tenant from seeking the removal of the offending clause. After all the tenant taking the initiative might find that transaction costs exceeded the amount of any loss resulting from the illegal clause. All of the rest of the tenants benefit, but the person bringing the suit would bear all costs of the proceeding. Thus the law provides that the plaintiff can recover damages of $ 500 or actual damages, whichever is greater. The winning plaintiff may also recover attorneys' fees. This reward may be sufficient to prompt an enterprising person to examine systematically rental contracts and sponsor one of the affected tenants to give notice in the hope that the landlord would not comply and that the $ 500 could then be collected.

Second, in case the above is not sufficient, the law also makes publishers of lease forms liable for any damages suffered by a landlord as a result of including an illegal provision. The leverage provided by the $ 500 and the publisher's liability are very relevant to the high information cost situation. It would be very costly to educate every tenant to be aware of the illegal clauses. But if leverage can be given to the few who become informed, all can benefit even though they remain ignorant of the law. This saves a lot of education costs. The key is to increase the ratio of gain to the individual to the cost of acting for the individual but to have the result of the action apply to all similar members of the group.

Another aspect of information costs is that of uncertainty. The problem is not necessarily unequal cost of acquiring information, but that it is inherently uncertain. The landlord may make a mistake in projecting costs for the lease period and thus find profit margins squeezed or eliminated. Thus some landlords included contract provisions allowing them to alter the lease unilaterally, the tenant's only recourse if the alteration were unsatifactory to him being to move. The new law prohibited clauses permitting such unilateral alteration, except for providing that rents could be increased to cover additional costs in operating the premises such as increases in property taxes, electricity, heating, insurance and the like. In effect, the profit margin may not be altered, but the tenant is exposed to correction of any mistaken predictions of operating costs over the life of the lease. In such cases, the legal issue is not whether to require a party with superior information to share it with those with higher information costs, but whether to alter the distribution of gains and losses arising from incorrect prediction of costs.

2. Exclusion Costs

To illustrate this type of interdependence with the case at hand, consider passage of the law itself as the good. It has the characteristic that if the law exists to benefit one member of the class of tenants, it benefits all. It is costly even impossible, to exclude those who did not contribute to passage of the law. Knowing this, tenants may not contribute to the expenses of lobbying for such a bill before the legislature. Even those who agree that their benefits would exceed their share of the costs may be opportunistic free riders. The lobbying effort may fail from lack of contributions.

Various approaches to unseat the free rider are possible. One is that a leader may emerge and bear the organizational costs at great personal hardship in the short run in hopes that the effort may be recognized by the electorate if the leader runs for office in a future election. Sometimes lobby groups are formed as an adjunct of another organization which makes a profit selling low exclusion cost goods. Such is common in agriculture where a farm organization sells farm supplies and memberships in the political pressure group at the same time. Or, a medical association sells advertising in its journal and uses the profits for lobbying (see Olson, 1965:chap. 6).

Sometimes there is enough sense of community solidarity and of something approaching patriotism that people do not act opportunistically. When people are related to each other in terms of learned status transactions, there is little opportunistic behavior, as people act habitually. In the present case, one of the major lobbying groups was a public interest lobbying group largely paid for by funds collected from university students, who are mostly renters. There are transaction costs in any voluntary fund raising just in contacting the possible donors. In this case, the university administration lowered the transaction costs by including on the tuition payment cards issued to each student a reminder that such lobbying groups existed and that money for them could be included in the tuition payment and would be remitted to the groups. This is becoming more common on government tax forms with an optional check-off advising the government to spend money for certain designated purposes. If too many groups were listed the reminder would lose its attention-raising effect, so the right to be so included is very valuable in overcoming collection transaction costs.

Sometimes the government allows groups to place what is in effect a private tax on certain activities. By law there might be a charge for each rental contract, which the landlord collects and remits to some private tenants' association to use for tenant education. Such checkoffs are common for promotion of U.S. generic agricultural products (Ward, et al., 1983). To maintain the appearance of voluntarism, the fee is refundable. But again, transaction costs become a factor and few will bother to ask for a refund of an individually small amount which nevertheless in sum may finance major group activities. Many methods to overcome the free rider create unwilling riders who are forced to contribute to something they actually do not consider worth the cost. But since the opportunistic free rider cannot be distinguished from the unwilling rider, property rights must decide whose interests count. Appeals to freedom do not help solve the issue since one person's freedom (liberty) is another person's exposure to free riders or group failure.

3. Joint-Impact Goods

Some goods have the characteristic that whatever physical quantity of good is available, an additional user can be added at zero marginal cost. This situation is the polar opposite of the incompatible use good. A new user can be added without subtracting from the utility of the previous user. This creates an interdependence over cost sharing. Everyone wants to be the marginal user and pay only the zero marginal cost, letting the intra-marginal users pay the original costs of producing the good. The passage of the law is a high exclusion cost good as previously discussed, and also a joint-impact good. It applies to one tenant or all at no extra cost in terms of lobbying.

Even if there were no problem with free riders there would be an argument over cost shares. Even if non-payers could be excluded, should they be excluded if they can use the good without adding to the costs? The law often leaves it up to the entrepreneur to formulate any price structure he or she wishes. Persons with a few options who do not vary their use much in response to price (inelastic demand) are charged a higher price than their opposities. Some may regard this price differentiation as fair while others may not. Perhaps the renters' lobbying association check-off is less for old and college age renters than for middle aged (presumably higher income) renters. The position derived from pricing policy is part of a tenants' opportunity set, for one's real wealth is a function of what prices one faces.

4. Peak Loads

The time pattern of consumption for many goods is uneven. This means that capacity built for the period of high demand is unused during slack periods. This capacity must be paid for. Are the users of the extra physical units to pay the full extra cost of the capacity or is the total cost to be spread equally as average cost for all users? In the case of housing in university towns there is a peak demand during the nine months of the regular school year and excess capacity during the summer. Leases might be offered only for a certain rate for the whole year in which case the peak users pay the average cost of providing the apartment and can rent out the space for whatever they can get during the summer. Or, the landlord may rent for a high rate for the regular term and a much reduced rate during the summer. The right to take the initiative on relative prices affects the prices facing different groups of renters. The law does not speak to the issue and the landlords tend to choose the latter alternative. They pick a pricing structure to maximize their profits, though an alternative set of prices might raise the same total revenues, but affect the welfare of regular and summer students in quite different ways.

5. Surpluses

Different units of a productive factor may have different productivity. As demand forces use of less productive inputs, any price covering the last used input will mean an extra surplus of return to the intra-marginal units. In the case of land as space, land near centres of economic activity is more productive than more distant sites. The more distant sites are more costly to utilize because of transportation costs. This means that if the same total expenditure is paid for the close-in site, it earns a surplus or an economic rent. Rent is earned in a market transaction since the price of the close-in site is bid up by people trying to avoid the transportation costs and there is not enough of it to go around.

The issue is one of pricing and allocation rights. If the market is used to allocate apartments close to centres of economic activity, their owners capture the surplus. The surplus could later be taxed away by the government after price has performed its allocation role. Or, if it is public housing, where administrative transactions are used, the most desired sites could be rented for the same price as the more distant. Some non-price rationing system could be used such as age, length of time on the waiting list, or who is a friend or pays a bribe to the housing official. Some American cities have tried to prevent rents from rising but none has ever tried to remove rental differences based on location for apartments which are otherwise of similar quality.

6. Conclusion

While hindsight is always better, a good institutional theory should have warned the writers of the Security Deposit Law that changing factor ownership of the deposit would not be enough to alter performance and return more of the deposit money to the tenant. If the only type of interdependence situation were created by incompatible use and bargaining power, then changing resource (factor) ownership and maintaining competition would have been sufficient. In the transaction over the deposit, bargaining inequality was hopefully rendered inoperative by prohibition of exchange. But when interdependence was also created by information and other transaction costs, additional legal structural variables became instrumental.

The provisions of the Truth in Renting Act reduced the ability of landlords to provide misinformation which was effective because of high information costs. Further, by reducing transaction costs for winning tenants, the law gave leverage to a few informed tenants to get rid of misinformation for all tenants.

Theory suggests what variables need to be controlled and what kinds of rights are relevant. But was the law successful? The Truth in Renting Act has greatly reduced the number of illegal clauses in rental contracts in multiple unit housing. Nevertheless, some landlords probably withhold deposits by bluff from unknowledgeable tenants. Even the right to be told that tenants have rights which should be investigated will not keep unaware tenants from exploitation. It is not in the power of law to solve all problems.

Theory provides no guarantees. It does allow experimentation to proceed less blindly. For example, in the case of a high exclusion cost good like the results of lobbying the government the theory-organized experience can suggest alternatives to try. Even if an institutional alternative has never been tried with tenant lobbying, experience suggests ways to control free riders. If one way is blocked for political or ideological reasons, it is helpful to have a theory to suggest other alternatives which serve the same function. The relevant experience need not even be as similar as another type of lobbying. Any type of high exclusion cost good such as benefits won from trade union bargaining may provide useful clues for new institutions to try. We may hope that institutional theory will continue to evolve so as to make available hypotheses relating situation, structure and performance.

Bibliography

Backhaus, Jürgen, and Hans G. Nutzinger (eds.) (1982) *Eigentumsrechte und Partizipation. Frankfurter Abhandlungen zu den gesamten Staatswissenschaften.* Vol. 2, Frankfurt: Haag and Herchen.

Commons, John R. (1950) *The Economics of Collective Action.* New York: MacMillan.

Heilbronner, Robert L. (1962) *The Making of Economic Society.* New Jersey: Prentice Hall. Englewood Cliffs.

Hohfeld, Wesley N. (1913) "Some Fundamental Legal Conceptions as Applied in Judicial Reasoning," 23 *Yale Law Journal* 16.

Olson, Mancur (1965) *The Logic of Collective Action.* Cambridge: Harvard.

Parsons, Kenneth (1942) "John R. Commons' Point of View," 18 *Journal of Land and Public Utility Economics* 245.

Polanyi, Karl (1957) *Trade and Market in the Early Empires.* Glencoe, Illinois: Free Press.

Samuels, Warren J. (1981) "Welfare Economics, Power, and Property," in W. J. Samuels and A. A. Schmid (eds.), *Law and Economics: An Institutional Perspective,* Boston: Martinus Nijhoff.

Schmid, A. Allan (1978) *Property, Power, and Public Choice, An Inquiry Into Law and Economics.* New York: Praeger.

Ward, Ronald W. et al. (1983) "Advertising, Promotion and Research," in W. J. Armbruster et al. (eds.), *Federal Marketing Programs In Agriculture.* Danville, Illinois: Interstate Printers.

Quality Regulation in Consumer Goods Markets: Theoretical Concepts and Practical Examples

Christian Joerges*
Bremen

Introduction

The theme of this paper no doubt calls for some material explanations, and presumably also for some information on the author's motives and interests. The objective context is complicated. Lawyers cannot associate any systematic legal field with "law of quality regulation", but rather perceive it in terms of a multiplicity of relevant subjects: guarantees in the law of contract, liability in competition and anti-trust law, public law permit procedures and other forms of product regulation[1]. This mixed situation, with all its legal difficulties, is very inaccessible for foreign lawyers, and is no doubt of only secondary interest in the context of a volume dealing with the relevance of economic theories for legal analyses. I shall therefore not make even a rudimentary attempt to provide systematic information on the German law of quality regulation. Instead, I shall concentrate on particular implications of my subject for legal theory. This leads me to the more personal context of the paper. The law of quality regulation seems to me to be a suitable field in which to discuss the theoretical attempts at identifying rationality structures of "post-modern" law. That such a discussion is on the agenda for intrinsic theoretical reasons has been shown by Gunther Teubner in his analysis of the changing structures of modern law (Teubner, 1982). What I want to show in this paper is that this discussion is dependent on the closest possible observation of concrete developments, that not only is Teubner's scepticism regarding interventionist law and materialised concepts of law confirmed but also that scepticism must sometimes be accompanied by theoretical endeavours towards new rationality structures.

The structure of the paper is intended to correspond to the approaches

* This article takes account of suggestions made in Florence and criticisms by Gert Brüggemeier, Reinhard Damm, Dieter Hart, Hans-W. Michlitz, Norbert Reich and Eike Schmidt in Bremen. This article remains, however, extremely imperfect and is meant as a discussion paper.

1 Brendel's underregarded work (1976) concentrates on the law of product liability and, as far as economic theory goes, on traditional price theory and welfare economics approaches.

sketched out above. An introductory section compares the treatment by economic theories of the quality problem to various regulatory approaches (I). On the basis of these insights into the problems of quality regulation, we proceed to a discussion of the rival legal conceptions of quality regulation. This discussion deals with the German debate, and thus distinguishes between competition law, interventionist and oppositional approaches (II–IV). The last section (V) does not present a final conclusion, but rather observations, theses and approaches which are intended as tentative.

1. Economic Theory and Legal Instruments of Quality Regulation

The quality regulation of consumer goods is an attractive field of study for lawyers with interdisciplinary interests. This interest lies above all in the fact that economic analyses themselves often suggest institutional measures for guaranteeing quality – economic theory and legal science thus meet in an area that overlaps both disciplines.

1.1. Quality and Economic Theory

(a) The whole difficulty surrounding quality regulation immediately becomes apparent when one considers the attempts at defining the concept of quality. As is often stated in marketing text-books, quality constitutes "a bundle of elements providing satisfaction... incorporating certain properties which contribute to the satisfaction of wants (in the broadest sense)". Quality is then a "multidimensional concept" providing the link between "production and the structure of individual wants" (Kupsch and Mathes, 1977:23). Such attempts at definition will be better understood if we first look at the miscellaneous nature of the cited "dimensions" of quality:

(1) One aspect of quality is the performance of products – their technical composition and usefulness. Obviously the conceptualisation of this aspect may present difficulty. One can read in the German Standard Specifications (DIN Norm) 55.350, which is a surprisingly similar formulation to § 459 (1) of the German Civil Code, that quality constitutes "the sum-total of the elements and characteristics of a product or of an activity contributing to the fulfillment of particular requirements".

(2). Such an objectivist concept of quality is, though, partially rejected by marketing theorists because of its inability to incorporate the combined efforts of marketing policy: advertising, sales methods, service, product range, information supplied, and so forth. Those who consider this whole performance of the producers' side tend to speak of an "economic" concept of quality and it is then only a short step before the price is also included as an integral part of the producers' performance: economic quality is synonymous with the relationship between price and total performance (Engelhardt, 1974:1801).

(3) The question of what constitutes a favourable relation between price and performance (i.e. high economic quality) leads us to the third dimension of the quality "phenomenon": what may appear to one person to constitute a favourable performance bundle, is to another merely an unnecessary luxury. This

subjective dimension is deeply rooted in economic theory. The quality of a product is determined by the measure of utility it provides. Utility, though, is an individualistic-subjectivistic concept which, taken to its logical conclusion, makes the comparability of goods an impossible task, since intersubjective criteria for quality are excluded a priori: a generally applicable gauge of individual preferences does not exist (Frank, 1976:142).

(4) Certainly, everyone is searching for a way out of this subjectivisation impasse. For economists, i.e. the marketing theorists, it is a matter of course that they propound the necessity of standardising production with a view to achieving economies of scale and that they suggest aligning quality performance to what the market demands (Klatt, 1961:19). In this context one speaks of a "socialisation of goals" (Klatt; 1965:16) – but would it not then be logical to extend this aspect of "socialisation" in order to include other factors, like environment protection, or energy consumption, for instance? Even though such societal factors have as yet not been systematised by economists in the various concepts, this in no way detracts from their actual relevance – by 1976 approximately 10 per cent of all new norms were based on their societal relevance, and by 1981 the proportion of socio-politically relevant standards had already reached approximately 50 (Kypke, 1982: Chap. 2.2 and 4.1).

(b) The social and political implications of quality regulation should already have made it clear that there can be no universally binding conceptual definitions of quality. Instead, all endeavours at definition must always have recourse to a theoretical framework and thus take preliminary decisions on the "appropriate" regulation of quality. Here it is sufficient to broadly characterise these tendencies and approaches in legal science which may be taken as starting points.

(1) The economists' propensity to employ a "broad" concept of quality, embracing both the technical and the economic performance on the producers' side and their taking into account consumer subjectivity in ideas of utility, points to the interpretation of quality as an optimisation problem. In this context, quality would be controlled by firms' quality policies on the one hand and external market forces on the other. The question of how competition based on quality differences is to be explained and to be evaluated from the point of view of competition policy is, however, not given a uniform answer. In other words, the respective concept of competition taken as a basis determines the extent to which competition is accepted as a control mechanism or otherwise governmental competition policy is expected to provide control over quality competition.

(2) Competition policy concepts tend in analysing market processes to concentrate on the behaviour of the producer's side. By contrast, the economics of information draw attention to a fact of central importance to the functionality of quality competition – the asymmetric distribution of discriminatory quality information. Producers possess far more information than even the best informed consumer especially, with regard to so-called "experience," "search" or "credence" goods. This seemingly trivial insight has far-reaching implications for competition policy and other forms of quality regulation (cf. for the following, Hauser 1979:756). With experience goods, whose quality the con-

sumer learns to judge in the course of using them, the "monopolistic" competition of brand-name producers is in turn dependent on repeat purchases and this certainly means an implicit quality guarantee for the purchases – and it would be questionable to fight the market power of such producers in the name of the icon of perfect competition. Where, however, product differentiation by brand offers no adequate quality guarantee, or where the market power of producers ought to be fought for competition policy reasons (for instance in the interest of newcomers' market chances), then quality guarantees can be provided only through other governmental or private institutions. The economics of information thus proves to be an instrument for the explanation and justification of regulatory measures.
(3) Phenomena of failure, as diagnosed by the economics of information, are also frequently used to justify preventive protective measures against health risks or strict liability norms against safety risks. The same is true of other external effects, for example the controversies in the environmental debate and attempts at a social evaluation of technology. Here we can not enter into a discussion about market failures (for the neo-classical tradition cf. Bator 1958:351), nor into a critique of the more recent attempts at replacing theories of market failure by economic analyses of regulatory failure (cf. Schueller, 1983:151). In the real world, at any rate, measures to protect health, safety and the environment appear as a rule to be the outcome of political processes, and the implementation of each individual measure comes into being from the various conflicts of goals between competing protective aims. It might be said that the discrepancies which become apparent here between economic theory and political process are essentially responsible for the continuing marginality, on the whole, of economic theory within administrative and judicial decision-making processes.

1.2. Quality and Legal System

The "law of quality regulation" does not yet exist as an established subject in legal study, though it performs a regulatory task that involves the legal system in many ways. Accordingly, any systematic description and analysis of quality law must inevitably have recourse to some new theoretical framework and accordingly neither legal science nor the economic theory contributions to the quality issue can reach consensus on the tasks of quality regulation. Here it is sufficient for us to begin by indicating a few parallels between the economic and the legal system.

(a) The market process continues to be the central institution of quality regulation; anti-trust and competition law, and other like measures serve to guarantee the functional conditions of markets, and count as the most important contribution of the law to the guaranteeing of quality interests. But in economic theory there are differing perspectives on competition which correspond to the variety of concepts of competition law and divergent interpretations of those fields of the civil law which concern the "economic quality" of the exchange of goods and services.

(b) There is also an extremely tight and unsystematic regulatory web administered by governmental, private and semi-governmental bodies:

- the legal system accepts and promotes much self-limitation on the producer side in labelling, guarantees, recommended contractual conditions and restrictions on competition. In the area of technical safety law it transforms the standards of privately constituted organisations into state law and similarly deals with the self-regulation of services by professional associations.
- with many experience and credence goods the role of the state has increased, e.g. the 1976 law on drugs (§§ 21 seq. AMG) replaced the earlier registration procedure by a licensing system; and in the area of auto safety regulation the law requires a road permit, which can also be issued separately for vehicle parts (§§ 18 seq., 22a StVZO). Another example is the correspondence course supervisory law of 1976 which introduced preventive controls in a service sector (and thereby evidently ruined a particular type of offer). In insurance law supervisory measures have been adopted over a long period of time and these in effect amount to nothing less than quality control. In other areas, product control has been limited to prohibitory arrangements in the nature of general clauses and authorisations banning the use of particular materials. Foodstuffs law in particular (§§ 8 seq. LMBG) follows this pattern.

(c) The multiplicity of quality regulations located at different levels has a disintegrating effect on the traditional approach to quality control. The regulatory influences have to be adjusted to each other thereby producing new, as it were, vertical, internal differentiations in the legal system oriented towards the various areas covered (Joerges, 1981:125; 1983:57) The legal assumption of control over quality regulation is further impeded because both in legislation and in the implementation of legislative programmes social and political actors, administrative authorities, and other institutions introduce conflicting goals into the process of law-making. The discrepancies between economic theory and political process have a parallel in the discrepancies between the regulatory models employed and the actual decisional processes.

1.3. Economic Theory and Law

(a) Quality regulation law opens up a wide area for interdisciplinary cooperation between economics and legal science. In all the contributions of economic theory to the functionality of the market, the phenomena of market failure and the possibilities of correcting it, one will find striking parallels in legal arrangements and institutions. It is therefore tempting to analyse the way legal science deals with these norms and institutions based on explicit or implicit economic premises, and ask what benefits the law and legal science might derive from intensified application of economic theories. With this in mind, three tendencies in the German legal debate will be discussed below. However a number of difficulties arising from the nature of the subject matter and from the state of debate in the literature will have to be accepted in the context of this discussion.

There has, to date, been practically no attempt to summarize systematically the complex network of quality regulations. Our recourse to approaches, that merely prescribe particular general orientations is therefore to be understood only as an expedient starting point, but one which is difficult to avoid.

The possibilities for cooperation between economic theory and legal science are largely determined by the premises on which an economic approach rests and the way in which legal concepts take up corresponding assumptions. The neo-classical competition theory of the Hayek type and the individualism of economic analysis of law clearly have a greater chance of being adopted than functionalist competition theories, information economy approaches or empirically weightier approaches of consumer sociology. It is an urgent task for interdisciplinary research to study these "distortions of competition" between rival approaches and where possible remove them. The argument followed below will however only deal in a cursory manner with the intrinsic theoretical difficulties of interdisciplinary efforts, and instead concentrate on the discrepancies between theoretical approaches and actual decision-making processes. This may explain the structure of the individual sections, each of which first sketches a particular approach, then points to some theoretical difficulties, and finally shows by examples how these difficulties are dealt with in practice. This procedure of confrontation between theory and practice rests in turn on prior theoretical considerations. These can only be presented as theses here. The theses are:

(1) The transformation of theoretically grounded concepts into legal decisions must itself be made the object of interdisciplinary research,

(2) One of the reasons for the discrepancies between theory and practice is the remoteness from reality of economic theories. "Practice as a discovery procedure", in which complex conflict situations are mastered in reality, cannot be discredited in the name of such theories.

(3) A reflective "legalisation" of such "practice as a discovery procedure" can avoid the impasses of materialisation concepts, without being limited merely to the elimination of functional disruptions.

2. Market Compatible Quality Control

In German legal debate the theoretical perspectives on the measures which are given the task of controlling the "economic quality" of goods and services, that dominate are those which supposedly embrace both the goals and the methods of legal regulation. According to such models the legal influence should remain as compatible with "the system" as possible. System congruency is defined as "market conformity", and we are thereby supplied with the explanation of why it is information and anti-trust policies which form the core of generally accepted interventions in the market process.

2.1. Competition and Information Policies

Just how fragile this conceptual unity of quality control measures based on market compatibility really is becomes readily apparent when a closer look at the theoretical premises and the concepts of competition and information policy is taken.

(a) We know that the dominant orientation of competition theory in Germany does not treat competition as a means for attaining policy objectives, but rather as a coordination mechanism whose effectiveness (workability) is evaluated by the behaviour of private actors on the market. The regulation of competition is dedicated to an *abstract* goal: its task is to open the way to "better" solutions, it is quite irrelevant whether this refers to better quality, a more favourable price, product innovation, or more favourable conditions of purchase etc. (Hoppmann, 1978:15). It is, though, precisely due to this abandoning of result-oriented goals that information policy, in isolating just one specific parameter of competitive behaviour, namely the quality of goods, is bound to conflict with the goals of anti-trust policy. But this main rival to the concept of free competition also inevitably runs into corresponding difficulties. When, in an appraisal of the workability of competition the criteria of structure, behaviour and result are employed, diverse aspects being attributed to each, it may just happen that competition and information policies are working to the same end; but this is purely coincidental, and there is no overriding conceptual orientation which can vouch for this conformity of aims.

(b) These insights also become apparent on a brief examination of the theoretical foundations of information policy and connected empirical research (cf. Assmann and Kübler, 1981:23). This can be demonstrated by two interrelated subjects. The first concerns the chances of consumers to arrive at an economically rational choice of quality. Much has been written about whether the price of a consumer product can serve as an indicator for quality. The findings have been disappointing all down the line (Diller, 1977; Dardis and Gieser, 1980) and the misallocations caused by "misguided consumer decisions" are immense (Beier, 1978). Such results are hardly surprising. They simply underline the fact that the freedoms to maneouvre on "imperfect markets" postulated by competition theory really do exist and that this scope in quality competition is exploited by individual firms in accordance with their view of economic rationality. The resulting question of which configuration of quality information actually would enable rational purchase decisions has proven to be an extraordinarily complex one. We know that consumers do heed test information, but it is certainly not possible to simply construct a positive correlation between the amount of information and a corresponding rationality in buying behaviour, nor is it possible to assume any congruence between individual preferences and the criteria used by "neutral" test institutes (Kaas and Toelle, 1981, Silberer et al., 1981).

(c) Here we are dealing with the paradoxical situation in which information policy increasingly clashes with the goals of anti-trust policy when it is more concerned with its own efficiency and as it becomes conscious of its effects – and this applies in principle to all measures aimed at facilitating the consumer's buying behaviour. Using as their example the tests conducted by the Product Testing Foundation "Warentest", Silberer et al. (1981) have attempted to clarify this aspect with empirical evidence and Czerwonka/Schoeppe (1981) have endeavoured to systematise the possible areas of conflict:

- quality information leads necessarily to a degree of standardisation – the rapporteur substitutes his own for the individual preferences of consumers;
- quality information is a "public good". Among the "free riders" of information policy measures is the producer, who can orient his production and sales policy to the criteria and findings of neutral quality tests;
- quality information has not only non-use benefits but also non-use costs: it can produce the effect of impeding innovation and favour enterprises with high turnover, thus tending to foster concentration. It can, indeed, even lead to the existence of "lemon" markets in the event that the test results are heeded only by the already quality-conscious and critical consumer groups who respond by "exit" rather than "voice";
- the independent status of information policy, moreover, makes it suitable for pursuing more far-reaching goals. Why should the power of information policy not, for instance, be employed in the service of environment policy (Silberer et al., 1981:16)?

If then, in view of all these problems empirical research and economic theory merely reveal a diversity of competing goals, but no coherent criteria of evaluation, what can be done by those interdisciplinarily committed lawyers who are so keen to avail themselves of the decision-making guidance proffered by economic theory?

2.2. Functions of Law

The most obvious way out is, of course, to seek theoretical approaches that promise to clear up the above-mentioned conflict of objectives. I have a suspicion that some of the trends in the economic analysis of law consistently oriented to the efficiency of production and allocation hold such a great appeal for lawyers not least because they apparently avoid the disputes over incommensurable conceptual aims and also because of the attractiveness of neo-classical competition theory of the Hayek type in Germany, an approach which offers the expectation that it will deliver a "unity" of the legal system overriding all disparities encountered in the individual fields. Be that as it may: the main burden of dealing with conflicting policies is currently borne by the judiciary – albeit only in the sense that vindication of judgment is drawn not from science, but from the realm of practice. The Warentest case serves to illustrate this problem-resolving strategy.

In its famous "Warentest II" decision of 9 December 1975 (BGHZ 65:325) the German Federal High Court rejected the firm's claim for damages against the Warentest Foundation on the grounds that its product had been wrongly assessed. The Court held that the test results could not to be controlled in relation of their objective correctness, but rather with regard to the seriousness of their intent. As a consequence of this ruling a quality assessment is to be viewed as a critique expressed by an especially accredited institution, which – even if a bitter pill – must be swallowed without complaining. The ruling of the High Court of March 11, 1982 (NJW 1982:1596) on the limitations placed on commercial advertising using test results is quite consistent with this. If within a test-batch of 22 cameras 10 are awarded the classification "very good" and 11 "good", then all advertising referring to the classification "good" must also include an indication of the relative quality rank termed "good" (§ 3 UWG). This ruling can be seen as being consistent particularly because it places the competitive use of test results in a specifically competitive context, thereby subjecting this use to more rigorous criteria than the testing procedure itself. By this differentiation the tests of the Foundation "Warentest" are shielded from being abused and thus the non-use costs of published results are lowered. To be sure, the cited case was a comparatively clear-cut one. A second issue raised in "Warentest II" was more complex: the plaintiff also complained that he had suffered damages as result of unduly positive assessments of competitor products.[2] Understandably we would be interested to hear how the High Court would rule on the complaint of a medium-sized firm whose own products were not included in a test at all and subsequently contended that the use of test results in advertising constitutes unfair advantage, since such advertising is only feasible for large companies thus giving them a competitive edge. I certainly do not want to speculate on the outcome of such a case, but simply to point out the way in which the judiciary justifies its approach in such matters. In the case of the "Warentest II" judgment, the High Court reminded the plaintiff that the programme applied in the testing of his product had been laid before a "programming committee" on which the manufacturer concerned had been represented, and that the plaintiff himself had attested that the programme had "clearly been thought out with great care and expertise" (BGHZ 65:326). In the ruling on advertising with test results, the High Court made explicit reference to the "recommendations of advertising with test results" issued on May 20, 1977 by none other than the Foundation Warentest (Stiftung Warentest, 1977:7) – and this reference may prove to be the key to a judicial solution of the problem. The background of these recommendations is illuminating. The Foundation was obliged under Article 14 of its statute to take action against firms incorporating test results in their advertising (Voigt, 1965), pursuant to the principles laid down on May 6, 1965 by the Central Committee of the Advertising Industry. However, interest in such advertising proved to be considerable. The Foundation "Warentest" perceived no legal means to counteract this growing trend and so it annulled the corresponding section of its statutes (Stiftung Warentest, 1975:51; 1977:7). Parallel to this there was an "official" modification of the standpoint of the Central Committee for the Advertising Industry (cf. Schönleber, 1982:39). At any rate, the recommendations of 1977 which replaced the ban on test advertising by a regulation on advertising practice drew only mild criticism from this body and met with the approval of consumer organisations (cf. Schönleber, 1982:44). My interpretation of this: the courts do not adjudicate by dint of their own juridical competency, but rather by means of ratifying the results of compromises negotiated or tolerated by pressure groups. Credence is given to this view by the fact that in instances where no such facilitation for

[2] From the reasoning in the decision on "good" tests it seems very likely that this would be an infringement of § 823 BGB (Cf. Brinkmann, 1983:94).

decision-making is available the courts have tended to remain non-committal. Consequently, firms whose advertising is hampered through their products not being included in tests must first endeavour to claim the non-use costs involved in direct negotiations with the "Warentest" foundation[3]; direct recourse to the courts seems to be of little use.

3. Market Failures, Interventionism, and the Substantive Rationality of Law

Due to its supposed compatibility with our economic order, the policy of consumer information enjoys widespread acclaim and support. However, at the same time – as was shown by the Warentest and test advertising cases – it generates conflicts of goals which are in effect resolved through bargaining processes: the only thing to be said in favour of this is that there would appear to be no other way. Of course, alternatives to these crude mitigation strategies have been propounded. The major one is the age-old means of state intervention. Even if we are to restrict ourselves to the realm of economic and legal theory it is not easy to incorporate the notion of intervention within a relatively representative and at the same time conceptually consistent approach. One can, however, identify three facets as being characteristic of the interventionist strategy: at the outset there is the detection of a "market failure"; arising from this, the plea for regulation by the state and the notion of the substantive rationality of regulatory intervention. All three of these facets can, of course, assume different forms. The very discovery of a market failure in the first place is dependent on the analytical tools which are applied to markets. The act of regulatory intervention can be either the domain of the law and the courts, or be placed within the realm of competence of special preventive or reactive administrative authorities; it can be concerned either directly with the sphere of production or with drawing up the conditions for services. The "substantive rationality" of legal norms can endeavour either to retain the *form* of conditional programmes, or it can act openly as politico-legal purposive programming (as "political administration"). The prerequisites for the success for substantive rationality would appear to favour the latter alternative; the realities of the political process usually end up in the establishment of the former one (on all this see Teubner, 1982:24, 28, 40, 51; Hart, 1984).

3.1. The Example of Planned Obsolescene

The interventionists in jurisprudence have never played a very significant role and it is quite difficult to find an example in which the characteristic elements of interventionism have either received theoretical scrutiny or have been worked out in any theoretical detail.[4] All this justifies a contribution concerned directly

[3] Cf. the report in the periodical impulse (1981: vol. 4, 34) according to which Warentest has stated its readiness to retest non-included products and give them a grading.

[4] For an informative survey of the German debate cf. Meier (1982:272, 292).

with the quality issue which illustrates concurrently not only the normative merits but also the practical drawbacks of interventionist strategies. I am referring to Ingo Schmidt's advocacy of a control of the "planned obsolescence" of consumer goods through the German Federal Cartel Agency (Bundeskartellamt) on the basis of § 22 GWB (Schmidt, 1971, 1976).

(a) The term "planned obsolescence" describes product strategies which aim at shortening the effective life of consumer durables by inducing the premature substitution of a product. Together with many other marketing theorists (Raffee and Wiedemann, 1980), Ingo Schmidt distinguishes between three configurations of this strategy: *qualitative* obsolescence entails the deliberate shortening of product life through the omission of known technological improvements; one speaks of *psychological* obsolescence when merely the appearance of a product and not its technical usefulness is altered to such an extent that consumers are enticed to purchase the new product; finally *functional-technical* utility decline is present when products which are still usable are made obsolete by innovations.

Of course, it is a matter of controversy whether such production policies exist at all (Roeper, 1976:72). On the one hand the weight of empirical evidence is great; on the other the theory of competition itself demonstrates that under certain conditions obsolescence strategies are perfectly compatible with the economic strategy to be expected of a rational producer (Stuyck, 1983:Chap. 2). This is then the core idea of Ingo Schmidt's thesis: the phenomenon of planned obsolescence indicates that the producers can unilaterally exploit opportunities which are insufficiently controlled by competition (Schmidt, 1971:870). This analysis then gives rise to policy proposals, two of which are worthy of particular mention. *De lege lata,* Ingo Schmidt, proposes that the Federal Cartel Agency should take action against dominant firms employing qualitative and psychological obsolescence strategies by means of both judicial writ and positive fiat on the basis of § 22 GWB; *de lege ferenda,* the protective purpose of anti-trust regulations (§ 28 Abs. 2 GWB) should be expanded by empowering the Bundeskartellamt to prescribe minimum standards *ex officio* (Schmidt, 1971:875; Rz. 36, 38).

(b) To anyone who has followed the long but vain efforts of the Bundeskartellamt to combat the most blatant instances of price abuse with even modest sanctions (cf. Hart and Joerges, 1980:196 seq.), it will hardly come as a surprise to hear that the Kartellamt is not exactly over-enthusiastic about becoming involved in disputes on obsolescence strategies and that Ingo Schmidt's proposals have found no echo in the amendments to the cartel law. The whole theoretical debate on anti-trust policy which the neo-classical school brought to bear against the discretionary functionalistic concept of competition applies equally well to Ingo Schmidt's quality control, and the practical difficulty in "applying" § 22 of the GWB with regard to the quality parameter would most certainly be even greater than in the case of price control. But here I do not want to return to such widely discussed objections which arise from competition theory and rule of law considerations. It is my view that two other more relevant points explain the reasons for Ingo Schmidt's lack of success. The first has to do with the conflict of policy goals that any attempt at the control of firms' quality policy must overcome. For instance, Ingo Schmidt himself mentions anticyclical considerations in favour of built-in obsolescence, but then hurriedly withdraws them in order to deal with possible conflicts of goals within the context of a functionalistic competition policy (Schmidt, 1971:871; 1976:Rz 9). This is much too simple. Certainly, one has to pose the question whether objectivised and normatively justifiable quality demands may not compete with environmental policy goals, and likewise bear in mind that the rationality criteria of anti-trust policy cannot easily be brought into line with normative political demands for the minimisation of safety hazards. The second point concerns the regulatory capacity which Ingo Schmidt wishes to assign to the Bundeskartellamt. This authority would already be overburdened with the interventionist provision of quality standards based on rationality criteria of competition policy; and it would be even more so if it had to coordinate competition policy standards with conflicting policy objectives.

3.2. The Transformation of Interventionist Law in "Practice as a Discovery Procedure"

The example of planned obsolescence is of exemplary importance. It fits perfectly into a whole series of decisions surrounding the efforts at an interventionist anti-trust law[5] in which the protection of entrepreneurial freedom and trust in ungoverned competition prevailed over performance-oriented concepts. It should be noted that this preference for a specific economic approach by no means rests upon some comparative evaluation of rival economic theories. I do not want to suggest, however, that the rejection of performance standards can be attributed either to the influence of pressure groups or to less visible power structures. Instead, responsibility for the failure of interventionist concepts of competition is more likely to lie with the excess strain put on them by the administration and the legal system. It is to be noted that the central area of product standardisation, namely the so-called technical safety law, has long had an established regulatory structure which takes account of this state of affairs.

Significantly, this regulation structure accomplishes its task even where legislation *formally* provides for more intensive state intervention (Schefold, 1983). The reference to such partly open, partly concealed mediations between governmental regulatory claims and private actors should not be misunderstood as a pure apology for this practice. It would equally be premature on the other hand to oppose the criticisms of interventionism purely on grounds of its legitimate goals. A critical discussion of the transformation outlined above of interventionist regulations should instead begin with their specific structures – which means developing rationality criteria for the procedures of cooperative law making. In the area of technical safety law such approaches can be found not only in the

[5] Cf. on § 22 GWB Hart and Joerges (1980:196); Spieß (1980); on § 26 (2) GWB cf. Joerges (1981:97), and IV 2 c below.

literature but also in case law. Product standardisation, in the Federal Republic is handled in practice by the 'Deutsches Institut für Normung' (DIN), a type of private quasi-agency, which is becoming increasingly involved in public debate, calling for standardisation work to be related to the economic and social consequences of technical development by seeking the institutional measures to take such decision-making criteria into account (Kypke, 1982:Chap. 10). In the most politically sensitive area of technical safety law, even "expertise" has in view of these developments plainly abandoned its neutrality. The Federal Constitutional Court has, at any rate, found in its Kalkar-decision that the reference in § 27 (2) (3) of the Atom act to the "latest state of science and technology" can empower the Court to request an opinion on scientifically disputed questions and therefore refer the responsibility for decision back to the legislature and his practical reason" (BVerfGE 49:89). We may not generalise from this example, since, as in the case of planned obsolescence, the economic and social implications of technical developments are in general of more modest dimensions. This area ought to contain unexploited opportunities for legal arrangements in the nature of "practice as a discovery procedure", as a decentralised procedure incorporating independent expertise and promoting participation opportunities for the institutions and social actors involved in this field.

4. Self-organised Interest Aggregation and Corporative Interest Bargaining

4.1. Consumer Self-Organisation as a Legal Policy Concept

Reservations regarding the abstract regulatory performance of the market and regarding specific interventions of the state and its bureaucracy inevitably lead to participatory approaches. The question is asked how consumers affected by quality standardisation can and should become involved in the process of establishing norms, in order to maintain their interests. Udo Reifner has formulated such approaches in the most decisive way as legal policy prospects. His theory of the "collective use of law" takes as its basis that the basic social conflict between capital and labour has shifted so much into the reproduction sector that the time has come for a collective implementation of "consumer value interests" by the consumers themselves. (For a brief description, cf. Reifner and Adler, 1981:346). We can merely allude here to the theoretical and practical weaknesses of these perspectives (in detail Joerges, 1981:24, 37, 46, 52). Can the problem of quality be reduced to a bipolarity of conflict of interests between producers and consumers, or is there not a much more complex conflict situation? Have Olson's theorems not so far withstood all objections to his methodological individualism and demonstrated the irresolvability of the "organisation question" (Olson, 1968)? If, then, one must expect a more or less "natural" organisational advantage for producer interests, and if selective incentives can at best contribute to the introduction of a further voice into the bargaining processes of organized interests: what consequences would the demand for consumer self-organisation and their incorporation in the process of law making and law implementation then have?[6]

4.2. The Example of Car Sales

Instead of systematically developing this approach, I should like to demonstrate their relevance by one example: the legal treatment of automobile sales systems. This is a quality regulation problem only in an extremely conventional sense. Legal measures in which the ultimate purchaser of a new car directly or indirectly is interested are concerned at once with the "economic quality" of the products offered, i.e. the contractual conditions of the ultimate purchaser (see a), with the position of his immediate contractual partner, i.e. the dealer (see b), and with the sales strategies of the manufacturers (see c). Three aspects of the current debate on the influence of law on the positions of the consumer, dealer and manufacturer should be particularly mentioned: i.e. the limited chances of a legal policy concept starting from the interests of ultimate consumers; the way the legal system deals with what economic theory offers; the factual significance of conflicts of goals arising from the relative independence of legal influence, according to specific criteria in each case (see d).

(a) The terms of sales for new cars are the outcome of partly successful and partly unsuccessful corporativist and interventionist influences. The corporativist elements are constituted by the negotiations between the Car-Repairers Central Association (ZdK), the Automobile Industry Association (VdA) and the Vehicle Importers Association (VdIK) with the German Automobile Club (ADAC).

The agreement reached between the dealers, manufacturers and driver associations was, as expected, ratified by the Bundeskartellamt[7]. Through this ratification the Bundeskartellamt gave up its powers under § 38 (1) No. 3 GWB of verifying the proposed recommended conditions on the basis of the criteria of the Standard Terms Act (AGBG) – a verification which following the state of case law and legal doctrine at the time of registration ought to have suggested a large number of changes (cf. only Schmitz, 1975). The task of further improvement of the outcome of negotiations between the associations involved, in the sense of improved consumer protection, therefore fell to the judiciary. Its reactions admittedly do not fall into a single interpretive scheme. In a highly regarded decision, the Federal High Court declared the so-called daily price clause (whereby the seller could change the selling price where the delivery times were over four months) to be invalid, and proposed that the producer allow purchasers a right to withdraw in the event of price changes (BGHZ 82:21). Among the points remaining open is the admissibility of the AGB provisions whereby the seller reserves the right to make "slight", "acceptable" model

[6] For a survey of the state of the debate in political sociology cf. Heinze (1981:41, 64).
[7] The recommended terms are reproduced in BAnz. Nr. 108/77 v. 14. 7. 1977. (1980).

changes (No. IV 5). According to the High Court decision of February 6, 1980 (NJW 1980:1097) a vehicle may at any rate be termed "factory new" only "if and insofar as the model of the vehicle continues to be produced unchanged" (so therefore they can be done if it is not manufactured in the current year!) Another unclear point is the effectiveness of the guarantee provisions (point VII of the recommended terms). (For a critique see Jung 1980; v. Westfalen, 1982). According to the BGH-decision of November 12, 1980 (BGHZ 78:369) it is established that the manufacture is contractually obliged to the client through the guarantee card – though whether this is clearly expressed in AGB (point VII. 20) is open to doubt. The High Court has now decided further that the purchaser may proceed against the manufacturer under § 823 Abs. 1 BGB, where a car is damaged because of defects in individual parts (BB 1983:462).

This state of the law is hard to interpret. Through the recommended terms on the part of the producer, competition through terms of offer is practically abolished – without thereby becoming transferred to the price (so at least the Bundeskartellamt found in WuW/E:1781 – "Original-VW-Ersatzteile II"). The recommended conditions have on the other hand already strengthened the consumers' legal position in the version accepted by the Bundeskartellamt, and their further piecemeal improvement through judicial intervention on the basis of AGBG has had wide-spread effect precisely because the terms of sale are uniform – judicial control can really achieve this (Micklitz, 1983:Chap. 1 III). But what rationality can this mixture of prior negotiations between associations and subsequent judicial correction claim?

(b) Judicial interventions whereby the contractual position of the final purchaser is improved by comparison with the corporatively negotiated recommended conditions have become biased against one negotiating partner. They have impaired the position of the dealers without at the same time being able to examine the relationship between the dealers and producers. This situation is unsatisfactory, if only because the dealers' behaviour towards the final purchaser is essentially determined by the dealer-manufacturer relationship. Thus, attempts by the trade to sell off out-of-date models as "new cars" will be seen in a kinder light when the trade in turn is obliged to meet corresponding purchase obligations. It is also clear that dealers will be more willing to do guarantee work the more generous is their compensation from the manufacturer (for an analysis of the corresponding conflict situation in American law cf. Macaulay, 1973:21).

The legal basis for control over the relationships between dealers and manufacturers is provided by the AGBG. The control task is formidable: the contract dealer agreement is a typical one for car sales, each consist of a network of regulations sometimes fifty pages long, on which the legal sections of the firms have been continually working for decades. One of these contractual creations, the one of Adam Opel AG, is at present the object of a suit brought by the association of German Opel-dealers. In this suit the dealers have attacked a number of one-sided rights which protect the manufacturer: the right to change the sales programme, the right to decide on the acceptance and execution of orders and on changes in the guarantee conditions, and the right to engage further contract dealers. The basis of interpretation, whereby Opel is to take its decisions by "fair judgment", was attacked as inadequate self-regulation. Further points of conflict arise in the context of the dealers' personal obligations to management and – of course – in relation to the provisions on termination and entitlement to compensation in the event of termination. In the first instance, dealers were successful on 14 out of a total of 17 complaints (LG Frankfurt a. M., judgment of April 27, 1982, ZIP 1982: 1224). Here we shall not go into details on the District-Court's grounds nor forecast the ultimate outcome of the suit, but consider in principle the difficulties of a legal solution of the conflict. These difficulties result first from the fact that the legal basis, § 9 AGBG, offers only a very vague basis for taking a decision. The concretisation of this general clause is, moreover, particularly difficult with a contract dealer agreement, because it is not a case of a "discrete transaction", but a "relational exchange", to use the terminology of Macneil (1981). It is a long term relationship which has to be adapted to changing contextual conditions. Control over such "general conditions of business" must therefore also be considered as control of a process of adjustment – the usual prescription of rights and duties is not enough. The difficulty of arriving at control criteria results also from the peculiar interest situation of the contract dealers themselves. From a legal point of view contract dealers are themselves entrepreneurs. But these firms are in fact integrated into the sales plans of their contractual partners – the binding relationships between dealers and manufacturers, controversial from the viewpoint of competition policy, are not an object of dispute in the Opel-suit. The issue in the control of contract dealer agreements in accordance with the AGBG is the status of an "entrepreneur-worker" that arises out of legal autonomy on the one hand and economic integration and dependency on the other.

(c) The incorporation of contract dealers into the sales strategies of manufacturers is controversial not only from point of view of fairness of contract terms, but also because of reasons of anti-trust law. The contract dealer systems in the automobile sector contain exclusive supply and purchasing obligations. They regulate in detail the image and the business practice of the authorised dealer – and not only the sale of new cars but also the provision of customer's service and repairs. From the anti-trust law point of view these contract dealer systems have long been regarded as essentially unimpeachable. In particular, there has been no serious attempt to break up the selective distribution of automobiles by use of § 26 Abs. 2 GWB, in the same way as was done against the specialist dealer links with the introduction of new forms of distribution in the retail trade. Nevertheless, the Bundeskartellamt has made an attempt to loosen up the contract dealers' rights as far as their spare parts go. The Kartellamt prohibited the Volkswagen-Werk AG from "compelling their contract dealers and contract workshops (VAG-Betriebe) to use only original spare parts of the VAG-Konzern for repairs to VW cars, to the extent that the VAG-Betriebe are thereby prevented from using spare parts manufactured by supplier firms of the VW-Konzern which have the same design as the parts used by the VW-Konzern under contractual supplier relationships in producing new vehicles and as original spare parts ('Identteile')..." (ruling of 21. 3. 1979, BKartA WuW/E:1781). This move by the Kartellamt has since failed. The trust panel of the Federal High Court found that the VW-Konzern marketing arrangements were worth protecting. There was a technical and economic connection between the new car, spare-part and repair business; VW must be in a position to take account of this connection in its sale systems and ought therefore to be able to exclude the use of spare parts that it has not checked on, at least on a random sample basis (ruling of November 11, 1981, BGHZ 81:322 – "Original-VW-Ersatzteile II").

The importance of this decision arises from the fact that the contractual provisions opposed by the Bundeskartellamt were the easiest points of attack from among all the restraints on competition in the contract dealer agreements. Accordingly, the High Court ruling has presumably taken the car industry contract dealer system out of range of competition policy at least until further notice. That makes the justification of the High Court position in the context of competition theory all the more interesting. One commentator (Köhler, 1982) identified the basis of the High Court decision as the theory of so-called group competition. According to this theory, the accustomed orientations of competition policy should be abandonend in favour of a new "structure oriented" policy accepting contractual cooperation within the economic system; in particular, cooperation within more or less thoroughly organised groups ought to be free from competition policy interventions (Tietz, 1981:101, see also Joerges et al. 1986: Ch. 5).

The philosophy of group competition in fact corresponds exactly to the car industry's self-perceptions, and the High Court decision may therefore be interpreted as the adoption of this concept. Meanwhile, competition theory has many other grounds for justifying this concept – these vary from the "coordination approach" of the von Hayek/Hoppman-School to Posner's laissez-faire approach to vertical restrictions (Heidrich, 1981; Posner, 1977; 1981). These possible justifications have received just as little attention by the High Court as have the competition policy critiques of vertical restraints in theory and practice (e.g. Swiss Monopoly Commission, 1978; Monopolies and Mergers Commission, 1982).

(d) This brings us back to three questions which were asked at the beginning of this section. The chances of a legal policy concept based directly on the interests of the ultimate consumer are evidently slight; these interests are taken into account in subsequent judicial correction of recommended conditions, but they cannot have any direct influence in the control of contract dealer agreements under the Standard Terms Act of 1976 or in competition policy. The influence of economic theory on the decisions taken is also arguable; there can in any case be no question of a search for such bases or for reflective handling of competing concepts in case law. Equally inadequate is the treatment of conflicts of goals between legal interventions in the various relationships. The pro-consumer decisions of the High Court do not include protective measures for the dealers against the manufacturers; the protection of authorised dealers against manufacturers is in turn not coordinated with the competition policy blessing given to the manufacturers' marketing conceptions.

In view of this situation, solutions should evidently be sought at two levels. What is required is analysis of the interdependence between the various legal influences *and* procedures for coordinating these measures. The difficulties posed by such a solution strategy are by no means insuperable. "Justified" aims of contract-law consumer protection might, where the trade is "excessively" burdened by them, lead to rights of redress against the manufacturer. The "appropriate" protection of the dealers' entrepreneurial independence might be given the form of a defence against "overdrawn" restraints on competition and coordinated with the anti-trust measures. The procedure for registering recommended conditions might offer an approach to early harmonisation of the interests of all groups concerned, and the relatively weak negotiating position of the consumers might be compensated for through the Bundeskartellamt's control powers (cf. Hart, 1983: section 4). Admittedly, the problem of giving concrete form to the criteria here described as general clauses still exists. "Cognitive" assistance can by all means be expected from economic theory, as Goldberg (1979) shows by the example of the termination of contract dealer agreements. Such assistance does not solve the decision-making problem, and is certainly not enough to overcome the strategic behaviour of those concerned in "theory selection" and its legal manifestation. But how else might one conceive of the interpretation and arbitration of conflicts of interests by those concerned in situations where there can be no universally binding criteria or "neutral" solutions deriving from them?

5. Summary

A conception that would structure the subject of quality law, present well-founded pronouncements on regulatory requirements, assign these regulatory requirements to the appropriate legal programmes and institutions and derive from all this statements on the function of the law, has not been promised. In conclusion the reasons for this reticence, together with the insights and approaches arising from the above arguments will be briefly summarised now.

5.1. Quality Law

Quality regulation constitutes a control problem, not only for economic theory but also for legal science and politics. It is a problem that is multidimensional in nature and burdened with incommensurable objectives. Quality expectations in exchange relationships deserve protection, safety requirements must be realised, and criteria of "social evaluation of technology" must be integrated. None of the legal conceptions examined above seems up to these tasks. Re-formalisations are clearly no longer applicable on the scale of society; interventionist programmes put too much strain on the cognitive and political powers of government and administration; appeals to a collective self-organisation of those concerned prove helpless. Despite all these difficulties, practice as discovery, under the pressure of its needs to make decisions, points the way to solution where theory has got stuck in the search for concepts. How are these "solutions" to be considered?

5.2. The Lessons of the Examples

No general statements can be justified by a few examples. Nevertheless it is noteworthy that in all the areas covered, structually similar solution patterns have prevailed over the legal conceptual notions.

(a) Of all the examples mentioned, the conflict between information and competition policy no doubt offers the greatest hope. In this context, the Stiftung Warentest constitutes a formally independent agency representing the interests of "latent" groups; here the civil law has attuned its theories to the specific tasks of that institution, here also conflicts are negotiated and mediated upon with interest groups concerned. But the uncomfortable question of whether judicial restraint, which the courts for good reason display, is sufficient to protect the institution against influence strategies of organised interests remains.

(b) In the case of planned obsolescence it is correct but too simple to diagnose the failure of interventionist legalization, and it is clear that norms relating to technical safety standards cannot be arrived at without consulting the expertise of the industry concerned. But immediately there arise the consequential problems of the referral techniques that take the burden off government and the law. The call for pluralisation or democratisation of decentralised decision-making is attractive. But can any conceivable representatives of social interests transcend the cognitive advantage of organised expertise?

(c) The example of legal control over car sales is particularly disquieting because uncoordinated legal measures are there taken to protect consumer, dealer and manufacturer interests, which in the pursuit of the goals may obstruct each other, and may end up in practice favouring the most powerful economic actors.

5.3. Legalization of Practice as a Discovery Procedure

From all this, the delegation of decision-making powers to social actors, the adoption of solutions arrived at in bargaining processes between groups concerned and the abandoning of legal intervention in the event of failure to agree, all prove to be extremely ambivalent developments. Nevertheless, in view of the failures of re-formalisation and of interventionism, the point is to adjust legal concepts to the structures that are developing. I do not wish to take any position on the macro-theoretical debate, i.e. of whether it is post-modernity that is taking shape in these developments or instead whether modernity should be treated as an uncompleted project for the law too. My "parti pris" can be found in the brief comments on the individual examples. It amounts to the attempt to open up the procedures of law-making to competing problem definitions and solutions, and to proposals from those concerned, and nevertheless to place the latter under a compulsion to reach agreement. This is not, as yet a "concept" for the "legalisation of practice as a discovery procedure".

Bibliography

ASSMANN, HEINZ-DIETER and FRIEDRICH KÜBLER (1981) *Staatliche Verbraucherinformation im Ordnungsgefüge des Privatrechts.* Königstein: Athenäum.

BATOR, FRANCIS M. (1958) "The Anatomy of Market Failure", 72 *The Quarterly Journal of Economics* 351.

BEIER, UDO (1978) "Entscheidungsbedingte Kaufkraftverluste: Formen, Umfang und verbraucherpolitische Relevanz", 4 *Zeitschrift für Verbraucherpolitik* 159.

BRENDEL, THOMAS (1976) *Qualitätsrecht. Die technisch-ökonomischen Implikationen der Produzentenhaftung.* Berlin: Duncker & Humblot.

BRINKMANN, WERNER (1983) "Die wettbewerbs- und deliktsrechtliche Bedeutung des Ranges in Warentests und Preisvergleichen", *Der Betriebs-Berater* 91.

CZERWONKA, CHRISTINE and GÜNTER SCHÖPPE (1981) "Verbraucherinformationspolitik und Funktionsfähigkeit des Wettbewerbs", *Wirtschaft und Wettbewerb* 165.

DARDIS, RACHEL and NANCY GIESER "Price and Quality of Durable Goods: Are They More Closely Related in the Seventies than in the Sixties?", 4 *Zeitschrift für Verbraucherpolitik* 238.

DILLER, HERMANN (1982) "Das Preisinteresse von Konsumenten", 34 *Schmalenbachs Zeitschrift für betriebswirtschaftliche Forschung* 315.

ENGELHARDT, WERNER-HANS (1974) "Qualitätspolitik", in: Bruno Tietz (ed.) *Handbuch der Absatzwirtschaft.* Stuttgart: Poeschel.

FRANK, JÜRGEN (1976) *Kritische Ökonomie.* Reinbek: Rowohlt.

GOLDBERG, VICTOR P. "The Law and Economics of Vertical Restrictions: A Relational Perspective", 58 *Texas Law Review* 91.

HART, DIETER (1984) "Zur konzeptionellen Entwicklung des Vertragsrechts", *Die Aktiengesellschaft* 66.

HART, DIETER and CHRISTIAN JOERGES (1980) "Verbraucherrecht und Marktökonomik: Eine Kritik ordnungstheoretischer Eingrenzungen der Verbraucherpolitik", in: H.-D. Assmann, G. Brüggemeier, D. Hart and Ch. Joerges (eds.), *Wirtschaftsrecht als Kritik des Privatrechts. Beiträge zur Privat- und Wirtschaftsrechtstheorie.* Königstein: Athenäum.

HAUSER, HEINZ (1979) "Qualitätsinformationen und Marktstrukturen", 32 *Kyklos* 739.

HEIDRICH, HOLGER (1981) *Konsumentenwissen und Wettbewerb. Die Marktprozesse bei dauerhaften Konsumgütern am Beispiel neuer und gebrauchter Personenkraftwagen.* Freiburg i. Br.: Haufe.

HEINZE, ROLF G. (1981) *Verbändepolitik und "Neo-Korporatismus": Zur politischen Soziologie organisierter Interessen.* Opladen: Westdeutscher Verlag.

HENNING, WERNER and JAN JARRE (1980) "Zur Praxis des Bundeskartellamtes bei Konditionenempfehlungen", *Der Betrieb* 1429.

HOPPMANN, ERICH (1978) *Das Konzept des wirksamen Presiwettbewerbs. Dargestellt am Beispiel der Arzneimittelmärkte.* Tübingen: Mohr.

JOERGES, CHRISTIAN (1981) *Verbraucherschutz als Rechtsproblem. Eine Untersuchung zum Stand der Theorie und zu den Entwicklungsperspektiven des Verbraucherrechts.* Heidelberg: Recht und Wirtschaft.

– (1983) "Der Schutz des Verbrauchers und die Einheit des Zivilrechts", *Die Aktiengesellschaft* 57.

JOERGES, CHRISTIAN, EUGEN HILLER, KNUT HOLZSCHECK and HANS-W. MICKLITZ (1986) *Vertriebspraktiken im Automobilersatzteilsektor. Ihre Auswirkungen auf die Interessen der Verbraucher.* Frankfurt a. M.: Lang.

JUNG, ECKHARD (1980) "Autogarantie-Arbeiten zum Null-Tarif", 49 *Deutsches Autorecht* 353.

KAAS, KLAUS-PETER and KLAUS TÖLLE (1981) "Der Einfluß von Warentestinformationen auf das Informationsverhalten von Konsumenten", 5 *Zeitschrift für Verbraucherpolitik* 239.

KLATT, SIGURD (1961) "Die Qualität als Objekt der Wirtschaftswissenschaft", 12 *Jahrbuch für Sozialwissenschaft* 19.

– (1965) *Die ökonomische Bedeutung der Qualität von Verkehrsleistungen*. Berlin: Duncker & Humblot.

KÖHLER, HELMUT (1982) "Individualwettbewerb und Gruppenwettbewerb", 146 *Zeitschrift für das gesamte Handelsrecht und Wirtschaftsrecht* 580.

KUPSCH, PETER and HEINZ D. MATHES (1977) "Determinanten der Qualitätsbeurteilung bei langlebigen Gebrauchsgütern", 23 *Jahrbuch der Absatz- und Verbrauchsforschung* 233.

KYPKE, ULRICH (1982) *Technische Normung und Verbraucherinteresse: Strukturelle, konzeptionelle und steuerungspolitische Probleme technischer Regelwerke*. Köln: Pahl-Rugenstein.

MACAULAY, STEWART (1973) "The Standardized Contracts of United States Automobile Manufacturers", in *International Encyclopedia of Comparative Law*. Tübingen: Mohr, Alphen: Sijthoff & Noordhoff.

MACNEIL, IAN R. (1981) "Economic Analysis of Contractual Relations" in P. Burrows and G. Veljanowski (eds.) *The Economic Approach to Law*. London: Butterworths.

MARBURGER, PETER (1981) "Das technische Risiko als Rechtsproblem", in *Bittburger Gespräche. Jahrbuch der Gesellschaft für Rechtspolitik*. Trier, München: Beck.

MEIER, CHRISTIAN J. (1982) "Über Entwicklung, Begriff und Aufgabe des Wirtschaftsrechts", *Zeitschrift für Schweizerisches Recht* I 267.

MICKLITZ, HANS-W. (1984) Der Reparaturvertrag. München: Schweitzer.

MITNICK, BARRY M. (1980) *The Political Economy of Regulation. Creating, Designing and Removing Regulatory Forms*. New York: Columbia University Press.

THE MONOPOLIES AND MERGERS COMMISSION (1982) *A Report on the matter of the existence or the possible existence of a complex monopoly situation in relation to the wholesale supply of motor car parts in the United Kingdom*. London: HMSO.

OLSON, MANCUR (1968) *Die Logik des kollektiven Handelns*. Tübingen: Mohr.

POSNER, RICHARD M. (1977) "The Rule of Reason and the Economic Approach: Reflections on the Sylvania Decision" 45 *University of Chicago Law Review* 1.

– (1981) "The Next Step in the Antitrust Treatment of Restricted Distribution: *Per Se* Legality", 48 *University of Chicago Law Review* 6.

RAFFÉE, HANS and KLAUS PETER WIEDMANN (1980) "Die Obsoleszenzkontroverse – Versuch einer Klärung", 34 *Schmalenbachs Zeitschrift für betriebswirtschaftliche Forschung* 149.

REIFNER, UDO and SABINE ADLER (1981) "Möglichkeiten für eine präventive und breitenwirksame Verbraucherberatung durch die Verbraucherzentralen", 5 *Zeitschrift für Verbraucherpolitik* 346.

RÖPER, BURKARDT (1976) *Gibt es geplanten Verschleiß?* Göttingen: Otto Schwartz & Co.

SCHEFOLD, DIAN (1983) "Verfassungsfragen zum Verhältnis von Erst- und Nachanmelder im Zulassungsverfahren von Arzneimitteln in Zuleeg", in: M. and D. Schefold (eds.) *Die Zweitanmelderproblematik*. Berlin: Reimer.

SCHMID, INGO (1971) "Obsoleszenz und Mißbrauch wirtschaftlicher Macht", *Wirtschaft und Wettbewerb* 868.

– "Geplanter Verschleiß" in ARBEITSGEMEINSCHAFT DER VERBRAUCHER/DEUTSCHER GEWERKSCHAFTSBUND (eds.) *Handbuch des Verbraucherrechts*. Neuwied: Luchterhand.

SCHMITZ, GÜNTHER (1975) "Die Reformbedürftigkeit der Bedingungen des Neuwagenkaufs", 44 *Deutsches Autorecht* 141.

SCHÖNLEBER, MARTIN (1982) *Die rechtliche Bewertung neutraler Warentests in der Werbung der Hersteller und Händler.* Diss. jur. Bremen.

SCHÜLLER, ALFRED (1983) "Property Rights, Theorie der Firma und wettbewerbliches Marktsystem", in: A. Schüller (ed.) *Property Rights und ökonomische Theorie.* München: Vahlen.

SCHWEIZERISCHE KARTELLKOMMISSION (1978) "Die Bedeutung der Alleinvertriebsverträge für den Wettbewerb in der Autobestandteilbranche", 13 *Veröffentlichungen der Schweizerischen Kartellkommission* 97.

SILBERER, GÜNTER, WOLFGANG FRITZ, HANS RAFFÉE, HARALD HILGER and FRIEDRICH FÖRSTER (1981) "Testwirkungen im Anbieter- und Konsumentenbereich" in G. Fleischmann (ed.) *Der kritische Verbraucher. Information – Organisation – Durchsetzung seiner Interessen.* Frankfurt a. M./New York: Campus.

SPIESS, HANS-JÜRGEN (1980) *Preismißbrauchsaufsicht über marktbeherrschende Unternehmen als ordnungspolitisches Problem? – Zur ordnungspolitischen Derogation einer wirtschaftspolitischen Norm.* Königstein: Athenäum.

STIFTUNG WARENTEST (1975) Jahresbericht der Stiftung Warentest. Berlin.

– (1977) Jahresbericht der Stiftung Warentest. Berlin.

STUYCK, JULES (1983) *Product Differenciation – The Legal Situation.* Deventer: Kluwer.

TEUBNER, GUNTHER (1979) "Neo-korporatistische Strategien rechtlicher Organisationssteuerung. Staatliche Strukturvorgaben für gesellschaftliche Verarbeitung politischer Konflikte", 10 *Zeitschrift für Parlamentsfragen* 487.

– (1982) "Reflexives Recht. Entwicklungsmodelle des Rechts in vergleichender Perspektive", 68 *Archiv für Rechts- und Sozialphilosophie* 13.

TIETZ, BRUNO (1981) *Der Gruppenwettbewerb als Element der Wettbewerbswirtschaft. Das Beispiel der Automobilwirtschaft.* Köln: Heymanns.

ULMER, PETER (1969) *Der Vertragshändler. Tatsachen und Rechtsfragen kaufmännischer Geschäftsbesorgung beim Absatz von Markenwaren.* München: Beck.

VOIGT, GÜNTER (1965) "Die 'Stiftung Warentest'", *Der Markenartikel* 3.

v. WESTPHALEN, FRIEDRICH GRAF (1982) "Herstellergarantie und Verkäufergewährleistung im Automobilbereich", 51 *Deutsches Autorecht* 51.

The Design and Performance of Long-Term Contracts

TERENCE DAINTITH
Firenze

Introduction

Besides offering general rationales for the legal recognition and enforcement of agreements (Romani, above), and seeking to explain particular rules and concepts used in contract law (Harris and Veljanovski, above), economic and social studies in the field of contract have also offered information and explanations about the *use* of contracts, or of given types of contracts. This paper aims to be a contribution to this class of contract literature: it is based on a study of the incidence, design and performance of long-term contracts ("LTCs") in the world iron ore market over the last 15–20 years.[1]

The paper should be seen as a by-product of the study, whose main purpose is to produce information about *effects* of employing long-term contracts which may have practical relevance for policy-making in the field of international trade in primary commodities. It starts from the assumption that instability in such trade, in terms of wide and rapid changes in prices or quantitites, has deleterious effects both for importers and exporters, and particularly for developing country exporters of such commodities. The acceptance of this view by policy-makers has since the Second World War led to the introduction of a variety of measures to stabilise markets or alleviate the effects of instability, requiring the intervention of governments or of international agencies in the operation of markets through such mechanisms as buffer stocks or schemes of compensatory finance. It may be, however, that governmental interventions could be reduced, or could operate more effectively, if parties were to contribute to the stabilisation of their own trading environment through appropriate contractual arrangements. What is appropriate may vary with the commodity: futures markets may help in the

[1] This study has been conducted jointly with Christopher D. Rogers, Senior Lecturer in Economics at the University of Dundee, Scotland, and has been financed by the United Kingdom Economic and Social Research Council under grant no. HR 7907/1. Factual information in this paper about the iron ore market and industry is based on Christopher Rogers' contributions to the study. Information on contracts and their performance is based on contracts communicated by participants in the market, on questionnaire responses, and on interviews.

case of homogeneous products with unambiguous prices, but are unlikely to develop where these qualities are absent (Streit, 1980). The initial assumption of the study was that, in the absence of such qualities, long-term contracts could have this stabilising effect. Testing this assumption has involved the construction of indices of stability of iron ore prices and quantities for each major exporting and importing country over the study period and over sub-periods within that time, and relating the results to the extent to which the iron ore trade of different countries at different times was conducted under long-term contracts, as opposed to being carried out on a short-term or spot basis. Simultaneously it has involved examining the contents of as wide a range as possible as long-term contracts, in order to check for significant variations (for example in the degree of price or quantity flexibility offered) over time and space; and examining performance of these contracts. These detailed investigations of contract terms and behaviour are vital to the correct interpretation of the statistical data. To take an extreme case, if it appeared that long-term contracts did not *in fact* constrain party behaviour in such matters as prices or quantities to any significant extent, then the reasons for any correlation between use of such contracts and market stability would have to be sought among factors other than the legal relation installed.

Two lines of development in the contract literature already referred to are of particular relevance to this investigation and may, in turn, be furthered by its findings. The first is concerned with the use of long-term contract as a link in the production chain. It considers when and why enterprises rely on such contracts for the procurement of materials or semi-finished goods, in preference to other forms of economic organisation such as backward integration (ownership of supply facilities) or short-term contracts; and also considers what the results of such reliance might be. This kind of discussion has perhaps been furthest advanced in the writings of Williamson, whose work on employment (1975), inflation (1978) and firm structure (especially vertical integration) (1971; 1975) has more recently led him to attempt to identify relationships between certain forms of contract and a characterisation of economic relations in terms of uncertainty, recurrence of transactions, and specificity of related investment (1979).

Drawing on the work of Macneil (1974, 1978, and see also 1981), who has developed the notion of "relational contracting" as counterweight and contrast to the "discrete single transaction" contract model of classical contract law and neoclassical economics, Williamson arranges contract forms along a spectrum ranging from the classical model at one end to what he calls "unified governance" (i.e. vertical integration) at the other. He expects to find classical contracting, as an expression of market governance, efficiently associated with recurrent or occasional transactions where no buyer-specific supplier investments are involved; where, however, investment is, or becomes, highly specific to transactions between the supplier and a given buyer ("idiosyncratic"), and these transactions are recurrent, Williamson expects to see "unified governance" occurring. As might be imagined, the area of greatest interest lies somewhere between these two extremes: here Williamson distinguishes a class of investment of mixed non-specific and idiosyncratic character (for example where the object of transaction is "customized" equipment or material) and suggests that *occasional* transactions of this type may be best subjected to "trilateral governance" contracts which make provision for third party determination of disputes, as by architects, arbitrators etc., while *recurrent* transactions may be the object of "bilateral governance", that is to say, of contracts or sequences of contracts which the parties will themselves take pains to maintain and to adjust to changing circumstances.

While the transaction-specific character of the investment, leading to its greatly reduced value in other applications, is the main factor which explain these departures from a classical contract model in which significant breach of contract terms leads naturally to litigation, or termination, or both, Williamson also attaches importance to other elements such as economies in communication costs between the parties (in terms of both knowledge and trust) which steadily increase as the contractual relation continues. Finally, given our concern with market stability, we should notice Williamson's view that within the framework of "bilateral governance" (which, I shall argue, is most relevant to the long-term contracts under examination), adjustments to contract quantities are normally much less problematic than adjustments to prices. He bases this both on the general observation that

> price adjustments have an unfortunate zero-sum quality, whereas proposals to increase, decrease, or delay delivery do not (1979:251)

and on the idea that where the product is specialised, the costs involved in switching supplies mean that there is little risk of opportunistic quantity adjustments, by buyers who have found cheaper suppliers elsewhere or sellers who have found better sales opportunities.

The characteristics of the iron ore market make it an excellent arena in which to work over Williamson's theories.[2] Iron ore is an indispensable raw material for steel-making. You cannot make steel without it: at the same time there is virtually no other use for iron ore. Deposits of ore are distributed throughout the world. Broadly speaking, ore is sold in three broad categories: lumps, fines, and pellets. Lumps, as the name indicates, are lumps of ore, from pea-size up, which can be used directly in the iron furnace. Fines are smaller particles, which require to be sintered, that is, fused by heat, before they can be so used. By reason of the fragility of sinter, sintering normally takes place at the steelworks, though the Japanese mills have recently thought it worthwhile to construct sintering works in the Philippines to process Australian fines before onward carriage to Japan. Obviously lumps are a higher value product, but they can only be produced by mines with an ore body of sufficient purity. Pellets are a bonded form of ore, sometimes manufactured at the mine, which contains additives and generally reduces processing costs at the furnace stage. Pelletisation is one solution to the marketing of ore from a low-grade but large and easy-to-work body of ore; the construction of pelleting plant, however, involves substantial additional invest-

[2] For another positive empirical test see Palay (1984).

ment. It is quite possible for individual steel-makers to vary their inputs as between lumps, pellets and sintered fines, though process readjustment costs will be incurred in the substitution of one type of ore for another, and in particular, steel-makers will hesitate before closing down their own sintering plant in order to use lumps or pellets.

In addition to these differences in physical presentation, ores from different mines will vary widely in terms of chemical composition. A key factor is obviously the richness of the ore, that is, the percentage of iron (Fe), and prices will normally be expressed on the basis of minimum and normal percentages of Fe per ton, or at so many cents per Fe percentage unit per ton. The presence of other elements such as manganese, alumina and silica, and their relative quantities in the ore, and of impurities such as phosphorous and sulphur, will also be important. Each steelmaker's facilities will operate best on a particular chemical "mix"; he will therefore seek to balance ores of different provenance and composition in order to maintain this mix. Two steel-makers with similar quantitative needs may thus be prepared to pay significantly different prices for the same cargo of ore.

This pronounced physical and chemical differentiation of the product by reference to the needs of individual buyers has prevented the emergence of reference grades, standards or contracts on which a commodity exchange type of trading could be based. Also militating against this type of open trading (and hence against stabilisation through futures markets) are the low value per ton of the product, the high costs of storage and, due to the evolution of the market in terms of the location of buyers and sellers, the high proportion of prices represented by freights. In 1982, for example, the price of 65 per cent Fe Brazilian ore c.i.f. at North Sea ports was $ 25.90 per tonne, while spot freights per cargo tonne for this journey averaged $ 5.40, a relatively low figure.

The steel industry, as already noted, is the iron ore industry's only signifcant customer. It grew up, first in Western Europe and later in the United States, round workable deposits of iron ore and coal. Steel mills controlled their own iron ore sources. There was little commercial trading in iron ore, and virtually none on an inter-regional basis. This situation continued until after the Second World War, from which time the depletion of US and West European ore reserves, and the emergence of Japan as a major steel-maker with inadequate domestic ore supplies, caused a rapid expansion of new sources of supply, with the exploitation of reserves in India, West Africa, Brazil and Australia. In 1955, 85 per cent of iron ore production took place in Europe, the United States and Canada; by 1977 this proportion had fallen to under 55 per cent. Most of the growth in this period has been in Australia and Brazil. In 1955 these two countries together accounted for under 2 per cent of world production and 3 per cent of exports. By 1980 these figures had risen, respectively, to 20 and 40 per cent. Trade in ore from these new sources has very largely – though not exclusively – been conducted with the Western countries, Japan, and one or two "new" steel-making countries like Korea. Despite a large increase, over the period since 1955, in its steel production, both in absolute terms and as a proportion of world production, the Communist world has remained self-sufficient in iron ore, East Europe drawing on steadily expanding Russian supplies and China being self-sufficient.

To summarise, with a first attempt at relating these facts to Williamson's transactions categories, we may say that this is a market of recurrent transactions in which there is a significant, but perhaps not determining, degree of investment specialisation. In such circumstances we might expect to find classical market contracting and relational contracting with bilateral governance as competing models for the industry. Also to be taken into account, however, is the virtually closed character of the market – the product has no alternative uses, the buyer has no alternative product – and the very small number of actual, and even potential, participants in that market. One of them has described the ore market as "intimate", a term which captures the small number of participants, their long-term interdependence, the closeness of their relationship and the discretion with which it is conducted. This feature appears in recent times to have shifted the balance firmly in favour of relational, as opposed to market contracting, as we shall see.

A second line of work was originated by Macaulay's pioneering 1963 paper, "Non-contractual Relations in Business: A Preliminary Study". In this paper, based mainly on a survey of firms operating in Wisconsin and of some lawyers advising them, Macaulay posed the question of the extent to which businessmen *used* contract law. He found that the amount of planning by businessmen for various contingencies was highly variable; that planning for legal sanctions, and treatment of defective performance, in particular, were minimal; that exchanges were commonly made without any agreement on terms and conditions being reached (especially where the parties were using standardised forms), or on legally unenforceable terms, so that there was no binding contract at all – and that parties frequently knew this, and were indifferent to it; that performance difficulties were regularly resolved without reference to contractual obligations; and that dispute settlement through litigation was extremely rare. In the heavily-lawyered society that is the United States these empirical findings seemed to need some explanation, which Macaulay found mainly in the availability of effective alternatives to contract: standardised or pre-tested products, for example; insurance; non-legal sanctions, such as intra-firm pressures for quality by salesmen on production staff, loss of future business, loss of trade reputation. He also stressed the heavy costs, both in money and in business relations terms, that might be involved in creating a detailed contract and, still more, in litigating to enforce one. In the light of all these factors, Macaulay found it necessary to conclude by explaining why contract should be used at all, stressing such points as the value of a detailed contract as a communication device within the buyer or seller enterprise, or in cases where there was a likelihood that significant problems would arise (as where complex performance over an extended period was called for); the existence of special relationships, such as the manufacturer-dealer franchise, in which the normal non-contractual controls might not operate; and the possible interest of third parties, like government, in seeing a formal contract concluded.

Subsequent empirical studies, in different legal cultures, have tended to confirm these findings (Beale and Dugdale, 1975; Kurczewski and Frieske, 1977). Reflecting on this later, Macaulay (1977) pointed out that despite all this empirical evidence to suggest the irrelevance of the classical contract process to the real world, the classical view of contract continued to dominate. What functions, then, did it serve? Two of his suggestions deserve mention here: the thought that contract's role may be as "the foundation for strategic manoeuvres in the game of negotiated settlement" (1977:515), and the idea that contract law might "crystallize business customs and provide a normative vocabulary, affecting expectations about what is fair" (1977:519).

The relevance of this line of work might at first sight appear to be limited, since it is clear that those engaged in the iron ore trade have for the most part conducted their business under quite detailed formal contracts. Macaulay gives us grounds to suspect, however, that the link between contractual stipulations and trading behaviour may be weak, and that factors other than a sense of contractual obligation may be determinant. In examining contractual performance in the iron ore market – which, as already explained, is a necessary step in relating market stability to long-term contract – we thus have the chance to test these suspicions in a new arena: that of major international raw material contracts.

1. The Incidence of Long-Term Contracts

We have seen that in the early days of the steel industry the normal mode of procurement of iron ore was through the ownership of the mine. As economic local supplies became exhausted, and mills began to look overseas for supplies, mill ownership of overseas mines became quite common: in the late nineteenth century, Swedish and Spanish mines were developed in this way by the British steel industry. United States mills undertook this kind of development in Canada and, later, in South America, and British mills were developing mines in Canada and West Africa in the middle years of this century. Most of these developments, however, did not involve 100 per cent ownership and management of the mine by a single mill: full vertical integration was seldom sought. The pattern of ownership and management was in fact often highly complex, particularly where United States mills were concerned. Mills formed themselves into consortia for the ownership of mines; individual mills would commonly have a less-than-controlling interest, and functions of mine management would often be undertaken by merchanting companies, which had carved out an important specialised role for themselves in the American industry, in such spheres as financing, transportation, sales, and mine management. This system was exported to South America also, though here it became more common for a single mill or, sometimes, a single merchanting company, to have a controlling share of the mining enterprise, as with Bethlehem Steel in Venezuela or Marcona in Peru.

In the post-Second World War expansion, ownership by steel mills played an even less important role. To be economic, the new mines needed to be large. Their output might considerably exceed the needs of any individual steel company; their financing might be beyond its capacity, which was in any event strained throughout the industry by the need to finance new production facilities. Other factors militating against procurement via ownership were the suspicions of some of the new host countries, especially Brazil and India, in regard to overseas ownership of their mineral resources; the active dislike of others, like Mauretania, and Venezuela and Peru, who expropriated private holdings in their iron ore and other mines; and the preference of the Japanese, who were emerging as a major influence in the industry, for procurement through contract rather than through overseas investment. In consequence, at the present day, ownership of mines outside the socialist bloc is essentially divided between two types of institution. On the one hand are the State mining companies, some of early foundation, like LKAB in Sweden, some the heritors of recent nationalisations, like Hierro Peru or SNIM in Mauretania. On the other side there are the mining consortia: here the role of steel mills is much reduced, being supplied by larger merchant company participations, and by the arrival of a major new actor in the industry, the specialist mining company (like Amax or Rio Tinto Zinc). Sole ownership by a steel company of a mine located overseas is now extremely rare.

Today, therefore, even where steel companies participate in mine development, the conditions for "unified governance" in Williamson's sense, involving direct intra-organisational transfer of ore from mine to mill, do not exist. Contract, of some kind, is thus the vehicle through which the mills must obtain their ores, even though the seller may be a joint venture company in which they themselves have an interest. Even where the consortium takes the form of an unincorporated joint venture the members will normally set up a joint sales agency company to which they sell their production and from which they buy their needs, rather than relying on direct separate disposal as is common in the oil industry.

In the phase of major development of the industry in the nineteen-sixties and early nineteen-seventies, the overwhelming preference, apparently of both buyers and sellers, was for procurement through long-term contracts: that is to say, contracts in which the quantities to be supplied (and normally the prices also) were fixed over a period of years. The traditional pattern of dealing in Europe for ore supplies other than those owned by steel companies – principally, supplies from Sweden – was one of short-term or spot contracts. The Japanese, when they entered the market, wanted greater security of supply than these contracts could provide, but as has been noted, were not anxious to invest heavily overseas in acquiring new mining capacity. Their preferred vehicle was the long-term supply contract, though the mills sometimes found it necessary to take small participations in mining consortia either themselves or through the Japanese merchant companies which acted as their trading agents. This mode of acquiring supplies quickly spread from the Japanese market so as to dominate non-socialist world iron ore trade, so that a safe estimate might now be that not less than 80 per cent of the ore entering such trade is sold on this basis. Such contracts appeared to offer advantages to all classes of buyers and sellers. For sellers, they offered a secure avenue for the disposal of output in a period of proliferation of supply sources. Where sellers, as was frequently the case, were undertaking new mine development, they also provided collateral for mine finance. For buyers, who in the nineteen-sixties and early seventies were looking forward to a period of continuing growth in steel demand, they guaranteed secure supplies of the right type through periods when the market might become very constricted, should mine development lag behind steel demand.

We may summarise these considerations in economic terms by saying that the reduction of uncertainty as to availability of appropriate supplies and access to appropriate markets in a time of expansion of both milling and mining capacity provided the main motivation for this massive resort to long-term contracting. By itself, the idea of buyer-specific investment seems insufficient to explain the dominance of this method of trade: appropriate mixes of ore inputs could be maintained by judicious short-term and spot buying, and the Swedish company LKAB showed over a long period that iron ore mining could prosper on the basis of such short-term arrangements. While in theory short-term contracting might have offered an alternative trading framework for the expanding industry, once long-term arrangements became established in a significant portion of this "intimate" market the attractiveness of short-term arrangements rapidly diminished due to the restriction of the variety and quantity of ore available on such terms. A snowball effect was thus initiated, which has continued, despite the vicissitudes that will be described, to the present day (even LKAB is now selling some ore on contracts extending over several years), and which it is hard to see being reversed in the absence of a complete breakdown of the LTC system.

On one view it may seem a little surprising that no such breakdown has taken place. Parties reduce uncertainty through long-term contracts by foreseeing a range of future possibilities and determining in advance their trading behaviour in such circumstances. One problem with this technique is the limited capacity of contracts to cope with future changes of circumstances of a kind or intensity which the parties did not foresee. If contracts are rigid enough to eliminate foreseen uncertainties they may break under the strain of unforeseen events. As we shall see in the next section, the LTCs of the late sixties and early seventies were rigid contracts. Since that time, moreover, the course of events affecting the iron ore market has been different in two fundamental respects from the expectations of the contracting parties.

In the first place, parties chose the US dollar as the numeraire, or money of account, in their contracts. Given the gold convertibility of the dollar and the international nature of the market one would not have expected anything else. In 1971, however, the gold convertibility of the dollar was suspended and the dollar later devalued against most other currencies. Within a short time most currencies were floating freely against one another. This introduced a quite unexpected element of instability in to the economic balance of the contracts, whose effects were exacerbated for most producers by a strong world inflation in the same period which exerted disproportionate pressures on their costs.

Secondly, in the nineteen-sixties and early seventies steelmakers were anticipating a lengthy period of continuing growth of demand for steel. But from 1970 to 1982 virtually no growth occurred: world production of crude steel in 1970 was 599.1 MT, in 1982 645.4 MT. The 1982 figure is *lower* than that for

1973. Moreover, during this period there has been significant growth in the steel output of new steelmaking countries (e.g. Korea, 1.16 MT in 1973, 11.76 MT in 1982; Taiwan, 0.54 MT in 1973, 4.15 MT in 1982),which has meant that the market shares of the large traditional buyers of iron ore in Europe and Japan have been squeezed even further. Japanese steel production declined from 119.32 MT in 1973 to 99.55 MT in 1982, EEC production in the same period from 151.11 MT to 111.28 MT. Steel companies, therefore, found themselves in need of far less iron ore than they had anticipated when concluding their LCTs in the sunny days of the nineteen-sixties and early seventies.

2. Content and Structure of the Long-Term Iron Ore Contract

To appreciate the nature and seriousness of the effect of these developments on the operation of LTCs we need to examine the structure and contents of such contracts. This is not easy: the industry is sensitive on questions of confidentiality, and a number of companies approached or interviewed refused even to disclose individual clauses of a technical character (e.g. force majeure, or arbitration) used in their contracts. Nonetheless, a substantial number of individual and *pro forma* contracts have been collected, on the basis of which it is possible to discern the general pattern to which the contracts conform, normal ways of dealing with common contractual issues and the range of variations around such norms, and, not least important, the way in which the framing of contracts has changed over time, in reponse to the developments of the nineteen-seventies which have been summarised above. There is certainly no such thing as a standard contract in the iron ore industry, and it is doubtful whether it can even be said that there is a "typical" one. To convey a fair impression of contractual contents, therefore, I propose first to identify and classify the main clauses which will appear in virtually every contract, and then to analyse in more detail those which are of particular interest here: the key commercial stipulations as to quantity and price on the one hand, and what I shall call "lawyers' law" stipulations on such matters as dispute settlement on the other. To illustrate this detailed examination, examples will consistently be drawn fron two specific contracts. The first, which will be referred to as Contract A, is an actual contract operative from the late sixties, and thus concluded before the unpredicted disturbances of the next decade. The second, Contract B, is a model contract drafted for use in the nineteen-eighties, that is, with the benefit of experience of this period. Naturally, where these contracts provide unusual solutions to the problems they confront, this will be indicated.

2.1. Contract Clauses in General

All long-term iron ore contracts will provide for the following matters:

(i) Term, quantity and price: these are examined in detail below.

(ii) Specification or quality: this will be expressed in terms of the chemical analysis of the ore, usually by reference to a minimum Fe content and maximum levels for impurities such as potassium and sulphur; to its maximum moisture content; and to its physical composition (size of particles). Non-conformity with specification will normally be dealt with by price adjustments (which may be on scales specified in advance in the contract), rather than by allowing the buyer any right of rejection. The buyer may, however, have the right to suspend shipments in the event of repeated quality failures.

(iii) Weight, sampling and analysis: cargoes need to be weighed, and sampled to ensure compliance with specification. For these purposes parties commonly, though not invariably, make reference to independent agents, such as draft surveyors. Recourse to an independent analyst, as umpire, is almost invariably provided for in the case where parties disagree as to the results of analysis. Actual reference to such third party decision in this field is regarded as a matter of routine, and not as a sign that a real dispute has arisen between the parties. Detailed terms of contracts in this area may also vary according to whether the ore is being shipped FOB (buyer's vessels) or C & F (seller's vessels).

(iv) Shipping arrangements: these will be set out in considerable detail, in the contract itself or in a schedule. Most contracts are on FOB terms: the buyer provides his own shipping. The contract will therefore stipulate arrangements for the scheduling and access of buyer's vessels, permissible delays in loading, and so on. FOB terms also mean that the buyer, rather than the seller, has *de facto* control over what quantities are taken and when. In the rarer case of C & F shipping, sellers will be concerned to ensure that their ships can discharge cargo speedily at buyer's nominated ports.

(v) Title, risk, and insurance: these provisions do not reflect the shipping arrangements made, but are a matter of negotiation. In an FOB contract, for example, risk may pass to the buyer on loading but title remain in the seller as security for payment.

(vi) Payment: payment by the establishment of an irrevocable letter of credit against which the seller can draw is probably the most usual form though contracts calling for cash payments are not uncommon.

(vii) *Force majeure*, arbitration, assignment, notices: these "lawyers' law" clauses are more fully discussed below.

In concentrating, for the purposes of more detailed analysis, on term, quantity and price clauses, and on the lawyers' law clauses, I would stress that this does not indicate the unimportance of the other types of clause, which might be compendiously labelled "technical". Such things as specification, sampling, shipping arrangements, and mode of payment are of great importance to the parties. Broadly speaking, however, these clauses will be similar in content – for transactions between identical parties – whatever the duration of the contract (with the exception of spot sales of single cargoes, which may be accomplished on the basis only of a telephone call and exchange of telexes). The clauses may well be drafted with greater care in LTCs and enter into greater detail. They may also be performed somewhat differently: buyers under a short-term contract may be readier to exercise a contractual right of cancellation for repeated sub-specification cargoes (if given) than buyers under LTCs, who may prefer to co-operate with sellers to remove the cause of the defect. Their general character, however, is not affected by the type of contract in which they are found. The opposite is true of the term, quantity and price clauses now to be analysed. Together, these characterise the LTC and express its essential features.

2.2. The Term and Quantity Clause

In both the sample contracts, term and quantity are stipulated in close conjunction in the same clause. Contract A, provides as follows:

Quantity

Seller hereby agrees to deliver to Buyer 1,667,000 dry long tons (one long ton to be 2,240 pounds) of Sized Lump Ore and 1,667,000 dry long tons of Iron Ore Fines (hereinafter sometimes collectively referred to as "Ore") during the period commencing October 1, 1969, and terminating September 30, 1979, according to the following annual delivery schedule:

Contract Year (Commencing on October 1 in any year and ending Sept. 30 in the next succeeding year)	*Quantity (Dry Long Tons)* *Sized Lump Ore*	*Iron Ore Fines*
1969	166,700	166,700
1970	166,700	166,700
1971	166,700	166,700
1972	166,700	166,700
1973	166,700	166,700
1974	166,700	166,700
1975	166,700	166,700
1976	166,700	166,700
1977	166,700	166,700
1978	166,700	166,700
Total	1,667,000	1,667,000

Buyer shall have the option to increase or decrease the annual delivery quantities referred to above for each contract year, except for 1968 contract year, by up to 15 per cent. Buyer shall notify Seller of any exercise of such option at least three months prior to the commencement of each contract year.

Buyer shall use its best efforts to exercise such option in a manner which will maintain an even ratio between Sized Lump Ore and Iron Ore Fines in any contract year.

Notwithstanding the above option to increase or decrease the annual delivery quantities, Buyer shall receive the total contract quantity for each grade by September 30, 1979.

Contract B provides:

Quantity

Seller shall sell and deliver to *Buyer* and *Buyer* shall buy, accept and pay for during the period beginning January 1st, 198 and ending December 31st, 198 , the following annual quantities of iron ore in metric tons:

198 through 198 annually:

Buyer shall have the right to decrease the quantity of to be delivered and accepted during the following year by up to 10 per cent, provided *Buyer* exercises this option by giving *Seller* notice in writing before August 1st of each preceding year.

The close association of term and quantity is no accident: it is the predetermination of their relationship which distinguishes the LTC from other arrangements. A long-term supply contract may be defined as one which stipulates the delivery of a given quantity of product over a given period of years. What period qualifies as "long" will depend both on the product and on the current circumstances of trade. In the oil industry today one year is long. In the iron ore market in the nineteen sixties and early seventies "long" generally connoted a span of at least ten years; now the consensus in the industry is rather for five, and this is the figure used in this paper as the minimum which justifies calling a contract long-term. Excluded from the category of LTCs for the purposes of this enquiry, therefore, are requirements and run-of-mine contracts, under which, respectively, the seller agrees to provide the whole or a given proportion of the buyer's requirements over a fixed period, and the buyer agrees to purchase the whole or a given proportion of the seller's mine output over such a period. Quantity obligations under such contracts will vary freely according to requirements and output respectively. They are not in fact encountered in arm's length iron ore trade, though the current mode of performance of iron ore LTCs is, as we shall see, hard to distinguish from that which would follow from requirements contracts.

Also excluded by definition (even though they are occasionally encountered) are evergreen contracts – that is, contracts which are automatically renewed unless one of the parties decides otherwise – with an initial fixed term of less than five years. Such contracts, even if their initial duration is as short as one or two years, may in fact last for very long periods; but by reason of the opportunities they provide for renegotiation on renewal they neither offer the security, nor impose the constraints, of the true LTC as above defined. The same is true, *a fortiori,* of short-term contracts not expressed to be evergreen, but which in fact succeed another in time within the framework of a long-term course of dealing between the parties: a much commoner pattern of trading in this market. Where evergreen contracts are used, or where such succession occurs, we may conveniently speak of long-term relations between the parties in question. Whether there has, *in fact,* been any difference between the behaviour of parties to LTCs and in long-term relations is a key element in the answer, in this context, to our general question about the significance of legally-binding obligations.

The fixed-term character of iron ore LTCs is generally quite stark, in the sense that a majority of contracts provides neither for a discontinuation of the contract before the expiry of the term for any reason other than continued *force majeure* nor for the renewal of the contract. The *force majeure* clause of contract A (below, pp. 179-80) is in fairly common form in providing that the party advised of (i.e. not invoking) *force majeure* may terminate the contract if the *force majeure* continues for 12 months. Contract B, unusually, does not provide for termination even under such circumstances. Both contracts are unusual in providing explicitly – even if not in rigid terms – for a possible renewal:

Contract A

Extension

It is the intention of both parties to extend this agreement to provide for delivery of additional Iron Ore beyond the contract period, subject to mutual agreement on price, tonnage and other terms and conditions for an extended period.

Contract B

Clause 1 – Quantity

This contract runs for the period January 1st 198 to December 31st 198 . On or before March 31st 198 , *Buyer* and *Seller* shall negotiate the quantities and period for which the contract could be extended.

In contrast, ways of expressing quantity stipulations are well represented by our two examples. While contract B fixes an annual quantity only, contract A fixes both total quantities of lumps and fines over the whole contract period, and a year-by-year schedule of quantities. Each contract also gives the buyer, only, an option to vary these quantities within specified limits: in B, down by 10 per cent in any year; in A, up or down by 15 per cent in any year. All contracts will have some such provision for limited variation of quantities in a given year at buyer's option (the fourchette). Where a total quantity is specified, as in contract A, the fourchette enables the buyer to smooth his intake of ore to reflect temporary surges or depressions in demand, to match the availability of shipping, and so on. In contract B the absence of an overall quantity provision means that the buyer may end up taking up to 10 per cent less than the cumulated annual totals provided. While this offers less security to the seller than the arrangement in contract A, there is an offsetting advantage in the absence of any upward revision option: with the normal two-way fourchette the seller is effectively compelled to install capacity sufficient to satisfy the full utilisation by the buyer of the upward option, capacity which may never be used.

Obviously the desire of buyers will be to obtain the greatest flexibility possible, but the width of the fourchette, and its impact on total quantities to be taken, will in the case of new mine developments be limited by the need for the contract to offer sufficient security to serve as collateral, *de jure* or *de facto*, for the raising of development finance. Lenders for iron ore development projects seem, however, to have been satisfied with a considerably weaker commitment on the part of buyers to take the contract quantities than has been the case in other mineral markets, notably that of natural gas, where it is common for lenders to insist on the inclusion in the contract of a "take or pay" provision whereunder buyers must pay the price of the commodity even if they choose not to take it. In the light of the experience of contract performance of quantity stipulations in the last decade, lenders may now be more demanding: LTCs relating to the biggest current iron ore development, at Carajas in Brazil, include an express warranty on the part of the buyer that in any year he will take at least 80 per cent of the nominal contract quantity. In other cases, where contracts are not linked to mine finance (e.g. renewal contracts for supplies from established mines), the opposite result in terms of contract provision has followed from this experience: buyers have secured the insertion of a "tonnage flexibility" clause permitting the unlimited downward revision of contract quantities in a given year either at the buyer's request, if he has difficulties with production or sales, or at the seller's, if he has difficulties in delivery. A form of the clause is reproduced as an Appendix. In most, if not all contracts such reductions affect total contract quantities also. In present circumstances of slack steel demand and substantial overcommitment on LTCs by some buyers (see below), this clause benefits only the buyer. If total quantities can be reduced by invoking the clause, it arguably changes the whole nature of the contract, converting it from a fixed-quantity LTC into a requirements contract. The significance of this change will be discussed in the concluding paragraphs of this paper.

2.3. The Price Clause

Here contracts A and B present an important contrast which reflects the date of their design.

Contract A

Price

Sized Lump Ore: US-$ 9.21 per dry long ton FOB spout trimmed, Fe 64.00% base
Fines: US-$ 7.52 per dry long ton FOB spout trimmed, Fe 64.00% base

The above-mentioned prices and terms specified hereunder shall be applicable to 833,333 dry long tons of Sized Lump Ore, 833,333 dry long tons of Iron Ore Fines stipulated in paragraph 2 hereinabove. The price and terms applicable to the remaining contract quantity of each grade shall be decided by mutual agreement by September 30, 1973.

Contract B

Price

The purchase price or prices C & F hold of vessel at those ports of discharge designated by *Buyer* applicable to annual deliveries of iron ore hereunder shall be determined from year to year by mutual agreement between the parties hereto. During the last quarter of each year, representatives of *Buyer* and *Seller* shall meet to establish in good faith the prices at those ports of discharge designated by *Buyer* which will be effective as to all deliveries called for under this contract during the following calendar year.

In order to establish said competitive prices the parties hereto shall, in good faith, take into account the worldwide price trends for ores comparable, from the standpoint of quantity and quality, with the ores to be delivered under this agreement, the effective or potential availability of said comparable ores at the ports of discharge designated by *Buyer*, the FOB prices of said comparable ores and the ocean freight from their ports of origin to the ports of discharge designated by *Buyer*. Bunker escalation clause shall also be discussed during this meeting. It is understood, however, that *Buyer* cannot ask to be granted a lower price, if said lower price for the same delivery period had previously been offered by *Seller* and was not accepted by *Buyer*. *Seller* is also free to sell trial shipments not exceeding 100,000 tons per customer without the necessity to adjust the price established between *Buyer* and *Seller*. As soon as agreement on price has been reached, *Buyer* and *Seller* shall execute a Supplemental Agreement hereto setting forth the C & F price or prices and discharging conditions applicable to deliveries to be made under this Contract during the following year.

All dues, duties and taxes relating to the iron ore or transportation levied in the country of origin shall be for the account of *Seller*. All dues, duties and taxes relating to the iron ore or transportation levied in the country of destination and/or country through which iron ore shall pass at *Buyer's* request shall be fore the account of *Buyer*. For the definition of C & F, wherever mentioned in this contract, the INCO terms are applicable.

Contract A, concluded in 1968, has a fixed price, subject to adjustment for quality, for half of the contract quantity of lumps and fines respectively. The price for the remainder is to be fixed by agreement not later than half-way through the contract period. Such a provision is common in LTCs concluded up to around 1974–75. Sometimes prices were fixed for a period of years (3–5 years), rather than by reference to a proportion of total quantity; sometimes more complex arrangements were made, with split prices for proportions of each year's quantities. Indexation has been rare, though some contracts have had prices tied to the price of a basket of ores, to pig iron prices, and so on. Contract B shows the effects of the instability of the nineteen-seventies: prices are to be negotiated annually. This contract sets out negotiating procedure and criteria more fully than most, but is silent on the important question of what happens if the parties fail to agree a price before the date when deliveries for a given year are due to start. In the absence of a specific provision, the price once agreed will presumably apply retrospectively to shipments made before agreement. The contract may however provide that where the price cannot be agreed, shipments for that year may be cancelled; or that, pending agreement, shipments are to continue at the previous year's price, with the new price, once agreed, being applied retrospectively only to a proportion of the ore so shipped. Some contracts smooth out annual fluctuations in prices by providing for review of the price of half the contract quantity every other year (the "brick pricing" system).

2.4. "Lawyers' Law" Clauses

Clauses of this type are few and simple in iron ore LTCs. Part of the reason, undoubtedly, is the small part played by lawyers in the design of these contracts, and, indeed, the limited value attached to legal advice by company personnel responsible for their negotiation and performance. Despite our advance indication of an interest in specifically legal questions, such as the design of *force majeure* clauses, lawyers were present at only three of the fifteen company visits so far conducted in the research for this study; in only one of the other cases did company representatives make any spontaneous reference to legal advice. The low visibility of lawyers in this business confirms impressions collected by the earlier investigations of Macaulay (1963) and Beale and Dugdale (1975) into contracts mainly of engineering firms in Wisconsin and Bristol respectively, but is perhaps more surprising in view of the international character of the market and the very large sums of money involved.

Two possible reasons may be suggested. First, though the iron ore market is worldwide in scope, the total number of companies operating as buyers or sellers within the main currents of trade is small, probably not more than fifty. Within these companies negotiations are conducted by senior people who develop close personal relationships. They may be able to rely more heavily on personal trust and on industry *mores,* and feel less need of legal protection, than operators in larger, more impersonal markets. Second, although the existence of an iron ore LTC probably signifies a degree of interdependence between the parties (adjustment of processing facilities to product specification, construction of suitable loading and unloading facilities, acquisition of necessary shipping, etc.) closer to that involved in a capital-sharing joint venture than in a spot sales transaction, the form of the LTC appears to have developed as the simple extension in time of the annual or spot contracts which were quite recently, as we have seen, the only arm's-length mode of trading. It consequently shares their simplicity and their heavy reliance on general rules and principles, whether legal or custom of the trade, for guidance in the unlikely event of dispute. Whatever the reasons may be, the simple form of this part of the LTC requires that we consider both the clauses that are found and those which we might expect to find, but do not.

It is hard to imagine an LTC without a *force majeure* clause. The purpose of the clause, it should be remembered, is to ensure, within limits, the continuation of the contract in circumstances which, under general law, might constitute a breach on the part of one party, might terminate the contract by reason of impossibility or unforeseen onerousness of performance, or warrant its *ex post facto* adjustment by a court. To avoid these uncertainties Contracts A and B each contain a *force majeure* clause, as follows:

Contract A

Force Majeure

Either party shall be relieved of and excused from its obligations to perform hereunder, during any period that its performance (including any performance required of Receivers, and/or vessels nominated and accepted under this contract) is prevented or delayed by inability to obtain a proper export or import license, act of God, war or threat of war, governmental restrictions or regulations, strike, fire, flood, or any other cause beyond the reasonable control of such party. In the event that such a force majeure condition occurs or is anticipated, the party directly affected shall advise the other by cable as promptly as possible and then submit a written advice of the force majeure condition, with evidence and proof if possible, within ten days after occurrence of such force majeure condition. Deliveries that would otherwise have been made hereunder during the period in which performance by either party is prevented shall be made by mutual agreement as soon as practicable following termination of this force majeure condition; provided, however, that if any such period continues for more than one hundred eighty (180) consecutive days, the party advised of the force majeure condition may, at its option, cancel the tonnage that would otherwise have been delivered during such period; also provided, however, that if any such period continues for more than twelve (12) months, the said party may, at its option, cancel the remainder of this contract.

Contract B

In the event that performance of this Contract by either party is delayed, interrupted or prevented by reason of force majeure including strikes, lockouts of any kind or other causes beyond the control of the party which is unable to perform, then the party concerned shall be excused from the performance of this contract while and to the extent that such party is delayed interrupted or prevented; it being understood that in the event of any such occurrence, both parties shall perform such of their respective duties and obligations as conditions may reasonably permit, and so far as reasonably practicable deliveries and receipts of the grade or grades of ore affected shall be prorated with other existing foreign obligations of *Seller* and *Buyer* as the case may be, provided that any quantities of iron ore not delivered and accepted as a result of such occurrence shall be cancelled except as the parties may otherwise agree in writing.

The party whose performance is affected by any such occurrence shall immediately notify the other party of the commencement hereof, defining exactly and precisely the nature of such occurrence and the expected duration and cessation.

These clauses excuse failure to perform in defined circumstances, and stipulate the results of such a failure: cancellation of tonnage under contract B, while contract A provides for postponement of tonnage, cancellation of tonnage and, finally, cancellation of contract, according to the length of time for which the *force majeure* condition prevails. The definition of *force majeure* events, while varying in particularity in the two contracts, is in both cases quite conventional and would exclude any possibility of claiming *force majeure* on the basis of major market changes as in cost of supply or level or product demand such as have in fact upset the economy of LTCs in the last decade.

With one exception only, all the contracts seen or discussed so far in this investigation have had an arbitration clause. These can vary quite widely in content, as our two examples show.

Contract A

Arbitration

Any dispute which may arise hereunder and which cannot be disposed of by mutual agreement shall be decided by arbitration in the United States of America, in accordance with current American Arbitration rules and procedures. Arbitration may be initiated by either party by giving thirty (30) days' notice in writing to the other of commencement of arbitration proceedings. Thereupon, a board of three (3) arbitrators shall be appointed, one of whom shall be chosen by Buyer, one by Seller, and a third by two (2) so chosen. If either Buyer or Seller fails to choose an arbitrator within fourteen (14) days after receiving notice of commencement of arbitration proceedings, or if the two arbitrators so chosen cannot agree upon a third arbitrator within fourteen (14) days after they have been so chosen, the American Arbitration Association shall, upon request of either party, appoint the arbitrator or arbitrators required to complete the board. The decision of the majority of the arbitrators shall be final and binding upon both parties.

Contract B

Arbitration

Any claim, dispute or controversy, with the exception of non-agreement on price, arising out of, or relative to this Contract, the activities performed under its terms or the breach thereof, that cannot be settled by mutual agreement between the contracting parties, shall be subject to arbitration in Paris in accordance with the rules of the International Chamber of Commerce, Paris, France.

Whenever the provisions of this Clause shall apply then the matter shall be referred for decision to three referees who shall be persons fitted by the possession of expert knowledge for such decision.

Each of the parties hereto shall be entitled to appoint one referee and the third one shall be nominated by mutual agreement between the parties or failing such agreement by the President for the time being of the International Chamber of Commerce. All such referees shall be deemed to be acting as experts and not as arbitrators and their decision shall be final and conclusive.

The parties hereby expressly state that this Clause shall be binding upon them despite the fact that it does not provide detailed guidelines for the decision of the referees.

Normally this clause will cover all save quality disputes, which have their own specialised settlement procedure (though note that contract B excludes arbitration on price matters), and will provide for a "neutral" arbitration in a third country, often according to International Chamber of Commerce or UNCITRAL rules. Arbitration is regarded as a last resort: we are not aware of any arbitration taking place under an iron ore LTC.

While assignment and notice clauses require no particular attention, a word should be said about two types of clause which one would ordinarily expect to find in any modern long-term international contract. The first is a governing law clause. Given that the parties to the contract inhabit different jurisdictions one would expect them to specify what system of law should govern their contractual relations. This might be a national system, whether of one of the parties or of a third country, or some "self-designed" law such as "the principles of law common to the legal systems of both parties" and other such formulae. Failure to specify a system will mean that the arbitrators, or any court before which a dispute is brought, will need to determine the question, applying rules which may vary from court to court and are far from predictable in their application. Contract A contains such a clause, under which substantive law of the State of California is to govern the construction and performance of the agreement. Contract B, by contrast omits any mention of governing law and such omission is in fact common in iron ore LTCs. In these cases, I think, parties consider the risks of litigation too remote to justify the risks of difficulty in reaching agreement inherent in the attempt to choose a governing law.

The second type of missing clause is a hardship, or general adjustment clause. Such clauses represent an attempt by parties to plan, on a broader scale than is offered by the traditional *force majeure* clause, for supervening events which may impede contract performance, Frequently, this attempt takes the form of provision of a mechanism for adjusting the contract (whether by negotiation or otherwise) in the event of hardship to one of the parties. A recent example is in the following form:

15. Mutual Collaboration
Both Buyer and Seller recognise a long-term relationship requires mutual collaboration and assistance should either Buyer or Seller suffer hardship or unfairness.

Both Buyer and Seller agree that they will make their best efforts to solve any problem due to any such circumstances in the spirit of mutual understanding and collaboration.

Even after the disturbances of the last decade, clauses like this appear to be unusual. A number of companies take the view that such an understanding has always been an unexpressed, but vital part of their relationships with their opposite numbers under LTCs, and that its contractual expression would not strengthen its force. At the same time even those companies which express this view most strongly – the Japanese, for example – have recently been anxious, where circumstances permitted, to formalise arrangements for dealing with certain types of "difficulty", such as collapse of finished product markets leading to lack of need for contracted quantities (the "tonnage flexibility" clause above referred to: see Appendix). The unilateral and discretionary character of this latter clause, however, arguably diasqualifies it from consideration as a real hardship clause, and rather represents, as suggested earlier, a basic change in the nature of the contract.

3. Performance under Iron Ore LTCs

The pre-1975 iron ore LTC, therefore, as represented here by Contract A, was a simple, rigid agreement not well adapted to survive the major disruptions of the market which have occurred in the last decade. The previous section, and Contract B, convey some impression about how parties drew lessons from this experience which they have applied, or will apply, in the drafting of new contracts. Already in the early nineteen-seventies, however, LTCs were in force which would cover a very high percentage of total iron ore demand up to 1985 or even beyond. The crucial question, therefore, is what happened to these contracts as a result of the collapse of the numeraire and the collapse of the steel market. Were they terminated? amended? breached? or, somehow, duly performed?

3.1. Currency Instability and Inflation

The dollar devaluation of 1971 occurred at a time when a substantial number of major contracts including, in particular, the first contracts covering the development of large Australian iron ore deposits, were in their first few years of operation under fixed price regimes. Between 1970 and 1974 the Australians were doubly hit: by a rapid domestic cost inflation (the Australian index of manufacturing prices rose 37 per cent in this period) and by US dollar devaluation of 25 per cent by reference to their own currency. Other sellers were luckier in that the devaluation of the dollar, in own currency terms, was small or even negative. It appears that the currency changes were recognised, on all sides, as a matter for industry concern. We do not have information about how all parties behaved, but the pattern in the Australia-Japan trade appears to have been as follows. The mines continued to deliver, while indicating that they must have higher prices if they were to be able to continue to operate. After negotiations the Japanese mills (which deal separately with each mining company, but negotiate as a cartel) agreed in 1973 to a price adjustment. This price adjustment was on the same basis for all sellers: in fact it did not fully compensate the Australians for their currency-related losses, and over-compensated the Indians, who were already receiving currency gains because the rupee had depreciated even faster than the US dollar. This adjustment was "covered", in the case of the Australian contracts, by a hardship memorandum signed the following year, whose central provisions are virtually identical to the "mutual collaboration" clause above cited. In the words of the Memorandum

> Buyer and Seller hereby reconfirm the same spirit of mutual co-operation and assistance and agree that in the event of future hardship or unfairness resulting from abnormal circumstances, as compared with those in existence at the time of the signing of the contracts, the two parties shall meet promptly and exert their best efforts to reach a solution to alleviate such hardship or unfairness, taking into account all relevant factors.

The 1973 price adjustment, and a further adjustment made in 1974, were incorporated as formal amendments to the contracts, but the hardship memorandum, it should be noted, was not. It appears to have been important to the buyers, at this stage, not to enter into such a legally binding commitment.

After another year it became clear that the inflationary pressures and currency instability which had brought about these adjustments were not quickly going to disappear. The Japanese, after a general contractual review, agreed to formalise the *de facto* situation by moving to a system of annual negotiation of prices, usually according to the "brick" system. The common procedure, incorporated in 1976 into already existing contracts and still persisting, is for the parties to agree, in respect of half the annual contract quantity, at the end of year 1, the price that will apply in years 2 and 3 and the date by which (and perhaps the broad criteria according to which) the price for years 4 and 5 should be agreed. A similar agreement will be reached at the end of year 2 in respect of the other half of the annual contract quantity. These agreements are then treated as amendments to the original contract. Though part of its raison d'être has been removed by this process, the hardship memorandum, where concluded, is still regarded as being in force so long as the original contract has not expired.

3.2. Steel Market Collapse

Before the steel market began to crumble in the mid-seventies it was the policy of European mills to acquire some 65–70 per cent of their needs under LTCs, either from their own mines or from third party sellers. The Japanese were even more committed to LTCs: in 1971 three major mills had a total intake of 80 MT of iron ore and were committed to LTCs with a total *basic* tonnage of 73.6 MT. Not surprisingly, therefore, when steel demand fell away, LTCs immediately came under stress. Buyers began to claim that they could take only quantities falling below (in some cases far below) the bottom limits of their contract fourchettes, or even to seek to cancel contracts completely. The degree of their distress of course varied, according to the weakness of their own market, the degree to which they were able to reduce their ore intake by cutting back on purchases under short-term contracts, their desire to protect their investment in captive mines, and their capacity, if buying as traders, to sell on excess ore on a spot or short-term basis. Also varying, it would appear, was the degree of their attachment to their existing LTCs, with European buyers (who were admittedly harder hit by the steel crisis in the first instance) much quicker to suggest radical solutions like cancellation.

In the face of this chorus of hardship, the overriding concern of all sellers was to keep their contracts alive. They strongly, and largely successfully, resisted buyers' proposals to terminate contracts or to suspend them indefinitely. A few contracts were unilaterally terminated – for example when a lucky buyer found that he could successfully allege continuing breach of specification – but for the most part what emerged was a situation in which buyers took what quantities they could, when they could, under their LTCs. Over the last five to ten years this has meant that most buyers are normally taking less than the minimum annual contract quantities. To indicate the current dimensions of the problem, in 1982 the three Japanese mills already referred to together took 69.25 MT under LTCs, as against a basic tonnage for these contracts of 111.8 MT and a minimum permitted tonnage of 101.6 MT.

Buyers will normally indicate to their sellers, at the beginning of the annual price negotiation, how much they intend to take, a figure which they may, or may not, adhere to in the course of the year (it will be remembered that most sales are FOB so that the buyer controls shipping). The tonnage which is "lost" in this way may be taken in a later year – this has rarely happened; it may be postponed to the end of the contract period, so that at this moment the contract is, in effect, extended in time; or it may simply be cancelled. The parties will not necessarily be explicit as to which of these alternatives is to operate. In contrast with the situation on prices, contracts have not been amended, other than on renewal (see below), to reflect this crisis situation. Sellers do not appear to regard buyers' failure to take a contracted annual quantity as in itself a significant breach of the contract, if indeed they regard it as a breach at all, but (with rare exceptions) they refuse to endorse the taking of lesser quantities by contract amendment or even by informal agreement, preferring to await the last years of the contract for a negotiation in which they will seek to recuperate "lost" tonnage through contract extension or quantity increase. So far, to my knowledge, cancellation of quantities has been agreed only in the context of a partial extension of a contract.

When Japanese mills came to renew their contracts, from about 1978 onwards, they insisted on formalising the *de facto* situation on liftings through the insertion of the "tonnage flexibility" clause (Appendix). We have already noted that whatever the quantities and fourchette written into the contract, this clause in effect turns the contract into one for requirements, rather than for fixed quantities. This is the factual situation obtaining even in those cases where the clause does not operate. One buyer, indeed, went so far as to say in interview that it was an unwritten rule that the buyer can only be asked to lift the tonnage he can reasonably be expected to consume, whatever his contractual commitments may be. Another such rule, which would certainly command widespread acceptance, is that every buyer must operate his programme of tonnage reductions fairly as between his different suppliers under LTCs. Fairness does not mean that all takings must be cut *pro rata:* sellers accept, within limits, the propensity of buyers to favour captive mines among their long-term sellers, and their need for appropriate mixes of ores for economical furnace operation. This principle of fairness is incorporated into the tonnage flexibility clause as a contractual obligation.

4. Conclusions

The experience of the iron ore industry in the last decade presents a wide range of lessons for the student of international trade and of contract law. Here I propose only to relate this experience to the ideas about contract advanced by Williamson and Macaulay, by briefly making a few points connected with the legal force of contracts and the utility of legally binding obligations.

1. The modern operation of the iron ore market seems in general terms to correspond to Williamson's expectations about the use of relational contracting. As already noted, however, the remarkable dominance of long-term contracting at the present time cannot be attributed solely to his key factor of recurrent idiosyncratic transactions, which is present in the iron ore industry, but in a fairly weak form. The origins of this dominance lie in the preference of some major actors in this intimate market for relational contracting, as opposed to unified governance (acquistion of mines), as a means of reducing supply uncertainties in a period of rapid growth; its consolidation we may trace first to the difficulty of maintaining viable short-term trading arrangements in a truncated market, and second to the reduction of total demand in the market to the point where many major buyers needed less ore than the minimum provided for under their LTCs. These elements of market structure and dynamics are touched on only lightly in Williamson's 1979 paper, and it would doubtless be helpful to examine other markets involving large recurrent transactions among a small number of actors to see if one can generalise as to the effect on contract choices of such additional factors.

2. The LTCs concluded in the early nineteen-seventies and before were a remarkably rigid set of documents, notwithstanding their importance in financial terms, and the length of the commitments they created. This rigidity is not wholly explicable by the need to use many of these contracts as collateral for financing purposes: contracts from other sectors, such as gas, while stricter in their "take or pay" obligations, usually attempt to provide in a controlled way for future changes in circumstances (see, e.g., Kemp (1983)). Williamson's suggestion that where parties are conscious of uncertainty they will react by providing an "elaborated governance apparatus, thereby facilitating more effective, sequential decision making" (1979:254) perhaps overrates the rationality of the parties. More specifically, one may offer an answer on a superficial level, in

line with the general conclusions of Macaulay (1963), by pointing to the minimal role of lawyers in the design of these contracts and their direct evolution from simple short-term contract forms. More profoundly, this absence from the scene of the conflict specialists that lawyers are suggests that the perspective of the parties at the time of conclusion of the contracts was one of co-operation rather than conflict, coupled with the assumption that such co-operation would of itself, without contractual stipulation, suffice to resolve any difficulties which might arise from changed circumstances. The presence of arbitration clauses in all these contracts at first sight suggests foresight of conflict or even Williamsons's category of "trilateral governance", but experience shows that parties do not in fact resort to arbitration as a mode of settlement. Incorporation of an arbitration clause, I would suggest, shows only that the parties wish to avoid the possibility that a dispute will come before the ordinary courts.

3. Despite their rigidity and lack of sophistication, iron ore LTCs are, with rare exceptions, still in place after a very violent shake-up in the industry. This remarkable result has been achieved at the expense of an almost total change in the character of the contracts in question. From fixed-term, fixed-quantity, fixed-price contracts, they have been converted into requirements contracts which may, through extension, have an indefinite term, with annually negotiated prices. This has been formally reflected in contract amendment only in regard to price, save where tonnage flexibility has been introduced through contract extension. In most cases, today, the parties are performing a relationship different from that written in the contract, in which non-contractual norms, like fairness in quantity reductions, may be more important than contractual ones. This experience may be interpreted in terms of Williamson's argument as manifesting the desire of parties to maintain as many elements of their long-term contractual relations as possible, even while altering some fundamental ones, in order to enjoy continuing advantages in terms of mutual knowledge and other "relational" values. The apparent desire of parties to provide formally for price negotiations, while leaving quantity negotiations to operate contrary to formal contractual requirements, could be seen as an interesting empirical demonstration of his feeling that quantity adjustments were less problematical than price ones (above, p. 166).

Other types of explanation might, however, also be offered. It could be argued that the pattern of contractual behaviour reflects changes in the relative bargaining strength of buyers and sellers. Buyers were forced to accede to sellers' demands for prices in excess of contract levels in 1973 and 1974 out of fear of a drying up of supplies in a market that still seemed to be in a phase of growth. Subsequent extra-contractual quantity reductions, and the arrival of tonnage flexibility, may be seen as expressions of the dominant position of buyers in a shrinking market, a position reinforced by the introduction – again at buyers' behest – of annual price negotiations as the means of securing price adjustments, rather than any kind of indexing system. The leading buyers – the Japanese and, to a lesser extent, the Germans – have thus attained a position where they can bargain on price with the threat of exercise of their contractual or extra-contractual discretion to reduce quantities, a discretion constrained only by nondiscrimination requirements of a type commonly associated, in domestic or Community law, with dominant enterprises. This situation, in which it has become artificial to make a rigid separation of quantity and price negotiations, offers ample scope for what Williamson would call "opportunistic" behaviour. In this connection it is worth noting that the Japanese mills appear to have deliberately enlarged their freedom of manoeuvre in the last few years by continuing to undertake new long-term purchase commitments even while taking below the minimum on existing contracts.

4. In the current – and continuing – state of the steel market, the only iron ore contracts likely to be performed strictly according to their terms are those incorporating annual price revisions and a tonnage flexibility clause. There must, however, be serious doubt about the practical enforceability of these contracts in the event of breach. Say a buyer refuses, in breach of his nondiscrimination obligation, to take any ore in a given year from a particular supplier under such a contract. In order to measure the seller's loss the court, or the arbitrator, will need to determine both what price the parties would (or should) have fixed *and* what quantity the buyer would (or should) have taken. Some courts and arbitrators might accept this double challenge: others might not. Without caricaturing too much we might say that the performable contracts may be unenforceable and the enforceable contracts may be unperformable. Yet in this unpromising situation, in which one might think that a series of annual contracts would serve the interests of the parties just as well, sellers cling tenaciously to the maintenance of existing LTCs and the creation of new ones, and the attitude of the major buyers is complaisant. Sellers and buyers alike, moreover, are very sensitive to questions of nomenclature, and clearly distinguish contractual elements in their relationship (agreements) from non-contractual ones (side letters, memoranda, and so on): they show none of the indifference to the existence of an identifiable contract manifested by some of the manufacturers interviewed by Macaulay, or by Beale and Dugdale. How are we to explain this attachment to contractual form? I would make three suggestions.

First, the LTC facilitates the dealings of buyer and seller with important third parties. It reassures lenders – even today, as the Carajas development shows. It offers tidy answers to governments anxious for a fair return on their natural resources.

Second, it provides a fairly comprehensive set of parameters for the parties' regular – or irregular – dealings and discussions. If problems arise, say on a matter like quality, the LTC offers a series of elements – price, quantity, shipping etc. – which, at least at the beginning of the negotiation, are fixed points of reference. In this way the contract may provide, albeit in a rather weak form, "the foundation for strategic manoevures in the game of negotiated settlement" to which Macaulay refers (Macaulay, 1977:515).

Third, and most important, the LTC creates a privileged trading relationship between the parties, which is of great importance in times of difficult markets, of glut or scarcity, in the sense that it reinforces, by rendering unambiguous, each party's claim to remain in business relations with the other. It thus gives better, but not absolute, security to the trading position of each party.

For this purpose, however, the legal quality that counts is not enforceability, but formality. By using this legal form the parties sanctify their intentions. As one seller puts it: "The legal contract... reinforces our moral position." In a glutted market for a product substantially interchangeable with those of one's competitors, and with a single, restricted set of buyers, a reinforced moral position must be a very valuable asset.

Appendix

Tonnage Flexibility

5. Quantity Flexibility:

(1) In the event difficulties prevent Buyers from receiving deliveries of the tonnage to be delivered under the Extension Contract, or in the event that Seller is unable to effect the delivery of the tonnage under the Extension Contract, Buyers may request Seller or Seller may request Buyers, forty-five days prior to the commencement of each contract year, to reduce the tonnage to be delivered in the said contract year, and the party receiving the request shall comply.

Furthermore, at the times when Buyers submit to Seller the tentative monthly shipping schedules covering the next quarter, Buyers or Seller may request for a revision of such reduction in tonnage and the party receiving such request shall give it serious consideration in recognition of the long-term contractual relationship between the parties in a spirit of mutual cooperation and assistance.

(2) In the event of a reduction in tonnage to be delivered under the Extension Contract in accordance with item 5(1) hereof at the request of Buyers, Buyers shall ensure that Seller is treated fairly so that no discrimination or disadvantage in the tonnage reduction shall occur compared with other major suppliers and shall exert their best efforts so as not to bring about any reduction in the Seller's share of iron ore purchases by Buyers from major suppliers which are each supplying iron ore to Buyers under similar conditions.

Similarly, in the event of such reduction being effected at the request of Seller, Seller shall ensure a fair treatment of Buyers so that no discrimination or disadvantage shall occur as compared with other users.

Bibliography

BEALE, HUGH and TONY DUGDALE (1976) "Contracts between Businessmen: Planning and the Use of Contractual Remedies", 2 *British Journal of Law and Society 45.*

KEMP, KAREN (1983) "Applying the Hardship Clause", 1 *Journal of Energy and Natural Resources Law* 119.

KURCZEWSKI, JACEK and KAZIMIERZ FRIESKE (1977) "Some Problems in the Legal Regulation of the Activities of Economic Institutions", 11 *Law and Society Review* 489.

MACAULAY, STEWART (1963) "Non-contractual Relations in Business: A preliminary study", 28 *American Sociological Review* 55.
– (1977) "Elegant Models, Empirical Pictures, and the Complexities of Contract", 11 *Law and Society Review* 507.
MACNEIL IAN (1974) "The Many Futures of Contracts", 47 *Southern California Law Review* 691.
– (1978) "Contracts: Adjustment of Long-term Contractual Relations under Classical, Neo-classical and Relational Contract Law", 72 *Northwestern University Law Review* 854.
– (1981) "Economic Analysis of Contractual Relations", in P. Burrows and C. G. Veljanowski (eds.) *The Economic Approach to Law*. London: Butterworths.
PALAY, THOMAS (1984) "Comparative Institutional Economics: The Governance of Rail Freight Contracting", 13 *Journal of Legal Studies* 265.
STREIT, MANFRED (1980) "On the Use of Futures Markets for Stabilization Purposes", 116 *Weltwirtschaftliches Archiv* 493.
WILLIAMSON, OLIVER, MICHAEL WACHTER and J. HARRIS (1975) "Understanding the Employment Relation: The Analysis of Idiosyncratic Exchange", 6 *Bell Journal of Economics* 250.
WILLIAMSON, OLIVER and MICHAEL WACHTER (1978) "Obligational Markets and the Mechanics of Inflation", 9 *Bell Journal of Economics* 549.
– (1971) "The Vertical Integration of Production: Market Failure Considerations", 61 *American Economic Review* 112.
– (1975) *Markets and Hierarchies: Analysis and Antitrust Implications*. New York: The Free Press.

IV.
Organisation

The Contribution of Economics to Legal Analysis: The Concept of the Firm

GERARD FARJAT*
Nice

As a proponent of economic law, I am profoundly convinced of the reality and appropriateness of the contribution made to legal analysis by the social sciences. The discipline of economic law emerged from the interpenetration of economics and legal science, in ideology, in theory and in social practice. There is a need for a new deal of the academic cards: in particular, the training of lawyers should be modified to take account of the contribution of economics to the functioning of the legal system. Furthermore, the contribution of economics to law is not confined to a purely auxiliary role, but should be taken further, into an enquiry in the legal system itself.

The concept of the firm is certainly, in French law, a fruitful field in which to raise these questions. On the one hand, because it allows a multiplicity of localised influences of economic analysis on law to be taken into account; but also because one may note a relative failure of legal theories – at least the more ambitious ones – of the firm. While company law (an assemblage of one-off solutions), and interfirm relations or those between firms and the State exist there is no legal concept of the firm.

What causes the difficulty here is that the firm is. to begin with, not a legal concept on which an approach might be based. Instead, it is the firm that has put its questions to lawyers (the firm as a subject in search of an author!), rather than lawyers who have enquired into the legitimacy of using economic concepts in legal science.

In fact, the right question is not so much what use is economics, but what question the lawyer ought to ask. In the area of the firm, it would seem that lawyers have instead let the problems be dictated to them.

We shall therefore first look at how the firm has forced open the doors of the law (with the doorkeepers' connivance). But this task calls for a critical balance-sheet, which we shall also draw up. The concept of firm will be employed, thereby, giving an opportunity for raising questions pertaining to the field of lawyers.

* Translated from the French by Iain Fraser.

I. Some Contributions by Economics to Company Law

In order to pick out significant possible contributions of polictical economy to legal analysis, one may look at all the elements that make up the legal system. The law appears as a *communications system* between *subjects*, acting through *norms* and *procedures*, and establishing *relationships* (rights and obligations) among these subjects. One might highlight political economy's contributions to these various elements by concentrating on the concept of the firm. The firm appears to some to be a new type of legal subject; in any case, new relationships among firms or between firms and the State, initially perceived as being economic, are being "legalised". Obviously, some legal norms refer to the economy; it is not merely in procedures that these changes are reflected. Ultimately, is it not law as a communications system that is affected?

1. Legal Subjects

In France it is the theme of "the firm as a nascent legal subject" that has "popularised" the concept of the firm: the latter is presented as a *rival to existing legal subjects*[1], i.e. the owners. The firm as a new "economic and social reality", as defined by economists, is considered as literally imposing itself on the legal system, which should take account of new interests (in particular those of wage earners). The very importance of the firm, regarded as "one of the foundations of our industrial, technological, scientific and urban society" (Champaud, 1971:1), is held to justify its promotion to legal subject. The clearest statement of economic determinism is from Jean Paillusseau: "the firm turns to its advantage mechanisms and techniques conceived in the past, to give life to a collectivity of associates", or again, "the power... which was organised in such a way as to permit representation of the associates, would be created by the need to administer and govern the firm. It would be organised according to the practice of company administration..." (Paillusseau, 1967). It is exceptional for the influence of *"scientific rationality"* on law to be asserted with such vigour.

2. Legal Relationships

The firm is the area of two types of relationship: first, the *internal relationships*, which initiated legal debate on the firm. The conflictual relationships between capital and labour had to be harmonised by a redistribution of rights within a new legal community: the firm. Another part of internal relationships is the distribution of power within commercial companies (shareholder representatives become directors so as to ensure sound economic management).

However, the main reason in France for such widespread use (outside labour law) of the concept of the firm is the existence of new potentially litigious relationships, this time *external relationships*, which first appear in the field of political economy. It is significant that an important circular on competition law

[1] The most notable work, which attracted great attention in French doctrine, is by Despax (1957).

treats certain relationships between firms – of union or dependency – as "economic links" (Circular, 14. 2. 1978, Dalloz 1978 Leg. 142). These are indeed initially "economic links", since they have not yet given rise to litigation, still less to statute, but subsequently they are "legalised".

On the nature of these relationships, some clarification is called for. The firm, and the relationships to which it gives rise, have developed, in the transition from an atomistic economy of isolated exploiters to a molecular economy centralised through large groups or the State (Farjat, 1982:90). Though State-firm relationships did not exist in the liberal epoch, there was an economic policy on the part of government, concerning both the behaviour or conduct and the structures of firms. Such a policy, whether authoritarian as a kind of economic *ordre public*, or by agreement as in a contractual or concerted economy, does in fact create new relationships. These relationships are, to be sure, initially "economic", based as they are on analyses of schemes, concepts etc. supplied by economic science and economic practice. The same is true of the relationships of the private economy. Examples are those between small, legally autonomous, firms and the big firms they supply with parts (subcontracting) or for whom they act as distributors (exclusive or selective distribution), or those between subsidiaries and the parent company. These are "economic links" which are sometimes not even formalised by a legal document[2].

Though, to begin with, these new relationships are essentially analysed and constructed by reference to economic science and practice, gradually, starting from these economic bases, law takes over.

3. Norms

The economic sciences supply law with numerous norms, or are offered the possibility of doing so. A few examples will suffice.

Many might be taken from French bankruptcy law. For instance, an Order of 23 September 1967 relating to the "economic and financial rehabilitation of certain firms" applies to firms "whose closure, being of such a nature as to cause serious harm to the national or regional economy, may be avoided on terms deemed compatible with creditors' interests". An economic and financial rehabilitation plan may be drawn up and imposed on the creditors under the supervision of the judges. More generally, as has been said, the bankruptcy procedures no longer really have the aim of ensuring the subjective rights of the creditors of a debtor that has suspended payment, but have become instruments for "restructuring flagging capital under the supervision of the State and of private economic authorities" (Boy *et al.*, 1982). Whereas in classical liberal law bankruptcy "was seen as the natural consequence" of a legal settlement of conflicts of rights, a new law which tends to favour economic analyses is taking shape. "Should the economic unit be eliminated, integrated (restructured), or saved, in terms of this or that economic interest?" (Farjat, 1982:112). Bankruptcy

[2] Not only when these links are founded upon economic dependence (the stronger partner has no need of a contract), but also where there are forms of equal collaboration (the partners wish to be able to break it off).

law, having turned into the law of firms in difficulty, no longer obeys a legal logic (termination of payment, creditors' rights) but economic diagnoses, strategies and policies, and it puts forward "remedies". A firm no longer *suspends payment but is put in that position,* by its banker, its major customer company or the group it depends on, following an economic strategy. There is therefore a multiplication of economic criteria – norms – in both the public (State aid) and private economy.

The multiplication of economic norms is equally clear in *competition law.* The basis for an opinion on the advisability or otherwise of an economic agreement is an "economic balance-sheet". Interference with competition is unpenalised where it has "the effect of furthering economic progress..." (Farjat, 1982:516).

4. Procedures

It might be thought that these would constitute the hinterland of law[3]. However, the emergence of inter-firm relationships established according to economic analyses and policies, and of economic norms, also affect procedures. In most of the socialist countries economic-law courts or tribunals have appeared (State arbitration in the USSR, the Contracts Tribunal in the GDR). In France and in Belgium the creation of an economic court or tribunal has been suggested (Jacquemin and Schrans, 1977:412). But even now the creation of new channels for settling conflicts can be noted. Special mention should be made of the various Commissions, originating in the US and employed in all free-economy countries (such as the Monopolies Commission or the Securities Exchange Commission).

One of the justifications put forward is the need to reproduce within these bodies the mechanisms of the market, the rules of the economic game. The Commissions, composed of "professionals", and of economic agents, are held to be inspired by the "natural" law of supply and demand. Introducing the State and its judges into this economic machinery would mean violating that natural law (!). As Schumpeter wrote, lawyers' ability to apply antitrust laws might be doubted. In any case, the question of the communications system is posed.

5. The Law as Communications System

This is the level where the question of a possible contribution of economics to legal analysis is decisively posed. The law, as a means of communication, is simultaneously a language, a set of ideas, concepts and modes of arguing and analysis, and institutions and techniques that enable the system to operate (bodies of lawyers, educational structures etc.). Let us think, for instance, of *"doctrine"*, which in France tends to be made into a source of law, and whose influence is in any case not negligible; its role is to constantly refine concepts, norms and procedures, for the better functioning of the system.

Has political economy an influence on the communications system?

Undoubtedly. A whole section of French doctrine specifically asserts the need

[3] As Goldman (1968:297) wrote about competition law: "... the law, if one still wishes it well, can proceed in only two ways: by creating categories or by instituting procedures".

for a new discipline that will guarantee political economy a privileged place in legal analysis: economic law, or company law[4]. "In some ways it is better not to be a lawyer in order to study economic law", as B. Chenot puts it (1965). This was also the position of the German founding fathers of economic law. It was likewise that of the Soviet founding fathers, one of whom maintained that Soviet economic law was "political economy translated into articles and paragraphs"[5]. In French-language doctrine, there are many authors who think that the explanation for the birth of economic law is a fundamental mutation in the law. According to Claude Champaud, "economic law is a specific legal feeling applied to a varied body of rules. Only the feeling is really new" (1967:215). "Economic law is a law of regrouping and synthesis, which enables lawyers to consider the needs of the economy in all their breadth and see what rules they have engendered... Thus, economic law may today be seen as a way of looking at – perhaps even feeling – legal problems in terms of economic needs", writes M. Vasseur (1959). "Economic law is, then, less a branch of legal science than an academic discipline formed by the links between legal sciences and economic sciences", write A. Jacquemin and G. Schrans (1974).

Applied to the firm, this notion amounts to the construction of a law on companies on the basis of management needs. This is precisely the idea of Jean Paillusseau (1967).

The attempt by doctrine to assign to law the role of servant of political economy clearly makes the law into an *instrument,* whereas previously it was regarded as a vehicle of religious or moral values, or as conveying values of its own (human rights, ownership). Let there be no doubt about it: in our present-day societies, the "ought", the "*sollen*", is constantly being taken from the social sciences, especially economics. Hence the frequent assertions of the law's "backwardness" or "maladaptation".

The law has, as it were, become "scientific", in two ways. On the one hand, it must make room for the social sciences (as, for instance, the sources of the concepts it uses); on the other hand, it is itself changing (in its methods of arguing: critical approach, appeal to dialectical analysis, "observation" of society using legal concepts, experimentation with legal innovations, etc.). It is not by chance that the legal system is coming apart, with a redistribution of topics around the specific "objects" concerned. This redistribution is taking place not only in connection with social topics such as the family or the economy, but even within these social areas, in terms of social distinctions external to the law: consumers, the environment, the firm, etc. What happens next is "legalisation". One must therefore enquire into the exact dimensions of the movement.

[4] The expression "business law" is sometimes also used to express the need for a new discipline.

[5] The words are from Stuchka, for many years people's commissar for justice, particularly at the creation of the USSR. Pachoukanis had a subtler analysis.

II. A Critical Balance-Sheet

It is not an easy task to give an opinion on the "movements" taking place between the two disciplines. A truly scientific attitude would necessitate putting oneself outside both systems, legal and economic. Knowledge of both, law and economics, is no guarantee of success – nor *a fortiori* is the knowledge of one of these disciplines. All we can give is the critical observations of a lawyer "open" to the economic sciences.

The first observation is that the impact of economics on the law is not so corrosive as is often claimed. Instead, economics acts as a reinforcement of the law.

The second series of observations will relate to the very ideal of a "contribution" by an academic discipline to the law. Without being specialised in epistemology, we feel that these "exchanges" between disciplines are suspect. This will not however prevent us from formulating a few methodological propositions.

1. Political economy as a reinforcement of law

Looking at French positive law, especially on the question of the firm, one finds that economics has not brought any "subversion" of the legal system. Instead, it would seem as if economics has tended to strengthen the bases of the legal system.

The firm has not become a legal subject in any country with a capitalist economy. The legal subject remains the proprietor, whether natural person or legal person. It cannot even be said that the proprietor's powers have been seriously reduced (except, very exceptionally, in the context of bankruptcy proceedings). It is significant that in company law judges scrupulously respect the principle of non-intervention in the administration of company affairs (de Juglart *et al.*, 1982:677), despite a few calls for action on the basis of doctrine. It is not conceivable, in a liberal economy based on private ownership of the means of production, for the owners of capital to be deprived of decision-making power. "There is, therefore, necessarily a duality between the legal person who is proprietor of the firm and the proprietor's economic unity and pre-eminence" (Farjat, 1982:104). It is significant that this duality ends only in the case of nationalisation (the public enterprise being then a legal subject).

Following one radical critical opinion, the concept of the firm is "the technocratic manifestation aimed at saving the essentials of capitalist domination" (Bourjol *et al.*, 1978:60). Georges Ripert had already in one of his works criticised the idea of ownership as a social function, calling it hypocrisy. For this convinced supporter of liberalism, owners ought to be defended as such, without pretending they are "functionaries". Having presented the owners as functionaries, one would now seek to present them as managers! The concept of enterprise and the references to management needs would then have essentially a *legitimising function*. This hypothesis merits serious consideration. As has been remarked, "Has this question of a dialogue between law and the social sciences... not come just in time to make up for the loss of credibility by the legitimation notions that legal thinking was traditionally based on?" (Ost and van de Kerchove, 1983:1). In a country like France where private property in the means of production is the object of considerable ideological dispute, it is not surprising for the social sciences to be called upon to contribute their support to the solutions of positive law. It seems to us beyond doubt that in labour law the various European debates have for half a century been essentially ideological in scope. By that we mean that the legal consequences for wage-earners' place within the firm have not reached the level of their aspirations.

However, the contribution of the social sciences is not exclusively "ideological", in the area of pure debate. The authors of the radical critical opinion mentioned above admit the existence of "profound changes in commercial law" and "traces of movement beyond the bourgeois legal form..." in French positive law (Bourjol *et al.*, 1978). If economic law is today "competing" with commercial law, that is because of the taking into account of public and collective interests the firm is recognised to have. The firm has "invaded the public space of economic law", it has been "deprivatised for reasons of public utility", as Claude Champaud notes (1979:1).

Even in labour law, where the practical consequences of recognition of the firm would be harder to reconcile with the basis of liberal law, some very partial reflections of the idea – such as works councils or restrictions on right of dismissal – are constraints on capital owners.

What seems probable to us is that *in very "legalised" or very "administered" societies it is the law and the State*[6]*, as the dominant modes of social control, that largely orient research in the social sciences and that build into their systems the "usable" results of these sciences.* We feel that in France at any rate "the law" in fact opens up to the social sciences only those areas it wants to. But this very area of thought, on establishing "relationships" between disciplines, calls for critical consideration.

2. Thoughts on the Contribution of the Sciences to Law

According to the most widespread approach, knowledge, and economic "discoveries", gradually impose themselves on law, which has an irritating tendency to lag behind economics. This approach is followed by many French lawyers who support economic law. But it was also that of proponents of labour law in the past. Thus, P. Durand denounced "the lagging of legal analysis behind social reality" and invited doctrine to go beyond the contribution of law and jurisprudence and seek support from sociology and political economy "at the frontiers of law" (1956:73). Going still further back, the Italian author Vivante stated in his 1893 treatise on commercial law that "one must consider commercial practice, dominated as it is by great economic laws, and make the study of law into an observational science".

This thinking, while we do not regard it as wrong, does call for a few observations, or even reservations.

[6] We are thinking of the industrialised liberal societies, for the law, and the socialist societies, for the State.

1. It is not accepted by the whole of doctrine. One section of French doctrine remains more or less explicitly attached to natural law, and therefore does not invoke the social sciences' aid to justify legal solutions. Those who invoke the social sciences and regret the slow development of law are often the lawyers promoting new branches of law that have difficulty in making headway: specialists in labour law, welfare law, consumer law, economic law etc. For nearly a century now developments in the law (especially those linked with the Welfare State) have always met a stumbling-block in a large part (probably a large majority) of the legal world and its "authorities" (such as Georges Ripert in France). But this attitude is in no way peculiar to the world of law. Liberal economists like Hayek, far from demanding that the law reflect or follow economic teachings, hope for a return to the "pure" law of the liberal heyday. In the view of liberal political economy, it is instead *the classical legal structures that ensure the economy's success* (private property, contractual freedom etc.).

2. One is, then, brought to considering, to each his own law, to each his own economics. In more scholarly fashion, many epistemologists analyse the science in a way that challenges the prevailing thinking. Scholars do not "discover" social "realities", but construct them using conceptual systems. There are several political economies. Doubtless, there are hardly any economic facts of "laws" convincingly obvious enough to impose a change in the law. The facts are, in a way, "constructed", and do not directly dictate a solution. There could not in any rigorous way be a genuine opposition of facts and law. There is always controversy, and each side has its own facts.

Thus, the idea of a systematic contribution to the law may be criticised. It smacks of an outdated "scientism". Finally, and more particularly, it is far too idealistic. It ignores the *social forces,* their *interests* and their differing *value judgements.*

Let us say clearly that today the advanced state of the social sciences does not allow any single legal solution to be presented as imposed by scientific analysis, by scientific rationality. When it comes to social relationships, to the economic interests of subjects, then material and moral values are always involved in a legal solution.

3. Methodological Propositions

The foregoing observations lead us to a first proposition which may sound banal; but since the banality concerns more the ideas than the practice, we shall repeat it. Researchers should display enormous prudence and profound relativism in formulating analyses, and still more, solutions.

Those who refuse the contributions of science or facts in the name of moral values or natural law ought, failing reference to the modern lessons of epistemology, to meditate on Pascal's saying: "he who makes the angel makes the beast". Those who invoke science should be aware that people may be executed or locked up in the name of science. The psychiatric hospital may be used as a punishment. And those who think that science may be either bourgeois or proletarian may develop police-state epistemologies. When it comes to the social sciences, the authority of science depends on bets, and of course those who *wager* have more to win than others!

Staying with the obvious, we shall in the second place point out that the various *disciplines* that analyse or construct social phenomena are *complementary*. In one sense it is absurd to ask whether economics can contribute to legal analysis or *vice versa*. The carving up of social "reality" according to disciplines is an artificial mutilation, however necessary in view of the inability of one researcher to cover the whole range of human phenomena.

The firm is a social phenomenon – a set of social relationships – founded on mechanisms that are analysed by various scientific disciplines (economics, sociology etc.) and according to differing value systems (those of unions, employers, management, workers etc.). It is also a locus of conflicts of interests. One should bear in mind that there is a constant dialectic between these various elements and systems and the law, which may favour one aspect or another, and itself have a very variable place in society.

These necessary, albeit vague, preliminaries may allow the formulation of more precise propositions on the relationships between economics and law.

1. One of the primary contributions of economics to legal analysis may paradoxically be maintaining law's important position in most industrialised societies, and *legitimising legal analysis as such*. The immense amount of "vulgar" economics (or sociology) diffused among the public at large and lawyers in particular creates a risk of falsification of legal analysis and of law's true place. But *while a little political economy* (especially that "creeping economics" that tends to pass itself off as "obvious") *may turn lawyers themselves away from the law, a lot of it may bring them back*. Tackling the economic disciplines gives one a healthy scepticism. If for no other reason, it shows one that there are several political economies, which always differ both in analyses and solutions.

This elementary observation ought to make lawyers extremely careful about using political economy. But beyond this, one has to recognise that the economic sciences may justify the – relative – autonomy of the law and its analytical tools.

One pointed illustration of this statement is that whereas French legal doctrine constantly refers to economists' formulas to define the legal concept of the firm, economists for their part have recourse to the concept of legal person to define the economic concept of the firm. What economists regard as the safest criterion of the firm is legal autonomy.

At a higher level, the law supplies, or helps to supply, important categories of political economy: the concept of ownership, and those of private and public. Surely even the fundamental distinction among contemporary economies rests upon the nature, whether private or public, of the ownership of the means of production?

The first methodological proposition that we feel may be agreed upon is as follows: *legal analysis may constitute one of the methods of analysing social reality in legalised societies*, or at the very least may be used in the same way as the social sciences. Lawyers wishing to make the law operate like a science ought to be saying that their specific contribution can be nothing other than legal. Using their own concepts, they can analyse, or construct, a part of social phenomena. On the basis of this view, they can greatly contribute towards the analysis conducted by economists. The precondition, however, is not to adopt the totally false analysis whereby the law is held to be an instrument or a "toolkit".

2. The second methodological proposition that may be put forward is that political economy, and the social sciences in general, necessarily have an influence on legal analysis through the "facts" that they "deliver". The most common task for lawyers is to characterise the concrete facts so as to bring them into their system. But the facts are not "raw", not directly legible using a legal code. *The social sciences, especially economics, constantly construct and destroy, or in one word modify, the facts that lawyers work on in producing law.*

3. Finally, economics may enrich and change the law itself, not merely the facts. Just as the law is not outside economics, so "economics is not outside law (or the legal relationship), but contributes to constituting it"[7].

Legal concepts are never purely "formal" (except, no doubt, as regards procedure) but correspond to "specific" or "substantive" elements. For instance, the right of ownership corresponds to very specific prerogatives *(usus, fructus, abusus).* If lawyers can characterise specific facts, it is because a relationship between the facts and the legal concepts exists.

Economic analyses may modify the categories of law, create new ones, bring new elements into the construction of a legal concept, and redistribute roles. This is the way we have seen political economy operating in our first part. But equally rich contributions from law to political economy could certainly be found – especially as regards the firm. If one economic lawyer who is "open" to economics has been led to defend the role of the law, it is because he has been able to note the flaws in political economy due to lack of knowledge in law.

Bibliography

Bourjol, Maurice et al. (1978) *Pour une critique du droit.* Maspero: P. U. G.

Boy, Laurence, Robert Guillaumond and Antoine Jeammaud (1982) *Droit des faillites et restructuration du capital.* Collection critique du droit. Grenoble: Presses Universitaires de Grenoble.

Champaud, Claude (1967) "Contribution à la définition du droit économique", Revue Dalloz 215.

– (1979) "Pouvoir public et entreprises défaillantes", *Humanisme et Entreprise* 1.

Chenot, Bernard (1965) *Organisation économique de l'Etat.* Paris: Dalloz.

Commaille, Jacques (1982) "Esquisse d'analyse des rapports entre droit et sociologie, les sociologies juridiques" *Revue interdisciplinaire d'études juridiques* 26.

de Juglart, Michel *et al.* (1982) *Traité de Droit Commercial* Vol. 2. (3rd ed.) Paris: Montchrestien.

Despax, Michel (1957) *L'entreprise et le droit.* Paris: Librairie Générale de Droit et de Jurisprudence.

[7] We are borrowing the formula (which he applies to politics) from Commaille (1982:26).

Durand, Paul (1956) "La connaissance du phénomène juridique et les tâches de la doctrine moderne", *Revue Dalloz* 73.

Farjat, Gerard (1982) *Droit économique*. Paris: Thémis.

Goldman, Berthold (1968) "Obstacle tenant au droit interne des sociétés", (Rapport), *Revue du Marché Commun* 297.

Jacquemin, Alex and Guy Schrans (1974) *Le droit économique*. Paris: Presses Universitaires de France.

– (1977) "Eléments structurels d'une magistrature économique", *Revue trimestrielle de droit commercial* 412.

Ost, François and Michel van de Kerchove (1983) *Jalons pour une épistémologie de la recherche interdisciplinaire en droit. Revue interdisciplinaire d'études juridiques*. Brussels: Faculté Universitaires Saint-Louis.

Paillusseau, Jean (1967) *La société anonyme, technique d'organisation de l'entreprise*. Paris: Sirey.

Vasseur, Michel (1959) *Le droit de la réforme des structures industrielles et des économies régionales*. Paris: Librairie Générale de Droit et de Jurisprudence.

Potential and Limits of Economic Analysis: The Constitution of the Firm

ERICH SCHANZE
Frankfurt

1. Characteristics and Limits of Economic Analysis

In his legal theory, Immanuel Kant rejects the articulation of a solely empirical theory of law by equating it graphically to the wooden head in a fable by Phaedrus: "A head which may be beautiful, but alas! it has no brains!" (Kant 1798:32). As part of the continuing search for substantive principles of justice, much current legal theory concerns itself with exploring the potential for and limits of an economic explanation of the legal order. This is, indeed, an unprecedented and often painful exercise. Economics – a science which relies on use of everyday terms such as "market" and "price" – may have a parvenu appearance compared to the body of classical theories which deal with the governance of human affairs. By operating on the basis of a model which assumes that the individual strives to maximize his own utility, economics obviously makes a virtue of selfishness[1]. The notion that institutions are not founded on ethical first principles, but rather are modalities for channeling transactions, and are themselves subjected to a selection process in a market place for institutions, appears to be the very realization of Burke's prediction that "the age of chivalry is gone. That of sophisters, calculators, and economists has succeeded and the glory of Europe is extinguished forever". Kenneth Arrow refers to Burke's dictum in his lecture on "The Limits of Organization". He goes on to say: "The rather dry, recondite calculation of gains and losses does not lead to great enthusiasm. It does not offer magic resolutions to difficult problems... Rationality, after all, has to do with means and ends and their relation. It does not specify what the ends are. It only tries to make us aware of the congruence or

[1] The concept of self-interest as the motivating force of institutional development is no specialty of neo-institutional economists. In his "Geist des römischen Rechts" (Spirit of Roman Law) (1852:292 seq.) the famous German jurist Rudolph von Jhering celebrates selfishness as "the true and moving force of classical Roman law": "Selfishness is the motive of Roman universality – selfishness... the basic pattern of the Roman character." Jhering goes on to describe Roman law as "the religion of selfishness." Within the liberal credo this is, of course, a self-fulfilling analysis.

dissonance between the two. So ultimately any value discussion must come to a rest temporarily on unanalyzed postulates. There is an infinite regress as we try to justify one value judgment in terms of supposedly deeper ones". (Arrow 1974:17).

There are, certainly, limits to an economic analysis of human behavior. I might briefly refer here to the short but impressive papers by Coase (1978) and Nutter (1979), who reject current pretensions of an economic "imperialism" within the social sciences. The seemingly higher degree of optimism expressed in a recent series of lectures by George Stigler (1980) rests on the firm conviction that the science of the self-interested individual should not be intermingled with ethical preoccupations.

To be explicit about this at the very beginning: I do not regard economic theory as an exclusive means of justifying individual or social action, and neither do I consider it to be the primary source of substantive principles for the guiding of human conduct. Economic theory should serve as a means of discovery, a means of understanding the institutional context of human conduct. Thus, economic theory could hardly replace the Kantian vision of an ethical order of human affairs, whether or not one wishes to accept the validity of the Kantian principles of moral decision-making. The analytical model includes, however, a number of important qualifications which demonstrate, in part, a structural affinity to the formality of Kantian ethics: the notion of basic respect for individual preferences and rational choice, and the insistence on clear definitions of individual entitlements. Additional features of the model include an understanding of institutions not as barriers, but rather as open-ended and variation-rich facilitative frameworks for individual and collective choices and related transactions; as well as the postulate that every institutional arrangement should be so defined that it tends to internalize the total cost associated with a given transaction or activity. For those who think in terms of hierarchies of stable norms, the most offensive characteristic of the model may be its general notion of an ever-changing equilibrium of institutional arrangements, selected through a process of substitution at the margin.

As in any theory, there are problem-prone interfaces between the model and reality. Important limits to the economic model lie in the conception of the individual wealth maximizer (who has in fact to deal with bounded rationality), in the problem of the initial assignment (or distribution) of rights, and in the relative vagueness of the magic term "preferences"[2], which, of course, can be used not only to analyze, but also to justify strange outcomes. Furthermore, the price system itself does not always function perfectly. If it is applied to the model under more complicated and more realistic assumptions than those of the near-perfect conditions of complete information, free competition and costless transactions, results are frequently imprecise or, at least, can be given only as a range of possible results within the boundaries of convex functions. The formal elegance of a marginal analysis operating with the Pareto and the Kaldor-Hicks criteria does not tell us, as Kenneth Boulding (1952) has noted in referring to the

[2] A classic and concise exposition of these problems is given in March's (1978:593 seq.) chapter on the treatment of tastes.

Pareto criterion, whether we are dealing with the tip of a mole's hill or the top of Mount Everest.

All of this, in my view, does not preclude our exploring the potential of economic analysis. It may be, though, that we have to be more modest in selecting our theories. Theories are, almost by definition, to be evaluated on the basis of their logic, coherence and completeness in explaining reality. A less rigid test may result from a traditional concern of economics: the test of the relative heuristic utility of the theory. It may even be enough to inquire on the basis of intuitive standards whether, in an obscure problem area, a particular theory produces a marginal net increase in clarification. In terms of this limited research standard, a theory may be said to be useful if it produces more scientific benefits than scientific cost. A theory may, of course, be barren in the sense that it only changes the semantics of a stated problem and is circular in substance. Certain uses of systems theory and semiotics have exhibited this kind of scientific sterility in the recent past. However, the kind of analysis presented in the *Journal of Law and Economics*, in the *Journal of Legal Studies*, in the *Bell Journal of Economics* and in many leading American law reviews, and more recently in the *International Journal of Law and Economics* and the *Zeitschrift für die gesamte Staatswissenschaft* can hardly be called a sterile part of economic and legal research. The renewed interest in the economic functions of legal institutions, or what might be broadly termed "neo-institutionalism", has had a substantial impact on both disciplines.

The development of *transactional economics*, inspired by the research of Coase and Williamson, may be regraded as one of the most important theoretical movements in economics since the development and reception of game theory (cf. Picot 1982). On the other hand, the economic impact of specific legal arrangements has recently become a central and explicit theme of legal theory and practice. It may well be that transactional economics – with its explicit recognition of institutions as essential variables, and not as remote circumstantial conditions in the anonymous world of the *ceteres pares* – will lead to a unification of legal and economic questions in a renewed tradition of political economy. However, a coherent picture is far from being established. Under the labels of "new institutional economics" and "economic analysis of law" one can find a wide variety of approaches which have a common core in the application of modern price theory to institutions, but which are otherwise so diverse that it is difficult to indicate further synoptic features. A survey of the different research approaches of some of the most well-known proponents of these theories may serve as an initial orientation.

Posner (1977) and his school are chiefly concerned with a "positive" analysis of the common law. They contrast the "efficiency" of judge-made rules to those imposed by regulatory measures. They are thus pursuing one theme of Coase's 1960 article, which pointed specifically to the economic logic of Victorian judge-made nuisance law.

Coase (1937, 1960) himself is obviously less interested in "proving" the efficiencies of judge-made law than in examining the empirical variety of modes of transacting in the light of cost considerations.

While the economist Coase emphasizes the economic functions of law, the lawyer/economist Calabresi (1970) stresses a more rational design of institutionalization in a law reform perspective. He also presents a general framework of regulatory modes (Calabresi/Melamed 1972) which was recently elaborated upon and clarified by Polinsky (1979, 1980).

Williamson (1975, 1980, 1984), and Schenk (1980, 1981), are interested in the macro-aspects of institutional design in a transactional economics perspective. While Williamson works mainly on the level of broad comparisons of the properties of institutional arrangements within the markets and hierarchies paradigm, Schenk uses the methodology of transactional economics to compare the constituent elements of political-economic systems.

2. The Coasean Approach

My interest focuses on an economic analysis of institutional variety, in the context of *economic law* (in the broad sense of the legal organization of subjects and objects of economic transactions). In this area, I am confident that discriminating between and selecting legal regimes on the basis of cost considerations may be a safe and productive analytical approach.

My current concern is to reexamine the basis for the analysis laid out by Coase in two seminal articles, the first on the theory of the firm (Coase 1937) and the second on the problem of social cost (Coase 1960). By emphasizing the starting point of the theory, I argue against the shorthand reception of the theory which found expression in the early expositions of the so-called "property rights theory", which has had a considerable influence on the reception of this body of learning particularly outside of the United States of America. This school is characterized by the attempt to follow *one* theme of Coase's 1960 article. It reconstructs every institutional setting as the outcome of an individual bargaining process, and discredits any arrangement which – at a first (or possibly a very shy second) glance – does not readily demonstrate the features that would intuitively follow from a hypothetical bargaining situation. A recent paper by Furubotn (1981) on codetermination is a good example of this kind of analysis.

Let us briefly reconsider the Coasean approach. The constitution of the firm is a most suitable topic because it is the explicit theme of Coase's pioneering article of 1937. For those interested in organizational problems of the firm, or its various legal guises, the article may prove to be disappointing. Coase (1937) is interested in the more general (generic) question of the structure and evolution of institutions. He develops a *theory* that the market and hierarchy are involved in a process of substitution at the margin which is guided by transaction cost considerations (Cf. Schanze 1981). In this view, it may be too costly to carry out a given quantity of transactions in an atomistic market; the particular system of internal directives employed by the firm may thereby save costs in organizing the allocation of resources. This theory of the evolution of the firm may be generalized as a *method* of evaluating the efficiency of a specific institutional regime. In using price theory as a method of institutional choice, Coase does not simply extend the neoclassical analysis to different objects. The method assumes institutional competition, but not in a frictionless world. Positive transaction costs are the key to institutional variation. A good illustration is Coase's note on the relation of market and planning:

It is easy to see when the State takes over the direction of an industry that, in planning it, it is doing something which was previously done by the price mechanism. What is usually not realised is that any business man in organising the relations between his departments is also doing something which could be organised through the price mechanism. There is therefore point in Mr. Durbin's answer to those who emphasise the problems involved in economic planning that the same problems have to be solved by business men in the competitive system. The important difference between these two cases is that economic planning is imposed on industry while firms arise voluntarily because they represent a more efficient method of organizing production. In a competitive system, there is an "optimum" amount of planning. (Coase, 1937:389 n. 3).

If Coase's view is valid, it changes the economic conception of legal institutions. In the neoclassical tradition, law is regarded as one constant constraining factor in the environment surrounding the economic decision. In the Coasean scenario, the economic decision implies a joint and unseverable evaluation of the product-specific and transaction-specific (institutional, informational or transportational) characteristics. If I interpret the scenario correctly, law is viewed as a *variable system* of alternative institutional arrangements, which alternatives are subject to *choice* according to cost considerations. Starting from this premise, the system has then to provide highly selective institutions which mobilize and facilitate transactions. The requisite variety and selectivity amongst institutions is again limited by cost considerations. Advantages of standardization of institutional design may offset advantages of extreme selectivity. Hence, in a system of rational institutional choice there is an equilibrium of standard conceptions (cogent and dispositive law, standard contracts trade or industry usages) and individual institutional variety[3].

Coase's article on social cost (1960) adds a further dimension to this mode of thought. In the earlier article Coase (1937) works from the perspective of a single actor who evaluates the cost and benefits of a particular institutional arrangement. In his famous demonstration that the conventional Pigouvian analysis of external effects is superficial, he shifts the focus to the interdependence of cost functions of parties who are in turn arranging for a Pareto-superior move. If one looks at the total cost of a given arrangement, the so-called "externality" becomes a part of the transaction costs. Coase teaches that costs cannot be

[3] In the liberal paradigm, the equilibrium of standard conceptions and individual institutional variety is understood as an antinomy of self-determination of the individual ("party autonomy") vs. state intervention ("regulation" in the conventional narrow meaning). This antinomy is not endorsed by the theory of regulation presented in this paper. Specific properties of state action are acknowledged, but they do not form a fundamental mark of distinction. The state is viewed as but one (important) actor among many actors who are involved in the process of institutional design and choice, and who thereby regulate transactions of their concern. For the various levels of public, private and intermediary regulation in present mixed economies, which we describe as systems of *organized interdependence*, see Mertens, Kirchner and Schanze (1982:71).

determined *ex ante* from a unilateral perspective, but that they are always the product of reciprocal consideration. In this manner, institutional choice becomes part of a reciprocal optimization process which considers the total value of production in the light of possible alternatives of transacting. Only in the neoclassical world of zero transaction costs is the initial definition of the institutional arrangement without allocative effects and, consequently, irrelevant. Such a conception is as strange as a model of the physical world based on an assumption of zero friction (Stigler 1972:12).

Obviously, this approach has consequences for institutional design in a world of positive transaction costs. An efficient legal system will be characterized not only by a state of equilibrium between opposing trends towards variety or standardization of institutions, but by two additional premises: a clear definition of entitlements emanating from the decision-making unit *(explicitness);* and the proposition that institutional arrangements should be so defined that they include the total cost of transacting, and thus internalize externalities *(internalization bias).* These two premises are normative *desiderata.* They have to be "produced" and "maintained" by the constitutional order; they are not automatic results of free market transactions (cf. Dahlmann 1979).

With respect to general forms of entitlements, modern economic analysis works with property rules (exclusive entitlements), liability rules (an infringement of rights is possible without prior consent, but requires compensation), and taxes and subsidies (Calabresi/Melamed 1972, Polinsky 1979, 1980). Taxes and subsidies are probably a variety of the more general modality of pooling and redistributing. These modalities have been tested using different qualified assumptions, such as assumptions of strategic behavior or of different levels of information (Polinsky 1979, 1980).

Following this line of economic analysis of law, I propose to view institutional evolution as a *dual process* of (1) *offering a broad variety of institutional designs* that have the properties of both explicitness and internalization bias (and thus reject those solutions which do not meet these requirements through political or professional consensus); and of (2) *choosing* between the so-defined institutional alternatives by actors whose purpose is to individualize the institutional environment of their concern (institutional choice).

If institutional designs are framed – as they are typically – as packages of normative arrangements, there may be institutional competition between these comprehensive normative entities. I will refer to this aspect under the rubric of "extrinsic analysis". By contrast, I will use the term "intrinsic analysis" to describe the selection of more individualized institutional components, or "institutional modules". Here, I envisage a structural or "macro" analysis, which I will briefly outline in this paper, and a "micro" analysis which would detail complex macro structures, and thereby reach the ordinary legal rule level in its most complex aspects.

3. The Constitution of the Firm

Let us now turn to the constitution of the large corporation. Given the complexity of all those legal relations relevant to the constitution of the corporation it is obvious that we are not dealing with a classic case of the application of theory to reality. A series of general propositions may be offered in our case simply by applying single elements of the theory[4].

3.1 Extrinsic Analysis: Markets for Institutions

I have already referred to Coase's general explanation of the nature of the firm, which may be called a mode of extrinsic analysis. According to this view, the market decides whether markets or firms are efficient in controlling a given set of transactions. A related scheme of analysis is applied by Manne (1967) to explain the process of institutional differentiation with reference to the concept of the corporation. Different corporate forms – from the large and publically-owned to the small, closely-held corporation – are regarded as responses to the different markets which control corporate inputs. In the case of the large corporation, Manne distinguishes three such markets: the market for capital, the market for securities, and the market for corporate control. In this vein Mertens and I have argued that the scheme of codetermination presented in the 1976 German Codetermination Act might create a new, fourth market controlling the large corporation – namely, a market for competing codetermined and non-codetermined business organizations (Mertens, Schanze 1979). The German solution, which permits a choice between the two forms of organization, is based on the principle of institutional design intended to encourage institutional variety.

Another kind of understanding of Coase's market/hierarchy paradigm is found in a recent article by Brinkmann and Kübler (1981). They argue that legislative action leading to institutional codetermination is a means of saving transaction costs, because it avoids complex bargaining about the issue. Furubotn (1981) and others (Pejovich 1978, Jensen, Meckling 1979) argue in turn that since codetermination rights are hardly created through voluntary arrangements between capital owners/managers and employees (an argument which would require more empirical scrutiny), the legal imposition of codetermination would be *per se* inefficient. Without assessing here the validity of these views, it is safe to say that both lines of argument depart from the Coasean analysis because they do not engage in real world comparisons between the costs of selectivity and of standardization[5]. In general I have argued elsewhere (Schanze 1983) that the current instrumentalism in the application of corporate laws may be explained as an effort to stress selectivity.

Extrinsic analysis of the kind demonstrated here may serve as a helpful general tool for explaining the coordinating properties of institutions and their relation to the relative availability of resources. An example which is relevant to the current issue of codetermination may illustrate the point. In the current discussion about the constitution of business enterprises it has become standard

[4] A basic summary of issues concerning the concept of the corporation is found in Posner (1977:289 seq.) see also the excellent collection of papers in Posner and Scott (1980).

[5] For detailed cost/benefit considerations concerning the German scheme of codetermination see e.g. Gäfgen (1981), Fleischmann (1983); for small corporations see Cable and FitzRoy (1980).

practice to ask why classical corporate law concentrates on the issue of organizing the financial capital input alone, instead of coordinating both financial and human capital (cf. Vanberg 1982). The textbook explanation resorts to the "invention" of limited liability, and its obvious advantages for capital suppliers. Under the protective umbrella of limited liability, risk-averse individuals were enabled to pool parts of their wealth and to share in the fruits of the whole investment. The analysis presented here suggests that we look at relative historical shortages of corporate inputs, and scrutinize their relative institutional development. At the time when corporate law developed, there was as short a supply of finance capital as there was of available institutional forms for pooling such capital. Modern saving and banking systems as well were as undeveloped as were methods of financing within the corporate format. The supply of human capital needed in the early phases of industrialization (workers, who could be trained on the job) was ample; the liberal labor contract existed as a standardized and cheap means of transacting. Moreover, innovation was carried out by outside inventors or by owner/investors.

The economic situation in which we find codetermination schemes is obviously different. Today, available modes of pooling and supplying capital for industrial ventures are manifold. The institutional framework is adapted to high mobility and allocative efficiency of capital flows; in this institutional perspective the supply of financial capital may be regarded as satisfactory. However, the obvious need for highly skilled and innovative human capital, and the perpetuation of trial and error procedures in the responses of institutions to this need, indicate the existence of an institutional scarcity which will likely stimulate alternative institutional means of integrating human capital of this kind into the firm. In this area we may not yet have created the requisite variety of institutional designs to permit an optimal institutional choice.

To generalize the point, complex resources such as capital, manpower and innovative skills cannot be defined simply in terms of a "physical" availability, but must also be defined as functions of the relative institutional development associated with such resources. Legal concepts may eventually reflect these specific institutional and physical "shortages" as they exist in a particular historical setting.

3.2 Intrinsic Analysis: The Nexus Model of the Corporation

Ownership of capital is central to the traditional legal concept of the corporation. The neo-institutional school of economists points out that the firm can hardly be explained as a function of one single input. Rather, they suggest that all relevant inputs should be considered. This has led to the elaboration of a fertile model of intrinsic analysis of the corporation: the "set of contracts" or "nexus" perspective of the firm (Alchian, Demsetz 1972; Jensen, Meckling 1976; Fama 1980).

Fama (1980:290) restates concisely:

> Each factor in a firm is owned by somebody. The firm is just the set of contracts covering the way inputs are joined to create outputs and the way receipts from outputs are shared

among inputs. In this "nexus of contracts" perspective, ownership of the firm is an irrelevant concept.

Fama (1980:289) summarizes his conclusions as follows:

We first set aside the typical presumption that a corporation has owners in any meaningful sense. The attractive concept of the entrepreneur is also laid to rest, at least for the purposes of the large modern corporation. Instead, the two functions usually attributed to the entrepreneur, management and risk bearing, are treated as naturally separate factors within the set of contracts called a firm. The firm is disciplined by competition from other firms, which forces the evolution of devices for efficiently monitoring the performance of the entire team and of its individual members. In addition, individual participants in the firm, and in particular its managers, face both the discipline and opportunities provided by the markets for their services, both within and outside of the firm.

The nexus theory does not recognize a vested priority of one single input. It thus may serve to describe both "capitalistic" and "laboristic" types of firms. Fama does not consider the problem of codetermination; rather, he addresses himself specifically to the problem of organizing the managerial input. He develops a theory that managerial behavior is not controlled by the grant of a residual claim, on the firm's receipts for its outputs, as Alchian and Demsetz (1972) asserted, but that managerial behavior is monitored by outside and inside markets for managers. Fleischmann (1983:24) uses this line of argument to explain why owner/entrepreneurs have introduced voluntary schemes of codetermination in Germany (cf. Cable, FitzRoy 1980), while German managers are likely to oppose such schemes:

An owner/entrepreneur who introduces codetermination may be irritated by being called on outsider in his market. However, as long as his customers accept his products, this negative judgment is likely to be irrelevant. Managers, who are dependent on their reputation on the market for managers, face a different situation. They are in a precarious situation if they do not observe the prevailing judgment of the business community.

In a more general way of course this statement reveals the importance of prevailing tastes in the formulation of institutional arrangements which will be attractive to a specific class of input owners.

3.3 Variation of the Nexus Model: A Research Program

The *conventional model* of the corporation starts from the assumption that the particular means of contributing financial capital to the productive unit will define the structure of the corporation. The corporation is viewed as an institutional scheme for organizing the interests of "owners" or equity contributors. This specific class of capital contributors and its institutional conception (common ownership/shareholding) forms the center of the organizational structure. All other inputs are integrated into this structure through specific "outside" markets (labor market, market for technical and administrative know-how, non-equity capital market, etc.). Some inputs are conceived as being "physically" integrated into the corporation (managers, employees) through special contracts (cf. Diagram 1: Business Corporation, conventional model).

Diagram 1: Business Corporation, conventional model

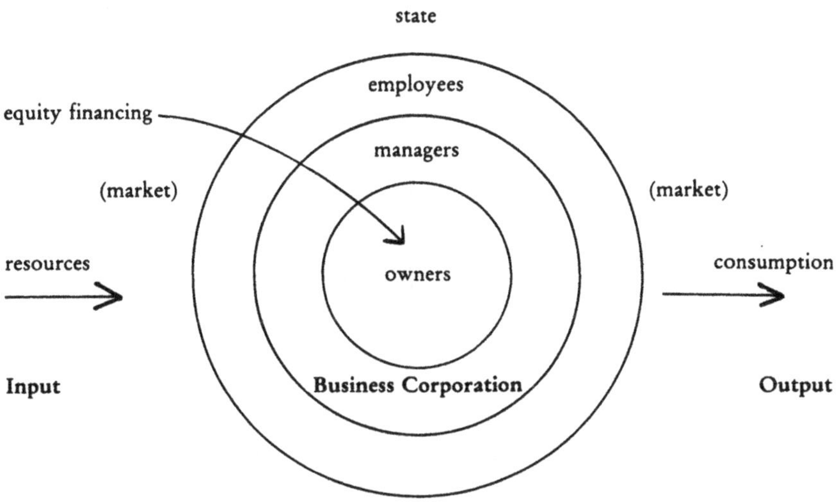

The *nexus model* of the firm discards the notion of a vested priority of one specific input. Rather, it stresses that all input/output relations should be analyzed as interlocking functions of the corporate concept. These relations are of course subject to change over time. During the last 200 years these functions have been modified, differentiated into subfunctions, or substituted through the process of institutional choice.

In Diagram 2, I have listed typical input/output relations relevant for the modern corporate nexus. I have distinguished eleven aggregate actors which typically engage in input/output relations with large corporations. They are listed clockwise as: the state; intermediary organizations; consumers; insurers against social and private liabilities; employees; labor managers; managers; shareholders; bondholders; banks; and productive input owners who sell hardware or software (such as e.g. patents) to the production unit.

In this model, the "constitution" of the corporation is defined by the constitution of the institutional "interfaces" of the various input/output relations. The initial nexus model as used by Alchian, Demsetz (1972), Jensen, Meckling (1976), and Fama (1980) relies solely on a *contractual* interface. In their conception every input/output relation is described as a contractual arrangement. This appears to be remnant of the early property rights theory. It has already been mentioned that modern economic analysis (Calabresi, Melamed 1972, Polinsky 1979, 1980) has replaced the original contract (or property rule) approach by working with a triple scheme consisting of property rules (contract), liability rules (decisions by a third party assessing the burden of economic losses caused by unilateral actions), and taxes/subsidies (creation of an authority for pooling and redistributing). These three basic options for regulating (in a

Diagram 2: Business Corporation, nexus model

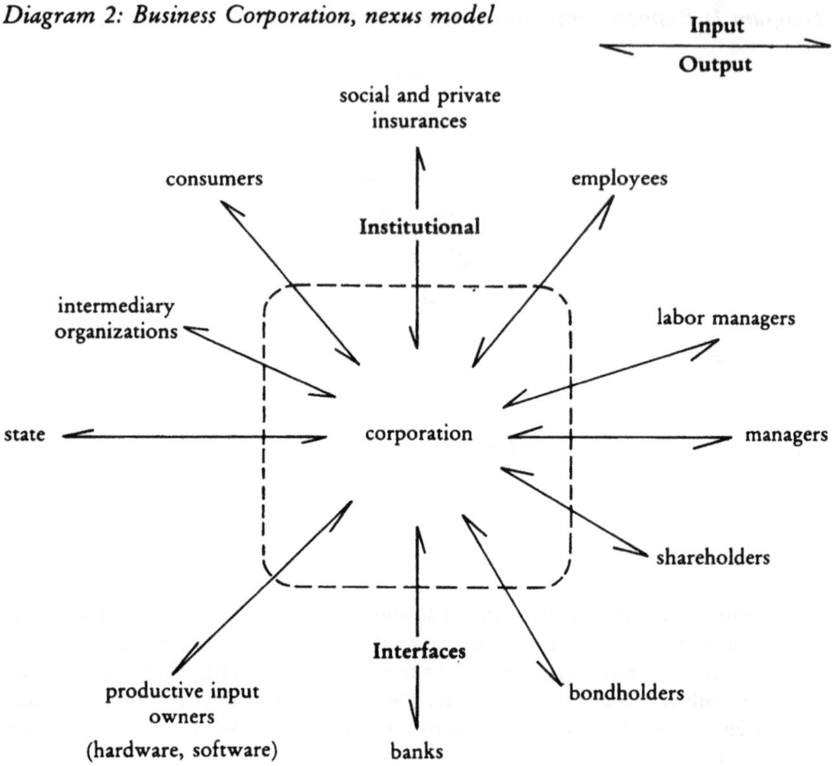

broad sense) an input/output relation relate to a *structural* triple scheme for describing the *constitutional modes of regulation*, i.e. the basic procedures which are employed in modern mixed economies to deal with legal issues of economic concern. Here, three legal modes of regulating institutional interfaces may be distinguished, displaying an affinity to the original triple scheme. These modes of regulation are

(1) *directive* (general laws, indicative, planning, administration),
(2) *contract* (ad hoc coordination), and
(3) *participation* (through representation and voting).

Every regulatory mode may have certain properties which will make it more or less efficient as applied to a particular transactional context. Of course, one could argue that a membership commitment, or even a directive (as, for example, an order to pool through taxation and to redistribute) might be considered a contract in a very broad sense (social contract). However, this does not seem to be a meaningful use of the term "contract", which in the strict sense should involve a punctual coordination of the interests of consenting parties. The concept presented here is elaborated in Diagram 3 (regulatory interface, state – corporation).

Diagram 3: Regulatory interface, state – corporation
structural (macro) level

Regulatory Modes	State Inputs	Corporate Outputs
general laws indicative planning public administration	resources and infrastructure (physical, institutional, human capital) general supervision statutory subsidies	taxes, production human capital civil liabilities for harmful activities
contract	*as above and/or:* performance supervision specific infrastructure specific subsidies	*as above and/or:* periodical control and revision rights corporate infrastructure specific taxes
corporate participation	*as above and/or:* capital management supervision through voting	*as above and/or:* dividends amenities for political/bureaucratic elites, remuneration supervisory and voting rights
intermediary organization	suasion	suasion

Extrinsic control mechanisms:
1. "market for states" (regions, industry locations)
   concerning resource endowment, infrastructure including laws
2. "market for corporations"
   concerning capital, technology, management capacity

I have chosen the state – corporation interface as a first illustration to demonstrate that, in this model, "public" inputs and outputs are analytically similar to classical "private" input/output relations. The state is viewed as a "super firm" (Coase 1960), producing specific corporate inputs and consuming specific corporate outputs. It is, however, constitutionally privileged in one respect: As an actor, it may make extensive use of the directive as a means of regulation (it may even be constitutionally bound to use this form exclusively as a matter of its prerogative, cf. Daintith 1979). In the actual practice of mixed economies, of course, there is ample evidence of contractual and participatory commitments of the state in various industries. This is particularly evident in the regulation of basic industries in developing countries (cf. Schanze 1981).

However, other actors concerned with classical private input/output relations also resort to directive and participatory modes of regulation if this appears to be an appropriate framework for structuring their specific relations. In his article on the nature of the firm, Coase (1937) has shown the economic logic of the substitution of market transactions through directed transactions and vice versa. The present mix of regulatory modes is also visible in the employee – corporation interface. Here, the classical private labor contract remains an important regulatory structure of the institutional interface. In addition, labor and management have created an intermediary structure of collective agreements, a structure which frequently assumes the characteristics of directive or quasi-legal arrangements. Moreover, the actors concerned have used legislation as a means of regulating some specific problem areas. Somtimes, the actors have also resorted to participatory regulation, in some cases to explicit codetermination. They have used this option to a varying degree depending on the organizational preferences of the actors in various countries and in various industries.

The plurality of actors and interfaces contained in the model demonstrates that a change in the institutional structure of one interface may have consequences for a multitude of input/output relations. Every change affects the institutional equilibrium and may require the adjustment of property rights as well as of positive and negative externalities in the complete nexus system. The Furubotn (1981) analysis, which views the introduction of participatory rights in the employee – corporation interface as an "attenuation" of property rights in the shareholder – corporation interface, arbitrarily isolates two interfaces and posits that there is a direct correlation between them. In so doing, it endorses the vested priority of equity ownership found in the conventional model of the business corporation, rather than working with the policy-neutral nexus model. Thus, it necessarily reaches normative conclusions.

It has been the purpose of this paper not to detail, but to outline a concept of positive inquiry into the constitution of the firm[6]. I have presented the economic nexus explanation of the firm combined with a scheme of basic institutional modes of regulating economic transactions as a program for future research. A full review and elaboration of the various institutional interfaces made in the terms offered by this model, I submit, could adequately demonstrate the interpretive potential of an economic analysis of institutions.

Bibliography

ALCHIAN, ARMEN A. and HAROLD DEMSETZ (1972) "Production, Information Costs, and Economic Organization", 62 *American Economic Review* 777.

ARROW, KENNETH J. (1974) *The Limits of Organization*. New York: Norton & Co.

ASSMANN, HEINZ-DIETER, CHRISTIAN KIRCHNER, and ERICH SCHANZE (Eds.) (1978) *Ökonomische Analyse des Rechts*. Kronberg: Athenäum.

BEHRENS, PETER (1985) "The Firm as a Complex Institution", 141 *Zeitschrift für die gesamte Staatswissenschaft* 62.

BOULDING, KENNETH E. (1952) *Welfare Economics*. Homewood, Ill.

BRINKMANN, TOMAS, and FRIEDRICH KÜBLER (1981) "Überlegungen zur ökonomischen Analyse von Unternehmensrecht", 137 *Zeitschrift für die gesamte Staatswissenschaft* 681.

[6] Other research perspectives on structural aspects of the corporate concept are developed by Kirchner (1983); by Picot (1982) and Behrens (1985).

CABLE, JOHN R., and FELIX R. FITZROY (1980) "Productive Efficiency, Incentives and Employee Participation: Some Preliminary Results for West Germany", 33 *Kyklos* 100.

CALABRESI, GUIDO and A. DOUGLAS MELAMED (1972) "Property Rules, Liability Rules, and Inalienability: One View of the Cathedral", 85 *Harvard Law Review* 1089.

COASE, RONALD H. (1937) "The Nature of the Firm", [n. s.] 4 *Economica* 386–405.

– (1960) "The Problem of Social Cost", 3 *Journal of Law and Economics* 1.

– (1978) "Economics and Contiguous Disciplines", 7 *Journal of Legal Studies* 201.

DAHLMAN, CARL J. (1979) "The Problem of Externality", 22 *Journal of Law and Economics* 141.

DAINTITH, TERENCE (1979) "Regulation by Contract: A New Prerogative?", 32 *Current Legal Problems* 41.

FAMA, EUGENE F. (1980) "Agency Problems and the Theory of the Firm", 88 *Journal of Political Economy* 288.

FLEISCHMANN, GERD (1983) "Mitbestimmung und Neue Politische Ökonomie", 2 *Jahrbuch für Neue Politische Ökonomie.*

FURUBOTN, EIRIK (1981) "Codetermination and the Efficient Partitioning of Ownership Rights in the Firm", 137 *Zeitschrift für die gesamte Staatswissenschaft* 702.

GÄFGEN, GÉRARD (1981) "Zur volkswirtschaftlichen Beurteilung der Entscheidungsteilnahme in Unternehmungen: Die deutsche Mitbestimmungsregelung als Beispiel", in H. Steinmann, G. Gäfgen and W. Blomeyer, *Die Kosten der Mitbestimmung*. Mannheim, Wien, Zürich: Bibliographisches Institut.

JENSEN, MICHAEL C. and WILLIAM H. MECKLING (1976) "Theory of the Firm: Managerial Behavior, Agency Costs and Ownership Structure", 3 *Journal of Financial Economics* 306.

– (1979) "Rights and Production Functions: An Application to Labor Managed Firms and Codetermination", 52 *Journal of Business* 469.

JHERING, RUDOLPH VON (1852) *Geist des römischen Rechts auf den verschiedenen Stufen seiner Entwicklung*. Erster Teil, Leipzig: Breitkopf und Härtel.

KANT, IMMANUEL (1798) *Metaphysische Anfangsgründe der Rechtslehre*. 2nd ed. Königsberg: Nicolovius.

KIRCHNER, CHRISTIAN (1983) "Ökonomische Analyse des Unternehmensrechts: Ein Forschungsansatz", 2 *Jahrbuch für Neue Politische Ökonomie* 137.

MANNE, HENRY G. (1967) "Our Two Corporation Systems: Law and Economics", 53 *Virginia Law Review* 259.

MARCH, JAMES G. (1978) "Bounded rationality, ambiguity, and the engineering of choice", 9 *Bell Journal of Economics* 587.

MERTENS, HANS-JOACHIM, CHRISTIAN KIRCHNER, and ERICH SCHANZE (1982) *Wirtschaftsrecht. Eine Problemorientierung*. 2nd ed. Opladen: Westdeutscher Verlag.

MERTENS, HANS-JOACHIM, and ERICH SCHANZE (1979) "The German Codetermination Act of 1976", 2 *Journal of Comparative Corporate Law and Securities Regulation* 75.

NUTTER, WARREN G. (1979) "On Economism", 22 *Journal of Law and Economics* 263.

PEJOVICH, SRETOZAR (1978) "Codetermination: A New Perspective for the West", in S. Pejovich, *The Codetermination Movement in the West*. Lexington, Mass.: Lexington.

PICOT, ARNOLD (1982) "Transaktionskostenansatz in der Organisationstheorie: Stand der Diskussion und Aussagewert", 42 *Die Betriebswirtschaft* 175.

POLINSKY, A. MITCHELL (1979) "Controlling Externalities and Protecting Entitlements: Property Rights, Liability Rule, and Tax Subsidy Approaches", 8 *Journal of Legal Studies* 1.

– (1980) "On the Choice Between Property Rules and Liability Rules", 18 *Economic Inquiry* 233.

POSNER, RICHARD A. (1977) *Economic Analysis of Law*. 2nd ed. Boston, Toronto: Little, Brown.

POSNER, RICHARD and KENNETH E. SCOTT (1980) *Economics of Corporation Law and Securities Regulation.* Boston, Toronto: Little, Brown.

SCHANZE, ERICH (1981a) "Forms of Agreement and the Joint Venture Practice", in Erich Schanze et al., *Mining Ventures in Developing Countries. Part 2: Analysis of Project Agreements.* Frankfurt: Metzner.

– (1981b) "Der Beitrag von Coase zu Recht und Ökonomie des Unternehmens", 137 *Zeitschrift für die gesamte Staatswissenschaft* 694.

– (1983) „Theorie des Unternehmens und Ökonomische Analyse des Rechts", 2 *Jahrbuch für Neue Politische Ökonomie* 161.

SCHENK, KARL-ERNST (1981) *Märkte, Hierarchien und Wettbewerb.* München: Vahlen.

– (1982) "'Institutional Choice' und Transaktionsökonomik – Perspektiven der systemanalytischen und industrieökonomischen Anwendung", in Karl-Ernst Schenk (ed.), *Studien zur politischen Ökonomie.* Stuttgart, New York: Fischer.

STIGLER, GEORGE J. (1972) "The Law and Economics of Public Policy: A Plea to the Scholars", 1 *Journal of Legal Studies* 1.

– (1980) "The Economist as Preacher; The Ethics of Competition: The Friendly Economists; The Ethics of Competition: The Unfriendly Critics" (Tanner Lectures at Harvard) Center for the Study of the Economy and the State Special Paper Series 001–003.

VANBERG, VICTOR (1982) "Das Unternehmen als Sozialverband. Zur Sozialtheorie der Unternehmung und zur juristischen Diskussion um ein neues Unternehmensrecht", 1 *Jahrbuch für Neue Politische Ökonomie* 276.

WILLIAMSON, OLIVER E. (1975) *Markets and Hierarchies: Analysis and Antitrust Implications.* New York, London.

– (1980) "Emergence of the Visible Hand. Implications for Industrial Organization", in Alfred D. Chandler and Herman Daems, *Managerial Hierarchies.* Cambridge, Mass., London: Harvard.

From Old to New Monism: An Approach to an Economic Theory of the "Constitution" of the Firm

DETLEF KRAUSE

Bremen

Introduction

The purpose of the following arguments is to give a brief outline of the idea of a new monism to be considered in the context of a discussion of a modern "constitution" of the firm[1]. New, as opposed to old monism refers to the idea that the core justification of the "constitution" of the classical capitalist firm should be kept, but on an enlightened generalised basis. Emphasis is laid upon the presentation of the theoretical foundations of a new monism. For this reason, no detailed reference is made to the literature on the subject of the "constitution" of the firm (Gärtner and Luder, 1979; Weitzig, 1979), and no means and ways can be shown on how to put the basic model of a new monism into practice.

1. Starting-Points and Extensions

1.1. Starting Points

(1) Scarcity and Efficiency

The economic problem at the root of the (capitalist) firm and the (capitalist) market system is scarcity. The prerequisite for reducing scarcity is efficiency (Eucken, 1959).

The phenomenon of scarcity has proved a concomitant symptom of evolutionary societies (Luhmann, 1970). Scarcity is defined as continuing situations of lack of means relative to human wants and needs to be satisfied. Scarcity means that it is impossible to satisfy in any case any need of any human being at any point of time. It does not matter what are the reasons of scarcity – for example: an absolute lack of natural resources, differentiation and expansion of human wants and needs – and everywhere scarcity can be understood as relative scarcity only, that is as relative to a set of varying causal conditions. Under condition of

[1] The term "constitution" stands for the institutionalised set of written or actual rules regulating organisational decision-making. The terms firm, enterprise, corporation and economic organisation are synonymously applied to a profit-making organisation.

relative scarcity, the societal institutions of firm and market can be looked upon as economic inventions whose task is to reduce relative scarcity (Demsetz, 1964; Krause, 1982b; Röpke, 1983) in a more efficient manner than previously. Reducing the gap between means and needs is not an end in itself. It serves the final end of satisfying the needs of the consumer or the needs of human beings (Hondrich, 1975).

Now one might suppose that nowadays there is no economic problem or problem of reducing relative scarcity left to be solved. One might suppose that the economic problem has been reduced to one of (world-wide) re-distribution of wealth and affluence. Even if this is so, it is not a valid basis for an attack against efficient economic institutions. It is a simple truth that you cannot have your cake and eat it. Hinting at other points of criticism, there is no irony in stating that charging our economised world for affluence and wastage, for damaging its very roots by environmental loads, in sum turns out to be the same as diagnosing increasing relative scarcity and along with this calling for even more economic efficiency to recover and maintain chances to need-satisfying actions.

Economic efficiency, induced by relative scarcity, in its narrowest meaning stands for natural or physical productivity. Difficulties arise if, due to the increasing complexity of societal division of activities, productive activities and their results are to be exposed to some kind of evaluation whether an objective or subjective standard of value or some other criterion seems to be appropriate. Then productivity expresses the relation of valued total output to single factor inputs (usually labour or capital) or to total factor input.

Apart from any more sophisticated considerations, one should acknowledge the functional usefulness of an abstractly defined general measure of economic activities in comparing all economic activities and their results by a common standard which provides each participant with equally obtainable, understandable and usable information, thereby maintaining the openness of the whole socio-economic system for any actual and even potential, as yet unknown, need-based activities. What is more, if there is no unique standard of value no measurement of different degrees of relative scarcity would be possible and, therefore, no efficient decision-making on resource allocation could take place. The only suitable standard of value available is represented by (market) price.

It follows that the term "economic efficiency" is best applied to any uniquely valued input-output or output-input relationship. This is the precondition of comparing different relationships directly and of finding out the most efficient alternative or of ranking different alternatives according to their relative efficiency.

In turn, the procedure of valuing alternative choices and of selecting the most advantageous alternative indicates economic rationality. By itself, economic rational action is relative resource-saving action and thereby action serving the possible maximum of satisfaction of human wants and needs.

Concepts of and means for reaching and sustaining efficiency are closely connected with concepts and conditions for establishing and maintaining human freedom of action (Friedman, 1976; Machlup, 1969). Making economic rational choices simply depends on the freedom to do so. Widespread freedom of choice furthers the chance of the best or most efficient alternative to be successful. Fundamentally understood, a system of actions which is open to any alternatives constitutes and enhances to the maximum the chances of each individual and each action unit to strive for its own aims without substantially restricting the respective chances of others. Welfare gains will be realised: freedom functions as a precondition of efficiency. On the other hand, reduction of relative scarcity widens the realm of human freedom of action. Any progress on the ladder of need-fulfilment implies more freedom of choice as to quantity as well as to quality: efficiency functions as a precondition of freedom.

Any "constitution" of the firm should meet the efficiency standard (Albach, 1981; Picot, 1981). One cannot, to give an adverse example, define efficiency as a result of inter-mediating processes within the framework of the firm where the processes themselves are not restricted by resource-saving constraints (Laske, 1979). Furthermore, it is one of the central objections to be raised against the current interest-oriented debate on the "constitution" of the firm (Brinkmann, 1983) that the reciprocity of freedom and efficiency is widely neglected.

(2) Market and Democracy

The central theoretical subject should be mentioned in advance: The topic is actions of actors or action units motivated by profit-orientation (the term profit is to be used very broadly), stimulated by competition, and mediated by generalised participative mechanisms such as market and voice.

The market mechanism is commonly viewed as applicable exclusively to the control of economic affairs, and the democratic mechanism, i.e. the mechanism of voice, is said to be applicable exclusively to the control of political affairs. Thus economics and political control could be understood as clearly distinguished areas of theoretical interest and practical arrangement. Such distinctions and separations, however, are neither justified by any difference of purposes to be pursued nor by any difference as to the regulative capacity of the mechanisms (Krause, 1982a).

To begin with, both market and democracy are modes of consensus-building and decision-making which indiscriminately meet the following requirements:

- they are open to the greatest possible variety of purposes a human being may conceive of and
- they are prepared to combine and to mediate a theoretically unlimited number of heterogeneous actions of a great number of heterogeneous actors or action units.

That is, both mechanisms satisfy the postulates of freedom and efficiency (Krause, 1982a). The prerequisite of freedom – in its general as well as in its more specific economic and political understanding – becomes tentatively satisfied by the degree of potential and real chances for participative choices if the mechanism of participative self-control functions effectively, i.e. if simultaneously it provokes and curbs self-seeking actions and thereby tends to reduce the accumulation and abuse of power. Efficiency, too, is an emergent property of market and democracy, since a largely unlimited effective participation results in increasing wealth.

Even more, both market and democracy are democratic mechanisms. Participation in the market system (choosing products/services or "economic" production programmes of goods and services) and in a political system (choosing parties/candidates or "political" production programmes of goods and services) should be equally looked upon as modes of democracy. As actual developments demonstrate, market democracy is increasingly accomplished by permanent voting procedures accompanied by expanding chances for voting. The same holds true for political democracy, where it becomes more and more customary to look at political voting and decision-making from an economic point of view (Frey, 1977). To go a little further, the economic element in calculating political consent (Downs, 1968) finds its equivalent in marketing as an intra-organisational strategy for building consensus (Paul 1977).

In addition, it would be too narrow a view to limit democracy to legally established rules conferring equal rights to participate by means of periodical or permanent elections. In contrast to formal democracy, functional democracy extends to processes to participative decision-making on the basis of competences required by the jobs or tasks to be performed (Hondrich, 1972). The concepts of formal and functional democracy are not mutually exclusive. On the contrary, they should be understood and handled as interrelated functionally.

Finally there is no persuasive criterion for discriminating between "economic" goods and services and "political" goods and services as a starting-point of associating to the different spheres of production different means and mechanisms of control.

In dealing with the "constitution" of the firm, the obvious overall consequence is that no restrictions should be allowed in relation to the alternative mechanisms of internal and external control (Alchian, 1975; Alchian & Demsetz, 1975).

1.2 Extensions

(1) Property Rights and Actors

The concept of property rights is usually presented as a consolidation of traditional microeconomic theory (Alchian and Demsetz, 1973; Demsetz, 1964; Furubotn and Pejovich, 1972). In this paper, however, the property rights approach is primarily introduced with the intention of gaining more profound insight into the conditions of allocation and distribution of scarce resources serving both freedom and efficiency within an economic organisation and in society (Hesse, 1983; Hutter, 1979; Krause, 1982b; Meyer, 1983).

Positively defined, property rights are rights to resources (see Figure 1). More precisely, property rights refer to rights to scarce resources. By resources I mean material or tangible resources as well as immaterial or intangible resources. Generally, rights to resources exist as bundles of rights to resources, that is to say, they consist of different rights to different resources. In this respect, the rights as such are of more interest than the resources as such. Likewise, the use of resources or the use of the rights to use resources is of more interest than the mere ownership of resources; and the idea of an optimal portfolio of property

Figure 1: The Property Rights – Concept

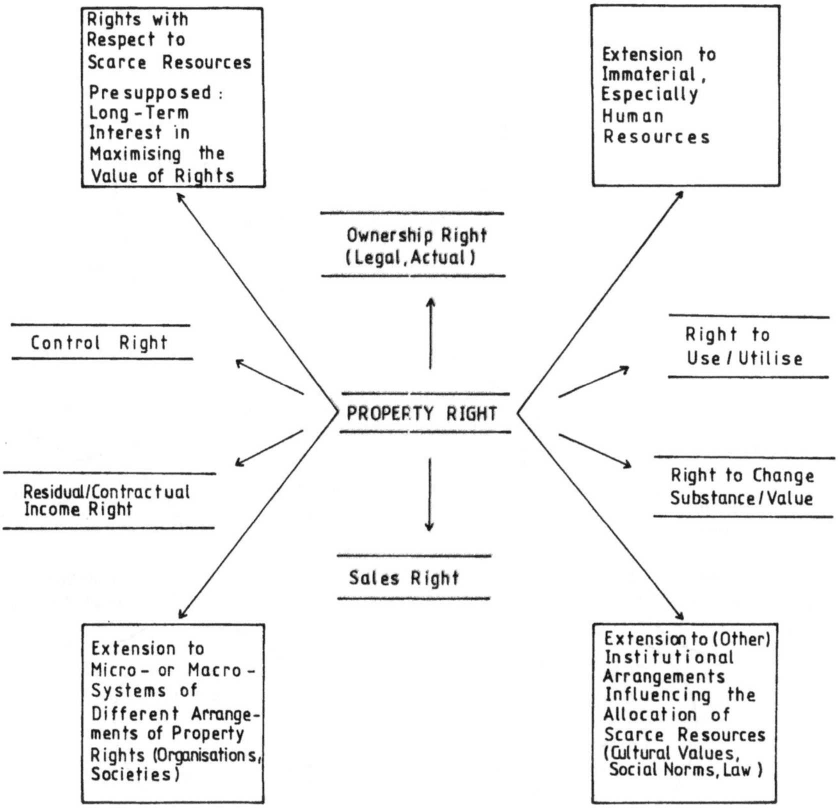

rights, aimed at maximising the total value of property rights, is of more interest than the value of the single resource as such.

To be sure, property rights represent a specific class of action rights, namely those which refer to the existence of scarce resources and pertain to their use. Thereby the property rights approach facilitates the conceptualisation of any use of resources (including material or tangible resources and, especially, human or intangible resources – later on referred to as physical and human capital) as a use of property rights. Therefore, the more or less static idea of the individual private ownership of resources is to be replaced by the more or less dynamic idea of different sets of different rights to resources, different bundles of property rights, which are differentially assigned and attributed. In this way it becomes possible and necessary to reflect more on actors and action units *as actors* rather than exclusively as the relevant holders of property rights.

Beyond all that, property rights turn out to be affected by (other) institutional

Figure 2: Analytical Outline of Elements Constituting the Structure of Organisationally-Bound Property Rights

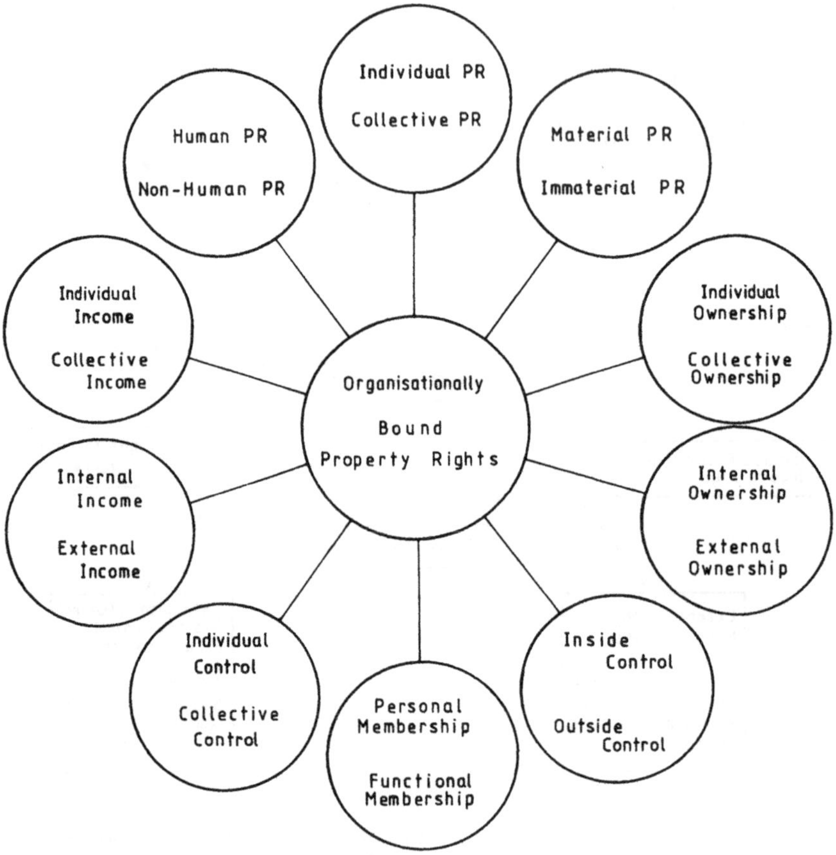

arrangements. The allocation and distribution of scarce resources is influenced by cultural values, social norms, the law, and the like.

Bringing together the different elements of the property rights concepts (for details see Figure 1 and Figure 2), an extended horizon for analysing efficiency emerges. It becomes convenient to look at different types of property rights and different total or sub-systems of property rights as alternative societal answers to the economic problem which are comparable with regard to efficiency (Demsetz, 1964; Meyer, 1983; Leipold, 1983). That is the salient point: property rights themselves and their institutionalised reality are seen as mile-stones on the road to (increased) efficiency and freedom (Roepke, 1983). Therefore, the property rights base of the firm as an economic organisation will reveal the firm in its true colours of efficiency (Pejovich, 1976; Jensen and Meckling, 1979; Picot, 1981).

The assumptions of freedom and efficiency and the search for an arrangement of property rights (from the level of society to the level of the individual firm) which does justice to these assumptions require a revised assessment of the relevant actors or action units.

In traditional theory, there is only one type of actor – the person or individual as a private actor. Admittedly, the same holds true for the prevailing theory of property rights. This approach derives from its origins a predominant concern with the importance of persons or individuals as private actors endowed with certain bundles of unattenuated property rights exchangeable by contracts (Furubotn & Pejovich, 1978). No doubt, there are no compelling, substantial objections to the brilliant societal invention of the positive, mutually reinforcing relationship between individual rights and individual motivation (Held, 1979) to preserve and augment these rights in pursuit of self-interest.

But this traditional concept tends to resort to individual or personal reductionism when faced with the phenomenon of collective actors (Olson, 1968). Really, to begin with, the concept of a personal identity of a formally organised and self-containing collective is a mere fiction since any collective, as such, has no consciousness. The real identity (of a formal organisation) as a collective actor originates both from the obvious relative functional autonomy of a formally organised collective (of persons) as against its external and internal environment (Raiser, 1969) and (which makes a significant difference) from the fact that formal entitlement to rights to act as a quasi-person (Ott, 1977) is granted regardless of (changeable) organisational memberships (Coleman, 1982; Luhmann, 1972). On further consideration, indeed, it becomes necessary to take into account certain differences between actions assigned to a fictitious person as such, actions of a fictitious person on behalf of its members, and actions of members carried out on behalf of a fictitious person.

To apply these findings to the property right-based theory of the "constitution" of the corporation: the well-known gap between individual and collective interest must be bridged by making the corporate interest the interest of corporate members by means of adequate allocation and distribution of property rights at the level of the corporation as a collective actor.

(2) Hierarchy and Voice

Obviously, a theoretically unlimited multitude of actions of a multitude of actors, based on property rights, and motivated by chances for gains, is best performed by a multitude of single contracts, provided the conditions for contractual stipulations are commonly known and calculable. Otherwise, the greater the complexity of the whole participative network, the smaller the probability of comprehensive and equal information on the part of the participants and the greater the degree of uncertainty in making efficient decisions.

Already this gives the reason for reflecting on alternative ways to allocate rights to scarce resources. The approximate idea is to organise the processing of information which is necessary to pool certain rights to resources. From the point of view of economising transaction costs alone, any kind of organised or coordinated economic activity will be a better alternative to that of action taken on an individual basis (Alchian, 1977; Bössmann, 1981; Coase, 1937; Manne, 1981). Information and communication deficiencies, in the case of atomistic conditions, are one important reason to recommend the model of pooling rights to resources, pooling property rights, as an efficient model of economic organisation. Other essential reasons are the advantages of larger scale production, the synergetic or multiplicative effects of pooled activities on productivity, and the limited original abilities of human beings to process information (bounded rationality).

Generalised, alternative choices of different mechanisms and forms of allocating scarce resources are available (Herder-Dorneich, 1980; Lindblom, 1980). Market and hierarchy is a typical alternative (Williamson, 1975; Schenk, 1981). Yet, it would be misleading to think of markets as unorganised and nonhierarchic institutions and to think of hierarchies, i.e. formally organised activities, as institutions without elements of market and competition. In the real world, markets are never completely unstructured (unorganised) and hierarchies never completely structured (hierarchically organised).

Furthermore, it is easy to identify positive relations between the comparatively high-structured type of economic organisation (hierarchy) and the comparatively low-structured type of economic organisation (market). Firms, as hierarchically organized economic organisations, come into existence and grow only to that point where savings of transaction costs tend to become zero. Markets, as economic organisations, gain ground as efficient multipliers of efficient actions to be performed in the course of socio-economic development; markets gain ground, inside and outside the more structured type of socio-economic organisation, if efficiency losses because of organisational slack occur. What is more, as current experience reveals, there is a one-way street neither to growing size of socio-economic organisations nor to growing regulative deficits of market and democracy and, therefore, there is certainly no one-way street to the predominance of hierarchy in society and economy.

The organisational failures approach which explicitly conceives of hierarchies and markets as different modes of organising economic activities efficiently (Williamson, 1975) is very similar to the exit and voice approach (Hirschman, 1970; Williamson, 1974) with the exception that the latter is tied to the existence and persistence of organisational membership, especially personal organisational membership.

In addition to the explanation of markets and hierarchies in terms of net advantages as to the value of property rights combined and exchanged, the recognition of voice as a functional equivalent to, and as a potential amplifier of, exit (i.e. market transaction) deepens our understanding of the way organised activities may be performed. Even the mechanism of exit itself may be applied to intra-organisational personnel movements in department and division, and in the plant. This could be called internal exit.

Voice, in itself an element of democracy, refers to all kinds of individually or collectively articulated discontent against organisational slack. Within the organisation, voice links up with participative marketing (Kirsch and Scholl, 1977) and with participation rights already established by legislation or other agreements.

Within markets, voice meets with the formation of consumer protest and with the use of countervailing and bargaining power (Gartner and Riessman, 1974).

2. Internalisation of Control: The Case of the Firm

Before turning more directly to the subject, the main consequences of the arguments developed so far should be summarised:

- Efficiency and freedom serve as basic conditions to be met in evaluating the "constitution" of the firm.
- In evaluating the "constitution" of the firm, market and democracy as well as market and hierarchy should be applied as organisation principles to be kept apart only to the extent that they structure economic activity.
- Exit and voice basically constitute likewise applicable mechanisms of allocating property rights efficiently, both on the level of the economy and on the level of the firm.

Each "constitution" of the firm should be analysed in terms of efficient arrangements or institutionalisations of property rights, whereby the pooled set of property rights interacts specifically with the total set of other factors affecting the use of property rights.

2.1 At the Outset: The Capitalist Firm

(1) The Basic Model to be Modified

According to traditional theory and to the reductionist property rights theory of the firm (Ridder-Aab, 1980; Schüller, 1983), an enterprise can be compared to an entrepreneur, in the sense that, for purposes of profit-making, a natural person or a small number of such persons invests capital (money invested taken as capital) in an activity in order to direct and supervise personally the use of the capital invested as well as to appropriate personally the fruits of investment (capital income, residual income).

The basic legitimation of this idea of a capitalist enterprise is straightforward: a behavioural justification is that the owner is best motivated to care for his property. Personal or individual (private) ownership, then, is regarded as the first prerequisite of efficiency. Indeed, human experience and societal experiments reveal the absence of any substitute for the positive relation between an actor's unattenuated ownership of resources and efficient actions. But this neither implies exclusive validity for the ownership of capital invested in the form of physical capital nor exclusive validity for individuals or persons as private actors.

Under conditions of permanent relative scarcity of resources, physical capital, as one of the resources needed, is supposed to be the key resource. Physical capital proves to be the resource with the highest degree of relative scarcity as it is indicated both by the ratio of factor prices (price of physical capital relative to the price of human capital) and by the substitutions of capital for labour thereby induced. A greater relative scarcity of physical capital, then, is said to represent a second prerequisite of efficiency. That the scarcity of physical capital has a bottleneck function is open to doubt. Surely, it is more important to secure an allocation of all kinds of capital, that is of all rights to resources, which guarantees the greatest possible difference between total valued capital input and total valued output of means. It also follows directly that no exclusive prerogative of rights to physical capital in controlling the use of resources at the level of the firm suggests itself.

As to the external control, the enterprise has to adjust its decisions to market imperatives (imperative consumer votes) which are primarily signalled by prices. There is nothing else to do but to transform (external) market signals into (internal) production decisions at once. Under condition of perfect competition, the scope of decisions to be made can be reduced to variations of factor employment (rights to resources "employed"). The capitalist enterprise reacts to market forces; it does a vicarious job. This is said to represent a third prerequisite of efficiency. The weak point of this reasoning, of course, is the assumption of a more or less perfect functioning of markets, that is the assumption of frictionless transmission of consumer votes via market into production decisions and derived decisions on factor or resource employment.

At first sight, the actual existence of widespread market imperfections and market regulations, as well as the fact that firms exercise influence on markets to a substantial degree, could be taken as proving the self-evident inadequacy of the pure model used to describe reality (Marris & Mueller, 1980; Williamson, 1975). There is some truth in it, yet one would be wrong to diagnose that a general decline of markets is accompanied by a general shift of market control over firms to that of control of firms over markets. Whatever the results of a thorough diagnosis might be, there are functional equivalents to bridge the gap between the pure model and complex reality without resorting to the intertwined strategies of internalisation of external interests on the level of the firm and of replacing market forces by political regulation (Böbel, 1982; Posner, 1975).

(2) The Goals of the Firm

The character of the firm as an economic organisation must be understood in its relation to consumer interests. It is the competitive structure of a market economy which turns profit-orientation into a means of surviving in competition and into a strong incentive for an efficient allocation of property rights on the level of the economy and on the level of the firm. Thus, the general goal of profit-making (Ortmann, 1976) is to be understood as a means of reducing relative scarcity and, what turns out to be the same, of satisfying the wants and needs of human beings in their role as consumers.

Formal goals, whether called utility (on the part of the consumers) or profit (on the part of producers), serve as functional instruments for a basically unlimited plurality of concrete material (tangible) and immaterial (intangible) goals. The formal character of a homogeneous abstract goal (utility, profit) is a necessary condition for the realisation of a plurality of heterogeneous concrete goals (goods, services).

It would be easy to oppose the ideas of formal goal-orientations and abstract mechanisms of mediating goal-oriented actions of self-seeking actors as preconditions of doing efficiently the job of reducing relative scarcity:

- One degree of under-determination stems from the nature of human wants and needs. Single needs or groups of homogeneous needs are satisfiable by different means. Heterogeneous needs or groups of heterogeneous needs may be served by identical means. In this respect, the firm or the producer may choose between any alternative compatible with profit-orientation.
- Another degree of under-determination concerns the transformation of external demands into internal demands. It is possible to choose between alternative modes of combining resources (property rights) within the economic organisation to reach externally given goals or bundle of goals.
- In this way a margin is left to the firm to influence, on its part, the consumer needs. That may result in decisions on products or product mixes and in ensuring allocations of property rights in a way which, in the end, may be more advantageous in terms of mere profit than in pure satisfaction of needs.

Whatever could be said against the basic model, could by no means, seriously effect its substance. In accordance with the imperatives of organising the allocation of property rights efficiently, one far-reaching extension must be brought about. It is no longer sufficient solely to attribute the job of profit-making to a natural person – the capitalist owner (of physical capital), the capitalist entrepreneur, the (capitalist) manager – it is also the economic organisation (the collective actor, the corporate actor) itself also which acts in the pursuit of interests to be satisfied by means of profit-making. The interest of the economic organisation (the corporate interest) is the satisfaction of consumer interests by means of profit-making.

As before, effective mechanisms of external and internal control are essential preconditions to keep the corporate interest in line with the (common) consumer interest. Only within these limits may discretion to follow external sub-goals (e.g. market share, sales target) or internal sub-goals (e.g. manager interests, labour interests), or both, exist. As recent empirical research confirms (Budde, Child, Francis and Kieser, 1982), the profit goal proves to be paramount. Purely and simply, only under the conditions of satisfying the profit goal may other goals become the objective function of the firm.

2.2. Property Rights and Membership Rights Specified

(1) Organisatonally Bound Property Rights

The question arises of how to contract and to allocate property rights on the level of an economic organisation, of how to organize the use of property rights within such an organisation.

As a first step, a short outline of the elements to be considered in constituting an organisational arrangement of property rights will be given (see Figure 2). The wreath of circles symbolises the different relevant subjects to be decided upon. Decisions are required on

- whether only non-human material property rights (e.g. rights to physical capital) or also immaterial human property rights (e.g. rights to human capital) are to be considered as equally relevant or not,
- whether only individual property rights or also collective property rights should be differentiated,
- how to handle ownership (individual vs. collective ownership, internal vs. external ownership) and control rights (individual vs. collective control, inside vs. outside control) and their relations to one another (Berle, 1959; Steinmann, Schreyögg, and Dütthorn, 1983),
- how to establish income rights (individual vs. collective income rights, internal vs. external income rights) relative to ownership and control rights,
- how to differentiate membership and membership rights.

Figure 3: Property Rights and Organisation

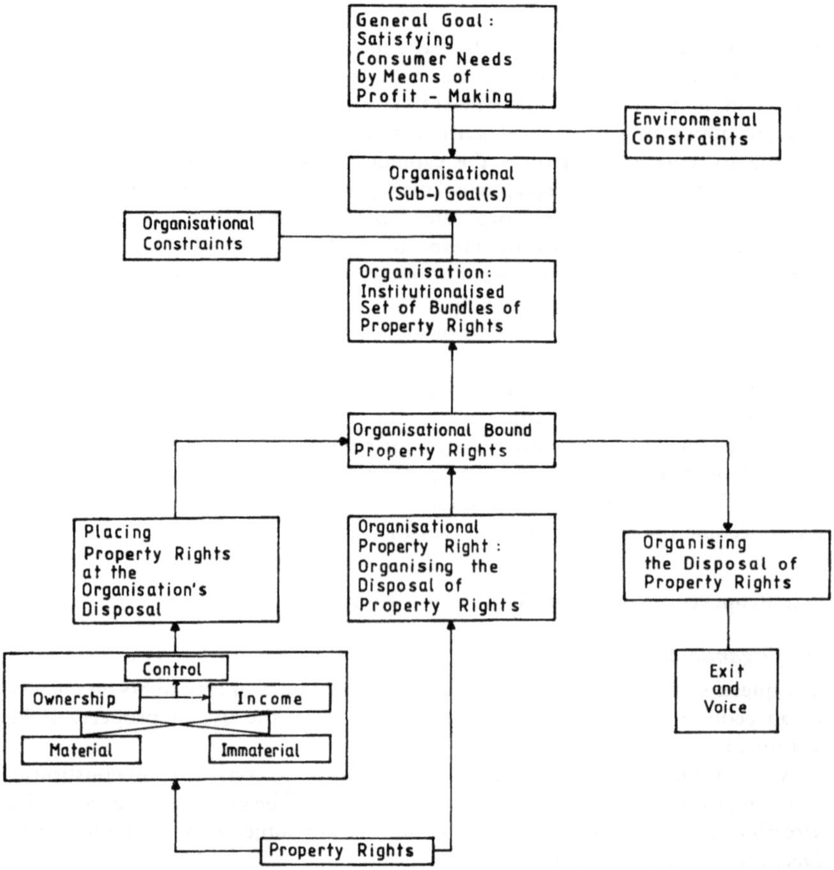

Each individual decision predetermines to a certain degree the range of points which have still to be decided upon. The main decisions to be made are whether

- to treat human capital as equal to physical capital as to their respective status as scarce resources,
- to treat collective actorship as functionally equal to individual or personal actorship.

On this broadened basis, the explanation of an economic organisation as the result of an organised pooling of rights to physical capital in order to save transaction costs needs only to be somewhat extended and modified (see Figure 3). Instead of clinging to individual rights to physical capital individual rights to human capital should be recognised as well. Instead of only focussing on rights to capital, the focus becomes property rights (as delineated in Figure 1). Moreover, the central point of interest is the placing of all property rights at the disposal of the organisation, as a result of which the disposal of the organisation itself can be looked upon as an organisational property right. Now it makes sense to speak of organisationally-bound property rights and to define the organisation as an organised institutionalised set of bundles of property rights. Organising the disposal of property rights means dividing property rights into sub-bundles and distributing them to the members of the organisation (and also to organisational sub-units and groups of organisational members): this is a property right practised by the members of the organisation.

The allocation of property rights to an organisation and the distribution of property rights within it – the latter not being exclusively predetermined by the former – should follow the final goal of contributing efficiently to the satisfaction of external wants and needs of human beings. Within this limit, the pursuit of external and internal sub-goals (also as intermediate means to the final end), including the specific interests of personal and functional members (also: as intermediate means to the final end), is not excluded.

(2) Resource-Based Organisational Membership

To repeat, the traditional view of the firm is based on the premise that ownership rights on physical capital are the sole basis of control rights (that is of the right to decide on the material goals of the firm and on the structure of the process of intra-organisational goal-attainment) and of income rights (that is of the right to decide on the distribution of the total residual income). The starting-point in defining organisational membership should, however, be the idea of organisationally-bound property rights (see Figure 4):

- The first leading supposition is the restriction of organisational membership to a resource base. Put plainly, to partake in the course of internal and external control of an economic organisation requires at least a resource-based interest based on grounds of having placed rights to resources at the disposal of such an organisation. The respective transfer of rights depends an contractual agreements.
- The second leading supposition is the differentiation between personal and functional membership. To be sure, the class of potential organisation mem-

Figure 4: Resource-Based Organisational Membership

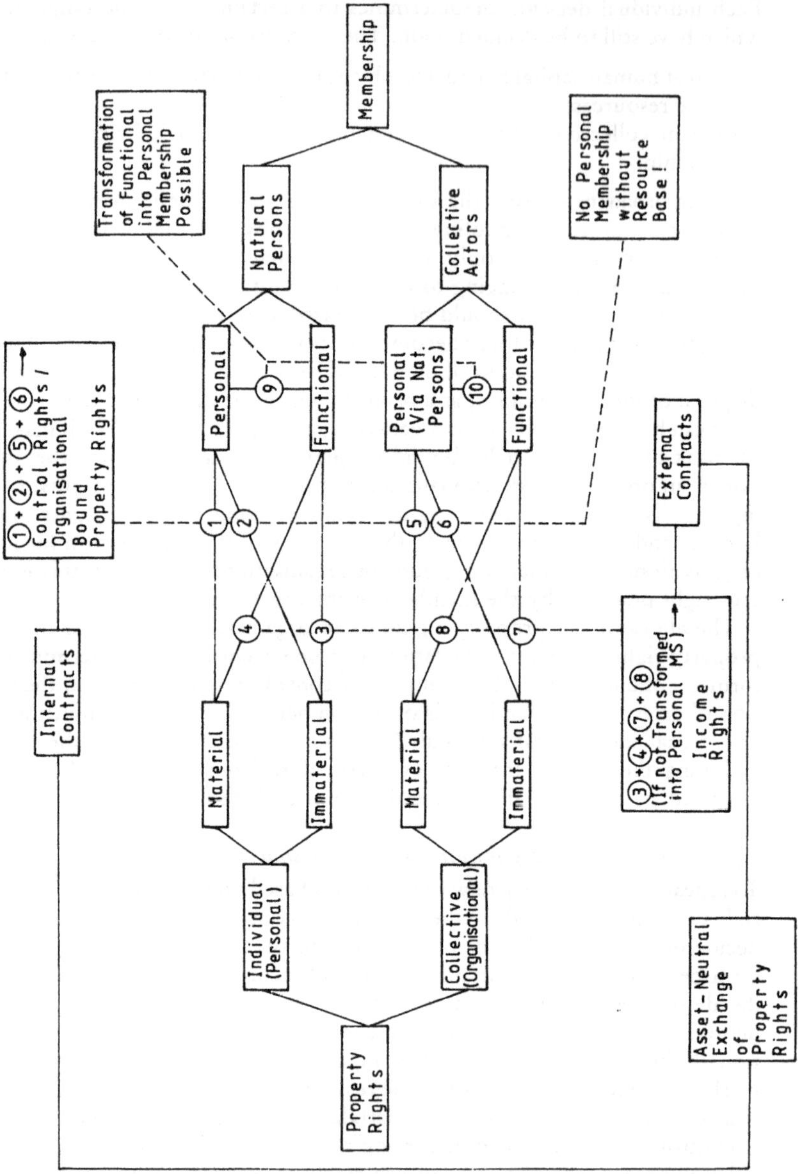

bers is made up of natural persons and of fictitious persons, and rights to be associated with organisational membership are composed of individually- and collectively-held material and immaterial rights.

- The third leading supposition is the restriction of immediate personal participation in decision-making at all organisational levels both to the condition of having placed rights to resources at the disposal of the organisation and to the proof of being competent to contribute to organisational goal-attainment.
- The fourth leading supposition refers to organisational membership on the whole, which is not only a matter dependent on a resource base but also and thereby dependent on certain rules of entry and exit. That is to say, that even personal membership, on the basis of human capital, should be handled according to the idea of asset-neutral exchange of property rights. In practice, this especially implies material participation (in assets, in profits) even if it does not treat rights to human capital in the same way as rights to physical capital.
- The fifth leading supposition concerns the control of the organisation. Direct, internal control rights should be based on personal membership only. Personal membership is defined, more or less vaguely, by formally institutionalised rules for participation in organisational decision-making at each level. External control rights rest on functional membership, whereas functional membership is defined by mere resource involvements without personal membership. External control rights are to be restricted to bring their indirect influence to bear on internal control by market forces only.

The overall message put forward by these principles of organisational membership is to preserve and to apply the idea of unattenuated rights to resources and the strong motivational forces associated with it as a means to maximise the value of resources at the (intra-)organisational level.

2.3. Dynamic Internal Allocation of Property Rights

Personal membership is the *conditio sine qua non* of becoming directly involved in the internal organisational processes of goal-oriented distribution and allocation of organisationally-bound property rights. Personal membership constitutes the right and the duty to use one's own human property rights (skills, knowledge, abilities) to contribute to efficient organisational goal-attainment.

As things stand, this structural basic condition is a necessary but not a sufficient one. Each structural arrangement of rights within an organisational framework ought to be enlivened by dynamic mechanisms inducing and sustaining effective participation, reducing internal organisational slack and curbing external organisational power.

On the level of the firm, market and hierarchy, as well as exit and voice, are well adopted to meet the requirements mentioned. The leading idea may be called positive multiple complementarity of market (exit) and hierarchy (voice) (see Figure 5). The organised interplay of market (market democracy) and hierarchy (political democracy) should result in increased internal complexity in order to reduce the external complexity to which the firm is exposed.

Figure 5: Internal Organisational Mechanisms of Allocating Property Rights

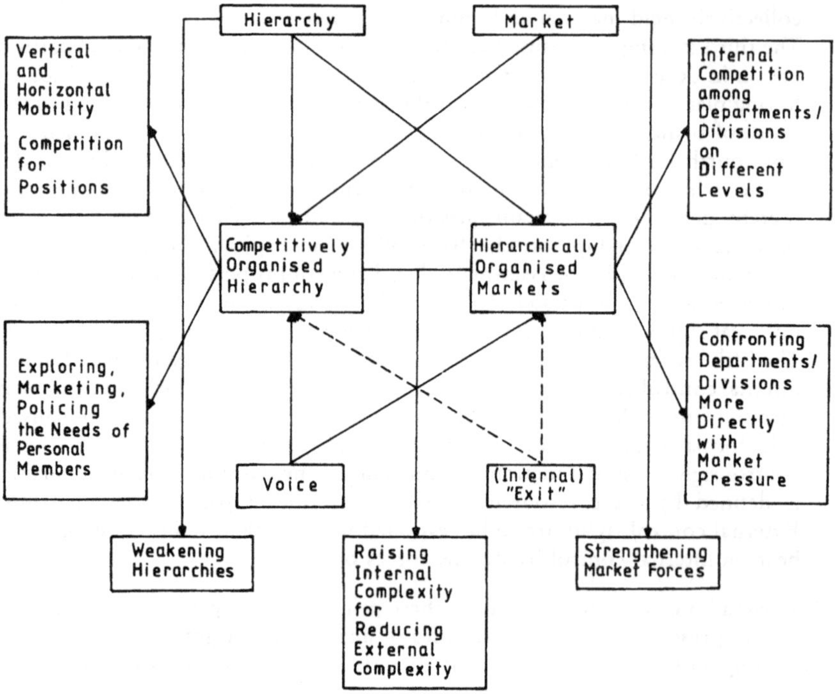

In detail:

- Both market and hierarchy as different means to organise allocative activities co-exist on the level of the economy and of a single economic organisation (Alchian, 1975; Alchian and Demsetz, 1975; Marris and Mueller, 1980).
- Markets inside economic organisations show features comparable to markets outside. They are hierarchically built and they differ in the degree to which they are separated from one another. In turn, hierarchies within an organisation separate internal markets from one another by different degrees. The internal structure of an organisation is double-faced. There is both a need for hierarchically organised markets and for competitively organised hierarchies.
- Exposing internal markets – as differentiated by organisational principles relying on functional division of labour – to external competitive pressure means lowering the hierarchical level of relations to relevant outside market segments (divisionalisation, project-organisation) (Marris and Mueller, 1980). Exposing internal markets to internal competitive pressure means furthering their competitive relations by such management principles as management by objectives or by building profit-centres.

- Exposing internal hierarchy – as differentiated according to the division of labour and occupations – to external competitive pressure means overcoming the segmentation of the internal labour market by allowing for competition for positions at all steps of the hierarchical ladder. Exposing internal hierarchy to internal competitive pressure (Hirschman, 1970) means to overcome the rigidities of horizontal and vertical mobility (internal exit) by exploring and marketing needs and offering incentives (Fleischmann, 1975; Kirsch and Scholl, 1977; Paul, 1979).
- Finally, it must be mentioned that all strategies of mobilising the use of property rights which rely on internal pressure should be accompanied by institutionalised opportunities for voice (rights, information channels). External voice by functional members and other interested persons and groups will also help to adapt the organisational use of property rights to the rule of efficiency.

2.4. Alternative Approaches to Corporate "Constitutions" Reviewed

(1) Alternative Monistic Approaches

Historical developments aside – e.g. the changes in the dominant position of land, capital, and labour as scarce key-resources – it is appropriate to systematise briefly the different models of allocating rights to physical or human capital or both:

- Rights to physical capital (i.e. money invested in equipment) exclusively serve as the basis of control and income rights. Rights to manpower, though nominally designated as rights to human capital (i.e. money invested in working abilities), only serve on a contractual basis as productive resources. This is the case of the pure capitalist firm.
- Rights to manpower, conceived as rights to human capital as productive resources, exclusively serve as basis of control and income rights. Rights to physical capital only serve, on a contractual basis, as productive resources. This model is neither discussed nor developed here.
- Rights to physical capital and to human capital, both being equally conceived as productive resources, include equal control and income rights and are employed by means of contract. Up to now, only some theoretical attention has been paid to this model (Steinbrenner, 1975).
- Rights to physical and to human capital, both being equally conceived as productive resources, include equal control and income rights. As to their use, both rights are placed at the disposal of the personal members of the firm on a contractual basis. This is the model advanced in this paper.
- Rights to manpower, whereby manpower is conceived as a productive resource but not as human capital, serve as the exclusive basis of control and income rights. In this case, rights to manpower are combined contractually. Their combination with rights to physical capital also rests on a contractual basis. This is the case of the pure "labourist" firm (Furubotn, 1976; Pejovich, 1976; Jensen and Meckling, 1979).

At first, it should be kept in mind that all these models, whether realised or not in some form or another, are strictly resource-based, and each one refers to rights to resources. Then, all models refer explicitly to rights to physical or human capital as a distinct class of rights to resources, namely rights to productive resources. It follows that, above all, the first four models adopt the premise of a close relation between rights to productive resources and the holder's "natural" interest in economising such rights.

(2) Alternative Non-Monistic Approaches

So-called dual and plural models (Steinmann and Gerum, 1978; Weitsig, 1979) have their roots in monistic models (see Figure 6). The prevailing argument runs as follows: if there are two different types of rights to resources, and if the rights to one type of resource are dependent on rights to the other, then a balance of power should be reached by power-sharing (Brinkmann, 1983). This is the basis of German codetermination. This is the root of works councils.

In fact, what happens in the case of codetermination is a reconciliation or a unification of the divergent interests of employees and employers (Chmielewicz, 1975). Heretofore, conflicting interests seem to have been mediated on behalf of the interest of the firm. Because, at first glance, both interest parties seem to be only interested in the interest of the firm, this might be a desirable result.

Looked at more closely, several defects become manifest (Wickenkamp, 1983). In the same manner as before, the parties follow their specific interest by using the interest of the firm as a means to satisfy their specific interests. Add to this that participation in decision-making on the grounds of being "merely" an employee lacks a substantial resource-based interest in the interest of the firm. Interest-specific action within the firm overlaps with complementary organised interests outside the firm which inherently works to reduce competition (e.g. interlocking directorates, union representatives on boards (Burt, Christman, and Kilburn, 1980; Poensgen, 1980). There are sufficient indications that the allied specific producer interest will be pursued to the detriment of the common consumer interest (Böhm, 1952). Dual models tend to absorb too much productive or economising energy (Prosi, 1978) in favour of interest mediation or producing a favourable climate of social peace (Tegtmeier, 1973). (For empirical evidence see Krause, 1985).

Multiplying the number of groups entitled to participate in organisational decision-making transforms dual into plural models. However, a remarkable difference between dual and plural models is easily overlooked. The argument for giving external interests, none of whom are entitled to substantial rights to productive resources and productive interests (Furubotn, 1981), influence to bear inside a firm marks the starting-point of making a firm a self-service instrument of privileged organisable and typically organised external interests at the expense of the common good.

It is possible to moderate the defects associated with dual and plural models by means of arranging secondary feed-backs to resource-specific interests (material participation, resource-related liabilities, setting standards of competence for participation in decision-making, and by means of implementing effective mech-

Figure 6: Interest-Based Approaches to Corporate "Constitutions"

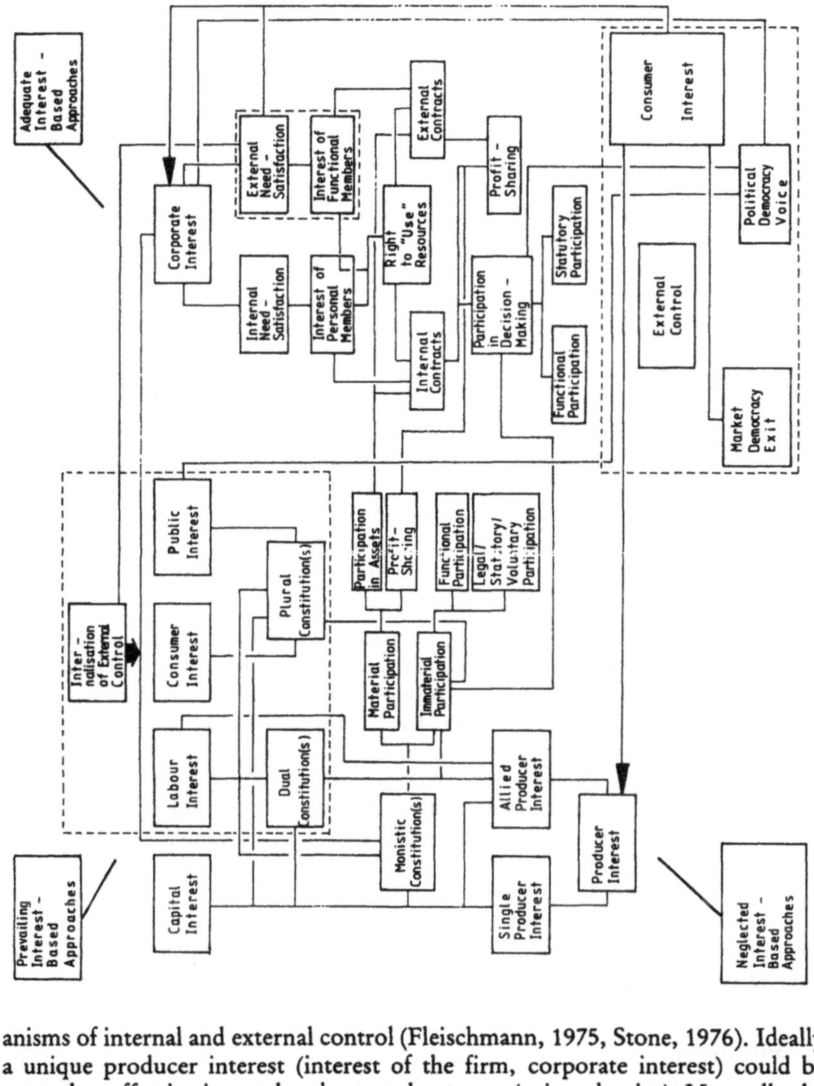

anisms of internal and external control (Fleischmann, 1975, Stone, 1976). Ideally a unique producer interest (interest of the firm, corporate interest) could be exerted to effective internal and external pressure (exit and voice). Normally the tendency to escape the powers of control, by defensively playing the cards of survival, at the expense of productive dynamics and by playing the card of settling conflicting interests at the expense of calling forth productive resource-based conflicts, will prevail.

Concerning the model of organisationally-bound property rights, the critical arguments referring to the role of effective control mechanisms remain valid. Moreover, this model is better equipped to deal with deficiencies stemming from the absence of ties to resource-based rights and interests.

2.5. The Big Corporation as a Public Institution?

One could argue that all the arguments developed so far do not affect big economic organisations (see Figure 7). There is a good deal of truth in this reasoning. The big corporation exercises:

- economic power (monopoly or oligopoly power),
- social power (socio-economic impacts on its large number of members and also on its socio-economic environment),
- political power (influences on communal, regional and central political authorities (Coleman, 1982; Ulrich, 1977).

The big corporation tends to avoid being controlled by external pressures. On the contrary, its strategy is to control external circumstances and to survive as a socio-economic and political institution at the expense of others.

Consequently it is plausible, to some degree, to favour the strategy of modifying the powerful position of a big corporation by the re-establishment of external control by means of direct participation of societal groups in decision-making, thereby establishing the corporation as a system of interest mediation (Steinmann and Gerum, 1978) and of multiple-determination procedures (Ulrich, 1977).

This solution, however, should not be presented as an exclusive one. If exaggerated, an unintended adverse effect might be brought about, i.e. a tendency to keep the firm in existence, just because of its far-reaching social and political impacts and against economic reason. The big corporation would then become a societally legitimised free rider at the expense of the society itself.

Therefore, before implementing a social system adopting extensively the principle of internalisation of external controls solutions should first be sought which rely on the extension and enlargement of internal control (implementing participative and competitive organisational structures and processes) and on the extension and enlargement of external control (by strengthening competitive mechanisms or procedures, by developing participative systems of information and communication reinforcing market powers and by giving effect to bargaining and countervailing powers).

3. Summary

A somewhat different view of the classical ideas of efficient welfare production gives some new insight into the main conditions relevant for a revised "constitution" of the firm as an economic institution. The essential elements used as the foundations are taken from the property rights approach, from the organisational failures approach (markets and hierarchies), and from the concept of exit and voice. The consideration of rights to resources (property rights) and

Figure 7: The Big Corporation: A Network of Influences

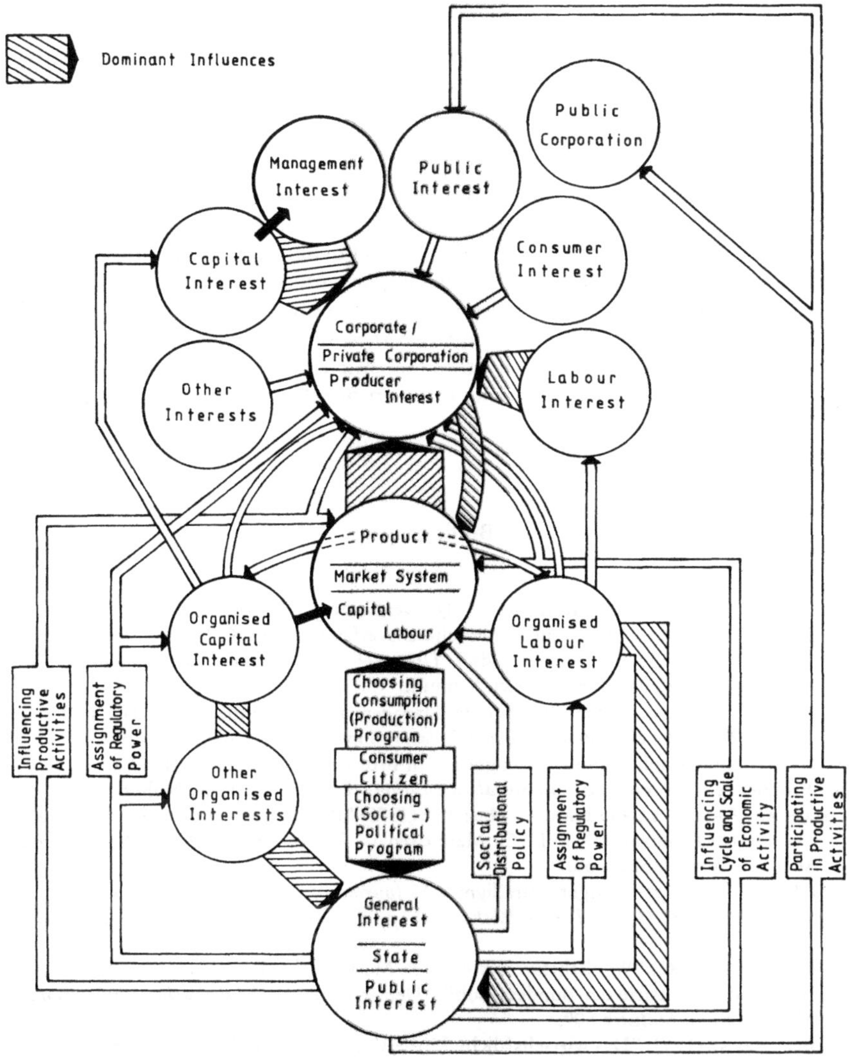

resource-based interests (interests in property rights) as basically intertwined elements which serve as foundation-stones of an economic organisation have turned out to be promising. Property rights to human and non-human resources are, therefore, to be taken into account on an equal basis. An extended view of the relevant actors is also called for, namely the acknowledgment of a collective or corporate actor following a collective or corporate interest. As heretofore, the main interest of the firm or the corporate interest is the satisfaction of the needs of consumers by means of profit-making. Next the essentials of organisational membership ought to be reconsidered. Organisational membership should be strictly tied to the precondition of having placed property rights at the disposal of an economic organisation, which can be viewed as an institutionalised set of contractually bound property rights. Now it becomes the job of the economic organisation, namely its members, to decide on the internal allocation of property rights that are available. In order to use property rights within an economic organisation efficiently, dynamic arrangements of property rights and control mechanisms through large-scale application of the means of internal exit and internal voice (i.e. the principles of market democracy and political market) prove to be possible and useful. In the end, an outline of a modified "constitution" of the firm, which could improve upon the reduced capitalist model as well as the "modern" dual and plural models comes into sight. Finally, the paper is, above all, predicated on the assumption that efficiency and freedom are emergent properties for solving the economic problem of relative scarcity to the greatest possible extent.

Bibliography

Albach, Horst (1981) "Verfassung folgt Verfassung. Ein organisationstheoretischer Beitrag zur Diskussion um die Unternehmensverfassung", in K. Bohr, J. Drukarczyk, H.-J. Drumm und G. Scherrer (eds.), *Unternehmensverfassung als Problem der Betriebswirtschaftslehre*. Berlin: Erich Schmidt.

Alchian, Armen A. (1975) "Corporate Management and Property Rights", in H. G. Manne (ed.), *The Economics of Legal Relationships*. St. Paul: West Publication.

– (1977) "Some Implications of Recognition of Property Rights Transaction Costs", in K. Brunner (ed.), *Economics and Social Institutions*. Boston: Martinus Nijhoff.

Alchian, Armen A., and Harold Demsetz (1975) "Production, Information Costs, and Economic Organization", in H. G. Manne (ed.), *The Economics of Legal Relationships*. St. Paul: West Publication.

– (1973) "The Property Rights Paradigm", 33 *Journal of Economic History* 16.

Berle, Adolf A. (1959) *Power Without Property*. New York, Harcourt: Brace and Company.

Böbel, Ingo (1982) "Wohlfahrtsverluste durch Marktmacht: Eine Untersuchung für den Bereich der Industrie der Bundesrepublik Deutschland", 197 *Jahrbücher für Nationalökonomie und Statistik* 509.

Böhm, Franz (1952) "Das wirtschaftliche Mitbestimmungsrecht der Arbeiter im Betrieb", 4 *Ordo* 21.

Bössmann, Eva (1981) "Weshalb gibt es Unternehmungen?", 137 *Zeitschrift für die gesamte Staatswissenschaft* 667.

Brinkmann, Thomas (1983) *Unternehmensinteresse und Unternehmensrechtsstruktur*. Frankfurt am Main: Peter Lang.

Budde, Andreas, John Child, Arthur Francis, and Alfred Kieser (1982) "Corporate Goals, Managerial Objectives, and Organizational Structures in British and West German Companies", 3 *Organization Studies* 1.

BURT, RONALD S., KENNETH P. CHRISTMAN, and HAROLD C. KILBURN jr. (1980) "Testing a Structural Theory of Corporate Cooptation: Interorganizational Directorate Ties as a Strategy for Avoiding Market Constraints on Profits", 45 *American Sociological Review* 821.

CHMIELEWICZ, KLAUS (1975) *Arbeitnehmerinteressen und Kapitalismuskritik in der Betriebswirtschaftslehre*. Reinbek b. Hamburg: Rowohlt.

COASE, RONALD H. (1937) "The Nature of the Firm", 4 *Economica* 386.

COLEMAN, JAMES S. (1982) *The Asymmetric Society*. Syracuse: Syracuse University Press.

DEMSETZ, HAROLD (1964) "The Exchange and Enforcement of Property Rights", 7 *Journal of Law and Economics* 11.

DOWNS, ANTHONY (1968) *Ökonomische Theorie der Demokratie*. Tübingen: J. C. B. Mohr.

EUCKEN, WALTER (1959) *Grundsätze der Wirtschaftspolitik*. Reinbek b. Hamburg: Rowohlt.

FREY, BRUNO S. (1977) *Moderne politische Ökonomie*. München: Piper.

FRIEDMAN, MILTON (1976) *Kapitalismus und Freiheit*. München: Deutscher Taschenbuch Verlag.

FURUBOTN, EIRIK G. (1981) "Codetermination and the Efficient Partitioning of Ownership Rights in the Firm", 137 *Zeitschrift für die gesamte Staatswissenschaft* 701.

– (1976) "The Long-Run Analysis of the Labor-Managed Firm: An Alternative Interpretation", 66 *American Economic Review* 104.

FURUBOTN, EIRIK G. and SVETOZAR PEJOVICH (1972) "Property Rights and Economic Theory: A Survey of Recent Literature", 10 *Journal of Economic Literature* 1137.

GÄRTNER, ULRICH and PETER LUDER (1979) *Ziele und Wege einer Demokratisierung der Wirtschaft*. Diessenhofen: Rüegger.

GARTNER, ALAN and FRANK RIESSMAN (1974) *The Service Society and the Consumer Vanguard*. New York: Harper & Row.

HELD, VIRGINIA (1979) "Property Rights and Interests", 46 *Social Research* 550.

HERDER-DORNEICH, PHILIPP (1980) "Substitution und Kombination von Ordnungen", in W. Dettling (ed.), *Die Zähmung des Leviathan*. Baden-Baden: Nomos.

HESSE, GÜNTER (1983) "Zur Erklärung der Änderung von Handlungsrechten mit Hilfe ökonomischer Theorie", in A. Schüller (ed.), *Property Rights und ökonomische Theorie*. München: Vahlen.

HIRSCHMAN, ALBERT O. (1970) *Exit, Voice, and Loyalty*. Cambridge, Mass.: Harvard University Press.

HONDRICH, KARL O. (1975) *Menschliche Bedürfnisse und soziale Steuerung*. Reinbek b. Hamburg: Rowohlt.

– (1972) *Demokratisierung und Leistungsgesellschaft*. Stuttgart: Kohlhammer.

HUTTER, MICHAEL (1979) *Die Gestaltung von Property Rights als Mittel gesellschaftlich-wirtschaftlicher Allokation*. Göttingen: Vandenhoeck & Ruprecht.

JENSEN, MICHAEL C., and WILLIAM H. MECKLING (1979) "Rights and Production Functions: An Application to Labor-Managed Firms and Codetermination", 52 *Journal of Business* 469.

KIRSCH, WERNER, and WOLFGANG SCHOLL (1977) "Demokratisierung – Gefährdung der Handlungsfähigkeit organisierter Führungssysteme?", 37 *Die Betriebswirtschaft* 235.

KRAUSE, DETLEF (1982a) "Lücken im ordnungsliberalen System: Exklusive Steuerungsrechte und exklusive Steuerungsmechanismen", in D. Krause, *Alternativen interner und externer Unternehmenssteuerung*. Bremen: Department of Social Sciences, University of Bremen.

– (1982b) "Property Rights und soziale Steuerung", in D. Krause, *Alternativen interner und externer Unternehmenssteuerung*. Bremen: Department of Social Sciences, University of Bremen.

– (1985) "Mitbestimmung und Effizienz", 25 *Sociologia Internationalis.*

LASKE, STEPHAN (1979) "Unternehmensinteresse und Mitbestimmung", 143 *Zeitschrift für das gesamte Handelsrecht und Wirtschaftsrecht* 173.

LEIPOLD, HELMUT (1983) "Der Einfluß von Property Rights auf hierarchische und marktliche Transaktionen in sozialistischen Wirtschaftssystemen", in A. Schüller (ed.), *Property Rights und ökonomische Theorie.* München: Vahlen.

LINDBLOM, CHARLES E. (1980) *Jenseits von Markt und Staat.* Stuttgart: Klett Cotta.

LUHMANN, NIKLAS (1972) *Funktionen und Folgen formaler Organisation.* Berlin: Duncker & Humblot.

– "Wirtschaft als soziales System", in N. Luhmann, *Soziologische Aufklärung.* Köln: Westdeutscher Verlag.

MACHLUP, FRITZ (1969) "Liberalism and the Choice of Freedoms", in E. Streissler et al. (eds.), *Roads to Freedom.* London: Routledge & Kegan Paul.

MANNE, HENRY G. (1981) "The Publicly Held Corporation as a Market Creation", 137 *Zeitschrift für die gesamte Sozialwissenschaft* 689.

MARRIS, ROBIN, and DENNIS C. MUELLER (1980) "The Corporation, Competition, and the Invisible hand", 18 *Journal of Economic Literature* 32.

MEYER, WILLI (1983) "Entwicklung und Bedeutung des Property Rights-Ansatzes in der Nationalökonomie", in A. Schüller (ed.), *Property Rights und ökonomische Theorie.* München: Vahlen.

OLSON, MANCUR (1968) *Die Logik kollektiven Handelns.* Tübingen: Mohr & Siebeck.

ORTMANN, GÜNTHER (1976) *Unternehmensziele als Ideologie.* Köln: Kiepenheuer & Witsch.

OTT, CLAUS (1977) *Recht und Realität der Unternehmenskorporation.* Tübingen: Mohr & Siebeck.

PAUL, GERD (1977) *Bedürfnisberücksichtigung durch Mitbestimmung.* München: Universität München.

PEJOVICH, SVETOZAR (1976) "The Capitalist Corporation and the Socialist Firm: A Study of Comparative Efficiency", 112 *Schweizerische Zeitschrift für Volkswirtschaft und Statistik* 1.

PICOT, ARNOLD (1981) "Der Beitrag der Theorie der Verfügungsrechte zur ökonomischen Analyse von Unternehmensverfassungen", in K. Bohr, J. Drukarczyk, H.-J. Drumm, and G. Scherrer (eds.), *Unternehmensverfassung als Problem der Betriebswirtschaftslehre.* Berlin: E. Schmidt.

POENSGEN, OTTO H. (1980) "Between Market and Hierarchy – The Role of Interlocking Directorates", 136 *Zeitschrift für die gesamte Staatswissenschaft* 209.

POSNER, RICHARD A. (1975) "The Social Costs of Monopoly and Regulation", 83 *Journal of Political Economy* 807.

PROSI, GERHARD (1978) *Volkswirtschaftliche Auswirkungen des Mitbestimmungsgesetzes 1976.* Köln: Bachem.

RAISER, THOMAS (1969) *Das Unternehmen als Organisation.* Berlin: Duncker & Humblot.

RIDDER-AAB, CHRISTA-MARIA (1980) *Die moderne Aktiengesellschaft im Lichte der Theorie der Eigentumsrechte.* Frankfurt: Campus.

RÖPKE, JOCHEN (1983) "Handlungsrechte und wirtschaftliche Entwicklung", in A. Schüller (ed.), *Property Rights und ökonomische Theorie.* München: Vahlen.

SCHENK, KARL-E. (1981) *Märkte, Hierarchie und Wettbewerb.* München: Beck.

SCHÜLLER, ALFRED (1978) "Property Rights, unternehmerische Legitimation und Wirtschaftsordnung", in K.-E. Schenk (ed.), *Ökonomische Verfügungsrechte und Allokationsmechanismen in Wirtschaftssystemen.* Berlin: Duncker & Humblot.

STEINBRENNER, HANS P. (1975) *Arbeitsorientierte Unternehmensverfassung.* Frankfurt: Campus.

STEINMANN, HORST, and ELMAR GERUM (1978) *Reform der Unternehmensverfassung*. Köln: Heymanns.

STEINMANN, HORST, GEORG SCHREYÖGG, and CAROLA DÜTTHORN (1983) "Managerkontrolle in deutschen Großunternehmen – 1972 und 1979", 53 *Zeitschrift für Betriebswirtschaft* 4.

STONE, CHRISTOPHER D. (1976) *Where the Law Ends*. New York: Harper & Row.

TEGTMEIER, WERNER (1973) *Wirkungen der Mitbestimmung der Arbeitnehmer*. Göttingen: Vandenhoeck & Ruprecht.

ULRICH, PETER (1977) *Die Großunternehmung als quasi-öffentliche Institution*. Stuttgart: Poeschel.

WEITZIG, JOACHIM K. (1979) *Gesellschaftsorientierte Unternehmenspolitik und Unternehmensverfassung*. Berlin: Walter de Gruyter.

WICKENKAMP, ROLF (1983) *Unternehmensmitbestimmung und Verfügungsrechte. Die paritätische Aufsichtsratsbesetzung nach dem Mitbestimmungsgesetz von 1976 im Lichte der ökonomischen Theorie der property rights*. Köln: Institut für Wirtschaftspolitik an der Universität zu Köln.

WILLIAMSON, OLIVER E. (1975) *Markets and Hierarchies*. New York: The Free Press.

– (1974) "Exit and Voice: Some Implications for the Study of the Modern Corporation", 13 *Social Science Information* 61.

Codetermination and Property Rights Theory

JÜRGEN GOTTHOLD
Bremen

Introduction

Because scholarly discussion by West German scholars has for so long been concerned with the subject of codetermination (examining its political, religious, moral, economic, etc. aspects) it is difficult to expect that any important new ideas on the subject would be developed using new terminologies. One would expect the same to be true for an analysis of the codetermination problem using the terms of the property rights theory.

Advocates of the property rights theory have made a pretentious claim: "microeconomic theory properly developed is the property rights approach" (Furubotn/Pejovich, 1972:1157); but this claim is in turn challenged by the hypothesis that the difference of this approach may be only terminological, that is to say that old problems are simply reappearing in new clothes (Eschenburg, 1978:9)[1]. For this reason there seems to be a certain scepticism about the potential for obtaining new insights using the property rights theory. However, a theory which presents traditional scientific knowledge in new terms will often facilitate the discarding of traditional modes of thought and thereby help penetrate an issue to its very core. Hence it is not a pointless exercise to re-examine the old subject of co-determination using new terminology. The current popularity of the property rights theory stems not only from that analytical possibility, but also from the fact that it provides answers to normative questions. That is the main reason for its popularity among many jurists. The primary thrust of my examination, by contrast, is to show that the answers given so far by the property rights theory are misleading.

For this purpose I will first contrast the positive theory of the firm as outlined by property rights theorists – that is, the "contractual theory" – with the traditional understanding of the firm as hierarchical organisation (section 1).

[1] Eschenburg (1978:9) also argues, that it should be "examined how far with the above claim ('micro-economic theory properly developed is the property rights approach') the challenge for a new theory is included, or if the provocation is only terminological, that is to say that old problems appear in a new guise.

Most of the authors fail to apply the contractual theory with any degree of consequence; only Fama's approach seems consequential and fruitful to me. Fama also conceives of the relationship between the capital owner and firm as a contractual one. This concept is outlined in section 2. The third section is concerned with the normative question of codetermination. Here, I discuss in particular Furubotn's view. For him, codetermination is an inefficient concept, because it is not a product of the market. In section 3,1 I ask the question, if and to what extent codetermination is not really the result of "voluntary exchange contracts." Section 3.2 attempts to clarify the significance of the efficiency concept. First, I recall the fact that it is an individualistic notion of efficiency, by means of which political recommendations can be deduced only with important reservations (3.2 a). Beyond this point, Furubotn's efficiency test differs from the traditional property rights theory efficiency test (3.2 b); I try to demonstrate that Furubotn's test is a tautological one (3.2 c). But the traditional efficiency test does not permit an evaluation of the efficiency of codetermination, either (3.2 d). My paper in particular discusses the main stream of property rights theory, in so far as its advocates treat the codetermination problem. However, in section 4, I try to set out the various analytical possibilities included in the concept, in order to explain in what way different codetermination arrangements in different countries can plausibly be attributed to different distributions of legal positions, namely to positive or negative sanctions linked to real opportunities by the legal system. These analytical possibilities have not yet been used by the advocates of the theory with regard to the codetermination problem. I am sceptical about scientific normative declarations; the structure of the property rights efficiency test is, however, especially appropriate for justifying the actual social situation. If normative declarations are to be made, it would seem reasonable to base such declarations on comparative studies, by searching for a connection between a country's corporation law and the appearence of different social conflicts. Normative answers necessitate moral criteria, and therefore my conclusions indicating this possible interrelation have taken on a somewhat moral tone.

1. The Firm as a Hierarchical Organisation and as a Set of Contracts in the Property Rights Theory

Traditionally, reflections on the structure of the firm start from the empirical observation that firms, or at least big firms, are hierarchical and bureaucratic organisations. Employees are incorporated into the organisation and are subject to the authority of the employer. This authority is usually explained by the rules of ownership of the means of production, which permit the owner (or his agent) to direct the workers. Somehow, there has remained something of a mystery surrounding the theoretical explanation that ownership of the means of production should convey the authority to direct other people. For example, Marx tried to shed light on that mystery by declaring the employment contract to be a sales contract[2]. His explanation becomes noticeably wordy and repetitious as he

[2] Under the wage contract the worker *sells* his working power to the employer. So, the

tries to make his concept clear to the reader: that an employment contract gives the same rights to a "purchaser" of working power as to the purchaser of goods. Nevertheless, the explanation is not quite convincing because the image is contrary to our everyday experience. The sale of a good and the contractual obligation to work are too obviously different.

Another possible means of dealing with the mystery of the authoritarian structure of the firm is chosen by the property rights theorists. They reject the empirical evidence for this structure and declare it to be a mere delusion. Normally, one could ignore theories which are not based on empirical evidence. I do not do so, because it is precisely these contradictory assertions which provide the possibility of posing interesting questions. Alchain and Demsetz deny the existence of employer authority and disciplinary power and, they only accept the contract between employer and employee – a contract which in principle is not different from other exchange agreements. These authors compare the employment contract to the regular purchase of provisions from the grocer. "The single consumer can assign his grocer to the task of obtaining whatever the customer can induce the grocer to provide at a price acceptable to both parties. That is precisely all that an employer can do to an employee." (Alchian/Demsetz, 1972:777). We now come to the contractual theory of the firm: "Contractual relations are the essence of the firm, not only with employees but with suppliers, customers, creditors etc." (Jensen/Meckling, 1972:310). Can we derive new perspectives on codetermination from this contractual theory of the firm?

2. The Contractual Theory of the Firm and the Position of the Capital Owner

It is typical of the contractual theory of the firm, presented by Alchian, Demsetz, Jensen, and Meckling, that it does not apply this approach with a view towards examining its consequences[3]. For example Alchian/Demsetz declare:

The essence of the classical firm is identified here as a contractual structure with: 1. joint input production; 2. several input owners; 3. one party who is common to all the contracts

existence of the authority to direct is not explained, but may be illustrated by a figurative comparison: "Der Kapitalist zahlt z. B. den Tagewert der Arbeitskraft. Ihr Gebrauch, wie der jeder anderen Ware, z. B. eines Pferdes, das er für einen Tag gemietet, gehört ihm also für den Tag. Dem Käufer gehört der Gebrauch der Ware, und der Besitzer der Arbeitskraft gibt in der Tat nur den von ihm verkauften Gebrauchswert, indem er seine Arbeitskraft gibt. Von dem Augenblick an, wo er in die Werkstätte des Kapitalisten trat, gehörte der Gebrauchswert seiner Arbeit, also ihr Gebrauch, die Arbeit dem Kapitalisten. Der Kapitalist hat durch den Kauf der Arbeitskraft die Arbeit selbst als lebendigen Gärungsstoff den toten ihm gleichfalls gehörigen Bildungselementen des Produktes einverleibt. Von seinem Standpunkt ist der Arbeitsprozeß nur die Konsumtion der von ihm gekauften Ware Arbeitskraft, die er jedoch nur konsumieren kann, indem er ihr Produktionsmittel zusetzt. Der Arbeitsprozeß ist ein Prozeß zwischen Dingen, die der Kapitalist gekauft hat, zwischen ihm gehörigen Dingen." (Marx, 1890:200).

[3] See Nutzinger (1978) for a more detailed criticism.

of the joint inputs; 4. who has the right to renegotiate any input's contract independently of contract with other input owners; 5. who holds the residual claim; and 6. who has the right to sell his central contractual residuals status. The central agent is called the firm's owner and the employer (Alchian/Demsetz, 1972:794).

Equating the owner, the entrepreneur and the central agent who is the central contractual partner of all contracts is typical of the approach of property rights theorists. This is the main device which allows the theory to be used ideologically: initially, property rights are interpreted differently from their normal juridical significance and defined as entitlements (for the notion see especially Calabresi/Melamed, 1972, and Schueller, 1978:30). Subsequently, property rights are suddenly transformed from entitlements into private ownership and identified with the provision of capital (see Krause, 1981:8), thereby eliminating the previously postulated liberality in the distribution of entitlement rights. It was advantageous for this approach to retain those traditional concepts which are important mainly for jurists, as they are especially influenced by the biases of their particular legal systems. Recently, however, we find a contractual concept of the firm which no longer attributes the central role to the owner (see Fama, 1980; obviously, Fama's political goal is ideological support for managers' rule, even in the context of this particular theory of the firm). Consequently, ownership of the firm is an irrelevant concept. The provision of capital is based upon contracts made with owners of capital in the same way that they are made with owners of other factors of production. As a consequence, Fama insists that the functions attributed to the capital owner (risk bearing) and the management functions are separate factors within the set of contracts called a firm. The firm purchases its services on different markets, and therefore those services respond to different market signals. Risk bearers are of course interested in the success of the firm. However, they realise that interest by diversifying their holdings among many firms on the capital market (following portfolio theory) and not by directly controlling the management. "On the other hand, the managers of a firm rent a substantial amount of wealth – their human capital – to the firm, and the rental market is likely to depend on the success or failure of the firm" (Fama, 1980:291, 292). From this market Fama deduces the motivation and control function for managers.

This contractual perspective of the firm has no answer to the question posed by Alchian and Demsetz about the identity of the central agent of the firm. This economic gap may be filled by introducing a juridical notion into economic thinking, rather than of the inverse process of engaging in an economic analysis of law. If one does not previously resolve the question of what entitlement rights are to be attributed to the individuals who are creating the firm via their contracts, one can follow the traditional juridical concept which ignores the actors and instead, recognizes the firm itself. Indeed, this is the conception of the corporation as a legal person who is the contractual partner of all contracts (without the foundation contract)[4]. This concept permits the distribution of

[4] The legal system, however, recognises other legal persons who do not depend on contract (as the foundation). Therefore, one can ignore the fact that, historically capital owners

entitlements or property rights in the firm – without preconceptions. The firm – as an economic organisation, not as a legal entity – appears now as a chain of contracts in time centred around the legal person as the central contractual partner. Contractual partners of this legal person are capital owners, managers and employees, but also lenders, suppliers, customers, lessors of land, buildings, machines; insurers, the social security system, the fiscal authority, and so on.

3. Furubotn's Formula of the Inefficiency of Codetermination in the Firm

This concept, which ignores the question of ownership of the firm, again makes it easier to decide who in the organisation will have the authority to decide certain questions, because the owners of capital shares are no longer preordained to hold those positions in which the most important decisions are made. Now, all partners of the contractual set which comprises the firm come into play. This perspective is surprising only to those whose view of the reality of the firm is obscured by the prevailing property ideology. At least for large West German corporations it is significant that important contractual partners of the firm (bank houses, insurers, customers and suppliers) – often even competitors – obtain positions on the supervisory board(s).

Despite the existence of these practical solutions to the problem of firm control it would be in conformity with the practice of German theorists to search for criteria in the "set of contracts' perspective for the distribution of authority (entitlements or property rights) in the firm. The theorists would assume the role of the patriarchal state in regulating all appropriate needs, for the *bonum commune* of its vassals. However, this reform-from-the-top view does not correspond to the Anglo-American concept of contract. Promoters of this concept believe that concern for the *bonum commune* will follow from the egoistic concern for individual interests. In the logic of the contract theory of the firm, the distribution of authority (property rights) in the firm should follow spontaneously from market processes. German economists adverse to codetermination use all their sophistry to prove again and again that codetermination is detrimental to the single firm and to the economy as a whole (see e.g. Prosi, 1978). Conversely, the market argument seems to be significant in American economic thinking since Furubotn (1981:705) argues that codetermination is inefficient (that is to say, a bad thing) only because it does not follow from market operations. "Actually, given the rarity of voluntary codetermination arrangements in the real world, it seems possible to conclude that codetermina-

have contracted in advance, which suggests grounds for considering them as central agents. Though, empirically too, they (more or less) lose this position by founding the legal person.

[5] See in more detail the Monopolkommission (1982:129). As an example the following figure is quoted: the 8 banks and insurance corporations, which belong to the "100 biggest firms" of the Federal Republic of Germany, in 1980 held 99 seats on the supervisory boards of the "100 biggest firms".

tion is an inefficient organisational form and one that emerges merely because a powerful special interest group is able to use the political system to effect a wealth transfer from others to themselves."

Is the assumption true then that codetermination is inefficient (a bad thing) simply because voluntary exchanges seldom transfer codetermination rights to employees?

This argument receives additional support from the fact that capital owners in practice will often waive the decision-making rights attributed to them by the legal system. In reality they often cede these rights to other contractual partners of the firm, mainly to the banks as lenders, but often also to important suppliers and customers. Following the efficiency notion of the property rights theory, this practice seems to be efficient and to support the view that giving such positions to employees is inefficient.

3.1 The Empirical Meaning of the Formula

We must consider, first, the question of whether it is empirically true that codetermination or decision-making rights authority, or property rights in the firm are in fact so seldom voluntarily vested in employees. The answer can only be given if we specify on which level these rights are executed. Obviously, decisions are not only made by the supervisory board. There is a large range of decisions to be made in the firm, decisions which are made by many people. For example, in German terminology we distinguish between codetermination on the enterprise level, on the plant level and on the level of the working place. Beyond that, employees – as well as other contractual partners of the firm, – have the possibilities of influencing the policy of the firm in the short or the long term, in important and trivial matters, without having that influence recognised or implemented by organised means. They can determine the content.of the firm's decisions only by means of contractual obligations, or simply by their real influence. From recent German anti-trust policy we can see examples of this latter phenomenon of demand power. Anti-trust policy has often been concerned with problems of this sort in the motor industry. There it is often the case that legally independent suppliers of automobile corporations, who bear the risk of their own firms, are so dependent on their customers that many management decisions are no longer made by their own staff, but by the personnel of the motor corporation. We find examples of similar dependency between borrowers and their banks, especially regarding investment decisions. But we need not go so far. Decisions are made on all levels of the firm's hierarchy, even on the lowest level. If one goes to the root of the question in this manner it is less clear that codetermination is a bad thing simply because it is not a spontaneous response to the market. Especially in the USA we find some examples of collective agreements which grant important control rights to the unions. (see Summers, 1979:262; Simitis, 1975:329). Let me also mention – as a very interesting example of this kind of contract – the collective agreement of 1973 between Fiat and the metal workers' union (F.L.M.), which stipulated obligations for the investment policy of the enterprise, and which committed Fiat to a gradual shift to the production of means of public transport. In the terminology of the property rights literature, through these contracts the unions acquire property rights in the firm. I mention an "internal" example of this transfer of property rights to the employees of a firm; 25 per cent of the members of worker councils, who are exempt from the normal obligations of their job, have attained this status not by legal rules, but by voluntary agreements. Assuming the argument that codetermination is efficient if voluntarily agreed upon, I have proved only that it is efficient in the cited cases, not that it is efficient in cases where it is not voluntarily agreed upon. And in this regard we note especially that codetermination on the boards of firms – so important for German labour unions – is very seldom contracted.

3.2 The Meaning of the Efficiency Concept in the Property Rights Theory

(a) Consequences of the Methodological Individualism and of Non-Profit Utility Ends of Capital Owners

The statement that capital owners only seldom grant positions on the board of management to employees now requires explanation, especially with regard to what is meant exactly when property rights theorists declare a certain arrangement of property right to be more or less efficient than another one. Economists such as Posner, Demsetz and Furubotn advocate a strictly individualistic concept: every exchange of goods or property rights which takes place improves efficiency because it would not have taken place otherwise, and therefore efficiency is a notion which results only from the individual notions of utility held by the contracting partners. A change in the arrangement of property rights by a voluntary exchange contract is efficient because the partners expect an improvement of their situations by this exchange. An exchange contract does not result from inefficiency if one or both of the parties does not expect an enhancement of his utility. This efficiency concept is linked exclusively to the individual goals of utility; it does not offer any insights about economic or social efficiency. This concept is far removed from the classical economists' idea of the welfare of the nation or from the neoclassical idea of an economic optimum for the society.

Let me make two remarks with regard to this thesis, which is central for the understanding of the entire property rights theory:

First: in economic theory there is only one convincing and exactly formulated model which clearly combines individual economic freedom, individual efficiency and economic efficiency: the model of perfect competition. The absence of reality inherent in that model is the starting point of the property rights theorists (see Pejovich, 1976). So far we find a general accord among economists.

Second: setting aside all other (unrealistic) assumptions, concepts of individual and economic efficiency conform according to economic theory only if the owners of the means of production use them exclusively for profit-maximising ends. If they pursue other utility goals when making their decisions thus affecting the profit-maximising goal, then individual and economic efficiency become distinct. Since property rights theorists claim that their theory has an immediate practical relevance, we must comment that capital owners who have more than just profit-maximising interests at stake will likely refrain from transferring their traditional rights to the employees. In this case, it seems realistic to assume that other utilities such as personal power, social prestige and the like will be important.

Thus, the pretentious assertion, "given the rarity of voluntary codetermination arrangements in the real world, it seems possible to conclude that codetermination is an inefficient organisational form" should be worded more banally, and more honestly, as follows: capital owners seldom renounce the rights attributed to them in the firm by the law simply because they do not like the idea, for whatever reason.

(b) The Difference between the Formula of Furubotn and the Voluntary Exchange Test of the Property Rights Theory

To understand the significance of Furubotn's efficiency formula it is useful to see how this formula differs from the voluntary exchange test normally used by property rights theorists. As is well known, this test responds to the question of whether a resource (or a property right) is more "valuable" in the hands of an individual A than in the hands of an individual B. The decision is made following this criterion: is A prepared to offer a price to B inducing him to sell the resource to A? This formulation is based on the assumption that A can use the resource to produce a more valuable output, as measured by the price consumers are willing to pay for it, and thereby earning a bigger profit for A than B would have earned (see Posner, 1977:10). Obviously, this approach differs from the voluntary exchange test used by Furubotn with regard to codetermination rights in two aspects. Furubotn does not ask: in whose hand would the rights be more "valuable"? When the rights are shifted from capital owner's to employee's hands, would the employees enjoy more profit than the capital owners previously had? He therefore fails to ask what is the price that workers are willing to pay. Instead, his question is: are capital owners willing to give away their rights to their employees, for the sole reason that they expect bigger profits for themselves by the operation?[6]

(c) The Tautological Character of Furubotn's Efficiency Test

Furubotn theoretically studies the question of why such donations of rights so seldom occur, although his observation itself is intended to be empirical. This theoretical study nevertheless leads to a tautology because of a basic assumption of the property rights theory. This basic assumption is: private property rights

[6] The difference from the traditional question of the property rights theory becomes very clear, if one reformulates as a typical example the conflict of land utilisation between farmer and railway corporation. The situation there is no longer that the farmer sells his land to the railway corporation, if the price offered is higher than the returns he can produce on the land. Rather, the situation, according to Furubotn's codetermination test, is as follows: the farmer gives away his land to the railway corporation, if thereby, he can produce higher returns on the land than before.

achieve an efficient use of scarce resources because of the incentive and control functions linked to them. But these incentive and control functions play their role only if the right to ***use*** a resource *(usus)* and the right to receive ***returns*** from its use *(usus fructus)* are attached to the same person. Therefore, ***ex definitione***, an exchange of property rights – transferring only the decision making power of how to use a resource, without transferring the claim on the residual income – always contains the risk of reducing efficiency. Indeed, that is the case in transferring codetermination rights where the profit claim remains in the exclusive possession of the capital owners. This tautology cannot be rejected simply by remarking that property rights theorists also study very extensively the partitioning of ownership entitelements among stockholders and managers and come to contrary results in that case. In fact, the formulations of the questions in the two cases are reversed: in the latter case the property rights theorists have to find an explanation for real "voluntary exchange contracts" which, according to the theory, should not have taken place. Different explanations are promoted (direct controls over managers, capital market forces, take-over operations, the market for management services) in order to fill this lacuna. The result of all these explanations is that the interest of stockholders and managers are characterised as more or less the same. The corresponding question in the codetermination case is: why and under what circumstances do capital owners really voluntarily waive their legal rights, transferring them to employees or unions, and under what circumstances may we expect or not expect such transfers? This question is not posed by the property rights theorists. However, the allegation of fundamentally different objectives of capital owners and employer renders the tautological conclusion inevitable[7].

(d) Possible Insight Resulting from the Traditional Property Rights Efficiency Test

If the efficiency test promoted by Furubotn leads to tautological results then we will instead briefly discuss the question of whether the traditional voluntary exchange test of the property rights theory may grant any insights into the codetermined firm. To understand the structure of the test we must recognize that it is based on a strange schizophrenia. On the one hand, one is asking for the most efficient distribution of property rights, assuming therefore that the legal system has not already resolved this issue. The contractual theory of the firm is meaningful only with this contradictory assumption of an unresolved legal situation – that is to say, it is meaningful if the property rights in the firm are not yet distributed. On the other hand, the problem posed by the undecided situation is that a voluntary agreement is then impossible, because exchange contracts postulate the initial distribution of legal rights. Theorists handle this dilemma by simulating market processes. It is not easy to conceive of such simulated markets. In our case we can construct a model in which we sell the

[7] See Furubotn (1981:707): "The core problem, of course, is that corporate employees will not normally maximise their welfare by accepting those production strategies that maximise the present value of the firm's income stream".

central agent's position by auction among all contractual parties which, according to the contractual theory, constitute the firm. The legal system must then attribute the central position (free of charge) to the party who bids the most in this situation. However, this test is confronted by the following difficulties:

First: the test brings to mind the "Als-ob-Wettbewerbs-Methode" ("as-if-competition-method") from anti-trust policy. Surely, the methodological difficulties encountered in anti-trust policy will be few compared with those to be expected in the voluntary exchange test, especially if one wishes to give recommendations for possible political action. However, the fundamental objections against the simulation of market processes are the same in both cases. Competition theorists, whose positions are close to the property rights theory, formulate it most precisely: "Competition, in principle cannot be simulated and the ability of economic theory to predict does not include the prediction of the particular economic performance of a specific market or firm ..." (Hoppmann, 1977:21, translated by the author).

Second: the second objection concerns the interdependency between willingness to pay – the only criterion that matters, according to the property rights theory – and the ability to pay. According to the normative statements of the property rights theory, the legal system should give the resources or property rights to the person for whom they are most valuable, as measured by the different prices different persons are willing to pay. The political consequences of this recommendation are easily expressed with the example that a slice of bread must be given to the millionaire to feed his dog – and not to the beggar who is dying of hunger – because the beggar is not able to pay, while the millionaire is willing to compensate the baker generously. We must accept similarly immoral answers when analysing the codetermination problem by these means, because the employees' ability to pay will always be lower in reality than the similar ability of capital owners. Therefore, applying the proposed efficiency test to the auction case we see that even supposing that the profit of the firm would be highest if the employees took the position of the central agent, the position could never in reality be attributed to them, because they are not sufficiently solvent to make the highest bid in the auction.

Third: the test only permits a comparison between the capital-managed firm and the labour-managed firm, but not between either of the above and the codetermined firm – this follows from my observations about the tautological character of the Furubotn test. For, as suggested above, the basic assumptions of the property rights theory necessarily lead to the conclusion that situations where control rights and income rights are partitioned are less efficient than other situations where both categories of rights are united in a single hand. Jensen and Meckling (1979:503), in attempting to study the efficiency of codetermination using the property rights theory test, avoid this difficulty by employing alternative assumptions: in the case of the German codetermination law, they consider that in the short run it is reasonable that the stockholders will have complete control over the affairs of the firm. In the long run it may be possible that codetermination will lead to a result at the other end of the spectrum – that is, codetermination could end up effectively turning the firm over to labour. Consequently, Jensen and Meckling analyse codetermination only in regard to these two possibilities: either the stockholders prevail in the firm, or the firm becomes labour-managed. Lacking the necessary analytical instruments, they do not study the complicated, real processes which may influence the efficiency of codetermined firms.

4. Conditions of Voluntary Transfers of Property Rights Within the Firm

As I mentioned above, from the standpoint of the property rights theory the most interesting question should be: Why are employees or their organisations voluntarily given entitlements (property rights) which were previously held by the capital owners or their reprensentatives (I mentioned some examples in paragraph 3.1) and under which conditions such transfers are to be expected? I will discuss this question in property right terms in this section. The result is likely to seem banal: such voluntary transfers are the result of the relations of economic power, of legal rules and of the socio-cultural context in which they take place.

In the framework of the property rights theory we should begin with the significance of legal rules. My considerations refer to the schizophrenic position, mentioned above, in that the theory assumes legal positions or property rights to be not yet distributed; but on the other hand, that the "voluntary exchange test" must assume these rights as fixed in advance, because otherwise exchange contracts are impossible. For the really interesting question one can now formulate the dilemma as follows: if the normative question of how entitlements shall be distributed anew according to the criteria of the property rights theory is to be answered, – the answer depends on what the legal system prescribes in other aspects of the situation.

The value (in the property rights meaning) of an entitlement or a mere opportunity is dependent on the bargaining position of the contracting parties, which itself depends on the entitlements attributed to the contracting parties in other respects. Therefore, how far shall the alteration of the legal rules go?

In traditional economic terminology, the results of bargaining processes or market processes were explained as resulting from differences in bargaining power or in market power. If one interprets the distribution of resources – the granting of such power – and the entitlements – whether and in which way these resources may be used – as a legal fixing of a distribution of property rights, there is no difference between the two approaches. The result of the "voluntary exchange test" depends on the bargaining power or the market power of the contracting partners, who in turn depend on the legal rules which determine their positions.

These considerations may be concretised by the examples of voluntary transfers of property rights to other contracting partners of the firm mentioned in paragraph 3.1. Let us begin with the case of demand power. According to the property rights theory behaviour and performance resulting from demand power are efficient because they follow from voluntary exchange contracts. It is clear that the situation has improved for the party with demand power by the redistribution of property rights. But why does the dependent party so "voluntarily" renounce rights hitherto attributed to it? Let us vary the previously existing distribution of property rights so that it is now forbidden for the firm with strong demand power to exercise its market power in the bargaining process. Now, I assume the result of the voluntary exchange test will be different, because the relative bargaining positions have been altered. The same test will lead to new and different results if the legal system allows the dependent enterprises to cartelise, and therefore collectivise the negotiations between suppliers and the demand-powerful firm. In every case the (anti-trust) recommendation would be that the legal situation should not change. The anti-trust recommendation would only depend on the starting position of the firms and would in each case justify the existing anti-trust regulations. In general terms according to Schmid:

"Efficiency calculations always depend on where you start, but they can never validate that starting place. Therefore, a cost benefit analysis of alternative rights is always a partial analysis. Efficiency calculations always presume some set of rights and therefore cannot be a guide to rights, unless the prior rights are legitimated" (Schmid, 1978:246).

Within the framework of the analysis, however, well-founded suppositions may be made about the particular way that certain legal rules influence the bargaining positions of the contracting partners, and thereby it may be possible to explain given bargaining results. So we can also find plausible reasons in the legal system for explaining why capital owners do or do not transfer certain property rights of the firm to the employees or their organisations.

For example, Summers explains the distribution of property rights in US firms between management and unions. According to him, two legal rules lead to the situation where the unions' influence in decision-making is limited to the subject of "conditions of employment", and unions thereby excluded from real management decisions:

> The effect of these two legal rules is that a union cannot use its economic strength to expand the area of participation beyond that described by the statute (wages, hours, and other terms and conditions of employment); but the employer can use his economic strength to limit participation to an area smaller than that described by the statute ... The important point is that the law does not require the employer to grant these broader participation rights nor permit the union to use its economic strength to compel the employer to grant them. But the law does permit the employer to use his economic strength to restrict the scope of participation (Summers, 1979, 263; see also Simitis, 1975:329).

In analysing "voluntary" transfers of property rights in the firm between capital and labour, and in deciding in which situations such transfers are to be expected, one has to know the bargaining positions of the two contracting partners in a world where the legal system has attributed the position of the "central agent" to the capital owners. Of course, the bargaining situation would be different, and would lead to different outcomes, if the legal system attributed the position of the "central agent" to the representatives of the employees, who now contracted with each individual shareholder, fixing the amount of input the shareholder would be allowed to make and the amount of renumeration he would receive; and, in addition, we might suppose that five or ten per cent of the existing capital is urgently searching for "employment". Actually, given the distribution of bargaining power between the single employee and the employer in the real world, we cannot expect that property rights in the firm are transferred to employees just at the moment of concluding an individual wage contract. In the real world, employees, after having contracted individually, now as a collective body have something to offer to their employers in exchange for property rights previously attributed to the capital owners by the legal system. The only asset employees have to sell is their factual collective possibility to boycott production (especially by strike and by other means of refusing to perform their contractual obligations). These factual possibilities become property rights in the firm in so far as they are positively sanctioned by the legal system. To that extent they are to be introduced into collective bargaining and may change the relative bargaining positions of employers and employees. How far the employees are ready and able to begin such collective actions is, of course dependent on many other factors, which we can also analyse in property rights terms (as for example, freedom of association). Here, however, we do not propose to take this argument to its logical conclusion.

From the American example we have learned how the inability to use these real possibilities for pursuing certain goals can arise. We can translate this into the terminology of the property rights theory as follows: the legal system denies the only entitlement, the only property right, to the American worker that he can offer to the employer in exchange for codetermination rights on the management level. Consequently, such contracts do not come into existence. One could argue in similar fashion concerning the "Friedenspflicht" ("peace-obligation") imposed on the work councils by the German Betriebsverfassungsgesetz (Works Councils Act).

As is well known, the ends for which German unions may strike are rather limited. The acceptance of codetermination rules is not included among these permissible ends. However an analysis of this institutional arrangement, and of others, in terms of the property rights theory is not possible in this paper.

Let me finish this section by referring to the historically developed sociocultural context of these different institutional arrangements to highlight another defect of the property rights theory. Property rights theorists have based their ideas on assumptions about human behavior which are supposed to be valid independently of all temporal and local differences in the real world. However, the sociocultural context of labour-management relation may be a determining factor particularly with regard to the codetermination problem. What I mean here may be explained by three events in the history of German codetermination. In 1916 worker committees were legally prescribed in all plants which produced goods important for warfare, in order to avoid riots which could have an adverse effect on the war efforts. In November 1918, a basic agreement between employer associations and unions was reached, where the employers accepted the unions as representatives of the working class and as parties of collective contracts, and where codetermination was accepted on the national and plant level. After World War II, the iron and steel industry accepted parity-codetermination on supervisory boards in order to exclude the more comprehensive claims for nationalisation of this industry. Linked to this development, the unions promoted the idea that the interests of employers and employees are not necessarily contradictory, and that therefore they were ready to assume co-responsibility for the single firm and for the economic development of the whole country, in the framework of a capitalistic system.

On the other hand, Summers summarises the corresponding situation in the USA as follows (1979:263):

"American employers have never accepted the view that workers or their representatives should have a voice in the decisions of management; they have always jealously guarded their management prerogatives. In bargaining with unions they have not only strongly resisted demands, which they saw as encroachment on their freedom to manage, but have directed major efforts toward elaborating the management prerogative clause in the contract ... Both unions and employers view each other as adversaries and collective bargaining as a process of confrontation. The union's emphasis is on pressing for more benefits for its members. It is not anxious to have a full voice in the decisions of management, for it would then be required to assume the responsibility of management".

In considering these two different societies, it would be deceptive to conclude, that on the basis of our assumptions about the behaviour of the parties concerned the same economic outcomes will result when codetermination rules are established.

5. Final Remarks

By employing the terminology of the property rights theory to pose positive questions about the codetermination problem, one can suggest plausible hypotheses about causal interrelationships between the legally sanctioned positions of employees, capital owners, etc. and contractual codetermination rules. In particular, the contractual theory of the firm enables us to formulate such hypotheses. What is new about such hypotheses, however, seems to be only that they now appear in the context and the terminology of micro-economics. Up to now, advocates of the property rights theory have not pursued that possibility. Investigation of the (causal) interrelationships between codetermination rules and economic outcomes also permits the elaboration of an analysis with pratical implications (see e.g. Backhaus, 1979). However, we currently have very litle empirically-based knowledge of the subject. Property rights theorists themselves have not yet treated the problem empirically; and I even doubt that, on the basis of the property rights theory, essential contributions can be made by empirical studies as long as the theory commences with marginally-differentiated assumptions about human behaviour.

The question *why* legal codeterminatin rules exist is the same for property right theorists as the normative question of whether such rules *shall* exist[8]. It is the possibility of producing normative answers to these questions which makes the property rights theory so fascinating for jurists. In this paper I have attempted to show that these answers may be misleading. For, the property rights theory accepts efficiency as its only normative criterion. If codetermination impairs efficiency, then Furbuton's evaluation becomes obvious – that it is an organisational form "that emerges merely because a powerful special interest group is able to use the political system to effect a wealth transfer from others to themselves." (Furubotn, 1981: 705). For that reason, I attempted to explain that the efficiency notion of the property rights theory has so little meaning that empirical conclusions cannot be drawn from it. In section 4 I also tried to draw attention to the fact that the structure of the property rights theory leads to results which legitimate different existing economic relations. In principle, the efficiency test can lead to as many efficient results as the cases that one can employ. The normative question – which result would be better? – nevertheless remains open. This question can only be answered by applying subjective values. Traditionally, economists have avoided the conflict by using the Pareto rule, or in other words: traditional economic thinking in that respect accepts the legal context as *data*. Property rights theorists try to lift this barrier. Hutter commented correctly: "If alterations in rules are allowed – just because otherwise the status quo would be advantaged – then all values become dependent on these differently validated rules". The question – which legal rule is better? – depends on the answer to the question: "Better for whom? (see also Schmid, 1978:250). Another rule, typically used by economists when dealing with the distribution of decision-making authority, stated that external costs will tend to be internalised. There are good arguments to be made, following this rule, that the codetermined firm should be favoured. This follows from the consideration that in this case a bad decision costs the employees more than it does the capital owners[9]. The property rights theory no longer openly accepts this rule, because here internalising costs would damage the producer of the external costs (Coase 1960:1; see also my more detailed critique, Gotthold, 1980:558). Therefore, the assertions of the rule are not studied in the codetermination case.

Are no answers to be given at all to the normative question of whether codetermination is a good or a bad thing? Instead of lecturing on the "Werturteilsstreit" of the positivism debate, I refer to ideas of Joan Robinson (1978:21).

[8] In another publication I commented in more detail on the following contradiction: that property rights theory attempts to analyse non-market social relations with the help of micro-economic approaches.
Microeconomical thinking leads all social processes back to individual decisions (see Gotthold, 1980:554).

[9] One enumerates, as employee's costs, the human capital and the investment in private households and social relations. In the case of firing, resulting from bad decision making, these investments are slightly devalued. In contrast to this, the investments of capital owner are often small, as Fama emphasises. The capital owner can protect himself from a loss in his participation by a timely sale of his securities on the capital market (for more detail see Backhaus, 1980:26).

According to her the most pertinent question for economics to answer is: "What characteristic of the private enterprise system is it that condemns the wealthiest nation that the world has ever seen to keeping an appreciable proportion of its population in perpetual ignorance and misery? The professional economists keep up a smoke-screen of "theorems" and "laws" and "trade-offs" that prevents questions such as that from being asked." I believe that the American property rights literature is a good example of such a shroud. If we attempt to pursue Joan Robinson's question, we would have to search for plausible hypotheses which would explain the attributes of American society as cited by her. A first (simplistic) hypothesis is that the distribution of social and economic power is responsible for the situation. To understand something about this problem, a study comparing the USA and the Federal Republic of Germany, and focussing on the relationship of employees' participation in the firm's decision with the distribution of social and economic power in the community could be a useful approach. Considering the complexity of the variables concerned, we will of course not find an answer which is objectively true. Hayek taught us to be sceptical about the potential of empirical proofs for establishing causal relations in complex interrelationships. He is content with an allusion to the history of civilisation for proving the superiority of a private market economy to other economic systems. (Hayek, 1968:350). The interrelation between the firm constitution (property rights in the firm), the distribution of social and economic power in a community, and the proportion of the population held in permanent ignorance and misery, is not likely to be proved in fact. But comparative studies, indeed, supported by plausible arguments, may point to such an interrelationship in more detail.

Bibliography

ALCHIAN, ARMEN, A. and HAROLD DEMSETZ, (1972) "Production, Information Costs and Economic Organization", 62 *The American Economic Review* 777.

BACKHAUS, JÜRGEN (1980) Funktionsfähigkeit der mitbestimmten Großunternehmung? in: Fakultät für Wirtschaftswissenschaften und Statistik, *Diskussionsbeiträge Serie A-Nr. 143*.

COASE, RONALD H. (1960) "The Problem of Social Cost", 3 *Journal of Law and Economics* 1.

ESCHENBURG, ROLF (1978) "Mikroökonomische Aspekte von Property Rights", in K.-E. Schenk (ed.) *Ökonomische Verfügungsrechte und Allokationsmechanismen in Wirtschaftssystemen*, Schriften des Vereins für Socialpolitik, NF. vol. 97, Berlin: Duncker & Humblot.

FAMA, EUGENE F. (1980) "Agency Problems and the Theory of the Firm", 88 *Journal of Political Economy* 288.

FURUBOTN, EIRIK G. (1980) "Codetermination and the Efficient Partioning of Ownership Rights in the Firm", 137 *Zeitschrift für die gesamte Staatswissenschaft* 702.

FURUBOTN, EIRIK G. and SVETOZAR PEJOVICH (1972) "Property Rights and Economic Theory: A Survey of Recent Literature", 10 *Journal of Economic Literature* 1137.

Gotthold, Jürgen (1980) "Zur ökonomischen Theorie des Eigentums. Eine kritische Einführung", 144 *Zeitschrift für das gesamte Handelsrecht und Wirtschaftsrecht* 545.

Hayek, Friedrich A. v. (1968) "Der Wettbewerb als Entdeckungsverfahren", in: F. A. v. Hayek, *Freiburger Studien*, Tübingen: J. C. B. Mohr.

Hoppmann, Erich (1977) *Marktmacht und Wettbewerb*. Tübingen: J. C. B. Mohr.

Hutter, Michael (1980) "Über eine Alternative zur neoklassischen ökonomischen Analyse des Rechts", 144 *Zeitschrift für das gesamte Handelsrecht und Wirtschaft* 612.

Jensen, Michael C. and William H. Meckling (1976) "Theory of the Firm: Managerial Behavior, Agency Costs and Ownership Structure", 3 *Journal of Financial Economics* 305.

– (1979) "Rights and Production Functions: An Application to Labor managed Firms and Codetermination", *Journal of Business* 469.

Krause, Detlev (1981) "Der Property-Rights-Ansatz: Überlegungen zu einem neuen Paradigma der Analyse gesellschaftlicher Steuerung", Manuskript Bremen.

Marx, Karl (1969) *Das Kapital* (K. Marx/F. Engels, Werke, Bd. 23). Berlin (Ost): Dietz-Verlag.

Monopolkommission (1982) *Fortschritte bei der Konzentrationserfassung, Hauptgutachten 1980/81*. Baden-Baden: Nomos.

Nutzinger, Hans G. (1978) "The Firm as a Social Institution: the Failure of the Countractarian Viewpoint", in: J. Backhaus, Th. Eger and H. G. Nutzinger (eds.), *Partizipation in Betrieb und Gesellschaft*. Frankfurt a.M.: Haag & Herchen.

Pejovich, Svetozar (1976) "The Capitalist Corporation and the Socialist Firm", 112 *Schweizerische Zeitschrift für Volkswirtschaft und Statistik* 1.

Posner, Richard A. (1977) *Economic Analysis of Law*. Boston, Toronto: Little, Brown and Company.

Prosi, Gerhard (1978) *Volkswirtschaftliche Auswirkungen des Mitbestimmungsgesetzes 1976*. Köln: Bachem.

Robinson, Joan (1978) *The Disintegration of Economics*, WSI-Studie zur Wirtschafts- und Sozialforschung, Nr. 38, Krise der ökonomischen Theorie-Krise der Wirtschaftspolitik. Köln: Bund-Verlag.

Schmid, A. Allen (1978) *Property, Power and Public Choice: An Inquiry into Law and Economics*. New York: Praeger.

Schueller, Alfred (1978) "Property Rights, unternehmerische Legitimation und Wirtschaftsordnung. Zum vermögenstheoretischen Ansatz einer allgemeinen Theorie der Unternehmung", in: K.-E. Schenk (ed.) *Ökonomische Verfügungsrechte und Allokationsmechanismen in Wirtschaftssystemen*. Schriften des Vereins für Socialpolitik, N.F. vol. 97. Berlin: Duncker & Humblot.

Simitis, Spiros (1975) "Von der institutionalisierten zur problembezogenen Mitbestimmung", 23 *Arbeit und Recht* 321.

Summers, Clyde, W. (1979) "Worker Participation in the United States and the Federal Republic. A Comparative Study from an American Perspective", 32 *Recht der Arbeit* 257.

Wagener, Hans-Jürgen (1979) *Zur Analyse von Wirtschaftssystemen*, Berlin: Springer.

Industrial Democracy Through Law?
Social Functions of Law in Institutional Innovations

GUNTHER TEUBNER

Bremen, Firenze

Introduction

What does the law learn when it is confronted with its own consequences? It is this feedback loop from legal norm to social consequence to legal norm which probably constitutes the most important contribution of social science thinking to legal argument. There is a tradition in legal methodology, the so-called teleological approach, which is very similar to this kind of argument. Legal norms are interpreted in the light of their purpose and one important consideration is the question if the purpose has been actually reached or not. However the teleological method is still an intra-legal device. It relates the legal norm to the legally-set purpose, be it the legislature's goal, be it the judge's reformulation of the legal purpose. In contrast, the consequentialist method I am following here is going a step beyond the law itself. It necessarily utilizes extra-legal modes of analysis and feeds them back into the legal argument. The basic argument has the following elements: (1) What is the basic legislative or judicial social purpose of a norm? What are the intended social effects on social behavior and social structure which are expected to follow the enactment and implementation of the legal norm? (2) To what degree have these goals been reached in the social reality? What are the side-effects, what are the unintended consequences of a legal norm in social reality? (3) How has one to reformulate the legal norm in the light of its social consequences?

For this type of legal argument, there are no limits as to academic speciality of the information involved. Social science information in the broadest sense is needed, be it of sociological, economic or psychological nature. However there is a special branch in legal sociology developing which could be in the position to develop common standards of argumentation. "Legal Effect Research" (Rechtswirkungsforschung) is concerned with the question what difference it makes if social fields are regulated by formal legal norms. This is an autonomous realm of legal sociology. It becomes part of a broader sociological jurisprudence, if the selection of criteria for this type of research is guided by legal regulatory intentions and if the results of that research are used for a reformulation of legal norms.

Empirical findings and theoretical insights are likewise suited to be used in this kind of legal reasoning. In the following I am going to use empirical materials as well as theoretical constructions in order to show how social science research on social effects of legal regulation can inform the law about what it is doing. I will concentrate on one of the most important experiments to change the character of organizations by means of law, the example of industrial democracy.

There are many roads to "Industrial Democracy". A lively academic discussion as well as numerous social experiments reveal a whole variety of approaches: Via work place participation, work councils, board representation, representation of public interests, pluralist constitution of the firm, collective bargaining systems, workers' self-management, socialization of enterprises. One road, which the German labor movement has chosen, leads via law, legislation and the legal process (e.g. Carnoy and Shearer, 1980). Guided by national bias and experience I want to follow the German road to Industrial Democracy and to describe some of the promising land it leads to as well as the darker areas it surpasses, its potential and limits, its direction, its traps, its detours. If we are interested in successful road construction work, what lessons can we learn from the peculiar German experience? The German road is peculiar, even extreme, in two respects. First, it does not lead through the somewhat muddy lower levels of workplace participation, but rather finds its way through the lofty heights of corporate hierarchies: work councils at the middle echelon as counterweight to managerial authority and representation of workers' interest at the top level of the corporation. Secondly, on this road we do not meet a spontaneous, eruptive, anarchic, unstructured flow of social and political movements but a highly disciplined traffic guided by complicated traffic rules and many, many traffic signs. A high degree of juridification of labor interest representation is the most conspicuous trait of German co-determination. Thus, one should attempt to exploit the German experience and ask the following questions: What are the actual social functions of legalized co-determination as opposed to official goals and political ideologies? What is the effective role of the law in strengthening participation, power equalization and industrial democracy?

I have two tentative answers to these questions which I will elaborate in this paper. The material I rely on is some empirical evidence about the factual consequences of co-determination and some pieces of theory on interest-mediation in industrial relations.

1. *Social functions:* The official doctrine, co-determination contributes to "economic democracy" through workers' participation is an excellent example for political rhetorics. The main function of co-determination lies neither in individual benefits for the workers nor in an enhancement of their political status as economic citizens. Rather, we have to look for relevant effects on the intra-organizational and inter-organizational level. Co-determination changes intra-organizational power relations resulting in a new form of co-management among capital and union elites. In addition, co-determination changes inter-organizational relations insofar as it contributes to a specific form of political ("neo-corporatist") organization in the relation between the economic and the political system.

2. *The role of law:* Due to their norm-centered perspective, lawyers tend to over-estimate the role of legal norms in promoting industrial democracy. Their occupation with decision procedures, formal competences, and standards of legal protection leads them to a problematic identification of formal democratic structures with real democratic processes. On the other hand, social scientists tend to under-estimate the role of law. They perceive law more or less exclusively as a dependent variable and concentrate on social, organizational, psychological conditions. Empirical evidence suggests that both approaches fail to take account of the specific potential and limits of law in its "protective" and its "facilitative" functions. In both respects, legal norms have turned out to be a decisive factor – if not the most decisive factor – in changing effectively intra-organizational as well as inter-organizational power structures.

In order to work out these theses, we cannot fruitfully discuss the complex interrelations between co-determination law and industrial democracy as a whole. Rather one has to distinguish carefully between different levels of social organization and to scrutinize the social functions of law and its potential for change separately on each of these levels. I propose to distinguish three levels: individual interaction, the organization of the firm, the economic system in its relation to society at large.

1. Individual Effects

An old tradition of thought relates co-determination primarily to the individual worker in the firm. His status as a subdued individual in the framework of hierarchical authority and industrial subordination should be transformed into the status of an "economic citizen". This perspective of co-determination is underlain by a concept of economic democracy that aims primarily at the participation of those concerned. Co-determination is conceived as an antidote against "alienation". This treatment of the co-determination idea in terms of the individual is widespread. In a number of variants co-determination is interpreted as compensation for social domination. Individual participation by workers – admittedly mediated through complicated representation mechanisms – is supposed to promote the worker's human dignity, humanize the world of work, give the worker a sense of involvement in his work, control managerial domination and also extend the realization of the democratic principle of participation in decision making to economic enterprises.

Indubitably individual democratic participation and humanization of the world of work constitute social policy goals of the highest rank. But there are certainly great doubts whether the function of institutionalized co-determination has really been grasped hereby.

International empirical studies have scrutinized again and again the democratizing effects of co-determination for the individual worker (see for summaries Blumberg 1968, Wilpert 1975, Batstone and Davies 1976, Wall & Lischeron 1977, Adams and Rummel 1977, IDE 1982). They concentrated on the questions: Does co-determination lead to a reduction of personal alienation? Does it increase workers' motivation which might result in higher productivity?

The findings are contradictory and ambivalent, however, altogether they suggest a rather skeptical assessment.

These findings show the following picture. In general, workers have a rather positive attitude towards co-determination. However, if it comes to details, the attitudes become more negative. As the relation between co-determination and satisfaction is concerned, Tannenbaum et al. found that in countries where workers' representatives had more influence, the workers did not have more satisfaction, trust, sense of responsibility or work motivation than in the other countries (Tannenbaum 1974). In addition, the attitude of workers as to the effects of the representative system is not too positive. In a recent cross-national comparison, less than fifty percent of workers and supervisors in each country showed a positive evaluation of the functioning of representative bodies (IDE 1982: VII, 15). Rather than to democratize the workers' situation, the representative bodies are perceived to function as part of the control structure of the organization (IDE 1982: VII, 13). In more detail, it turned out that rank and file employees do not know much about the work of their representatives. Their attitude to personal involvement is lack of interest, indifference or even apathy. They assess the influence of the representative bodies as rather marginal. Streeck (1984) concludes as follows: "Workers under parity co-determination were as much subject to hierarchical control as workers everywhere else, the organization of their work continued to be determined by impersonal mechanisms beyond their influence and understanding, and their attitudes toward their work did not differ in any perceptible way from that of workers in other industries".

If we contrast these somewhat depressing findings to the high aspirations connected with co-determination, we have to admit that in this respect, political goals and actual social function do not coincide. Due to the large social distance between individual interaction at the workplace and organizational decision making in the corporate hierarchy, co-determination through worker representatives in corporate bodies is clearly not a suited means to achieve the goals of participatory democracy. There are other means which may have some success on the individual level: job enrichment, autonomous working groups, rotation system, and other ways of direct workplace democracy. In vain, however, we will look for democratizing effects of co-determination on this level. Its main social functions should instead be identified rather on the intra-organizational and inter-organizational levels. Thus, co-determination law should give up this orientation toward a non-suited purpose and concentrate its regulatory powers on the other.

2. Organizational Effects

Co-determination law plays a much more important role in the complicated power relations of intra-organizational decision making. Co-determination law seems to change considerably the distribution of power and influence, the goal structure of the organization and the structures of the capital-labor conflict.

2.1 Power and Influence

At first sight, co-determination law does not seem to matter very much. Although complicated rules, procedures, competencies and conflict resolution bodies are created these institutionalized patterns are only rarely used. Open, formalized conflict with decision by vote is only seldom. For example, Tegtmeyer (1973:88) reports that most of the supervisory board decisions were taken unanimously. And the Biedenkopf report (1970:130) contains data according to which only very rarely the "neutral" member of the board had to give the decisive vote. Thus, it might seem that the new legal machinery is not accepted and utilized for the labor interests. Does law only have symbolic functions?

Looking closer to the real decision making processes, the picture changes drastically. Indeed, open conflict is seldom, the legal machinery for conflict resolution is only used as a last resort. However, what happens is a change of informal negotiating processes. And there we can identify the most important albeit indirect effect of the law. The formula is "bargaining in the shadow of the law" (Mnookin and Kornhauser 1979). Management and labor representatives deal with each other by anticipating the power distribution in formal conflicts. The legal rules of co-determination have changed these power relations drastically. The increase of formal decision making power from practically nil to parity positions for the workers influences considerably the actual day-to-day behavior of management and labor. It does so not directly by the new procedures and rules, but by the changed formal positions which are anticipated in the ongoing negotiations. Matters of political conflict are discussed in informal meetings between labor and management before the formal board meeting takes place. And many issues even do not reach that stage of informal negotation since management tries to adapt to anticipated labor positions in order to avoid conflict (Tegtmeyer, 1973:126). Finally, labor representatives are often consulted even if legally it is not required (Streeck, 1984:23).

In a recent empirical study the direct and indirect effects of law in changing the actual power and influence structure have been scrutinized in a comparative way (IDE, 1982:VI). Economic organizations through all the countries are highly hierarchical. Co-determination does not abolish the hierarchy, but it modifies the power-distribution in a considerable way. It does so directly by granting a legal "meta-power" through the re-distribution of control rights and, indirectly by restricting the power of competing groups. Granting legal power to representative bodies does not only increase their influence, but diminishes at the same time the power of top-management.

It seems that the indirect effects of co-determination law (changes in negotiation power) are much more important than the direct effects (installation of a conflict resolution system). This impression is strengthened if one looks to the effects which co-determination had on the union's position as a whole. Streeck (1984:9) has argued that co-determination law has an indirect effect of strengthening the positions of unions in the respective industries in regard to three aspects: (1) Union control over the personnel department made it possible to recruit union members in a way very similar to a closed shop. As a consequence the density ratio of union membership had increased drastically in the coal and steel industry. (2) The presence of a full-time union official on the supervisory board strengthened the crucial contacts between union headquarters and the workforce in the enterprises. (3) Under conditions of parity co-determination, there occurred a practical fusion of the works council and the "external" union. These indications of a relative improvement of the unions bargaining position through law suggests that one indeed should concentrate the attention on indirect effects if one wants to assess functions of co-determination law.

Moreover, if we attempt to compare and evaluate the relative influence of legal norms on power distribution as opposed to structural and organizational variables the IDE-study confronts us with a rather surprising result. Social scientists occupied with worker participation have tended to expect a rather minimal influence of formal legal norms. For example, personal variables like high education of the workers are classically treated as crucial for organizational participation (Lipset et al. 1956, 127). Moreover, technology and organizational structure are seen as the main predictors for power distribution in the organization (Evan 1977). Others stress organizational factors like the size of the organization (Blau and Schoenherr 1971). Quite in contrast to these expectations, the authors of IDE conclude "that institutional norms relating to medium term decisions seems to be the most important instrument of power equalization and of further democratization of those work organizations . . ." All the other contextual variables – personal attributes of employees (skill, education, unionization), technological contingencies (automation, complexity), organizational contingencies (differentiation, formalization, control), economic and environmental contingencies – turned out to have much less influence on power distribution within the organization. It seems the law has only two serious competitors in changing effectively the power structure: "mobilization" of workers, their active participation in unions, labor actions and workers representative bodies and, second, strong outside influence within supervisory bodies. The policy lesson to be learned is a more "voluntaristic" approach to industrial democracy. It seems to be conditioned much more by human action – law, mobilization, outside influence – than by existent technological, structural and economic conditions.

2.2 Goal structure

Quite apart from those effects on power structures, co-determination law has a different function which we can call the "internalization of external conflicts" (Teubner, 1978:228). Without co-determination, workers' interests are mainly channelled through labor market structures and inter-organizational negotiations. In the collective bargaining system, labor-management conflicts are a matter of external relations. Insofar as co-determination shifts decisions and conflict resolutions to intra-organizational boards with labor representation, the industrial conflict becomes (partially) internalized into the economic organization itself. This changes the medium of communication: The collective bargaining system works via economic market mechanism – in Hirschman's terminology via "exit"-mechanisms – while co-determination leads to a politization of the conflicts, to the dominance of "voice" mechanisms. Moreover, the goal structure of the organization changes considerably. Workers' interests like job security, easiness of work, cushioning of rationalization are no longer external cost factors which must be minimized but a legitimate goal for the intra-organizational decision process itself (Luhmann 1966:8). This change in the goal structure leads to the partial internalization of the labor market into the organization and by its transformation into organizational manpower-planning and the creation of internal labor markets in large organization. Since labor interests arrived at a more prominent place in the goal hierarchy, management was put under constraints to develop mechanisms that would reduce the exhibition of labor to the fluctuations of the external labor market. Streeck (1984:30) argues that in this respect co-determination has not only created a problem for enterprises but also offered a solution. The new solutions, manpower planning and internal labor market were possible since co-determination "has provided the organizational instruments to cope with such rigidities without major losses in efficiency" (Streeck, 1984).

2.3 Capital-Labor Conflict

Thus, co-determination has changed the conditions of the labor-capital conflict. The great ideological battle on secular issues is transformed into nitty-gritty divergences which have to be dealt with on a rather trivial basis of day-to-day arrangements. And it creates a conflict solving mechanism which a German scholar has labeled as a "stroke of genius of modern social systems" ("Geniestreich moderner Sozialordnungen", Lutter 1982:567): the "dual loyalty" of interest representatives. While many empirical studies analyze the amount of frustration and alienation on the side of work councils, labor board representatives and labor directors, who suffer psychically from the role-tensions they are exposed to, one should not forget the other side of the coin. It is an old sociological insight that intra-role conflicts can serve as a link between highly divergent social interests (e.g. Stouffers 1949, Dahrendorf 1958). The structural conflict is "personalized", is transformed into a burdensome personal problem and the dual loyalties compel the individual to search for – socially and psychically – bearable solutions, compromises and temporary arrangements. Thus, we can generalize about the role the law is playing in this respect. The law which has created this conflict situation can, in a way ease the role-tensions without abolishing them. By granting formal power to the representative it legitimizes the ambivalent position he occupies and his desire to "balance antagonist interests".

The effects of co-determination law in this respect are, however, even more pervasive. They are not confined to change the conditions of conflict from antagonistic confrontation to stabilized compromise, they change the very structure of management. In the long run, the role of labor is not limited to the role of a pressure group influencing management by negotiations and threatening with sanctions backed by social power. Rather, the very combination of the work council system, the supervisory board representation and the collective bargaining system leads to mutually reinforcing effects and results in a kind of co-management between capital and labor. Tegtmeyer (1973:150) concludes that the main consequence of co-determination is a "joint and integrated decision-making process". The effect of the law is for capital and for labor a reciprocal internalization of interests. Streeck (1984:35) speaks of a "mutual incorporation of capital and labor by which labor internalizes the interests of capital just as capital internalizes those of labor, with the result that works council and management become subsystems of an integrated, internally differentiated system of industrial government which increasingly supersedes the traditionally dualistic class-based system of industrial relations".

3. Economic and Societal Effects

If we change now the system reference from the organization to the economic system in its interaction with other functional subsystems – especially politics and law – we realize that co-determination stands in strong contrast to principles of economic rationality. Co-determination relies on voting procedures, on pressure politics, on bureaucratic hierarchy, on negotiating and power balancing mechanisms, which are not compatible with economic principles of profit-maximation, with market-structures and with money as the economic communication mechanism.

3.1 Contradiction to the Prevailing Orientation

This politization of the economy through law is the conspicuous target for fundamental critique. Either, co-determination is supposed to destroy effectively economic rationality (Prosi, 1976) or co-determination is said to be one of the last tricks of capitalism: corruption of labor through pseudo-participation (Deppe 1969). Both positions have their merits by revealing important partial aspects of co-determination. Indeed co-determination flatly contradicts pure economic principles. The question is only to what degree and with what results. Indeed, co-determination changes the attitude of labor, from "conflictory" strategies to "cooperative" ones. Again, the question is only to what degree and with what effects. Both positions in a way tend to over-generalize their concrete observation of "market corruption" or "labor corruption". However, they fail to analyze the potential and limits of those phenomena by a closer analysis of the relations between market and organization.

If the relations between market and organization are defined by conditions of perfect competition, co-determination does not matter. Under perfect competition the constraints of the market on the organization are so strong that there is only one best solution. However, under conditions of market-imperfections – concentration, oligopolization – those constraints become weaker and management gains a considerable discretionary power in its decisions (e.g. Lindblom, 1977:152). And precisely this discretionary power is the main target of co-determination. Again, it is precisely the range of discretion which gives a limited justification to the liberal and to the leftist critique. Economic rationality is impaired, however not by co-determination, but by the very existence of managerial discretion which is due to market-imperfections. On the other hand, labor gets "corrupted" insofar as labor representatives have to bend to economic constraints, but this is only true for decisions outside the room of discretion. Insofar as management has gained discretionary power, labor with a strong formalized position within the enterprise possesses the power to make "non-corrupted" demands for the workers' interest. From the perspective of organization-market-relations it becomes clear that a description of co-determination as a total politization of the economy is just as inadequate as describing it in terms of corporate corruption of authentic labor interests. The crucial point is partiality. Economic rationality remains the prevailing principle, however it is modified to a certain degree by countervailing institutions which work as "built-in" contradictions to the prevailing orientation (Luhmann 1966:15).

3.2 Neo-Corporatist Coordination Mechanism

What then is the social function of co-determination if it represents a built-in contradiction to economic rationality? It is our thesis that the function of co-determination can be understood only in terms of differentiation and integration. Co-determination serves as one of the main integrative devices in a society which is characterized by extreme functional differentiation. The most conspicuous trait of differentiation processes is the high degree of functional autonomy the economic system has gained. This gives rise to the secular problem: How can the societal integration of the economy be carried out without losing the advantages of high differentiation. Even more: Do we have to conceive the relation between differentiation and integration as a zero-sum-game, where winning for one part means losing for the other? Or is there a possibility of integrative devices which not only maintain a given degree of differentiation but which support even increasing differentiation? (Willke 1978:228; 1983).

The interesting point about co-determination law is its indirect control technique as opposed to interventionist direct control. It is the specifity of co-determination law that the state does not intervene with external controls, for example with regulations of the market structure, with instruments of global steering, with legalization of corporate behavior, or with a direct politization of economic action. Rather it relies on indirect means of control, as an external stimulation of internal self-regulation. The crucial point is that state law changes the internal structure of the corporation by redistributing property rights, however by maintaining the economic principles of corporate autonomy and decentralized coordination. In this respect, co-determination represents one possible answer of how to integrate economic large scale organization politically without subduing them to direct state control which would end in de-differentiating tendencies.

Viewed in this perspective, co-determination has its main function clearly neither on the level of individual participation, nor on the intra-organizational level of labor-management-relations, but on the societal level as a re-integrating mechanism. It is not only a peculiar element of company law, but forms part of a whole ensemble of coordination mechanisms. Co-determination is the lowest echelon in a system of coordination mechanisms for which political scientists have coined the term "neo-corporatist syndrome" (Schmitter, 1974; Alemann 1981). This is a form of political organization in which organized business and organized labor are directly involved in state decisions and at the same time serve as implementation mechanisms for governments' economic policies.

Neo-corporatist arrangements should be clearly distinguished from "state-corporatism" on the one side and "interest group pluralism" on the other side. In Schmitter's terms (Schmitter 1974, 1979) "pluralism can be defined as a system of interest mediation in which the constituent units are organized in an unspecified number of multiple, voluntary, competitive, nonhierarchically ordered and self-determined (as to type or scope of interest) categories that are not specifically licensed, recognized or otherwise controlled in leadership election or interest articulation by the state and that do not exercise a monopoly of representational activity within their respective categories. Corporatism can be defined as a system of interest intermediation in which the constituent units are organized into a limited number of singular, compulsory, noncompetitive, hierarchically ordered, and functionally differentiated categories recognized or licensed (if not created) by the state and granted a deliberate representational monopoly within the respective categories in exchange for observing certain controls on their selection of leaders and articulation of demands and supports."

While these definitions show the difference between pluralism and corporatism, the difference between state corporatism and societal corporatism can be shown for each element of the definition of corporatism. In societal corporatism, the limitation of number, the singularity and the compulsory character of the collectives are due to social processes, through competition, cooptation, social pressures and interorganizational arrangement. In contrast, state corporatism creates these elements by deliberate government restriction, state-imposed eradication of multiplicity and through means of the law. Again, their non-competitive and hierarchical character, their functional differentiation, under conditions of societal corporatism is produced by internal processes of oligarchization and bureaucratization and not by state-imposed regulation of their internal structure and their external relations. Finally, societal corporatism produces recognition by the state and representational monopoly by imposition from below upon public officials, and not as privilege granted from above by the state as a condition for association formation and continuous operation. In more abstract terms of differentiation and integration, the differences can be caught in the following way. Both of them represent attempts of integrating a differentiated society. Due to its pervasive politization of society through state-dominated organizations, state corporatism tends however to decrease differentiation and autonomy of social subsystems, while societal corporatism which is based on state-independent social power resources tends to maintain or even increase social differentiation and subsystem autonomy.

Co-determination should be understood as an important mechanism of neo-corporatist structures which permeate on different levels of coordination between politics and economy (Erd, 1982:149). The neo-corporatist syndrome should no doubt be looked at as a whole. Such attunement processes take place at least at three levels: (1) The macro level of major economic policy decisions on incomes policy, tax policy and price policy, negotiated among the summit bodies of the economy, the trade unions and government bodies, (2) the meso level of regional and sectoral structure policy and the relationship between employer associations and trade unions (3), the micro level of the enterprise, via co-determination processes and public involvement, which mediate between the systems for distributing the firm's yield (company law profit distribution and collectively bargained wages). The relations between those three levels are the object of a controversial discussion today. On the one side, the thesis is put forward that legalized co-determination is a supportive structure if not a pre-requisite for a highly developed corporatism (Erd, 1982). This is contested by the counter-thesis that a highly developed corporatist structure on the macro-level is largely independent of micro-participation on the firm level, even that both mechanisms tend to work into different directions (Dittrich, 1983:89).

It should be realized that the integrative achievements of such neo-corporatist structures are bought at a certain price. For neo-corporatist negotiation systems in general and for co-determination in particular it is true that they carry with themselves consequential problems which can be circumscribed by "social closure". Centralization of decisions, the bureaucratization of organizations, the isolation of the negotiating elites, are some of the dysfunctional consequences of neo-corporatist procedures. In regard to co-determination it has been observed that the very installation of neo-corporatist mechanisms on the micro-level tends to have adverse effects on neo-corporatist mechanisms themselves, on the meso-level and on the macro-level. The more successful cooperation between capital and labor on the level of the organization transforms them into a collaborative "productivity coalition" the more they tend to exploit their environment and the less they are open to successful external regulation (Streeck, 1984:40). That means that co-determination which was intended by the union movement to be one part of a social planning system may become more and more resistent to the quasi-planning of neo-corporatist coordination. This poses threats to the interest aggregation process in labor unions as well as to labor policies and income policies of governments. Whether a solution out of this paradoxical situation can be found is an open question.

What are the institutional consequences? Firstly they would always have to relate the company constitution to the total context of neo-corporatist mediatory mechanisms at the various levels. Co-determination would have to be precisely aligned on this, also from the legal standpoint. In this view co-determination law would have to be separated from its individual or interest group related interpretation and reoriented towards this kind of social control concept. This would have consequences that would extend into the questions of the position in co-determination law of the trade-unions, of information and accountability obligations, of the delimitation of co-determination and collective bargaining system and of the institutional link of the organizations and their internal structures. Secondly, this approach would have implications particularly for state participation in co-determination models. If neo-corporatist coordination is to work successfuly, it has to be made sure that a coordination exists between coordinating mechanisms. If this can be achieved by close integration or contrary by an increasing separation again is an open question.

Bibliography

ADAMS, R. J. and C. H. RUMMEL (1977) "Workers' Participation in Management in West Germany – Impact on the Worker, the Enterprise and the Trade Union," 8 *Industrial Relations Journal* 4.

ALEMANN, ULRICH VON (1981) *Neokorporatismus*. Frankfurt, New York: Campus.

BATSTONE, ERIC and PAUL DAVIES (1976) *Industrial Democracy: European Experience*. London: Her Majesty's Stationary Office.

BIEDENKOPF, KURT (1970) *Mitbestimmung im Unternehmen*. Bericht der Sachverständigen-Kommission zur Auswertung der bisherigen Erfahrungen bei der Mitbestimmung (Mitbestimmungskommission). Bonn: Heger.

BLAU. PETER M. and RICHARD A. SCHÖNHERR (1971) *The Structure of Organizations*. New York: Basic Books.

BLUMBERG, PAUL (1968) *Industrial Democracy: The Sociology of Participation*. New York: Schocken.

CARNOY, MARTIN and DEREK SHEARER (1980) *Economic Democracy. The Challenge of the 1980s*. New York: Sharpe.

DAHRENDORF, RALF (1958) *Homo Sociologicus*. Opladen: Westdeutscher Verlag.

DEPPE, FRANK, *et al.* (1969) *Kritik der Mitbestimmung. Partnerschaft oder Klassenkampf?* Frankfurt: Suhrkamp.

DITTRICH, WALTER (1983) "Mitbestimmung. Eine korporatistische Strategie?," in: K. Armingeon *et al.* (eds.) *Neokorporatistische Politik in Westeuropa*, Konstanz: Universität.

ERD, RAINER (1982) "Die Modernisierung des Arbeitsrechts im korporatistischen Verbund," 12 *Probleme des Klassenkampfes* 149.

EVAN, WILLIAM (1977) "Hierarchy, Alienation, Commitment and Organizational Effectiveness," 30 *Human Relations* 77.

IDE RESEARCH GROUP (1982) *Industrial Democracy in Europe – Kooperation und Partizipation in Industrieunternehmen Europas.* Oxford: Oxford University Press.

LINDBLOM, CHARLES E. (1977) *Politics and Markets. The World's Political Economic Systems*. New York: Basic Books.

LIPSET, SEYMOUR M., MARTIN TROW and JAMES COLEMAN (1956) *Union Democracy. The Internal Politics of the International Typographical Union*. Glencoe, Ill.: Garden City, Doubleday Anchor Books.

LUHMANN, NIKLAS (1966) "Worker Participation and Decision Making." Arbeitspapier zum "Jablona Round Table Meeting" (International Political Science Association).

LUTTER, MARCUS (1982) "Rolle und Recht," in *Europäisches Rechtsdenken in Geschichte und Gegenwart*. München: Beck.

MNOOKIN, ROBERT H. and LEWIS KORNHAUSER (1979) "Bargaining in the Shadow of the Law. The Case of Divorce," 88 *Yale Law Journal* 950.

PROSI, GERHARD (1976) *Volkswirtschaftliche Auswirkungen des Mitbestimmungsgesetzes*. Köln: Bachem.

SCHMITTER, PHILIP C. (1974) "Still the Century of Corporatism?," in F. B. Pike and T. Stritch (eds.), *The New Corporatism. Social-Political Structures in the Iberian World.* London: University of Notre Dame Press.

– (1979) "Modes of Interest Intermediation and Models of Societal Change in Western Europe," 10 *Comparative Political Studies* 7.

STOUFFERS, SAMUEL A. (1949) "An Analysis of Conflicting Social Norms," 14 *American Sociological Review* 707.

STREECK, WOLFGANG, (1984) "Co-determination: The Fourth Decade", *International Yearbook of Organizational Democracy*, Vol. II, International Perspectives on Organizational Democracy. London: Wiley.

TANNENBAUM, ARNOLD S. *et al.* (1974) *Hierarchy in Organizations. An International Comparison.* San Francisco: Jossey/Bass.

TEGTMEYER, WERNER (1973) *Wirkungen der Mitbestimmung der Arbeitnehmer.* Göttingen: Vandenhoeck und Rupprecht.

TEUBNER, GUNTHER (1978) "Mitbestimmung – Gesellschaftliche Steuerung durch Organisationsrecht?" 26 *Arbeit und Recht* 296.

WALL, TOBY D. and JOSEPH LISCHERON (1977) *Worker Participation. A Critique of the Literature and Some Fresh Evidence.* London: McGraw Hill.

WILLKE, HELMUT (1978) "Zum Problem der Integration komplexer Sozialsysteme," 30 *Kölner Zeitschrift für Soziologie und Sozialpsychologie* 228.

– (1983) *Entzauberung des Staates.* Königstein: Athenäum.

WILPERT, BERNHARD (1975) "Research on Industrial Democracy: The German Case," 5 *Industrial Relations Journal* 53.

Federal Aspects of Corporate Law and Economic Theory

RICHARD M. BUXBAUM

Berkeley

Introduction

Economic theory still enjoys an uneasy relationship with legal doctrine (Buxbaum, 1984). It can be an aid to understanding, and thus to the proper formulation of good doctrine; it can also be an aid for mystification, and thus to the legitimation of good, bad or indifferent doctrine (see Cooter, 1982). The one thing it probably cannot do is itself to prescribe the good;[1] but at its most useful it should assist the law-maker and law-applier in transforming the prescribed value into the prescribed action.

A particularly fruitful example of this tension-filled relationship is the economic analysis of legal rules in the field of economic law and within that in the area of company or enterprise law. If the production of aggregate wealth – the efficient allocation of resources – has any claim to being a primary social value, it is in this field of law that it should find expression. This is not to say that in economic law or in interprise law efficiency is destined to be the primary let alone sole value statement, but that its competing claim to consideration is inherent in the subject matter in a visible and significant sense. Efficiency considerations exist in and can illuminate criminal law and family law, but more as marginal corrections of exorbitant efforts to implement other values. In at least the company and perhaps the enterprise area of economic law the situation rather is reversed.

This is a typically American way of looking at the field – it derives from the English utilitarian heritage and not from the Continental concern with productive activity as a major element of human liberty. For present purposes, however,

[1] But there is the possibility – whether seen as opportunity or risk – that the "microeconomic morality in which value is perceived as strictly individual, private and subjective" best characterizes the Anglo-American common law as a value system; cf. Michelman (1980:137, 139, 151). As Michelman elsewhere points out (1978), this is easily characterizable as a normative concept.

For the most explicit recent claim of a common law value system – that of private wealth maximization facilitation – see Posner (1980). For a critical rejection of the concept, see Dworkin (1980).

this difference in provenance can be ignored. The subject under discussion is not the basic question of economic freedom in the sphere of human activity generally, but the narrower question of the usefulness of certain quite specific economic theories to quite specific enterprise law issues. The two specific theorems to be discussed are the so-called efficient capital market and corporate control market hypotheses, and a pair of related theories focusing more specifically on federalism in economic affairs – the public choice theorem and the slightly broader bundle of public finance theories. The latter two are reviewed because of their common concern with the political and legal implications of federalism. They are applied, in the following discussion, to the specifically federal aspects of enterprise law, a matter of substantial concern both to the existing legal order in the United States and to the evolving legal order of the European Community.

The economic theory-legal doctrine relationship within which these theories will be analyzed is that existing in the United States. Therefore, a doctrinal presentation of American jurisprudence and (for reasons to be given, only secondarily) of American legislation is the center of the legal component of this discussion. Before this is undertaken, however, a few qualifications about the comparative value of the effort are necessary. They stem from two important cultural distinctions, which however well-known need always to be emphasized: one of history and one of institutions.

1. Historical and Institutional Background

1.1. History

The American experience with the unification of corporate law does not provide directly useful lessons for current or even prospective European harmonization and unification efforts. The difference in hierarchical government organization between the American states early bound into a federal union and the European nations transferring only some governmental powers to a federal organization on a revocable basis is too great to allow such direct comparability, quite apart from deeper differences in the degree to which the respective units possess a shared language and history. Admittedly, the one area exhibiting a common goal if not yet a common experience is that of economic union. It is therefore not surprising that of all American legal developments, those in economic law – company law and even enterprise law not least within that category – should most interest European legal scholars as providing useful analogical lessons. There is also a deeper if less articulated reason for this interest. Economic union is or may be the pathbreaker to more pervasive federal developments. Jean Monnet's famous vision of a politically united Europe echoes the experience of the American colonies: As Justice Rutledge felicitously phrased the colonists' fate, "[T]hey founded a nation, although they had set out only to reduce trade restrictions."[2]

[2] See (Justice) Rutledge (1947), as quoted in *EEOC* v. *Wyoming*, 103 S. Ct. 1054 (1983) (Stevens, J., concurring). Another well-known recent call echoes that experience, too – that of Max Frisch: "Wir riefen Arbeiter, und es kamen Menschen."

In these circumstances, an inquiry into the relation between the institutional concerns of federal organization and the social concerns of economic organization should interest legal scholars of both systems, no matter how historically qualified the inquiry's value may be. The following discussion of course can do no more than begin that inquiry, and even then is limited to the company law or at most to certain aspects of the enterprise law sector of the entire field. Nevertheless, some currently useful hypotheses can be gained from even a limited and preliminary discussion.

Two important points of difference between the two systems should be stated at the outset. The American Constitution does not ensrhine any particular form of economic organization. The nation (and not only the state) is constitutionally obliged to compensate any person for property taken by it, but then is free to embark on any form of mercantilist or socialist form of enterprise activity its representatives may choose (U.S. Constitution, Amendment XIV). It is less clear whether the Treaty of Rome is as neutral towards the form of economic organization the European Communities (or at least the original European Economic Community portion thereof) may choose to adopt.

The second point of difference concerns the legal *instrumentarium* available to the federal government for the achievement of politically desired levels of centralized law in the field of enterprise activity. The rules for accomplishing this purpose were embodied in the original Constitution at a level of detail that is missing from the organic acts constituting the European Common Market. This difference resides not so much in the substantive as in the procedural or institutional provisions. The substantive provisions – a strong grant of affirmative legislative power to the central government in matters bearing on interstate and foreign commerce (Article I, Section 8, part 3), and a strongly worded Supremacy Clause giving preemptive power to federal legislation enacted under the commerce clause (Article VI, part 2) – are perhaps somewhat more explicit than their parallels in the Treaty of Rome but not qualitatively different. Different is the institutional material, preeminently the establishment of a federal supreme court and the authorization, immediately used, for legislative establishment of a federal court system (Article III, Section 1).

1.2 Institutions – and Their History

Even these institutional provisions, however, do not themselves differ dramatically from those of the Rome Treaty. One needs to add the historical and political context to round out the picture. Courts and their role are the institutional variant earlier alluded to in warning about the legal-cultural limits on the transferability of the American discussion to Europe. This institutional variant, however, also has its own historical aspect.

The recently coined aphorism that the early Union was a "government of courts and parties", (Skowronek, 1982), expresses the point in shorthand fashion. The social reasons why these, and not traditional European state instruments, early were and long remained the primary American forms of government are in general well understood and in any event lie beyond the scope of this discussion. The way in which this context bears on the early legal developments that set the still-enduring framework for the role of federal actors and policies in government regulation of economic activity does, however, need brief explanation.

The importance of courts in this government of courts and parties is reflected in the substantive importance of the three early Supreme Court decisions that created the federal component of the American "economic constitution." In *Marbury v. Madison*[3] the Supreme Court arrogated to itself the right to declare federal laws unconstitutional and thus to nullify them. In *McCullough v. Maryland*[4] it declared its right to nullify state law that it interpreted as violating the federal Constitution. And in *Gibbons v. Ogden*[5] it laid down for future use the doctrine that the federal Commerce Clause, standing by itself and without the support of specific federal legislation enacted under its authority, could bar state legislation interpreted to be inconsistent with the "common market" envisaged by that clause. It is an important insight into the role of the Supreme Court in the federal government structure to realize that this decision established a court-controlled "negative Commerce Clause" well before events required the full development of a legislature-controlled "affirmative Commerce Clause".

For almost a century after the formation of the Union, the preemptive thrust of federal economic legislation was not of major concern. Except for a few problems of infrastructure development, the United States had not yet faced the need for a "national order" (Wiebe, 1967:xiii); not even the Civil War brought more than temporary centralizing legislation into play though it did hasten the technological changes that soon would set the stage for the march of federal legislation. When that march did begin, it was again the Supreme Court which led the way. It created both affirmative federal jurisdiction through its slowly expanding view of permissible federal action under the affirmative Commerce Clause and it used that legislation aggressively to preempt potentially conflicting state regulation under the Supremacy Clause.

It is no surprise, of course, that the economic activity whose facilitation or regulation was at stake was to an ever greater degree carried out by private corporations, and by ever larger ones. Early restrictions on the right of corporations – creatures of a particular state – to function on a nationwide basis soon were swept aside as these two aspects of the Commerce Clause achieved greater scope and power. The corporations' right to function under this national banner was more important than their right to be treated as other persons for the purpose of enjoying the protection of the due process and equal protection clauses of the 14th Amendment. The decisions establishing that right did, however, plant the seeds for a future development of substantial importance today, the imposition of a "free enterprise" economic philosophy on the states through the division of powers jurisprudence of the Supreme Court as this jurisprudence grew from the affirmative and negative Commerce Clause cases.

[3] 1 Cranch. (3 U.S.) 137 (1803).

[4] 4 Wheat. (17 U.S.) 316 (1819).

[5] 9 Wheat. (22 U.S.) 1 (1824).

Looking back at these developments from the middle of the Great Depression, and with the intention of buttressing the Supreme Court's maximal interpretation of the Commerce Clause as permitting the widest scope of regulatory legislation thereunder, Justice – then still Professor – Frankfurter coined a well-known aphorism: "So far as the states were concerned, if Congress chose not to regulate, *laissez faire* was the regulator" (Frankfurter, 1937:100). Institutional as well as ideological factors were at work in shaping the reality he so characterized. Since the states clearly were the subordinate partner in the federal partnership, only their regulatory or restrictive, not their facilitative or enabling lawmaking could create a tension between the two legal systems. Freedom offered by the junior partner is a problem for the affirmative Commerce Clause only; i.e., it takes explicit federal law to override or collide with state inaction, and the reach of that law into relatively local spheres is a question of the scope of the affirmative Commerce Clause. Only when the federal regime is the *laissez faire* one, and by definition devoid of specific legislation, can a "negative" collision arise between the federal sphere of inaction and a state regime of regulatory action.

Recent Supreme Court jurisprudence, by a court a majority of whose members are committed to a fairly explicit liberal economic philosophy, has brought this lesson home. Two examples illustrate this new confirmation of an older perception and will be briefly discussed here, though this will require a detour into some rather technical corporation law concepts.

In Edgar v. MITE Corp.,[6] the Court invalidated a typical state law regulating the phenomenon of tender offers or takeover bids. A tender offer is an offer by one entity, made directly to the shareholders of another, to purchase all or more frequently only a controlling part of that stock, usually in exchange for securities of the offeror though sometimes for cash. Various tax, financial and tactical considerations cause these offers to be made suddenly – especially if they are not made in cooperation with the management of the target company – and to be open only for a limited period of time. They are often followed by a second stage full-scale merger between the offeror and the target company; indeed, a plan to proceed to that stage often is publicly announced as part of the tender offer. In part because the offeror would then be in control of the target company and could dictate the terms of the second exchange offer, shareholders of the target company reasonably may feel themselves to be under a mild form of economic duress already from the start, and thus feel obliged to tender their shares pursuant to that first offer under less than truly voluntary conditions. In addition other groups interested in the target company, particularly its workforce and its locally dependent communities, may as "outsiders" fear the consequences of the control shift.

Federal law regulates the takeover phenomenon, but only from the standpoint of investor protection; and does this, pursuant to the general philosophy of securities regulation, simply by ensuring adequate disclosure of material infor-

[6] 457 U.S. 624 (1982).

mation to the solicited shareholders of the target company.[7] It provides no substantive review let alone control of such mergers except for an important but specialized review from the perspective of antitrust regulation.[8] As a result, many states enacted a specialized form of traditional "blue sky" regulation to subject proposed mergers and takeover bids to regulatory scrutiny, usually from the viewpoint of more paternalistic investor protection though in fact and in their procedures a concern with workplace protection was clearly apparent. It is this legislation which the Supreme Court struck down, in part on the ground that the jurisdictional claim at least of the actual statute under consideration was exorbitant, and in part because even the delay in the completion of tender offers brought about by that resolution, by constraining shareholders in their right to dispose of holdings on the stock market, interfered with the efficient allocation of resources.[9] In those two grounds the institutional and the ideological strands of the negative Commerce Clause jurisprudence are perfectly reproduced.

The second example is a preemption case, in which the Supremacy Clause is used to give a federal statute preemptive effect over an arguably conflicting state regulation. In *Southland Stores, Inc. v. Keating*,[10] the Supreme Court struck down a provision of a state statute which had forbidden recourse to arbitration in disputes arising from a franchise agreement. Because franchise contracts create investor protection problems similar to those created by purely passive investment in securities, California subjected them to state regulatory scrutiny much in the manner of the "blue sky" regulation of ordinary issues of securities. It has long been an article of faith at both federal and state levels that certain issues of public law are too important to be left to private dispute resolution between parties one of whom is the beneficiary of that public law.[11] Securities regulation is the classic example of that situation, and the non-arbitrability of securities regulation problems indeed is a federal doctrine, and a court-created doctrine at that.[12] Accordingly, the state followed a clear and long accepted policy when it forbade arbitration of such investment-related franchise disputes.

Despite the 50-year history of this doctrine, however, the Supreme Court decided that the Federal Arbitration Act of 1925, which removes the bar on the enforceability of agreements to submit future disputes to arbitration for all contracts involving interstate commerce, has with the passage of time and liberal interpretation of its terms sufficiently taken on the cast of a substantive federal policy in favor of arbitration to preempt the described state provision. While a desire to reduce the overload of the federal judiciary in the area of diversity jurisdiction may have played a role in this surprising decision, it is a clear example of the present Court's distaste for "excessive regulation" of enterprise activity, in some ways even more clearly an example of the ideological side of this institutional-ideological jurisprudence than is *Edgar v. MITE*.

[7] Williams Act, 15 U.S.C.A. Secs. 78m(d)-(e), n(d)-(f).
[8] This is the function of the Hart-Scott-Rodino Act, 15 U.S.C.A. Sec 18 (a).
[9] *Edgar v. MITE Corporation*, 475 U.S. 624 (1982).
[10] 104 S. Ct. 852 (1984).
[11] See the early and influential statements of this position in Kronstein (1944:36).
[12] *Wilko v. Swan*, 346 U.S. 427 (1953).

2. The Role of Economic Theory

2.1 The Institutional Problem of Economic Analysis

It is now appropriate, at the start of the actual inquiry into the role of economic theory in the formulation of legal doctrine, to revert to the original warning that institutional as well as historical particularities limit the comparative utility of any such examination. The courts are the institutional particularity; and that is so for institutional as well as for the just-described historical reasons.

American judges, and not only federal judges, enjoy great autonomy, in doctrinal as well as in political terms. Much legislative not to mention regulatory power now resides in them, in part yielded in part seized. In many areas of public law neither the authority nor the expertise of the executive branch holds them in awe; and the legislative branch, when it is not kept at bay by constitution-conjuring, plays over the courts like summer lightning, with more rumbles than strikes. With the partial exception of foreign relations,[13] the *raison d'état* no longer evokes their respect; while the argument that "you haven't read the cables" not only has been dissipated by the fitful quality of decisions made by those who have, but is not legitimate when those cables – that information – have been or are supposed to have been submitted in evidence to the courts.

Paradoxically, however, the awe before authority and competence which has been dissipated in this secularized judicial setting when claimed by the state is reentering the courts when claimed by the corporation. "You haven't met a payroll" is the new *parole*, and the *raison d'entreprise* the new constraint. It is not a constraint generated by the force of economic analysis (Buxbaum, 1984). It stems, rather, from institutional inexperience with the interior functioning of ever larger and perhaps ever more complex private economic actors, and from institutional fears of causing harm by interfering with mechanisms that, unlike public mechanisms, are not (yet?) found to be transparent and are thus not (yet?) adequately understood. This new constraint is aggravated by the courts' reluctance to embark on these difficult journeys at the instigation of politically and economically unaccountable complainants. The accident that much corporate-related litigation is contingent fee litigation, and that the often nominal plaintiff can be little more than a passport for the attorney's entry into this litigation arena and its private rewards, can understandably, if inappropriately, contribute to judicial acceptance of various arguments permitting serious inquiry into the merits of the particular dispute.

In this situation economic theory, or at least those economic theories that purport to demonstrate the adequacy of various markets to control various types of corporate behavior, can play an important and potentially dangerous role both to confirm and to mask this institutional *non liquet* position. It therefore becomes all the more important to analyze their validity and their utility in the

[13] *Dames & Morre v. Regan*, 453 U.S. 654 (1981); and compare *tel Oren v. Libyan Arab Republic*, 726 F. 2d 774 (D.C. Cir. 1984) with *Filartiga v. Pena-Irala*, 630 F. 2d 876 (2d Cir. 1980). But cf. Trimble (1984:317).

formulation of legal doctrine. The two Supreme Court opinions just discussed, and in particular the transaction at issue in *Edgar v. MITE*, provide an opportunity for at least a first, limited effort in that direction.

2.2 Efficiency-Apotheosizing Hypotheses: The Takeover Bid Phenomenon As a Case Study

If modern efficiency theorems provide the scientific basis for a legal rule based on liberal economic principles, it should be possible to test the results in these two paradigmatic cases from that perspective. Two candidates for the role have been presented in recent years; one has been explicitly adopted by the Court, the other by inference.

(1) The Efficient Capital Market and the Market for Control

(a) Statement

The efficiency-enhancing role of takeover bids has been much discussed recently, (see Easterbrook and Fischel, 1981:116; Gilson, 1981:819). That role or possibility itself rests upon a concept known as the efficient capital market hypothesis, which suggests that the market price of a stock reflects all material information known about the issuing company and absorbs information efficiently.[14] In its weak form this represents no more than the tautological observation that available information is reflected in market prices; in its strong form it suggests that even secret, inside information reaches the market quickly because of the activities of insiders as understood by those financial intermediaries whose competitive business it is to learn or and react to all company-specific information as quickly as possible. Indeed, this is the concept that in turn led Manne to recommend that insider trading be allowed because of its salutary institutional effect on a functioning stock market (Manne, 1966).

The efficient tender offer hypothesis suggests that on the assumptions of the efficient capital market hypothesis, a tender offer at a price above the market price typically or at least frequently demonstrates that at least in the eyes of the offeror, the resources of the target company are not being managed to their optimal use (Fischel, 1978). The reason for the inefficient current use of the resources is irrelevant; it may lie in the ability of the offeror to combine them with other resources in a synergistic way, or in the poor quality of current management. The important point of the tender offer is its efficiency check on current management of those resources. This is an important benefit to investors, whose ability to monitor or to replace current management through use of their aggregate voting power is relatively weak if not illusory. Therefore, tender offers, especially hostile ones, should be encouraged, not hindered.

As the argument of *Edgar v. MITE* demonstrates, a simplistic version of this

[14] The original statement of this thesis in its developed form is that of Fama (1970:383). For recent consideration of its implications in the field of securities regulation generally, see Easterbrook (1982:308).

theorem was adopted by the Supreme Court.[15] It is a theorem which the lawmaker of course could override; efficiency is not a right but only a necessity, sometimes not the only or even the most important necessity. The Court, however, did not rest its conclusion upon the argument that the federal tender offer legislation in fact had chosen this efficiency theorem and by doing so demonstrated its hostility to overriding state legislation; Justice White, the author of the plurality opinion, did so but failed to carry his colleagues. The majority rather based this conclusion upon the far more powerful basis of its own, quasi-legislative interpretation of the negative Commerce Clause. It is the Constitution, in short, which according to the Supreme Court embodies this present-day version of Social Darwinism.

(b) Critique

The efficient market for control theorem, built upon an efficient capital market hypothesis, can be criticized from a position which shares a concern with allocative efficiency as well as from a base of other values. The latter are illustrated by a statute which would explicitly subject takeovers to regulatory approval on the basis of distributive justice or *other non-efficiency related* values, such as a workplace protection test. The suspicion that such considerations lurk behind state takeover bid control statutes probably played a part in the result if not the reasoning in *Edgar v. MITE*. This analysis, however, is beyond the scope of this paper and will not be reviewed here.[16] It replicates, the effort to extend the scope of traditional company law to the concerns suggested by the term 'enterprise law.'

The critique from within an efficiency frame of reference, however, while narrower is more central to traditionally defined company law, being limited to the investor (owner) – management relationship. It can be argued, though not yet conclusively demonstrated, that efficiency considerations do not necessarily require maximum freedom for takeover efforts even apart from disclosure requirements. The major arguments have to do with the actual ability of even organized stock markets to fulfill their value-determining function, and the particular methods by which takeover bids may coerce target company shareholders to accept offers against their will.[17]

The stock market issue arises because of the question whether the much-noted separation of ownership and management, which has separated the governance from the financial aspects of share ownership, operates to constrain or to augment management's control over the price of the factor capital. The power of large corporations, powerful in their product market setting, to bargain with other factor providers let alone with customers at least as equal if not as dominant parties is not seriously debated in general, no matter how it can be debated in (important) detail.[18] Only as to the 'price' of stocks in trading markets is this general argument not accepted, not even in general. Yet it can be argued,

[15] 457 U.S. 624 (1982).

[16] The argument on this basis is presented in Buxbaum (1984a).

[17] On the following, see the extended analysis in Buxbaum (1984).

[18] For the major works bridging the gap between antitrust-oriented industrial organization

and supported by at least suggestive evidence, that the same "organizational surplus" which the modern large corporation has captured from its external relations can be used to insulate it at least in substantial part in its "internal" relation to the price of its own shares.

The bidder in a takeover may act not because of an expectation that the target's operations might be more efficiently structured but for two other basic reasons. The target's stock may be "institutionally" undervalued because of dysfunctional stock markets (effect of institutional holdings; of target management's ability to capture "excessive" proportions of profits; of owners' dysfunctional short-range expectations of management; of owners' change in risk aversion weighting because of the increasing transferability between different forms of surplus investment; etc.) (see in particular Lowenstein 1983:249 and Coffee 1985:1145). Only a few of these causes may signal suboptimal use of resources in the sense of "efficient takeover bids." The bidder also may act, or because of the first set of causes may be free to act, for reasons unrelated to efficiency, but stemming instead from internal power or prestige motives, or from the dysfunctionally easy availability of external credit to underwrite the bid, and so forth.

All of these are at this stage only categorical arguments, not factually buttressed; but if credible even to a degree, they may well undermine the efficiency argument that favors of maximum freedom to engage in these transactions. The bidding process may, of course, in some or even in many cases generate wealth transfers from the owners of bidders (or of their banks) to the owners of target companies, (see Bebchuk, 1982:1034; Gilson, 1981:853). That, however, is both a different justification and one much more randomly applicable than the asserted efficiency justification.

(2) *Public Choice Theory*

(a) Statement

Another important economic theorem supporting *laissez faire* economic policies also might be considered. Associated at least as to its legal policy implications with Buchanan,[19] it suggests that just as competition among suppliers of private goods ensures the efficient allocation of resources via mechanisms associated with the "invisible hand", so competition among providers of public goods may under specified circumstances achieve efficiency in the allocation of resources. It lies in the nature of public goods that ordinary pricing signals from their users do not function to allocate resources to their respective production efficiently, for reasons associated with positive externalities and the free rider phenomenon. On the other hand, informational and bureaucratic distortions associated with

literature and this "internalization" of market power in management structure and function, see Chandler (1977), and the more economics-oriented Marris (1964), and Williamson (1975). See also Williamson (1981, 1983).

[19] The concept is generally taken to have originated with Samuelson (1954:387), and to have been developed by Musgrave (1959). It then was used extensively for its public policy implications, including legal implications, in Buchanan (1968).

command decisions to produce public goods also prevent or at least fail to ensure the efficient allocation of resources. Thus, where some market-mimicking signals can be developed, an effort to use them in these decisional processes should be encouraged.

One special aspect of this concept is relevant to the law-making process itself. A state with a monopoly of the law-making power may be less attuned or less inclined to the efficient production of public goods than one which itself needs to compete with equal sovereigns for the attraction and retention of private productive resources, be they human or capital resources.[20] The issue involves law in two ways: as a condition for consideration of the problem (monopoly over the law-making authority); and in its substantive sense as the public good under discussion, either in and of itself or as a preliminary necessary condition for the production of some other public good. Underlying the entire concept, of course, is the call for recognition of the fact that distributive goals of public authority are not costless, a call that in turn can reflect either a truism or a specific value orientation concerning the myriad potential conflicts between allocative and distributive social goals.

As it happens, proponents of the latter vision of this concept have used it in exactly the area of concern here, the question of competence to enact corporation law (see Winter, 1978; Kitch, 1982). It is a well-known though endlessly debated situation that under judicially evolved choices of law principles, the law of the state of incorporation is taken to govern the internal affairs of the corporation – the relation among shareholders, between shareholders and the corporation, and between directors (management) and the corporation[21]. As a result, a race of laxity (of rules in favor of managerial supremacy) began in the latter part of the 19th Century, a race which by the 1960's had been won by the state of Delaware (Conard, 1976:14; Cary, 1974). Inevitably calls for either federal corporation law or for federal minimum standards as a floor to state corporation law were again heard, as they had been from time to time in the past (Cary, 1974). This time, in defense of the position that Delaware law could not be so one-sided as was claimed or investors long ago would have signalled their displeasure by investing in non-Delaware corporations, the new argument borrowed from public choice theory was available. It weaves together the categorical concept of the public choice position and a type of efficient market position similar to the one previously described. The combination was well stated by Professor (now Judge) *Winter*:

Neither Delaware's code nor the case law interpreting it is perfect – no code is ... But in the case of corporation codes there is a mechanism which, over time, reasonably guarantees to shareholders and management alike a proper legal system to govern their relation in the

[20] Winter (1978) argues that it is precisely this monopoly which is to be feared, whereas competition among the states would lead to an "improvement" (in facilitation of private transactions leading to efficient resource allocation) of each state's performance. This concept is explicitly applied to the states of the early American Union, as a guide to the development of the Common Market, in Kitch (1981).

[21] For the traditional American doctrine, see Restatement (Second), Conflict of Laws Secs. 296–310 (1971); cf. Conrad (1976:14).

capital market. That process is the very one reviled by proponents of federal intervention: competition among the states for corporate charters.

A state that rigs its corporation code so as to reduce the yield to shareholders will spawn corporations which are less attractive as investment opportunities than comparable corporations chartered in other states or countries ...

Considerations of the capital market make it not in the interest of management to seek out a corporate legal system that fails to protect investors, and the competition among states for charters is generally a contest to determine which legal system provides an optimal return for both interests. Only through that competition between legal systems can we perceive which legal rules are most appropriate for the capital market. Once a single legal system governs that market, we can no longer compare investor reaction. Ironically, in view of the conventional wisdom, the greater danger is not that states will compete for charters but that they will not. (Winter, 1978:43).

Before the implications of this approach for state tender offer statutes are considered, two comments about the significance of *Winter's* comments in their own context may be appropriate. Considering the ease with which an existing corporation may reincorporate in another state by the simple art of voting therefor, the choice of law principle in essence permits "the corporation" to choose its own internally governing law as in the case of any contract, and to apply the new law even to preexisting internal relationships. Secondly, considering the institutional realities of large company structures, this is a decision initiated by management, and ratified by shareholders under the same conditions of apathy and *anomie* as characterize their investment relationships generally (Buxbaum, 1984).

(b) Critique

That, in turn, leads to the underlying problem with expecting the law-making competition among states to signify anything. The limited and partial "investment" of any given shareholder's totality of passions and interests in his minor diversion of occasional surplus savings to a pool comprised of millions of fellow shareholders, and the relative fungibility of the 500 or so conglomerate pools among which this kind of investment choice can be varied, make the image of states fine-tuning their laws to accommodate vibrant and alert investors with significant interests at stake more of a caricature than a model.

The real problem, in other words, is the proper characterization of shareholders as producers to be controlled or consumers to be protected; i.e., as powerful actors enjoying the less than fully competitive structure of markets or as weak actors facing those structures (Buxbaum, 1984). The harmony of managers' and investors' interests as they benefit from their corporations' power in the marketplace does not guarantee a harmony of interests as they seek to apportion the fruits of that power between themselves. That commonplace observation underlies federal investor protection legislation which, in its embodiment in the federal securities laws, concentrates on full disclosure to present or potential investors of company-specific material information. It also underlies state shareholder protection legislation (and especially jurisprudence), which concentrates on substantive legal rules concerning governance (as well as some investment) problems[22].

[22] This contrast in approach is well expressed in the early cases involving the effort to

This implies, however, that the state needs to be free to disregard the unequal parties' distorted though contractual choice of law process; which in turn means disregarding, if necessary, the traditional orientation of the law governing the internal affairs of the corporation to the state of incorporation. Otherwise, the state's choice of appropriate policies as a matter of substantive law would be rendered meaningless. In the actual field of contract law, for example, substantive rules protecting the weaker party have been supplemented either by statutory choice of law rules (as in the case of explicit consumer legislation) or by judicially initiated common law revision of choice of law doctrine in favor of the forum state or the state with the most significant relation to the transaction (as has happened particularly when the forum state's statutes or precedents have embraced new substantive contract doctrines such as adhesion rules and the like)[23].

It is just here, however, that the corporation law proponents of public choice doctrine protest state claims. The already described tender offer legislation is the occasion of the following effort to deny state competence to legislate, again from Winter; and it again reveals a questionable admixture of competitive capital and management market assumptions with public choice insights:

> Takeover statutes, however, although they involve trading in shares, regulate the market for management control and may well serve as a vehicle for monopolization even at the state level ... In these circumstances, profit maximizing on behalf of the corporation – that is, providing for easy takeovers – may not be in managements' economic self-interest.
>
> The competition among states for charters may provide inadequate protection in the case of takeover statutes. Existing management of many corporations can be expected to lobby for such laws, and the ability to reincorporate without difficulty may pressure states into passing takeover statutes to prevent or to induce reincorporation ...
>
> ... Takeover laws apply not only to corporations chartered in a state but to all firms that have their principal offices there. Because they apply even when all shareholders reside elsewhere or are scatterd among the states, the competition for charters is not the significant factor in the state's legislative judgment ...
>
> The extraterritorial features of takeover statutes restrain the competition among state legal systems for corporate charters ...
>
> There is, therefore, a case for federal regulation protecting competition in the market for management control ... (Winter, 1978:43).

This is an argument against any state claim of legislative or subject matter jurisdiction breaching the extreme "party autonomy" notions of contract that underlie the classical choice of law doctrine in the substantive field of contract and corporation law.

As such, it flies in the face of two major modern perceptions: the general recognition that contract law in its substance may have to interfere at least in

insinuate "internal governance" rules into federal securities regulation doctrine via the protean implied tort remedy derived from SEC Rule 10b–5. See particularly the discussion in the contrasting cases of *O'Neill v. Maytag*, 339 F. 2d 764 (2d Cir. 1964) and *Ruckle v. Roto American Corporation*, 339 F. 2d 24 (2d Cir. 1964). Cf. generally the succinct overview in Jennings and Marsh (1982:944).

[23] This is most explicitly suggested in Professor Cavers' "better rule" conflicts principle; see Cavers (1965); see also the recent but more traditional approach of Kozyris (1985:1).

those exchange relations that are not the expressions of socially and economically uncoerced will;[24] and the special recognition that corporations are substantial and enduring institutions and therefore poor candidates for the unreflective application of principles of contract law and party autonomy, even to their internal governance (Buxbaum, 1984). In the latter case the probable inequality of bargaining power is not a necessary condition; that is, even equal parties joining to create a corporation may have to be subjected to special legal rules because of those rules' spillover or reflexive benefits to third parties.

2.3 Fiscal Federalism Theory: Political Economy and Legal Doctrine

Under these circumstances the "competition between states" to produce "efficient law" cannot be limited to the production of laws that in effect and in their own substance and goal merely reproduce efficiency.

It is to this argument that the well-known categorization of governmental fiscal goals/functions in a federal system is particularly appropriate. This approach, developed by Musgrave,[25] separately identifies allocative, distributive and stabilizing goals, and suggests both categorical and empirical reasons why the state or the nation may be better positioned to enact laws pursuing one or another of these goals. It supports the public choice argument in tendency, but makes clear that matters of degree, not of kind, are critical to a fiscally sound division of powers in this area (Musgrave and Musgrave, 1976:627).

In tendency, the stabilizing goal of a price policy may be easily defeated by the influx of goods from outside the subordinate state sovereign's borders[26].

Countermeasures, placing imports under the same constraint, would relatively quickly lead to interference with a constitutional mandate favoring free commerce and the condemnation of such state legislation. The allocative (or efficiency-supporting) goal of overcoming market failures by providing a public good as infrastructure (a fire department, a road, a school), by contrast, may be attainable relatively easily within such a state without the need for extraterritorial supplemental measures. This depends simply on the congruence between the benefit area and the tax-imposing political unit. In that case the constitutional warning against interference with national commerce is less often triggered.

This approach can be applied to the intangible spheres of commerce at issue in company law such as trade in shares of stock, and to the even more removed concepts of markets in control or in information. It helps to identify the degree to which state regulation infringes upon companies, investors and markets

[24] The general recognition and acceptance of this principle is reflected in the well-known Article 2–302 of the Uniform Commercial Code, with its Civilian-derived "good faith performance of contracts" norm.

[25] For this important categorization of governmental policies/goals, see Musgrave and Musgrave (1976, chaps. 1, 29, 30).

[26] See Musgrave and Musgrave (1976), and Oates (1972:7). For a demostration of the essentially factual nature of resource mobility and state control accomodation, see Inman and Rubinfeld (1979:1662).

elsewhere, and thus to identify the elements of market impact on the one hand and of state interests on the other, whose "balancing", to put it inexactly, it is the function of the courts to achieve under the discretion claimed for them by the Supreme Court's traditional Commerce Clause doctrine.

The emphasis on the state's interest as one element of this process, highlighted by this fiscal theory's categorization of goals, also is a useful reminder that no one of the three values is primary in constitutional value terms. Each of the three goals is in a categorical sense a legitimate expression of sovereignty, however that may in turn be subject to the further constraint of federalism (see Buxbaum, 1984a). Indeed, one might argue more generally that of the three goals of economic legislation – efficiency, distribution and stabilization – efficiency is the one that in a free enterprise system cannot be commanded but only observed. It is the outcome of market forces which in turn function within the distributive and stabilizing framework – i.e., the property or entitlement framework – set by law.

If that is so, or even if there prevails only the special situation of a modern legal system struggling to maintain a free economic order against the exigent institutional distortions that threaten to create order in the name of freedom, the role of the states as competing providers of those public goods called laws needs to be honored beyond the minimal conditions suggested by Winter. The states' role legitimately involves more than the providing of a facilitative regime; i.e., a regime of freedom of contract. By definition, therefore, it involves a larger jurisdictional claim in the corporation law field under discussion than that easily avoidable claim to govern only "its" corporations which Winter allows it. Some extraterritorial sphere of influence is an inevitable component of the very concept of state law once the states' right to attempt to promulgate norms with distributional or stabilization goals is acknowledged.

This acknowledgement is missing in the distinction between legitimate (facilitative/territorial) and illegitimate (distributive/extraterritorial) use of state legislative power posited by Winter; and it is missing in the absolutist view of an interference with national commerce posited by *Edgar v. MITE*. Winter argues that an unholy alliance among self-aggrandizing managements may lure states to enact exorbitantly extraterritorial protective legislation. In turn this will block the ordinary signalling effect of "wrong" laws. This justifies their constitutional prohibition (Winter, 1978:44; Romano, 1985). While Winter does not explicitly argue for a stringent or absolute prohibition, the logic of his approach seems to leave little room for a moderate approach to that issue[27]. The probability that investment will flee from states whose takeover legislation sends investors a disinvestment signal is refuted on the ground that the law cannot be avoided by shifting the investment elsewhere, without any consideration of the cost to a state of embarking on such an adventure (and without recognition of the equally

[27] This absolute constraint assumption ("no extraterritorial spillover") is implicit in recent criticism of the Supreme Court's continued exemption of mandatory direct state cartelization of private producers from the Sherman Act; see Easterbrook (1983:23).

important fact that most actual takeover legislation required substantial investor or workforce connection to the state before it applied)[28].

That cost, of disinvestment, might take longer to hit home than the immediately apparent cost of watching local companies reincorporate elsewhere; but it is also much more significant than the latter. Reincorporation removes no real assets or investment, disinvestment by definition does. If "competition in the production of law" among states is to be taken seriously – if the public choice theorem is to be honored – then the risktaking inherent in the very concept of competition cannot be avoided.

3. Conclusion

If *Edgar v. MITE*[29] and *Southland Stores v. Keating*[30] are expressions of the public choice theorem, they teach an extremely sterile form thereof. The states are free to be impotent, and may only compete to maximize that freedom.

That is not the tradition of Commerce Clause doctrine, which as to inadvertent state restraints teaches that the courts should by some imperfect (i.e., political) calculus balance the legitimate aim of the state enactment against the amount or seriousness of the restraint thereby imposed on the channels of interstate commerce[31]. By apotheosizing the day-to-day trading in securities as quintessential commerce, the Supreme Court gives excessive weight to the burden aspect, a matter I do not further pursue here (see Buxbaum, 1984a). By denigrating the aims of the state legislation – indeed, by purporting to find none[32] – the court completes the fashioning of an absolute bar to state regulation of enterprise activity if that regulation focusses on the stock market for its implementation. That is the use of "competition" as a shibboleth, not as a social value.

It is not necessary to go so far in turn as to limit the Commerce Clause to acting only as a self-enforcing mechanism of state experimentation – the revenge of the marketplace as it were. The lesson of "overreach" may be learned in the long run, but in the meanwhile substantial damage to the free flow of interstate capital, goods and services may result. The political judgment granted the Supreme Court by virtue of its reading of the Commerce Clause permits it to intervene whenever the mobility of factor flows, human and material, is significantly restrained by unrestrained state regulation. That may well depend more on the extraterritorial claim of the state regulation than on anything else, but certainly it should not depend on whether the goal of the state enactment – if at

[28] See the review in Comment (1982:689).

[29] 457 U.S. 624 (1982).

[30] 104 S. Ct. 852 (1984).

[31] *Pike v. Bruce Church, Inc.*, 397 U.S. 142 (1970). See Eule (1982:425); Maltz (1981:47).

[32] The Court reduced the state interest in the "weighing" of state goal v. interstate commerce constraint to zero, by declaring it already fully provided for in the Williams Act (though the majority did not find that the Williams Act preempted state regulation as such), *Edgar v. MITE*, 457 U.S. 624 (1982) at 644.

all legitimate under traditional "police power" concepts – is distributive or facilitative of existing entitlements (see Buxbaum, 1984a).

In that sense, the distinction observed by Winter can be useful. But the ciritical difference of approach is exactly the difference of degree. The values postulated by the Commerce Clause are political values of nationhood, not particular economic values[33]. The discretion first arrogated by and now legitimately residing in the Supreme Court is a discretion animated and legitimated by that primacy of political values. It is not an appropriate use thereof to enshrine a particular economic philosophy in an absolutist position of primacy as the governing norm for the federal intergovernmental relationship.

Whether this interpretation of recent American developments in the interaction of economic theory and legal doctrine has any relevance to the European discussion of legal integration is hard to judge. Many differences in the respective stages of already achieved economic and political integration stand in the way of an easy transferability of experience or evaluation. What probably remains common ground, however, is the rhetorical aspect of the interplay between economic theory and legal doctrine, a critical understanding of which is as essential a tool of legal education and legal schorlarship as it is of education and scholarship in the social sciences.

Bibliography

BEBCHUK, LUCIAN (1982) "The Case for Facilitating Competing Tender Offers", 95 *Harvard Law Review* 1028.

BUCHANAN, JAMES M. (1968) *The Demand and Supply of Public Goods*. Chicago: McNally.

BUXBAUM, RICHARD (1984) "Corporate Governance, Economic Theory and Legal Doctrine", 45 *Ohio State Law Review* 515.

– (1984a) "Federalism and Company Law", 82 *Michigan Law Review* 1163.

CARY, WILLIAM L. (1974) "Federalism and Corporate Law: Reflections upon Delaware", 88 *Yale Law Journal* 663.

CAVERS, DAVID F. (1965) *The Choice-of-Law Process*. Ann Arbor: University of Michigan Press.

CHANDLER, ALFRED D. (1977) *The Visible Hand – The Managerial Revolution in American Business*. Cambridge MA.: Harvard University Press.

COFFE, JOHN (1985) "Regulating the Market for Corporate Control: A Critical Assessment of the Tender Offer's Role in Corporate Governance", 85 *Columbia Law Review* 1145.

COMMENT (1982) "Empirical Research Project, Blue Sky Laws and the State Takeover Statutes: New Importance for an Old Battleground", 7 *Journal of Corporate Law* 689.

CONARD, ALFRED (1976) *Corporations in Perspective*. Mineola, N. Y.: Foundation Press.

COOTER, ROBERT (1982) "Law and the Imperialism of Economics: An Introduction to the Economic Analysis of Law and a Review of the Major Books", 29 *University of California Los Angeles Law Review* 1260.

DWORKIN, RONALD (1980) "Is Wealth a Value?" 9 *Journal of Legal Studies* 191.

[33] See authorities cited *supra* footnote: 26.

EASTERBROOK, FRANK H. (1982) "Insider Trading, Secret Agents, Evidentiary Privileges, and the Production of Information", *Supreme Court Review* 308.

– (1983) "Antitrust and the Economics of Federalism", 26 *Journal of Law and Economics* 23.

EASTERBROOK, FRANK and DANIEL R. FISCHEL (1981) "The Proper Role of a Target's Management in Responding to a Tender Offer", 94 *Harvard Law Review* 1161.

EULE, JULIAN N. (1982) "Laying the Dormant Commerce Clause to Rest", 91 *Yale Law Journal* 425.

FAMA, EUGENE F. (1970) "Efficient Capital Markets: A Review of Theory and Empircal Work", 25 *Journal of Finance* 383.

FISCHEL, DANIEL R. (1978) "Efficient Capital Market Theory, the Market for Corporate Control and the Regulation of Cash Tender Offers", 57 *Texas Law Review* 1.

FRANKFURTER, FELIX (1937) *The Commerce Clause under Marshall, Taney and Waite*. Chapel Hill: The University of North Carolina Press.

GILSON, RONALD J. (1981) "A Structural Approach to Corporations: The Case Against Defensive Tactics in Tender Offers", 33 *Stanford Law Review* 819.

INMAN, ROBERT J. and DANIEL L. RUBINFELD (1979) "The Judicial Pursuit of Local Fiscal Equity", 92 *Harvard Law Review* 1612.

JENNINGS, RICHARD and HAROLD MARSH (1982) *Securities Regulation, Cases and Materials* (5th ed.). Mineola, N. Y.: Foundation Press.

KITCH, EDMUND W. (1981) "Regulation and the American Common Market" in D. Tarlock (ed.) Regulation, Federalism, and *Interstate Commerce*. Cambridge/Mass.: Oelgeschlager, Gunn and Hain.

– (1982) "Regulation, the American Common Market and Public Choice", 6 *Harvard Journal of Law and Public Policy* (Special Issue) 119.

KOZYRIS, JOHN (1985) "Corporate Wars and Choice of Law", *Duke Law Journal 1*.

KRONSTEIN, HEINRICH (1944) "Business Arbitration – Instrument of Private Government", 54 *Yale Law Journal* 36.

LOWENSTEIN, LOUIS (1983) "Pruning Deadwood in Hostile Takeovers: A Proposal for Legislation", 83 *Columbia Law Review* 249.

MALTZ, EARL M. (1981) "How Much Regulation Is Too Much – An Examination of Commerce Clause Jurisprudence", 50 *George Washington Law Review* 47.

MANNE, HENRY G. (1966) *Insider Trading and the Stock Market*. New York: Free Press.

MARRIS, ROBIN (1964) *The Economic Theory of 'Managerial' Capitalism*. London: Macmillan, 1964.

MICHELMAN, FRANK (1978) "Norms and Normativity in the Economic Theory of Law" 62 *Minnesota Law Review* 1015.

– (1980) "Microeconomic Appraisal of Constitutional Law: A Methodological Preface", in D. Rubinfeld *Essays on the Law and Economics of Local Governments*. Washington: Urban Institute.

MUSGRAVE, RICHARD A. (1959) *The Theory of Public Finance: A Study in Public Economy*. New York: McGraw-Hill.

MUSGRAVE, RICHARD A. and PEGGY B. MUSGRAVE (1976) *Public Finance in Theory and Practice*. New York: McGraw-Hill.

OATES, WALLACE E. (1972) *Fiscal Federalism*. New York: Harcourt Brace Jovanovich.

POSNER, RICHARD (1980) "The Ethical and Political Basis of the Efficiency Norm in Common Law Adjudication", 8 *Hofstra Law Review* 487.

ROMANO, (1985) "Some Pieces of the Incorporation Puzzle", *Stanford Law and Economics Program, Working Paper No 19*.

RUTLEDGE, WILEY (1947) *A Declaration of Legal Faith*. Lawrence: University of Kansas Press.

Samuelson, Paul A. (1954) "The Pure Theory of Public Expenditure" 36 *Review of Economics and Statistics* 387.

Skowronek, Stephen (1982) *Building a New American State: the Expansion of National Administrative Capacities, 1877–1920*. New York: Cambridge University Press.

Trimble, Phillip R. (1984) "Foreign Policy Frustrated – *Dames & Moore*, Claims Court Jurisdictions and a New Raid on the Treasury", 84 *Columbia Law Review* 317.

Wiebe, Richard H. (1967) *The Search for Order* 1877–1920. New York: Hill and Wang.

Williamson, Oliver (1975) *Markets and Hierarchies*. New York: Free Press.

– (1981) "The Modern Corporation: Origins, Evolutions, Attributes" 19 *Journal of Economic Literature* 1537.

– (1983) "Organization Form, Residual Claimants, and Corporate Control", 26 *Journal of Law and Economics* 351.

Winter, Ralph (1978) *Government and the Corporation*. Washington: American Enterprise Institute for Public Policy Research.

Authors' Biographical Sketches

ALBERT, HANS, Professor of Sociology and Philosophy of Science; born 1921; Dr. rer. pol., University of Köln 1952; Professor, University of Mannheim 1963–; *Author*: Ökonomische Ideologie und politische Theorie, 1954, 2nd ed. 1972; Marktsoziologie und Entscheidungslogik, 1967; Traktat über kritische Vernunft, 1968, 4th ed. 1980 (English: Treatise on Critical Reason, Princeton 1985); Transzendentale Träumereien, 1975; Aufklärung und Steuerung, 1976; Traktat über rationale Praxis, 1978; Das Elend der Theologie, 1979; Die Wissenschaft und die Fehlbarkeit der Vernunft, 1982; various articles in professional journals.

BUXBAUM, RICHARD M., Professor of Law; born 1930; A. B. 1950, LL. B. 1952, Cornell University; LL. M. 1953, University of California, Berkeley; Private Practice, 1953–61; Professor of Law, School of Law University of California at Berkeley 1961–; Visiting Professor, University of Michigan School of Law 1965, University of Köln Faculty of Law 1966, University of Frankfurt Faculty of Law 1970, 1979. *Author*: Corporations – Cases and Materials, 5th ed. 1979; Die Bedeutung der privaten Klage als Mittel zur Durchsetzung wirtschaftspolitischer Rechtsnormen, 1972; Legal Harmonization and the Business Enterprise (with Hopt), forthcoming; articles in various American and European professional journals.

DAINTITH, TERENCE, Professor of Law; born 1942; M. A. Oxford University, 1968; Barrister, Lincoln's Inn, 1966; Associate in Law, University of California at Berkeley (Boalt Hall), 1963–64; Lecturer in Constitutional Law, University of Edinburgh, 1964–72; Professor of Public Law, 1972–83, and Director, Centre for Petroleum and Mineral Law Studies, 1977–83, University of Dundee; Professor of Law, European University Institute, 1981–; *Author*: The Economic Law of the United Kingdom, 1974; (with G. D. M. Willoughby) United Kingdom Oil and Gas Law, 1977, 2nd ed. 1984; (with L. Hancher) Energy Strategy in Europe: The Legal Framework, 1986.

FARJAT, GÉRARD, Professor of Law; born 1929; Advocate 1954; Judge 1957; Assistant at the University of Dijon 1958; Dr. jur. 1961, Agregation (private law) 1963; Professor of Law, University of Phnom-Penh (Cambodia) 1963; Professor of Law, University of Nice, 1967, University of Tunis 1974, Nice 1976–; President of Association Internationale de Droit Economique; *Author*: L'ordre public économique 1963; Droit économique 1971; Droit privé de l'économie, théorie des obligations 1975; Droit économique, 2nd ed., 1982; Réflexions sur les codes de conduite privés (in: Le droit des relations économiques internationales, Etudes B. Goldman, 1982).

GOTTHOLD, JÜRGEN, Professor of Law; born 1943; Referendar, University of Marburg 1966; Diplômes d'Etudes Supérieures de Droit Comparé 1967; Diplom-Volkswirt, Marburg 1970; Dr. jur., University of Marburg 1976; Employee of the Bundeskartellamt Berlin 1971–73; Referent für Stadtentwicklungsplanung Marburg 1973–78; Lecturer University of Marburg 1977–78; Professor of Economic Analysis of Law University of Bremen 1979–85; town conncillor at Marburg 1985–; *Author*: Wirtschaftliche Entwicklung und Verfassungsrecht, 1975; Macht und Wettbewerb in der Wirtschaft, 1975; Stadtentwicklung zwischen Krise und Planung, 1978; various articles in professional journals and collective publications.

HARRIS, DONALD RENSHAW, Director of the Centre for Socio-Legal Studies, University of Oxford 1975–; born 1928; B. A. (Classics 1949), LL. B. 1951, LL. M. 1952, University of New Zealand; B. C. L. 1955; M. A. 1956 University of Oxford, Balliol College; Barrister-at-law, New Zealand, 1952; Inner Temple, England, 1958; Legal practice, Auckland, New Zealand, 1950–53, 1955–56; Tutorial Fellow in Jurisprudence, Balliol College, Oxford, 1956–76 (also Senior Tutor 1962–66; Estates Bursar 1967–72; Senior Research Fellow, Balliol College 1977–; Member of Faculties of Law and Social Studies, University of Oxford. Visiting Professor (Lecturer or Fellow) at Universities of Auckland 1963, Western Ontario 1968–69, Illinois 1980, Research School of Social Sciences, Australian National, 1981, Tokyo, 1983 and Faculty of Law, Australian National, 1984. *Author or Editor* (with others): Chitty on Contracts (2 vols.) 22nd to 25th eds. 1983; Benjamin's Sale of Goods 1st and 2nd eds. 1981; Compensation and Support for Illness and Injury, 1984. Chapters in various collections; and articles in professional journals.

JOERGES, CHRISTIAN, Professor of Law; born 1943; Referendar, University of Frankfurt, 1966; Research Fellow, Institute for International and Foreign Trade Law, Georgetown University Law Center, Washington, D. C. 1966–67; Dr. jur., University of Frankfurt, 1970; Assessor, Wiesbaden 1971; Associate Professor, University of Frankfurt, 1973; Professor of Law, University of Bremen, 1974–; Co-Director, Centre for European Legal Policy, Bremen 1983–; Fellow, Netherlands Institute for Advanced Study in the Humanities and Social Sciences, Wassenaar, 1985–86; *Author*: Zum Funktionswandel des Kollisionsrechts, 1971; Bereicherungsrecht als Wirtschaftsrecht, 1977; Verbraucherschutz als Rechtsproblem, 1981; Vertriebspraktiken im Automobilersatzteilsektor (with Hiller, Holzscheck, Micklitz); various articles in professional journals and collective publications.

KRAUSE, DETLEF, Professor of Social Sciences; born 1940; Diplom-Sozialwissenschaftler, University of Bochum, 1969; Dr. rer. pol. (oec.), University of Marburg/Lahn, 1972; Professor of Social Sciences, University of Bremen, 1974–;

Author: Theorie des Humanvermögens, 1972; (with others) Bildungsökonomik und Hochschulplanung, 1976; Arbeitsteilung und Arbeitsorganisation, 1977; (with others) Tätigkeitsfelder und Qualifikationen von Wirtschafts-, Sozial-, Ingenieur- und Naturwissenschaftlern, 1981; Alternativen externer und interner Unternehmenssteuerung, 1982; various articles in professional journals and collective publications.

ROMANI, FRANCO, Professor of Political Economy; born 1935; Degree in Jurisprudence, University of Pavia, 1958; Lecturer University of York 1966–67; Professor of Public Finance, University of Siena, 1968–74; Professor of Public Finance, University of Rome, 1974–76; Professor of Political Economy, University of Rome 1976–; *Author*: Gli incrementi patrimoniali e l'imposta sul reddito, 1964; *Co-Editor*: Analisi economica ed interpretazione giuridica, 1982; various articles in academic journals.

SCHANZE, ERICH, Visiting Professor for German and Foreign Private and Commercial Law, University of Frankfurt 1985, and Associate, Institute for Foreign and International Trade Law (AIW-Institut) Frankfurt; born 1942; Referendar, University of Frankfurt 1967; Tutor, Edinburgh University 1967; LL. M., Harvard Law School 1969; Assessor, Wiesbaden 1972; Dr. iur., University of Frankfurt 1975; Visiting Scholar, Stanford Law School 1978; Visiting Associate Professor of Law, University of Chicago Law School 1980; Habilitation, University of Frankfurt 1984. *Author*: Einmanngesellschaft und Durchgriffshaftung 1975; (with Mertens and Kirchner) Wirtschaftsrecht 1978 (2nd ed. 1982); (with Assmann and Kirchner) Ökonomische Analyse des Rechts 1978; (with Kirchner, Bartels and others) Mining Ventures in Developing Countries (three volumes) 1979, 1981, 1981; (with Jaenicke and Hauser) A Joint Venture Agreement for Seabed Mining 1981; Investitionsverträge im internationalen Wirtschaftsrecht 1985; various articles in professional journals.

SCHMID, A. ALLAN, Professor of Agricultural Economics; born 1935; B. S. University of Nebraska 1956; M. S. and Ph. D., University of Wisconsin, 1959; Professor of Agricultural Economics, Michigan State University, 1956–; Visiting Scholar, Resources for the Future, 1964; Visiting Professor, Economic and Social Research Institute, Dublin, 1981; University of Perugia, Italy, 1985; Consultant to Institut National de la Récherche Agronomique, France, 1974; U.S. Congress Office of Technology Assessment, 1984; *Author*: Property, Power and Public Choice, 1978; (with Warren Samuels) Law and Economics, 1981.

TEUBNER, GUNTHER, Professor of Private Law and Sociology of Law; born 1944; Referendar, University of Tübingen, 1967; Dr. iur., University of Tübingen, 1970; Assessor, Stuttgart 1971; M. A. in Sociology of Law, Berkeley, 1974; Habilitation in Law, University of Tübingen, 1977; Privatdozent, University of Frankfurt, 1977; Professor of Law, University of Bremen, 1977–; European University Institute, Florence, Italy, 1981–; Head of Law Department, 1984; Visiting Professor, University of California at Berkeley, 1980–81;

Author: Standards und Direktiven in Generalklauseln, 1971; Public Status of Private Associations, 1974; Gegenseitige Vertragsuntreue, 1975; Organisationsdemokratie und Verbandsverfassung, 1978; *Co-author*: Alternativ-Kommentar zum BGB, 1979–81; *Editor*: Corporate Governance and Directors' Liabilities, 1985; Dilemmas of Law in the Welfare State, 1986; various articles in professional journals and collective publications.

TRUBEK, DAVID M., Professor of Law; born 1935; B. A. 1957, Wisconsin; LL. B. 1961, Yale; Note and Comment Editor, Yale Law Journal; Admitted CT, 1962; Law Clerk, Judge Charles Clark, U.S. Ct. App. 2d Cir., 1961–62; Attorney-Advisor, Agency for International Development, 1962–64; Legal Adv. & Cf., Off. of Housing and Urban Development, U.S. AID Mission to Brazil, Rio de Janeiro, 1964–66; Assistant Professor, Yale, 1966–67; Associate Professor, 1967–73; Professor of Law, Wisconsin, 1973–; Director of the Institute for Legal Studies; Visiting Professor at the European University Institute, Florence, 1982, Cardozo Law School and New School for Social Research, New York, 1984–85, University of Texas Law School, 1985. *Author*: Law, Planning and the Development of the Brazilian Capital Market, 1971; O Mercado de Capitais e os Incentivos Fiscais, 1971; Final Report of the Civil Litigation Research Project (3 vols.), 1983; Consumer Law, Common Markets and Federalism in Europe and the United States (with Bourgognie). *Editor*: Special Issue on Civil Litigation and Dispute Processing, 1980; various ariticles in professional journals and collective books.

VELJANOVSKI, CENTO, born 1953; degrees in law and economics, B. Ec., D. Phil.; Faculty member at the Centre for Socio-Legal Studies, Oxford, 1978–84; Lecturer in law and economics, University College, London, 1985–; visiting appointments in Law Faculties in Universities in North America and Australia. *Author*: (with P. Burrows) The Economic Approach to Law 1981; The New Law and Economics 1983; (with W. Bishop) Choice by Cable: The Economics of a New Era in Television 1982; (with A. Ogus) Readings in the Economics of Law and Regulation, 1984; various articles in professional journals and collective publications.

WIETHÖLTER, RUDOLF, Professor of Private, Commercial and Business Law, born 1929; Referendar, Köln, 1952; College of Europe, Bruges, 1952–53; Dr. iur., University of Köln, 1955; Assessor, Düsseldorf, 1956; Senior Research Associate in Law, University of California at Berkeley, 1958–59; Habilitation, University of Köln, 1960; Professor of Law, University of Frankfurt, 1963–; Visiting Professor, Louisiana State University, Baton Rouge, 1964. *Author*: Einseitige Kollisionsnormen als Grundlage des Internationalen Privatrechts, 1956; Der Rechtfertigungsgrund des verkehrsrichtigen Verhaltens, 1960; Interessen und Organisation der Aktiengesellschaft im amerikanischen und deutschen Recht, 1961; Rechtswissenschaft, 1968; various articles in professional journals and collective publications.

Index

Bei Fragen zur Produktsicherheit wenden Sie sich bitte an:
If you have any questions regarding product safety,
please contact:

Walter de Gruyter GmbH
Genthiner Straße 13
10785 Berlin
productsafety@degruyterbrill.com

Accounting, Finance, Sustainability, Governance & Fraud: Theory and Application

Series Editor

Kıymet Tunca Çalıyurt, Centre for Forensic Accounting Research and Enterprise, School of Finance and Management, SOAS University of London, London, Türkiye

This Scopus indexed series acts as a forum for book publications on current research arising from debates about key topics that have emerged from global economic crises during the past several years. The importance of governance and the will to deal with corruption, fraud, and bad practice, are themes featured in volumes published in the series. These topics are not only of concern to businesses and their investors, but also to governments and supranational organizations, such as the United Nations and the European Union. Accounting, Finance, Sustainability, Governance & Fraud: Theory and Application takes on a distinctive perspective to explore crucial issues that currently have little or no coverage. Thus the series integrates both theoretical developments and practical experiences to feature themes that are topical, or are deemed to become topical within a short time. The series welcomes interdisciplinary research covering the topics of accounting, auditing, governance, and fraud.

İnci Polat
Editor

Aviation Innovation

Cutting-Edge Processes and Experiential Applications

Springer

Editor
İnci Polat
Department of Aviation Management
Süleyman Demirel University
Isparta, Türkiye

ISSN 2509-7873 ISSN 2509-7881 (electronic)
Accounting, Finance, Sustainability, Governance & Fraud: Theory and Application
ISBN 978-981-96-7267-7 ISBN 978-981-96-7265-3 (eBook)
https://doi.org/10.1007/978-981-96-7265-3

Translation from the Turkish language edition: "Havacılıkta Yenilik Süreçleri ve Deneyimsel Uygulamalar" by İnci Polat, © Editor and Authors 2020. Published by Paradigma Akademi. All Rights Reserved.

This Springer imprint is published by the registered company Springer Nature Singapore Pte Ltd.
The registered company address is: 152 Beach Road, #21-01/04 Gateway East, Singapore 189721, Singapore

Foreword

İbrahim Kırcova

The concept of innovation is one of the foremost agenda items in almost all sectors today. Businesses now focus on long-term goals such as creating value for stakeholders, sustaining existence, and achieving sustainability, abandoning traditional goals like short-term profitability and growth. Consequently, competition is largely conducted through the prism of innovation, encompassing product and service development, processes, organizational structures, and business models. The aviation sector stands out as one of the industries where innovation is prolific, given the intense competition it experiences. In this sector, where a multitude of interconnected complex services are offered to customers, businesses strive to build long-term relationships based on loyalty with their customers and thus create value.

In the aviation sector, innovation processes are predominantly crafted around the idea of providing customers with a unique travel experience. Brands that excel in delivering the best travel experience take a step ahead, directing all efforts toward exceeding customer expectations by offering exceptional services. In this context, all service processes are redesigned based on variables such as quality, customer satisfaction, speed, safety, convenience, cost, and sustainability. Different experiences are tailored for different customer profiles.

This approach, centered on customer experience, has become one of the prominent concepts in marketing literature in recent years. Customer experience design is a discipline where marketers from different backgrounds come together to work collaboratively. Especially in recent years, with the increasing impact of technological innovations in the aviation sector, services have undergone a qualitative transformation. New concepts such as big data, the metaverse, personalization, gamification, artificial intelligence, and machine learning have begun to be integrated into the experience design processes.

This book, titled "Aviation Innovation: Cutting-Edge Processes and Experiential Applications," prepared under the editorship of Dr. İnci Polat, meticulously addresses different dimensions of innovation processes in carefully selected topic headings. All academics contributing to the book have aimed to deliver the latest information to readers by including extensive and up-to-date literature reviews in their chapters. Sector-specific applications are individually addressed in each chapter, and experiential design based on innovation is comprehensively explained in all its dimensions. This book is not only for university students but is also designed to meet the academic knowledge needs of managers in marketing departments in the industry. It fills a gap in the field with its quality publications.

We sincerely congratulate all the academics who contributed to the preparation of the topics in the book for successfully preparing such a high-quality work. Furthermore, we extend heartfelt thanks to Dr. İnci Polat, the editor of the book, for her meticulous work from the selection of topics to the preparation of the book for printing and reaching the readers, setting an example of careful work for the entire marketing academia and the aviation industry.

Cihan Çobanoğlu

The airline industry enables millions of people to travel globally and locally, contributing significantly to tourism and tourism revenues through direct and indirect effects. In today's world, where experiential innovations are gaining momentum, the book "Aviation Innovation: Cutting-Edge Processes and Experiential Applications," which focuses on the aviation industry in terms of its interactions with different areas and technologies, can be considered not only as filling a gap in the literature but also as an important bedside book for practitioners and managers. Congratulations to all the academics who contributed to the book and Editor Dr. İnci Polat for bringing this wonderful idea to life.

Ozlem Atalık

I wholeheartedly wish the book "Aviation Innovation: Cutting-Edge Processes and Experiential Applications," created and presented to the aviation community by my former successful student, now esteemed colleague İnci Polat Sesliokuyucu, with whom our paths crossed in 2012, to be auspicious and successful. The book fills an important gap in the literature of the field.

Yıldız Teknik Üniversitesi İİBF İşletme Bölümü, İbrahim Kırcova
Davutpaşa Kampüsü Esenler
Istanbul, Türkiye

University of South Florida, Muma College of Business Cihan Çobanoğlu
School of Hospitality and Tourism Management
Tampa, FL, USA

Faculty of Aeronautics and Astronautics Ozlem Atalık
Department of Aviation Management
Eskişehir Technical University
Eskişehir, Türkiye

Contents

List of Figures

List of Tables

About the Editor

İnci Polat was born in Gaziantep (1985). She graduated from Celal Bayar University School of Applied Sciences, Department of International Trade (2009). She received her master's degree from Gaziantep University, Department of International Trade and Logistics (2012). She completed her PhD at Anadolu University, Department of Civil Aviation Management (2018). She worked as a Research Assistant at Gaziantep University (2009–2019). She is currently an Associate Professor at Süleyman Demirel University in the Department of Aviation Management, School of Civil Aviation. Since September 2023, she has also been conducting post-doctoral research at Embry-Riddle Aeronautical University, O'Maley College of Business (USA), focusing on customer experience and service design in aviation. Her main research interests are airline marketing, service innovation, service design, and environmental sustainability.

Part I
Introduction

Chapter 1
Approaching Innovation in Aviation Through an Experiential Lens

İnci Polat

Abstract I am pleased to present the first book of a two-volume series, *Aviation Innovation: Cutting-Edge Processes and Experiential Applications*. As the sole editor, this inaugural volume focuses on the transformative role of innovation in the aviation industry, examining the advanced technologies and experiential strategies that are shaping the future of air travel. This book lays the foundation for the series by addressing key themes such as sustainability, technological advancements, and customer-centric approaches, offering valuable insights for academics and industry professionals alike.

Keywords Innovation in aviation · Experiential applications · Advanced technologies · Customer experience

1.1 Introduction

The aviation industry symbolizes progress and global connectivity, uniting people, cultures, and economies worldwide. It is a field that has revolutionized transportation and driven technological advancements and economic development on a global scale. Aviation has been at the forefront of innovation for decades, from engineering

---

This book is a translation of some parts of the book, which was published in Turkish and whose information is given below. Havacılıkta Yenilik Süreçleri ve Deneyimsel Uygulamalar. https://www.paradigmaakademiyayinlari.com/8561/havacilikta-yenilik-surecleri-ve-deneyimsel-uygulamalar/

İ. Polat (✉)
Department of Aviation Management, Süleyman Demirel University, Isparta, Türkiye

O'Maley College of Business, Embry-Riddle Aeronautical University, Daytona Beach, FL, USA
e-mail: inciseliokuyucu@sdu.edu.tr

İ. Polat (ed.), *Aviation Innovation*, Accounting, Finance, Sustainability, Governance & Fraud: Theory and Application,
https://doi.org/10.1007/978-981-96-7265-3_1

breakthroughs like jet propulsion and lightweight materials to sophisticated customer service systems and state-of-the-art airport infrastructure (Lappas and Kourousis 2016; Soonthodu et al. 2022). These innovations have reshaped modern travel and transformed how societies interact and conduct business.

Despite its legacy of innovation, the industry today finds itself at a pivotal moment, facing various complex challenges. Rapidly evolving customer expectations demand personalized, seamless, and technologically enhanced travel experiences (Murman et al. 2016; Taneja 2017). Meanwhile, the mounting urgency of environmental concerns, such as reducing carbon emissions and combating climate change, places immense pressure on aviation stakeholders to adopt sustainable practices (Raman et al. 2024). Additionally, integrating disruptive technologies—from artificial intelligence to blockchain—requires a recalibration of traditional operational models. These challenges are further compounded by external factors such as economic instability, geopolitical tensions, and the lingering effects of global disruptions like the COVID-19 pandemic.

In this rapidly changing landscape, innovation is no longer a luxury but a necessity for survival and growth. Airlines, airports, and related organizations must continuously evolve to remain competitive, ensuring their services are efficient, sustainable, and customer-centric. Travelers are no longer satisfied with merely reaching their destinations; they increasingly seek meaningful and engaging experiences throughout their journey. This shift has elevated experiential innovation to a critical priority, where the focus is on creating value through memorable and personalized interactions.

This book, *Aviation Innovation: Cutting-Edge Processes and Experiential Applications*, is a comprehensive exploration of how the aviation sector is leveraging innovation to address these pressing challenges. It delves into the transformative role of cutting-edge processes and experiential strategies in shaping the industry's future. Drawing on a blend of theoretical frameworks and real-world applications, the book examines how aviation stakeholders embrace advanced technologies, rethink traditional business models, and foster creative problem-solving approaches to deliver exceptional value.

At the heart of this book is the concept of experiential innovation. This involves designing solutions that improve functionality and efficiency and resonate emotionally with travelers, creating lasting impressions and fostering loyalty. The chapters explore how experiential innovation bridges the gap between technology and human-centric design, emphasizing the importance of balancing operational excellence with customer satisfaction.

This book addresses key topics such as the adoption of advanced technologies, the strategic use of big data, and the application of design thinking, providing a roadmap for navigating the complexities of the aviation landscape. It highlights the importance of collaboration among stakeholders, from airlines and airports to policymakers and technology providers, in achieving shared goals such as sustainability, resilience, and competitiveness.

As the aviation industry navigates an era of unprecedented change, this book is a timely resource for academics, industry professionals, and policymakers alike.

It offers a forward-looking perspective on the opportunities and challenges ahead, showcasing how innovation can drive meaningful progress in a world where adaptability and creativity are paramount. By exploring the transformative power of cutting-edge processes and experiential applications, this book aims to inspire a new vision for the future of aviation—a future defined by innovation, sustainability, and human-centered solutions.

The second chapter explores experiential applications in aviation innovation as key drivers of industry transformation. This chapter discusses how innovative customer experiences and operational advancements contribute to competitive advantage. The focus is placed on the intersection of technology and service design, illustrating how these elements create value for stakeholders.

The third chapter examines disruptive innovation in aviation's experiential processes. The chapter highlights how the industry adapts to changing market dynamics and consumer preferences by integrating new technologies. It emphasizes the importance of proactive innovation management in navigating challenges and maintaining a competitive edge.

The fourth chapter's subject is technology's role in experiential processes in aviation. This chapter investigates how advancements such as augmented reality, virtual reality, and artificial intelligence are reshaping customer experiences. Through case studies and theoretical frameworks, it provides insights into how technology enhances operational efficiency and personalization.

The fifth chapter discusses the application of big data in the airline industry. The chapter explores how data-driven decision-making supports strategic planning, optimizes operations, and improves customer satisfaction. It also highlights the ethical considerations and challenges associated with utilizing large datasets in aviation.

The sixth chapter focuses on applying design thinking to experiential processes in aviation. This chapter demonstrates how creative problem-solving methodologies can improve service quality, enhance customer satisfaction, and foster innovation. Examples of successful implementations in the aviation industry illustrate these concepts.

Finally, the seventh chapter analyzes experiential applications in business model innovation in aviation. This chapter examines how airlines and airports are evolving their business models to meet the demands of sustainability, efficiency, and customer-centric strategies. It highlights the importance of adaptability and continuous improvement in achieving long-term success.

References

Lappas I, Kourousis KI (2016) Anticipating the need for new skills for the future aerospace and aviation professionals. J Aerosp Technol Manag 8:232–241

Murman E, Allen T, Bozdogan K, Cutcher-Gershenfeld J, McManus H, Nightingale D et al (2016) Lean enterprise value: insights from MIT's lean aerospace initiative. Springer

Raman R, Gunasekar S, Dávid LD, Nedungadi P (2024) Aligning sustainable aviation fuel research with sustainable development goals: trends and thematic analysis. Energy Rep 12:2642–2652
Soonthodu S, Wahab IN, Hassan A (2022) Technology application usage in aviation industry in Asia. In: Handbook of technology application in tourism in Asia. Springer Nature Singapore, Singapore, pp 313–341
Taneja NK (2017) 21st century airlines: connecting the dots. Routledge, London

İnci Polat was born in Gaziantep (1985). She graduated from Celal Bayar University School of Applied Sciences, Department of International Trade (2009). She received her master's degree from Gaziantep University, Department of International Trade and Logistics (2012). She completed her PhD at Anadolu University, Department of Civil Aviation Management (2018). She worked as a Research Assistant at Gaziantep University (2009–2019). She is currently an Associate Professor at Süleyman Demirel University in the Department of Aviation Management, School of Civil Aviation. Since September 2023, she has also been conducting post-doctoral research at Embry-Riddle Aeronautical University, O'Maley College of Business (USA), focusing on customer experience and service design in aviation. Her main research interests are airline marketing, service innovation, service design, and environmental sustainability.

Part II
Innovation in the Aviation Sector

Chapter 2
Exploring Innovation Through Experiential Applications in Aviation

Inan Eryilmaz

Abstract The chapter examines the concept of innovation, particularly in aviation. Innovation, defined as introducing new or significantly improved products, processes, marketing methods, or organizational practices, is essential for economic development and competitive advantage. The chapter highlights the historical evolution of the term and its vital role in modern business strategies, emphasizing the need for effective innovation management. In aviation, innovation spans from technological advancements to enhancing customer experiences and operational efficiencies. The chapter underscores the industry's technological leader role and spillover effects across various sectors. Furthermore, it discusses the challenges and opportunities in managing innovation processes, particularly in dynamic and crisis-prone environments such as global pandemics. The aviation industry's innovation efforts, including experiential innovations like customer service enhancements and airport efficiency, are crucial for maintaining competitive edges and addressing environmental concerns.

Keywords Aviation innovation · Innovation management · Experimental applications · Technological advancements · Customer experience

2.1 Introduction

The concept of innovation, which ranks first in economic development and development prescription, is stated as the engine of the capitalist system in the work *Capitalism, Socialism and Democracy* by Schumpeter (1942), one of the important economists of the twentieth century, and is described as the dynamo of change. Countries are taking steps to develop innovation within the framework of the

I. Eryilmaz (✉)
Department of Aviation Management, Süleyman Demirel University, Isparta, Türkiye
e-mail: inaneryilmaz@sdu.edu.tr

İ. Polat (ed.), *Aviation Innovation*, Accounting, Finance, Sustainability, Governance & Fraud: Theory and Application,
https://doi.org/10.1007/978-981-96-7265-3_2

techno-economic paradigm every passing day to create new opportunities with economic growth to gain and maintain competitiveness.

The word "innovation," which is derived from the Latin word "innovatus," is frequently used as "innovation" in the national literature, similar to its original usage, but it is also used to mean novelty, innovativeness, improvement, and renovation. The Turkish Language Association dictionary, as for that, gives the equivalent of the word as "innovation" (TDK 2022). Researchers who use the word as innovation state that the concept is a technical term that is widely used just like the word "technology" (Durna 2002). Some researchers, on the other hand, state that the word innovation does not fully meet the economic emphasis in the word "improvement" (Elçi 2006: 1).

From the second half of the twentieth century, the concept of innovation, which has been frequently discussed in the academic literature and in the discourse of management and marketing gurus, has traces of social change. The rapid change in market structure and customer expectations and the progressing intense competition in all industries have led businesses to renew themselves and produce innovation, and the continuity of businesses has changed depending on their capacity to produce and manage innovation (Boer and During 2001). However, very few businesses that only produce innovation have survived. This situation has revealed the importance of managing the innovation process and its aftermath as much as producing innovation.

Although innovation is vital for the sustainability of businesses, it is the management of existing innovation that is essential. The success of innovation management strategies depends on the coordination between all functions of the business as a whole and the dissemination of innovation as a culture (Ventura and Soyuer 2016: 41). By this means, innovation management practices will be directly related to the performance and success of innovation (Babkin et al. 2015). However, it remains unclear which innovation management model will make businesses successful. In this sense, although the innovation activities of enterprises vary according to their fields of activity, universal innovation management practices independent of context are discussed in the literature (Du Plessis and Pretorius 2017).

In order for businesses to keep up with change, they need to literally run. In this sense, it is of great importance that they act flexibly and dynamically, using all functions of information technology and becoming open to innovation (Ratten et al. 2017). In this context, compared to many other sectors, the aviation industry has been the pioneer of innovation and the flag bearer of technological and service innovation with its ability to spill over to different sectors. In this section, the importance of innovation for businesses will be reviewed, and innovation management and innovation culture will be discussed. In addition, the process and impact of innovation in the aviation context and the place of experiential practices in aviation will be addressed.

2.1.1 Definition of Innovation

Many researches have been conducted on the concept of innovation, and different definitions and classifications have been made under the influence of the periodic active paradigm. In a study examining the evolution of the concept of innovation over a period of 40 years, it is underlined that definitions, classifications, additions, and deletions of the concept vary according to the perception and perspective of the authors (Rowley et al. 2011). The changing paradigm was also observed in another study. Prior to 1960, innovation was built on making inventions and creating new products (Ortt and Duin 2008), and businesses allocated resources to R&D activities (Hidalgo and Albors 2008). However, today, it is seen that innovation and sustainability of existing innovation cannot be solved by focusing only on R&D processes. For this reason, R&D processes have been focused on new business models formed within the framework of new markets and customer expectations and experiences, and it has been understood that the inclusion of the innovation process as a whole will enable effective and efficient businesses.

According to the internationally accepted Oslo guidelines published jointly by the OECD and Eurostat, which are frequently cited in research on the concept, innovation is defined as "the implementation of a new and significantly changed product (goods or services) or process, a new marketing method, or a new organizational method in business practices, workplace organization and relations with the external environment" (OECD 2005: 50–51). The practices and methods mentioned in the definition and described as new refer to all organizational, financial, technological, scientific, and commercial steps (OECD 2005: 50–51). According to another important definition, innovation is the process of transforming new ideas into value-creating outputs (Ansal 2013: 75).

There are many definitions of innovation. When these definitions are reviewed, it is seen that each of them evaluates the concept from their own point of view, but they basically focus on similar results. Innovation, defined by Lane et al. (2013: 10) as abstract or concrete ideas related to production, emerges as a result of the combination of concepts such as product, market, technology, and business (Boer and During 2001: 84). While the definitions discussed in technical aspects focus on production outputs and commercial results (Hult et al. 2004; Salavou 2004), innovation evaluated in the social context focuses on positive change in human attitudes and behaviors (Durna 2002). The definitions of the concept reveal that innovation has a holistic character beyond both technical and sociological details.

According to Schumpeter (1942), cited in the introduction to the chapter, innovations are different and novel combinations of the following situations:

- Developing a new product or introducing products with new features
- Developing a new production method or technique
- Expanding into a new market
- Obtaining new or alternative sources of raw materials
- Running the organization with a new management

Schumpeter defines innovation as putting new solutions into practice. Undoubtedly, his definition is valuable as it is the beginning of a discussion about the importance of innovation in the economy. However, Schumpeter focused on technical innovation and its reflection on the economy. He is therefore the author of the concept of "creative destruction," which is conceptualized as the continuous destruction of old structures and the continuous development of new, more efficient structures, and states that industrial mutation can only ensure the continuity of the economy. According to twenty-first-century management guru Peter F. Drucker, innovation is the entrepreneur's special tool, but by means of these tools, an opportunity to establish a new business or providing new services is enabled. It is stated that there is no need for anything technical or even material in Drucker's innovation. In this sense, putting into practice new or significantly improved solutions related to process, marketing, or organizational system is considered innovation (Drucker 1986: 110).

2.2 Importance of Innovation

Today, innovation is synonymous with progress and modernity in all areas, from the social sphere to the education system, science, and economy. Innovation not only generates new solutions that contribute to competitive advantage in the market and thus raise the economic level but also contributes to social development and a high quality of life. Steve Jobs, the founding CEO of Apple, emphasized the individual, organizational, and national importance of innovation by saying, "Innovation is the difference between leaders and followers." The confirmation of this can be seen in many data showing that most of the projects based on innovation and high technologies are implemented in the USA, and thus the US economy leads the world economy. This situation has caused other countries not to drop the concept of innovation from their agenda, but to allocate more and more resources for R&D and innovation every year (Witkowski 2009). Moreover, in order to reduce the gap between itself and the USA in the field of economic development, the European Union is putting implementations into practice to increase the industrial and technological mobility of the qualified labor force beyond its borders by seeking solutions similar to the US immigration policy.

The emphasis on innovation continues to evolve through systematic research, experimentation, and the ultimate testing of management practices and experience. Day by day it becomes increasingly difficult to follow a rapidly developing and interdisciplinary field. In the field of general business and economic research, there are more than 200 active research centers worldwide, and around 5000 articles are produced each year, many of which are relevant to innovation management (Baden-Fuller and Mangematin 2013). In more specialized areas of technology and innovation management, 120 research centers worldwide publish hundreds of articles each year (Bhupatiraju et al. 2012).

In this sense, some classifications are made by taking into account the context of the published research. In this taxonomy, which considers innovation processes in four different contexts, the first two are divided according to the internal environment of the business and the last two according to the external environment (Kotler 2002).

- Type of innovation (e.g., incremental, radical, transformational)
- Type of organization (e.g., centralized, decentralized, functional, organic)
- Type of industry (e.g., high-tech, supplier-driven, fast-moving consumer goods)
- Country/culture type (e.g., egalitarian, authoritarian)

2.3 Innovation in Aviation

The concept of innovation is undoubtedly of great importance for the aviation industry, as it is in every industry. Especially, technological progress in aviation has shown a spillover effect to many different sectors. In this respect, the frequency of academic studies on innovation in the aviation industry has increased. According to a search made on the Web of Science database using the keywords "aviation" and "innovation," the number of scientific research has increased from around 100 in 2014 to nearly 400 by the end of 2021 (see Fig. 2.1).

The air transportation industry is also constantly changing with rapid growth in both traffic and passenger expectations (Chambers 2007). Even though consumer trends, changes in safety and security, and global problems such as Covid-19 have made air transportation difficult at times, it has continued to innovate with new products, services, processes, strategies, and business models to remain competitive (Graham 2013).

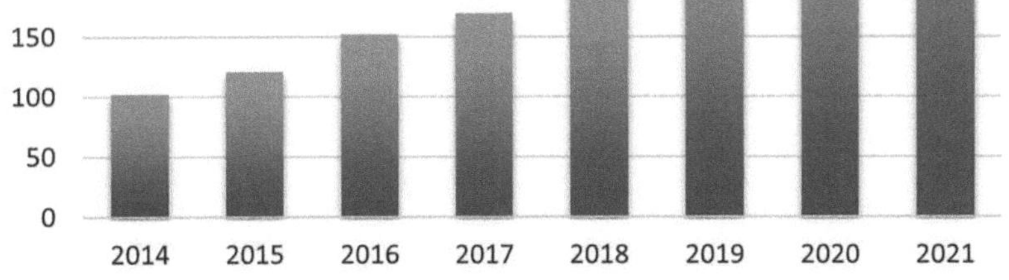

Fig. 2.1 The number of scientific research on aviation and innovation by years

Innovation is the creation of added value through new ideas, methods, or products (Merriam-Webster 2017). It is through the interaction of technology, market, and organization that competitive advantage can be achieved by producing and offering new products and services (Tidd and Bessant 2013). In this regard, aviation businesses invest a significant number of resources particularly in technological innovation (Kılıç et al. 2021). This situation also stands out in the research on aviation (Fig. 2.2). In this context, while the concepts of aviation and innovation are the keywords in the search of research articles on the Web of Science database without time constraint, it is seen that the research based on the concept of innovation are mostly carried out on engineering, materials, environmental sciences, and energy. In a search on the ScienceDirect database using similar keywords between 2005 and 2015, the areas where studies on innovation in air transport are seen more frequently are the aircraft industry (energy efficiency, industrial process, and noise and pollutant emission reduction), airlines (business model, Information Technologies (IT), and planning and management), policies (sustainable transportation, incentive mechanisms, and societal expectations), and airports (security, self-financing, and air traffic control and projects) (Caetano and Clautono 2019).

Aviation research conducted on innovation, which is the dynamo of the economy, shows changes in the axis of country distribution as well. It is seen that research on innovation in aviation is increasing outside the USA and Europe, which are the centers of international aviation. A similar increase is seen in the academic publications containing the keywords aviation and innovation of China, which has increased its investments in regional aircraft production and space studies, especially in the recent period (Fig. 2.3).

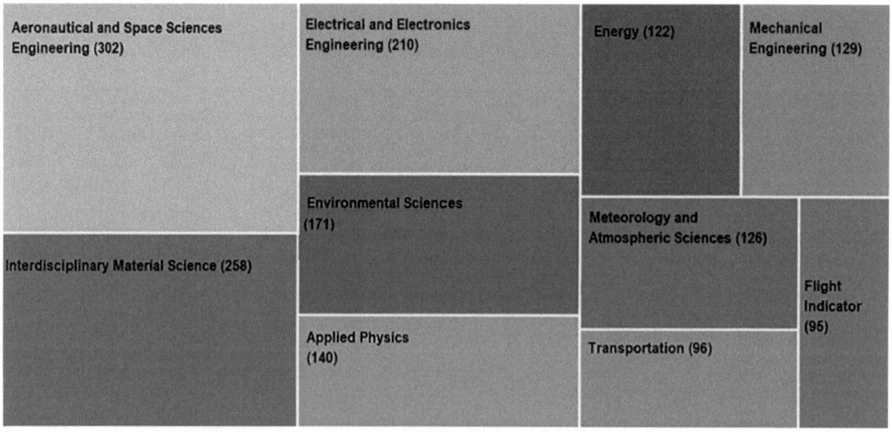

Fig. 2.2 Research areas on aviation and innovation

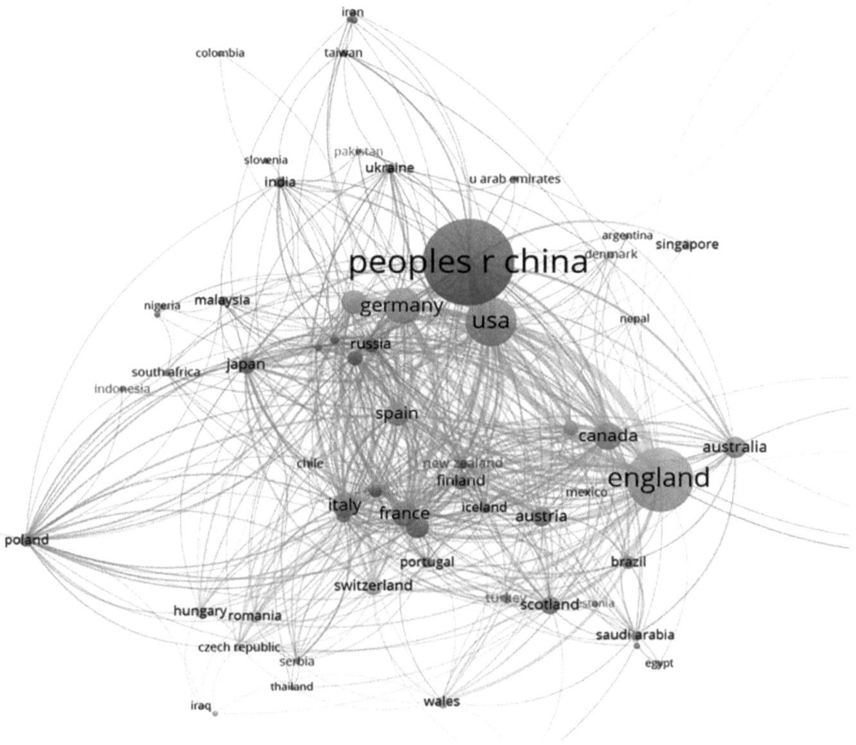

Fig. 2.3 Distribution of aviation and innovation research across countries

2.4 Creating Innovation in the Experiential Process in Aviation

Many innovation efforts focus on new propositions (Berry and Carbone 2007). However, innovation practices are shifting the focus towards value created from products and services and, essentially, the experience (Prahalad and Ramaswamy 2004). In this sense, as the main component of business activities, customer experience takes place on the basis of modern marketing approaches. In the process of gaining and retaining customers, it is essential to create a positive customer experience (Chesbrough et al. 2018). Customer experience management is a strategic process for managing the total customer experience with a service, product, business, or organization. In essence, customer experience is a mental response to direct and indirect communication that includes all aspects of a business's products and services (Prahalad and Ramaswamy 2004). In this sense, experience is an interactive process triggered by stimuli such as brand, communication, and environment; continues as emotional, cognitive, and behavioral responses; and is remembered for better or worse (Jain et al. 2017). The process, which should focus on creating a unique, attractive, and memorable experience, plays an important role in achieving financial and nonfinancial performance of the business. In a study conducted on multinational enterprises, it is indicated that 89% of large-scale enterprises have a competitive plan based on customer experience (Keiningham et al. 2017).

Today, the transport sector is one of the pillars of balanced and sustainable development in countries, as transportation networks are closely linked to important components such as economy, security, and justice. The study of economic and social development shows that there is a direct relationship between the development of transportation and the achievement of a higher rate of economic growth. In other words, as the value added in the transportation sector increases, GDP increases (Mataleh and Pirzad 2019).

The airline industry is undergoing dynamic change, facing many challenges such as cost reduction, demand shortages during global crises, and keeping up with rapidly changing quality standards (Sabrina et al. 2013). This situation is changing customer perceptions and expectations of service quality. With the increase in volume and the presence of low-cost carriers, airfares are significantly decreasing. Intense competition and therefore more alternatives for the customer generate efforts to differentiate in various markets in order to meet increasing demands. One of the important strategies in this sense is the process of creating a positive customer experience, which is one of the determining factors on the loyalty coefficient of customers. According to IATA's report, customers who have a positive customer service experience are 16% more likely to remain loyal to the airline in the coming year compared to those who do not. It is reported that, conversely, those who have a negative customer service experience are 24% less likely to remain loyal over the next year compared to other customers (IATA 2011).

Airports are the first and last point of contact for international guests in the country they are visiting. For this reason, services need to be processed efficiently at an airport to ensure that travel times are optimized and leisure time is utilized in the commercial areas of the airport (Gatersleben and Van der Weij 1999). In parallel with innovation implementations in air transportation, innovations in airport design are also made. Innovation in airport design has a crucial role in the aviation safety chain, linking airline safety with passenger safety and customer freight. How to solve big problems such as the growth of airports, reaching the optimal limits of their capacity, insufficient runways, etc. confronts us as an important problem. Efforts have been made to address this problem by renovating, improving, or making some additions to the airport and its facilities. However, the future concepts of modern airports are envisioned to address three key elements based on innovation:

- More comfortable use of passengers
- High level of capacity and quality increase
- Air operations: reducing the environmental impact on nature
- Maintaining clean energy projects and airport facilities

In a study that holistically assessed research conducted between 2000 and 2019 on how innovations have shaped the aviation industry worldwide, making it more efficient, agile, sustainable, and safe, industry innovations were categorized into five main groups. These are:

(i) Aircraft technology innovations that create value in terms of efficiency and sustainability
(ii) Innovation in passenger services to create personalized services and enhance the customer experience
(iii) In-flight innovation to create value in terms of safety and security environment
(iv) Innovation in business and operations management to improve procedures and revenue
(v) From the point of view Aviation 4.0, automation and big data, including general applications (cyber-physical systems, Internet of Things (IoT), and cloud computing) that add value to Aviation 4.0 (see Fig. 2.4) (Pereira et al. 2022)

When Fig. 2.4 is reviewed, it was found that, within the context of the experiential process, value is often created in passenger services towards more personalized service that improves the customer experience. Innovations in this category have helped industry embrace a more seamless and automated journey and address the needs and problems of passengers at airports. Difficulties in check-in, boarding, and baggage claim services have been addressed by automated systems, allowing faster procedures to be implemented. In addition, innovations in passenger services have enabled the improvement of identification processes, especially at checkpoints,

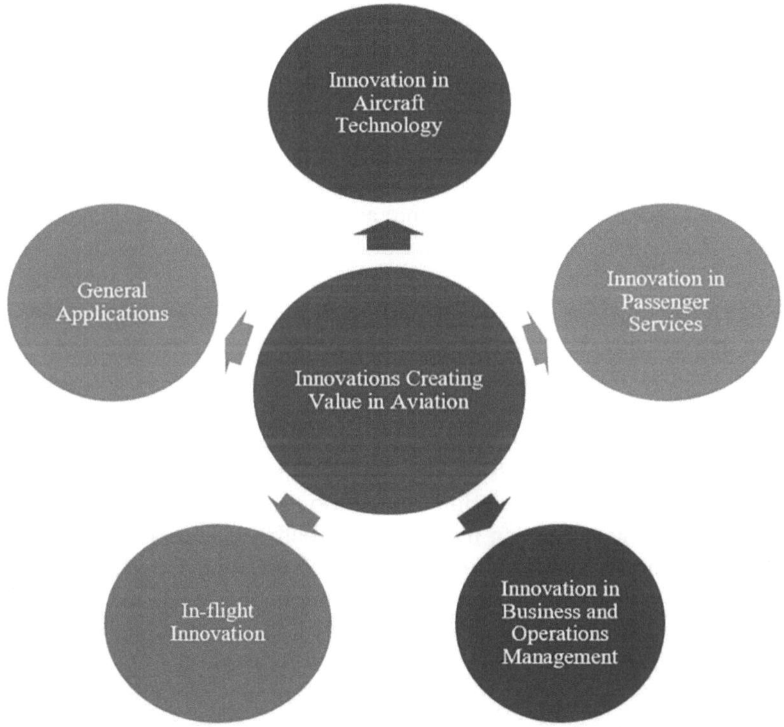

Fig. 2.4 Overall assessment of innovations creating value in aviation (source adapted from Pereira, B.A. et al., 2022)

allowing for more in-flight experiences. For example, technological advances in the early 2000s, such as the ability to verify passengers using facial, fingerprint, and iris recognition, or a combination of these methods, have allowed passengers to speed through queues and facilitate connections to flights (Photonics 2001). It has also provided better entertainment for passenger cabins, offering Wi-Fi and improved device connectivity and onboard streaming services (Garcia 2017).

Mobile internet services, kiosks, automated gates, and innovations in smart airports that provide a sense of control over the entire travel process have all focused on the experiential process (Halder 2013; Martin-Domingo and Martín 2016).

2.5 Conclusion

The continuity of businesses is possible through the construction and management of the innovation process. However, this process reserves a structure that is influenced by multiple factors, varies according to the context of the business, and therefore needs to be handled holistically. Innovation in the aviation industry, which has a direct and indirect impact on many sectors, creates a spillover effect on different layers. This effect is not limited only to innovations achieved in products and technology. Process, method, and service experience innovation are also included in this scope.

Many of today's businesses are trying to respond to both global competitors and sudden changes such as pandemics by making changes and innovations in all their areas of activity. They have to recognize and manage threats, in a way; they have to survive by creating different opportunities from crises. During the pandemic, especially the retail sector turned the crisis into an opportunity with technological innovation solutions and innovations in distribution services. Businesses that create and manage innovation such as mergers, joint ventures, new forms of organization, new technologies and products, new business processes, and e-business initiatives have been able to overcome the current global crisis. The aviation industry has also tried to alleviate the deep crisis caused by the pandemic, especially in air passenger transportation, by moving the center of gravity to the cargo area.

Most attempts to better explain what factors drive innovation in the aviation sector have been technology-based approaches. Against the background of international concerns about global warming, in addition to rising oil prices, airlines are again focusing on energy-saving innovations in both technologies and operations. However, Budd and Vorley (2013), in their research focusing on technological innovation in aviation, emphasized that aircraft technologies developed rapidly in the 1950s and 1960s (mostly jet engines), but the pace has slowed since the 1970s due to limitations related to improving engine and aerodynamic efficiency, and that the direction of innovation has been in passenger transportation due to the deregulations.

Global crises and economic bottlenecks are expected to continue in the future, as they have at certain periods in the past. These challenging conditions should not hinder the growth of airports, which have a significant impact on development, employment opportunities, and economic development (Carrier and Fiig 2018). In the success of airports, on the other hand, it is vital to consider not only the physical but also the impact on the value creation process. However, it should not be overlooked that the meaning and creation process of value has shifted from a product-, service-, and business-centered perspective to personalized consumer experiences that occur within the business and in foreign markets (Chesbrough et al. 2018).

Value creation depends on an organization's ability to make innovation successfully. For this reason, not only internal but also external factors need to be considered. In order to improve innovation and value creation, businesses need to provide the perspectives of stakeholders and internal support from the organization. They must also meet the existing needs or desires of their customers by offering a more comprehensive range of attractive goods and services. In this sense, the aviation industry strives to continuously improve value creation, efficiency, safety and security, operational and management capabilities, new customer experiences, and sustainability for its different areas and focuses on differentiation by creating new opportunities for airports and airlines (Husted et al. 2015; Liu et al. 2017; Polat 2021).

In this sense, innovations in the aviation industry, made especially in the last 20 years, have brought multifaceted benefits to the aviation industry at all levels.

When innovations are evaluated at the micro, meso, and macro levels, there have been many innovations actualized in the passenger experience, including most notably in passenger booking, ticketing, boarding passes, baggage drop-off, and in-flight comfort and entertainment experiences. In addition, long-range airplanes with new engines have shortened flight distances and times. At the meso level (organizations), airports and airlines have benefited from a range of technologies, mostly related to efficiencies in aircraft, engines, fuel, traffic management, safety and security procedures, maintenance, and predictive operations. Thus, they have developed more efficient and sustainable business models. Finally, at the macro level, stakeholders and supply chain networks have deepened and institutionalized the sector and businesses by introducing innovations such as better communication, IT integration, operations management, and the use of on-site services.

The management and implementation of national innovation strategies is critical for success in sustaining innovation in aviation. The process of developing a national strategy requires adequate involvement of stakeholders, including business, academia, social partners, and other key actors. As many policies affect innovation, it is important that they are in rapport not only at the central government level but also between central and local governments, many of which actively support innovation. The development and implementation of innovation policies makes a holistic contribution, including building trust in government actions and ensuring stakeholder support for policy actions.

Popper (1959) underlines that a good theory should be simple, measured, and realistic. As a result of the systematic review of the concepts of aviation and innovation presented in this chapter, it is concluded that this is a very fragmented area of research lacking scientific consolidation within its paradigmatic structure. Therefore, more research focusing on innovation transformation and development in aviation is needed.

References

Ansal H (2013) In *Açık inovasyon* (Open Innovation), Yeni paradigma (New Paradigm). Optimist Yayım, İstanbul, pp 75–91
Babkin AV, Lipatnikov VS, Muraveva SV (2015) Assessing the impact of innovation strategies and R&D costs on the performance of IT companies. Procedia Soc Behav Sci 207:749–758
Baden-Fuller C, Mangematin V (2013) Business models: a challenging agenda. Strateg Organ 11(4):418–427
Berry LL, Carbone LP (2007) Building loyalty through experience management. Qual Prog 40(9):26–32
Bhupatiraju S, Nomaler Ö, Triulzi G, Verspagen B (2012) Knowledge flows-analyzing the core literature of innovation, entrepreneurship, and science and technology studies. Res Policy 41(7):1205–1218
Boer H, During WE (2001) Innovation, what innovation? A comparison between product, process and organizational innovation. Int J Technol Manag 22(1/2/3):83–107
Budd L, Vorley T (2013) Airlines, apps, and business travel: a critical examination. Res Transp Bus Manag 9:41–49
Caetano M, Cláudio J (2019) Innovation system in air transport management. J Inf Syst Technol Manag 16. https://doi.org/10.4301/s1807-1775201916010
Carrier E, Fiig T (2018) Special issue: future of airline revenue management. J Revenue Pricing Manag 17(2):45–47
Chambers RD (2007) Tackling uncertainty in airport design: a real options approach. Doctoral dissertation, Massachusetts Institute of Technology, Engineering Systems Division, Technology and Policy Program
Chesbrough H, Lettl C, Ritter T (2018) Value creation and value capture in open innovation: value creation and value capture. J Prod Innov Manag 35(6):930–938
Drucker PF (1986) Innovation and entrepreneurship: practice and principles. Simon and Schuster, New York
Du Plessis MJ, Pretorius MW (2017) Towards a better understanding of the key elements driving the innovativeness of the mineral resources industry: a literature review. International Conference on Management of Engineering and Technology, PICMET 2017:1–11
Durna U (2002) Yenilik yönetimi. Nobel Yayın Dağıtım, Ankara
Elçi S (2006) İnovasyon Kalkınmanın ve Rekabetin Anahtarı. Pelit Yayınları, İstanbul
Garcia M (2017) 10 years on, airlines begin to see the benefits of inflight wifi. https://www.phocuswire.com/10-years-on-airlines-begin-to-see-the-benefits-of-inflight-wifi. Accessed 13 Mar 2023
Gatersleben MR, Van der Weij SW (1999) Analysis and simulation of passenger flows in an airport terminal. In: Proceedings of the 31st conference on Winter simulation: Simulation—a bridge to the future, vol 2. pp 1226–1231
Graham A (2013) Managing airports, 4th edn. Routledge, London
Halder V (2013) Innovations in supply chain in aviation industry. UPES Manag Rev 2(1):21–30
Hidalgo A, Albors J (2008) Innovation management techniques and tools: a review from theory and practice. R&D Manag 38(2):113–127
Hult T, Ketchen D, Slater S (2004) Information processing, knowledge development, and strategic supply chain performance. Acad Manag J 47(2):241–253
Husted BW, Allen DB, Kock N (2015) Value creation through social strategy. Bus Soc 54(2):147–186
International Air Transport Association (IATA) (2011) Vision 2050 report. Singapore, 12 February 2011
Jain R, Aagja J, Bagdare S (2017) Customer experience – a review and research agenda. J Serv Theory Pract 27(3):642–666
Keiningham T, Ball J, Benoit S, Bruce HL, Buoye A, Dzenkovska J, Zaki M (2017) The interplay of customer experience and commitment. J Serv Mark 31(2):148–160

Kiliç S, Ucler C, Martin-Domingo L (2021) Innovation at airports: a systematic literature review (2000–2019). Aviation 25(3):220–231

Kotler P (2002) Marketing management. analysis, planning, implementation, and Control, 11th edn. Prentice-Hall, Englewood Cliffs, NJ

Lane K, McCormack T, Richardson M (2013) Resilient leaders: essential for organizational innovation. Int J Organ Innov 6(2):7–25

Liu Y, Kreimeier M, Stumpf E, Zhou Y, Liu H (2017) Overview of recent endeavors on personal aerial vehicles: a focus on the US and Europe-led research activities. Prog Aerosp Sci 91:53–66

Martin-Domingo L, Martin JC (2016) Airport mobile internet an innovation. J Air Transp Manag 55:102–112

Mataleh M, Pirzad A (2019) Investigating the impact of customer relationship management, service quality and brand image on customer loyalty (case study: airlines of the islamic republic of iran), fifth national conference on applied research in management and accounting, Tehran, In Persian

Merriam-Webster (2017) Innovation. https://www.merriam-webster.com/thesaurus/innovation. Accessed 05 Aug 2022

OECD-Eurostat (2005) Oslo manual guidelines for collecting and interpreting innovation data, 3rd edn. http://www.oecd.org/sti/inno/2367580pdf. Accessed 02 Aug 2022

Ortt JR, Duin PA (2008) The evolution of innovation management towards contextual innovation. Eur J Innov Manag 11(4):522–538

Pereira BA, Lohmann G, Houghton L (2022) Technology trajectory in aviation: innovations leading to value creation (2000–2019). Int J Innov Stud 6(3):128–141

Photonics (2001) EyeTicket announces congressional request of $2.75 million. www.photonics.com/Articles/EyeTicket_ Announces_Congressional_ Request_of/a9548. Accessed 12 Aug 2022

Polat İ (2021) Value co-creation and passenger loyalty in the context of the DART model: the mediating role of perceived service newness. J Aviation 5(2):219–229

Popper K (1959) The logic of scientific discovery. Routledge, London

Prahalad CK, Ramaswamy V (2004) Co-creation experiences: the next practice in value creation. J Interact Mark 18(3):5–14

Ratten V, Ferreira JJ, Fernandes CI (2017) Innovation management – current trends and future directions. Int J Innov Learn 22(2):135–155

Rowley J, Baregheh A, Sambrook S (2011) Towards an innovation-type mapping tool. Manag Decis 49(1):73–86

Sabrina S, Patrick S, Thomas C (2013) Business model innovation in the aviation industry. Int J Prod Dev 18(3/4):286–310

Salavou H (2004) The concept innovativeness: should we need to focus? Eur J Innov Manag 7(1):33–44

Schumpeter JA (1942) Capitalism, socialism, and democracy, vol 36. Harper & Row, New York, pp 132–145

TDK (2022). https://sozluk.gov.tr. Accessed 02 Aug 2022

Tidd J, Bessant J (2013) Integrating technological, market and organizational change, 5th edn. Wiley

Ventura K, Soyuer H (2016). İşletmelerde Yenilik Yönetimi ve Araştırma Geliştirme- Pazarlama-Üretim Entegrasyonunda Bilgiye Dayalı Yenilik Yaklaşımı. Ege Akademik Bakış, 16 (Özel Sayı), 41–50.

Witkowski K (2009) The innovations for sustainable development. CO-MAT-TECH 2009, Industrial Engineering, Management and Quality for 21st century, 17th International Scientific Conference, Trnava

Inan Eryilmaz was born in Ankara and completed his primary and secondary education in Ankara. Between 2005 and 2020, he did his duty in the Land Aviation Units of the Turkish Armed Forces on aircraft maintenance, quality control and maintenance planning. During his service in the Turkish Armed Forces, he received his bachelor's degree from Anadolu University, Department of Business Administration (2009), master's degree from the Department of Management and Organization (2012) and doctorate degree from the Department of Business Administration (2017). In 2020, he became an Associate Professor in the field of Management and Strategy. Between 2019 and 2021, he worked at Maltepe University Aircraft Technology program. He continues to work as a faculty member at Süleyman Demirel University, School of Civil Aviation, Department of Aviation Management (2021–). Dr. Eryilmaz, who continues his research on leadership, motivation, organizational strength, human factors in aviation and team resource management, is the editor-in-chief of the Journal of Aviation Research (JAR) and area editor of the Journal of Aviation.

Chapter 3
Disruptive Innovation in Aviation's Experiential Processes

Ali Emre Sarılgan

Abstract This chapter examines disruptive innovation in the aviation sector, focusing on its experiential practices. Disruptive innovation, particularly in the airline transportation industry, signifies innovations that create significant changes and transform market structures. The chapter discusses examples, such as the low-cost carrier model, detailing how these innovations emerge and impact existing businesses. It also explores how technological advancements and new business models can shape the future evolution of the aviation industry. Potential future innovations, such as pilotless (automated) airplanes, fully automated airports, and alternative fuel airplanes, are also discussed in this context.

Keywords Disruptive innovation · Aviation sector · Low-cost carrier · Technological advancements · Business models

3.1 Introduction

The only thing that has not changed for billions of years since the world's creation is "change." In today's world, where even the day before and the day after are different, it is inconceivable that a global business line, such as airline transportation, is not affected by changes in the world. When considering the stages that the airline transportation industry has gone through from the onset of its development during World War II to the present day, it is seen that it is one of the rare sectors closely intertwined with the concept of "disruptive innovation." In this intensely competitive environment, airline companies are trying to better understand the market and develop strategies that will carry them one step ahead of their competitors in order

A. E. Sarılgan (✉)
Faculty of Aviation and Astronautics, Department of Aviation Management, Eskişehir Technical University, Eskisehir, Türkiye
e-mail: aesarilgan@eskisehir.edu.tr

İ. Polat (ed.), *Aviation Innovation*, Accounting, Finance, Sustainability, Governance & Fraud: Theory and Application,
https://doi.org/10.1007/978-981-96-7265-3_3

to maintain their existence. The fact that there have been 208 articles published on the concept of disruptive innovation in SSCI journals between 1995 and 2019 demonstrates the popularity of this concept worldwide (Si and Chen 2020). This chapter aims to examine experiential practices based on disruptive innovation in aviation by providing a conceptual framework for disruptive innovation. In this way, the aim is to contribute to Turkish literature on a topic that has been studied so much, that is, disruptive innovation.

3.2 Disruptive Technology and Innovation

The concept of "innovation," which is translated into Turkish as "novelty," needs to meet some specific conditions in order to be disruptive. Today, almost every innovation activity is referred to as disruptive innovation, and this causes information pollution. Before disruptive innovation, it is important to know what the concept of innovation is. Innovation is the use of new techniques and practices in cultural, administrative, and social environments (Şahin 2021).

The concept of disruptive technology or disruptive innovation was first mentioned by Clayton Christensen in 1900s in his book named *Innovator's Dilemma*. According to this concept, "because successful businesses focus on their existing customers and business models, they ignore alternative business models, strategies, new technologies and approaches, causing new businesses to enter these areas." And consequently, it was stated that the current situation could not be sustained due to the demand for the product, causing a disruptive effect. Christensen and Raynor (2003) cited discount stores, low-cost airlines, and online sales of products and services such as vacations, books, education, etc. as examples of disruptive innovations. Over time, disruptive innovation has been developed to include not only innovations but also products and business models. While existing businesses in the market focus on the most profitable or what they see as the most profitable part of the market, newly established businesses offer cheaper, simpler, preferable products and services, which can be accepted in the market and lead to the collapse of dominant businesses in the market. While there are different approaches to whether a new business deserves the label "disruptive," it is a fact that many of today's popular innovation concepts cannot be explained by this approach.

In the twenty-first century, where the pace of technological, political, and societal change has increased incomparably with regard to previous periods, not every change can be labeled "disruptive innovation." Business managers have to sustain growth with the help of the threat posed by disruptive innovation and constantly evolving technologies. The environment in emerging markets can give countenance to disruptive innovation. This is because product design and business model changes that substantially reduce costs are often serve as a prerequisite to unlock a market segment for a customer with limited disposable income in these markets. Large numbers of early adopters with lower expectations can enable the development of disruptive innovations for developed markets in a cheaper and faster manner

(Williamson et al. 2013). An example of this can be seen in the transportation industry in Brazil, where the use of flex-fuel vehicles, which account for approximately 35% of the fuel market, has created a pioneering source of innovation in sustainable biofuels. Subsequently, this practice has been applied in the Asian and African markets as well. Bharti Airtel, a mobile telecommunications business in India that incorporated innovative marketing, pricing, and billing systems specifically tailored to serve low-income consumers, revolutionized the markets of around 20 countries in Asia and Africa (Angelo 2012).

Disruptive innovation can result not only from new technologies that exceed the performance of the current dominant technology in a market but also from changes in business models or service processes that offer superior or new value to consumers (Christensen 2006). Markides further clarifies this classification and classifies disruptive innovations into three parts: technological, business model, and radical product innovations (Markides 2006). These different types of disruptive innovations can all follow similar processes to capture the existing market and have similar disruptive effects on existing businesses in the market.

Analyzing the disruptive innovations developed by Chinese enterprises, Yin and Williamson (2011) categorized disruptive innovation into three classes: cost innovation, application innovation, and business model innovation. Cost innovation refers to restructuring the cost structure in new ways to deliver superior quality at lower cost to customers. Application innovation is defined as finding innovative applications for existing technology or products. Business model innovation, on the other hand, involves fast and low-cost practices to change one of the four key components of the business model (customer value proposition, profit formula, key resources, or new processes) (Wan et al. 2015).

Kalfaoğlu and Akgemci (2020) listed the characteristics of disruptive innovation as follows:

(i) Focusing on previously unmet needs
(ii) Being nonstandard
(iii) Create new niche markets
(iv) Value creation
(v) Being a catalyst for change

Brands such as Facebook, Uber, Amazon, Airbnb, Booking.com, and iPhone have demonstrated the importance of innovation by offering products and services that change people's daily habits. Although there is confusion in the literature about whether every successful business is "disruptive innovation" or not, disruptive innovation, as understood from the definition, is an approach in which small businesses focus on markets that large businesses do not attach importance to and overlook and reinforce their success by moving to a higher product service group. Within the framework of this approach, small businesses add the customers of big businesses to their own portfolio through disruptive innovation.

It is also seen that innovations that are often called disruptive innovation in literature are actually sustainable innovations. Sustainable innovation is the efforts of dominant enterprises in the market to improve their products and services. The improvements made by television manufacturers to improve image quality and the new features added by cell phone manufacturers to new models can be given as examples of this situation. In addition, the Apple brand, by becoming a competitor to laptops, has become the main tool for accessing the internet, challenging the laptop market and bringing the internet to the pocket—this can also be called disruptive innovation (Sonmucid's Blog 2022).

Disruptive innovation occurs when small businesses focus on markets ignored by existing businesses and offer products/services at affordable prices; over time other consumers begin to prefer these businesses. Disruptive innovation occurs when businesses gain share in submarket shares or newly emerging markets. Businesses in the market compete to produce better quality goods or services in order to satisfy customers in segments with higher profitability. These businesses neglect consumers at the bottom of the market, and thus, businesses that enter the market from the bottom of the market eventually move towards more profitable segments of the market, posing a threat to existing businesses. Disruptive innovation is common in low-price markets with relatively cheap prices. New businesses are often attracted to these markets because of the lack of importance attached to markets with low profits. Other markets where disruptive innovation is seen are newly emerging (newly created) markets. It is the process of turning nonconsumers into consumers. Photocopiers can be given as an example. Disruptive innovation is a process where businesses, often using a different business model, introduce a simpler, more affordable, or more convenient product or service that eventually displaces established market leaders. Some disruptive innovations succeed, while others do not. If a business applying disruptive innovation enters the market, the existing business should continue to operate for a period of time (Dünya Gazetesi 2022).

The concept of innovation, which is classified in different ways by experts, can be analyzed in three classes: disruptive innovation, radical innovation, and incremental innovation. While radical innovation refers to the revolutionary change of existing technology with a high degree of new technology, incremental innovation

Table 3.1 Innovation classes (*Source* Wang et al. 2022)

Characteristics	Disruptive innovation	Radical innovation	Incremental innovation
Scope	Involves products, services, or business models	Involves products or services	Involves products or services
Process	It initially meets the needs of non-mainstream customers and eventually meets the needs of mainstream customers through continuous improvement	It focuses on satisfying emerging and mainstream customers with revolutionary breakthroughs	Focuses on satisfying core customers with small improvements
Technology	It involves a new technology, involving new technology or combinations or simplifications of existing technologies	It uses current technological methods, which is a revolutionary change of current technology	It uses existing technological methods, which is a slow, imperceptible change of current technology

refers to the renewal or minor improvement of existing technology and involves a low degree of new know-how (Wang et al. 2022) (see Table 3.1).

According to Christensen, disruptive innovation occurs when "a small business enters a market having lesser resources in a submarket segment then gradually rises to the top market and eventually controls the market." Disruptive innovation is also referred to as low-end disruptive innovation or new-market disruptive innovation (Otike et al. 2022).

- *New market disruptive innovation*: Small businesses come from the bottom of the market and offer products and services to a market ignored by established businesses.
- *Low-level disruptive innovation*: Entrants often focus on the customers who are underserved. For this reason, businesses that first offer low-quality goods and services gradually develop their products and services for the high-quality goods and services group.

3.3 Disruptive Innovation Process

The process of disruptive innovation starts with businesses entering the market they want to hold on to. Then, businesses develop here and enter the main market, and when they enter the main market, they realize this innovation in the main market. Customers in the main market show interest in the new product/service, and the established business in the market develops and implements new strategies at the point where the demand for its products/services decreases. If the strategies implemented by the business do not work, disruptive innovation is realized. The stages in disruptive innovation are shown in Fig. 3.1.

Disruptive technologies enable new markets to emerge. Disruptive products are often simpler and cheaper, with lower profit margins. However, disruptive technologies typically emerge first in emerging or insignificant markets. Moreover, the most profitable customers of leading businesses often do not want and do not initially use products/services based on disruptive technologies.

"Disruptive innovation" is a process. Businesses that can be characterized as disruptive develop business models that are quite different from the way traditional businesses do business. Not every disruptive innovation may become successful. Trying to understand customers; putting oneself in the shoes of the customer; by being together with customers; and following their experiences with a product/service first-hand provide more qualified information than any qualitative or quantitative study. From time to time, the concept of disruptive innovation and the concept of sustainable innovation are confused with each other. Increasing the competitiveness of businesses, innovations made in product/service performance are defined as sustainable innovation. With the improvements made in products, it is aimed to increase the profit of the enterprises (Bilge 2017).

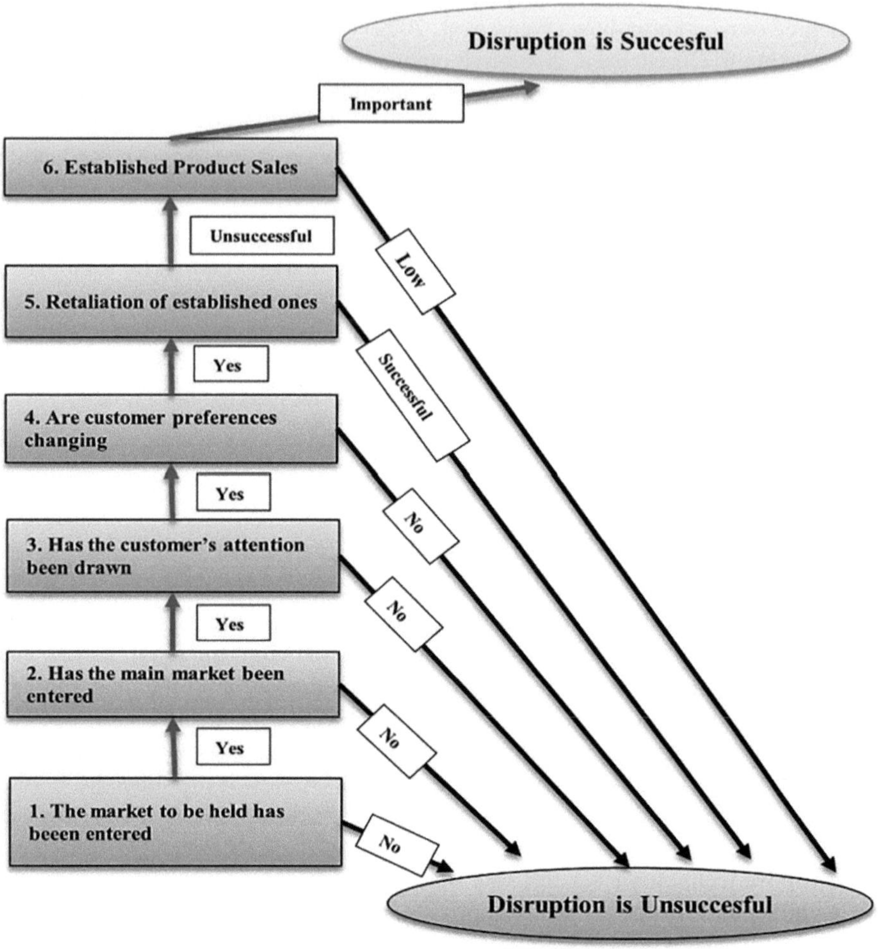

Fig. 3.1 Six stages of disruptive process (*Source* Reagan 2014)

3.3.1 Implementations Not Considered Within the Scope of Disruptive Innovation

Today, there are many innovations that have changed the structure of markets. Some of them are Uber, Wikipedia, Airbnb, iPhone, Netflix, Starlink, and Tesla (electric cars). But can Uber be considered a disruptive innovation according to this theory? Uber is one of the leading examples of innovation, even though it does not feed on the low-level market and does not create new markets. Although it later diversified into various customer segments such as Uber Select and Uber Green, its main idea is to offer an alternative to taxi service without owning a taxi. Similarly, Wikipedia is a free online encyclopedia written by volunteers, although it has driven traditional encyclopedias out of the market. Airbnb has likewise brought about huge changes in the accommodation sector. The process that started with three friends renting out three inflatable beds in the appropriate section of their homes has evolved into a billion-dollar system with millions of reservations today. Although it is an innovation that has a huge impact on the accommodation industry, experts do not call it a disruptive innovation because it does not fit the definition.

iPhone, a brand that combines the use of the phone and the internet and offers numerous security and ease of use with its proprietary operating system, is not considered a disruptive innovation because it does not meet the above definition, even though it offers major developments that have changed the habits of mobile phone and internet use.

Netflix, which rented movies by mail when it was first established, later became a global organization by moving its services to the online platform. In this way, it took market share from other businesses such as cinema and television. Starlink aims to become the world's global internet provider to provide internet service much faster and from space. Its revolutionary practices do not fall within the scope of disruptive innovation for similar reasons.

Tesla (electric cars) is the first business to materialize large-scale production of cars powered by fuel cells that charge with electricity instead of fossil fuels. Of course, although this is an innovation that has changed the structure of the automobile market worldwide, it does not qualify as a disruptive innovation because it does not meet the abovementioned characteristics.

3.3.2 Experiential Practices in Disruptive Innovation in Aviation

Airline transportation is an intensely competitive sector in which a small number of businesses operate and international rules and laws are applied. Starting in 1903 with the flight of the first heavier-than-air aircraft, airline transportation has grown day by day with the transportation of mail, cargo, and passengers and has become a sector serving more than 4.5 billion passengers before the Covid-19 crisis (ATAG 2021). In line with these developments, it has become one of the main elements of globalization, trade, and tourism in the world.

Naturally, many innovations have taken place in the airline transportation industry since its inception. Some of them can be listed as follows: cabin pressurization, radar technology, hub-and-spoke flight network structure, deicing, e-ticketing, jet engine, computerized reservation systems, airport security systems, low-cost airlines, internet, kiosks, chip technology in passports, etc. These innovations have enabled the air transportation industry to evolve day by day to its current strategic position. Yet, there are also innovations that are still in their infancy. Some of these are artificial intelligence, alternative fuels, etc. Especially today, various studies are carried out for automation at airports. Automation efforts are accelerating in tasks such as check-in, maintenance, cleaning, and baggage delivery. London Heathrow Airport has invested 6.5 million pounds in 72 automated baggage claim areas and automated baggage loading units (WNS 2022).

Although experts rank the importance of innovations in the air transportation industry over the last century differently, the first thing that comes to mind when we think of disruptive innovation is the low-cost carrier business model. The low-cost carrier business model is a business model implemented by Pacific Southwest Airlines in the 1960s before the liberalization of airline transportation in the USA in the late 1970s. After the liberalization (Deregulation Act) in 1978, the model re-implemented by Southwest Airlines is one of the first examples that come to mind when it comes to disruptive innovation, which first became widespread in the USA and then all over the world.

The functioning of the business model is characterized by a number of features, such as providing passengers with all services for a fee other than the flight itself, point-to-point flights, the use of a single type of aircraft, rapid preparation of the aircraft for the next flight, and intensive use of aircraft (until late in the evening). This business model, which was first implemented in the USA, then in Europe and Asia, and became successful, has been implemented in Turkey since 2005. In the low-cost business model, as mentioned earlier in the concept of disruptive innovation, affordable tickets were offered to the lowest segment of the airline passenger market, the market segment that does not generate high revenues, which the major airlines do not care about. In the market where they focus on high-revenue passenger segments, the low-cost airline business model has been successful in this sub-passenger segment and has become a competitor to traditional airlines over time. To understand this better, it is necessary to know the developments in the airline transportation market in the USA and the world in the 1970s. The 1970s was a period of strict price and frequency restrictions in airline transportation. In the USA, the largest market in the world (at that time), the civil aviation authority determined pricing by allocating flight lines to airline operators. Airline operators operated on these predetermined set prices (without price competition), trying to create differences in service quality (live piano concerts, buffet meals, etc.). In the rest of the world, on the other hand, mostly state-owned traditional airline companies operated in a non-competitive market structure with various mutual agreements.

The idea of a low-cost airline business model, which was born in the 1960s but could not become widespread due to various constraints, could be implemented in the late 1970s due to the favorable legal environment. The main idea of the low-cost airline business model is to offer passengers all services other than flight services (such as catering, free baggage allowance, seat number, etc.) for a fee and to offer cheap tickets to the market by reducing costs through practices such as uniform service class on aircraft, frequent seating, intensive aircraft use, etc. It has targeted price-sensitive passengers (both airplane and bus travelers), due to the ticket prices being 50–70% cheaper (those were not given importance by traditional carriers and were considered unprofitable for the business).

Airline companies used to sell tickets through global distribution systems, which are called traditional distribution channels, via travel agencies and ticket sales agencies. As might be expected, since the owners of these global distribution channels are major airlines, higher ticket prices were prioritized and displayed prominently on the screen. With the development of the internet, traditional airlines were able to overcome this distribution monopoly barrier and offer their tickets to the market. At the rise of the jet age, computers were not developed yet, and airline operations were very complicated. In the 1950s, the average reservation took 90 min. The system developed by American Airlines reduced this to 1.2 s. In the twentieth century, with the emergence of the low-cost business model, a disruption (disruptive innovation) took place in travel and reservation services due to the internet. Alaska Airlines became the first airline to sell tickets online in 1995 and actualized the first online check-in in 1998 (IGT 2022).

After liberalization in the USA in 1975, the number of passengers increased from 205 million to 927 million in 2019, while the occupancy rate increased from 54% to 85%. Taking inflation into account, the average domestic ticket price declined from around $560 in 1990 to around $370 in 2019 (Investopedia 2022). Subsequently, in all markets where liberalization was implemented (Europe, Asia, Turkey, etc.), prices have similarly fallen, while occupancy rates and passenger numbers have increased. The low-cost airline business model is the best example of disruptive innovation in airline businesses. It has made customers out of passengers who are willing to pay low ticket prices that nobody cares about, and over time, it has attracted other passengers who can afford to pay high ticket prices but do not want to pay them, with its high service quality, on-time arrival and departure, etc. Many traditional airlines were adversely affected by this situation and either lost their market share or had to exit the market.

In 2019, the low-cost airline business model carried 31% of the total number of passengers in the world, serving 1.4 billion passengers (ICAO 2022). While the contribution of the low-cost airline business model to regions, countries, tourism, and the economy is a separate topic of study, its impact and popularity are increasing day by day. When defining the concept of disruptive innovation within the scope of the low-cost airline business model, the example of Southwest Airlines is often used as a low-cost airline (LCA). Southwest Airlines started flights with low service standards. For this reason, it was able to provide the same service at about 50% more affordable prices. In the beginning, the managers of large airline companies did not want to spend time and resources on a business that targeted bus passengers with no airline service.

Southwest Airlines' simple, cheap, and convenient business model:

- Fast aircraft turnaround (getting the aircraft ready from one flight to the next).
- No catering on board (only peanuts).
- Not giving seat numbers (first one on board sits where they want).
- Paid baggage.
- Highly motivated staff.
- Heavy use of airplane.
- Uniform fleet.
- Unique mileage program (based on the number of flights, not distance flown).

- The use of secondary airports (low landing and take-off fees, uncrowded, flights can be organized at any time, etc.) has succeeded in providing services at low prices.

As the airline grew stronger over time, initially competing with buses, it became competitive with full-service, traditional airlines and even reached the level of capturing their market. Over time, Southwest Airlines has expanded its services depending on passenger demands and needs. These are:

- Priority boarding
- Free ticket exchange
- Earning miles from credit cards
- In-flight internet, etc., thus enhancing its disruptive capabilities by adding the requirements of business travelers

As a result, the number of passengers increased, and it became the largest domestic airline in the USA. It has become one of the largest players in the world with more than 700 aircraft and nearly 500 aircraft orders. Another example of disruptive innovation in airline transportation is the long-distance low-cost airline (LDLCA). The success of the low-cost business model on short- and medium-distance flights has changed the structure of the air transportation industry. Enterprises such as Ryanair, easyJet, AirAsia, Peach, Wizz Air, and Pegasus have gained significant market share on short- and medium-distance routes against existing traditional (network) carriers.

While low-cost and traditional airline business models, which became the established players in the market by applying disruptive innovation, are converging to each other, the feasibility of the LDLCA business model previously discussed in the market began to be questioned in the industry. Despite the structural differences between LCA and LDLCA operations, new aircraft types along with advancing technology have paved the way for this business model. Airlines such as Norwegian, AirAsia X, Scoot, and Jetstar have proven their success in the market. Carriers operating in this business model target all passenger groups. They also focus on operating at low costs and minimizing complexity. They try to increase their occupancy rates by feeding their own hubs with short- and medium-distance flights. LDLCA is a different business model that brings a new understanding to long-distance passenger transportation. All of the abovementioned points are fulfilled by the LDLCA business model. Of the 31 LDLCAs established from the past to the present, 16 continue to operate (Albers et al. 2020). Innovations in aircraft technology have made it possible to reach longer distances with less fuel. With the development of the A321XLR-type aircraft, long-range, low-capacity routes have started to be served. Besides, the use of new-generation aircraft (B787, A321XLR, and A330Neo) on medium- and long-distance routes has paved the way for cheap ticket sales by providing a fuel advantage of approximately 20% (Noticias 2022).

3.4 Conclusion

Change will continue without stopping for businesses and institutions that are open to change and innovation. In airline businesses, on the other hand, the rate of change is fast and effective due to advanced technology, well-educated workforce, high profit, competition, etc. Although not every innovation is a disruptive innovation, being open to innovations and following innovations are among the issues that every business should attach importance to in today's world. It is not easy to accept new ideas easily, especially for large, corporate businesses. For example, when we look at the story of Turkcell's founding, when the idea was taken to the country's largest businesses, no one leaned towards the idea. The group that accepted the idea soon became one of the biggest groups in Turkey. Similarly, Kodak, which did not find the idea of photocopying suitable, lost the market to Xerox. Similar factors have also led to the shift of the watch industry's center from Switzerland to Japan. After the invention of the digital watch, Swiss businesses that did not like the idea had to cede the market to Seiko after a while. Disruptive innovation is a process, and small businesses that see gaps in submarket segments eventually capture the competitor's customers. It is important to remember that not all innovation is disruptive innovation. Although there are many studies on disruptive innovation in the literature, according to a small number of authors, disruptive innovation is not characterized as a theory and model. There are also those who consider this concept as an idea (Dünya Gazetesi 2022).

Due to its reliance on high technology, openness to international competition, and intense market rivalry, the air transportation industry is one of the sectors where the concept of innovation is most intensely observed. Disruptive innovation, on the other hand, has brought about fundamental changes affecting the structure of the air transportation industry, with the entry of "low-cost airlines" and later "long-distance low-cost airlines," after technology enabled access to new niche markets. In the future, many developments in the fields of "innovation" and "disruptive innovation" are expected to occur as technological advances are applied to the air transportation industry. Examples include pilotless (automated) airplanes, fully automated airports, and alternative fuel (hydrogen, electric, etc.) airplanes.

References

Albers S, Daft J, Stabenow S, Rundshagen V (2020) The long-haul low-cost airline business model: a disruptive innovation perspective. J Air Transp Manag 89:101878

Angelo C (2012) Growth of ethanol fuel stalls in Brazil. Nature 491(7426):646–647

ATAG (2021) Facts&figures. https://www.atag.org/facts-figures.html. Retrieved 22 Aug 2022

Bilge B (2017) Yıkıcı Teknolojilerin Belirlenmesi, Savunma Bilimleri Dergisi. J Defense Sci 16(1). ISSN (Basılı): 1303-6831 ISSN (Online): 2148-1776, Mayıs/May 2017

Christensen CM (2006) The ongoing process of building a theory of disruption. J Prod Innov Manag 23(1):39–55

Christensen CM, Raynor ME (2003) The innovator's solution: creating and sustaining successful growth. Harvard Business School Press, Boston
Dünya Gazetesi (2022) Disruptive methodology and innovation. March 10. https://www.dunya.com/kose-yazisi/yikici-yontembilim-ve-yenilesim/438771. Retrieved 13 Sept 2022
ICAO (2022) The world of air transport in 2019. https://www.icao.int/annual-report-2019/Pages/the-world-of-air-transport-in-2019.aspx. Retrieved 18 Sept 2022
IGT Solutions (2022) The potential of disruptive technologies in aviation. https://www.igtsolutions.com/blog/the-potential-of-disruptive-technologies-in-aviation/. Retrieved 22 Aug 2022
Investopedia (2022) An economic analysis of the low-cost airline Industry. https://www.investopedia.com/articles/investing/022916/economic-analysis-lowcost-airline-industry-luvdal.asp. Retrieved 10 Aug 2022
Kalfaoglu S, Akgemci T (2020) Disruptive innovation and managerial issues in business administration. Eğitim Yayınevi, pp 99–108
Markides C (2006) Disruptive innovation: in need of better theory. J Prod Innov Manag 23:19–25. https://doi.org/10.1111/j.1540-5885.2005.00177.x
Noticias (2022) A320neo: Leaping into fuel efficiency. https://www.noticiaslatamsales.com/noticias/january-2011/a320neo-leaping-fuel-efficiency/. Retrieved 12 Aug 2022
Otike F, Barát ÁH, Kiszl P (2022) Innovation strategies in academic libraries using business entrepreneurial theories: analysis of competing values framework and disruptive innovation theory. J Acad Librariansh 48(4):102537
Reagan JL (2014) Predicting disruptive innovation: which factors determine success? Doctoral dissertation, Shenandoah University
Si S, Chen H (2020) A literature review of disruptive innovation: what it is, how it works and where it goes. J Eng Technol Manag 56:101568
Sonmucid's Blog (2022) The driving force of new era, disruptive innovation. https://sonmucid.wordpress.com/2018/03/10/yeni-cagin-itici-gucu-yikici-inovasyon/. Retrieved 13 Sept 2022
Şahin Z (2021) Asset sharing business model and innovation the case of Uber and Airbnb. Hiperlink Yayın, Istanbul
Wan F, Williamson PJ, Yin E (2015) Antecedents and implications of disruptive innovation: evidence from China. Technovation 39:94–104
Wang C, Qureshi I, Guo F, Zhang Q (2022) Corporate social responsibility and disruptive innovation: the moderating effects of environmental turbulence. J Bus Res 139:1435–1450
Williamson PJ, Ramamurti R, Fleury A, Fleury MTL (eds) (2013) The competitive advantage of emerging market multinationals. Cambridge University Press
WNS (2022) Top 5 trends disrupting the airline industry. https://www.wns.com/perspectives/articles/articledetail/46/top-5-trends-disrupting-the-airline-industry. Retrieved 12 Aug 2022
Yin E, Williamson PJ (2011) Competitiveness of Chinese emerging multinationals through new approaches to innovation. In: International Conference 'Re-assessing Emerging Market Multinationals' Evolving Competitive Advantages', Cambridge, UK, pp 25–27

Ali Emre Sarılgan (Dr.) was born in Eskisehir (1975). He graduated from Anadolu University, Department of Civil Air Transportation Management (1998). He received his master's degree from Anadolu University, Department of Civil Aviation Management (2001). He completed his PhD at Anadolu University, Department of Civil Aviation Management (2008). He is currently working as an Assistant Professor at Eskisehir Technical University, Faculty of Aviation and Space Sciences, Department of Aviation Management. His main research interests are airline management, air cargo, tourism transportation and environmental sustainability.

Chapter 4
Using Technology in Experiential Process in Aviation

Savas S. Ateş and Ezgi Filazoglu

Abstract Since the early twenty-first century, rapidly advancing technological innovations have fundamentally transformed business and marketing strategies. Advanced technologies such as holograms, artificial intelligence (AI), virtual reality (VR), augmented reality (AR), mixed reality, and the metaverse have reshaped customer experiences. Experiential marketing applications with robots and 3D printers offer innovative solutions in service delivery. New technologies like information technology and the Internet of Things (IoT) have significantly contributed to the service sector, while the Internet and online marketing have transformed business operations and customer relationships. Airports and airlines are leveraging these technologies to provide unique experiences to customers and popularize experiential marketing practices. Digital maturity models play a crucial role in businesses' digital transformation processes, with elements such as digital culture, technology, operations, and strategy being decisive in this process. The potential returns of technological investments and the balance between humans and technology are critical factors in the success of service delivery. This holistic perspective underscores the strategic importance of technology in marketing and the service sector, helping businesses gain a competitive edge in the digital age.

Keywords Experiential marketing · Hologram marketing · Artificial intelligence · Virtual reality · Augmented reality · Mixed reality · Metaverse marketing · Robot services · 3D printers · Internet of Things

S. S. Ateş
Eskisehir, Türkiye

E. Filazoglu (✉)
Gozen Air Services, Istanbul, Türkiye

İ. Polat (ed.), *Aviation Innovation*, Accounting, Finance, Sustainability, Governance & Fraud: Theory and Application,
https://doi.org/10.1007/978-981-96-7265-3_4

4.1 Introduction

Especially as of the twenty-first century, the world has progressed very rapidly in a technological sense. Due to the innovations in the historical process that has developed until today, a technological ecosystem evolving from simple automation systems which make life easier to self-moving autonomous vehicles has emerged. As a result of this, new breakthroughs have emerged in parallel with the development of technology in the areas of production and marketing, which are the basic functions of business. Almost each and every new technology has been used by businesses in the areas of marketing and advertising to offer different experiences to customers. The use of new technologies has enabled businesses to identify new marketing strategies and has accelerated the transition from traditional marketing to experiential marketing. With today's technological infrastructure, experiential marketing has the potential to change the balance in competition, by going beyond product or service marketing and by aiming to provide customers with an unforgettable experience. The important point here is to use these rapidly developing technological innovations for the right customer at the right time. In experiential marketing, the realization of accurate market segmentation of consumers, appropriate experience design, and timely delivery to the target audience are important for achieving success. As in many other industries, experiential marketing practices have started to be seen in the aviation industry as well. Airports and airline enterprises offer different experiences to their customers with the help of technological developments. This study focuses on the role of technology in the experiential processes in aviation. How airlines and airports use technology in experiential marketing has been explained with examples.

4.2 The Importance of Technology in Service Systems

As a result of the increase in people's desires and needs over time, the concept of service marketing has gained more importance. In order for service marketing to be carried out in a healthy way, some factors need to be considered. These are (Öz 2017):

- Defining the target market
- Selecting the target market and conducting market research
- Developing services that will appeal to the market
- Convincing the market for these services
- Monitoring changes in purchasing behavior in the market

As a result of these mentioned factors, businesses have to develop new marketing strategies to sustain their activities. In this case, the most important element that can help them develop strong strategies is technology.

The use of technology in service delivery can provide convenience to both customers and service providers. However, the important point here is to provide the right technology at the right time, as the capacity and willingness of the individuals being served are very important in the adoption of the technology offered. According to the study of Walker et al., even if individuals have sufficient capacity, they may not want to use new technologies in a service purchase. On the other hand, some individuals who accept service delivery supported by technologies may not be able to use these technologies even if they want to use them due to capacity (age, education, health status, etc.). Therefore, it is necessary to know the target customer group well before determining which technologies should be used in service delivery (2002).

The rapid development of technology has increased the use of different technologies in service delivery. However, some problems that need to be solved have also emerged. For example, whether high-cost technological investments will provide a significant return for businesses or how to balance the use of people and technology in service delivery stand out as important problems to be solved (Aydın 2005).

In service delivery, the moments of "service encounters" are very important. These moments create interaction between the customer and the business. These encounters can be of different lengths. For example, short encounters, such as getting gasoline at a gas station, or long-term experiences, such as those at Disneyland, which include rides, shows, and brand stores, can be called service encounters. Although encounters play a different role in each of these examples, in each case, the experienced individual encounter can be critical in determining the customer's future behavior towards the business (Bitner et al. 2000). "Touching" customers in some part of the service delivery system provides an advantage for customers to evaluate the service provider. These "touching" moments give customers an idea about service quality (Baron and Harris 1995). As a result of the influence of technology at a great pace on the service sector, a technology component to Kotler's (1994) service marketing triangle was added by Parasuraman (1996). Thus, by adding a new dimension to the two-dimensional service marketing triangle model, it was turned into a three-dimensional pyramid. This change made in the model is shown in Fig. 4.1.

According to Kotler's service marketing triangle, there are different types of marketing. The first one is external marketing between the business and customers. External marketing takes place between the business and its employees. The concept of 4Ps (product, promotion, price, place), which is called the marketing mix and explained as product, price, promotion, and distribution channels, is highly important. Internal marketing, on the other hand, sees employees as internal customers. In order to better serve external customers, it is necessary to provide internal customers with appropriate training, support, motivation, and rewards. In interactive (i.e., conversational) marketing, on the other hand, the goal is to leave a good impression on customers when they interact with business employees. According to Parasuraman, the widespread use of technology in the process of product or service purchase has necessitated the addition of a technology component to the service marketing triangle, because technology now serves as an important juncture in the purchase and sale of products or services. For this reason, business-technology,

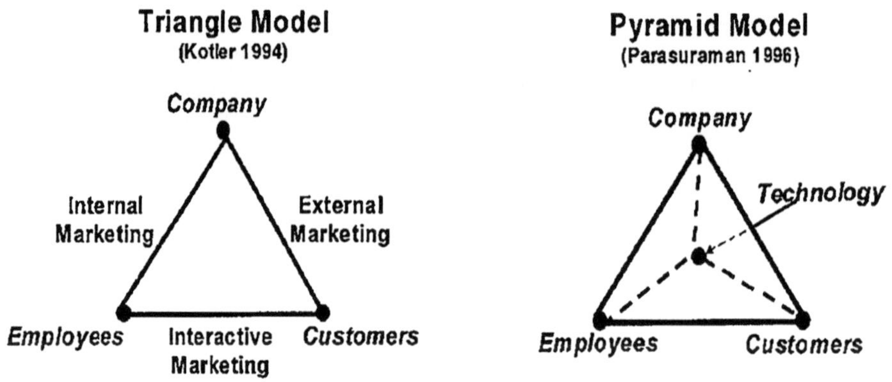

Fig. 4.1 Transition from the service marketing triangle to the service marketing pyramid (*Source* Parasuraman and Grewal 2000)

technology-employee, and technology-customer relationships have become important issues to be emphasized (Parasuraman and Grewal 2000).

The introduction of the service marketing pyramid in the literature has brought a new perspective to the marketing field. For example, Padgett and Mulvey (2007), in their study, mentioned that the service marketing pyramid affected the market positioning strategies of businesses. This is because the technology variable added to the equation has caused businesses to reconsider their market positioning strategies. For example, integrating a new technology into an established market can be challenging. For this reason, three important factors should be considered. These are (Padgett and Mulvey 2007):

- Differentiating service interaction: It should be emphasized how the business engages in interactions for differentiation. These characteristics should be clearly presented.
- Communicating relevant customer values: Businesses should emphasize the values appropriate to the services they provide. For example, the values emphasized by a business that uses self-service applications and businesses that use human consultants should be different.
- Correlating technology to customer value realization: The benefits of technology in creating customer value should be emphasized.

4.3 Technologies Affecting the Service Sector

Economic, social, environmental, or technological changes in the world have made markets dynamic. In case of unexpected situations, businesses should foresee the change and respond quickly, because rapid reaction is important for the survival of businesses. Technology is one of the important changes that influence marketing relationships (Zineldin 2000).

First, it would be useful to talk about the effects of information technologies on marketing. Major breakthroughs in information technologies take place on the basis of technologies, such as the Internet of Things (IoT), artificial intelligence (AI), big data, etc., that have emerged in recent years. Possibly the first disruptive development in the history of information technologies was the Internet. The Internet and the World Wide Web (www) have dramatically changed the way enterprises carry on business and their customer relations policies by changing both market opportunities and the information technologies. The Internet has created new market opportunities by eliminating existing business models (McCollum 1997). The most important benefit of the Internet with respect to marketing is that it enables online marketing. Websites have emerged that go beyond the traditional marketing mix (4Ps) and provide online functionality, convey information and emotions, share tips, and promote products. These websites affect the decision-making process of customers by providing a platform for enterprises and customers to meet (Constantinides 2004). Online shopping has developed rapidly, especially in the twenty-first century, due to the intense work schedule of most people. Due to the Internet, stores have changed shape and become global. Online stores try to evoke the physical resemblance of the purchase to the customer and allow them to do so without coming to the store from wherever they want (Singh and Sailo 2013).

4.4 The Relationship of Experiential Marketing and Technology

Bernd Schmitt, who is seen as the first person to introduce the concept of experiential marketing into the literature, mentioned in his 1999 study that experiential marketing will replace traditional marketing. The main reason for this change is that traditional marketing is a result of the industrial age and appeals to this age. In addition, due to today's age of branding and communication, the marketing technique that can appeal to the customer is experiential marketing (Schmitt 1999).

Urdea and Constantin (2021), in their study, revealed which steps should be followed in order to implement experiential marketing. The first step to focus on when developing an experiential marketing strategy is to create a concept that attracts the customer's attention and includes different experiences (Fig. 4.2). This is because, unlike before, customers want to encounter unexpected innovations, and marketing experts are trying to create contact points in line with expectations. Technology is the key for creating new experiences in this regard. In addition, protecting the health of customers and adapting to changing conditions in all kinds of marketing activities during the Covid-19 pandemic have been key issues considered from a marketing perspective. The second step in developing an experiential marketing strategy is the selection of a set of technological tools that can enhance communication with customers and result in higher customer engagement. The factors driving digitalization are rapid technological progress, increasing need for comfort, and the desire for

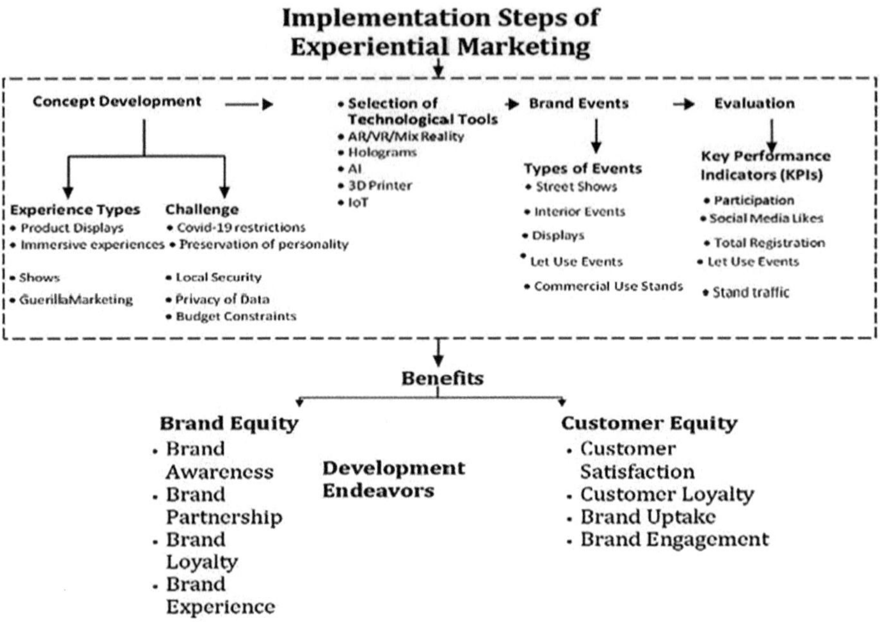

Fig. 4.2 Implementation steps of experiential marketing (*Source* Urdea and Constantin 2021)

a secure environment. One of the biggest advantages of virtual platforms is the ability to reach more customers.

Animations, product tests, holograms, augmented reality (AR) applications, the IoT, and AI are among the applications that can be used in experiential marketing. The third step refers to brand activation based on experiential events that aim to interact with consumers. Test drives, road shows, in-store events, exhibitions, and fairs are examples of brand activations. As a final step, it is important to evaluate the aftermath of the events. In order to overcome the competition, it is necessary to evaluate the impact of the events on consumers' perception and plan future activities. To make all these assessments, it is necessary to identify some key performance indicators. Indicators such as customers' opinions, behaviors, product market performance, financial results, and social media can be used to evaluate the customer experience (Urdea and Constantin 2021).

4.5 Determining the Technological Maturity Level

The technological maturity level of businesses aiming to do experiential marketing is one of the important issues. The definition of digital maturity, which comprises technological maturity, is the adequate response of a business to changes in the technological field, achieving digital successes in business processes, as well as the development of technological competencies of the staff. Businesses targeting to increase their technological maturity levels undergo digital transformation in all areas of their activities (Aslanova and Kulichkina 2020).

In order to maintain competitive advantage in an increasingly digitalized environment, today's businesses seek to assess their level of digital maturity. Given this situation, numerous digital maturity models designed to assess the digital state of a business have emerged during the last few years. Largely developed and published by practitioners, it remains unclear whether these models are academically valuable (Thordsen et al. 2020). Teichert (2019) reviewed many studies and identified the most common digital maturity domains. These areas are shown in Table 4.1.

Table 4.1 Most common digital maturity domains (*Source* Teichert 2019)

Digital maturity domain	Characteristics
Digital culture	It creates the characteristics that accelerate digital transformation, such as risk-taking, testing, learning, being customer-oriented, and openness to change
Technology	This includes information communication and information technology architecture/systems. New digitalization-based systems, digital data processing, etc. are some of them
Operations and procedures	Factors such as digitalization of processes, automation and flexibility/agility, bringing processes to an industrialized standard, and operational excellence are important
Digital strategy	Developing/executing a strategy that uses digital technology to do business in new ways, long-term orientation, digital transformation linked to business strategy, and Industry 4.0 roadmap are important for digital maturity in digital strategy
Organization	Management structure/practices that support digital business, cross-functional collaboration, digital skills built across the organization, defined digitalization-related roles/tasks, adequate resource allocation, cross-functional teams to implement digital business priorities, flexible communities, and agile management are indicators of an organization's digital maturity
Digital skills	Digital skills, expertise, experience, and interest; staff dedicated to Industry 4.0; employees' information communication technologies competencies; data-enhanced decision-making; openness to new technologies; and employees' access to digital skills/expertise when needed are seen as the indicators of reaching maturity with regard to digital skills
Innovation	Capabilities that enable a more flexible/agile way of working, developing disruptive business models, using agile methods, engaging the customer in the innovation process, financing the innovation, and regularly executed innovation are important steps to achieve digital maturity
Customer insight and experience	Benefiting the customer from digitalization; personalization of products/services; using digital services to interact with customers; focusing on customer value; digitalization of customer touch-points; creating value from data; and customer engagement and empowerment are important maturity indicators for customer insight and experience

(continued)

Table 4.1 (continued)

Digital maturity domain	Characteristics
Management	To ensure the comprehensive/reliable execution of the digital strategy, everyone empowered to think creatively and innovate should adopt a systematic approach to innovation/change management. It is also important to ensure participation at different hierarchical levels, adherence to standards and regulations, and adequate resource allocation. These characteristics are important for management to achieve digital maturity
Vision	It is important for the organization to effectuate its prioritized digital vision and for all staff to work in line with the digital vision to ensure digital maturity as a vision
Digital ecosystem	Organizations operate as part of a digital ecosystem; digitization/integration of vertical/horizontal value chains, digital connectivity with the business network, interoperable technology platforms, and providing new/highly customizable solutions configured by end users are important to ensure maturity in the digital ecosystem
Leadership	The leadership team learns new technologies, leaders have a long-term convincing vision, and leaders actively identify and realize new opportunities, foster collaboration, and ensure central coordination for Industry 4.0 or digital transformation. Thus, digital maturity can be achieved
Compatibility and safety	IT security, digital security, IT compliance within the organization and for stakeholders, assessment of risk factors, risk management, optimizing the value chain network for compliance, and avoiding unauthorized access are important for ensuring digital maturity for compliance and security
Products and services	Smart products/services, digitization of product/service offerings, distributed data analytics for personalization, data-based services, and digital features are important in achieving digital maturity for products and services
Business model	By developing new and groundbreaking business models, integrated customer solutions across the supply chain, and a digital product/service portfolio with software, network (M2M), and key differentiating data, digital initiatives generate value and expand business models. Thus, achieving digital maturity in business models can become easier

4.6 Experiential Marketing Technologies Used in Aviation

The history of in-flight entertainment systems dates back to the 1920s. The first movie to be seen on an airplane was *Howdy Chicago*, which was shown on an 11-passenger seaplane in 1921, as shown in Fig. 4.3 (Groening 2013).

However, due to strict regulations in aviation, it lasted until 1988 for the first in-flight entertainment system to be tested. With the marketing strategy implemented by Northwest Orient Airlines, the use of in-flight entertainment systems on Boeing 747s quickly became popular, and the airline expanded it to its entire fleet (Wilson 2022). Airline and airport enterprises continue to offer new marketing experiences to their domestic and international customers by using today's technologies. The main experiential marketing technologies used in aviation today can be listed as follows:

Fig. 4.3 The first in-flight entertainment system (*Source* Mullen 2017)

- Three-dimensional (3D) image technologies
  a) Holograms
  b) VR
  c) AR
  d) Immersive reality (mixed reality)
  e) Metaverse
- Robotic technologies
  a) Robots
  b) Autonomous and semiautonomous devices
  c) 3D printers
- Software and hardware technologies
  a) IoT
  b) AI
  c) Machine learning (ML) (artificial learning)
  d) Deep learning (DL)

4.6.1 3D Image Technologies

3D image production methods started before electronic systems. Optical illusions that started with holograms were supported by 3D glasses in parallel with the development of electronic devices. The sensors added to these technologies have increased the perception level of the images presented to the customer.

Holograms
Holography is a technique that allows a wave front to be recorded and then reconstructed. Holography is known as the best method for producing three-dimensional images (Işık 2014). Holography is done by superimposing a second wave front on the wave front. Apart from image processing, it is also used in many areas, from sound to information transmission. The use of holograms is one of the newest technologies in aviation. In hologram systems used through VR glasses, the information required for flight operations can be easily delivered to airline and airport customers. For example, Microsoft HoloLens is a holographic computer that does not depend on any additional hardware known in this sector (Microsoft 2022). On this hardware, there is a platform that enables the use of applications related to VR, AR, and mixed reality. In this experience, special glasses and headsets such as HoloLens are used to access holographic images seen through computers that interact with the real-world environment. The difference between this technology and VR is that the connection with the real world cannot be delinked. Hologram technology enables hands-free viewing of the data required in the real world (Brown 2018). Since 2005, 2D and 3D holograms have been used in airports to manage customer services (Photograph 3.2). At airports, hologram customer representatives existing at the airport serve for static operations such as security information and passenger guidance (Beale 2012). For businesses, the substitution of customer representatives with hologram technology is seen as a tool to reduce costs in routine work. In addition, with the developing technology, interactive smart holograms are used with AI (AI) technologies. For example, the "Magic Mirror" application at Istanbul Airport uses technology that allows customers to see how watches, clothes, or makeup products will look on them without physically trying them on. Magic Mirror technology aims to enhance customer experience (Kali 2017) (Fig. 4.4).

One of the areas where hologram technology is used for internal customers in aviation is cockpits. In systems called "heads-up" displays, critical flight data and instructions can be displayed on the windshield of the cockpit. This makes it easier to access information and reduces distractions for pilots. The use of holograms is not limited to the cockpit.

Virtual Reality (VR)
VR is a computer-based 3D simulation system. This simulation is a simulated experience that can be similar to or completely different from the real world (Burdea and Coiffet 2008). The main features of VR technology comprise the 3I: Immersion, Interaction, and Imagination (Fig. 4.5). The immersion aspect of VR is the feature that makes the virtual real and allows a user to feel immersed in a virtual environment and completely separated from the real world (Burdea and Coiffet 2008). The visual aspects implemented using today's 3D computer graphics vary depending on the quality of the tools used to isolate the user's visual senses. In the near future, with the advancement of simulation technologies, the user will be able to smell or taste objects in addition to seeing, hearing, and feeling them. Secondly, the interaction feature is normally considered a dynamic feature to help the user not only see, hear, or feel virtual objects but also interact with them. By interacting in real time

Fig. 4.4 Hologram technology used for managing customer services (*Source* Beale 2012)

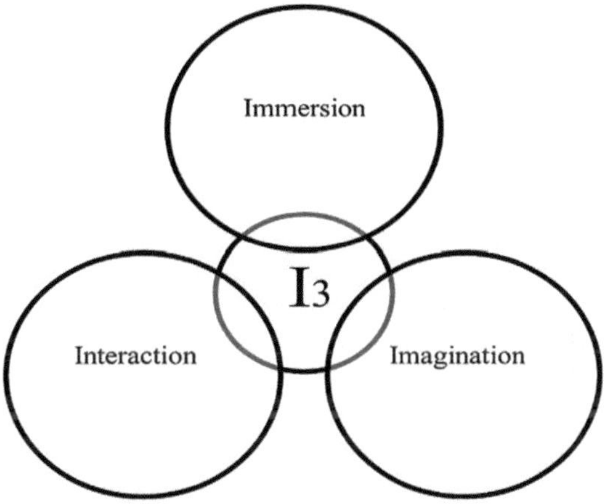

Fig. 4.5 The main features of VR technology (*Source* Burdea and Coiffet 2008)

with other people as well as with objects, the user can change the state of a virtual environment, and the objects in it, and thus deeply immerse themselves in the virtual world. Finally, a virtual world is often designed to serve a purpose or offer a specific application. With today's technologies, it has not been possible to model the whole world. How a virtual world with all its objects and people behaves and works depends on the imagination of its designers. But despite all the different designs of virtual worlds, realistic simulation, interaction, and real-time communication are always necessary (Nguyen 2014).

One of the businesses creating VR-enabled systems for the aviation industry is providing VR content to passengers in the concourse of Rome Fiumicino Airport in

Fig. 4.6 In-flight use of VR technologies (*Source* VRWorldTech 2022)

partnership with the ground handling provider Aviapartner. The VR experience offered by the Inflight VR enterprise at the airport offers passengers different experiences, including shopping, travel experiences, 3D cinema, and games. Another experiential marketing initiative by Emirates took place at Dubai International Airport in early 2022. Similarly, Etihad Airways offered this experience to its passengers in the first and business class lounges at Abu Dhabi International Airport. While airline companies also increase customer satisfaction with small screens behind the seat in in-flight entertainment systems, some airline companies have started to offer VR glasses to their customers as a different experience (Fig. 4.6).

Çelebi Ground Handling Services uses VR technology experience not only for airline passengers but also for its employees (internal customers). They provide training by increasing the internal customer experience with different scenarios in the VR environment they have prepared for apron safety. VR technologies can be utilized in depth in the context of aviation trainings. VR systems can be used not only as testing and validation environments but also as a training environment for passengers who encounter such an interface for the first time (Sportillo et al. 2017). By using VR technologies, airline companies take safety trainings given in the cabin to a different dimension and increase the internal and external customer experience, as shown in Fig. 4.7 (DPVR 2021).

Augmented Reality (AR)

AR is defined as an experience in which computer-generated perceptual structure information is presented to the user interactively in a real-world environment. It is the overlay of three-dimensional objects produced by software on computer-generated content in the real world. It is based on the principle that the objects that exist in the real world create sensorial harmony with visual, auditory, tactile, olfactory, and complex emotional systems (somatosensorial) (Cipresso et al. 2018). AR

Fig. 4.7 VR applications used in cabin training (*Source* DPVR 2021)

can be defined as a system that includes three basic features. These features can be described as a combination of real and virtual worlds, real-time interaction, and three-dimensional registration of virtual and real objects. The superimposed sensory information can be either constructive (i.e., an addition to the natural environment) or destructive (i.e., a masking of the natural environment). This experience is given immaculately interwoven with the physical world so that it is perceived as an immersive aspect of the real environment (Rosenberg 1992).

AR elements are a live, direct, or indirect view of a physical, real-world environment, complete with computer-generated sensory inputs such as audio, video, graphics, or GPS data. Since AR is superimposed on our own world, it allows the user the same freedom as in normal life. AR uses your existing reality and adds to it using some kind of device (Pehlivan 2020). London Heathrow Airport has partnered with luxury brands such as Chanel with its "beauty spaceship" (Fig. 4.8). Thus, it enabled shoppers to try the products virtually (Reed Smith 2022). They enhanced customer experiences by recommending different components to passengers with smart mirror technologies.

In 2019, Airbus and Microsoft reached an agreement to use AR in aircraft production. According to the statement made by Airbus, the aim of this cooperation is to produce faster aircraft and to ensure that employees are better equipped (Fig. 4.9). With the first development made within the scope of this partnership, airline maintenance staff and cabin crews were given the opportunity to receive training in a 3D environment. This is done through a program that allows them to access virtual work instructions through HoloLens without the need to receive physical instructions (Bishop 2019; Scammell 2018).

In addition to all these, there are studies on the use of AR systems in air traffic control. According to the study by Han et al. (2019), the workload of air traffic controllers is expected to increase due to the steady rise in air traffic. Hologram systems

Fig. 4.8 Beauty spaceship application at Heathrow Airport (*Source* Tan-Gillies 2021)

Fig. 4.9 Example of AR technology used in aircraft manufacturing (*Source* Bishop 2019)

can be utilized to present complex navigation data to controllers effectively. This system is provided in a form that can be used in real operational environments with a head-mounted transparent display installed with a controller to provide structured job support. In addition, this system offers a new experience by increasing efficiency, as it can be controlled firsthand by air traffic controllers (Han et al. 2019).

Immersive Reality (Mixed Reality)
One of the components necessary to interact with VR environments is immersive interfaces. By using this technology, interfaces for new generation customer behavior can be created. By means of immersive interface technology, it becomes possible to show marketing-oriented information to airport or airline customers, and data can be collected without distraction. Immersive virtual environments are usually accessed through head-mounted displays, so that isometric mappings of changes in users' head movements can be made through the cameras in the virtual world. On

Fig. 4.10 Cabin interior immersive reality applications (*Source* Max Planck Institute 2014)

these screens, head, hand, and body positions are also measured, and feedback is provided. Thus, a simulation of activities such as walking, running, and driving a car can be created in a virtual environment. This technology can also enable individuals with mobility limitations to move in the virtual world (Bruder et al. 2012).

In order to increase passenger comfort in different application scenarios, immersive reality applications are used in aircraft cabins. Passengers can experience a different flight experience with immersive reality in the narrow and cramped aircraft cabin. By means of the goggle technology used for this purpose, passengers can see beyond the area where the plane moves and experience the sensation of flying (Photograph 3.7). Different experiences for those who are afraid of heights and turbulence have also been developed using these technologies (Max Planck Institute 2014) (Fig. 4.10).

Metaverse

The Metaverse is a post-reality universe, a continuous and persistent multiuser environment that combines physical reality with digital virtuality. It is based on the convergence of virtual environments, digital objects, and technologies that enable multisensory interactions with people, such as VR and AR. The Metaverse is a network of multiuser 3D and interconnected social environments (Mystakidis 2021). Studies on the use of the Metaverse universe in the field of aviation are available in literature. For example, Siyaev and Jo (2021) in their study suggested that it may be more cost-effective to work on a virtual copy of the aircraft in aircraft maintenance training. In this study, the “Aircraft Maintenance Metaverse” of the Boeing aircraft was proposed, which can meet in a common maintenance area equipped with virtual assets specific to the Boeing 737. The metaverse, which is completely virtual and can replace expensive physical aircrafts costing hundreds of millions of dollars, is a cost-effective solution for institutions providing training on older aircraft models (Siyaev and Jo 2021). In addition, pilot training in the virtual world can also create an important experience for internal customers. Besides all these, the aviation industry, which had a difficult period especially during the Covid-19 pandemic, had

Fig. 4.11 Qatar Airways metaverse online check-in service (*Source* Qatar Airways 2022)

to find new marketing techniques to attract external customers. One of the most important of these has been to use the virtual world. For example, a virtual queue was created at Los Angeles Airport, and customers did not need to be physically present there. By partnering with luxury brands, London Heathrow Airport has enabled shoppers to try products virtually. Qatar Airways launched QVerse, a VR program that allows passengers to tour the inside of airplanes while sitting at home (Reed Smith 2022). Qatar Airways has entered the meta-universe with the world's first MetaHuman cabin crew with "QVerse" VR (Fig. 4.11). Passengers were offered the experience of online check-in services in the meta-universe (Qatar Airways 2022).

Airbus has designed an innovative marketing and customer experience using the metaverse to redesign and elevate the passenger experience from departure to arrival (HeroX 2022).

4.6.2 Robotic Technologies

Advances in computer processors, scientific studies on electronic components, and new products have led to major leap in robotics over the last 20 years.

Robots

A robot is a machine that can perform a complex set of actions automatically, specifically programmed by a computer. A robot can be guided by an external controller or the controller embedded within the robot. Devices designed for human interaction are called cobots (collaborative robots). Humanoid robots are robots that are anatomically designed to resemble the human anatomy. For example, Sophia is a robot developed by Hanson Robotics, a Hong Kong-based company that produces humanoid robots. Sophia, who was granted citizenship by Saudi Arabia, became the world's first robot citizen (CNN 2017). Humanoid robots are made to awaken the human form.

Fig. 4.12 The world's first robot-staffed hotel (*Source* Rajesh 2015)

Fig. 4.13 Istanbul Airport robot assistant fleet (*Source* Taskiran 2019)

In the service sector, one of the most well-known examples of robot use in customer experiences is the Henn na Hotel in Nagasaki, Japan (Fig. 4.12). The hotel, where all employees from cleaners to receptionists are robots, offers a different technological experience to its customers with technological additions such as air-conditioning that adjusts to the body temperature of the guests (Rajesh 2015). Ivanov et al. (2017) conducted research on the adoption of robots and service automation by tourism and hospitality businesses.

There is a fleet of assistant robots at Istanbul Airport. The blue robot in this fleet can communicate verbally with customers. When the robot speaks, its mouth area lights up, and it can blink its eyes. Two robotic arms are also attached to hold objects and message signals. A touch screen attached to the robot's chest allows customers to interact with the machine (Fig. 4.13). The robot has a barcode reader to read airplane tickets and display flight information (Taskiran 2019).

Autonomous and Semiautonomous Devices

It seems probable that vehicles without human intervention will appear in the near future. Since autonomous cars will not require constant supervision, it is considered that the driver will be free to engage in a secondary activity such as talking to passengers, reading a book, or using a smartphone or tablet. For these scenarios to be actualized, the following are necessary:

- The "Control Transfer" system, which enables the automatic driving control to be taken over from the human,
- The "Takeover" system, in which the automated driving system warns the driver to take over control immediately,
- The "Driving Authorization" system, which is used by the human driver when he or she wants to leave the control to the autonomous vehicle

Designing airline travel, where the passenger leaves the door of their home and arrives at the door of their home at their final destination, increases passenger comfort. By putting the "Autonomous Shuttle" project into practice in Turkey, İGA plans to transfer passengers from the parking lot to the terminal using driverless electric midibuses (Fig. 4.14).

In addition to this implementation, autonomous valet service was started at Gatwick Airport in London to increase parking capacity (Fig. 4.15). In order to save time for passengers and increase comfort, the cars of passengers arriving at the airport are transported to the parking lot by autonomous robots. It is estimated that this practice will increase parking capacity by 50%.

3D Printers

3D printing is a technology that adds material to produce the part and is therefore also called additive manufacturing. Similar to how a 2D printer prints line by line with ink, 3D printers produce a 3D object layer by layer with a special printing

Fig. 4.14 Example of a vehicle that enables passengers to transfer from the parking lot to the terminal (*Source* Kaplanseren 2018)

Fig. 4.15 Autonomous valet service at airports (*Source* Gökyüzü Haberci 2019)

Fig. 4.16 Experiential marketing model with BMW iX 3D printer model (*Source* BMW 2021)

material (Oropallo and Piegl 2016). One of the first examples of using 3D printers in experiential marketing was actualized by BMW with the BMW iX model during the pandemic restriction period (Fig. 4.16). At the beginning of 2021, when the company could not set up a stand and offer test drive, it sent car models to its customers who requested it, which they could print at home using 3D printers.

3D printers have started to be used by domestic customers in the field of aviation. Particularly in the field of aircraft production and maintenance, their use has become widespread. Faster and simpler production saves both time and money. In addition, the weight reduction of the parts made from lighter materials is seen as another benefit. If the parts produced meet the standards set by aviation authorities, a great convenience in terms of parts supply in the aviation industry can be achieved (GE Additive 2022).

Fig. 4.17 İGA Airport tower 3D printer printout model (*Source* 3D Ocean 2022)

In the field of marketing, the introduction of 3D printing technologies for visual marketing purposes enables enterprises to create large and small visual advertising products that are not just images on a wall, but actual 3D representations of the product, often in super-sized form. For example, in the United States, life-size sculptures of famous "Rugby" athletes were created by a 3D printer business to engage people with the brand through experience (Evanhaim 2019). A similar campaign in the field of aviation with 3D models of airplanes or airports can positively affect customers' brand perceptions (Fig. 4.17).

4.6.3 Software and Hardware Technologies

IoT

The IoT technology, which started to emerge gradually in the 1940s, has gained momentum over time. According to Moore's Law, it is thought that computer processing power will double every 1½ to 2 years. However, today it is understood that this rate has increased geometrically. As if to prove the accuracy of this law, the processing power, memory size, and network capacity of computers are growing exponentially, while costs are decreasing at a similar rate. One of the waves of innovation over the years is the IoT. This disruptive innovation, based on the real-time networking of objects and subjects, has been constantly evolving since the advent of computers (Kagermann 2014).

The concept of the IoT was first used in a presentation made by Kevin Ashton in 1999 (Ashton 2009). However, the first use of this technology dates to a project at Cambridge University in 1991. In this study, images of a coffee machine were shared over the Internet using a camera system. The researchers of this project started from the idea in Tom Igoe's book *Making Things Talk*. According to the project, people and smart objects used in daily life will be placed on the same communication layer. Thus, they will be able to learn and cooperate with each other (Mansilla et al. 2012; Gökrem and Bozuklu 2016).

In the IoT, data and services enable any technological device to exchange information at high speeds with any device or person anywhere in the world. The most up-to-date information about the state of individual devices and their environment can be received at any time. Technology infrastructure can be monitored and operated even over huge physical distances. Networking enables simultaneous control and optimal coordination of a wide range of complex technological processes. In the future, smart navigation systems in cars, buses, trains, and other vehicles will share information about traffic volumes and disruptions to local public transportation services and will enable the management of traffic in tomorrow's cities autonomously. It will also be possible to connect production systems and business processes in factories and enterprises, from ordering to outbound logistics, in real time and across different enterprises (Kagermann 2014). IoT technology, which integrates wireless sensor networks with traditional communication networks, provides a platform for remote management and monitoring of related equipment. When this technology is integrated into intelligent transportation systems, an organic combination of vehicle management technologies and Intelligent Transportation Systems (ITS) is achieved. This combination makes transportation more reliable, safer, and faster. On the other hand, it also plays an important role in reducing transportation costs (Zhang and Tan 2021).

There are three components that form the basis of IoT architecture. These are hardware, middleware, and presentation layer. The hardware consists of sensor nodes, embedded operating system, and interface circuitry. The middleware performs the tasks of data storage, analysis, and resource processing. The presentation layer, on the other hand, consists of effective visualization tools that are compatible with various platforms for different applications and present data in an understandable way to the end user (Shafique et al. 2020). IoT technology, which has many areas of use, collects data with the help of sensors. This data creates big data. Big data is stored in cloud computing systems. They are analyzed through ML (Gökrem and Bozuklu 2016).

In experiential marketing, smart labels and QR tag applications that customers can scan with their phones have already been implemented in many sectors. Customers can be directed to products of their own interest, personalized discounts, interesting product information, and even in-store experiences. It enables geofencing for customer targeting using GPS data. For example, Burger King, by using its mobile app, aims to gain a marketing advantage over its competitor, McDonald's. Customers who turned on the active location services of the Burger King mobile application, if they were within 600 m of McDonald's, were given the opportunity to order hamburgers at a discount for a limited time. Thus, by using IoT, the enterprise ensured more preferability against its competitor (Kantor 2018). At the annual Smart Airport Technology Conference and Exhibition hosted by the Hong Kong

Airport Authority, IoT-enabled terminal facilities were introduced, and products for customer experiences were exhibited (MotherApp 2018).

Since the introduction of the first 1G system in 1981, a new mobile network technology has emerged almost every 10 years. 1G technology provided a mass mobile telephony service. 2G has created a globally interoperable environment. It also enabled reliable mobile telephony and SMS text messaging. 3G's high-speed data transfer capability made it easier to download information from the Internet. Providing significant improvements in data capacity and speed, 4G has made online platforms and high-speed mobile Internet services available to the masses. 5G technology, on the other hand, is the most powerful cellular wireless network, with extraordinary data capabilities, unlimited call volumes, and endless data broadcasting (Attaran 2021). The fifth-generation (5G) mobile networks, which are expected to form the mobile communication infrastructure of the future, can be defined as faster and having a higher capacity than existing systems (4.5G). 5G, which has low latency, has a wide range of capabilities. 5G can perform all activities such as object-to-object communication, providing information and entertainment services like 4G does, operations using Wi-Fi and Bluetooth, reporting technical problems to manufacturers, and updating firmware (Krasniqi and Hajrizi 2016). IoT bridges digital and physical environments. Within the scope of smart factories, autonomous vehicles, smart buildings, smart cities, and IoT-connected industrial applications, more automation and autonomous decisions are required than ever before. Faster resources are required to cope with the massive amounts of data generated when collecting and analyzing information. 5G is capable of providing the functions needed for various tasks in the IoT field and beyond, such as reliability, low latency, and mobility (I-SCOOP 2018).

IoT is an important resource that can solve the complexity of passenger management at airports. The use of biometric systems equipped with built-in tracking mechanisms facilitates passenger tracking and helps airports monitor real-time passenger traffic. However, IoT can be used to develop systems that can detect passengers by the way they walk (Libson 2022). IoT solutions in smart airports help to overcome the issue of lost luggage, which has always been a major area of dissatisfaction for airline customers. Finding lost luggage is incredibly easy with IoT beacon technology and its ongoing connectivity. These beacons integrate with the airport's cellular network and track the location of baggage at all touchpoints in real time. At the same time, these beacons enable passengers to track their belongings from check-in to the cargo hold, which is instrumental in reducing the number of lost baggage. For example, Hong Kong International Airport (HKIA) has made its baggage handling system smart with RFID technology (Libson 2022). In another example, JetBlue, a US-based airline, has provided an automated check-in function by automatically assigning passengers a ticket and seat 24 h before their flight. The seats to be assigned for the passenger are selected after carefully analyzing their booking patterns and behavior.

Flight delays are an annoying problem and cause huge losses, but with IoT at airports, authorities can effectively monitor weather conditions and prevent flight delays. They track weather updates and share forecasts with internal and external customers. It thus connects weather monitoring beacons across runways. This can help improve flight management and save costs. Besides, connected surveillance can save passengers a lot of time and convenience by informing them about delays and stoppages (Libson 2022).

Artificial Intelligence (AI), Machine Learning (ML), and Deep Learning (DL) AI is a branch of science and technology that creates intelligent machines and computer programs to perform various tasks that require human intelligence. AI has made people's lives more productive by being used in areas such as education, law, health, security, etc. The AI of the future will undoubtedly have many more features than the current one. It is thought that it will work more similarly to human intelligence and may even be capable of taking over a CEO position. AI brings innovations in health, transportation, e-commerce, and many other areas. The upcoming innovations are expected to have a major impact on people's lives and future generations (Sivasubramanian 2021).

The development of AI technology has led to the concept of ML. ML is an evolving branch of computational algorithms designed to mimic human intelligence by learning from the surrounding environment. Techniques based on ML have been successfully applied in various fields ranging from spacecraft engineering, finance, entertainment, biomedical, and medical applications (El Naga and Murphy 2015). Traditional ML techniques were limited in their ability to process natural data in their raw forms. For many years, building a pattern recognition or ML system, a technology that transforms raw data into a suitable internal representation or feature vector, has not been produced. With DL, a number of methods have been developed that allow a machine to be fed with raw data and automatically discover what is needed for detection and classification (LeCun et al. 2015).

Big data is used for AI, ML, and DL. Big data refers to data sets that are large, complex, and having diverse structures. To store, analyze, and visualize these large data sets is difficult. This is where big data analytics steps in. To analyze big data in a way that will benefit businesses or individuals and put them ahead of the competition, big data analytics is used (Sagiroglu and Sinanc 2013). Before the big data revolution, businesses could not store all their archives for long periods of time and could not manage huge data sets efficiently. The limited storage capacity of traditional technologies was expensive, even though they had solid management tools. They also lacked the scalability, flexibility, and performance needed in the big data context. Big data management paves the way for new methods and technologies to process, analyze, secure, and provide granular access to massive amounts of data sets (Oussous et al. 2018).

Today, the transformation of marketing is actualized by using big data in businesses with consumer analytics. Many sources, mainly the social networking platforms, are used to provide big data. Enterprises transform consumer behavior into experiential marketing in three stages by using mobile applications (Erevelles et al. 2016):

- They collect and store data as big data
- They draw consumer insights from big data
- Leverage consumer insights to develop dynamic/adaptive capabilities

The aviation industry generates a huge amount of data on a daily basis, but most of the data is not in an organized manner. The biggest challenge faced by various airlines is the integration of customer information stored on hard disks. For example, airlines can retrieve passenger data from the following sources (TechVidan 2022):

- Online transaction habits when booking tickets
- Search data from websites and apps
- Data from customer service
- Response to offers/discounts
- Travel history

It is important to recognize that each customer has their own needs. Some customers may be time-sensitive; others may be price-sensitive. Some customers place more importance on comfort and luxury, while for others these are not important. For this reason, airlines can produce various offers to appeal to different segments. Depending on the offer, airlines can price their tickets. This different pricing strategy helps to maximize revenue from each customer. Big data analysis based on AI and ML helps to understand the customer's travel behavior, willingness to pay, etc. The customer's preferred flight destinations, search history for products and services, hotels reviewed, etc. are analyzed with AI and ML, and individual marketing can be done with customized offers.

Customized offers always attract customers and help increase customer satisfaction and loyalty. Boxever, for example, is a customer intelligence and personalized marketing platform in the travel industry. This business serves a variety of clients, helping them prepare personalized offers for their customers. Boxever makes a marketing plan for its client regarding rental cars that need to be returned to dealerships and sends personalized emails to its customers. As a result, this business received more than $1 million in bookings per week with the help of email communications (TechVidan 2022).

One of the technologies used to ensure data security and the security of data produced in the virtual world is Blockchain applications. Although there is no common opinion on its definition in both academia and industry, blockchain is a collection of data elements in which data blocks are linked together to form a chain, secured using cryptography. Once the information is entered into the blockchain, it cannot be changed or deleted (Kakavand et al. 2017; Zhan 2020). The security of the documents used by passengers at the airport is provided by blockchain applications.

4.7 Conclusion

Aviation's transition from traditional marketing to experiential marketing has paralleled the development of technology. Aviation is one of the pioneering industries that first experienced many technologies. The rapid development of technology has also increased the use of different technologies in service delivery. For this reason, the service marketing triangle has shifted to the service marketing pyramid, and technology has been added to the process. This is because the economic, social, environmental, and technological changes in the world make the markets dynamic. The technological maturity levels of businesses that aim to provide experiential marketing to their internal and external customers is one of the important issues. Starting with airplane entertainment systems, airline passenger experiences have gained another dimension with 3D image technologies. It is estimated that the developing metaverse technology will create a new market all over the world. The aviation industry will also offer these technologies as new experiences to customers in sales and distribution channels. Robotic tools and next-generation AI software used in the marketing process have helped the transition to personalized marketing in customer experiences. Intensively used software saves personal data in large data pools and enables effective marketing to the target market. DL and ML algorithms can be effective in choosing the right marketing channels and pricing by modeling the behavior and purchasing habits of consumers. Internal and external stakeholders of the industry, especially airline companies, are increasingly using this software.

References

3D Ocean (2022) Istanbul Airport Tower (Tower of İstanbul 3rd Airport). https://3docean.net/item/istanbul-airport-tower-istanbul-3-havaliman-kulesi/22596800?irgwc=1&clickid=0sQyL02s0xyNTOAVqs3wbUHyUkDRY5QhEX9A180&iradid=275988&irpid=1300154&iradtype=ONLINE_TRACKING_LINK&irmptype=mediapartner&mp_value1=&utm_campaign=af_impact_r. Accessed 03 Sept 2022

Ashton K (2009) That 'Internet of Things' thing. RFID J

Aslanova I, Kulichkina A (2020) Digital maturity: definition and model. Adv Econ Bus Manag Res 138:443–449

Attaran M (2021) The impact of 5G on the evolution of intelligent automation and industry digitization. J Ambient Intell Human Comput

Aydın G (2005) Hizmet Sunumunda Teknoloji Kullanımı ve Müşteri Adaptasyonu. J Manag Econ Res:185–204

Baron S, Harris K (1995) Service Encounters. 48–75

Beale S (2012) Airport virtual assistant hologram at Newark Liberty International Airport. https://laughingsquid.com/airport-virtual-assistant-hologram-at-newark-liberty-international-airport/. Accessed 05 Sept 2022

Bishop T (2019) Airbus and Microsoft team up to sell holographic tech to airlines, defense and aerospace companies. https://www.geekwire.com/2019/airbus-microsoft-team-sell-holographic-tech-airlines-defense-aerospace-companies/. Accessed 30 Aug 2022

Bitner MJ, Brown S, Meuter M (2000) Technology infusion in service encounters. J Acad Mark Sci 28(1):138–149

BMW (2021) BMW IX. https://www.bmw.com.tr/tr_TR/all-models/bmw-i/bmw-ix/2021/bmw-ix.html? Accessed 02 Sept 2022

Brown L (2018) Augmenting the next generation of aviation professionals by training with holograms. Uniting Aviation: https://unitingaviation.com/news/capacity-efficiency/augmenting-aviation-training-with-holograms/. Accessed 03 Sept 2022

Bruder G, Interrante V, Phillips L, Steinicke F (2012) Redirecting walking and driving for natural navigation in immersive virtual environments. IEEE Trans Vis Comput Graph 18(4):538–545

Burdea GC, Coiffet P (2008) Virtual reality technology. IEEE Press

Cipresso P, Giglioli IA, Raya MA, Riva G (2018) The past, present, and future of virtual and augmented reality research: a network and cluster analysis of the literature. Front Psychol. https://doi.org/10.3389/fpsyg.2018.02086

CNN (2017) Dünya'nın ilk robot vatandaşı Suudi Arabistanlı. CNN News Turkish. https://www.bbc.com/turkce/haberler-dunya-41780346. Accessed 01 Sept 2022

Constantinides E (2004) Influencing the online consumer's behavior: the Web experience. Internet Res 14(2):111–126

DPVR (2021) 5 Airline industry trends using virtual reality hardware and software. https://www.dpvr.com/en/5-airline-industry-trends-using-virtual-reality-hardware-and-software/?srsltid=AfmBOooRjFhLktUr1Sa2vPpDxX71foEnnRGie5dap6WrzzeuuMrMQILy. Accessed 01 Sept 2022

El Naga I, Murphy M (2015) What is machine learning? In: El Naqa IM (ed) Machine learning in radiation oncology. Springer, pp 3–11

Erevelles S, Fukawa N, Swayne L (2016) Big Data consumer analytics and the transformation of marketing. J Bus Res 69(2):897–904. https://doi.org/10.1016/j.jbusres.2015.07.001

Evanhaim ND (2019) From retail to entertainment, 3D printing is changing everything. 3D Printing Media Network: https://www.3dprintingmedia.network/retail-entertainment-3d-printing-massivit/. Accessed 07 Sept 2022

GE Additive (2022) Aviation and aerospace industry. GE Additive: https://www.geaerospace.com/?_ga=2.43858087.341853124.1735600172-1835482902.1735600172&_gl=1*mjax3p*_ga*MTgzNTQ4MjkwMi4xNzM1NjAwMTcy*_ga_M2Q4NS0CLZ*MTczNTYwMDE3Mi4xLjAuMTczNTYwMDE3Mi42MC4wLjA. Accessed 08 Sept 2022

Gökrem L, Bozuklu M (2016) Nesnelerin İnterneti: Yapılan Çalışmalar ve Ülkemizdeki Mevcut Durum. Gaziosmanpaşa Scientif Stud J:47–68

Gökyüzü Haberci (2019) Havalimanı'nda robot vale: https://www.gokyuzuhaberci.com/havalimani-nda-robot-valevideo-46276.html. Accessed 08 Sept 2022

Groening S (2013) Aerial screens. Hist Technol, 284–303. https://doi.org/10.1080/07341512.2013.858523. Accessed 09 Sept 2022

Han K, Shah SH, Lee JW (2019) Holographic mixed reality system for air traffic control and management. Appl Sci 9(16)

HeroX (2022) Airbus to explore future of travel through metaverse; Crowdsources with HeroX. PRNewswire: https://www.herox.com/press-release/67. Accessed 01 Sept 2022

I-SCOOP (2018) 5G and IoT: the mobile broadband future of IoT. i-scoop.eu: https://www.i--scoop.eu/internet-of-things-iot/5g-iot/. Accessed 07 Sept 2022

Ivanov D, Tsipoulanidis A, Schönberger J (2017) Global supply chain and operations management. Springer Nature

Işık V (2014) Holografik Sanatta Kullanılan Hologram Çeşitleri. Elektronik Sosyal Bilimler Dergisi 13(49):366–385

Kagermann H (2014) Change through digitization—value creation in the age of Industry 4.0. Manag Permanent Change, pp 23–45

Kakavand H, Kost De Sevres N, Chilton B (2017) The blockchain revolution: an analysis of regulation and technology related to distributed ledger technologies. SSRN Electron J

Kali Z (2017) İGA'dan Akıllı Havalimanı için son teknoloji uygulamaları. https://www.aeroportist.com/igadan-akilli-havalimani-icin-son-teknoloji-uygulamalari/. Accessed 08 Sept 2022

Kantor M (2018) Burgers for a penny, and the power of location intelligence. https://www.esri.com/about/newsroom/publications/wherenext/burger-king-marketing-campaign/. Accessed 02 Sept 2022

Kaplanseren E (2018) Shield. Yeni Havalimanı Teknolojide de Birinci: https://www.posta.com.tr/yazarlar/erdal-kaplanseren/yeni-havalimani-teknolojide-de-birinci-2055061. Accessed 08 Sept 2022

Krasniqi X, Hajrizi E (2016) Use of IoT technology to drive the automotive industry from connected to full autonomous vehicles. IFAC Papers Online 49(29):269–274

Kotler P (1994) Reconceptualizing marketing: an interview with Philip Kotler. Eur Manag J 12(4):353–361
LeCun Y, Bengio Y, Hinton G (2015) Deep Learning. Nature 521:436–444
Libson S (2022) IoT-ushering-new-era-smart-airports. https://www.kellton.com/kellton-tech-blog/iot-ushering-new-era-smart-airports. Accessed 01 Sept 2022
Mansilla D, Armentia J, Ipina D (2012) Fighting against vampire appliances through eco-aware things. Sixth International Conference on Innovative Mobile and Internet Services, Ubiquitous Computing
Max Planck Institute (2014) VR-HYPERSPACE – FLIGHT COMFORT IN VIRTUAL REALITY. https://tuebingen.mpg.de/en/detail/vr-hyperspace-flight-comfort-in-virtual-reality/. Accessed 01 Sept 2022
McCollum T (1997) Making Internet work for you. Nation's Business:7–13
Microsoft (2022) Microsoft HoloLens. https://docs.microsoft.com/en-us/hololens/hololens2-hardware. Accessed 01 Sept 2022
MotherApp (2018) Internet of Things (IoT) Smart Airport Solution Showcase 2018. https://motherapp.com/internet-of-things-iot-smart-airport-showcase-2018/. Accessed 05 Sept 2022
Mullen K (2017) This is what one of the first in-flight movies looked like in-flight movies have come a long way. On August 10, 2022 Huff Post: https://www.huffpost.com/entry/first-in-flight-movie_n_5505182. Accessed 30 Aug 2022.
Mystakidis S (2021) Metaverse. Encyclopedia:486–497
Nguyen HT (2014) Proposition of new metaphors and techniques for 3D interaction and navigation preserving immersion and facilitating collaboration between distant users. INSA de Rennes
Oropallo W, Piegl L (2016) Ten challenges in 3D printing. Eng Comput 32:135–148
Oussous A, Benjelloun F-Z, Lahcen A, Belfkih S (2018) Big data technologies: a survey. J King Saud Univ Comp Inf Sci 30(4):431–448
Öz F (2017) Hizmet ve Hizmet Pazarlaması Kavramı. In: Onaran B, Özmen A (eds) Hizmet Pazarlaması: Stratejik Bir Yaklaşımla (5). EFİL YAYINEVİ, Ankara
Padgett D, Mulvey M (2007) Differentiation via technology: strategic positioning of services following the introduction of disruptive technology. J Retail 83:375–391
Parasuraman A (1996) Understanding and leveraging the role of customer service in external, interactive and internal marketing. In: Frontiers in Services Conference, Nashville, TN (No. 1996/10, p. 3)
Parasuraman A, Grewal D (2000) The impact of technology on the quality-value-loyalty chain: a research agenda. J Acad Mark Sci 28(1):168–174
Pehlivan G (2020) VR AR MR Terimlerinin Farkları Nelerdir? Codemodeon. https://codemodeon.com/tr/vr-ar-mr-terimlerinin-farklari-nelerdir/. Accessed 30 Aug 2022
Qatar Airways (2022) Qverse. On boarding - business: https://www.qatarairways.com/html/redirect/QR/qverse/check-in?lang=en. Accessed 01 Sept 2024
Rajesh M (2015) Inside Japan's first robot-staffed hotel. The Guardian. T: https://www.theguardian.com/travel/2015/aug/14/japan-henn-na-hotel-staffed-by-robots. Accessed 30 Aug 2022
Reed Smith (2022) Aviation in the metaverse: breaking the reality barrier. reedsmith.com: https://www.reedsmith.com/en/perspectives/metaverse/2022/08/aviation-in-the-metaverse-breaking-the-reality-barrier. Accessed 30 Aug 2022
Rosenberg LB (1992). https://upload.wikimedia.org/wikipedia/commons/2/2c/Virtual_Fixtures_USAF_Report_%281992%29_EXCERPT_n.pdf. Defense Technical Information Center Armstrong Laboratory. https://apps.dtic.mil/sti/pdfs/ADA292450.pdf. Accessed 10 Aug 2022
Sagiroglu S, Sinanc D (2013) Big data: a review. International Conference on Collaboration Technologies and Systems (Cts):42–47
Scammell R (2018) Holography improves heads-up displays for aircraft pilots. Airforce-Technology: https://bit.ly/3sjfVgh. Accessed 01 Sept 2022
Schmitt B (1999) Experiential marketing. J Mark Manag 15(1–3):53–67

Shafique K, Khawaja B, Sabir F, Qazi S (2020) Internet of Things (IoT) for next-generation smart systems: a review of current challenges, future trends and prospects for emerging 5G-IoT scenarios. Special Section on Antenna and Propagation for 5G and Beyond
Singh A, Sailo M (2013) Consumer behavior in online shopping: a study of Aizawl. Int J Bus Manag Res 1(3):45–49
Sivasubramanian M (2021) Artificial intelligence's impact on our everyday lives. In: Karthikeyan J, Hie TS, Jin NY (eds) Learning outcomes of classroom research. L Ordine Nuovo Publication, New Delhi, pp 1–9
Siyaev A, Jo G-S (2021) Neuro-symbolic speech understanding in aircraft maintenance metaverse. IEEE Access 9:154484–154499
Sportillo D, Paljic A, Boukhris M, Fuchs P, Ojeda L, Roussarie V (2017) An immersive virtual reality system for semi- autonomous driving simulation: a comparison between realistic and 6-DoF controller-based interaction. Proceedings of the 9th International Conference on Computer and Automation Engineering, pp 6–10
Tan-Gillies H (2021) On location with a travel retail 'quaternity': Chanel N°5 Spaceship lifts off at Heathrow. The Moodie Davitt Report: https://moodiedavittreport.com/on-location-with-a-travel-retail-quaternity-chanel-n5-spaceship-lifts-off-at-heathrow/. Accessed 10 Aug 2022
Taskiran İ (2019) Havalimanındaki danışma robotlarına yoğun ilgi. Anadolu Ajansı. https://www.aa.com.tr/tr/turkiye/havalimanindaki-danisma-robotlarina-yogun-ilgi-/1552721. Accessed 02 Sept 2022
TechVidan (2022) Sky is the limit for big data analytics in the aviation industry. https://techvidvan.com/tutorials/big-data-aviation/. Accessed 01 Sept 2022
Teichert R (2019) Digital transformation maturity: a systematic review of literature. Acta Universitatis Agriculturae et Silviculturae Mendelianae Brunensis:1673–1687
Thordsen T, Murawski M, Bick M (2020) How to measure digitalization? A critical evaluation of digital maturity models. Responsible design, implementation and use of information and communication technology. Lecture Notes in Computer Science, pp 358–369
Urdea A-M, Constantin C (2021) Experts' perspective on the development of experientialmarketing strategy: implementation steps, benefits, and challenges. J Risk Financ Managment
VRWorldTech (2022) Iberia trials VR on select flights. Magazine Virtual Reality World Technologies. Accessed 30 Aug 2022
Walker R, Craig-Lees M, Hecker R, Francis H (2002) Technology- enabled service delivery: an investigation of reasons affecting customer adoption and rejection. Int J Serv Ind Manag 13(1):91–106
Wilson BJ (2022) In-flight entertainment has come a long way. Honeywell Aerospace Blog. https://aerospace.honeywell.com/us/en/about-us/blogs/inflight-entertainment-has-come-a-long-way. Accessed 10 Aug 2022
Zhan Y (2020) Blockchain. In: Shen X, Lin X, Zhang K (eds) Encyclopedia of Wireless Networks (115). Springer
Zhang D, Tan P (2021) Internet of things and intelligent transportation system. J Phys: Conference Series
Zineldin M (2000) Beyond relationship marketing: technologicalship marketing. Mark Intell Plan 18(1):9–23

Savas S. Ateş graduated from Anadolu University, School of Civil Aviation, Air Transportation Management in 2004. Between 2004 and 2005, he worked as a dispatch (flight operations) specialist at Onur Airlines for 1 year. Between 2005 and 2007, he worked as assistant manager at Eskisehir Hasan Polatkan Airport. He started his academic career as a research assistant at Anadolu University School of Civil Aviation at the end of 2007. He graduated from Anadolu University Institute of Social Sciences Civil Aviation Management Master's Program in 2008 with the thesis on "Airport master planning approaches and research on different applications." He graduated from the PhD program of the same department in 2013 with his thesis titled "Decision support system model proposal for reducing delays in the operational processes of aviation enterprises and its application at Atatürk Airport". In 2014, he was appointed as an Assistant Professor at Anadolu University, Faculty of Aviation and Space Sciences, Department of Aviation Management. Between 2015 and 2016, he worked as the Assistant Director of the Aviation Museum at Anadolu University. Between 2016 and 2020, he served as the Deputy Dean of the Faculty of Aviation and Aeronautics and SHY147 Basic Training Maintenance Organization. Since 2015, he has been working as an Assistant Academic Coordinator in the Aviation Management Program of the Open Education Faculty and since 2020; he has been a member of the Board of Directors of Eskisehir Technical University Open and Distance Education Application Center.

Ezgi Filazoglu was born in Adana (1995). She graduated from Anadolu University, Faculty of Aviation and Space Sciences, Department of Aviation Management (2018). She received her master's degree from Eskisehir Technical University, Department of Aviation Management (2022). She worked as Dispatcher at Adana HAVAŞ station (2018–2019). She worked as a Research Assistant at Nisantasi University (2020–2022). She is currently working as a System Support Specialist at Gozen Digital Aviation (2022–...). Main research interests: new approaches in aviation education, the relationship between technological developments and aviation, PAT area safety and intelligent transportation systems.

Chapter 5
Utilizing Online-Centered Big Data in the Airline Industry

Bahri Baran Kocak

Abstract Data is the most valuable fuel for marketing activities today. Thus, the level of competition in the markets has increased the importance of data in the airline industry, as in all other industries. With the development and spread of online technologies, the highly needed data by airlines started to be produced by consumers in online environments. In this regard, one of the shortest ways to determine the reactions and changes in consumer behavior phenomenon is to collect, process, and analyze big data that could be derived from consumer online activities. This chapter aims to provide a literature review on the application of online consumer-based big data in airline marketing and to create a research agenda. In this context, the current chapter presents the sustainable contributions of the use of big data in the airline industry. Moreover, big data analytics, web analytics, social media analytics, sentiment analysis, and search engine optimization are also presented in detail. Finally, the chapter concludes by presenting insights into the direction of online consumer data that airlines could leverage in their marketing efforts.

Keywords Business models · Airline · Online big data · Marketing · Consumer behavior · Social media analytics · Search engine optimization

5.1 Introduction

In the last period when the modern industry has become integrated with information systems, the amount of data reaching extraordinary levels, such as 1000 exabits (1 billion gigabits) per year, has become more important than ever for businesses with its usage, application, and information output (Yin and Kaynak 2015). The contribution of the studies in both physical sciences, which includes important disciplines

B. B. Kocak (✉)
Aviation Management Department, Dicle University, Diyarbakir, Türkiye
e-mail: bahribaran.kocak@dicle.edu.tr

İ. Polat (ed.), *Aviation Innovation*, Accounting, Finance, Sustainability, Governance & Fraud: Theory and Application,
https://doi.org/10.1007/978-981-96-7265-3_5

such as engineering and medicine, and social sciences, which examine human behavior and relationships, to various sectors is through the effective acquisition, classification, and analysis of data and the presentation of the results with correct interpretations. These problems that IT managers frequently face have brought the concept of "big data" into our lives (Davenport et al. 2012). Big data, which has created the need for wide-scale use, ranging from Internet providers to businesses and even individuals, is defined as "the acquisition, storage, management and analysis processes of data sets beyond the possibilities offered by traditional database tools" (Cui et al. 2016). It consists of five fundamental components: volume, diversity, speed, value, and accuracy. Bulk data generated by various organizations and communities, including online channels, represents volume and diversity; instantaneous flow of data without any manipulation or filtering represents speed and accuracy; and accurate data that provides useful, reliable, and precise returns across disciplines, including institutions and academia, represents value (Yin and Kaynak 2015).

In the past, data obtained from the environment as a result of surveys and observations has been made available to businesses and researchers in much easier ways with the help of information processing machines with technological development. The data sources to be processed are basically divided into two classes: internal sources, such as sales, customer, website, survey, and market research data to manage the daily operations of organizations, and external data, such as social networking applications, various websites, search engine data, location, and signal-based external data in the online environment (Blazquez and Domenech 2018). From the perspective of businesses, it has become possible to develop products and services and respond quickly to change by taking advantage of big data with systems that provide instant information flow from their environment (Davenport et al. 2012). As a matter of fact, a significant number of organizations, Google being in the first place, that deal with massive volume of data related to e-commerce and social networking applications benefit from this situation, and when necessary, they can improve their business activities and stand out in business decision-making processes by using big data analytics and traditional methods together. In addition to these acquired advantages, the use of big data supports business decisions and saves cost and time (Alam et al. 2014).

Considering the need for businesses to gain customer-oriented behavior in today's markets, where unlimited products and services have become almost copies of each other, brands that want to gain competitive opportunities may need consumer feedback to improve their products and services in accordance with human needs in these expanding, globalized markets. It is known that big data has an important role in modern industrial development, especially in risk management and finance, in the context of machines, cloud-based solutions, and business management, considering the customer factor (Yin and Kaynak 2015). The airline industry, where consumer needs are at the forefront, is among these industries that depend on the rational use of data (Chung et al. 2020). The transformation of data into information, especially used in marketing efforts, is an integral part of business intelligence and can provide professional competitive advantage in decision-making processes as well (Hedin et al. 2014).

Airline companies may need some consumer data in order to provide innovations or improvements in their products and services to satisfy passengers. For the data needed, it is possible to utilize online tools, where passengers reflect their research, desires, and experiences before, during, and after travel. In the relevant process, many data such as potential passengers' search engine queries, website access results, reservations, and purchase statistics as well as their social media comments are important in understanding and analyzing behaviors and making decisions that will bring profit to the business. Among those using customer-oriented big data in the sector, well-established businesses stand out. For example, United Airlines analyzed its passengers' past trips and purchasing behavior using a big data approach and increased its revenues by 15%. Delta Air Lines, on the other hand, has tried to increase customer satisfaction with its baggage locator application that uses instantaneous big data flow. Another airline company, Southwest, uses passenger-generated text (Rijmenam 2013) and voice-based big data to improve customer service receiving help from important organizations such as NASA (Duke 2017). In addition to service improvement, big data is becoming advantageous for airlines to forecast demand, build brand awareness, produce compelling content, and increase the effectiveness of social media pages (Menon et al. 2019) and for more positive marketing outcomes (Tsai and Men 2013).

A review of the literature reveals that although there are extensive studies on the airline industry's use of big data (Izzo 2019; Hausladen and Schosser 2020; Mohamed and Al-Azab 2021), little attention has been paid to its importance and its relationship with the airline industry, especially in the context of online consumer behavior (Chen et al. 2016; Knorr 2019; Tian et al. 2019). To fill this gap, in the following sections of the study, the types of online consumer-based big data in airline marketing, its application areas and contributions to marketing efforts, and the suggestions for future research will be presented.

5.2 Online Customer-Centric Big Data in the Airline Industry

The speed and spread of technological advancements have paved the way for new communication channels and consumption approaches, leading to more complex consumer behavior and making it almost imperative for marketers to have access to richer, faster, and more diverse consumer data. Sustainable competitiveness of brands, especially in the markets in which they operate, depends on their dynamic adaptation to the competition by allocating a significant portion of their physical, human, and organizational capital to the collection, storage, and presume of big data (Erevelles et al. 2016). In the aviation industry, data can be obtained from flights, airport operations, meteorological conditions, airline information, economic indicators, safety presentations, and aircraft and passenger information (Andronie 2015). Although the information that airlines store in their databases is important for operational and management purposes (Sumathi et al. 2017), the increase in the amount of data from various sources has made different data structures useful for decision-making. This situation is related to the structured data created by the diversity of the dimensions of big data and refers to the tables that airline companies keep ready for use in their databases. To examine other data structures that need to be considered, semi-structured data are texts taking place in the web environment that can only be structured by natural language processing or information derivation methods, while unstructured data are structures such as text, image, audio, video, and message content that are mostly produced by social media applications in the online environment and require strong programming knowledge to process (Rusu et al. 2013).

However, when we consider the issue from the perspective of airline marketing and customer relationship management, it is possible to reach meaningful results by filtering the collected online data and positively improve the services in this direction. It is possible to obtain online consumer-centric big data from airline website statistics (Mohamed and Al-Azab 2021), web search engines, social media channels, and mobile location data (Schosser 2020). Before moving on to these data types and application areas that businesses accumulate in traditional or online (cloud technologies) databases, it is necessary to mention big data analytics, which includes the process of transforming data into meaningful information.

Big data analytics, which is used in decision-making in many industries to develop future-oriented strategies, increase revenues with low costs, and achieve competitive difference and value in innovation approach (LaValle et al. 2011), is one of the most important auxiliary tools both in aviation literature (Chung et al. 2020) and in operations and service management (Aarthy et al. 2021). Once a business gains access to useful data, the process of applying big data analytics which requires specialized analytical skills (Aktan 2018), to process structured, semi-structured, and unstructured data at hand with a holistic approach for reaching the information that will provide assistance in taking strategic decisions, can be defined as the application of analytical capabilities to big data (Russom 2011). Big data analytics basically consists of four stages, as shown in Fig. 5.1 (Almaslamani et al. 2020).

To apply the process to the airline industry, it is important to determine the purposes for which big data will be used. For example, the amount of stock to be kept in in-cabin catering services should be related to the estimated number of passengers. Otherwise, these stocks of perishable foods may be wasted, and costs may increase. Therefore, when purchasing inventory, airline managers may want to estimate the number of passengers arriving in the coming periods. In partnership with the marketing and finance departments, they would then ask the relevant managers to determine the number of passengers likely to be hosted in the next 6 months and make a presentation. In line with this objective, an airline company will require various types of data such as daily, weekly, or monthly passenger counts, website statistics, search engine queries by passengers, surveys, frequent flyer program

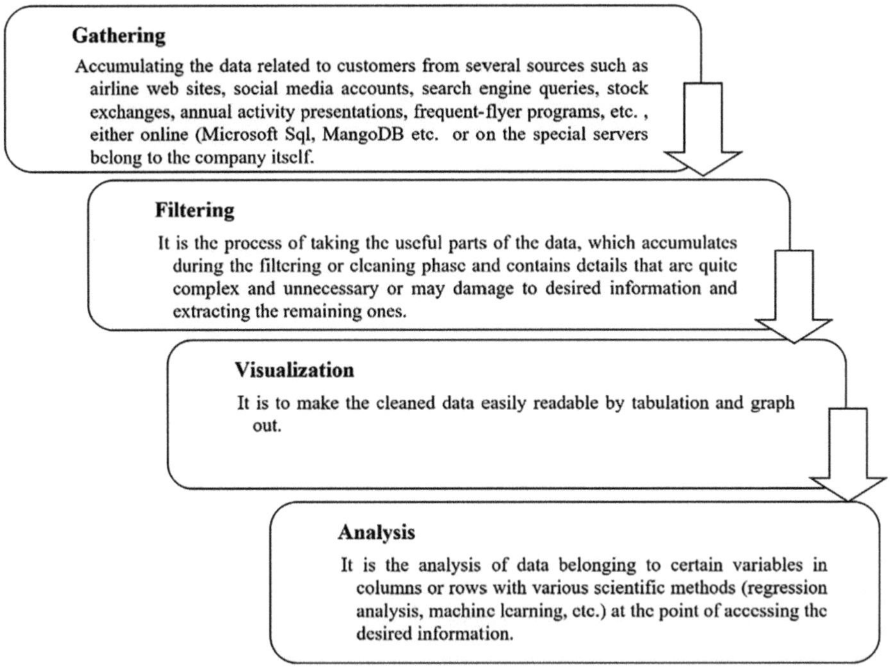

Fig. 5.1 The process of big data analytics (*Source* Almaslamani et al. 2020)

results, reservation records, and historical inventory levels within the cabin from past periods. Once the company has collected the acquired data into relevant databases, it will need to clean it, as there will be unnecessary bulk variables, including consumer identity information and hobbies. The desired variables should then be placed in columns in Microsoft Excel tables, such as date, number of passengers, stock quantity, etc., and the first graphs needed should be created. Thus, the big data will have an easy-to-understand visualization before the analysis is applied. In the last step of big data analytics, analysis and presentation, the airline company will consider the amount of inventory as the dependent variable and will be able to predict the number of passengers for the next period by using regression or machine learning methods on independent variables, such as the number of passengers and website statistics. As a result, after the stages of big data analytics are completed, it will be possible to present the desired information to the management in line with the objectives.

Although big data analytics provides many benefits to airline companies such as product/service development, consumer experience/loyalty building, forecasting capability, decision support, price differentiation, opening new routes, personnel management, and performance measurement by benchmarking against competitors, managing the increasing amount of data, insufficient knowledge in data science, privacy/security concerns, and a lack of sufficient qualified human resources are among the major problems in the industry (Mohamed and Al-Azab 2021). Despite all these advantages and disadvantages, it is necessary to consider the sectoral contribution of big data analytics by recognizing that big data is one of today's realities within the scope of competition and sustainability (Aktan 2018). Big data, which is among the first auxiliary resources of the airline industry, is used to understand the online consumer behavior needed, while the role of big data analytics in the analysis part is quite high (Holland et al. 2020).

5.3 Web Analytics in Airline Industry

The spread and utilization of Internet technology and websites among the masses, coupled with the tracking of "logs" that represent individuals' entries and exits on specific websites, and the big data brought by this traffic have given rise to the concept of web analytics. The emergence of various websites in the early 2000s was one of the key factors contributing to the popularity of web analytics (Kaushik 2007). In the new business understanding brought about by globalization, brands deliver their products and services to their consumers in a world without borders, even through their websites. While fulfilling all these efforts, they can collect many data from consumers through their websites, especially through surveys, in order to improve their marketing capabilities. More importantly, website metrics that reflect consumers' shopping experiences and personal characteristics are among the indispensable variables of web analytics. Website metrics can be obtained from users (number of logins, number of users, etc.) and devices (operating system, IP address, cookies, etc.) (Esen and Türkay 2017).

Website usage has emerged as a revenue booster for airline companies in ticket sales (IdeaWorks 2012; Díaz and Martin-Consuegra, 2016). However, ever-changing consumer behaviors have an impact on online habits. For example, while the seasonal conditions are important for airline sales, according to 2024 data, 53% of these sales were made through websites (IATA 2024). Therefore, the importance of website traffic and the use of data derived from this traffic have the potential to increase airline revenues, albeit indirectly.

According to the annual web traffic data of the transportation industry published by Similarweb, it was determined that online travel agencies (such as Kayak, Skyscanner, etc.) surpassed airline businesses in terms of page traffic and website access, which had declined during Covid-19 but gained an upward trend in 2022. A significant portion of it was organic or direct through web search engines. However, although global geopolitical and economic bottlenecks have had a negative impact on airline transportation website access, it has also been observed that this case has caused a significant increase in web traffic for low-cost airlines (Krueger 2022). The impact of online technologies on the industry has encouraged the use of web analytics. The process of tracking, analyzing, and presenting data obtained from the web can be referred to as web analytics (Mohamed and Al-Azab 2021).

Due to being part of a service-intensive industry, airline companies' website presentations encompass informational content (flight status, prices, baggage, ticket sales reservations, car rental, hotels, transportation status, etc.), usability features (updates, site map, language options, search tools, etc.), business status (about us, company history, privacy, investor relations, etc.), design/visual aesthetics, engagement (feedback, social networks, loyalty programs, etc.), and reciprocity principles (customer service, promotions, and news) (Díaz and Martin-Consuegra 2016). Depending on the design and management of their websites, airline companies can benefit from these electronic services in terms of financial profitability, consumer satisfaction, availability, and accessibility (Harison and Boonstra 2008). Therefore, directing or attracting online traffic to the airline website is a highly important marketing activity and can have a positive impact on brand awareness (Sakas and Giannakopoulos 2021). However, knowing the sources of traffic directed to the website will be useful in performing web analytics and determining the points where marketing efforts will be directed. In general, it is possible to say that users access websites in four different ways (Longden 2020):

(i) *Direct traffic*: It refers to Internet users accessing the page by typing the URL address of the airline website without using any search engine. In web analytics applications, direct traffic is determined from browsers or link clicks in word processing software such as Microsoft Word/Excel.
(ii) *Referral traffic*: It refers to users who access the page by clicking on links from other websites. It also proves that the referral page mentioned on the website is considered safe by Google.
(iii) *Social traffic*: It refers to traffic that comes from social networking applications (such as Twitter, Facebook, Instagram, etc.). It is also a reflection of brand awareness when users access the website by clicking on the links attached to the messages sent through the applications.
(iv) *Organic traffic*: This type of traffic occurs when access to a website results from search engine queries. With search engine optimization (SEO) applications as an output of the business's marketing efforts, the web page can be ranked highly to provide the best results for user searches.

Looking at airline applications in web analytics, it can be said that digital marketing effectiveness is closely related to the increase in the traffic types mentioned above. In fact, recent studies on airline brands have found that desktop website usage is positively correlated with organic, direct, and referral traffic, while mobile usage may have a negative relationship with the aforementioned traffic (Sakas and Giannakopoulos 2021). Moreover, it has been determined that access to the pages of airline companies that offer paid campaigns on crowdsourcing websites increases consumer engagement, and this is positively correlated with organic traffic (Sakas and Reklitis 2021). Although increasing website traffic is clearly important for airline companies, different strategies may need to be generated for each type of traffic. For direct traffic, providing brand awareness and placing the customer at the center by increasing the quality of service can offer memorable solutions. For referral traffic, quality content production and support from blog or forum networks can be obtained. For social traffic, encouraging followers on social media platforms to like, share, or interact with a post can lead them to click on links. For organic traffic, SEO assistance can be obtained, as mentioned earlier (Longden 2020).

5.4 The Applications of Social Media Analytics in Airline Industry

With the emergence of Web 2.0 technology, user-generated content has created a general concept that today includes blogs, content communities, social networking sites, virtual games, and virtual social worlds. This concept and application area, known as social media, has led to radical changes in both brands taking place online and classical business understanding and business practices (Kaplan and Haeinlein 2010). This situation has sparked research interest for various disciplines in both academic and computer science circles and has led to the growing significance of an application area known as social media analytics. In general terms, social media analytics can be defined as collecting, monitoring, analyzing, summarizing, and visualizing social media data with an application suitable for special requests in line with the development and evaluation of informational tools (Zeng et al. 2010).

Based on 2022 data, 65,000 photographs are shared per minute on Instagram, while 90 million comments are made annually on Goodreads (Statista 2022a). These data are a sign that the big data generated by social media reached incredible amounts and dimensions, and it is clear that the data obtained from here will show significant differences in product, brand, and marketing research. Hence, as it was aforementioned, before processing the big data, just like in web analytics, it is necessary to know which metrics are involved in the data gathered from social media. The basic metrics to be used for social media analytics can be listed as the sender information (ID number, geographical location, name, and profile photo); the message (post text, image, emoji, hashtag, and link); the date the post was published; the number of likes, shares, views, and comments; the post received; and finally the date the data was captured by the researcher. When viewed from a technical standpoint, these metrics used in data and text mining can be used in extremely rich application tools, in managerial decision-making processes, forecasting, and the development of new applications, within a concept known as social media intelligence (Zeng et al. 2010). In the processes of acquisition, understanding, and presentation, social media analytics techniques include sentiment analysis, social network analysis (Fan and Gordon 2014), and engagement analysis (Akter et al. 2016).

Social media analytics techniques are frequently used in the airline industry, where consumer and brand concepts are especially prominent. In fact, research shows that 87% of airline executives have embraced the use of social media analytics to provide in-depth information about consumers, with advantages such as instant feedback, trend spotting, competitive analysis, and crisis management gaining importance (Genylabs 2022).

5.4.1 Sentiment Analysis

Sentiment analysis, which has become an efficient research field in the early 2000s and is used to meet industrial needs with natural language processing techniques, is a field that examines the opinions, attitudes, and emotions of the public about products, services, organizations, individuals, events, issues, and their attributes (Liu 2012). This technique, in which comments on social media are frequently used, is simply based on labeling user comments on a brand as positive or negative and teaching these labels to machine learning algorithms to automatically classify all posts (Cambria 2016). In general terms, the steps to be applied during sentiment analysis are gathering, text preprocessing, and classification (Adeva et al. 2014; Koçak and Atalık 2019):

- *Gathering*: It is the process of extracting data (metrics) to be used for analysis from social media applications by means of application interfaces, labeling the posts according to the sentiments they contain, and separating them into training (data to be taught to the machine) and test data (machine output).
- *Text preprocessing*: It is the process of taking tagged consumer submissions through natural language processing and converting them into machine-understandable digital form.
- *Classification*: It is the process of classifying the sentiments previously taught to the machine with learning algorithms.

Recent studies are identifying sentiments of consumers based on the dimensions of services in their posts in the airline industry. This technique is referred to as feature-based sentiment analysis (Ashi et al. 2018). Although sentiment analysis applications are encountered in the airline industry (Wan and Gao 2015; Rane and Kumar 2018; Koçak and Atalık 2019; Chang et al. 2022), these studies use various machine learning and deep learning techniques and compare algorithms in order to provide the most objective classification results, which airline managers can use in future decision-making processes.

5.4.2 Social Network Analysis

In our everyday lives, we are socialized by our family, friends, the environments in which we interact with them, and other members of society whom we meet and get to know through these environments. In this way, we can get a rough idea of how extensive our social network is. Similarly, we can meet these people on social media applications, make new friends, and have the opportunity to expand our circle. Social networks encompass relationships and interactions among individuals, groups, and organizations (government, foundations, businesses, etc.) as well (Tabassum et al. 2018). Social network analysis, which is seen as a form of developing social capital in communication and brand strategies, can be used by marketing

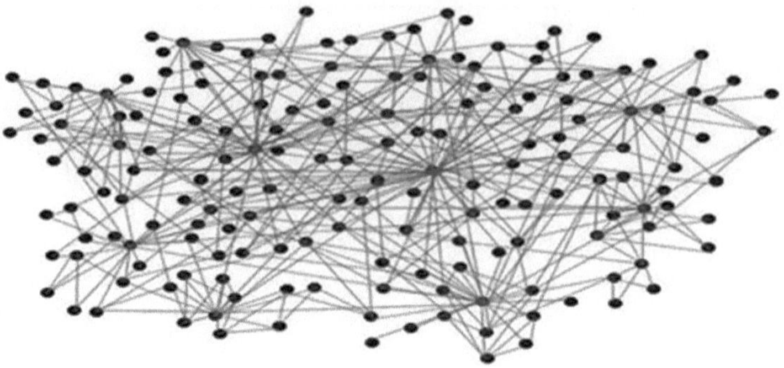

Fig. 5.2 Social network map (*Source* Miguélez 2020)

researchers to track and analyze customer relationships and the development of these relationships (Antoniadis and Charmantzi 2016). The visual representation of a social network structure consists of nodes/blobs representing individuals/organizations and ribbons (links) depicting the relationships among them (Fig. 5.2).

In social network analysis, in addition to information about individuals, what needs to be taken into account are the direction, strength, degree, closeness, and togetherness of the ribbons that connect the nodes, that is, the direction, strength, degree, closeness, and togetherness of the relationship. The direction of the ribbon can occur directly and unilaterally in social media when one user tags another user, or it can take indirect forms when two users are part of the same community, creating non-direct connections. The strength of a ribbon can gain weight through a user tagging another user (brand or consumer) once or multiple times. Similarly, the number of social media communities a user belongs to determines the degree of the ribbons, while closeness can vary based on a user's direct/indirect connection to another user. Togetherness depends on the number of communities a user is close to. In addition to these applied techniques, it is also possible to determine community structures by clustering, using algorithms and optimization methods (Tabassum et al. 2018). When airline applications of social network analysis are examined, depending on consumer behaviors and characteristics, the interest of communities in the brand can be determined by text mining and clustering analysis (Punel and Ermagun 2018), and meaningful results can be obtained regarding which social media applications provide more effective results for the services (Wibisono and Ruldeviyani 2021).

5.4.3 Participation Analysis

Consumer participation behavior can be defined as the psychological state exhibited by a customer who engages in an interactive co-creation process with a brand that is central to a service relationship (Brodie et al. 2011). Consumer participation in social media can occur in the form of following the brand, liking, sharing, or commenting on posts (de Vries et al. 2012; Cvijikj and Michahelles 2013). It is important to understand consumers' participation behaviors on social media to ensure brand loyalty (Hapsari et al. 2017) and to see the results of marketing efforts, such as advertising, promotion, and communication (Tsai and Men 2013). Determining what incentivizes consumers to participate can help businesses to adopt the right communication and marketing strategies.

Participation analytics on social media can be used by businesses to determine how much participation they receive on which types of posts. As a matter of fact, although many studies in the literature list the reasons that push consumers to participate as content type (informational, social, entertaining, etc.), presentation type (video, image, etc.), and link usage (Cvijikj and Michahelles 2013; Luarn et al. 2015; Demmers et al. 2020), recent studies reveal that technical content such as psycholinguistics focusing on grammatical structure (Labrecque et al. 2020; Koçak 2021) and emoji usage (Koçak 2022a) can also affect participation behavior. Some studies suggest that, especially in the airline industry, content strategies can significantly affect participation and draw attention (Leung et al. 2013; Menon et al. 2019; Koçak 2021, 2022a, b).

The participation analysis process generally involves capturing airline posts with social media metrics, classifying the post content with independent reviewers' opinions, and analyzing the relationship between interaction and content corresponding to each tagged post with various statistical methods. In the process, Kappa statistics can be used for reviewers' agreement among themselves, and correlation and various regression methods (multiple linear, Poisson, negative binomial, etc.) can be used to explore the relationship between content and interaction (Menon et al. 2019; Demmers et al. 2020; Koçak 2021, 2022a, b).

5.4.4 Search Engine Applications in Airline Industry

Access to information is at the forefront of the services offered by the Internet. As a matter of fact, while the information offered saves time, power, and other costs for users, it has also changed the classic information-seeking behavior of consumers such as turning to mass media and sales consultants (Peterson and Merino 2003). Search engines are among the leading services that facilitate searching on the Internet. Based on 2022 data, Google has overtaken Yandex, Yahoo, Bing, and Baidu in the search engine market, with a share of 83% (Statista 2022b). The daily search volume conducted solely on Google exceeds 3.5 billion (Google Statistics 2022); thus, this massive volume of data is capturing the attention of businesses as well, and it is widely used in numerous research studies to uncover consumer behavior in information search. The free availability of statistics on search engine queries through Google's trends service (trends.google.com) brings opportunities to researchers from all segments of society and industries ranging from health (Brigo et al. 2014) to employment (Naccarato et al. 2018) and from finance (Preis et al. 2013) to tourism (Önder and Gunter 2016).

Researchers who use statistics on search engine queries to learn about instant search behavior related to ticketing and booking without the need for transportation agencies (Little et al. 2011) can use the results for advertising (Schultz 2020) and content marketing (Penela et al. 2017). It is possible to say that search engine research in the airline industry is generally focused on demand forecasting and understanding passenger behavior. Demand forecasting is an area of research that tries to reveal the number of passengers that airline companies will host in the future; it enables the realization of pinpoint pricing strategies by using resources accurately. Moreover, increasing forecast accuracy allows the industry to avoid economic fluctuations and unnecessary investments (Suh and Ryerson 2019). The steps to be followed when forecasting demand with search engine queries are similar to big data analytics processes and may differ methodologically at some points.

(v) *Identifying keywords*: This is the step where the search queries related to the sector are revealed using the search engine optimization methods mentioned earlier (Önder and Gunter 2016).

(vi) *Search engine and obtaining demand data*: Depending on the keywords selected from the search engine page, the periodic search index and data indicating the demand for the airline are obtained. Search results are indexed between 1 and 100. Demand, on the other hand, consists of periodic data such as the number of passengers, paid passenger kilometers, and seat kilometers supplied taking place in the airline's annual financial presentations.

(vii) *Statistical analysis*: At this stage of the process, the relationship between search engine queries and the amount of demand is determined by correlation or causality analysis, and then future demand is predicted from historical data using methods such as auto-regressive models, machine learning, and deep learning (Yu et al. 2019).

(viii) *Visualization and presentation*: This is the stage where periodic graphs of search engine queries in comparison with demand are visualized with forecasts and made ready for presentation.

When research on demand forecasting using search engine queries is reviewed, it has been observed that short-term forecasts for the airline industry yield positive results (Park et al. 2017). Understanding why and how online consumer queries occur can contribute to the design of airline websites (Broder 2002), keyword selection decisions that can bring the page to the top of search queries (Koçak 2020), and consumer profiling in general (Nagar and Suleman 2019). In his study, Koçak (2020) examined the word variations associated with the query "ticket" on Google and found that passengers use the search engine to access transactional results, such as downloading mobile applications, printing tickets, or accessing airline websites. He concluded that this behavior, which is described as navigational search, varies seasonally.

5.5 Conclusion

Consumer culture, which is one of the results of industrial development, has brought the need for information to the forefront for both businesses and consumers and has enabled them to make use of online technologies to meet this need. The big data generated by online consumer is being collected, analyzed, visualized, and presented by researchers in a utilitarian approach by researchers to improve marketing efforts and generate new strategies. Airline companies taking place in a competitive industry, on the other hand, can reference to big data analytics to keep up with innovations and make rational decisions. In particular, passenger data is an important source of reference for improving and developing services and can be obtained in different structures from the online environment. Thus, passengers' information-seeking behaviors, processes of accessing products and services, general profiles, wants, and needs can be understood. When using online consumer data in the airline industry, questions regarding the purpose of the data, the sources from which it will be obtained, its size, the methods by which it will be analyzed, and how it should be presented have gained importance. Within the scope of the reviewed literature, problems and solutions generated for airline businesses can be listed as follows:

- To increase website rankings in search engines, increase page traffic (Krueger 2022), get the return on digital marketing efforts (Sakas and Giannakopoulos 2021), Web analytics, crowdsourcing (Sakas and Reklitis 2021), for increasing ticket sales and reservations (IdeaWorks 2012; Díaz and Martin-Consuegra 2016), SEO applications, fuzzy logic, and correlation and regression analyses (Sakas and Giannakopoulos 2021).
- Social media analytics, natural language processing in sentiment analysis, machine/deep learning, and multidimensional analysis techniques (Adeva et al. 2014; Koçak and Atalık 2019) in order to determine the general public opinion about airline brands, products, and services (Liu 2012) and to reveal the dominance of the brand in a competitive environment (Koçak and Atalık 2019).
- To identify the overall passenger profile, manage/track customer relationships (Antoniadis and Charmantzi 2016), understand consumer behavior, and learn the sequence of activities in airline online applications, clustering, mapping, and optimization algorithms in social network analytics (Tabassum et al. 2018; Punel and Ermagun 2018).
- Participation analysis, correlation analysis, and multiple regression analysis in social media analytics (Menon et al. 2019; Koçak 2022a, b) to see the online response to airline marketing efforts, especially advertising and communication, and to ensure brand loyalty (Hapsari et al. 2017; Tsai and Men 2013).
- Keyword identification with SEO to search engine analytics correlation regression (Önder and Gunter 2016) analysis of variance (Koçak 2020) causality analysis and artificial and deep learning algorithms (Yu et al. 2019) can be used to determine the instantaneous behavior of passengers and predict demand

When examining the literature on big data offered by Internet technology, it is possible to say that its applications in the airline industry are limited. As a matter of fact, tourism applications, which are among the connected sectors, also utilize big data applications through passengers flying and give an idea into the usage of big data in the airline industry. Studies on the use of online passenger data in the development of marketing strategies stand out in the recent literature.

In the service industry, determining the wants, needs, attitudes, and purchasing behaviors of passengers instantly and making predictions in this direction are very important in the highly dynamic airline market. It will be beneficial to increase the use of online consumer data in the airline industry in the coming years and to intensify the interest in storage, security, and IT departments in this direction. Moreover, testing artificial and deep learning algorithms to increase the success of demand forecasting with new applications and investigating passenger behavior towards different operating systems, web applications, and search engines will contribute to the industry by expanding the existing literature.

References

Aarthy CCJ, Narayanan MB, Kumar GR, Jayasundaram J, Saikrishna S, Kumar CR (2021) Big data analytics and anintelligent aviation information management system. Turkish J Comp Math Educ 12(11):4328–4340

Adeva JG, Atxa JP, Carrillo MU, Zengotitabengoa EA (2014) Automatic text classification to support systematic reviews inmedicine. Expert Syst Appl 41(4):1498–1508

Aktan E (2018) Büyük veri: Uygulama alanları, analitiği ve güvenlik boyutu. Bilgi Yönetimi 1(1):1–22

Akter S, Bhattacharyya M, Wamba SF, Aditya S (2016) How does social media analytics create value? J Organ End User Comput (JOEUC) 28(3):1–9

Alam JR, Sajid A, Talib R, Niaz M (2014) A review on the role of big data in business. Int J Comput Sci Mob Comput 3(4):446–453

Almaslamani F, Abuhussein R, Saleet H, AbuHilal L, Santarisi N (2020) Using big data analytics to design an intelligent market basket-case study at same mall. Int J Eng Res Technol 13:3444–3455

Andronie M (2015) Airline applications of business intelligence systems. Incas Bull 7(3):153

Antoniadis I, Charmantzi A (2016) Social network analysis and social capital in marketing: theory and practical implementation. Int J Technol Mark 11(3):344–359

Ashi MM, Siddiqui MA, Nadeem F (2018) Pre-trained word embeddings for Arabic aspect-based sentiment analysis of airline tweets. In: International Conference on Advanced Intelligent Systems and Informatics. Springer, Cham, pp 241–251

Blazquez D, Domenech J (2018) Big Data sources and methods for social and economic analyses. Technol Forecast Soc Chang 130:99–113

Brigo F, Lochner P, Tezzon F, Nardone R (2014) Web search behavior for multiple sclerosis: an info demiological study. Multiple Sclerosis and Related Disorders 3(4):440–443

Broder A (2002) A taxonomy of web search. ACM Sigir forum 36(2):3–10

Brodie RJ, Hollebeek LD, Jurič B, Ilič A (2011) Customer engagement: conceptual domain, fundamental propositions, and implications for research. J Serv Res 14(3):252–271

Cambria E (2016) Affective computing and sentiment analysis. IEEE Intell Syst 31(2):102–107

Chang YC, Ku CH, Le Nguyen DD (2022) Predicting aspect-based sentiment using deep learning and information visualization: the impact of COVID-19 on the airline industry. Inf Manag 59(2):103587
Chen S, Huang Y, Huang W (2016) Big data analytics on aviation social media: the case of china southern airlines on Sina Weibo. In: 2016 IEEE second international conference on big data computing service and applications (BigDataService). IEEE, pp 152–155
Chung SH, Ma HL, Hansen M, Choi TM (2020) Data science and analytics in aviation. Transp Res Part E Logist Transp Rev 134:101837
Cui L, Yu FR, Yan Q (2016) When big data meets software-defined networking: SDN for big data and big data for SDN. IEEE Netw 30(1):58–65
Cvijikj IP, Michahelles F (2013) Online engagement factors on Facebook brand pages. Soc Netw Anal Min 3(4):843–861. https://doi.org/10.1007/s13278-013-0098-8
Davenport TH, Barth P, Bean R (2012) How Big Data is different. MIT Sloan Manag Rev 54(1):43–46
de Vries L, Gensleer S, Leeflang PS (2012) Popularity of brand posts on brand fan pages: an investigation of the effects of social media marketing. J Interact Mark 26(2):83–91
Demmers J, Weltevreden JW, van Dolen WM (2020) Consumer engagement with brand posts on social media in consecutive stages of the customer journey. Int J Electron Commer 24(1):53–77
Díaz E, Martín-Consuegra D (2016) A latent class segmentation analysis of airlines based on website evaluation. J Air Transp Manag 55:20–40
Duke A (2017) Bigdata: a game changer in the business world. https://www.linkedin.com/pulse/big-data-game-changer-business-world-ashley-byrd. Accessed 21 Sept 2022
Erevelles S, Fukawa N, Swayne L (2016) Big Data consumer analytics and the transformation of marketing. J Bus Res 69(2):897–904
Esen MF, Türkay B (2017) Turizm Endüstrilerinde Büyük Veri Kullanımı (Big Data Applications in Tourism). J Tour Gastron Stud 5(4):92–115
Fan W, Gordon MD (2014) The power of social media analytics. Commun ACM 57(6):74–81
Genylabs (2022) How social media analytics helps the airline industry. https://genylabs.io/how-social-media-analytics-helps-the-airline-industry/. Accessed 14 Aug 2022
Google Statistics (2022) Google Search Statistics https://www.internetlivestats.com/google-search-statistics/. Accessed 15 Aug 2022
Hapsari R, Clemes MD, Dean D (2017) The impact of service quality, customer engagement and selected marketing constructs on airline passenger loyalty. Int J Qual Serv Sci 9(1):21–40
Harison E, Boonstra A (2008) Reaching new altitudes in e-commerce: assessing the performance of airline websites. J Air Transp Manag 14(2):92–98
Hausladen I, Schosser M (2020) Towards a maturity model for big data analytics in airline network planning. J Air Transp Manag 82:101721
Hedin H, Hirvensalo I, Vaarnas M (2014) The handbook of market intelligence: understand, compete and grow in global markets. Wiley
Holland CP, Thornton SC, Naudé P (2020) B2B analytics in the airline market: harnessing the power of consumer big data. Ind Mark Manag 86:52–64
IdeaWorks (2012) Ryanair – the godfather of ancillary revenue. http://www.ideaworkscompany.com/wp-content/uploads/2012/05/021908. AnalysisRyanairAncillary20081.pdf. Accessed 10 Aug 2022
IATA (2024) Global Passenger Survey (GPS). https://www.iata.org/en/publications/manuals/global-passenger-survey/. Accessed 28 Nov 2024
Izzo F (2019) Management transition to big data analytics: exploratory study on airline industry. Int Bus Res 12(10):48–56
Kaplan AM, Haenlein M (2010) Users of the world, unite! The challenges and opportunities of social media. Bus Horizons 53(1):59–68
Kaushik A (2007) Web analytics: an hour a day. Wiley
Knorr A (2019) Big Data, customer relationship and revenue management in the airline industry: what future role for frequent flyer programs? Rev Integr Bus Econ Res 8(2):38–51

Koçak BB (2020) Exploring and identification of passengers' web search goals using "ticket" related queries in the airline market: a Google trends study. Pazarlama ve Pazarlama Araştırmaları Dergisi 13(3):443–460

Koçak BB (2021) Fly "Withus"! Impact of consumer-brand relationship on consumer engagement: an empirical investigation on Turkish Airline Instagram pages. Tüketici ve Tüketim Araştırmaları Dergisi 13(2):253–282

Koçak BB (2022a) More than thousand words!: Emoji engagement on Turkish Airline Instagram pages. In: Cases on developing effective research plans for communications and information science. IGI Global, pp 251–267

Koçak BB (2022b) Improving consumer engagement with airline brands: a case of SKYTRAX 100's YouTube pages. J Intern Appl Manag 13(1):1–19

Koçak BB, Atalık Ö (2019) Perceptual maps of Turkish airline services for different periods using supervised machine learning approach and multidimensional scaling. Int J Sustain Aviation 5(3):205–229

Krueger R (2022) Similar web travel report: strong rebound for online bookings. https://www.similarweb.com/corp/blog/insights/similarweb-travel-report-strong-rebound-for-online-bookings/. Accessed 31 Jul 2022

Labrecque LI, Swani K, Stephen AT (2020) The impact of pronoun choices on consumer engagement actions: exploring top global brands' social media communications. Psychol Mark 37(6):796–814

LaValle S, Lesser E, Shockley R, Hopkins MS, Kruschwitz N (2011) Bigdata, analytics and the path from insights to value. MIT Sloan Manag Rev 52(2):21–32

Leung R, Schuckert M, Yeung E (2013) Attracting user social media engagement: a study of three budget airlines Facebook pages. In: Information and communication technologies in Tourism. Springer, Berlin, pp 195–206

Little R, Williams C, Yost J (2011) Airline travel: a history of information-seeking behavior by leisure and business passengers. In: Aspray W, Hayes BM (eds) Everyday information: the evolution of seeking in America. MIT Press, Cambridge, pp 121–156

Liu B (2012) Sentiment analysis and opinion mining. Synthesis Lect Hum Lang Technol 5(1):1–167

Longden K (2020) What are the different types of website traffic? https://activeinternetmarketing.co.uk/what-are-the-different-types-of-website-traffic/. Accessed 11 Aug 2022

Luarn P, Lin YF, Chiu YP (2015) Influence of Facebook brand-page posts on online engagement. Online Inf Rev 39(4):505–519

Menon RV, Sigurdsson V, Larsen NM, Fagerstrøm A, Sørensen H, Marteinsdottir HG, Foxall GR (2019) How to grow brand post engagement on Facebook and Twitter for airlines? An empirical investigation of design and content factors. J Air Transp Manag 79:101678

Miguélez A (2020) Graph theory applied to social media analysis. https://opensistemas.com/en/graph-theory-applied-to-social-media-analysis/. Accessed 14 Aug 2022

Mohamed HAES, Al-Azab MR (2021) Big Data analytics in airlines: opportunities and challenges. J Assoc Arab Univ Tour Hospitality 21(4):73–108

Naccarato A, Falorsi S, Loriga S, Pierini A (2018) Combining official and Google Trends data to forecast the Italian youth unemployment rate. Technol Forecast Soc Chang 130:114–122

Nagar J, Suleman H (2019) Using signal processing to investigate user web search behavior on topics of interest with multiple periodicities. Proceedings of Asia-Pacific Library and Information Education and Practice (A-LIEP), November 4–7, 2019, Kuala Lumpur, Malaysia

Önder I, Gunter U (2016) Forecasting tourism demand with Google trends for a major European city destination. Tour Anal 21(2–3):203–220

Park S, Lee J, Song W (2017) Short-term forecasting of Japanese tourist inflow to South Korea using Google trends data. J Travel Tour Mark 34(3):357–368

Penela CG, de Luca P, Pegan G (2017) Insights from Google search user-generated data: a study on European Wine in the US Market. Contributoin Conference proceedings XIVSIM conference: "Il marketing disuccesso, impreseenti persone. pp 1–7

Peterson RA, Merino MC (2003) Consumer information search behavior and the Internet. Psychol Mark 20(2):99–121
Preis T, Moat HS, Stanley HE (2013) Quantifying trading behavior in financial markets using Google Trends. Sci Rep 3:1684
Punel A, Ermagun A (2018) Using Twitter network to detect market segments in the airline industry. J Air Transp Manag 73:67–76
Rane A, Kumar A (2018) Sentiment classification system of Twitter data for US airline service analysis. In: 2018 IEEE 42nd Annual Computer Software and Applications Conference (COMPSAC), vol 1. IEEE, pp 769–773
Rijmenam M (2013) Southwest airlines uses big data to deliver excellent customer service. https://www.thedigitalspeaker.com/southwest-airlines-uses-big-data-to-deliver-excellent-customer-service/. Accessed 21 Sept 2022
Russom P (2011) Big data analytics. TDWI best practices report, fourth quarter 19(4):1–34
Rusu O, Halcu I, Grigoriu O, Neculoiu G, Sandulescu V, Marinescu M, Marinescu V (2013) Converting unstructured and semi-structured data into knowledge. In: 2013 11th RoEduNet International Conference. IEEE, pp 1–4
Sakas DP, Giannakopoulos NT (2021) Big data contribution in desktop and mobile devices comparison, regarding airlines' digital brand name effect. Big Data Cogn Comput 5(4):48
Sakas DP, Reklitis DP (2021) The impact of organic traffic of crowd sourcing platforms on airlines' website traffic and user engagement. Sustainability 13(16):8850
Schosser M (2020) Big data opportunities for airline network planning. In: Big Data to improve strategic network planning in airlines. Springer Gabler, Wiesbaden, pp 195–259
Schultz CD (2020) Informational, transactional, and navigational need of information: relevance of search intention in search engine advertising. Inf Retr J 23:117–135
Statista (2022a) User generated content. https://www.statista.com/topics/1716/user-generated-content/#topicHeaderwrapper. Accessed 14 Aug 2022
Statista (2022b) Worldwide market share of search engines. https://www.statista.com/statistics/216573/worldwide-market-share-of-search-engines/. Accessed 15 Aug 2022
Suh DY, Ryerson MS (2019) Forecast to grow: aviation demand forecasting in an era of demand uncertainty and optimism bias. Transp Res Part E Logist Transp Rev 128:400–416
Sumathi N, Gokulakrishnan S, Kaushik Ramana S, Muralitharan R, Kamal CV (2017) Application of Big Data systems to airline management. Int J Latest Technol Eng Manag Appl Sci (IJLTEMAS) 6(12):129–132
Tabassum S, Pereira FS, Fernandes S, Gama J (2018) Social network analysis: an overview. Wiley Interdiscipl Rev Data Mining Knowl Discov 8(5):e1256
Tian X, He W, Tang C, Li L, Xu H, Selover D (2019) A new approach of social media analytics to predict service quality: evidence from the airline industry. J Enterprise Inf Manag 33(1):51–70
Wibisono AI, Ruldeviyani Y (2021) Detecting social media influencers of airline services through social network analysis on Twitter: a case study of the Indonesian Airline Industry. In: 2021 3rd East Indonesia Conference on Computer and Information Technology (EIConCIT). IEEE, pp 314–319
Tsai W, Men LR (2013) Motivations and antecedents of consumer engagement with brand pages on social networking sites. J Interact Advert 13(2):76–87. https://doi.org/10.1080/15252019.2013.826549
Wan Y, Gao Q (2015) An ensemble sentiment classification system of twitter data for airline services analysis. 2015 IEEE International Conference on Data Mining Workshop (ICDMW). https://doi.org/10.1109/ICDMW37719.2015
Yin S, Kaynak O (2015) Big data for modern industry: challenges and trends [point of view]. Proc IEEE 103(2):143–146
Yu L, Zhao Y, Tang L, Yang Z (2019) Online big data-driven oil consumption forecasting with Google trends. Int J Forecast 35(1):213–223
Zeng D, Chen H, Lusch R, Li SH (2010) Social media analytics and intelligence. IEEE Intell Syst 25(6):13–16

Bahri Baran Kocak was born in Dogubayazit (1983). He graduated from Anadolu University, Department of Aviation Management (2012). He completed his PhD at Anadolu University Institute of Social Sciences, Department of Civil Aviation Management (2018). The author, who works as a faculty member at Dicle University School of Civil Aviation, Department of Aviation Management, is interested in scientific fields such as marketing, communication, social media, artificial learning and psycholinguistics, as well as fiction-literature.

Chapter 6
Applying Design Thinking to Aviation's Experiential Processes

İnci Polat and Scott C. Ambrose

Abstract This chapter discusses the significant role of design thinking in enhancing aviation's experiential processes. It emphasizes the evolution of design from a singular creative process to a multidisciplinary interaction across various fields. Design thinking is highlighted as a flexible, human-centered approach that integrates the needs of users, the possibilities of technology, and business requirements. The chapter outlines the principles, stages, methods, and tools of design thinking, including user-driven engagement, problem-solving, iteration, interdisciplinary collaboration, tolerance for uncertainty, and the blend of rationality and intuition. Case studies from Airbus, All Nippon Airways, Air New Zealand, and American Airlines illustrate successful applications of design thinking in the aviation industry, showing its potential to drive innovation and improve customer experiences.

Keywords Service design · Design thinking · Human-centered design · Innovation · Customer experience

6.1 Introduction

Over the last century, the concept of design has undergone significant changes from a predominantly individual creative process to a multidisciplinary process of interaction across disciplines such as engineering, medicine, information technology,

İ. Polat (✉)
Department of Aviation Management, Süleyman Demirel University, Isparta, Türkiye

O'Maley College of Business, Embry-Riddle Aeronautical University, Daytona Beach, FL, USA
e-mail: inciseliokuyucu@sdu.edu.tr

S. C. Ambrose
David B. O'Maley College of Business, Embry-Riddle Aeronautical University, Daytona Beach, FL, USA
e-mail: scott.ambrose@erau.edu

İ. Polat (ed.), *Aviation Innovation*, Accounting, Finance, Sustainability, Governance & Fraud: Theory and Application,
https://doi.org/10.1007/978-981-96-7265-3_6

education, economics, and social sciences (Badke-Schaub 2022). In their book *Change by Design* (2011), Brown and Katz state that the problems we face in today's society, industry, and environment are too complex to be solved by the methods used in the past. Brown and Katz (2011) identify the need for change in design as the main challenge of the twenty-first century. This change indicates that design thinking will respond with the concepts of flexibility and adaptability, which are much closer to the needs of the complex world of business and management, rather than with the hierarchical and cost-effective nature of design. Thus, design thinking challenges the focus on the omnipotent designer and the products as solutions. Design is advocated as a "collaborative endeavor where the design process is spread across various participating stakeholders and competencies" (Bjögvinsson et al. 2012). Due to the increasing competition in the global market and rapidly changing demands of the market, organizations need to innovate. Such business challenges have been supported by the design thinking approach, which attracts the interest of both designers and non-designers (Seidel and Fixson 2013). Service design emphasizes that organizations need to look beyond traditional thinking concepts, such as "single entity" or "tangible products," and focus on the design strategy of holistic experiences (Bitner et al. 2008). It is known that the underlying aim of this thinking is to create not only an integrated, enjoyable, and memorable experience for customers but also a viable, efficient, and effective solution for providers. Design thinking can thus be described as a human-centered, iterative problem-solving approach that involves stakeholders from diverse backgrounds. In contrast to linear innovation approaches, design thinking is not a rigid process but a framework that combines creative and analytical modes of reasoning, specific mindsets, and a variety of applied tools and techniques (Liedtka 2015). Ingle (2013) defines design thinking as "an egalitarian skill set that can be learned, practiced and advocated by professionals across sectors and job titles." It shows that the talent and creativity of all businesses should be harnessed and that a good idea does not care who has it (Flynn et al. 2003). The reason most of the existing publications on design thinking have been oriented towards practitioners rather than academics until now is due to a lack of theoretical foundation (Johansson-Sköldberg et al. 2013). In this context, this chapter of the book aims to contribute to the literature on customer experience in aviation from a design thinking perspective.

6.2 Design Thinking

Design thinking has been defined as a meaningful approach to overcoming problems (Buchanan 1992). According to Nelson and Stolterman (2014), design does not aim to solve a problem with a final answer, but to create a positive contribution to the current situation. In this way, design differs significantly from ordinary problem-solving. Designers aim to contribute to the existing situation through their designs, rather than seeing the world as a place where they need to discover the perfect design. Design is therefore seen as an exploratory activity where mistakes are made and then corrected (Leinonen and Gazulla 2014). Tim Brown, president and CEO of IDEO, defines design thinking as "a human-centered innovation approach that leverages the designer's toolkit to integrate the needs of people, the possibilities of technology, and the requirements for business success" (Brown 2008). The embrace of design thinking has played a significant role in Apple's position as one of the leading innovative companies. Design thinking is a solution-oriented process used to achieve innovation while taking into consideration the consumer at the center of all development phases (Elmansy 2016).

Since individuals, processes, interactions, and structures are strongly intertwined when design thinking is viewed in an institutional context, there is an integrative perspective for conceptualization. Marx (2022) has presented an elaborated and comprehensive list of defining elements, using existing conceptualizations related to design thinking (Micheli et al. 2019; Liedtka 2020; Magistretti et al. 2021), and developed Table 6.1 by grouping the overarching domains into relevant groups. Table 6.1 consists of inclusive domains defined by the compilation of studies, including user-driven and engagement, problem-solving, iteration and experimentation, interdisciplinary collaboration, tolerance for uncertainty and failure, and the blending of rationality and intuition. The elements that define the problem-solving domain include encouraging problem-solving by reframing the problem, building existing capabilities to solve new problems, assessing and prioritizing needed capabilities or problem-solving, and allowing for immediate solutions. The example shows that each domain involves the integration of individual, interactional, structural, and process-related elements (Marx 2022).

Human-centered design (HCD) involves a dynamic and reflective process of observing people to understand their needs, desires, and motivations and to propose a desirable state or outcome. Human-centered design is defined as an approach that models end-user behavior and seeks to design platforms, products, and services that are intuitive, desirable, and commercially viable. The purpose of this design is to develop empathy for others in order to make insightful decisions and take effective actions. The basic principles of human-centered design are given in Fig. 6.1 (Beausoleil 2022).

Norman and Verganti (2014) define human-centered design as "an iterative research cycle, often characterized by observations, an ideation phase, and rapid prototyping and testing." According to the authors, while human-centered design is playing an important role in incremental innovation, it is not a driving force of radical innovation. Instead, (i) technological change and (ii) a change in the meaning of products or technologies for people are discussed as the main sources of radical innovation. The process of human-centered design involves a careful analysis of the needs of a person or even a society. In addition to learning and implementing human-centered design methods, businesses need to collaborate in order to develop innovative products, services, and platforms. The digitalization of everyday life by the rapid evolution of online technologies has led to the differentiation of traditional approaches in designing creative collaboration and culture. Digital design thinking has also extended traditional concepts of design thinking to encompass both digital environments and tools and collaborative approaches to innovation and creativity. With that being said, digital design thinking is defined as a cognitive process of "collective creativity" supported by digital platforms, updating it to encompass the types of social creativity enabled by digital networks (Nakakoji et al. 2000; Lee et al. 2020).

Table 6.1 Factors of corporate design thinking (Source: Marx 2022)

Domain	The element of design thinking
User-driven and engagement	• Deep understanding of user needs • Inclusion of different perspectives • Providing user-driven criteria for assessment • Create emotional engagement • Inviting ownership and participation • Empathize with users • Looking at sociocultural trends
Problem-solving	• Encouraging problem-solving by reframing the problem • Building existing capabilities to solve new problems • Assessing and prioritizing needed capabilities related to problem-solving • Allowing for immediate solutions
Iteration and experimentation	• Alternatives that combine multiple solutions • Directing and execution of an action • Prototyping and testing • Iteration between the idea of exploration and experimentation
Interdisciplinary collaboration	• Dialog-based conversations • Broadening the perspective of teams • Involving key stakeholders outside the core team • Promote harmony between different perspectives • Expanding access to networks and resources and increasing the aspiration to co-create • Involving experts • Decentralization of responsibility • Intermediation knowledge
Tolerance for uncertainty and failure	• Fostering a mindset inspired by possibilities • Reducing the visibility of errors • Increasing the psychological safety • Releasing uncertainty • Learning by doing • Creative trust
Blending of rationality and intuition	• Logical and rational reasoning • Reducing prejudices • Deductive thinking • Inductive thinking • Avoidant thinking • Pure mind

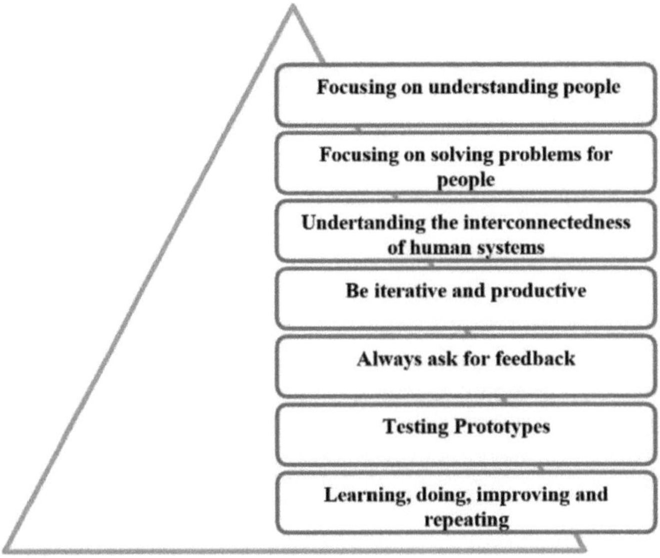

Fig. 6.1 The basic principles of human-centered design (Source adapted by the authors)

6.3 Different Approaches in Design Thinking

Brown is defining design thinking as "a discipline that uses the designer's sensibility and methods to match people's needs with what is technologically possible and what is a practicable business strategy can turn into customer value and market opportunity" (Brown 2008). Within the framework of business design, human-centered design methods, including customer insights provided by ethnographic methods when spreadsheets and big data analytical tools are insufficient, are used. Stakeholder-centered design, on the other hand, is an approach to designing desirable, commercially practicable platforms, products, and services that model both end-user and ecosystem member behavior (Beausoleil 2022). This approach is largely a response to the increasing complexity of modern technology and modern commerce. This complexity takes many forms. Sometimes, software at the heart of a product needs to be integrated with hardware and made intuitive and simple from the user's point of view. Sometimes the problem at hand is multifaceted: when considering how much more difficult it is to reinvent a healthcare system than to design a shoe, the business environment is so volatile that an organization needs to try more than one way to survive (Kolko 2015; Badke-Schaub 2022). Thus, Brown (2009) highlights three key propositions of design thinking:

(i) Design thinking is equally concerned with designing products and spaces as it is with more abstract problems such as the design of systems or services. Systems and services are now more important to the client and therefore to the designer.

(ii) Design thinking is a disruptive innovation to gain competitive advantage in the global market. This statement does not provide new insights, nor does it point to new behavioral strategies, as previously claimed. In fact, although it has been a long time since practitioners in engineering design developed the first methodologies aimed at supporting the design process and hence the development of innovative products, Osborn (1952) identified three key steps – fact finding, idea finding, and solution finding – to arrive at a creative and successful outcome.

(iii) Design thinking is human-/user-centered. The value of design thinking is not limited to industries or people tasked with designing products who are supposedly creative. On the contrary, considered in the abstract, it is often a powerful tool for solving multifaceted problems, such as "improving the guest experience in a hotel," helping customers save more money, or developing a persuasive narrative for public service campaigns.

The design process also adopts innovative design tools as needed and finds its place in a globalized design ecosystem (Singh and Gu 2012). These new design paradigms for the digital age are summarized under three headings: creativity, collaboration, and culture (Fig. 6.2).

Creativity in design thinking emphasizes computational design which is using a variety of strategies and complex cognitive activities. Creative ideas offer not only new or unexpected solutions but also useful, efficient, and valuable solutions

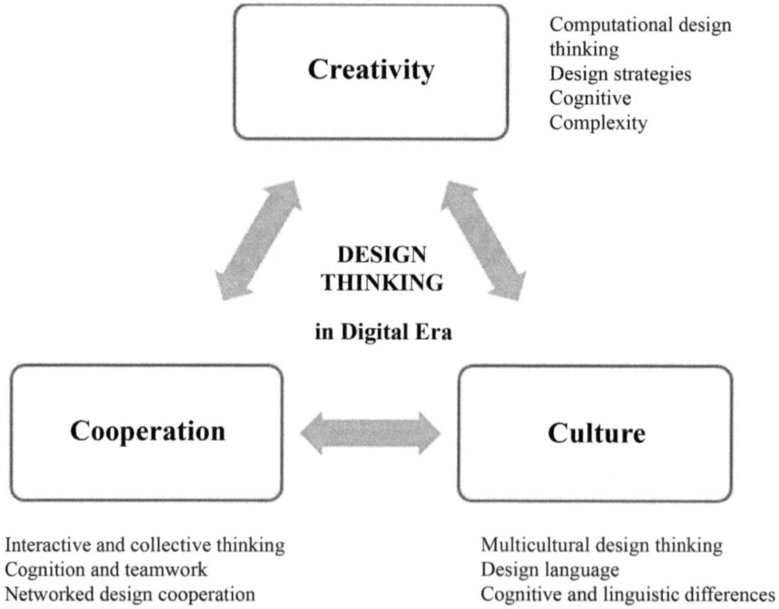

Fig. 6.2 Themes in design thinking for the digital age (Source: Lee et al. 2020)

(Georgiev and Georgiev 2018). Kryssanov et al. (2001) define creativity as a combination of novelty and convenience. Although design thinking is sometimes confused with creative thinking in cognitive research, there is a common alternative perspective that argues design thinking pursues innovation rather than creativity. This case stems from the idea that design processes and products are measurable and manageable in terms of the levels of innovation they develop. In contrast, creativity has often been seen as a mysterious area of complex human activity, difficult to understand and subjective. Therefore, some people argue that creativity is not a product of design thinking, because strategic and deliberate thinking leads to innovation. This disagreement partly explains why past research on design thinking has been limited to studying explicit cognitive processes and products. Thus, creativity and innovation are often understood as closely related concepts in design, as is the interrelationship between aesthetic and technical values (Lee et al. 2020). Collaboration in design thinking refers to interactive and collective thinking, teamwork, and networked design collaboration. Mobile and pervasive computing enables interactive and collective design thinking by continuously building and sharing creative processes and products (Lee et al. 2013). Collaboration provided in the design process and especially through the use of digital tools is an area that requires further research. Culture in design thinking is concerned with designing and thinking in multicultural contexts, encompassing design language and cognitive and linguistic differences in design thinking. Although some existing theories in design thinking need to be questioned before they "melt into thin air" as progress is made in the field, the aim is to develop new knowledge and ideas, not necessarily to erase old ones.

Unlike other approaches, design thinking focuses on the nature of the problem as much as it aims to find a solution. However, by aiming for "better" rather than "best," it moves away from identifying the single best solution. Figure 6.3 shows the four steps that define design thinking as it is best applied to marketing strategy. It outlines the tools to be used in each of the four steps: observe, learn, design, and validate. Although different design thinking approaches use different terminology for the various steps or differentiate the activities in different ways, the underlying philosophy remains the same (Diderich, 2020a, b) (Table 6.2).

When questioning design research, not only aesthetics and usability are considered, but much broader and fundamental issues are taken into account. For example,

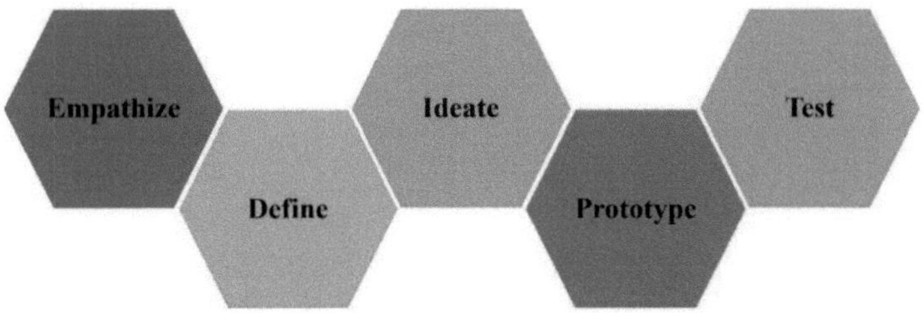

Fig. 6.3 The design thinking model proposed by Stanford Design School (Source: d.school 2022)

Table 6.2 The four quadrants that define the design thinking approach (Source: Diderich, 2020a, b)

Past/ present	*(1) Observe* • Observation • Negotiation • Mind mapping • Answering the five why questions	*(2) Learning* • Classification of information • Determining the analogies • Identification of the persons • Documenting customer journeys and value chains
Future	*(3) Design* • Generating Ideas • Brainstorming • Prototyping • Creating models	*(4) Verification* • Hypothesize • Testing • Running the simulations • A/B test
	Thinking different **Discovery analysis**	**Common thinking** **Confirmatory synthesis**

Hyysalo (2009) categorizes design at five different levels. The design of the power button of a cell phone can be cited as an example of different levels of design.

(i) At the first level, *design is about details*. For example, the design of the power button of a mobile phone, its physical shape, icon, and color are the design of details.
(ii) The second level is *user interface design*. Deciding that one has to hold down the power button for 1 s, after which the phone gives feedback with a vibration saying that it has started, is an example of user interface design.
(iii) At the third level of design, *the interest is on the systems*. The logic that the phone will keep its setting even if it is switched off is the design of the entire software system running on the phone.
(iv) The fourth level of *design involves social issues*. The functionality on the power button of a cell phone that makes it possible to put it into silent mode or meeting mode is a decision that pays attention to the social contexts in which the phone is used.
(v) The fifth level of *design considers wider societal consequences*. The decision to turn off the power button to make it impossible to track the phone may have been made to protect the user's privacy.

Decisions made at different levels of design are not made disjointly but are interdependent and influence each other. The complexity of design requires research and the ability to see and analyze both the whole and the details (Leinonen and Gazulla 2014).

6.4 The Stages of Design Thinking

According to the d.school approach, which is prominent in the application and teaching of design thinking at the Hasso Plattner Institute of Design at Stanford, there are five stages in the design thinking process (Interaction Design Foundation 2002); these are as follows:

- *Empathizing* with users
- *Defining* the needs, problems, and insights of users
- Challenging assumptions and *ideating* for innovative solutions
- *Developing* prototypes to start producing solutions
- *Testing* the solutions

The initial steps of design thinking can be described as the birthplace of the human-centered philosophy. Before starting to imagine the solutions, it is necessary to empathize with users and identify their problems.

In general, design thinking is a five-phase development process consisting of empathizing, defining, idea generating, prototyping, and testing (Fig. 6.3).

6.4.1 First Phase: Empathize

Empathizing is the first phase of design thinking. In this phase, a lot of time may need to be spent understanding the users, as well as their needs and goals. This phase is necessary to know the psychological and emotional levels of people, to interact with them and gain real insights, leaving aside the designer's assumptions (Durga 2022). This first phase is about understanding the problem at hand. Observations, interviews, and measurements are some of the key tools used to gain an objective, nonjudgmental view of the challenge at hand. The key elements here are empathy and customer centricity (Diderich 2020a, b).

6.4.2 Second Phase: Define

All findings collected during the empathizing phase are critically reviewed to solve and define the problem. It is important to review critically the problem from a user-centered perspective (Durga 2022). The defining phase of the design process is about providing clarity and focalization to the design space. The aim of the definition phase is to create a meaningful and actionable perspective. This phase is also an effort to synthesize findings with insights. The final viewpoint should combine these three elements of user, need, and insight, guiding the rest of the design process towards an actionable standpoint (Balcaitis 2019).

6.4.3 Third Phase: Ideate

The idea generation phase is the key point in the design thinking process. It is where the problem or challenge is defined. Prototype solutions may not achieve their goals without a clear definition. For this reason, various design thinking tools can be applied to analyze the research data collected from the previous phase using different field research methods. The idea allows the design team to translate the knowledge they gained during inspiration, the first stage of the design thinking process, into a concrete model or prototype. This clear definition of the problem puts the team at the center of the design process, as they can see, touch, evaluate, and brainstorm different challenges related to the newly generated ideas. Generating idea takes place in the middle of the design thinking process, as it links the inspiration research phase, which helps us investigate the problem at hand, with the implementation phase, which transforms prototypes into a product or service. In this middle phase, the design team is allowed to visualize, brainstorm, and evaluate the ideas to arrive at a viable choice. While the design thinking tools and methods at this phase vary depending on the type of expected outcome, which could be a product or service, they differ according to the design process requirements between brainstorming and evaluation tools (Elmansy 2022).

The idea generation phase is a phase where a lot of creativity is involved. Here, the designer tries to challenge established beliefs that may prove to be wrong from time to time. At the end of this phase, the designer should proceed by narrowing down ideas from large to very small (, Durga 2022). When viewed from the perspective of the aviation industry, the mantra "fail early, fail often" can be a frightening concept for any aviation product, because there is a tendency to think of failure as a loss of an airplane or a loss of life. However, this adage is designed to be applied in the idea generation and refinement phase of design thinking. During the idea generation and refinement phase, the more ideas that can be prototyped and tested, the more feedback will be generated, which leads to a better understanding of how to solve a problem over time. It is important to understand that design thinking as an innovation process takes place before the final product development process, so the testing phase does not imply qualification or certification testing. This phase of design thinking means testing the product or concept with customers in their own environment to ensure that the final design receives all appropriate input from its users (Damlo 2018).

6.4.4 Fourth Phase: Prototype

The fourth phase, prototype development, is where several ideas selected from the previous phase are tested to see if the visibility of the products is received. This phase is basically an improvised model of the product that takes into account the solutions of the previous phases. This is a highly crucial step in cross validating each solution. Thus, the constraints and flaws are captured and eliminated at this phase. However, in the prototype development phase, more improvisations can be made depending on the reliability of the result and achieving the final prototype. It can even be redesigned or rejected (Durga 2022). Prototype development is prepared and used to explore, evaluate, and communicate service ideas during different activities in the service design process. Through prototypes, the design team can make connections and quickly identify important aspects of a new concept, explore different alternative solutions, and evaluate which one might work in everyday reality. Prototypes can also be used as a communication tool to improve collaboration with users, as well as to persuade or inspire them (Stickdorn et al. 2018).

6.4.5 Fifth Phase: Test

The testing phase is the last phase, following the prototype phase. The testing phase involves a process where feedback is requested on the prototypes created. At this phase, prototypes are shown to users, and this provides another opportunity to empathize with the people they are designed (Balcaitis 2019). It is difficult to conclude that testing is the end of design thinking. This is because sometimes, to redefine the original problem, after the testing phase, if necessary, until a suitable solution is obtained, all the previous phases may have to be repeated (Durga 2022). It is important to note that the five phases are not always sequential. While not necessarily following a specific sequence, these phases can often occur in parallel and recur iteratively. It is therefore important not to think of phases as a hierarchical or step-by-step process. Instead, it is necessary to understand this as an overview of the phases that contribute to an innovative project, rather than sequential steps (Interaction Design Foundation 2002).

6.5 Design Thinking Methods and Tools

Understanding how design thinking methods and tools support innovation is becoming an increasingly important area that has received little attention in existing research. The need for design thinking methods and tools that encompass both convergent and divergent types of thinking is in line with the holistic nature of design thinking (Chasanidou et al. 2015). Design thinking provides systematic design activities and useful tools to integrate tangible and intangible touch points and effectively conduct value creation. These include the creation of a research wall, persona, stakeholder map, customer journey map, service plan, business model canvas, and service prototype.

6.5.1 Research Wall

A research wall is a data analysis tool that enables the researcher to visualize all relevant data on a physical wall, define distinctive patterns, and organize them into different categories based on the patterns. The research wall facilitates data organization using post-it notes that can be freely moved or removed. Any data collected can consist of interviews, photographs, or information collected from different research tools. The research wall is an important tool for creating shared value, as it can be made visible for everyone on the team to return and reassess data (Stickdorn et al. 2018). This tool is also in coordination with client insights into the customer journey, which includes their experience and their emotions throughout the experience. The research wall also helps to break down and visualize the large pool of data obtained from in-depth interviews (Anh 2020). The team writes all research-related notes on single post-it notes and organizes them on the wall to begin to identify clusters, related themes, and key information that can inform and inspire the design process. The wall allows for a structured placement of all notes, listing all the notes of each interviewee (which helps to identify people and cross-patterns) or all the points of each step of the journey (which helps to analyze an experience and pain points) (Service Design Tools, 2022a).

6.5.2 Persona

A persona is a profile that represents a specific group of people, such as a group of customers or users, a market segment, a subset of employees, or any other stakeholder group. The persona method can help identify the needs and desires of the user. A persona is "a representation of a user that aims to simplify communication and project decision-making by selecting project rules that fit real propositions" (Junior and Filgueiras 2005). Although personas are fictional, they help to make groups with similar service needs more understandable. Personas should be research-based and represent a group of people with common needs or common behavioral patterns. This tool helps a team to get on the same page, empathize with client groups, put themselves in the shoes of different stakeholders, understand their needs, and review their tasks. Personas are a useful reference throughout the entire design process. They can become empathetic descriptions that are defined and shared in a way that everyone can work together, about a business's customers or target groups. Some businesses even have life-size cardboard cutouts of personas. They can bring them to meetings to include a particular perspective (Stickdorn et al. 2018).

Personas are a tool, based on fictional characters that help to personalize and humanize the abstract idea of a group of users. Carved out from insights derived from observational activities, personas allow exemplifying certain characteristics of a product or service user. While a persona is not a representation of a concrete target group, it seeks to elicit deeper insights regarding the various experiences that users have, with the goal of being a driving force for generating ideas about how to improve those experiences (Liedtka and Ogilvie 2011). The persona method is used to reflect the human perspective of design thinking with the purposes of developing marketing products, communication, and service design. Personas can be used in the empathizing or describing phases of design thinking. An example of a software tool for creating personas is Smaply, a web service that hosts and delivers personas and other methods, such as stakeholder maps and customer journey maps. Smaply offers several options for identifying people, including ready-made avatars, quotes, collaboration options, and absorbing visualizations (Chasanidou et al. 2015).

6.5.3 Stakeholder Map

A stakeholder map shows the various stakeholders involved in an experience. The stakeholder map basically seeks to answer the question, "Who are the most important people and organizations involved in an experience?" By representing different customer groups or individuals, front stage and backstage employees or departments, and partner organizations, as well as other stakeholders that may have a direct or indirect impact on the experience, the interaction between these various groups can be diagrammed and analyzed. Stakeholder maps help to understand which stakeholders are involved in this ecosystem, reveal the relationships between these stakeholders, identify informal networks or frictions between stakeholders, and find unseen business opportunities. Stakeholder maps enable a design team to actively redesign a system by adding or removing specific stakeholders, creating, changing, or intentionally strengthening or weakening relationships between stakeholders (Stickdorn et al. 2018).

During the customer journey, customers interact with a variety of internal and external stakeholders. While customers often interact with websites, applications, machines, platforms, and more, they often do not realize which stakeholders are involved in this process until they think about who is responsible for these systems and who is involved in processing their information. The stakeholder map attempts to identify all parties involved in the problem statement. It is a fact that identifying extreme users is important in projects related to design thinking. Experience with stakeholder mapping shows that it is important to define the term "stakeholder" broadly. For example, in a business-to-business setting, it is essential to include the end customer as a stakeholder (Brenner et al. 2016).

6.5.4 Customer Journey Map

The customer journey is the end-to-end path a customer takes to complete a transaction with a business. For this reason, it is very important for businesses to manage the customer journey and therefore the customer experience. For this, the customer journey is usually mapped. Mapping the customer journey provides a good opportunity to design and manage the customer experience. To map the customer journey, it is necessary to follow each path like the customer and document the steps from beginning to end. Customer experience mapping is the strategic process of visually planning and organizing all customer interactions, activities, and engagements along a customer journey with a brand. It covers every touch point and almost everything from the first touch point to the last interaction. An intelligent customer experience platform helps map the customer journey through detailed customer journey maps to capture real moments (Stickdorn et al. 2018). The study about customer journeys reflects a mix of relevant perspectives rather than a single widely accepted customer journey perspective. Some see customer journeys as clearly delimited service processes with clear starting and ending points, while others see customer journeys as more open-ended processes comparable to customer loyalty steps (Nichita et al. 2013). The customer journey map helps to identify opportunities for service innovation and problem areas in the service improvement process (Krippendorff 2005).

By implementing the customer journey, it is possible for businesses to obtain the customer's perspective on the service process (Følstad and Kvale 2018). Lemon and Verhoef (2016) define the customer experience in three stages: pre-purchase, during-purchase, and post-purchase. Each phase has different touch points that affect the overall customer experience. These phases may include several touch points, some of which belong to the business or brand. A touch point is defined as "an instance or potential point of contact or interaction between a customer and a service provider." Customer touch points are any point of contact between a business and a customer via email, call center, business website, etc. A customer journey map is a powerful tool to tell a story and visualize the customer experience from different touch points and at a holistic level. Since organizations rarely observe the entire customer experience from the customer's perspective, they are often inundated with inconsistent information and guessed assumptions from different data sources. A customer journey map makes it easier for each stakeholder and department of an organization to understand customer needs at different touch points and develop a shared vision to improve the customer experience as a whole (Kaplan 2016).

6.5.5 *Service Blueprint*

The service blueprint, introduced by Shostack (1984), is a template that shows the steps and flows of service delivery related to the roles of stakeholders and the process. Service blueprint illustrates the actions between customers and service providers during service delivery. The service blueprint is a process-oriented method of design thinking for work and technical perspectives and shows all actions, including technical activities. Such a plan can benefit designers in the innovation process, such as identifying a phase, by showing a sequence of actions of both front stage tasks (actions visible to the customer) and backstage tasks (actions invisible to the customer). A web-based tool for plan diagrams is Creately, based on the first version of the service blueprint made by Shostack.

6.5.6 *Business Model Canvas*

The business model canvas provides a simple template for drawing a business model using nine basic building blocks. These nine building blocks include customer segments; value propositions; channels such as communication, distribution, and sales; customer relationships; revenue streams; key resources; key activities; key partnerships; and cost structure (Osterwalder et al. 2011). The business model canvas can be used to understand the impact of various options on the employee and customer experience as well as the impact on the business. In addition, businesses can also use it to map their competitors and compare their business models with their own. In this way, the business model canvas can also give businesses an idea about where they need to differentiate from the competition (Stickdorn et al. 2018). Businesses should embed their value proposition into a suitable business model in order to create value, and to do so, they should be able to utilize the business model canvas, which is a tool that explains how your organization creates, offers, and captures value. The business model canvas and the value proposition canvas integrate perfectly. The value proposition canvas is referred to as an add-on to the business model canvas, which allows a closer look at the details of how businesses create value for customers (Osterwalder et al. 2015).

6.5.7 *Service Prototype*

The aim of service prototyping is to replicate as much as possible the final experience of interacting with the service in order to test and validate all design options. The complexity in the simulation comes from the fact that the entire journey touching different service components is verified, as the service only exists after it has been delivered and the experience of using a specific touch point (such as a mobile app) can be relative during testing. This is always challenging, especially when there are physical locations or interactions with the service personnel involved. The more the service expands between different touch points, the more the service prototype needs to be organized as one big "staging" with a specific plan to follow (Service Design Tools, 2022b).

The mix of techniques and visualization tools used in service design practice focuses mainly on the need to represent and manage the complexity of the elements that make up service systems and processes. Design phases therefore require both abstract representations that support the description of this complexity and realistic representations that give visibility to equally abstract and fundamental elements such as atmosphere and experience (Diana et al. 2012). The methods and tools in a design thinker's toolbox cannot be easily assigned to single steps in a micro or macro process. Thus, the experienced design thinker uses the ones that are appropriate to the situation from a pool comprising more than 100 methods (Brenner et al. 2016).

6.6 Design Thinking Within the Framework of Innovation

The principle "Innovation is made by people, for people" is a guiding principle for design thinking as a process as well as for all other principles. Design thinking is a deeply human-centered method. Human needs are at the heart of every innovation, and if these needs cannot be met by the new solution, the innovation process must be repeated. As a result of the human-centeredness of design thinking, the various steps of the innovation process are conducted differently from traditional innovation processes. These steps and environments include the interaction, emergence, and resolution of conflicts throughout the process, as well as the physical spaces where the innovation process takes place, which should reflect a different "nature" in their spatial design (Brenner et al. 2016).

Design thinking is a progressive field that recognizes the impact of new technologies and ideas. Parametric design offers an innovative way of generating new design solutions based on algorithmic thinking. In particular, design thinking with parameters and rules in parametric design is examined in terms of its capacity to generate and develop innovative or original ideas (Lee et al. 2015). Elmansy (2016) explores different design thinking models in design thinking articles, including the IDEO model, the d.school model, and the IBM design thinking model, stating that most of these models show the goal of achieving innovation through three main factors (Fig. 6.4).

(i) *User desirability*: The product should meet the needs of the consumer by solving everyday problems through a user-centered process. This can be achieved through a deep understanding of the user and an empathetic design process that can only be realized by putting oneself in the shoes of the consumer (using tools such as an empathetic personality map).

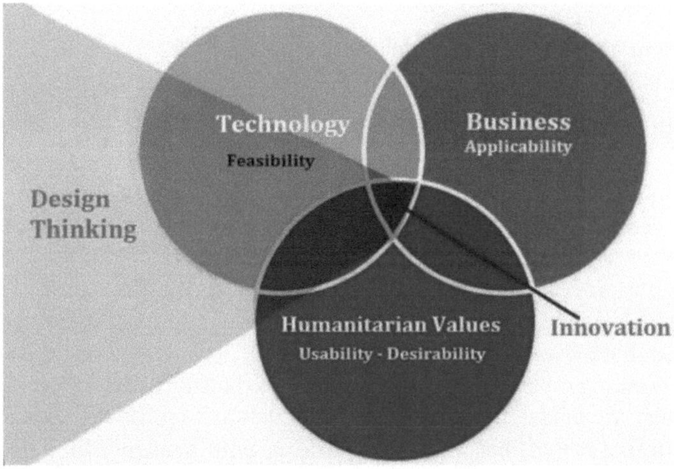

Fig. 6.4 The relationship between design thinking and innovation (Source: Elmansy 2016)

(ii) *Market applicability*: Successful products require an integrated marketing strategy that identifies the target segment and builds the product brand that is suitable for this target segment. Tools such as the business model canvas can help to understand the project and create a business strategy for the project. In addition, tools such as SWOT analysis help to understand the strengths, weaknesses, opportunities, and threats of a given product.

(iii) *Technology feasibility*: Technology provides state-of-the-art tools for designers to innovate and develop products that meet today's needs. Technology should be embraced throughout the development process, including the prototype phase, where a visual presentation of the product to the team is made (Elmansy 2016).

Johansson-Sköldberg et al. (2013) put forward the view that design thinking in management is the best way to be innovative, while in the field of design, the design thinking method may be overlooked or underestimated, despite its long history of academic development and debate. Design for innovation thinking indicates that it requires a mindset that recognizes contradictory elements in products, services, and customer experiences and knows how to deal with the tensions between them. F. Scott Fitzgerald (1936) stated, "The test of a first-rate intelligence is the ability to hold two contradictory ideas in mind at the same time and yet retain the functional one" – a prerequisite for design thinking in innovation. Thus, the design thinking mindset requires keeping in mind the elements that appear contradictory in the following tensions (Prud'homme van Reine 2017):

- Analysis versus imagination
- User empathy towards the passion for the organization's products
- Functionalism versus aesthetic ways of knowing
- Closed and open approaches to innovation

- Coherence versus pragmatism
- Experiment against linear planning
- Collaboration versus individual idea generation
- Encouraging everyone to participate against the determination
- Creating immediate benefits versus exploring possibilities of what could be

Brown and Katz (2011) identified a set of tools to help designers move forward, which they call the "three domains of innovation." The first is "inspiration," defined as the problem or opportunity that motivates the search for solutions. The second is "ideation," the process of generating, developing, and testing ideas. The third is "implementation," which is the path from project idea to market. Brown and Katz (2011) argue that these skills need to be distributed across organizations; in particular, design thinking needs to move "upstream" to the executive suites where strategic decisions are made. Design-focused innovation requires an exploratory and integrative mindset that blends critical thinking with strategic thinking, curiosity, and empathy with analysis and creative synthesis.

This mindset is expressed as a set of assumptions, methods, and beliefs held by one or more individuals or groups of people. A mindset is a mental map that originates from one's worldview or philosophy and is expressed in attitudes and actions and plays a critical role in how challenges are dealt with. As can be seen in Table 6.3, mindsets for design-focused innovation consist of learning mindset, development mindset, creative mindset, and design mindset (Beausoleil 2022).

Table 6.3 The mindsets for design thinking (Source: Beausoleil 2022)

Mindset	Definition	Verification questions
Learning mindset	It is known that failure has something to teach us and that everything learned contributes to growth. Every great success requires a kind of struggle	• Are you curious? • Are you brave? • Do you love to learn?
Development mindset	It is having the desire to work hard and explore new things to overcome challenges and grow	• Do you seek new experiences? • Are you determined? • Do you see problems as opportunities?
Creative mindset	It is living with an attitude that allows you to think, feel, and express creatively, confidently, and consistently	• Do you have imagination? • Can you express yourself? • Do you make your thoughts visible?
Design mindset	It is seeing and feeling a need or problem and trying to solve it The design mindset combines learning and creative mindsets to propose new futures	• Do you see things that others do not see? • Do you empathize with others? • Do you experiment with ideas?

6.7 Service Design Implementations in Experiential Processes in Aviation

6.7.1 *Airbus*

Bastian Schaefer, Airbus's chief innovation officer, decided it was time to take a fresh look at the business' old problems when innovation in the aerospace industry began to stagnate. Schaefer's team reached out to Autodesk, a 3D design and engineering enterprise, hoping to give Airbus new movements. Working together, the two businesses focused on what passengers really want from a flight and how "comfort" means different things to different people. For some passengers, comfort meant the freedom to use technology to work, play, and collaborate, while for others it was defined as greater accessibility, privacy, or simply more space. Starting from a human-centered focus, the organized teams began to identify opportunities to improve aircraft design while aiming to maximize the flight experience. Autodesk emphasized the need to move away from traditional engineering approaches to resolve the design constraints associated with the project. Using Autodesk's "generative design" technology, the Airbus team established the design parameters and then explored all possible permutations of the solution found to identify the best option. This design also demonstrated that the resulting reduction in fuel use would reduce CO_2 emissions by up to 166 metric tons per aircraft per year. Airbus is using generative design tools to reconfigure many more parts with the aim of creating a bionic aircraft in the future. Although the teams at Airbus and Autodesk seemed to be taking a technical approach to a technical problem, they were only able to solve it by taking a human-centered approach. In this way, design thinking has helped the teams identify the right problem to be solved in order to find the best possible solution to implement and to use the innovative technology (ExperiencePoint 2022).

6.7.2 *All Nippon Airways: Digital Design Laboratory*

Faced with the challenges of a stagnant industry and a risk-averse cultural context, All Nippon Airways (ANA), Japan's largest airline, sought ways to address these challenges by establishing a Digital Design Lab (DDL) in April 2016. ANA has focused on creating and experimenting with concepts that can reimagine business or industry in general. Since the very beginning, ANA has been a rare private enterprise in an industry that is predominantly controlled by state-sponsored enterprises. Given the context of a cumbersome aviation industry and traditional Japanese society, this case is not seen as the right approach to running a business in Japan. Therefore, it is worth taking a closer look at DDL, as it can give an insight into what businesses in Japan or businesses in the aviation industry might look like in the future (Fig. 6.5).

Fig. 6.5 Core team of DDL (Source: Lehtonen et al. 2016)

The DDL consists of five people with diverse backgrounds, from Millennials and Baby Boomers to hospitality experts, engineers, and internal innovators. Working as a team, DDL focuses on questions or issues that could transform ANA in the future, such as avatars, AR, VR, drones, etc. DDL ambassadors meet regularly to discuss emerging issues and challenges within the organization, as well as how to disseminate DDL's outputs to the ANA. In doing this, they not only serve to identify best practices and current challenges for DDL across the organization but are also regularly convened by DDL to help disseminate knowledge and ideas across DDL's wider stakeholder network. By means of traditionally characterizing Japanese businesses, this situation has encouraged employees at all levels of responsibility to intervene when they encounter nonfunctioning processes. However, the focus of DDL is to go beyond optimizing the present, focusing mostly on the future.

For ANA and DDL, design thinking reinforces the DNA of the business. DDL and its application of design thinking provide the business with tools and methods to clarify its essence through concrete, yet experimental, initiatives such as the WonderFLY platform. The WonderFLY platform offers individuals and teams the opportunity to see if their ideas have potential among ANA's loyal customers. At this stage, as WonderFLY is in its infancy, it is somewhat difficult to analyze how this platform has changed or will change ANA. Nevertheless, DDL and WonderFLY should be seen as designer-informed propositions for how things can be organized. Indeed, many businesses especially in Japan appear to adopt design thinking at a superficial level, which indicates that their focus is on copying and following the process; consequently, they may be at risk of neglecting their initial competitive advantages (Lehtonen et al. 2016).

6.7.3 Air New Zealand: Design Thinking in Practice

Located in the South Pacific, New Zealand is an island treasure far from most of the world. Air New Zealand, New Zealand's national and flag carrier airline, is known for connecting people to this small corner of the world and specialized in long-haul flying. In the mid-2000s, the main carrier Air New Zealand was looking to reinvigorate the cabin experience. Knowing that their passengers prefer and are more interested in flying in the front of the cabin, Air New Zealand was trying to revamp their customer experience for the large proportion of people who fly in the back of the plane, especially over long distances. How could they make the experience more comfortable and relaxing for their valued customers? To help them figure this out, Air New Zealand turned to IDEO, the business founded by David Kelley based on design thinking. Many people consider David Kelley to be the father of the design thinking movement. At IDEO, design thinking is defined as "a human-centered approach to innovation that leverages the designer's toolkit to integrate the needs of people, the possibilities of technology, and the requirements for business success." At its core, design thinking starts with empathy for the customer and aims to solve customer-related problems using technology that can help a business thrive. But few people know that David Kelley started in aviation as an engineer at Boeing. In fact, he is the one who designed the "restroom occupied" sign on airplanes. He found a solution to the very real problem of passengers waiting in unsafe lines in the aisles without knowing if a restroom was available. This low-tech solution is still used today by airlines all over the world. Hence, it was only natural that Air New Zealand turned to IDEO for help in designing a better customer experience.

After years of testing different designs in a secret warehouse, Air New Zealand introduced the SkyCouch (Fig. 6.6) in 2010, as the result of their partnership with IDEO. Designed primarily for couples or parents traveling with young children, a

Fig. 6.6 Air New Zealand's SkyCouch application (Source: Air New Zealand 2022)

special leg rest was created that allows three side-by-side passenger seats to transform into a flat sofa. Dubbed "Cuddle Class" by Scott McCartney of *The Wall Street Journal's* "Middle Seat" column, Air New Zealand designers have succeeded in creating product innovation on board aircraft that has been neglected by airlines for years. How did they do it? By doing what many marketing persons fail to do: that is, they simply "observed" people. In terms of marketing, observing people in their natural environment is called ethnographic research. Researchers saw families and couples bending their bodies in all sorts of ways, with an open seat next to them to be more comfortable. With a healthy dose of empathy for the customer and a willingness to see things from their perspective, Air New Zealand was able to create a unique and award-winning product. SkyCouch is so unique that Air New Zealand even managed to get a patent on the footrest design. Therefore, you may also see a variant of the SkyCouch on other airlines, but other airlines need to buy the licensing rights from Air New Zealand in order to be able to offer the similar product. As long as the airline does not compete on direct routes, Air New Zealand was willing to sell SkyCouch. Azul of Brazil is one such airline that markets SkySofa.

Air New Zealand does not rely on their success, as they always aim to stay one step ahead of the competition. The airline has spent the last few years developing a new product called SkyNest (Fig. 6.7), which offers up to six bunk-style sleeping compartments in its economy cabins. Once again, starting from one of the core principles of design thinking – customer empathy – Air New Zealand is preparing to introduce this latest innovation for passenger sleep and restoration in 2024. Who says airlines can't develop new products that truly improve the customer experience on board (Ambrose and Waguespack 2021)?

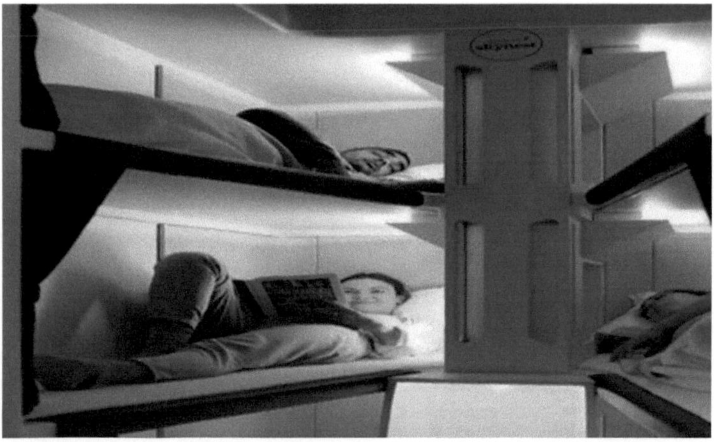

Fig. 6.7 Air New Zealand's SkyNest application (Source: Air New Zealand 2022)

6.7.4 American Airlines: Design Thinking Workshop

As one of the world's largest airlines, American Airlines has a history of complex mergers and acquisitions that have significantly impacted the airline's culture, priorities, and methodologies for getting things done. American Airlines made one of these methodological changes in 2018 in an attempt to become a more design-focused organization. Over the course of a year, the digital team at American Airlines fully adopted agile and design thinking practices into their workflows. But they were aware that they needed more than what was already available, and they knew they needed help becoming more efficient in their new design-focused process. Drawn, a boutique brand development agency specializing in creating meaningful experiences, hosted eight members of American Airlines' digital design team for a workshop demonstrating design thinking methodology and applied this work to real-world problems that American Airlines needed to solve. Drawn provided some instantaneous insights about brand and cultures of enterprises through design thinking methodology while also guiding them over the course of the process by establishing the groundwork to adapt these new approaches into their daily process. Thus, Drawn has used design thinking to help the world's largest airline enterprise solve their real-world problems (Fig. 6.8).

Among all the insights gained from the workshop, American Airlines highlighted at the top of the list their newfound ability to understand that their team was part of a much larger whole that needed to function as a cohesive unit. To be sure that they were designing solutions with the right jobs to do, they discovered how their teams align into the whole flight experience, how their roles impacted the overall reality of the business, how they could help creating a better connective tissue between the various pieces they worked with, and how they needed to spend more time with customers. As it is in this example as well, for using design thinking effectively, it needs to find a context within an organizational system that works coherently towards a goal (Drawn 2022).

Fig. 6.8 A design thinking workshop for American Airlines (Source: Drawn 2022)

6.8 Conclusion

It can be confusing for those with hardly earned design degrees to define a role for themselves, and it seems equally difficult to ask managers to think like designers. But having this perspective is seen as an inevitable consequence of the maturing field of design thinking. The fact that airline businesses are also interested in design thinking, which Bruce Mau calls “the big change” and which seems to be in harmony with the spirit of the times, makes it necessary for every employee of the airline to think like designers. Design thinking is valued for its capacity to generate innovative ideas and solutions that have the potential to transform society and industry (Brown 2009; Martin and Martin 2009; Neumeier 2009; Lee et al. 2020). For managers in the aviation industry, as in any field, applying design thinking when going through a creative problem-solving process, seeking new opportunities, or trying to overcome challenges will provide significant benefits. Aviation managers who take a deeper look at the dynamics and power of the design thinking process and tools will make rapid progress in facilitating and participating in innovation processes. However, managers need to incorporate collaboration, multidisciplinary, and bidirectional thinking into their understanding of the use of design thinking tools. More collaborative strategies and engagement tools will be necessary, given the fact that organizations are encouraged to adopt design thinking in teams where people may not have prior experience with such methods (Seidel and Fixson 2013; Chasanidou et al. 2015).

Moreover, as the aviation industry continues to evolve, embracing design thinking will be critical in addressing future challenges and capitalizing on emerging opportunities. The adoption of design thinking not only fosters creativity and innovation but also enhances the ability of aviation organizations to remain agile and responsive to the ever-changing demands of the market. By prioritizing empathy, collaboration, and iterative problem-solving, aviation managers can lead their teams towards creating more meaningful and impactful experiences for both passengers and stakeholders. Ultimately, integrating design thinking into the core of aviation management practices will pave the way for sustained growth, improved customer satisfaction, and a more resilient industry capable of thriving in the face of uncertainty and disruption.

References

Air New Zealand (2022). https://www.airnewzealandnewsroom.com/press-release-2022-airnz-offers-best-sleep-in-the-sky. Accessed 5 Oct 2022

Ambrose S, Waguespack B (2021) Fundamentals of airline marketing. Routledge

Anh L (2020) Developing customer experience with Integrify©. Master thesis, International Sales and Marketing, Haaga-Helia University of Applied Sciences

Badke-Schaub P (2022) Design thinking between myth and methodology. In: Different perspectives in design thinking. CRC Press, pp 1–5

Balcaitis R (2019) Design thinking models. Stanford d.school. https://empathizeit.com/design-thinking-models-stanford-d-school/. Accessed 15 Aug 2022

Beausoleil AM (2022) Business design method Step 1: Start. In: Business design thinking and doing. Palgrave Macmillan, Cham, pp 29–47

Bitner MJ, Ostrom AL, Morgan FN (2008) Service blueprinting: a practical technique for service innovation. California Management Review 50(3):66–94

Bjögvinsson E, Ehn P, Hillgren PA (2012) Design things and design thinking: contemporary participatory design challenges. Design Issues 28(3):101–116

Brenner W, Uebernickel F, Abrell T (2016) Design thinking as mindset, process, and toolbox. In: Design thinking for innovation. Springer, Cham, pp 3–21

Brown T (2008) Design thinking. Harvard Business Review 86(6):84

Brown T (2009) Change by design: how design thinking creates new alternatives for business and society. HarperCollins, New York, NY

Brown T, Katz B (2011) Change by design. Journal of Product Innovation Management 28(3):381–383

Buchanan R (1992) Wicked problems in design thinking. Design Issues 8(2):5–21

Chasanidou D, Gasparini AA, Lee E (2015) Design thinking methods and tools for innovation. In: Design, user experience, and usability: design discourse. Springer, Cham, pp 12–23

Damlo C (2018) Design thinking for aerospace systems innovations. https://medium.com/igniting-innovation/design-thinking-for-aerospace-systems-innovations-ca3c4dee60b4. Accessed 2 Aug 2022

Diana C, Pacenti E, Tassi R (2012) Visualtiles: communication tools for (service) design. In: Conference Proceedings ServDes. 2009; DeThinking Service; ReThinking Design; Oslo, Norway, 24–26 November 2009 (No. 059). Linköping University Electronic Press, pp 65–76

Diderich C (2020a) Recognizing key insights that make design thinking valuable to strategy. In: Design thinking for strategy. Springer, Cham, pp 15–28

Diderich C (2020b) Understanding the need for a new approach to strategy development. In: Design thinking for strategy. Springer, Cham, pp 3–14

Drawn (2022) A design thinking workshop for American Airlines. https://drawn.agency/our-work/american-airlines/. Accessed 12 Aug 2022

Durga AK (2022) Tools for design thinking. In: Design thinking. CRC Press, pp 3–13

Elmansy R (2016) Design thinking case study: innovation at Apple. https://www.designorate.com/design-thinking-case-study-innovation-at-apple. Accessed 30 July 2022

Elmansy R (2022) Design thinking tools for ideation. https://www.designorate.com/ideation-design-thinking-tools/. Accessed 30 July 2022

Experiencepoint (2022) Airbus. https://blog.experiencepoint.com/airbus-design-thinking-leads-to-new-solutions. Accessed 15 Aug 2022

Flynn M, Dooley L, O'sullivan D, Cormican K (2003) Idea management for organisational innovation. International Journal of Innovation Management 7(04):417–442

Følstad A, Kvale K (2018) Customer journeys: a systematic literature review. Journal of Service Theory and Practice 28(2):196–227. https://doi.org/10.1108/JSTP-11-2014-0261

Georgiev GV, Georgiev DD (2018) Enhancing user creativity: semantic measures for idea generation. Knowledge-Based Systems 151:1–15

Hyysalo S (2009) Figuring technologies, users, and designers: steps towards an adequate vocabulary for design-use relation. Use of science and technology in business: exploring the impact of using activity for systems, organizations, and people, eds. Frans

Ingle BR (2013) Design thinking for entrepreneurs and small businesses: putting the power of design to work. Apress, Berkeley

Interaction Design Foundation (2002) The basics of user experience design. https://www.interaction-design.org/ebook. Accessed 15 Aug 2022

Johansson-Sköldberg U, Woodilla J, Çetinkaya M (2013) Design thinking: past, present and possible futures. Creativity and Innovation Management 22(2):121–146

Junior PTA, Filgueiras LVL (2005) User modeling with personas. In: Proceedings of the 2005 Latin American conference on Human-computer interaction. pp 277–282
Kaplan K (2016) Nielsen Norman Group: customer journey mapping. https://www.nngroup.com/articles/customer-journey-mapping/. Accessed 18 Aug 2022
Kolko J (2015) Design thinking comes of age. https://hbr.org/2015/09/design-thinking-comes-of-age. Accessed 3 August 2022
Krippendorff K (2005) The semantic turn: a new foundation for design. Taylor and Francis, Boca Raton, FL, USA
Kryssanov VV, Tamaki H, Kitamura S (2001) Understanding design fundamentals: how synthesis and analysis drive creativity, resulting in emergence. Artificial Intelligence in Engineering 15(4):329–342
Lee JH, Gu N, Ostwald MJ (2015) Creativity and parametric design? Comparing designer's cognitive approaches with assessed levels of creativity. International Journal of Design Creativity and Innovation 3(2):78–94
Lee JH, Kim MJ, Maher ML (2013) Designing for interactive and collective mobile creativity. In: Proceedings of the 9th ACM Conference on Creativity & Cognition. pp 345–348
Lee JH, Ostwald MJ, Gu N (2020) Design thinking and the digital ecosystem. In: Design thinking: creativity, collaboration and culture. Springer, Cham, pp 165–188
Lehtonen MJ, Kajitani K, Paukku M (2016) Be rebellious! How ANA is utilizing design thinking to connect its past with its future. https://thisisdesignthinking.net/2016/12/ana-design-thinking-japan/. Accessed 1 Aug 2022
Leinonen T, Gazulla ED (2014) Design thinking and collaborative learning. Comunicar. Media Education Research Journal 22(1)
Lemon KN, Verhoef PC (2016) Understanding customer experience throughout the customer journey. Journal of Marketing 80(6):69–96
Liedtka J, Ogilvie T (2011) Designing for growth: a design thinking tool kit for managers. Columbia University Press
Liedtka J (2015) Perspective: linking design thinking with innovation outcomes through cognitive bias reduction. Journal of Product Innovation Management 32(6):925–938
Liedtka J (2020) Putting technology in its place: design thinking's social technology at work. California Management Review 62(2):53–83
Magistretti S, Ardito L, Messeni Petruzzelli A (2021) Framing the microfoundations of design thinking as a dynamic capability for innovation: reconciling theory and practice. Journal of Product Innovation Management 38(6):645–667
Martin R, Martin RL (2009) The design of business: why design thinking is the next competitive advantage. Harvard Business Press
Marx C (2022) Design thinking for digital transformation: reconciling theory and practice. In: Design Thinking Research. Springer, Cham, pp 57–77
Micheli P, Wilner SJ, Bhatti SH, Mura M, Beverland MB (2019) Doing design thinking: conceptual review, synthesis, and research agenda. Journal of Product Innovation Management 36(2):124–148
Nakakoji K, Yamamoto Y, Takada S, Reeves BN (2000) Two-dimensional spatial positioning as a means for reflection in design. In: Proceedings of the 3rd conference on designing interactive systems: processes, practices, methods, and techniques. pp 145–154
Nelson HG, Stolterman E (2014) The design way: intentional change in an unpredictable world. MIT Press
Neumeier M (2009) The designful company: how to build a culture of nonstop innovation. Peachpit Press
Nichita ME, Vulpoi M, Toader G (2013) Knowledge management and customer relationship management for accounting services companies. Chinese Business Review 12(6)
Norman DA, Verganti R (2014) Incremental and radical innovation: design research vs. technology and meaning change. Design Issues 30(1):78–96

Osborn AF (1952) Wake up your mind: 101 ways to develop creativeness. Charles Scribner's Sons, New York, London

Osterwalder A, Pigneur Y, Bernarda G, Smith A (2015) Value proposition design: how to create products and services customers want. Wiley

Osterwalder A, Pigneur Y, Oliveira MAY, Ferreira JJP (2011) Business model generation: a handbook for visionaries, game changers and challengers. African Journal of Business Management 5(7):22–30

Prud'homme van Reine P (2017) The culture of design thinking for innovation. Journal of Innovation Management 5(2):56–80

Scott Fitzgerald F (1936) The crack-up. Esquire 5(February):41–64

Seidel VP, Fixson SK (2013) Adopting design thinking in novice multidisciplinary teams: the application and limits of design methods and reflexive practices. Journal of Product Innovation Management 30:19–33

Service Design Tools (2022a) Synthesis wall. https://servicedesigntools.org/tools/synthesis-wall. Accessed 13 Sept 2022

Service Design Tools (2022b) Service prototype. https://servicedesigntools.org/tools/service-prototype. Accessed 13 Sept 2022

Shostack L (1984) Designing services that deliver. Harvard Business Review 62(1):133–139

Singh V, Gu N (2012) Towards an integrated generative design framework. Design Studies 33(2):185–207

Stanford Design School (d.school) (2022) A design thinking process. https://web.stanford.edu/class/me113/d_thinking.html. Accessed 16 Sept 2022

Stickdorn M, Hormess ME, Lawrence A, Schneider J (2018) This is service design doing: applying service design thinking in the real world. O'Reilly Media

İnci Polat was born in Gaziantep (1985). She graduated from Celal Bayar University School of Applied Sciences, Department of International Trade (2009). She received her master's degree from Gaziantep University, Department of International Trade and Logistics (2012). She completed her PhD at Anadolu University, Department of Civil Aviation Management (2018). She worked as a Research Assistant at Gaziantep University (2009–2019). She is currently an Associate Professor at Süleyman Demirel University in the Department of Aviation Management, School of Civil Aviation. Since September 2023, she has also been conducting post-doctoral research at Embry-Riddle Aeronautical University, O'Maley College of Business (USA), focusing on customer experience and service design in aviation. Her main research interests are airline marketing, service innovation, service design, and environmental sustainability.

Scott C. Ambrose is an Associate Professor of Marketing at the David B. O'Maley School of Business at Embry-Riddle Aeronautical University. He graduated from Kennesaw State University with a Doctor of Business Administration in Marketing. He teaches core courses in marketing and sales besides an MBA course in airline marketing. He has articles published in academic journals such as Industrial Marketing Management, Journal of Business Research, Journal of Personal Selling and Sales Management, Marketing Management Journal and Journal of Selling. He has worked in various marketing roles at Delta Air Lines, primarily in program development, and has presented seminars on airline marketing to airlines around the world. He was awarded the Excellence in Research Award by the David B. O'Maley School of Business at Embry-Riddle Aeronautical University in 2018–2019 and the Best Academician award by Tej Gupta in 2022. He is a member of the editorial review board of Marketing Management Journal.

Chapter 7
Experiential Applications in Business Model Innovation in Aviation

Rukiye Sonmez

Abstract The business model, which is depicted as bringing together all the activities of the firms in components and making all the elements work in harmony, is seen as essential. Although not all firms have a business model, firms that have established a business model gain an advantage by adding more value than their competitors. This chapter has focused on business model innovation in the aviation industry. The chapter aims to design a business model that can create an advantage in the aviation industry and also provides experiential applications of business model innovation to avoid imitation by competitors and ensure the sustainability of the advantage gained. In this context, this chapter has included the definition of the business model concept, the difference between business model and competitive strategy, the creation of a successful business model, the ability of a business model to provide competitive advantage, the well-known business model classification in the aviation industry, and the business model innovation and its applications in the aviation industry. As a result, once the success of the business model has been confirmed, it should have the ability to be innovated based on the value created, the collaborations established, the problem solution that improves consumers' lives, the technology developed, and innovation. In this way, the business model that alters the standards in the industry and the way of doing business will increase both competitive advantage and firm performance.

Keywords Business models · Business model innovation · Aviation industry · Aviation management · Competitive strategy

---

R. Sonmez (✉)
Canakkale Onsekiz Mart University, Canakkale, Türkiye
e-mail: rsonmez@comu.edu.tr

İ. Polat (ed.), *Aviation Innovation*, Accounting, Finance, Sustainability, Governance & Fraud: Theory and Application,
https://doi.org/10.1007/978-981-96-7265-3_7

7.1 Introduction

The concept of business model is frequently encountered in literature and practice and is a subject that attracts attention across different disciplines, such as entrepreneurship and marketing. As Morris et al. (2005) pointed out, since the concept is sometimes used interchangeably with concepts such as competitive strategy, strategy, revenue model, and economic model, it conduces to conceptual confusion. Magretta (2002), on the other hand, states that in today's business world, business model and strategy are among the most carelessly used concepts, which can be stretched to mean anything and ultimately lose their meaning. As long as the boundaries of the concepts and what they mean are not defined, the uncertainty about the idea continues. In this chapter, firstly, the conceptual framework is touched on, and the differences between the concept of business model and competitive strategy are mentioned. Then, the creation of a successful business model is discussed. Finally, an analysis is made through examples of business models applied in aviation.

7.2 The Concept of Business Model

Before moving on to the definition of the concept, when it is said "Model," the term brings to mind the image of a white board full of mathematical formulas (Magretta 2002). Although the concept is not expressed numerically, the business model shows activities just like the components of an equation, which are juxtaposed in harmony with each other. With the story analogy made by Magretta (2002), we can briefly define the concept of business models as stories that explain how firms work. Creating a business model means writing a new story. In order to create this story, the assumptions in the story need to be correct, and the parts of a business need to describe how they will come together in harmony.

A strong business model contains in itself all the elements of a good story, such as concretely described characters, valid reasons, a plot that allows the creation of value to be delineated, and an idea of value to be developed. This story is a variation on an old story, a reworking of universal themes that reflect the human experience. New business models, on the other hand, are variations of the overall value chain that underpins all firms (Magretta 2002: 4).

Definitions of the concept, influenced by the development of the Internet and Internet-related e-commerce activities, focus on explaining how a firm will make money (Stewart and Zhao 2000). The business model shows the design of transaction content, structure, and management in a way that creates value through the leveraging of business opportunities (Amit and Zott 2001).

A business model provides data and other evidence that shows the logic of the business and how a firm creates and delivers value to customers. It also outlines the architecture of revenues, costs, and profits that deliver that value (Teece 2010: 173).

The business model is when a firm transcends its own boundaries through a system of interdependent activities by creating value together with its partners (Zott and Amit 2010). We can say that a business model is an important innovation hub and a significant source of value creation for the firm and its suppliers, partners, and customers (Amit and Zott 2001).

7.3 The Relationship Between Business Model Innovation and Competitive Strategy

While the business model includes the parts and the concord between them, it does not include competition, the most important dimension of performance. This is the task of strategy (Magretta 2002). It is the competitive strategy that enables the firm to gain competitive advantage despite having many advantages and weaknesses compared to its competitors. Although there are different classifications of competitive strategies, they are generally categorized as cost leadership, diversification, and focus strategies (Porter 1985). A good business model should be complemented by the firm's appropriate competitive strategy (Magretta 2002) and should be a reflection of its realized strategies (Casadesus-Masanell and Ricart 2009).

To see the difference between business model and strategy, it is enough to look at the dynamics of the sector. For example, the success of Walmart operating in the retail sector comes from its competitive strategy rather than its business model. Since the mid-1950s, the discount market model emerged and was implemented by a number of grocery chains. The aim was to keep prices lower by reducing costs. The store was designed for a large customer base, saving money on decoration. The number of employees was reduced, and the work that should have been done by the employees was transferred to the customers. When Sam Walton saw this and founded Walmart in 1962, he built this existing business model in a different way. In Walton's own words, the part that made the difference was "opening big stores in small towns that everyone else ignored," and he predicted that consumers would shop in their own towns at lower prices rather than in these towns. It also avoided the threat of potential competitors due to a town could not afford more than one large supermarket. By creating value for its customers in terms of pricing as well, it promised to offer national brands at low prices every day. Competitors focused on private labels, secondary brands, and promotions. By implementing innovative practices such as procurement, logistics, and information management, a focus on efficiency has been given priority, resulting in cost reduction (Magretta 2002).

In the airline sector, which is a competitive market, competition should also be included in the business model components, since it has the power to change and affect all components in the airline model in terms of competition strategies and related activities (Şengür and Şengür 2012).

The business model cannot be separated from creativity and innovation. In building the way a business is done, creativity plays the large part. A way of doing business that has not been thought of before in the sector and bringing together a chain of value-creating activities are the products of a new problem-solving method of ingeniousness. Although supporting the business model with creativity strengthens the structure, it is not enough. It is important to support these structures and elements with technology infrastructure and to follow technological change.

In fast-changing sectors, the value proposition made must also be updated and new values introduced. In order to realize this update in a timely manner, it is crucial to create a network of collaborators that contribute to shared value creation. A business model can be quickly copied by competitors. However, if the model is integrated with the elements listed above, it becomes very difficult to imitate. It is necessary to weave the business model like embroidery to create a whole from motifs.

Firms can compete with their business models and create value with effective models (Zott et al. 2011). They should respond quickly to increasing competition and environmental changes by increasing innovation and innovativeness and especially by developing new business models (Loon et al. 2020).

7.4 Business Model Innovation

Either for a new venture or an established white shoe firm, a good business model remains essential (Magretta 2002). For success, a business model should be created, which will change the standards of the sector and the way of doing business in the industry. Doing the way other companies do will not provide a competitive advantage. A successful business model is also a source of competitive advantage (Zott et al. 2011) and is often propounded to strengthen and complement the core competence. It is not enough for the business model to be new for the firm. It should also be new for the industry or market or a game-changer. Otherwise, creating a new business model will only be a waste of time and cost (Johnson et al. 2010).

Building a successful business model, the following characteristics should be questioned:

- Changing sector standards.
- Offering one or more values to the customer.
- Effective resolution of at least one of the customer issues.
- Strengthening basic skills.
- Continuous updating of technological infrastructure and technological developments.
- Focusing on the big picture and the whole, where all parts are brought together in harmony.
- A business model that cannot be copied, imitated, or substituted.
- Protecting the model through competitive strategy and tactics.
- Existence of effective and efficient activities.
- Synthesizing the model with the innovative product or service.
- Leveraging the power of collaboration and alliances in value creation.
- Strengthening the model with technological infrastructure and continuing technology development in the process.

- Profit-making.
- On one hand, differentiating pursuant to the competitors; on the other hand, having balanced costs in internal processes.
- Responsibility towards society.
- It is a question of whether it is sustainable in the long run.

Success depends on the management's ability to examine the model in depth and even to renew it (Magretta 2002). The existing model should be updated over time, even if it is simple and minor revisions. Especially today, when consumer wants and needs are changing rapidly, ways to increase the value offered should be explored by questioning how the value is created. The extent to which the business model complies with the above-mentioned features should be evaluated periodically.

To profit from innovation, they need to excel not only in product innovation but also in business model innovation and understanding customer needs and technological trajectories as well as business design options. Developing a successful business model is not enough to gain competitive advantage, as imitation is often easy: a business model that is differentiated and difficult to imitate but effective and efficient is more likely to be profitable. Only then can there be a path to competitive advantage (Teece 2010: 173).

The most practical way to find a successful business model is to take a proven business model and apply it in a different country. It can also be adapted to a different sector if synthesized with creativity. If there is no contextual incompatibility, this is a very practical and guaranteed path to success. However, since it is easy to imitate, it will not provide a competitive advantage unless it is renewed.

7.5 Business Model in Aviation

There are many external environmental parameters affecting the airline industry. Economic, political, legal, technological, and international environments are the main parameters. For example, demand changes according to the economic conjuncture. During periods of economic recession and crisis, business and leisure travel decreases. It is also highly influenced by the domestic environment and other sectors (such as tourism, information technologies). The main parameters belonging to all of these can be multiplied as national and international aviation regulation and supervision bodies, aircraft manufacturers and lessors, aviation training institutions, tour operators and tourism companies, fuel oil manufacturers, technical maintenance and service, ground services, epidemics, natural disasters, war, etc.

The scope of the business model is not limited to the internal and external environmental factors of the firm but provides a holistic view of all firm activities (Schneider et al. 2013).

Companies do not always present their business model openly to the environment. But this does not mean that the business model cannot be known. Phrases that express their strategic position such as strategy, vision, mission, and values are important. Information about the ways of doing business, as well as the definition and boundaries of the business, can provide some evidence about business models (Sengur and Sengur 2017: 3).

Although there is a general categorization, as mentioned in the definition of business model, a model that differentiates itself from its competitors in the sector, offers a new value proposition, and reconstructs the way of doing business in the sector can be described as a business model. One of the confusing points here is that novelty stems from innovation. However, without business model innovation, the standards of the sector can be changed with the complexity of the value proposition without the need for product or service innovation.

Today, with rapid technological transformations and business model change, innovation is the most important element of an effective business strategy for competing airlines. Air transportation is recognized as one of the most important services in terms of its social and economic benefits. The aviation sector has always made a significant contribution to global economic growth and expansion (Heiets et al. 2019). As the aviation industry liberalized around the world and with the effect of globalization, many different models were sought to gain competitive advantage. As the result of testing these models, by the 2000s, a competitive separation was seen between traditional full-service providers and low-cost providers. Over time, this divergence accelerated and changed (Thomas 2014). Subsequently, regional and non-scheduled airline business models were added to this distinction, resulting in a general classification.

7.5.1 Full-Service Provider Business Model

The full-service carriers (FSC) business model is a type of business model that uses a differentiation strategy as a competitive strategy to provide flights to large hub airports. Companies applying this business model use the hub-and-spoke model to combine flights from large-scale and major cities by connecting with feeder routes. They use different aircraft types for different types of mixed flight operations, ranging from short-distance, medium-distance, and long-distance routes (Hunter 2006). This model provides both high quality and a wide variety of services.

Airline companies implementing the FSC business model compete fiercely with companies implementing the same business model with their diversified services, such as frequent flight scheduling, the quality of service they provide to passengers in terms of flight flexibility, and a high service image. In addition, they provide passengers with comprehensive in-flight services, a wide range of ground handling services, and the use of major airports (Heiets et al. 2019).

Airlines with this business model operate connecting flights with one or more home bases. They generally prefer direct (point to point) flights from one destination to another. Figure 7.1 shows a simple hub-and-spoke flight network. There are flights to nine different cities, and all cities are connected to city H. This route network is likened to the hub of a bicycle wheel, hence its name. The city of H, which is at the hub, has been chosen as the central station due to its central geographical location. Any station is at most one stop away from all other stations. This is an

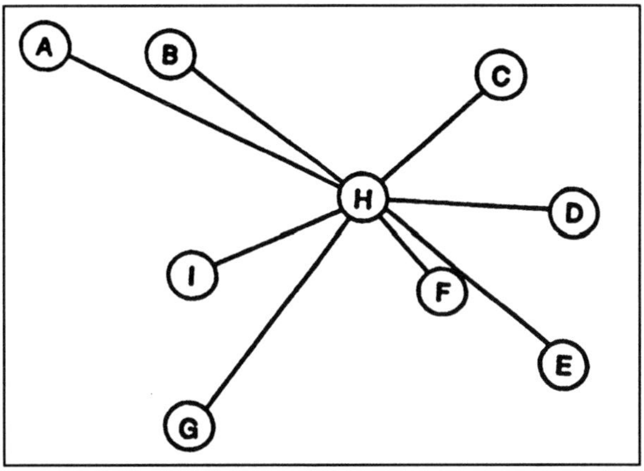

Fig. 7.1 Hub-and-spoke flight network (Source: Oum and Tretheway 1990)

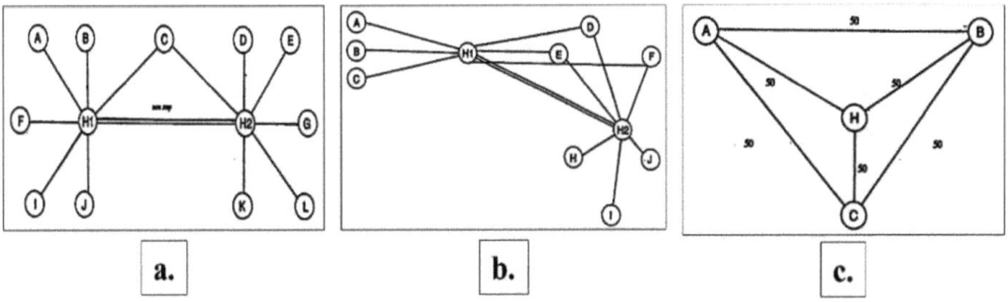

Fig. 7.2 Multi-hub-and-spoke flight network (Source: Oum and Tretheway 1990)

idealized hub-and-spoke (point to point) network (Oum and Tretheway 1990). This model increases the service life of airplanes and provides advantages such as nonstop flights and expansion into new markets.

Figure 7.2a shows a type of multi-hub network, where hubs (H1, H2) are connected by nonstop flights and each hub has several connecting stations. Figure 7.2b shows another example of multi-hubs, often used by large network carriers, where some destinations connected to the hub are combined.

Figure 7.2c is a nonstop network, where all cities in a network are connected by nonstop flights or single-stop flights through a hub. However, the nonstop network can result in low traffic levels on each route. For example, each pair of cities in a 4-station network is capable of supporting 50 passengers per day (Oum and Tretheway 1990).

7.5.2 *Low-Cost Airlines Business Model*

The low-cost carrier (LCC) business model is a model developed by airlines to compete with established full-service provider carriers in the industry by offering low fares in order to sustain and remain competitive in the market (Gerede 2015).

The first airline to adopt this new business model and be regarded as a role model and a long-standing example of success is Southwest Airlines. Historically, this airline generates higher revenues per passenger mile at lower costs compared to other airlines practicing the LCC business model (Azadian and Vasigh 2019). However, it can be said that Ryanair is the best airline that has achieved success by reducing costs and offering its services to its passengers only in the simplest form.

In Ryanair's business model, no network connection service is provided. Tickets for its passengers connecting to other flights are also not sold. Since there are no connecting passengers, it is easier to manage the inventory of seats available for sale. Since short-distance flights are preferred, passengers need luggage in fewer numbers (Tretheway 2004). Ryanair offers about 25 percent of its seats for free, but generates revenue from cross-selling and additional services such as seat reservations and priority boarding. For this purpose, products such as food, card games, perfume, and MP3 players are sold during the flight. It also generates revenue from third parties in return for advertisements during the flight (Girotra and Netessine 2014).

The low-cost airline business model achieves cost advantages in almost every activity by focusing only on core activities and eliminating other additional services. Thus, it offers lower ticket prices to its passengers and charges additional fees for additional services. For cost advantage, by having a single type of aircraft in its fleet, the airline gains advantages in issues such as training, the number and skills of flight crew, maintenance, and repair costs. They prefer point-to-point flights from secondary airports. However, Azadian and Vasigh's (2019) study comparing traditional airlines and the LCC business model shows a notable change in Southwest's business model. They argue that Southwest is increasingly adopting practices expected of traditional airlines today. For example, Southwest serves larger airports where it is in direct competition with traditional airlines. Similarly, it is expanding its operations and increasing the number of cities it focuses on. Although not officially recognized as hubs, it focuses on the representative hubs of cities in the business model of traditional airlines. The common assumption is that while full-service carriers prefer "hub and spoke" networks, low-cost carriers prefer point-to-point networks (Lange and Bier 2019).

7.5.3 Regional Airline Business Model

The regional airline business model is a business model that focuses on one or a few specific regions, which is both cost-effective and flexible. Airlines adopting this model operate by finding niche markets (Bieger et al. 2002).

Having implemented the regional airline business model, Borajet was oriented towards short-distance flights. For this reason, instead of constantly adding new destinations to its flight network, Borajet was flying to other destinations from the newly added destination. For example, Borajet launched TRNC flights from Trabzon and Kayseri shortly after obtaining permission to fly to TRNC. In fact, the cooperation they started with AnadoluJet, which applies the low-cost airline business model, has evolved into a Code Share Agreement. For this reason, Borajet purchased three airplanes with a high number of seats that were incompatible with its business model and rented them to AnadoluJet. Some authors in the literature argue that the regional airline business model cannot keep up with today's competitive conditions and has succumbed to the business model of low-cost airlines.

7.5.4 Charter Airline Business Model

In the charter airline business model, airline firms assume operational responsibility by selling all (full charter) or a certain number of aircraft seats (split charter) to tour companies or tourism agencies. There is no direct communication with passengers. Non-scheduled (charter) airlines carry out their operations seasonally. Since they do not operate in the winter season, they spend this period mainly by renting their aircraft on wet lease (Aldemir 2018). Price competition is essential in this business model, which mostly serves the tourism demand and market and operates when demand arises. While marketing expenses are low, passenger loading factors are high (Arıkan 1998). It is a model that offers simple service with as low costs as possible (Şengür and Şengür 2012). The airlines operating in the charter airline business model in Turkey are Freebird, Corendon, and Tailwind.

According to Thomas (2014), the airline industry is centered on three models, and firms can be pioneers in one of these models or can transition from one to the other. One of these models, ultra-low-cost carriers (ULCC), shown in Fig. 7.3, focuses on creating new demand with low ticket fares. The second, the Hybrid low-cost model, is a value center attracting interest for its service orientation. The last, Premium Full-Service Carrier (PFSC) model, on the other hand, emphasizes and differentiates a holistic passenger experience.

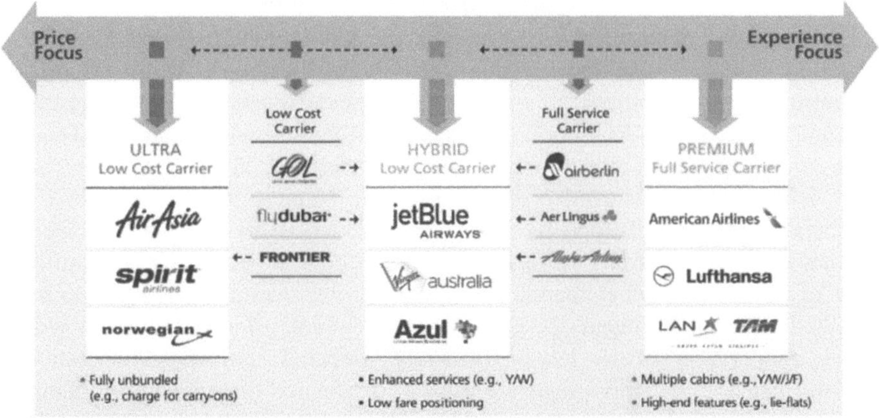

Fig. 7.3 The business models in the airline industry (Source: Thomas 2014)

Although the distinction between business models in the airline industry has started to lose its clarity due to factors such as cost pressures, liberalization, and global competition, these general business models are considered to be a guide for airlines that are new entrants to the industry, in the process of business model change, and trying to strengthen their competitive position (Şengür and Şengür 2012).

7.6 Business Model Innovation Based on Customer Experience in Aviation: Examples and Applications

Generally, companies in the same sector in the same line of activity produce the same product or offer the same service. In the value proposition offered to the customer, even if the product or service is the same compared to the competitor, the value created for the customer is different, and it is necessary to analyze the element or elements that create this value well. In the 1960s, Ray Kroc, the owner of McDonald's, realized that selling hamburgers at low margins would not generate the desired return and realized that the real value creation was the real estate value of the stores. Realizing where the real value lay was a turning point for McDonald's (Kadaster 2017).

These value propositions can be imitated by competitors in a short time. For this reason, in addition to offering a value proposition, transforming it into a business model, i.e., business model innovation, is very important for companies to increase their performance. This innovation allows for collaboration with competitors, diversification when the local market is saturated, immediate response to the demands and needs of new customers, and rapid exploitation of new opportunities when they arise. However, understanding the creation of new and innovative business models has become a necessity for both researchers and managers (Loon et al. 2020).

Figure 7.4 illustrates a business model innovation in the context of aircraft maintenance, repair, and overhaul (MRO). MRO business model innovation is influenced by two external drivers: the characteristics of the aircraft manufacturing industry and the structural characteristics of the airline sector. Both dimensions of the business model in this sector show change behavior with customer value proposition and intrinsic value creation. As a result, two types of business model innovation have emerged among MRO service providers: customer benefit-oriented and shared value-oriented business model innovation (Schneider et al. 2013).

In Table 7.1, the innovative elements of the business model of Etihad and Emirates Airlines, which apply a full-service provider business model, are given on the canvas table. Accordingly, it can be said that both airlines are quite similar in terms of business model elements. However, Emirates Airlines has flights to more than 70 destinations compared to Etihad Airways and develops its activities worldwide in cooperation with the low-cost airline Flydubai. Through this cooperation, it realizes integrated network cooperation with coordinated flight planning. They are developing their hubs by harmonizing their systems and operations to provide a seamless travel experience at the ultra-modern airport. In addition, Etihad and Emirates Airlines have collaborations with each other such as frequent flyer

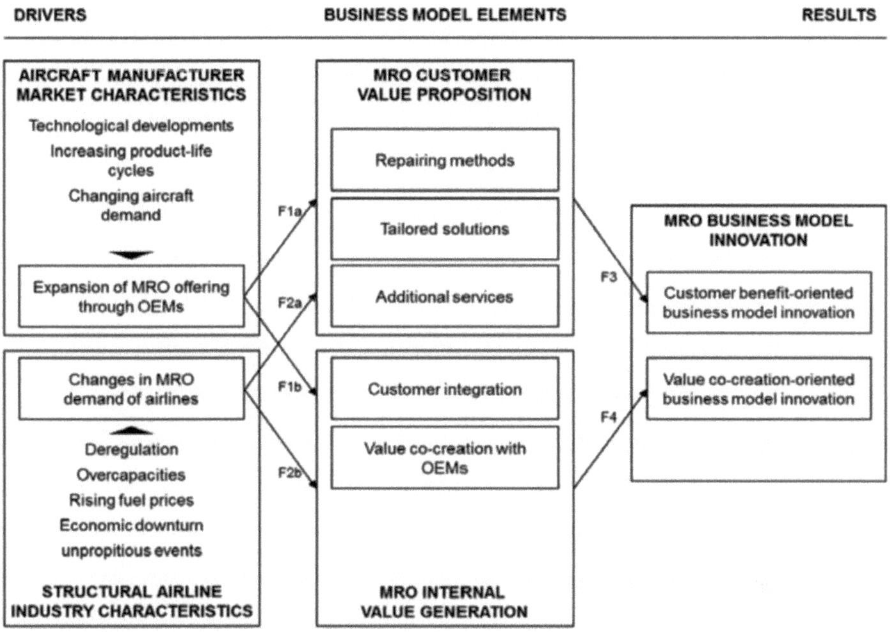

Fig. 7.4 Business model innovation in the MRO context (Source: Schneider et al. 2013)

program, cooperation in aviation safety, and access to new destinations (Heiets et al. 2019).

Today, one of the innovative models mentioned within the scope of business model innovation is the environmentalist models applied in various sectors as "Green" business model or sustainable business model. In the aviation industry, green business models lead to renewable energy sources, such as algae-based fuels and fuels produced from waste. Leading airlines in this regard are Air France and KLM.

Airline companies need to refuel anywhere on their flights between continents. They therefore aim to create local value chains on each continent. Such global supply chains require large amounts of capital, which can only be achieved through policy initiatives of airline alliances that unite aircraft manufacturers, associated industries, regulatory bodies and governments. Initiatives in this area include the Brazilian Aviation Biofuels Alliance (ABRABA); a consortium of European airlines led by Airbus and biofuel conversion technology providers; the Sustainable Aviation Fuel Users Group (SAFUG), an Australian consortium led by Qantas, comprising 21 airlines, 3 aircraft manufacturers, and 1 biofuel conversion technology provider; and the European Commission's Sustainable Pathway for Alternative Fuels and Energy in Aviation (SWAFEA) (Nair and Paulose 2014).

Among the investments made in this field, the first commercial facility was established in Germany in 2021 to produce synthetic aviation fuel (kerosene), known as environmentally friendly, which reduces the carbon footprint of flights (Euronews 2021). The first flight on biofuel belonged to Virgin Atlantic airline in

Table 7.1 Business model canvas: a comparative analysis of Etihad and Emirates airlines (Source: Heiets et al. 2019)

Blocks of business model canvas	Emirates Airlines	Etihad Airways
Key partners	Aircraft manufacturers Airports Banks Hotels and car rentals Retail and lifestyle companies Food suppliers Sponsorship Codeshare (21 agreements)	Aircraft manufacturers Airports Banks Hotels and car rentals Retail and lifestyle companies Food suppliers Sponsorship Codeshare (51 agreements)
Key activities	Operations Maintenance Marketing Customer service Security and safety Recruitment Catering Training Financials Planning (innovation as part of mission) Management (chief digital and innovation officer Emirates Group) Coordination Engineering	Operations Maintenance Marketing Customer service Security and safety Recruitment Catering Training Financials Planning Management (new management structure) Coordination Engineering
Value propositions	A world force in tourism Excellent service High quality of service New technology Operates more than 3500 flights per week across six continents A major player in the airfreight industry Personal entertainment systems in all seats. The first airline to offer passengers a facility to use their mobile phones The 2018 Innovators Awards	High quality of service New technology Skytrax Award 2018 (Best First Class in the Middle East) Excellence Award 2017 (Best First Class and Best Long-Haul Airline) Inflight Middle East Awards 2017 (Innovation in Commercial Airline Cabins) Innovation in commercial airline Hala Group
Customer relationships	Skywards business rewards Customer experience Security Brand awareness Trust Social media Network (more than 160 destinations in over 85 countries)	Skywards business rewards Customer experience Security Brand awareness Trust In-flight entertainment Network (more than 91 destinations in over 53 countries)

(continued)

Table 7.1 (continued)

Blocks of business model canvas	Emirates Airlines	Etihad Airways
Customer segments (fare structure)	First to offer mobile phone service Private-class suites First class Business class Economy class	The residence First class Business class Economy class
Key recourses	Routes Staff Brand IT platform Network Fleet (one of the youngest in the world) Wide body fleet Hub locations Emirates SkyCargo's (innovation lab)	Routes Brand Shared code agreements Fleet (one of the youngest in the world) Hub locations iCargo technology platform Etihad Innovation Centre
Channels (sales and distribution)	Website Airports Travel agencies Aggregators Social media Mobile app Chatbot	Website Airports Travel agencies Aggregators Social media Mobile app Chatbot
Cost structure	Jet fuel Staff-related cost Aircraft operating leases Depreciation and amortization Sales and marketing Handling In-flight catering and related costs Overflying Facilities and IT-related costs Aircraft maintenance Landing and parking Cost of goods sold Crew layover Corporate overheads	Jet fuel Staff-related cost Aircraft operating leases Commission Sales and marketing Handling In-flight catering and related costs Overflying Aircraft maintenance Landing and parking Insurance Reservation expenses Start-up costs
Revenue streams	Passenger revenue Cargo revenue Excess baggage Sale of goods Hotel operations Others transport revenue Non-transport revenue	Passenger revenue Cargo revenue Non-scheduled chartered Duty-free income Excess baggage Destinations and leisure

2008. This partially bio fueled aircraft took off from Heathrow Airport in England and landed in Amsterdam, the capital of the Netherlands (dünya.com 2008).

In Turkey, as well, Turkish Airlines started using sustainable aviation fuel on the Istanbul Airport to Paris Charles De Gaulle route. Biofuel will be used once a week in the first phase. It is then planned to expand it in increasing frequencies and different destinations. Due to cleaner combustion, greenhouse gas emissions will be reduced by approximately 87 percent compared to conventional kerosene fuel at the same rate, and global greenhouse gas emissions will also be reduced (THY 2021).

7.7 Conclusion

Although airline business models are presented under several categories, the business model is actually the unique story of the company. This story, consisting of interconnected patterns, exhibits the value creation that is different from other firms. These patterns prevent the value created from being easily copied by competitors. However, since replicability is not impossible, the business model needs to create synergies through various collaborations, and new values need to be added continuously. In order for the business model to provide sustainable competitive advantage, it may need to be renewed or even radically changed over time.

This innovation also needs to be addressed in a systematic way (Pceples, 2003). Business model innovation is very important for firms today to develop and improve their performance.

Business model innovation enables collaboration with competitors, diversification when the local market reaches saturation, meeting the demands and needs of new customers as soon as they are encountered, and quick seizing of new opportunities when they arise (Loon et al., 2020). The timing of this innovation is possible through environmental analysis. Changes in the internal and external environment are evaluated and added to the value creation process. In particular, changes that have occurred or may occur in customer wants and needs should be carefully reviewed.

Every company creates value with the products or services it produces. However, in today's conditions, the value created by production alone is not sufficient. A combination of several values or a value proposition offered by the business model is required.

References

Aldemir HÖ (2018) Türkiye'deki Charter/Tarifesiz Havayollarının Rekabet Yaklaşımının Miles ve Snow'un Rekabet Tipolojisine Göre İncelenmesi. J Transp Logist 3(2):1–12

Amit R, Zott C (2001) Value creation in e-business. Strateg Manag J 22(6–7):493–520

Arıkan İ (1998) Havayolu Ulaşımı ile Turizm İlişkisi ve Havaalanları. Anatolia: Turizm Araştırmaları Dergisi 9(2):46–54

Azadian F, Vasigh B (2019) The blurring lines between full-service network carriers and low-cost carriers: a financial perspective on business model convergence. Transp Policy 75:19–26. https://doi.org/10.1016/j.tranpol.2018.12.012
Bieger T, Döring T, Laesser C (2002) Transformation of business models in the airline industry–impact on tourism. In Air transport and tourism, 52nd Congress: 49–83
Casadesus-Masanell R, Ricart JE (2009) From strategy to business models and to tactics. Long Range Plan 43(2–3):195–215
Dünya Gazetesi (2008). https://www.dunya.com/ekonomi/biyo-yakitla-ilk-ucus-haberi-41529. Accessed 12 Aug 2022
Euronews (2021). https://tr.euronews.com/2021/10/04/iklim-krizi-almanya-cevre-dostu-sentetik-ucak-yak-t-icin-ilk-tesisi-kurdu. Accessed 12 Aug 2022
Gerede E (2015) Havayolu Taşımacılığı ve Ekonomik Düzenlemeler Teori ve Türkiye Uygulaması. Sivil Havacılık Genel Müdürlüğü Yayınları, Ankara
Girotra K, Netessine S (2014) Four paths to business model innovation. Harv Bus Rev 92(7):96–103
Heiets I, Spivakovskyy S, Spivakovska T (2019) Innovative business models for full cycle operating airlines. Int J Bus Perform Manag 20(4):356. https://doi.org/10.1504/IJBPM.2019.105246
Hunter L (2006) 'Low cost airlines: business model and employment relations'. Eur Manag J 24(5):315–321
Johnson MW, Christensen CM, Kagermann H (2010) İş Modelinizi Yeniden Yaratmak. Harv Bus Rev. (Translated by: İlker, G.). MESS Publications, İstanbul
Kadaster P (2017) The founder: disruption from French fries to franchises. Harv Bus Rev
Lange A, Bier T (2019) Airline business models and their network structures (6. bs). Bundesvereinigung Logistik (BVL) e.V. https://doi.org/10.23773/2019_6
Loon M, Otaye-Ebede L, Stewart J (2020) Thriving in the new normal: the HR microfoundations of capabilities for business model innovation. An integrated literature review. J Manag Stud 57(3)
Magretta J (2002) Why Business Models Matter. Harv Bus Rev:3–8
Morris M, Schindehutte M, Allen J (2005) The entrepreneur's business model: toward a unified perspective. J Bus Res 58(6):726–735
Nair S, Paulose H (2014) Emergence of green business models: the case of algae biofuel for aviation. Energy Policy 65:175–184
Oum TH, Tretheway MW (1990) Airline hub and spoke systems. J Transp Res Forum 30(2):380–393
Peeples E (2003) Yeniliği Esinlendirmek. Harv Bus Rev:97–118. Yenilikçilik, (Translated by: Ahmet Kardam), MESS Publications, İstanbul
Porter ME (1985) Competitive advantage: creating and sustaining superior performance. Free Pres, New York
Schneider S, Spieth P, Clauss T (2013) Business model innovation in the aviation industry. Int J Prod Dev 18(3/4):286. https://doi.org/10.1504/IJPD.2013.055010
Şengür Y, Şengür FK (2012) Airline business models: a conceptual analysis, 20th National Management and Organization Congress, Izmir-Türkiye May 2012
Sengur Y, Sengur FK (2017) Airlines define their business models: a content analysis. World Rev Intermodal Transp Res 6(2):141–154
Stewart DA, Zhao Q (2000) Internet marketing, business models and public policy. J Public Policy Mark 19(2):287–296
Teece DJ (2010) Business models, business strategy and innovation. Long Range Plan 43(2–3):172–194. https://doi.org/10.1016/j.lrp.2009.07.003
Thomas J (2014) Aviation insights review (AIR): the future of airline business models – which will win? Executive Insights XVI(34) L.E.K. Consulting
Tretheway MW (2004) Distortions of airline revenues: why the network airline business model is broken. J Air Transp Manag 10(1):3–14. https://doi.org/10.1016/j.jairtraman.2003.10.010
Turkish Airlines Sustainability report, 2021
Zott C, Amit R (2010) Business model design: an activity system perspective. Long Range Plan 43(2–3):216–226
Zott C, Amit R, Massa L (2011) The business model: recent developments and future research. J Manag 37(4):1019–1042

Rukiye Sonmez She completed her undergraduate education at Adnan Menderes University, Department of Business Administration in 2006. Then, she completed her master's degree in business administration at Canakkale Onsekiz Mart University Institute of Social Sciences in 2011 and her doctorate in Management and Organization at Canakkale Onsekiz Mart University Institute of Social Sciences, Department of Business Administration in 2017. Between 2008–2017, she worked as a research assistant at Canakkale Onsekiz Mart University, Faculty of Economics and Administrative Sciences, Department of Business Administration. In 2018, she started to work as an Assistant Professor in the Department of Finance and Banking, Biga Faculty of Applied Sciences of the same university and continues to work. Her research interests and academic studies include airline management, business model, competitive dynamics, competitive behavior, moves and retaliation, strategic alliances and sustainable competitive advantage.

Index

İ. Polat (ed.), *Aviation Innovation*, Accounting, Finance, Sustainability, Governance & Fraud: Theory and Application,
https://doi.org/10.1007/978-981-96-7265-3

MIX
Papier aus verantwortungsvollen Quellen
Paper from responsible sources
FSC® C105338

If you have any concerns about our products,
you can contact us on
ProductSafety@springernature.com

In case Publisher is established outside the EU,
the EU authorized representative is:
Springer Nature Customer Service Center GmbH
Europaplatz 3, 69115 Heidelberg, Germany

Printed by Libri Plureos GmbH
in Hamburg, Germany